Sea of Blood

A Military History of the Partisan Movement in Yugoslavia 1941-1945

Gaj Trifković

Helion & Company Limited

To Goran Despotović, the best friend to all wartime Yugoslavia researchers

Helion & Company Limited
Unit 8 Amherst Business Centre
Budbrooke Road
Warwick
CV34 5WE
England
Tel. 01926 499 619
Email: info@helion.co.uk
Website: www.helion.co.uk
Twitter: @helionbooks
Visit our blog at blog.helion.co.uk

Published by Helion & Company 2022
Designed and typeset by Mary Woolley, Battlefield Design (www.battlefield-design.co.uk)
Cover designed by Paul Hewitt, Battlefield Design (www.battlefield-design.co.uk)

Cover Image: Group of Partisans from the 4th Montenegrin Proletarian Brigade, 1942/43 (courtesy of Museum of Yugoslavia, Belgrade, item no. III-4910).

ISBN 978-1-914059-94-0

British Library Cataloguing-in-Publication Data.
A catalogue record for this book is available from the British Library.

Contents

List of Maps

Abbreviations

AA	Anti-Aircraft
AAS	*Armeeabteilung Serbien* (Army Detachment Serbia)
AC	Army Corps
AT	Anti-Tank
AVNOJ	*Antifašističko vijeće narodnog oslobođenja Jugoslavije* (Anti-fascist Council of People's Liberation of Yugoslavia)
BAB	Bulgarian Armored Brigade
BAF	Balkan Air Force
BBC	British Broadcasting Corporation
Bde.	Brigade
BDO	*Befehlshaber der Ordnungspolizei* (Commander of Order Police)
BDTK	*Befehlshaber der deutschen Truppen in Kroatien* (Commander of German Troops in Croatia)
BhS	*Befehlshaber Serbien* (Commanding Officer in Serbia)
BID	Bulgarian Infantry Division
BIR	Bulgarian infantry regiment
BKP	*Българска Комунистическа Партия* (Bulgarian Communist Party)
BLO	British Liaison Officer
BOC	Bulgarian Occupation Corps
Btl.	Battalion
BA	Bulgarian Army
CB	Cavalry Brigade
CCB	Cossack Cavalry Brigade
CCC	Cossack Cavalry Corps
CCD	Cossack Cavalry Division
CCNN	*Camicie Nere* (Blackshirts)
CK	*Centralni komitet* (Central Committee)
COIN	Counterinsurgency
CO	Commanding Officer
CoS	*Commando Supremo* (Armed Forces High Command)
Coy.	Company
Cpt.	Captain
DČD	*Dinarska četnička divizija* (Dinara Chetnik Division)
Div.	Division

DGA	*Deutscher General in Agram* (German General in Zagreb)
DVJ	*Dobrovoljačka vojska Jugoslavije* (Volunteer Army of Yugoslavia)
EG	*Einsatzgruppe* (Action Group)
EK	*Einsatzkommando* (Action Squad)
ESDM	*Einsatzstaffel der deutschen Mannschaft* (Action Squad of German Militia)
FB	Fortress Brigade
FFK	*Fliegerführer Kroatien* (Air Commander Croatia)
FJB	*Fallschirmjäger-Bataillon* (Parachute Battalion)
FK	*Feldkommandatur* (Area Command)
GAC	Group of Assault Corps
GEGC	German Ethnic Group in Croatia
GHQ	General Headquarters
GMC	Guards Mechanized Corps
GOC	*Glavni obavještajni centar* (Main Intelligence Center)
GoD	Group of Detachments
GOG	*Glavna operativna grupa* (Main Operational Group)
GR	Grenadier Regiment
GVD	*Grupa vazduhoplovnih divizija* (Group of Air Divisions)
HD	*Hrvatska divizija* (Croatian Division)
HDB	*Hrvatsko domobranstvo* (Croatian Home Guard)
HGE/F	*Heeresgruppe* E/F (Army Group E/F)
HKdo	*Höheres Kommando zur besonderen Verwendung* (Higher Command for Special Purposes)
HOS	*Hrvatske oružane snage* (Croatian Armed Forces)
HSS	*Hrvatska seljačka stranka* (Croatian Peasant Party)
HSSPF	*Höhere SS und Polizeiführer Serbien* (Higher SS and Police Leader Serbia)
HUD	*Hrvatska udarna divizija* (Croatian Assault Division)
ID	Infantry Division
IR	Infantry Regiment
ITA	Italian Army
JB	*Jäger* Brigade
JD	*Jäger* Division
JOG	*Južna operativna grupa* (Southern Operational Group)
JRR	*Jäger* Reserve Regiment
KIA, WIA, MIA	Killed, Wounded, Missing-in-action
KK	*Kreiskommandantur* [District Command]
KM	*Kriegsmarine*
KNOJ	*Korpus narodne odbrane Jugoslavije* (Corps of People's Defense of Yugoslavia)
KPH	*Komunistička partija Hrvatske* (Communist Party of Croatia)
KPJ	*Komunistička partija Jugoslavije* (Communist Party of Yugoslavia)
KPS	*Komunistička partija Slovenije* (Communist Party of Slovenia)
LMG	Light Machine Gun

LSB	*Landesschützen-Bataillon* (territorial defense battalion)
LSR	*Landesschützen-Regiment* (territorial defense regiment)
LW	*Luftwaffe*
LWFD	*Luftwaffe* Field Division
MBSO	*Militärbefehlshaber Südost* (Military Commander Southeast)
MFK	*Montenegrinisches Freiwilligen-Korps* (Montenegrin Volunteer Corps)
MG	Machine Gun
MHQ	Main Headquarters
MoD	Ministry of Defense
MoI	Ministry of Interior
MTB	Mountain Brigade
MTC	Mountain Corps
MTD	Mountain Division
MK	*Mjesni komitet* (Town Committee)
MVAC	*Milizia volontaria anticomunista* (Voluntary Anti-communist Militia)
NB	*Naoružani brod* (Armed Boat)
NDH	*Nezavisna država Hrvatska* (Independent State of Croatia)
NOB	*Narodnooslobodilačka borba* (People's Liberation Struggle)
NOO	*Narodnooslobodilački odbor* (People's Liberation Council)
NOP	*Narodnooslobodilački pokret* (People's Liberation Movement)
NOR	*Narodnooslobodilački rat* (People's Liberation War)
NOVJ	*Narodnooslobodilačka vojska Jugoslavije* (People's Liberation Army of Yugoslavia)
NOVJD	NOVJ Division
NOVJC	NOVJ Corps
NKOJ	*Nacionalni komitet oslobođenja Jugoslavije* (National Committee of Liberation of Yugoslavia)
NSKK	*Nationalsozialistisches Kraftfahrkorps* (National Socialist Motor Corps)
OBSO	*Oberbefehlshaber Südost* (Commander-in-Chief Southeast)
OF	*Osvobodilna fronta* (Liberation Front)
OG	Operational Group
OGD	Operational Group of Divisions
OHQ	Operational Headquarters
OK	*Okružni komitet* (District Committee)
OKH	*Oberkommando des Heeres* (Army High Command)
OKW	*Oberkommando der Wehrmacht* (Wehrmacht High Command)
OOB	Order of Battle
OPL	Operational Party Leadership
OSS	Office of Strategic Services
OZ	Operational Zone
OZNA	*Odjeljenje za zaštitu naroda* (Department for the Protection of the People)

PČ	*Patrolni čamac* (Patrol Boat)
PCI	*Partito Comunista Italiano* (Italian Communist Party)
PK	*Pokrajinski komitet* (Provincial Committee)
PNF	*Partito Nazionale Fascista* (National Fascist Party)
POS	*Pomorski obalni sektor* (Naval Coastal Sector)
POW	Prisoner of War
PPK	*Protiv pete kolone* (Anti-Fifth-Column)
PR	Police Regiment
PTS	*Poglavnikov tjelesni sdrug* (Poglavnik's Bodyguard Brigade)
PzAOK	*Panzer-Armee-Oberkommando* (Panzer Army)
PzC	Panzer Corps
PzD	Panzer Division
PzGD	Panzergrenadier Division
PzGR	Panzergrenadier Regiment
PzR	Panzer Regiment
QM	Quartermaster
RA	*Regia Aeronautica* (Royal Air Force)
RAF	Royal Air Force
RC	Reserve Corps
REGS	*Regio Esercito* General Staff
RD	Reserve Division
RFSS	*Reichsführer SS* (Reich Leader-SS)
R&R	Rest and Recuperation
POG	*Primorska operativna grupa* (Coastal Operational Group)
RC	Rifle Corps
RD	Rifle Division
RPB	Reserve Police Battalion
Rgt.	Regiment
RMT	Reserve Mountain Division
RMTR	Reserve Mountain Regiment
RSHA	*Reichssicherheitshauptamt* (Reich Main Security Office)
RSI	*Repubblica Sociale Italiana* (Italian Social Republic)
RSK	*Rusisches Schutzkorps* (Russian Protective Corps)
RSSC	Railway Security Staff Croatia
SD	*Sicherheitsdienst* (Security Service)
SDIR	Supplement to Daily Intelligence Report
SHQ	Supreme Headquarters
SFK	*Serbisches Freiwilligenkorps* (Serbian Volunteer Corps)
SIPO	*Sicherheitspolizei* (Security Police)
SKOJ	*Savez komunističke omladine Jugoslavije* (Union of Communist Youth of Yugoslavia)
SMD	South Morava Detachment
s.Qu	*Sichere Quelle* (Safe Source)
SR	Security Regiment
SSW	*Serbische Staatswache* (Serbian State Guard)

TB	Tank Brigade
UAB	Ustasha Active Brigade
UDB	*Uprava državne bezbednosti* (Directorate of State Security)
UF	Ukrainian Front
UV	*Ustaška vojnica* (Ustasha Militia)
USAAF	United States Army Air Force
VDV	*Vojska državne varnosti* (Army of State Security)
VMRO	*Вътрешна Македонска Революционна Организация* (Internal Macedonian Revolutionary Organization)
VOS	*Varnostno-obveščevalna služba* (Intelligence and Security Service)
WBSO	*Wehrmachtsbefehlshaber Südost* (Wehrmacht High Command Southeast)
WK	*Wehrkreis* (Military District)
ZAPOLI	*Zapovjedništvo operativnog područja Lika* (Lika Operational Area Command)

Spelling & Pronunciation

All names are given in the original spelling, except geographic names with standard Anglicizations, like Belgrade (instead of Beograd), Syrmia (instead of Srem/Srijem), or Munich (instead of München).

Pronunciation guide for non-standard letters

Letter	**Pronounced as**
C; c	tz in blitz
Č/Ć; č/ć	ch in chocolate
Dž/Đ; dž/đ	G in George
J; j	y in yes
LJ; lj	ly in will you
NJ; nj	ny in canyon
Š; š	sh in ship
Ž; ž	J in Jacques

Introduction

"We have spilled a sea of blood for the brotherhood and unity of our peoples" was the punchline of Josip Broz Tito's famous speech given on 7 May 1962 at Split, Croatia.[1] The line contains two references to the main pillars of collective identity in Federative People's (later Socialist Federative) Republic of Yugoslavia. "A sea of blood" is probably the most succinct and apt definition of "People's Liberation War/Struggle" (*Narodnooslobodilački rat/borba*, commonly abbreviated to NOR/NOB), as the Second World War was officially known during the Socialist period. The conflict fought on the Yugoslav territory was an incredibly complex and brutal affair. It was a war of liberation, but also an ideological, civil, and even religious war, which ultimately devoured over one million lives (ca. 6.5 percent of the pre-war population). Between one-fourth and one-fifth of the victims belonged to People's Liberation Movement (*Narodnooslobodilački pokret*, NOP), a massive, popular organization led by Tito and the Communists. The second reference was to "Brotherhood and Unity" (*bratstvo i jedinstvo*), a concept of equality and harmonious relations between the country's many ethnic and religious groups. Promulgated already before the war, it became the NOP's rallying cry and played a major role in the movement's success. As we know, the society that was (at least nominally) based on these elevated principles outlived its founder by a mere decade before relapsing into a terrible conflict. Yugoslavia is gone for good, but the impact of the war that took place on its territory roughly eighty years ago can very much be felt today.

Let us now take a brief look at the primary and secondary sources pertaining to the Second World War in Yugoslavia. The Partisans actually left a rather large paper trail behind, a remarkable fact considering the perils of underground resistance and guerrilla life. For example, the central archives of the highest NOP and Communist Party bodies in Slovenia fell into Italian hands on two occasions in 1941 and 1942. The papers belonging to the supreme command of the movement vanished during the retreat from Serbia in late 1941. On lower levels, losses could result from more prosaic reasons. The Kalnik Detachment's documents were at one point placed in metal milk containers for safekeeping and buried. As soon as the shooting stopped, someone dug them up, threw away the contents and used them for the original purpose. Nevertheless, by the early 1970s, the central Yugoslav military archival repository alone managed to amass over 219 meters of documents of Partisan provenance.[2] A large part of these was published in the

1 The relevant part of Tito's speech is available at https://www.youtube.com/watch?v=BKp0tlOEpso (accessed 5.11.2021).

2 *Dokumenti ljudske revolucije u Sloveniji* (Ljubljana: Inštitut za zgodovino delavskega gibanja/Arhiv Republike Slovenije, 1962-2012), Vol. I, p. 6 [hereafter *DLRS*/volume/page]; *Josip Broz Tito–Sabrana*

first four decades after the war (see below), and they will be consulted extensively throughout this book. As far as the German records are concerned, our most important sources include the microfilmed (and recently digitized) documents in the possession of the US National Archives and Records Administration (NARA). The problem is is that very few documents on divisional level and below are available for the period after 1943, corps level after mid-1944, and army group level in 1945. The gaps can be partially filled by the ULTRA decrypts from the UK's National Archives and the recently released "booty documents" from Russia's central military repository. The Archives of Armed Forces in Belgrade, Serbia, contain numerous statements given by captured German servicemen, which proved invaluable in reconstructing the final months of the war.

Being the single most important event in the history of the "second Yugoslavia", the NOR was made into the central theme of the domestic historiography. From 1952 to 1974, the central publishing house of Yugoslav People's Army published a total of about 500 monographs, 140 of which dealt with the NOR.[3] By the end of the Socialist era, the number of books, articles, brochures, and newspaper serials covering nearly every aspect of the war could be measured in thousands. Although there are tendencies to simply dismiss these works as "Communist propaganda", the truth is, as always, far more nuanced. First, ideological coloring was present right up until the demise of the state, and the researcher simply has to accept this fact and learn to properly read these works. The intensity of the coloring and self-censorship varied greatly depending on the period and individual authors, but, on the whole, it can be said that it gradually decreased over the years. At the same time, the overall level of historians' professionalism and quality of their work steadily improved. For example, the early unit monographs were little more than a collection of heavily embellished wartime anecdotes; the later books, on the contrary, were largely written according to the established academic practices. Some sensitive topics, such as war crimes or Tito's role as supreme commander, never received proper (re-)evaluation. The bottom line is: if the focus of one's research lies on classic military history, then Yugoslav works are still a *sine qua non*. They can be considered reliable in terms of "technical" data, such as troop movements, dates, and course of engagements. Consequently, they will be quoted extensively throughout this book. This refers in particular to the official account of the war, *Oslobodilački rat naroda Jugoslavije 1941-1945*, published in Belgrade between 1957 and 1965. Together with the somewhat younger *Pregled operacija na jugoslovenskom ratištu* by Mladenko Colić, they still represent the main source for reconstructing the course of operations in the field.

Perhaps the greatest contribution of Yugoslav historiography to the research of the Second World War lay in publication of primary sources. By far the most important and ambitious of these projects was *Zbornik dokumenata i podataka o narodnooslobodilačkom ratu naroda Jugoslavije* (Collection of Documents and Data on the People's Liberation War of Yugoslav Peoples). The collection–which "simply has to be seen to be believed" (George Lepre)–is made up of 15 volumes with 173 books, the first of which appeared in 1949 and the final one in 1986. It is divided along geographical (e.g. Operations in Macedonia, Operations in Croatia, etc.),

djela (Belgrade: Komunist, 1981-89), Vol. VIII, p. 273; Vladimir Kapun, "Međimurci na Kalniku", in *Sjeverozapadna Hrvatska u narodnooslobodilačkoj borbi i socijalističkoj revoluciji: zbornik* (Varaždin: zajednica općina, 1976), p. 552; *Vojna Enciklopedija* (Belgrade: Redakcija Vojne enciklopedije, 1970-76), Vol. X, p. 581.

3 Ibid.

thematic (e.g. Yugoslav Air Force During NOR), and national lines (e.g. Documents of German Reich, Documents of Horthy's Hungary, etc.). Content and technical-wise, the *Zbornik* followed Yugoslav trends. The early books contained the barest minimum of editorial polishing; later on, the footnotes and explanations became so extensive that they are almost as valuable as the documents themselves. Touchy subjects were dealt with in a variety of ways, usually by avoiding them altogether, or by simply replacing the individual "problematic" references with ellipsis. Luckily for us, the censors were not interested in purely military-operational matters, so these shortcomings will practically have no impact on the manuscript at hand. Apart from the *Zbornik*, other notable collections of documents include those dealing with the provinces of Dalmatia, Slavonia, and Northwestern Croatia (each with ten books), Collected Works of Josip Broz Tito (23 books dealing with the period October 1940-July 1945), and Documents of Central Organs of Communist Party of Yugoslavia–NOR and Revolution (also 23 books). Of the regional collections, the one on Dalmatia probably offers the most, with some of its books having up to 1,800 pages. Among else, they contain a large number of Axis documents of various provenance, which is crucial to the proper understanding of the war and occupation. The Tito collection represents a valuable addition to those volumes of the *Zbornik* dealing with the Partisan high command; the Party collection offers a detailed insight into the functioning of this organization, and therefore the entire People's Liberation Movement, during the war. A note on the reliability of Yugoslav documents: the rumors, widely circulated especially during the 1990s, according to which the Communist forged documents in order to support their narrative of the war have never been proved. As mentioned above, there were far more subtle ways of hiding embarrassing details. The fact that the genuine documents contained more than enough discriminating evidence against their domestic enemies made forging unnecessary.

The hopes that the demise of Socialism in the early 1990s would lead to an open discussion on the Second World War in Yugoslavia were quickly dashed. The "Communist" narrative was, to a large part, simply replaced by by a new narrative based on the now-dominant right-wing politics and the closely related revisionism. The research of the topic was further compounded by the general drop in academic standards caused by the Yugoslav Wars and Transition. Moreover, there was an understandable tendency among historians to explore new, previously neglected topics and escape from Thucydides' extended "tower of political history".[4] As a result, the study of the military side of the conflict was very much relegated to the sidelines. An article or a monograph would appear from time to time, throwing new light on a particular episode or an aspect of the war; no attempts were made to write an updated, general history of the conflict.

As far as the literature in English and German is concerned, the situation is as follows. In the Anglo-Saxon world, the authors have traditionally given more attention to the political side of the conflict. This refers primarily to the relations between Great Britain and various Yugoslav factions, as well as the activities of intelligence services, Western Allied aid program, etc. Regarding operational matters, only naval and air activities over Yugoslavia received a limited coverage. An overview of military operations in the Balkans published by the US Army in 1954 is so flawed, that it probably did more harm than good. In recent decades, Ben Shepherd made a valuable contribution to our understanding of the functioning of the Wehrmacht's counterinsurgency

4 John H. Arnold, *History: A Very Short Introduction* (Oxford: Oxford University Press [hereafter OUP], 2000), p. 34.

(COIN) practices on the ground. Jozo Tomasevich's volumes on the Serbian royalists and Axis occupation of the country are simply unavoidable, although they contain comparatively little information on purely military matters. The armed forces of the Croat puppet state have not yet been the subject of a full-length academic monograph in English; this unfortunate gap is partially filled by Henry L. deZeng IV's series of excellent articles hosted on the "Axis History" website. Of the works published in German, especially relevant are the monographs on several army and Waffen-SS divisions that fought in Yugoslavia, largely authored by their former members. The study of the topic received a major boost with the publication of Klaus Schmider's *Partisanenkrieg in Jugoslawien* at the beginning of the 2000s. The book, an instant classic, represents an overview of the "guerrilla phase" of the war from the Axis perspective with an accent on strategic-operational issues. A few general observations on the non-Yugoslav literature. On the upside, authors were not bound by unwritten rules of conduct as in Yugoslavia, and were free to draw their own conclusions and present them in the manner they saw fit. As such, their works are very useful in pinpointing the potentially controversial episodes of the war. On the downside, older works are often heavily biased (especially if written by veterans) or reflect the Cold War tensions present at the time of their writing. Overall, the biggest shortcoming of foreign books and articles is the scant use of Yugoslav sources; it was caused, in part, by the language barrier and difficulties in gaining access to archival holdings. The Yugoslavs did little to entice foreign interest in their side of the story: only a handful of works dealing with the NOB, usually containing only general information and a few select documents, were translated into English and other world languages.

This volume will hopefully help fill some of the gaps mentioned above. It is conceived as the first academic overview of the Second World War in Yugoslavia written in English, and the first such work in any language since the end of the Socialist era. The "Sea of Blood" is unapologetically military-historical in nature, and for a good reason. The neglect of this branch of historiography has led to the paradoxical situation whereby detailed studies exist on gender and economic aspects, or on individual ethnic groups, yet no basic timeline of the conflict in the classical sense. In other words, a proper "frame" for all these valuable jigsaw pieces is missing. Building a clear picture of the military potential of the Partisan movement is crucial for understanding the Yugoslav policy of the great powers from this period. The average history enthusiast from the English-speaking world has probably heard of the Communist-led guerrillas in the Balkans, but not much more. Those with a modicum of knowledge on the region know that the arch-monarchist Winston Churchill decided to support Tito and his followers because they were the ones "who were killing the most Germans". The information on who precisely was doing the killing, when and where was the killing taking place, and how many were actually killed, has simply not been available until now. This unfortunate situation led to the impression that the Partisans were a semi-illegal group of conspirators who were propelled to power through backdoor scheming and only as a result of a deal between the Big Three. There can be no doubt that their ultimate triumph had to be approved by Moscow, London, and Washington, but the fact remains that the Partisans secured their status and foreign support through continuous four-year struggle and huge sacrifices made for the common cause.

The formation, development, and functioning of the NOP's armed branch, its operations and inner organization, will be the main topic of this book. The centerpiece of the old Yugoslav narrative of the war were the "Seven Offensives", major Axis attempts to destroy the bulk of the Partisan army and kill or capture Tito. Some very senior Partisan commanders have complained of the fact fairly early on that this simplistic construct had essentially hijacked the history of the war and obscured its immense complexity. "If the Germans had seven offensives, we had two thousand and seven", observed one of them[5], referring to the Partisans' doctrine of constant activity that ultimately proved to be the key ingredient of their success. This book will try to do justice to this fact by devoting as much space as possible to the events that took place in the "secondary" sectors and actions carried out by the NOP's provincial forces (i.e. those not directly subordinated to the movement's high command). Descriptions will vary in length: for example, more space will be devoted to the alleged collusion between the Partisans and Croatian fascists from March 1942 than to "Third Enemy Offensive", a relatively straightforward operation that has already been sufficiently explained elsewhere. Since Communist Party of Yugoslavia (*Komunistička partija Jugoslavije*, KPJ) was also waging a revolutionary war aimed at creating a socialist state, politics were inseparable from military matters, and will be mentioned as needed. The same goes for the NOP's relations with the outside world, since they had a huge impact on the movement's fortunes. War crimes are, unfortunately, an intrinsic part of the Yugoslav story, and can simply not be omitted, especially as they played an important role in insurgency and counter-insurgency strategies on both sides of the front. As this book is primarily conceived as a brief overview of the war in its entirety, considerable space will be devoted to the organization and tactics of the Partisans' many enemies. This refers primarily to the armies of the senior Axis partners (most notably the Germans, but also Italians, and, to a lesser extent, Bulgarians), but also to the most important domestic factions, such as the Serbian royalists and Croatian fascists.

The reader will note that this book makes frequent use of statistics. Although not a great fun to read, their presence is necessary for two reasons. First, numbers save words, which is very convenient when writing a single-volume project regardless of the topic. Second, numbers are necessary in order to convey the dynamic and intensity of the Yugoslav insurgency and understand what the killing from Churchill's quote actually meant. This book is not conceived as a reference work. The Axis launched literally hundreds of anti-guerrilla operations; providing a complete order-of-battle for each one of them would require, at the very least, one very thick volume. The same goes for the operations carried out by the Partisans. The fact is that units above battalion level rarely operated as single entities. All sides made extensive use of ad-hoc formations built for specific purpose from whatever men and weapons happened to be available at the time. As we are more interested in understanding the essence of the guerrilla warfare in Yugoslavia and internal mechanisms of opposing armies, precise designations of individual units (i.e. "X Battalion of the Y Regiment") will often be replaced by more general terms (i.e. "one battalion of the Z Division"); similarly, a task force composed of four battalions will often be referred to as "an equivalent of a reinforced regiment". The Germans, in particular, adhered to combined-arms approach and always added artillery and support services to their infantry; this fact will usually not be emphasized. Finally, a note on losses: the propensity to inflate enemy casualties and to cite these inflated figures in contemporary reports and books written later on is a trait common to soldiers and historians alike. It applied to both Partisan citizen-officers and Wehrmacht's professionals, to Yugoslav and non-Yugoslav authors in equal measure. In consequence, the notoriously unreliable claims concerning "enemy dead and wounded" will not

5 Peko Dapčević, "Završne operacije za oslobođenje Jugoslavije", in *Za pobjedu i slobodu. Završne operacije za oslobođenje Jugoslavije: učesnici govore* (Belgrade: Vojnoizdavački i novinski centar [hereafter VINC], 1986), pp. 95-96.

be included in the text. Instead, the carnage will be measured by quoting "own losses" and the much more tangible categories of prisoners and captured arms.

This book is divided into seven chapters; each of them is further divided into sub-chapters organized along temporal/geographical (e.g. "Winter Operations in Eastern Bosnia") and thematic lines (e.g. "Foča Reforms"). The first chapter covers the initial stage of the uprising that was ultimately cut short by the Axis autumn offensive in Serbia. Chapter two covers the first six months of 1942 and the change in Partisans' fortunes caused by both external pressure and their own errors. The central topic of the third chapter is the shift of the focal point of the war to the western parts of the Croatian puppet state (July-December 1942). Chapter four contains details on what is probably the most dramatic period of the war, marked by massive Axis offensives designed to destroy the main Partisan task force in Croatia, Bosnia-Herzegovina, and Montenegro (January-June 1943). The next, fifth, chapter covers the operations leading to, and following, the Italian surrender of September 1943. Chapter six deals with the Partisans' return to Serbia (March-September 1944) and their attempts to build a solid base there in expectation of the Red Army's arrival. Chapter seven covers the Soviet intervention in Yugoslavia, and the long and difficult voyage made by the increasingly regularized Partisan army towards the country's western borders (October 1944-May 1945). The "Closing Thoughts" brings the summary of the findings and also contains a brief discussion on the effectiveness of the Partisans' war efforts. Appendix one speaks of the human cost of the war with a special accent on military losses of the major belligerents, while Appendix two contains numerical data on the Soviet and Allied material aid to the NOP. Appendix three contains organizational charts of the Partisan army 1941-45.

Members of the NOP's armed branch will usually be referred to as "Partisans" or "fighters" (*borci*). "Guerrillas" or "insurgents" will also be used, but it should be noted that these terms can also apply to all armed rebels against the Axis in the early phase of the war regardless of their politics. The German military term *Jäger* will not be translated to "light infantry", as is sometimes done in the English-speaking world, but retained in the original. The term "Wehrmacht" originally referred to the German armed forces in their entirety, including the army, navy, and air force; unless stated otherwise, however, it will be used as a synonym for the ground component. Abbreviations will be used extensively throughout this book, especially in the footnotes. For example, "/Pol." will denote a report originating from the political section, "/QM" will denote quartermaster, "/Intel." intelligence, and so on. "Bde." will stand for brigade, "Btl." for battalion, "Coy." for company. All date and time information will be given in the following format: 8 May 1945, 0100 hours.

A note on footnotes: while writing the manuscript, I adhered rather rigidly to the principle one paragraph-one footnote. After going through it several times, I could not help but notice the presence of huge, unwieldy blocks of text. I therefore decided to break them up for the sake of better readability without disentangling the complex, massive footnotes that accompany them. As a result, a footnote will usually cover all the text between itself and the preceding footnote, regardless of whether it is one paragraph or more. I hope the readers - especially fellow historians - will forgive me for this slight, but necessary departure from the good practice of the trade.

Last but not the least, I would like to thank Miloš Bojanić, Goran Despotović, Dr. Federica Saini Fasanotti, Stefan Gužvica, George Lepre, Dr. Bisser Petrov, and Dr. Roberto Trajkovski for providing me with materials and technical assistance. A special thanks goes to Ivan Živančević, as well as Radovan Cukić (Museum of Yugoslavia, Belgrade), for their tireless efforts in the search for the best solution for the title cover. Needless to say, the author alone bears full responsibility for the possible errors and shortcomings of this work.

1

Uprising – Tide (July - December 1941)

1.1 Before Storm (April-June 1941)

At 2100 hours on 17 April 1941, in the damaged royal palace in Belgrade, representatives of High Command of the Kingdom of Yugoslavia's armed forces and European Axis powers signed the instrument of truce, thus bringing an end to the so-called "April War" after only twelve days of fighting. The signing effectively signaled the demise of the "First Yugoslavia" after only 23 years of existence. In 1918, the Kingdom of Montenegro and the former Austro-Hungarian provinces in the Balkans merged with Kingdom of Serbia to form Kingdom of Serbs, Croats, and Slovenes, a parliamentary monarchy under the Serbian Karađorđević dynasty. The new country had a surface of 247,542 km^2, and the richness of its landscape–including everything from frozen Alpine peaks in the northwest and fertile plains in the northeast to barren Dinaric Alps and primeval forests in the interior, and hot, Mediterranean coastline in the south–was matched only by its ethnic, religious, and cultural diversity. The main ethnic groups, whose members in theory enjoyed full civil rights, included Serbs, Croats, and Slovenes, as well as those deemed as such by the authorities like Montenegrins, Macedonians, and Muslims of Slavic origin. Combined, they made up only three-quarters of the population, which the estimates from 1941 put at 15,900,000 people. The remainder consisted of politically and socially largely disenfranchised minorities, including Albanians, Hungarians, Bulgarians, Romanians, Gypsies, Jews, Turks, and most notably, over half-a-million Ethnic Germans, the *Volksdeutsche.* Croats and Slovenes were overwhelmingly Catholic, Serbs were Orthodox, and there was a sizable Muslim population in Bosnia and Herzegovina, Sandžak, and Kosovo.

Throughout its brief existence, the kingdom was in a state of perpetual political crisis. The main point of contention between Croat and Serb political representatives was the issue of the state's internal organization, with the former pushing for more autonomy for their own part of the country, and the latter largely advocating a strong central government. In 1929, King Aleksandar I used the political instability as a pretext for abolishing political parties and instituting a personal dictatorship, coupled with the reforms aimed at creating a unitary state and a supra-ethnic Yugoslav identity. Although his death in Marseilles in 1934 at the hands of Croatian and Macedonian-Bulgarian ultra-nationalists paved the way for the return to parliamentary life in 1935 and for the creation of a semi-autonomous Croatian entity within Yugoslavia in 1939, political and ethnic tensions remained high. Constant political bickering, compounded by other problems such as widespread corruption and nepotism, did little to improve the country's economic base, which had been fragile from the start. Despite the increased pace of industrialization in the decade immediately preceding the war, the society remained overwhelmingly agrarian, with around three-quarters of the population living in the countryside. In 1931, there were only 25 urban centers with 20,000 or more inhabitants (Belgrade had close to 240,000; Zagreb 186,000; Subotica 100,000; Sarajevo 78,000; Skopje 68,000; Ljubljana 60,000). In terms of education and medical care the kingdom ranked among the worst in Europe: that same year, about 45 percent of the population was illiterate, and by 1939, the health insurance coverage amounted to only 7.5 percent. These deficiencies were particularly pronounced in the country's rugged interior, where rural communities continued with their traditional style of life, barely touched by the changes brought by the modern age.[1]

As an army represents a mirror image of the society from which it is drawn, the abysmal performance of the Yugoslav armed forces during the April War cannot come as a surprise. Even with the military spending hovering between one-fifth and one-fourth of an already strained budget, and despite frantic efforts to both boost domestic production of hardware and acquire arms from abroad in the late 1930s, the army remained ill-equipped to fight a modern war. For example, almost a half of altogether 7,000 artillery pieces were of obsolete type; the same goes for 265 out of 416 aircraft, and 60 out of 110 tanks. Nevertheless, the defeat can only partly be explained by shortages of equipment. Much more important was the total failure of the officer corps to rise to the occasion and provide clear military and political leadership. The higher ranks were dominated by veterans of the victorious Serbian army of 1914-18. Resting on its laurels, they thought the next conflict could be fought and won by repeating proven methods from the past. Consequently, Yugoslav plans called for a strategic retreat to Northern Greece in order to hook up with the Allies there, just as it had been the case in 1915-16. Apparently, little thought was given to the fact that the Axis were now in a much better position to cut off the retreat thanks to the availability of strong mechanized forces. Moreover, the royal Yugoslav Army was an ethnically mixed force. The reliability of non-Serb formations could not always be guaranteed, as witnessed by several instances of armed mutiny by Croatian recruits. Even Serbs turned out to be much less motivated to fight and die than their forefathers amidst the total confusion and lack of leadership from above caused by the sudden fury of the Axis onslaught. Yet the greatest flaw in the Yugoslav planning was the decision to deploy 27 out of altogether 31 infantry divisions (sing. ID) to the country's 3,000 km-long border. Motivated by internal political considerations and reasons of prestige, this move had stretched the army to breaking point and effectively made the creation of in-depth defenses impossible. Finally, both the senior echelons of the officer corps and the kingdom's political elites lost all credibility with the people, first by allowing the country to be drawn into the Tripartite Pact (25 March 1941), and then by launching a pro-Allied *coup d'état* two days later without having a clear and cohesive foreign

1 Branko Petranović, *Istorija Jugoslavije 1918-1988* (Belgrade: Nolit, 1988), Vol. I, pp. 64-65, 67-68, 70, 74, 324. For general information on Kingdom of Yugoslavia see John R. Lampe, *Yugoslavia as History: Twice there was a country* (Cambridge, UK: Cambridge University Press [hereinafter: CUP], 2000), pp. 101-200, and Sabrina P. Ramet, *The Three Yugoslavias: State-Building and Legitimation, 1918—2005* (Bloomington, IN: Indiana University Press, 2006), pp. 35-77, 79-111.

Map 1: Axis Partition of Yugoslavia.

policy strategy for the future. On 14-15 April, the 18-year-old King Peter I, accompanied by the government, left the country, as it turned out, for good.[2]

The German dictator felt personally insulted by Yugoslavia's sudden change of heart and became determined not only to punish the Balkan upstart, but to wipe it off the political map of Europe. Once the operations in the field had been concluded, diplomats in Berlin, Rome, Budapest, and Sofia set about translating the wishes of their respective masters into reality. The result was a veritable farrago of annexed territories, occupation zones, protectorates, condominiums, and spheres of influence, fittingly called "Hitler's New Disorder" by Steven K. Pavlowitch.

German territorial claims were limited to Slovenia proper, where ancient Habsburg lands of Upper Carniola (German: Oberkrain; Slovene: Gorenjska), Lower Styria (Untersteiermark/Štajerska), as well as parts of Lower Carniola (Unterkrain/Dolenjska) and Prekmurje, were placed under the Nazi governors of the neighboring Austrian provinces of Carinthia and Styria. Although these Slovene territories would never be formally annexed, for all practical purposes they became a part of the Third Reich. The Nazis immediately started a wide-reaching Germanization program, which included the planned expulsion of up to 260,000 Slovenes to Germany and other parts of Yugoslavia. Although the scheme would soon be scraped due to technical difficulties and constantly deteriorating situation in the entire region, it is estimated that some 80,000 people were forced to leave their homes. Needless to say, such heavy-handed denationalization polices helped turn Slovenia into a favorable breeding ground for resistance movements. In military-administrative respect, the country came under the auspices of XVIII Military District in Salzburg (*Wehrkreis XVIII*, WK), but the army would remain in the background during the initial phase of the occupation. Security tasks during this period would largely be carried out by the gendarmerie and police, whose members made up the majority of the estimated 13,600 armed personnel deployed in the country in the early summer of 1941.[3]

In terms of geopolitical and economic importance, the title of "crown jewel" of the German-dominated Western Balkans undoubtedly belonged to Serbia. Cut back to the borders predating the First Balkans War of 1912, the country was placed under the direct rule of the Wehrmacht. The army had a threefold task: keeping in check the unruly population, known for its guerrilla heritage and strong patriotic/nationalist feelings; securing the uninterrupted flow of traffic on the Danube and along the Serbian part of the all-important railway line linking Germany's southern border with Greece; enabling the exploitation of the country's substantial ore deposits and other economic assets.[4] In order to facilitate the administration of the country, the Germans formed the Serbian Commissary Government, and allowed it a force of close to 2,000 gendarmes.

2 Velimir Terzić, *Slom Kraljevine Jugoslavije 1941: uzroci i posledice poraza* (Belgrade: Narodna knjiga, 1982), Vol. II, pp. 122, 124, 129, 137-8, 143-5, 163, 170; Milan Miljkić, "12 dana otpora", *Odbrana*, Special Issue No. 166 (1.4.2017), pp. 1-32.

3 Zdravko Klanjšček, *Narodnooslobodilački rat u Sloveniji 1941-1945* (Belgrade: Vojnoistorijski institut [hereinafter: VII], 1984), pp. 34-35.

4 The Germans made sure that the new borders were drawn in a way that suited their economic interests: Northern Kosovo, with its vast Trepča mines, was not a part of the Italian zone like the remainder of the province, but came under the auspices of the German occupation apparatus in Serbia proper. Where border-tampering was not possible (e.g. in Macedonia, and in Herzegovina), the Germans were granted special exploitation rights.

Map 2: Occupied Eastern Yugoslavia.

The province of Banat was turned over to the local Ethnic German community, together with the right to form village militias and their own police battalions.[5]

Commanding Officer in Serbia (*Befehlshaber Serbien*, BhS)[6] stood at the apex of the entire occupation apparatus, including all its civilian, military, paramilitary, and security branches. The responsibility for day-to-day army operations rested with LXV Higher Command for Special Purposes *(Höheres Kommando zur besonderen Verwendung LXV*, HKdo LXV), corps-level formation with three infantry divisions (the 704th, 714th, and 717th IDs). In addition, each of the four area administrative commands (*Feldkommandatur*, FK) had one territorial defense battalion (*Landesschützen-Bataillon*, LSB) attached to it; they were used for guarding important objects, such as POW camps, bridges, and factories. All these units were of low quality and were of limited value even for purely defensive tasks. The divisions were raised as security, rather than front-line formations, a part of the so-called "15th Mobilization Wave" They had only two instead of usual three infantry regiments, and only rudimentary support services, so that their strength amounted to barely 6,000 men apiece. To make matters worse, these men were largely poorly trained reservists who were well past their military prime (most of them were born between 1907 and 1913). The soldiers belonging to the LSBs were older still, and thus even less suitable for active duty; one report read that they become utterly exhausted or footsore after marching only 10 km. The strength of the Wehrmacht contingent in late August 1941 is estimated at some 22,500 effectives.[7]

The remaining 8,600 or so German troops present in the region[8] were deployed in Independent State of Croatia (*Nezavisna država Hrvatska*, NDH), which encompassed the territory of today's Croatia, Bosnia and Herzegovina, and parts of Serbia (the province of Syrmia). The NDH was proclaimed on 10 April 1941 in Zagreb by erstwhile émigrés, members of the ultra-nationalist organization "Ustasha" (plural: Ustashe; literary meaning "the insurgent") which stood behind the already mentioned assassination of the Yugoslav king Aleksandar I. Despite originally being protégés of Rome, and having even accepted an Italian prince as their future king, by the end

5 Milan Borković, *Kvislinška uprava u Srbiji 1941-1944* (Belgrade: Sloboda, 1979), Vol. I, p. 42; Mirna Zakić, *Ethnic Germans and National-Socialism in Yugoslavia in World War II* (Cambridge, UK: CUP, 2017), pp. 145-48.

6 The title and responsibilities of this office changed several times until March 1942, when it was finally decided to concentrate all power in the person of Commanding General and Commanding Officer in Serbia (*Kommandierender General und Befehlshaber Serbien*). For clarity's sake, the abbreviation "BhS" will be used for the entire period up to summer 1943; see Klaus Schmider, *Partisanenkrieg in Jugoslawien 1941-1944* (Hamburg: E. S. Mittler & Sohn, 2002), pp. 581-83. The Serbian command was answerable to Wehrmacht High Command Southeast (the HQ of the 12th Army) [*Wehrmachtsbefehlshaber*, WBSO/AOK 12] in Thessaloniki.

7 Ibid, pp. 32-33, 586; United States National Archives and Records Administration, College Park, Maryland; Record Group 242, Microfilm Series T-315, Roll 2262, frame 67, 717th ID to XI Army Corps [AC] (27.5.1941)[hereinafter: NARA/microfilm series/roll/frame (if available), document title; if no original title is available, a provisional one will be provided in square brackets]; NARA/T315/2258/1426, History of 714th ID (undated); NARA/T315/1242, 104th *Jäger* Division [JD], Bandit Fighting in Central Sector (29.4.1943).

8 The 718th ID plus smaller attached units, all under the command of HKdo LXV: NARA/T501/251, Quartermaster [QM]/BhS, Appendix 11 to War Diary (August 1941). The Wehrmacht had its own representative with the NDH government, German General in Zagreb (*Deutscher General in Agram*, DGA). As was frequently the case with German agencies, this one would also change its name several times; for the sake of clarity, the abbreviation "DGA" will be used throughout this work.

of the year the Ustashe had completely drifted into the German sphere of influence. Their fiefdom stood on shaky legs from the very start: Italy annexed parts of Dalmatia and kept a large troop contingent in its occupation zone (at the NDH's expense), which stretched from the coast to the gates of Zagreb and Sarajevo. Unlike the Italians, the Germans had no territorial claims, but were very interested in the Herzegovinian bauxite ore, industrial products, and the railway line Zagreb–Belgrade. Furthermore, the NDH agreed to provide laborers for German factories and volunteers for the Eastern Front. Although heavy, these burdens were not life-threatening to the new state; Ustashe domestic policies, ironically, were. Bent on creating an ethnically homogeneous society, they would launch a war of annihilation against the Serbs, who constituted a full third of the country's population. This was one of the defining moments in the history of the Second World War in the Balkans, as it would transform the quiet backwater of the occupied Europe into a hotbed of guerrilla activity and an insoluble problem for the Axis.

The NDH was totally unprepared for waging any kind of counterinsurgency (COIN) campaign. By the beginning of summer, the regular army, Croatian Home Guard (*Hrvatsko domobranstvo*, HDB), had altogether five divisional commands and a host of smaller units, the total strength of which did not exceed ca. 44,000 men. Although basic needs in arms and equipment were covered from captured Yugoslav stocks[9], the HDB was short on virtually everything else, especially competent officers and motivated rank-and-file. The regime in Zagreb could also count on Ustasha Militia (*Ustaška vojnica*, UV), a Blackshirt-like party armed force created around a small number of original Ustasha émigrés; by late 1941, the UV had 10-15,000 volunteer members, and a privileged access to state funds. Last but not the least, the Gendarmerie (*Oružništvo*) had some 6,000 members spread across the breadth and width of the country in spring of 1941.[10]

Fascist Italy was bountifully rewarded for its partaking in the demise of the South Slav kingdom that once was the main barrier to Rome's expansionist plans in the region. The Italian "fifth shore" (*quinta sponda*), which had consisted of Albania before the war, now encompassed almost the entire Yugoslav coastline, and more. In the north, Italy annexed the remaining part of Slovenia (Inner, and the best part of Lower Carniola/Notranjska and Dolenjska) and named it Ljubljana Province. Rome's sphere of influence in the NDH was divided into three zones. Zone I (Northern Dalmatia, and some islands in Croatian Littoral and in Southern Dalmatia) was directly annexed. In Zone II, which stretched up to 70 km inland from the coast, the NDH was forbidden from maintaining any military installations; it is therefore usually referred to as "Demilitarized Zone". From there to the demarcation line with the Germans there was an additional belt of territory, named Zone III. In military respect, this entire area came under the jurisdiction of the Italian 2nd Army (2nd ITA), a force whose size dwarfed all other armies in the Balkans: on 1 August 1941 it had close to 230,000 soldiers. Its operational arm was divided into

9 By 1 December 1941, the Germans had, among else, captured: 448,000 rifles and carbines; 14,600 machine guns (MGs); 242 mortars; 1,999 cannon; 78 tanks. For the complete list see *Zbornik*/XII/1/756-59, 5th Military-Technical Staff to BhS (13.12.1941).

10 Jozo Tomasevich, *War and Revolution in Yugoslavia, 1941-1945: Occupation and Collaboration* (Stanford, CA: Stanford University Press, 2001), pp. 420-21, 424-27; for a general history of the NDH see ibid., pp. 233-510; Bogdan Krizman, *Pavelić između Hitlera i Musolinija* (Zagreb: Globus, 1980), p. 236; Schmider, *Partisanenkrieg*, p. 588; Terzić, *Slom*, pp. 576-7; H.L. deZeng IV, "Introduction to the Croatian Gendarmerie", http://www.axishistory.com/axis-nations/croatia/379-croatia-ustasha/croatia-ustasha-units/8198-introduction-to-the-croatian-gendarmerie (accessed 16.3.2018).

three army corps: the XI (the 21st ID "Granatieri di Sardegna" and 14th "Isonzo") was deployed in Slovenia; the V (the 57th "Lombardia", 13th "Re") in northwestern Croatia; the VI (the 15th "Bergamo", 12th "Sassari", 32nd "Marche") in Dalmatia and its hinterland. Furthermore, the "Celere" Corps, with a seat in Istria, had one of its divisions (the 1st Fast Division "Eugenio di Savoia") deployed southwest of the NDH's capital. Italy was also granted possession of Montenegro, and had Kosovo and western parts of Macedonia annexed to its Greater Albanian protectorate. These territories were occupied by the units of the 9th Army (headquartered in Tirana): the XVII AC's 18th ID "Messina" was deployed in the former, and the XIV AC's two divisions (the 38th "Puglie", and 41st "Firenze") in the latter. According to Yugoslav estimates, these forces numbered some 41,000 Italians and 5,000 Albanian auxiliaries.[11]

For junior Axis partners, campaign against Yugoslavia was all about settling old scores with Serbia. Bulgaria fought its western neighbor four times in less than 60 years. The main prize, Vardar Macedonia, which had been won and lost in the wars of 1912-13 and 1915-18, was now seemingly firmly in Bulgarian hands. The province was first occupied by the Bulgarian 5th Army in mid-April 1941 and then formally annexed. Although front-line divisions were soon replaced by lower-quality garrison units (the 14th and 15th IDs, and the 1st Cavalry Brigade [CB]), the authorities were confident that pro-Yugoslav sentiments of the local population could be kept in check by a strong and well-articulated police force consisting of 4,000 men. The Bulgarians also annexed the extreme southeastern corner of Serbia (the area around Vranje and Pirot) and secured it by parts of the 1st and 14th IDs.[12]

Despite having publicly pledged to uphold "perpetual peace and eternal friendship" with the Yugoslav Kingdom in December 1940, Horthy's Hungary readily availed herself of the opportunity to reclaim the territories lost to its southern neighbor in the aftermath of the First World War. By mid-April 1941, the Hungarian V AC had occupied the province of Bačka with the force of three infantry (the 13th-15th) and one cavalry (the 2nd) brigades. Croatian provinces north of the Drava (Baranja and Međimurje) were likewise occupied by two battalions each from the IV and III AC, respectively. The list of new Hungarian possessions was complete with the acquisition of Prekmurje, part of Slovenia located on the left bank of the Mura/Mur River. After first going through a phase of military, and than a phase of civilian rule, all these lands were formally annexed by early 1942.[13]

Reactions to the occupation differed. The majority of Croats welcomed the creation of their own state, but the honeymoon with the new regime would turn out to be very short. Some minorities, like the Albanians, who had been treated as second-class citizens in Yugoslavia, were now given preferential treatment by the occupier and were therefore content with the new scheme of things. The Serbs (and other Yugoslav-oriented citizens), who had lost the most, had the best reason to contemplate resistance. The fact was, however, that the recent disaster had come so swiftly, and was so complete, that the whole nation had found itself virtually paralyzed.

11 *Oslobodilački rat naroda Jugoslavije* (Belgrade: Vojnoizdavački zavod [hereinafter: VIZ], 1957-65), Vol. I, pp. 30-34, 49-50; Terzić, *Slom*, pp. 585, 597; Schmider, *Partisanenkrieg*, p. 587.

12 Boro Mitrovski, Venceslav Glišić, Tomo Ristovski, *Bugarska vojska u Jugoslaviji 1941-1945.* (Belgrade: Međunarodna politika, 1971), pp. 24-29; Živojin Nikolić-Brka, *Jugoistočna Srbija u Narodnooslobodilačkom ratu i revoluciji, 1941-1945* (Belgrade: Narodna knjiga, 1979), pp. 19, 43.

13 "Tekst ugovora o prijateljstvu između Kraljevine Jugoslavije i Kraljevine Mađarske", *Politika*, 13.12.1940; Terzić, *Slom*, p. 599; Tomasevich, *Occupation*, pp. 169-70.

With the king and the government in exile, the bulk of their trained menfolk taken to POW camps in Germany and Italy, the remaining officers in hiding, and prewar elites (priests, politicians, gendarmes, etc.) scattered, the prospects of a successful struggle against the invader looked bleak. To be sure, armed incidents began occurring throughout the land practically as soon as the war was over. Most of these were caused by small bands of Yugoslav soldiers who managed to avoid capture, or gangs of highwaymen, the existence of which "was nothing new in the Balkans"[14]. Some incidents were quite serious and ominous of what was yet to come. On 21 April 1941, the village of Dobrić in Western Serbia was torched after a routine search had gone awry, whereby one German serviceman was killed and two were injured. A couple of weeks later, inhabitants of several Serb villages in the vicinity of Sanski Most in Western Bosnia chased away a group of Ustashe who tried to confiscate their weapons, wounding several of them in the process. The NDH authorities then asked the German 132nd ID for help, which subsequently dispatched a battalion-sized battle group to the scene. In a firefight that lasted about two hours, and which involved the use of artillery, the rebels were forced to surrender. As a reprisal for the wounding of three of its soldiers, the division shot and hanged 27 hostages.[15]

All of these incidents were highly localized affairs, a spontaneous reaction rather than a premeditated action against the "new disorder". There was only one organization left which survived the war intact and was being capable of conducting organized resistance in the entire country. The KPJ had been founded in 1919 and went to become the fourth-strongest party in the parliament after the elections of 1920. Fearing its rising influence and increasingly radical program, the royal authorities used the Communist-instigated strikes as a pretext to place the Party outside the law that very same year. In reaction, two young Communists assassinated the interior minister, an event which started an all-out war against the KPJ. For the next 15 or so years, the Party struggled to survive, as membership plummeted, its leaders being exiled, jailed, or even ending up dead in police custody. Worst of all, the Party was riven with factionalism and internal discord. By mid-1930s Moscow was seriously contemplating abolishing it altogether. At the same time, the vast majority of Yugoslav Communists living in the USSR perished in the Stalinist purges. When the dust settled, the KPJ had a new leadership. Already in 1937, the 45-year-old Croat-Slovene metal worker and professional revolutionary named Josip Broz (known in Comintern circles as "Walter", and soon to be known as "Tito" to everyone else) managed to get himself appointed organizational secretary. By the time he had become secretary-general in January 1939, he had largely succeeded in getting the Party back on its feet. Tito "bolshevized" the KPJ, rooted out factionalism, instilled discipline and rigid hierarchy, and achieved financial self-sufficiency.[16]

In matters of foreign policy, the KPJ–and this is not readily discernible from historiography of the Socialist era–closely toed whichever line the Comintern chose to pursue at any given moment. The Party was advocating the dismemberment of Kingdom of Yugoslavia, the "dungeon of peoples" as it was called, prior to the introduction of "Popular Front" concept in 1935. It was at this time that the KPJ embraced the idea of a united South Slav state, and began

14 NARA/T315/2236/507-08, 60th Motorized Division, Situation Report (17.5.1941).

15 NARA/T501/245/117-30, BhS, Incidents (entries April-July 1941); Dušan Lukač, *Ustanak u Bosanskoj Krajini* (Belgrade: VIZ, 1969), pp. 61-62.

16 Ivo Banac, *With Stalin against Tito: Cominformist Splits in Yugoslav Communism* (Ithaca, NY: Cornell University Press, 1988), pp. 50-51, 61, 67-69.

advocating partnership with other political parties in order to stem the ever-growing tide of fascism. The signing of the Molotov-Ribbentrop Pact in August 1939 brought about a shocking U-turn in the Soviet foreign policy. Dumbfounded but disciplined, the Yugoslavs dutifully began referring to the new European conflict as "imperialist war" between two equally bad sides, and stepped up their propaganda calling for the maintenance of neutrality and an alliance with the USSR. On 27 March 1941, the Communists joined the spontaneous outpouring of anti-Axis sentiment in the aftermath of the military coup. Tito cabled to Moscow, among else, that the Party was demanding the annulment of the Tripartite Pact, and that it was "organizing nation-wide resistance to a German-Italian invasion of Yugoslavia and to England's attempts to draw Yugoslavia into the war on its side". Entirely in line with the Soviet policy at the time, the Comintern responded by cautioning Tito and the Central Committee (*Centralni komitet*, CK) not to "give way to momentary inclinations" and let themselves be "carried away by sensational and outwardly effective actions". Their job, so the secretary-general of the Comintern, Georgi Dimitrov, was to conserve cadres, and quietly, but resolutely, continue bolstering the Party influence in the army and among the masses.[17]

The only remaining way for the KPJ to do that during the April War was to have its members join the army. On 10 April 1941, the CK concluded that, in the likely case of defeat, the Party should basically remain on war footing. Tito himself was made the head of the newly formed Military Commission (later renamed Military Committee), and he called upon the soldiers to hide or retain their weapons for future use. On the 15th, the CK issued a fiery proclamation in which it blamed the bourgeoisie for the country's predicament and appealed to the population with a mix of patriotic and class slogans not to reconcile themselves with the present situation (meaning the occupation, and the creation of the NDH). Some three weeks later, each one of the KPJ's provincial leaderships was ordered to form its own military committee with the task of preparing the membership for war. Throughout May and June, Tito was reporting on dangerous, yet favorable working conditions in the country, of the Party's undiminished functionality and its increased prestige, and on widespread disaffection with the current state of affairs. This, however, did not mean that the Yugoslav Communists were willing to step out of line and compromise Josif V. Stalin's delicate policy of not provoking Adolf Hitler. Stretched between patriotic sentiments and the "internationalist duty", the Communists chose the latter: on 13 May, Tito informed Moscow that the Party was organizing combat detachments, educating military cadres, and preparing an armed uprising "in the case of an attack on the USSR".[18]

Although never explicitly described as such by Yugoslav historiography, the relations between the Communists and occupation authorities during the entire *interregnum* period were of icy, but neutral nature. According to one German police report from Banat, the Communists avoided attacking the Wehrmacht or engaging in sabotage activity. Likewise, gendarmerie in Štajerska noted that even the large workers' community in the local mines had been "absolutely

17 Miroljub Vasić, "Komunistička internacionala i KPJ (1929-1941)", *Istorija dvadesetog veka* [hereinafter: IDV], 11:1-2 (1993), pp. 147-54; *The Diary of Georgi Dimitrov*, 1933-1949 (London: Yale University Press, 2003), pp. 152-54 ([entries for] 28-9.3.1941).

18 Geoffrey Swain, *Tito: A Political Biography* (New York: I. B. Tauris, 2010), p. 30; Branko Petranović, Momčilo Zečević, (eds.), *Jugoslavija 1918.-1988: tematska zbirka dokumenata* (Belgrade: Rad, 1988), pp. 490-92, "Peoples of Yugoslavia!" (15.4.1941); Miroljub Vasić, "Ustanak u Jugoslaviji 1941. godine i Kominterna", *IDV*, 14:2 (1996), pp. 146-47.

loyal and made no public displays of hostility". In Serbia, German security apparatus monitored Communist activities, but made no effort, say, to re-arrest the Party members and sympathizers who had been freed after 27 March by the new Yugoslav government. Even if they had wanted to, this task would be almost impossible to complete, for the same government had also made another concession to the KPJ by ordering the destruction of the Communist card index belonging to the Belgrade police. NDH authorities retained in jail those Communists "inherited" from the royal police but refrained from making mass arrests of their own. In this respect, the detention of seven members of the KPJ in Travnik, Central Bosnia, on 30 April was an exception, rather than a rule.[19]

When the news of the commencement of Operation "Barbarossa" was announced on the morning of 22 June 1941, both sides were probably relieved that the charade was over; the long-awaited showdown had finally arrived. On the same day, the Germans and collaborationists began rounding up all known Communists, and the CK KPJ issued a proclamation calling for unity among workers, citizens, and peasants of Yugoslavia in the upcoming battle against fascism. After receiving Comintern's call to arms (it took four days to smuggle the cable from Zagreb, the seat of the Comintern's clandestine wireless station, to Belgrade, where secretary-general and his entourage were at the moment), Tito cabled back on the 27th that the Party was preparing a "people's uprising", asking for a green light from Moscow. A reply from "Grandpa" (nickname for the Comintern HQ), dated 1 July, authorized a full-blown guerrilla war behind Axis lines, demanding that the enemy should feel like "in a besieged fortress". On a meeting of the Politburo on 4 July 1941–held presumably as soon as the authorization arrived–it was decided to commence with armed operations immediately. The date signaled the beginning of "People's Liberation War" and would be celebrated for the next half-a-century as "The Fighter's Day" (*Dan borca*).[20]

The magnitude of the task standing before the KPJ was immense. Compared to the multitude of foes, whose combined strength went into hundreds of thousands, the Party's initial manpower potential was minuscule: anywhere between 8 and 12,000 card-carrying members (not certain if the latter figure included the candidates for full membership), and between 30 and 50,000 members of the Communist youth organization (*Savez komunističke omladine Jugoslavije*, SKOJ). The future guerrillas enjoyed several advantages, however. First, the insurgency would be waged across occupied Yugoslavia, regardless of the new borders drawn in the aftermath of the April War. This meant that Tito had all the prerogatives of a theater commander, including the ability to exercise full authority and synchronize actions on a truly strategic level; this was more than any of his Axis counterparts could boast of. Second, the membership of the above-mentioned organizations was, for the most part, well-versed in techniques of underground work. The ability to move stealthily, or communicate in secrecy, which had been practiced for decades in peacetime, could now be put to use in order to build and operate a clandestine army. For all

19 *Zbornik*/I/17/28, Report of police prefecture Veliki Bečkerek (15.1.1942); *Zbornik*/VI/1/270, Gendarmerie Trbovlje, Report (15.7.1941); Directorate of State Security [*Uprava državne bezbednosti*, UDB] for Serbia, Interrogation of Božidar Bećarević, p. 12 (8.6.1949). Original in Historical Archives of Belgrade [hereinafter: IAB], copy in the possession of the author; Ćamil Kazazović, *Travnik u Narodnooslobodilačkom ratu* (Zenica: Naša riječ, 1969), Vol. I, pp. 45-49; Marko Attila Hoare, *The Bosnian Muslims in the Second World War: a History* (London: Hurst & Company, 2013), p. 69.

20 Swain, *Tito*, pp. 33-34; Vasić, *Ustanak*, pp. 148-49.

those who had not served in the regular army, the Party organized short courses, usually led by the more experienced members, but also by individual NCOs and officers of the royal army. Third, the Communists would not go in entirely unarmed. The German efforts at disarming the population and securing the weapons belonging to the former Yugoslav army were haphazard, at best. This was largely due to the precipitous withdrawal of the original, numerically strong occupation contingent in preparation for the attack on the USSR, but also due to plain carelessness and overconfidence. In a much-related anecdote from April 1941, a German NCO overtakes the baggage train of a Yugoslav artillery battalion, orders it to surrender in the nearest town, and then drives away without even having disarmed the Yugoslav officer present; as soon as the German drove off, the officer simply disbanded his unit, each man leaving the field fully equipped. The weapons-gathering program, launched by the KPJ while the war still lasted, managed to secure almost 23,000 rifles, close to 1,500 pistols, 550 MGs, over 3,000,000 rounds of small-arms ammunition, and even five pieces of artillery.[21]

Owing to his position of secretary-general, but also to great personal charisma, Tito commanded unquestionable loyalty from his subordinates. Establishing the true extent of his military talents, on the other hand, is a difficult job. His heavily embellished war record remained untouchable almost until the end of the Socialist era. In the tide of revisionism that swept the region in the 1990s and thereafter, Tito is usually represented as being little more than a political schemer. His soldierly skills are often dismissed with an anecdote from 1941, related by his close companion and a later dissident Milovan Đilas, according to which the supreme commander had difficulty reading a map. Tito was no stranger to war: he served as a decorated NCO in the Austro-Hungarian army, first on the Serbian, and then on the Eastern Front before being captured by the Russians in 1915. Koča Popović, one of the premier soldiers of the war who later parted ways with Tito over Yugoslavia's inner politics, called his erstwhile superior "a true *condotierre*", who had "all the makings of an authentic leader", adding that "no one would have performed better in the top-tier position". In addition to his organizational skills and an eye for competence, his greatest talent lay in the realm of grand strategy: there was hardly a war-winning decision that he did not either instigate or approve. Đilas confirms this in his memoirs, and also adds that Tito performed his duties with vigilance and industry despite inadequate knowledge "and rashness". The latter, combined with his short temper, made him less than ideal in the role of field commander, and had very nearly ruined the army on several occasions. He usually gave faraway headquarters great latitude in implementation of the Party line but would not hesitate to take direct control over units in his immediate vicinity, often disrupting the already existing chains of command. Later in the war, as technical conditions improved, Tito would try to micromanage day-to-day operations of entire armies by wireless, with predictably adverse consequences.[22]

As far as the other CK members were concerned, Đilas wrote that only one (Sreten Žujović-Crni) had penchant for military affairs; others were and remained primarily "political workers", although with time "all learned something about warfare". The few people who did possess

21 Nikola Anić, Sekula Joksimović, Mirko Gutić, *Narodnooslobodilačka vojska Jugoslavije: pregled razvoja oružanih snaga Narodnooslobilačkog pokreta 1941.-1945.* (Belgrade: VII, 1982), pp. 12, 17-19; Aleksandar Nenadović, *Razgovori s Kočom* (Zagreb: Globus, 1989), pp. 34-36.

22 Milovan Djilas, *Wartime* (New York: Harcourt Brace Jovanovich, 1977), pp. 92, 183; Swain, *Tito*, p. 7; Nenadović, *Razgovori*, pp. 131-32.

either practical knowledge of the inner functioning of armed formations, or any recent combat experience, came from two groups. The first group consisted of a very small number of professionals from the royal army, mostly junior officers and NCOs, who decided to swim against the current and join the Communist-led guerrillas. The second group consisted of some 250 veterans of the Spanish Republican Army who succeeded in making the arduous journey back to Yugoslavia after Franco's victory through French detention camps and Third Reich itself. Among the "Spaniards" (*Španci*), as they were known, there were also those who had received military training in Moscow prior to being sent to the peninsula. The Iberian fighters would form the backbone of the command cadre of the insurgents' army, with no less than 30 of them becoming generals by the end of the war; 130 lost their lives. According to some outsiders, their overall contribution to the war effort had, indeed, been valuable, but not decisive. Very few of them had actually had any experience with guerrilla warfare, given that the war between the Nationalists and Loyalists was fought by and large in a regular manner. The "Spaniards" were also said to be dogmatic in the application of the tactics they learned overseas without taking into account specific set of circumstances they were now encountering in their homeland. Moreover, these veterans formed a closed clique, an elitist circle whose members were often favored over others on grounds of their pedigree alone. These "others" were soon to become the third and the most numerous group of guerrilla leaders; it consisted of grassroots KPJ members and local sympathizers, whose previously hidden martial qualities had now come to the fore.[23]

Their discipline and dedication (or fanaticism) notwithstanding, it would be wrong to imagine the KPJ and its affiliates as some sort of a warrior monk order, or a bunch of unwavering automatons. The Communist organization was made up of all kinds of people, each with hers/his own unique personality, life story, and particular set of strengths and weaknesses. In the course of time, some would become disillusioned by the war, lose faith in the old ideals, or even renege on them entirely. An untold number of Party members was interrogated and tortured by the Axis from 1941 to 1945. Unsurprisingly, many buckled under the tremendous strain and revealed everything they knew. In Banat, for instance, this happened even with two members of the provincial leadership. There were also those who went one step further and became active and willing collaborators, like one of the heads of the SKOJ in the same part of the country. He was first employed as agent-provocateur, and then openly as a police associate; as a reward for his many services, he was evacuated to Germany in late 1943. Sometimes, outside pressure was not needed at all. In early September 1941, a high-ranking member of the KPJ's branch from Belgrade's southern suburbs approached the Nazi Security Service (*Sicherheitsdienst*, SD) and offered cooperation; he feared for his safety after he had twice failed to carry out sabotage orders from above. This episode may have been connected with the devastating blow administered to the capital's underground organization later the same month by a captured member of the SKOJ's highest body. Apparently not even those who had fulfilled their "internationalist duty" were immune from treachery: one "Spaniard" who had returned to Dalmatia in early fall of 1941 was executed two years later as a Gestapo spy.[24]

23 Djilas, *Wartime*, p. 184; Anić, Joksimović, Gutić, *Narodnooslobodilačka*, p. 106; Vjeran Pavlaković, *Yugoslav Volunteers in the Spanish Civil War* (Belgrade: Rosa Luxemburg Stifung Southeast Europe, 2016), pp. 69-81, 89; Pavle Jakšić, *Nad uspomenama* (Belgrade: Rad, 1990), Vol. I, pp. 238-40.

24 Đorđe Momčilović, *Banat u Narodnooslobodilačkom ratu* (Belgrade: Vojnoizdavački zavod [hereinafter: VIZ], 1977), pp. 143-44, 187; *Nemačka obaveštajna služba* (Belgrade: Savezni sekretarijat unutrašnjih

1.2 "Urban Phase" of Uprising

Before moving on to the guerrilla campaign in the Serbian countryside, a few lines should be devoted to the earliest form of the KPJ's armed struggle, the "urban phase" of the uprising. Being ardent students of the history of the Bolshevik Party, but also of the Paris Commune, the Yugoslav Communists were certain that the decisive battles of the war against the occupier would be fought on the barricades in Belgrade and other towns and cities across the country. KPJ members also fervently hoped that these shots would signal the beginning of the revolution; they had been preparing for such an occasion for years using the Comintern-inspired manuals and even Lenin's famous "Tasks of Revolutionary Army Contingents" and his "Letter to the Fighting Committee" from 1905. Despite Moscow's explicit warnings that the present war was not about social change but the defeat of fascism, the Yugoslavs firmly believed that such scenario would take place in a matter of months, just as soon as the Red Army appeared on the country's borders. This shockingly naïve assessment, based on the almost childish belief in the superiority of the Soviet state and its armed forces, permeated the entire Party, from top to bottom. Although more cautious than his young lieutenants, Tito also believed that the Nazi Germany would not last longer than six months. On the other hand, there were several practical reasons speaking in favor of an urban campaign. The majority of KPJ members was already concentrated in cities and towns, knew the terrain well, and had support facilities (hideouts, sympathetic doctors, etc.) at their disposal. Unlike in the rural areas, actions could therefore be organized quickly, which was something the Comintern was insisting on. Third, acts of resistance in cities, even the smallest ones like writing slogans on walls, were likely to produce a much greater propaganda effect than if they had taken place in the countryside. The last point was very important, for the Party had just began to emerge from the shadows, having an ambition to become the leading political force in the divided country. At this stage, a successful marketing campaign was as important as a successful campaign in the field.[25]

Belgrade and its environs was the center of the Communist-led urban insurgency. During the first two months of the war, small assault teams consisting mostly of SKOJ members carried out some 50 acts of sabotage. Already on 4 July, Radio Belgrade went off-air for an hour-and-a-half due to the cutting of power lines. Probably the most serious of these incidents took place on 27 July, when 23 older German vehicles were lost to arson attacks. The resistance did not shy away from assassinations or open shootouts. During August, resistance fighters wounded two infamous police detectives and killed a police informant. Yet the most spectacular action of the Belgrade "illegals" (*ilegalci*), made known to the wider Yugoslav public through the immensely popular 1970s' TV-series "Otpisani" ("The Written-Off"), involved the rescue of the Politburo member Aleksandar Ranković on 29 July. "Taciturn and unruffled", Ranković's calm demeanor

poslova, 1959), Vol. IV, pp. 826-27; NARA/T314/1531/299-300, *Einsatzkommando* [EK] Belgrad/Abt. IV E, Report (2.9.1941); Jovan Marjanović, *Beograd* (Belgrade: Nolit, 1964), pp. 167-73; *Narodnooslobodilačka borba u Dalmaciji 1941-1945.: zbornik dokumenata* (Split: Institut za historiju radničkog pokreta Dalmacije [hereinafter: IHRPD], 1981-86), Vol. I, p. 250 [hereinafter: *Dalmacija*/volume/page].

25 Branko Petranović, *Srbija u Drugom svetskom ratu* (Belgrade: VINC, 1992), pp. 149-50, 167; Aleksei Timofejev, *Rusi i Drugi svetski rat u Jugoslaviji* (Belgrade: Institut za noviju istoriju Srbije [hereinafter: INIS], 2010), p. 193; Interview with Milovan Đilas in TV-documentary *"Jugoslavija u ratu 1941-1945"*, Episode 5 (Radio-televizija [hereinafter: RTV] Beograd, 1991-92).

hid a person possessed of great physical courage and exceptional organizational talent, but also of stomach for dirty work. In the near future he would become Tito's right hand-man and the head of the all-powerful secret police, but now he lay wounded, under guard, in a Belgrade hospital after being caught preparing an attack on the main radio transmitter. A specially organized task force of 50-60 fighters, armed with pistols, sealed off and broke into the hospital, killed a Serbian gendarme and a German serviceman, and fled the scene with the valuable prisoner.[26]

The NOP's underground organizations in other urban centers across occupied Yugoslavia were active as well. On 19 July 1941, a group of resistance fighters overcame the gendarmerie guard on the airfield at Jagodina, burned one and damaged several other aircraft. On 3 August, a bomb attack on "Park" Hotel in Niš killed one and wounded five German soldiers. Four days later, hay and leather depots in Kragujevac caught fire, "undoubtedly an act of sabotage." On 29 July, a bomb exploded in the main railway maintenance facility in Sarajevo. Zagreb, the capital of the NDH, was hit as well: already on 17 July, 3,000 bales of hay went up in flames in a depot belonging to the Wehrmacht. The next two months saw at least five serious incidents, including two attacks with hand grenades and pistols on Luftwaffe personnel (two killed, three wounded) and Ustashe units (at least 40 wounded), and an explosion in the main post office that resulted in a temporary breakdown in direct telephone communications with the Reich.[27] In Ljubljana, distribution of leaflets and writing of slogans were being increasingly complemented by armed actions. In addition to cutting telephone wires and setting off an explosive charge underneath a passing train, the resistance made two attempts on the lives of Italian servicemen (two killed, one wounded), and one on the former Yugoslav General Leo Rupnik, who survived and ultimately became the leading collaborationist in the province. The capital of Dalmatia was also turning into a dangerous place for the *Regio Esercito*: three separate attacks in Split on 14-15 September claimed one dead and ten wounded. About a month later, the resistance threw bombs on several targets in the city, wounding at least nine soldiers. Yet the deadliest attack of them all came on 9 November, when the Yugoslavs showered the passing music band of the 51st Infantry Regiment (IR) with hand grenades, wounding 29 men.[28]

Engaging in urban warfare helped increase the NOP's visibility, at the same time showing that Axis rule was far from being secure even in the centers of their newly acquired empires. On the other hand, the campaign was clearly running out of steam by the beginning of autumn 1941. Limited in the freedom of movement and facing a numerically strong and active enemy, the guerrillas were increasingly becoming the proverbial "fish in a barrel". Staffed by some very competent detectives who were now uninhibited by prewar scruples, the collaborationist police forces in the NDH and in Serbia repeatedly achieved break-ins into underground organizations, costing the NOP hundreds of members. Furthermore, every sabotage or assassination attempt

26 Slavko Vukčević, *Borbe i otpori u okupiranim gradovima Jugoslavije 1941-1945.* (Belgrade: VII, 1985), p. 95; Marjanović, *Beograd*, pp. 112-14, 117-19, 121-24, 133-34; NARA/T501/245/205, 207 (BhS, Incidents, 27, 29.7.29141), 526 (BhS, War diary, 4.7.1941); NARA/T312/425, WBSO, Daily report (7.8.1941); F.W.D. Deakin, *The Embattled Mountain* (New York: OUP, 1971), pp. 89-90.

27 NARA/T312/425, WBSO, Daily reports (4, 9, 22.8, and 15.9.1941); NARA/T315/2265/56, 718th ID, War diary (16.7.1941); *Zbornik*/IV/1/542, 4th NDH Gendarmerie Regiment [Rgt.], Intelligence report (6.8.1941); Vukčević, *Borbe*, pp. 124-25; NARA/T501/266/264, DGA to Wehrmacht High Command [*Oberkommando der Wehrmacht*, OKW] (4.10.1941).

28 See the Italian 2nd Army's internal reports in *Zbornik*/XIII/1/481, 485, 497, 517, 525, 527, 547, 575 (9, 15, 18, 25, 30, 29.9; 7 and 20.10.1941, respectively), and 735 (10.11.1941).

was now being punished with draconian reprisals against the civilian population, who could not understand how a burnt car or a stack of hay could be worth a dozen human lives or more. Bomb attacks in public spaces sometimes led to deaths and injuries among innocent bystanders. After a child (ironically, of a Party sympathizer) had accidentally been killed by a shrapnel in Split, the Italians made the most of it by mobilizing the public opinion against the resistance, and even giving the victim a ceremonial funeral.[29]

In short, the cost of the urban campaign was beginning to outstrip its usefulness. Consequently, both the main provincial HQ and Tito's staff would leave Belgrade for the countryside by mid-September 1941, signaling the shift in favor of a classic guerrilla campaign. The pace of transition differed from province to province. In Croatia, the belief in the "barricade tactics" was seemingly stronger than elsewhere. This prompted a senior Politburo member to comment that the local leadership effectively wanted to divided the war into two separate phases, first the "sabotage" (i.e. urban), followed by the "guerrilla", when in fact they should be parallel and complementary. Obstinate belief in old revolutionary methods and a speedy Soviet victory manifested itself in the use of out-of-place measures, and even resulted in abstinence from armed actions. For example, several Party cells in Dalmatia, Macedonia, and Bosnia organized strikes of factory workers, hardly an appropriate response to the standing orders calling for a total, uncompromising war against the Axis. Going even further, the KPJ committee in Zenica refused a direct order to sabotage the city's massive iron foundries, saying that the industry will be needed intact for the Socialist era, which would arrive shortly on Red Army tanks.[30]

Needless to say, the end of the street campaign did not mean the end of NOP's activities in urban surroundings in general. The Party was determined not to leave any sizable town without its presence and would keep reconstituting local cells and committees after each police raid until the very end of the war. Provincial leaderships preferred working in cities until enemy pressure became absolutely unbearable: the CK of the Communist Party of Croatia (*Komunistička partija Hrvatske*, KPH)[31] stayed in Zagreb until mid-March 1942, and the Macedonian provincial committee (*Pokrajinski komitet*, PK) vacated Skopje in April 1943. Thanks to the fact that the Italians' influence in Ljubljana barely reached beyond the confines of their barracks, the Slovenian leadership felt safe in the city until May 1942. The Serbian PK insisted in leading from Belgrade, and managed, incredibly, to stay undetected for the duration of its stay, which ended only in late 1943.

After 1941, the NOP would occasionally strike back against individual collaborators or police agents, but turned most of its energies to non-violent activities. Cities kept supplying a trickle of recruits to guerrilla detachments for the duration of the conflict, and served as relay stations for couriers, which was especially important during the first half of the war when W/T sets were few and far in between. They represented a source of money, food, and clothing, which were partly donated through the "People's Aid" (*Narodna pomoć*) program, but also of hard-to-obtain items: "We have received [...] your package", wrote Tito to Tempo, who was in Sarajevo at that time

29 Ibid., p. 473, Police HQ Split to Prefect of Split (29.10.1941); *Zbornik*/V/2/14-16, Rade Končar to Vlado Popović (10.11.1941).

30 *Zbornik*/II/1/30, Edvard Kardelj to Tito (2.8.1941); Vukčević, *Borbe*, pp. 64-6; Svetozar Vukmanović-Tempo, *Revolucija koja teče: memoari* (Belgrade: Komunist, 1971), Vol. I, pp. 198-99.

31 In 1937, the Comintern authorized the creation of the nominally autonomous Croatian and Slovenian (*Komunistička partija Slovenije*, KPS) branches of the KPJ.

(late February 1942), "[including] some cigarettes, 40 batteries, and 70 lemons for the hospital."[32] Lastly, towns and cities were hives of intelligence activity, especially in the NDH, where the NOP had many sympathizers within the civilian and military apparatus. Maintaining these liaisons was extremely risky. In early fall of 1941, the underground organization in Petrovaradin had recruited a *Domobranstvo* officer who helped them steal a considerable amount of arms and ammunition (including 38 crates of rifle cartridges and two cartloads of explosives) and store them in the underground cellars beneath the town's renowned fortress. In an attempt to widen the circle of conspirators, the officer contacted a colleague of his, who, however, immediately informed the NDH authorities. In the subsequent raid, the police not only secured the supplies, but captured 27 members of the resistance, most of whom were executed later on.[33]

1.3 Partisan Offensive in Serbia (July-September 1941)

The fateful Politburo meeting of 4 July 1941 produced little in the way of detailed guidelines concerning the conduct of the war. The main thing was to start forming guerrilla groups in the countryside and send them into fight as soon as possible. Unlike some other Yugoslav factions, the NOP attached greatest importance to the idea of constant armed action. In their eyes, this concept had no alternative for it was widely believed that the war against the USSR was the war against the Slavs in general; a Nazi victory would not only mean "suppression of socialism and democracy for decades to come, maybe even a whole century"[34], but the reduction of Yugoslav peoples to abject servitude, if not biological extinction. In this light, the question of reprisals against civilians caused by guerrilla attacks was of secondary importance. In one of his instructions to Montenegrin leadership, Tito wrote that the enemy could be forced to relinquish the use of reprisals, this "natural weapon" of his, only by the force of arms, and not by passivity or backing down. Successful armed actions, regardless of their scope, would wrest the population out of lethargy caused by the April catastrophe, and help establish the NOP as the only force in the country worth following. This approach was based on common logic: victories meant more weapons and prestige, which in turn brought new recruits, all of which resulted in an ever-growing army, and ever more ambitious operations. Apart from being the only way to gather experience, combat also helped weed out cowards, and increased camaraderie and self-confidence; furthermore, it was an excellent cure for idleness, that arch-enemy of every army.[35]

Although there is no equivocal evidence for the claim (originating from their contemporary enemies and often found in revisionist literature) that the Communists planned and carried out their raids with the express purpose of provoking reprisals against civilians, their leadership was certainly aware of their potential usefulness. The top Slovenian functionary, Edvard Kardelj,

32 *Zbornik*/II/1/398, Tito to Tempo (20.2.1942).

33 *Zbornik*/I/17/15-18, NDH Gendarmerie Petrovaradin to town commandant (October 1941). The already cited Vukčević, *Borbe*, offers a good overview of all aspects of NOP's activities in occupied cities across Yugoslavia. Much more information is available in works pertaining to individual places. Every self-respecting municipality in the Socialist Yugoslavia took pains to publish its own WW2 history; see, for instance, *Sarajevo u revoluciji* (Sarajevo: Istorijski arhiv Sarajevo, 1976-81), Vols. I-IV, or *Zagreb 1941-1945.: zbornik sjećanja* (Zagreb: Školska knjiga, 1982-84), Vols. I-IV.

34 Tempo, *Revolucija*, Vol. I, p. 187.

35 *Zbornik*/III/1/229, CK KPJ to PK Montenegro, 10.11.1941; *Zbornik*/II/1/342, Tito to Jahorina Detachment [Det.] (13.2.1942).

dealt with this problem with remarkable candidness (or cynicism) in one of his letters to Tito. Commenting on the fear of reprisals expressed by some of his fellow members in Croatia, Kardelj wrote that "in war, we must not fear the destruction of entire villages. The terror will without fail lead to armed action". Expounding further on his theory, he suggested the Communists form joint units with the members of the most popular pre-war political party in this part of the country, the Croatian Peasant Party (*Hrvatska seljačka stranka*, HSS): "The [Axis] terror against the followers of Maček [Vladko Maček, the head of the HSS] will bring entire Croatia on its feet."[36]

On the other hand–and this is oft forgotten–the Communists were still an unknown quantity, especially in the rural areas; if they were to lead a people's uprising, they had to earn the people's trust, and this was certainly not to be achieved by allowing the Axis to murder and burn with impunity. The protection of towns and villages "from fascist depredations" was listed as one of the main tasks of the nascent Partisan detachments in the very first issue of the official bulletin of Tito's HQ from mid-August 1941. In January of the following year, the secretary-general had again instructed the subordinated commands on all levels to intercept enemy punitive expeditions, for "this will earn you political prestige". Their first duty was to conserve the army's strength, but not at any price: in April 1942, the Croatian leadership criticized some of its subordinates for leaving a region without making even a token effort to protect the villages there, something the local population "will rightly blame you for". It was not unusual for Montenegrin Partisans to evacuate exposed villages before carrying out an ambush or act of sabotage.[37]

The most important technical conclusion of the meeting on 4 July 1941 was to send out a number of high-ranking Party functionaries to various parts of the country in order to assure the smooth implementation of instructions from the top. In this way, the already mentioned Edvard Kardelj, the bespectacled former school teacher-turned-Marxist-theoretician, was chosen for Slovenia (he was already there at the time of the meeting); the dark-complexioned Moscow veteran Sreten Žujović-Crni was to remain in his native Serbia; the short-tempered, 29-year-old Montenegrin Svetozar Vukmanović-Tempo got Bosnia and Herzegovina; the Party's main propagandist and Tito's protégé Milovan Đilas was to take over in his native Montenegro; Vlado Popović, another compatriot of Tempo and Đilas and a former captain of the Spanish Republican Army, was made responsible for Croatia. These "delegates" or "instructors", as they were known at the time, were also acting as representatives of the highest military command of the movement, formed out of the existing Military Committee of the CK KPJ. Neither the command, nor the army still had a fixed name. As Đilas later remembered, the word "Partisan" was not even mentioned at the time, and would not become the official name for the members of the KPJ-sponsored armed formations at least until the middle of the month. The word itself was borrowed from the Russian language for want of a suitable native word (the word *četnik*, normally used to describe an irregular fighter, was already taken). The high command went by at least three different names before settling for Main Headquarters of People's Liberation Partisan

36 Ibid., p. 31, Edvard Kardelj to Tito (2.8.1941). Perhaps the most remarkable fact about the letter is that it was printed in the official collection of wartime documents at the time when Kardelj was the foreign minister and one of the top-tier officials in Yugoslavia.

37 *Zbornik*/II/1/12, [Tito's HQ], Bulletin no. 1 (10.8.1941); see also the Supreme HQ's (SHQ) instructions from early 1942 in *Zbornik*/II/2/178, 200, and 236; *Zbornik*/V/4/118, MHQ Croatia to Banija Det. (25.4.1942); *Zbornik*/III/9/130, 2nd Coy./"13th July" Btl. to Durmitor Det. (13.2.1942).

Detachments of Yugoslavia (*Glavni štab Narodnooslobodilačkih partizanskih odreda Jugoslavije*) at the beginning of August. The official motto of the movement, "Death to Fascism–Freedom to the People!" (*Smrt fašizmu – sloboda narodu!*), was introduced on the same occasion.[38]

On 8 July 1941, Žujović and three other members left Belgrade for the area of Aranđelovac with orders to set up a special military HQ for Serbia. Due to communication difficulties, its zone of responsibility would remain confined to the western parts of the country; war efforts in other regions would be steered by the KPJ's provincial leadership through plenipotentiaries. Žujović found several groups of men and women who had organized themselves into nuclei of future *odredi* ("detachments"), the basic building block of the Partisan army. These groups were small: for example, Tamnava Company, formed near Obrenovac on the last day of June, had 18 members, and the Partisan *logor* ("camp") near Aranđelovac on 1 July had 40. They were made up of Communists, SKOJ members, and sympathizers, most of whom had fled from towns and cities. The decision to go to war was not taken easily: even some Party members prevaricated, suddenly called in sick, or said they had to tend to their fields and businesses. The peasants were reserved: they wanted to see how these new guerrillas would fare in action before joining them.[39]

And the first blood had already been drawn: on 7 July 1941, a dozen or so Partisans of Rađevo Company came to the village of Bela Crkva, outside Krupanj, held an anti-German rally, and left. Upon hearing that two Serbian gendarmes had come to investigate, the group returned to the village with the intention of disarming them. The gendarmes responded to the calls for surrender with a similar demand, after which they were both shot dead by Živorad Jovanović, the leader of the guerrillas and a veteran of Spain. The choice of this, and not some other, perhaps more suitable incident for the all-Yugoslav holiday called "The Day of the Uprising" (*Dan ustanka*) was in all probability motivated by propaganda considerations. The beginning of the armed struggle had to appear directly linked to the meeting of 4 July, and had to take place there, where Politburo and Tito were located at the time. It also cemented the symbolic, leading role of Serbia in the struggle against the invader and in the Yugoslav revolution.[40]

Throughout July 1941, KPJ bodies on all levels were working feverishly on building up the military organization. As a rule of thumb, each district committee (*okružni komitet*, OK) was responsible for raising one detachment. In Serbia and elsewhere, detachments were named after their native regions, and would occasionally wear the name of an especially deserving fallen comrade (i.e. Čačak Partisan Detachment "Dr Dragiša Mišović"), revolutionary heroes of the past (Grahovo-Peulje Detachment "Gavrilo Princip"), or the present (Detachment "Buđoni", named after the Soviet Marshal Semyon M. Budyonny). By the end of the month, 12

38 The traditional dating places the creation of the main military command under this name to 27 June 1941, but documentary evidence is lacking: Venceslav Glišić, Gojko Miljanić, *Rukovođenje Narodnooslobodilačkom borbom u Srbiji 1941-1945.* (Belgrade: Institut za savremenu istoriju [hereinafter: ISI], 1994), p. 32; Djilas, *Wartime*, p. 8; Tempo, *Revolucija*, Vol. I, pp. 184, 189; *Oslobodilački*, Vol. I, p. 42.

39 Glišić, Miljanić, *Rukovođenje*, pp. 36, 38; Milosav Bojić, *Posavski partizanski odred: Posavina u oružanom ustanku* (Belgrade: VINC, 1987), p. 79; Milivoje Stanković, *Prvi šumadijski partizanski odred* (Belgrade: Narodna knjiga, 1983), p. 113.

40 NARA/T501/245/159, BhS, Incidents (8.7.1941); Petranović, *Srbija*, p. 182. The gendarmes were rehabilitated in 2009 as "ideological-political" victims of "violence and persecution" practiced by the members of the Partisan movement: "Žandarmi iz Bele Crkve žrtve ideološkog terora", *Politika*, 2.1.2009: http://www.politika.rs/sr/clanak/69738/Drustvo/Zandarmi-iz-Bele-Crkve-zrtve-ideoloskog-terora (accessed on 25.3.2018).

detachments had been formed in Western Serbia, Šumadija, and Pomoravlje, and one in Eastern Serbia; in the remainder of the country, the guerrillas remained organized in smaller groups and camps. The fact that a detachment existed did not automatically mean it was carrying out armed actions: there were wide swaths of territory still virtually untouched by the insurgency. The Serbian PK was forced to issue a circular on 20 July reminding the entire Party membership of the great sacrifices that were being made by the Soviet people, and of do-or-die situation facing all patriots in Yugoslavia; at the same time, the letter demanded that the Partisans go over to the offensive at once.[41]

Some units, like the Posavina Detachment, did not need reminding. Between 11 and 31 July, the detachment carried out 12 actions, including blowing up two bridges in a single night, holding four political rallies, issuing a warning to a spy, conducting a successful "punitive expedition" against a former member of the unit, cutting telephone wires on two occasions, and precluding some villagers from selling their horses to the Germans ("great political success"). The Partisans also disarmed one group of five gendarmes, gave chase to another, and exchanged a few pot-shots with the third. On the last day of July, however, the detachment had two clashes with gendarmes, including one that involved 30+ men on both sides. By the end of the day, two gendarmes were captured (subsequently stripped of their clothes and set free), and three were killed. The unit's losses were limited to one member of the staff, shot dead by a local mayor who refused to surrender himself and his radio set to the guerrillas.[42]

The events mentioned in the above-cited report are representative of the type of activities the Serbian Partisans, and, to a large extent, the Communist-led guerrillas in general, engaged in during the first weeks of the uprising. These early actions could be considered low-risk, entry-level jobs aimed at winning experience, booty, and prestige, and strengthening inner cohesion. All six armed encounters the Posavina Detachment had were with the collaborationist authorities. From a military standpoint, the choice was reasonable: that was the only enemy whom the numerically weak, inexperienced, and badly armed Partisans could take on with a reasonable chance of success. The Germans, no matter how over-aged or ill-equipped they were according to Wehrmacht standards, were still better to avoid. In July 1941, the 714th ID recorded 33 guerrilla-related incidents in its sector, but lost only two men killed, and two men wounded in action (KIA, WIA). The 704th ID experienced a temporary loss of six men (captured and then released), and had very nearly lost one of its regimental commanders, General Adalbert Lontschar, when his car was fired upon near Valjevo. Although some of their native collocutors spoke of 30,000 rebels, and they themselves of "a real communist uprising", the occupation authorities in Belgrade felt that no army reinforcements were needed at the time, and that the police forces alone (most notably the newly arrived 64th Reserve Police Battalion [RPB]) could

41 Glišić, Miljanić, *Rukovođenje*, pp. 33-34, 37; *Sjeverozapdna Hrvatska u narodnooslobodilačkoj borbi i revoluciji: građa 1941.-1945.* (Zagreb: Savjet za izdavanje "Građe za povijest NOP-a i socijalističke revolucije u sjeverozapadnoj Hrvatskoj 1941-1945", 1981-89), Vol. I, p. 216, Leaflet (6.9.1941) [hereinafter: *SZH*/volume/page]; *Zbornik*/I/2/29-30, PK Serbia, Circular (20.7.1941).

42 *Zbornik*/I/1/52-53, Posavina Det., Activity report (1-14.8.1941); *Zbornik*/I/21/19-20, [Serbian] Commissariat of Interior, Monthly report on enemy activity (31.7.1941).

deal with the troubles. Fearing the negative propaganda fallout that would result even from smallest setbacks on the battlefield, the Wehrmacht was ordered to stay out of the fight.[43]

These rosy assessments had to be revised only several weeks later on account of the rapidly deteriorating situation. For instance, the 714th ID recorded almost three times as many incidents (85) in August as in the preceding month. According to BhS' own and incomplete statistics, there were 59 acts of sabotage or attacks on railways, 24 attacks on gendarmerie stations, 96 on communal offices and other administrative objects, nine on mines and factories, 24 cases of sabotage on telephone wires, and three more on road bridges. Illustrative of the growing strength and self-confidence of the guerrillas was the sharp increase in the number of attacks on the Wehrmacht (16), usually in the form of ambushes on single vehicles, resulting in the loss of altogether 59 KIA, 138 WIA, and seven missing in action (MIA).[44] Guerrilla activity now engulfed entire Serbia: in its eastern and southeastern parts, which had hitherto been largely quiet, there were now seven active Partisan detachments. The main area of activity was, as before, in the west, where their actions were no longer carried out for actions' sake alone. Already in late July, Tito formulated a broad-stroke plan calling for the establishment of a large "liberated territory" (*slobodna teritorija*). There, the snowball effect of guerrilla actions, already palpable, could be used to incite a true popular uprising. After corresponding with Žujović, Tito stuck with his original choice, Western Serbia, or more precisely the Western Morava Valley and upper and middle sections of the Drina. This area was chosen not only because of its suitable geographical position (proximity to Bosnia, Syrmia, and Montenegro) and rugged terrain, but also because of its long rebellious tradition and the presence of "allies".[45]

The term "allies" in this case referred to another guerrilla movement that was just beginning to develop in Serbia, the nationalist Chetniks. Deriving their name from the irregular bands that originally fought the Ottomans in Macedonia at the turn of the century, the group was founded around the former general staff colonel of Yugoslav Army, Dragoljub-Draža Mihailović. He and his small band of followers (mostly army personnel and gendarmes) evaded capture during the April War, and found refuge on Mount Ravna Gora near Valjevo in May 1941. Deciding on the course of resistance in order to restore the monarchy, Mihailović spent the next two months setting up his organization, receiving volunteers, and establishing links with other like-minded officers and collaborationist officials. He was firmly resolved not to start an uprising without the prospect of help from abroad, ideally in the form of Western Allied invasion. The appearance of the Communist armed formations and their attacks on gendarmerie stations and communal offices were therefore greeted with deep suspicion. In the beginning, the Partisans had largely ignored the monarchists, but this began to change during August, not least because of the increasingly friendly relations between the USSR and the British, the protecting power of the exiled Yugoslav government. Also fearing the possibility that the occupier might try to win over

43 NARA/T315/2258/224, 714th ID/Oper., Activity report (1.5-31.7.1941); NARA/T315/2236/94, 99, 704th ID, War diary (12, 18.7.1941); NARA/T175/126, BhS/Admin. to WBSO (23.7.1941); NARA/T314/1531/244, BhS to Army High Command [*Oberkommando des Heeres*, OKH] (3.8.1941).

44 NARA/T315/2258/174, 714th ID/Oper., Activity report (1-31.8.1941); NARA/T501/246, Ten-day reports (11, 21, and 31.81941).

45 *Glišić, Miljanić, Rukovođenje, pp.* 37, 39-40.

the nationalists, the Communist leadership in Serbia decided to try to form an alliance with them, or at least "neutralize them in a given moment".[46]

As a consequence, the Chetniks and Partisans held a series of talks on all levels during August 1941. On a meeting between Mihailović and a representative of the Serbian PK, both sides agreed not to attack each other, mutually acknowledged each other's freedom of action, including the provision that the Chetniks would join the fight at the moment of their own choosing. Behind the scenes, royalist officers were united in concern over the growing Communist influence in the country, but divided on which course to take on this issue. Some advocated launching a pre-emptive strike against what was in effect their main ideological foe; others favored joining the uprising. The latter were motivated not only by patriotic feelings and the desire to retrieve their badly-damaged reputations (a popular nickname for officers in the aftermath of the April War was *svileni*, meaning "the silky ones"), but also believed that this was the only way to retain at least some influence among the masses. It should be noted that the monarchists, despite their anti-communism, largely shared the prevailing pan-Slavic sentiment and the belief that the Soviets would soon be on the Danube.[47]

On 31 August 1941, one of these "activist" officers, Lieutenant-Colonel Veselin Misita, stormed the border town of Loznica, taking 93 Germans prisoner. The attack was most likely not sanctioned by Mihailović and was kept secret from the local Partisans. After that, the Chetniks (soon to be joined by a small Partisan contingent) turned their attention to the nearby spa place Banja Koviljača. Although the garrison, consisting of two companies of the 718th ID, had repulsed all attacks, it was nevertheless ordered to withdraw across the Drina on 6 September. Their compatriots at the town of Krupanj, some 20 km to the southeast, were neither as tough, nor as lucky. On 3 September, the Chetnik detachments of Lieutenant Ratko Martinović and Orthodox priest Vladimir Zečević (both of whom would soon become Partisan commanders) started their attack in cooperation with the Partisan Valjevo Detachment after the garrison had turned down a surrender ultimatum. The Germans first tried to hold their ground, and then attempted a breakout with the help of the newly-arrived dive bombers[48], but ultimately failed at both. On the 4th, the Yugoslavs celebrated their greatest victory yet: at the price of six KIA and 12 WIA, they took almost the entire garrison captive together with eight mortars, 22 light machine guns (LMGs), 92 pieces of small arms, plus a lot of other equipment and supplies. All in all, the Krupanj affair cost the 704th ID seven KIA, 20 WIA, and 172 MIA. Commenting on this unique situation in the occupied Europe, a lieutenant in the HKdo LXV wrote:

46 *Zbornik*/I/20/25, PK Serbia to OK Valjevo (8.8.1941).

47 Jozo Tomasevich, *War and Revolution in Yugoslavia, 1941-1945: The Chetniks* (Stanford, CA: Stanford University Press, 1975), pp. 122-26, 135-36, 138; Simon Trew, *Britain, Mihailović, and the Chetniks, 1941-1942* (London: Macmillan Press LTD, 1998), pp. 60-62; Petranović, *Srbija*, pp. 161, 186; Veselin Đuretić, *Saveznici i jugoslovenska ratna drama* (Belgrade: self-pub., 1988), Vol. I, p. 48.

48 In addition to a dozen or so transport, courier, and reconnaissance airplanes, the *Luftwaffe* (LW) operated a squadron of "Junkers" Ju-87 dive bombers over Serbia from early September to early November 1941; in this period, the squadron flew ca. 1,000 sorties. In early October, the air contingent (including the 5th Instrument Flight School) had a personnel strength of 1,272 men, the main bases being at Zemun and Niš, with subsidiary ones at Pančevo and Kraljevo: Vojislav V. Mikić, *Nemačka avijacija u Jugoslaviji 1941-1945* (Belgrade: VII, 1998), pp. 66, 84, 90; NARA/T501/246, 10th LW Field salvage staff to BhS (6.10.1941).

> The shit the bandits are dealing out is just beyond belief now. Today a general told us that two companies (!) have been missing for fourteen days (!!!) Just imagine that!! Two companies taken prisoner!!! With five officers and so on!!! We're searching for them with aircraft, day and night!!! You just want to scream right at the heavens!!!!![49]

Bearing in mind the fate of Krupanj and Loznica, the WBSO forbade the divisions to maintain garrisons with a force of less than one battalion. However, this measure failed to secure the grip on the western parts of the country: the battalions were fighting in virtual isolation, having dozens of kilometers of guerrilla-infested countryside between themselves and their sources of supplies and reinforcements. Bowing to the inevitable, the high command decided to evacuate the upper reaches of the Western Morava during the last decade of September 1941. As a result, the Partisans and Chetniks entered Užice and Požega on the 21st, and Čačak 10 days later. The insurgents used a stratagem to capture Gornji Milanovac on 29 September, bagging yet another full company of prisoners from the 920th LSB.

Cunning alone, however, would not be enough for two major garrisons in the Western Morava Valley, which the Germans were determined to defend at all costs. The insurgents tried to take Kruševac by storm on 26 September but failed, killing some two dozen enemy soldiers in the process. Further west, the two guerrilla movements also laid siege to Kraljevo, a strategically important railhead near the confluence of the Ibar and Western Morava. Attacks on urban centers were occurring in other parts of the country as well. Veliko Gradište in northeastern Serbia fell on 20 September, resulting in the capture of a handful of German officials. Fearing the insurgents would use the place to obstruct the traffic on the Danube, the Wehrmacht responded, in part, by launching air strikes.[50] In addition to these large-scale actions, the campaign of standard guerrilla attacks was reaching its crescendo. In only one week (13-19 September), authorities registered 20 attacks on gendarmerie stations, five on mines, 30 on ships, bridges, and other public objects, 80 on railway installations, and no less than 127 on communal offices. One particularly bloody incident occurred on 16 September when an ambush on a passenger train near Palilula produced 10 German soldiers KIA, and 12 more WIA.[51]

1.4 Conference at Stolice: Early Partisan Army

By mid-September 1941, the uprising had become too complex to be conducted from afar. On the 16th, Tito left his villa hideout in Belgrade and headed for the guerrilla-held territory on

49 Ratko Martinović, *Od Ravne gore do Vrhovnog štaba* (Belgrade: Rad, 1979), EPUB version, chapter "With the Partisans"; Milovan Batanović Batan, "Podrinjski partizanski odred", in *Ustanak naroda jugoslavije 1941.* (Belgrade: Vojno delo, 1964), Vol. I, pp. 190-92; NARA/T315/2265/998-1002, 3rd Battalion/738th IR [hereinafter: III/738th IR], Summary after-action report (9.9.1941); NARA/T315/2237/837, 704th ID, Appendix 7 to report no. 407/41 (12.9.1941); Ben Shepherd, *Hitler's Soldiers: The German Army in the Third Reich* (London: Yale University Press, 2018), EPUB edition, chapter ten, footnote 41.

50 NARA/T501/246, WBSO, Quelling the Serbian uprising (5.9.1941); ibid., Statement by Peter Strüder (23.9.1941); Schmider, *Partisanenkrieg*, pp. 65-74; NARA/T501/250/983-84, Statement by Franz Egger (22.10.1941).

51 NARA/T175/233, Chief of Security Police [*Sicherheitspolizei*, SIPO] and SD, Event report USSR no. 90 (21.9.1941); NARA/T312/425, WBSO, Daily report (17.9.1941).

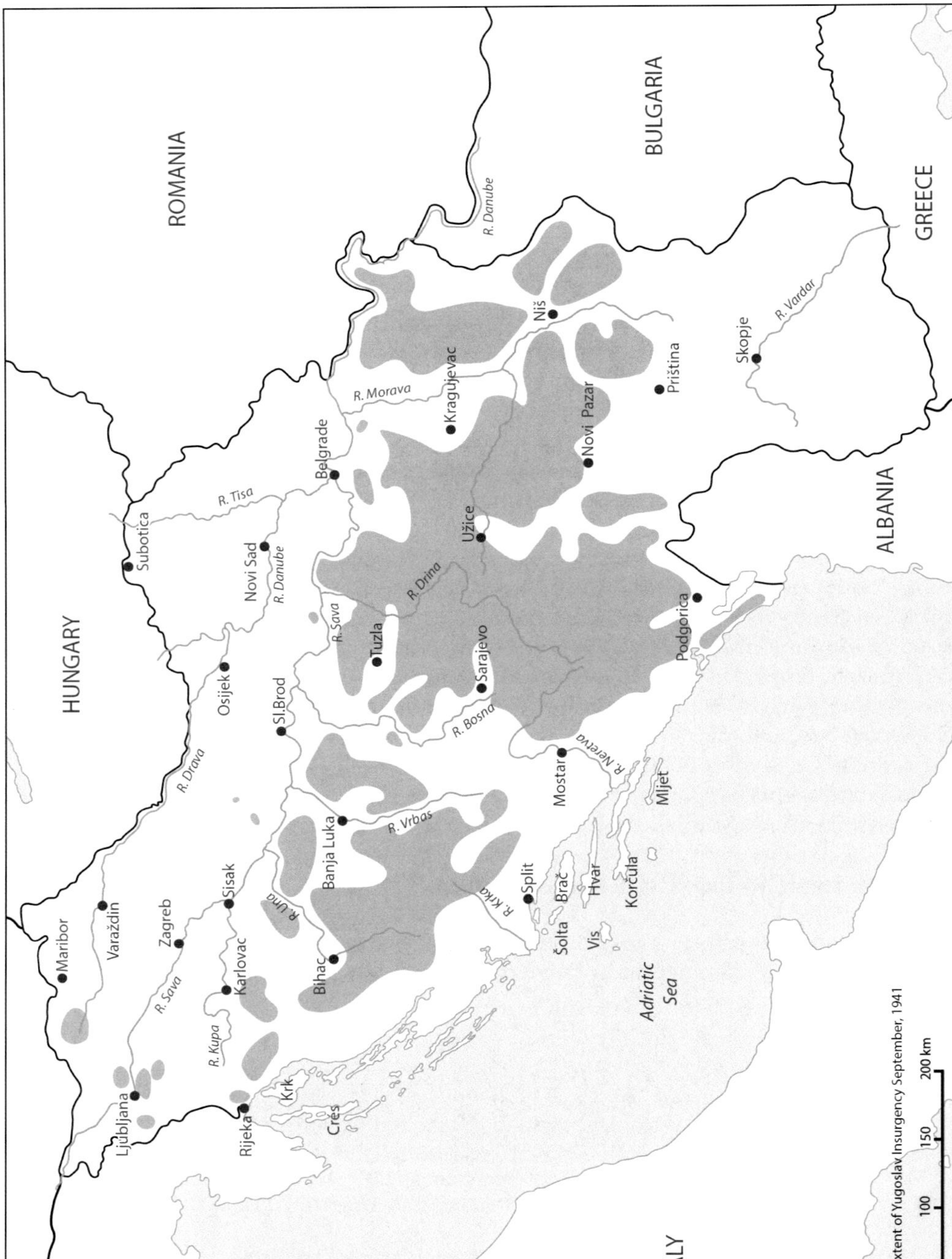

Map 3: Extent of Yugoslav insurgency (September 1941).

the outskirts of Valjevo. Ten days later he opened the conference of the Main HQ and the CK in the small village of Stolice near Krupanj. Present were delegates from all provincial commands save Macedonia; they had been informed of the conference weeks in advance in order to give them enough time to make such a long and arduous journey. The topics for discussion included military operations, competences of various HQs, division of operational areas, and structure of military formations, all "in preparation for the autumn campaign."[52] Rather than being a simple council of war, the conference turned out to be an important step in the revolutionary and state-building drive, which was just beginning to gain steam. It marked the start of the process of regularization, aimed at transforming the guerrilla bands into a full-blown–and internationally recognized–army of the future Yugoslav republic.

First, the organization of the Partisan army needed streamlining on the national level. In Serbia, the detachments were divided into companies and platoons; the same case was in Slovenia, only the basic unit was not called detachment, but company. Practically each separate command in Croatia and Bosnia had its own organization: battalions or even companies could be divided into detachments, sometimes with "sections" added in between as an extra level. Confusion was just as great with regard to the names of these commands. Some HQs began to style themselves "brigades" (e.g. Drvar Brigade, Bosnian-Herzegovinian Brigade), others contemplated using the reactionary-sounding term "regiment" for a multi-battalion unit, and some went further still, as illustrated by the existence of the short-lived Krajina Division in Western Bosnia. It should be noted that these names were purely cosmetic and did not reflect a change in the static, territorial nature of these commands. The Montenegrin military leadership showed itself capable of simultaneously imitating the Soviet model and respecting the ways and customs of the old. One set of guidelines from early October 1941 called the basic unit of the army "rifle company", and envisaged the creation of "moto-mechanized" units (all contemporary Red Army terms). On the other hand, the biggest formations of the army, each comprised of several brigades, were to be called "detachments", which was derived from Montenegrin tradition. Likewise, the peculiarities of the country's clan society were to be honored when forming new companies. According to the new regulations issued at Stolice, all these arrangements were to be discarded in favor of a unified structure valid for the entire country. From now on, the detachment would be the biggest formation, divided into two to four battalions, and these in turn into three companies of three platoons each. If required by operational necessity, two or more detachments could be combined into a group. At this time, Tito was against forming bigger permanent units, as well as the usgae of terms such as "brigade" or "division" for territorial commands. Each Yugoslav province would receive its own provincial Main HQ, which in turn would be answerable to the recently-christened *Vrhovni štab* (Supreme HQ, SHQ) and its Supreme Commander (*Vrhovni komandant*).[53]

52 All information on the conclusions of the conference come from Anić, Joksimović, Gutić, *Narodnooslobodilačka*, pp.63-69, unless stated otherwise.

53 *Zbornik*/IV/1/70 (Sarajevo Area HQ to PK Bosnia-Herzegovina, 22.8.1941); 169-70 (Drvar Brigade to OK Bosanska Krajina, 2.9.1941), 480 (Romanija Btl. to Sarajevo Brigade [Bde.], 27.9.1941); *Zbornik*/IV/2/83; *Zbornik*/V/1/107-11, Minutes of conference of delegates from Kordun and Banija (19-20.9.1941); *Zbornik*/III/1/50-57, MHQ for Montenegro, Sandžak and Boka [hereinafter: MHQ/PK Montenegro], Organization and structure of people's Partisan army (October 1941).

The conference also established the size and composition of staffs in Partisan units. The commander and the political commissar (*politkom*) now received deputies and each unit a quartermaster, a doctor, and a communications detail. The role of political commissars was discussed in more detail. Their official title changed several times; during the summer of 1941, they were called "political secretaries" in parts of Bosnia, and "persons for liaison with the people" in Montenegro. Their functions, on the contrary, remained largely the same throughout the war. In short, the commissar was responsible for all aspects of the inner life of a unit. Among else, he was tasked with upholding and popularizing the Party line, rooting out spies and ditherers, and overseeing political and cultural activities. The commissar was equal to the commander in rights and obligations, and privy to operational planning, but the latter had the final word in all purely military matters. In the early phase of the war the commissar was also responsible for running the day-to-day activities of the Party cell in his unit; after Stolice, these duties would be taken over by the deputy-commissar. It sounds incredible, but being a member of the KPJ was not necessarily a prerequisite for becoming a political officer. Partisan documents from Montenegro reveal that the office could also be held by some highly unlikely candidates like a former gendarmerie officer, or even a theologian. The answer to the riddle lies in the fact that the commissars, as well as commanders, were at first not appointed, but elected by their fellow fighters. This practice was something the Communists had to tolerate in those parts of the country where their influence with the rank-and-file was still weak. In Eastern Herzegovina in October 1941, for instance, the local HQ felt that any attempt to impose the choice of commissars would prove "very unpopular" and could even be exploited by the enemy. Wherever the grip on the insurgent masses was tight enough, the practice was discouraged, but the dismantling of the old system would last well into 1942.[54]

The *politkom* was also responsible for promoting the unique Partisan *esprit-de-corps*. The NOP's credo was based on a combination of patriotic and class motives, including the liberation of the homeland from a vicious oppressor and his native lackeys, freedom and emancipation for all Yugoslav peoples (including those living beyond the country's borders), but also the promise of a happier post-war life for all under the slogan "There will be no going back to the old ways" (*nema više povratka na staro*). Such a noble agenda would require noble men, and the KPJ embarked on an experiment not unlike the one conducted by Gustavus Adolphus II in 1630s. The king wanted to establish his native Sweden not only as the premier military, but also as premier moral power of Europe by fielding a truly Christian army which, unlike all other armies at the time, did not murder, burn, or pillage. In the Yugoslav version, Protestant teachings were replaced by the idea of the one and only true people's army that protected the weak regardless of their origin and punished only the guilty. Every individual who was accepted to this chosen band was required to submit to the special brand of discipline that was not based on coercion and intimidation ("like in the old army"), but on voluntary, conscious acceptance of the rules. The fighter had to be brave and obedient in combat, but also decent towards the

54 *Zbornik*/IX/1/6 (1st Btl. "Sloboda", Order no. 4, 20.8.141), 16-17 ([MHQ Slovenia], Tasks of *politkoms*, August 1941), 18 (PK Montenegro, Instructions, August 1941), 41-45 (Drvar Bde./Pol., Instructions, 7.10.1941); *Zbornik*/III/4/9-10 (MHQ Montenegro, To all people and units, 22.7.1941), 86 (Diary of Savo Orović, December 1941); *Zbornik*/III/1/203-04, Lovćen Det. to MHQ Montenegro (27.11.1941); *Zbornik*/IV/2/14, Herzegovina Det. to Tempo (2.10.1941); *Zbornik*/V/2/90, MHQ Croatia to Lika group of detachments [GoD] (1.12.1941).

captured enemy; off the battlefield, he (or she) was expected to treat civilians and their property with respect, maintain good relations with his comrades, and abstain from alcohol and carnal activities. The cult of discipline, long established in the militarized Communist milieu, was immediately transplanted to the new army. Infractions were usually punished by a relatively narrow palette of sanctions, determined by individual units and territorial commands. For example, according to "Penal Provisions" of the Posavina Detachment, published in October 1941, lesser transgressions could be punished only by a reprimand or a transfer to another unit; also mentioned are assignment to menial duties, forced labor, or expulsion from the army (also from the Party if the transgressor was a member).

However, one aspect of the "revolutionary justice" that captured the most attention and decidedly shaped the public image of the Partisans in the decades to come was the application of death sentence. Although the guerrillas usually did not shoot their own "for a pair of plucked plums", as the popular saying went, there can be no doubt that the highest penalty was meted out liberally for disciplinary infractions. In addition to practical considerations, like the lack of holding facilities, the Partisans turned to this form of punishment not least because of its symbolism and propaganda value. Carried out whenever possible after a short public trial, the sentence conveyed the resolve of the Partisans to live up to their self-proclaimed principles and cleanse their own ranks of criminal elements. Although deeply flawed from today's standpoint, these trials were something new amidst the orgy of indiscriminate violence practiced by all other factions, and symbolically satisfied the ordinary people's thirst for swift justice.[55] Although the Partisans, like the Swedes, had failed in the attempt to create a sinless army (as we shall see, the Communist-led guerrillas had more than their own share of war crimes), the credo was not simply a dead letter or a propaganda ploy, as witnessed by the constantly rising levels of popular support and ultimately, by the victory itself.

This might be the place to mention an episode from the early days of the uprising when the Partisan efforts in Serbia were plagued by the appearance of gangs of common criminals who attempted to ply their trade under the red banner. One of them had even taken the nickname Čaruga after the famous Slavonian outlaw who robbed the rich and gave to the poor in the immediate aftermath of the First World War, all in the name of the world revolution. The "new" Čaruga and his men were accepted into one of the companies of the Kosmaj Detachment. Very soon they had practically taken over the outfit, rendering it militarily useless. After their misdeeds (rape included) had been discovered, Čaruga and others were brought to trial. Considering him the proverbial "our scoundrel" on account of his alleged communist leanings, the judges decided not to shoot him, but to simply expel him and his minions from the army (he would nonetheless end up liquidated later the same year). Another criminal, a certain Tanda, profited from both outwardly embracing the Partisan cause and from the time spent in penitentiaries, where he came to know many Communists. After being allowed to join a company of the Kragujevac Detachment, Tanda and his group went on about their business of extortion, murder, and robbery. Ultimately, a delegate of the MHQ Serbia ordered the gang

55 Russel F. Weigley, *The Age of Battles: The Quest for Decisive Warfare from Breitenfeld to Waterloo* (London: Pimlico, 1993), p. 27; *Zbornik*/VI/1/22-31, MHQ Slovenia, Partisan canon (mid-July 1941); *Zbornik*/V/1/69-75, Role and tasks of Partisan detachments (September 1941); *Zbornik*/I/1/161-65, Posavina Det., Penal provisions (October 1941); for an example of a verdict handed down by a Partisan tribunal in Bosnia see *Zbornik*/I/1/353-54, Notice to comrades (18.9.1941).

disarmed and put on trial, with the ringleader and one of his closest accomplices ending up in front of a firing squad, two or three others expelled, and the rest allowed to stay with the ranks. More notably, the commander and *politkom* responsible for the admittance of these criminals into the army ("the most repugnant and dirty stain on the honor of the Party") received a suspended death sentence.[56]

In order to further strengthen the sense of belonging, but also to make the army as regular in both substance and appearance as possible, the SHQ introduced a special set of regulations. Official insignia was to be a five-pointed red star, which every fighter had to wear on his cap alongside the national tricolor (red-blue-white for the Serbs, red-white-blue for the Croats, etc.). The Partisans also had a new, unified text of the military oath, which replaced all local versions. First introduced by the Spaniards, the clenched-fist salute now became the official greeting of the NOP. One other Spanish tradition, however, did not hold; the term "guerrilla" (*gerilac*), still used in some parts of the country (e.g. Croatia), was definitely discarded in favor of *partizan*.[57]

The Stolice conference also reaffirmed the primacy of guerrilla tactics. Tito issued three sets of short training guidelines for the entire army. Given that the NOP was overwhelmingly made up of youth who did not have a chance to finish the compulsory army service, the first document dealt with the basics, including weapons training, sabotage and ambush techniques. The second set dealt with attacking populated places. The emphasis was placed on infiltration tactics, good intelligence, and speed; the attackers were reminded of the need to isolate the objective from the outside world by cutting telephone wires, destroying roads, and laying ambushes. The latter two methods were also to be employed for the defense of liberated territories, the subject of the third document. Realizing the guerrillas were still not prepared for a muzzle-to-muzzle confrontation with the regulars, the SHQ cautioned against holding classic defensive lines, or getting embroiled into protracted sieges, as had already happened in Serbia and elsewhere. The articles served as a basis for locally issued tactical manuals, some of which could be very detailed, like "Short Course for Partisan Commanders", written in Slovenia in the closing months of 1941.[58] The training should take place whenever the circumstances allow; it should not be based on "too much talking and explaining" in classrooms, but take place outdoors, and be diversified and practical. The instructions also made clear that the army could not hope for professional help from abroad; consequently, one should always be on a lookout for promising officer-candidates from the ranks of ordinary fighters. Beginning in mid-October at the latest, individual detachments organized short courses where NCOs would learn to solve simple tactical tasks like moving under enemy fire, placing of automatic weapons, making flanking attacks, etc. The best candidates would then be promoted to company commanders.[59]

56 *Zbornik*/I/2/58 (Kosmaj Det., Activity report, 29.8.1941), 77, 157-59 (Svetislav Stefanović-Ćeća to PK Serbia, 30.8.1941 and beginning of October 1941, respectively). For more examples of death sentences for indiscipline see ibid., p. 116 (Belić Company [Coy.], Activity report, 5.9.1941), and *Zbornik*/I/1/41 (Report to PK Serbia from Šabac area, 14.8.1941), 166 (2nd Btl./Posavina Det. [hereinafter: II/Posavina Det.] to all companies, 4.10.1941).

57 *Enciklopedija* Vol. VII, p. 239; *Zbornik*/II/1/64, Tito to Rade Končar (12.9.1941).

58 Tito's instructions are reproduced in full in Ibid., pp. 68-77; the Slovene manual can be found in *Zbornik*/VI/1/173-236.

59 *Zbornik*/IV/2/104 (MHQ Bosnia-Herzegovina, Circular, 19.10.1941), 111-12 (Kalinovik Det. to Prača Btl., 30.10.1941); *Zbornik*/I/1/194, I/Kragujevac Det. to 1st Coy. (11.10.1941).

By the time the conference ended, the Partisan army in Serbia consisted of 24 detachments (four were disbanded in the meantime), with an estimated 14,000 fighters. This was still largely a volunteer force, although the Partisans had already started experimenting with conscription; in the area of Paraćin in Central Serbia, it was carried out with such heavy-handedness that it provoked a pro-Axis backlash. Nevertheless, the Communist-led guerrillas could feel satisfied with the progress they had made in the past three months. Small, almost conspiratorial bands of Party members and sympathizers had become large, decently militarized formations made up of people from all layers of society. The Kragujevac Detachment had doubled in strength in a mere two weeks between 22 September and 5 October, and that was before the recruitment drive had even begun. The already mentioned 2nd Battalion of the Posavina Detachment (whose overall strength in this period is estimated at 1,500-2,200 men) had 645 fighters, 172 of whom were workers, 439 peasants, 24 intellectuals, and 10 soldiers; almost exactly one-half of them had served in the old army (328), including five reserve officers, and 14 reserve NCOs. The battalion was fully armed with infantry weapons; each fighter had some 50 rounds with him, and the battalion reserve amounted to some 10,000 rounds.[60]

The army's overall ammunition situation was far from satisfactory. The above-cited figures were just about sufficient for ordinary guerrilla activity, but protracted firefights were out of the question. The Partisans thought they had found the solution to this problem in Užice. The Germans did not only leave intact a vast ammunition depot with over 29,000,000 rounds of rifle ammunition of various calibers, but also the local arms factory, together with its tools and raw materials. By the end of November 1941, the factory would produce up to 20,000 rifles (one of them would even end up as a gift to Stalin in 1944), and an additional 2,700,000 cartridges. These supplies did not serve only to keep the fires of the uprising burning in Serbia, but were sent to the guerrillas in Eastern Bosnia as well. The two remaining factories in Užice and the host of smaller workshops spread throughout the liberated territory in the Western Morava Valley provided other badly needed products, like boots (altogether 2,000 pairs not counting the traditional peasant footwear, *opanci*), clothing (1,000 sets a day in late November 1941), and even cigarettes (some 200 tons of tobacco had been found in the town of Bajina Bašta). Last but not the least, the capture of Užice turned the NOP into a financial superpower: an estimated 45-55,000,000 dinars were found in the vaults of the local branch of the national bank (for comparison: in late December 1941, a kilogram of potatoes in Belgrade sold for eight dinars).

Speaking of finances, the movement acquired its revenues chiefly through confiscations and contributions. The latter came in variety of forms. Voluntary donations were commonplace and would sometimes come from unlikely quarters: "This national-liberation war really works miracles [...] If I told you who [agreed to donate the money], you would be surprised", wrote Kardelj to Tito about the situation in Ljubljana, where rich merchants and other *bourgeois* placed their resources at the NOP's disposal. "People's Tax" was introduced in Slovenia already in 1941; rates ranged from a symbolic one lira per month to 10 percent of income. The movement's provincial authorities began raising war loans that some year, and the practice would continue well into 1944; "People's Liberation Loan" was launched on a national level in early 1943.

60 *Zbornik*/I/2/152-53, Instructor of PK Serbia, Report on Pomoravlje district (9.10.1941); *Zbornik*/I/1/152 (Užice Det., Order, 30.9.1941), 169, 190-91 (II/Posavina Det., Weekly reports, 28.9-4.10., and 4-11.10.1941), 180 (Kragujevac Det., Weekly report, 26.9-5.10.1941); *Enciklopedija*, Vol. VII, p. 199; Bojić, *Posavski*, p. 233.

The financing of the war effort from December 1944 to May 1945 was secured by a series of short interim budgets, each covering a period one to three months. When all other sources of money got exhausted, the Yugoslav Communists resorted to time-tested methods of their Old Bolshevik idols: "During the last month [we] took 1,400,000 lire from state banks at gun point", concluded Kardelj his financial report from late 1942.[61]

1.5 German Counteroffensive in Serbia (September-December 1941)

The Wehrmacht contingent in Serbia was utterly unprepared for the situation they were facing in July 1941 but sought nevertheless to counter the threat with active campaigning. The first German anti-guerrilla operation in Yugoslavia, named "Gamsbock" took place already on 14 July, and it would be followed by literary hundreds of others in the following four years. The operation involved six to seven companies of troops from the 749th IR/717th ID and 724th IR/704th ID, which were sent on a wild goose chase after a non-existent group of 3,000 irregulars in the vicinity of Čačak. The 714th ID, on the contrary, pulled off a major coup when it surprised and routed two Partisan companies south of Smederevska Palanka, killing or capturing over 30 guerrillas (17-20 July). The growth of the uprising during this period is attested by the fact that the Germans saw themselves compelled to send no less than seven reinforced infantry battalions from all three divisions against the Partisans around Mount Kosmaj. The operation lasted for two days (8-9 August) and yielded meager results in relation to the force engaged: 18 killed and 13 captured guerrillas, together with 10 pieces of infantry weapons (the Partisan sources speak of 13 KIA and only one captured).[62]

After a month or so of fighting, the Germans could size up their foe, but also analyze their own first steps in the sphere of COIN operations. The Germans had thus learned the need to have their weapons always at a ready; to go in as lightly as possible, leaving the gas mask and entrenching tool behind; to carry as many hand grenades and ammunition as possible; to take artillery or heavy infantry weapons whenever practicable; to improve mobility by adding extra trucks and pack animals. Owing to the increasing number of ambushes on single vehicles, in mid-August the HKdo LXV ordered the creation of convoys, all of which should have at least five vehicles and one automatic weapon.

The concept of the *Jagdkommando*, or hunting detachment, was introduced at the same time. Each of these entirely motorized units was to be made up of 30-50 heavily-armed, hand-picked men whose task was not only to react quickly to enemy attacks, but to take the fight to the

61 NARA/T501/246, Užice munitions depot (20.9.1941); Milovan Djilas, *Conversations with Stalin* (Harmondsworth, UK: Penguin Books, 1967), p. 16; Milica Bodrožić, "Radnička klasa užičkog kraja u ratu i revoluciji 1941. godine", in *Užička republika* (Belgrade: NIRO Eksport-Pres, 1978), Vol. I, pp. 95-96; Sreten Sokić, "Karakter društveno-ekonomskih odnosa u Užičkoj republici", in ibid., p. 285; Miloš Timotijević, "Sudbina srebra Užičke republike", *Godišnjak za društevnu istoriju*, 1 (2018), pp. 59-64; *Enciklopedija*, Vol. II, p. 772, and Vol. VIII, pp. 39-40; *Zbornik*/II/7/90-91, Kardelj to Tito (14.12.1942).

62 NARA/T315/2262/131-2, 749th IR, Report [operation] "Gamsbock" (15.7.1941); NARA/T315/2258/199-201 (714th ID, Report "Kosmaj", 11.8.1941), 228 (714th ID/Oper., Activity Report, 1.5.-31.7.1941); Aleksandar Vitorović, *Srbija u narodnooslobodilačkoj borbi: Centralna Srbija* (Belgrade: Nolit, 1967), pp. 110-11; Dragoslav Dimitrijević-Beli, *Kosmajski partizani* (Belgrade: Beogradski izdavačko-grafički zavod [hereinafter: BIGZ], 1983, Vol. I, pp. 103-07.

guerrillas, pursue them relentlessly and destroy their bases. Each of the recently created battalion operational sectors was to have one to two such units based in all permanent strongpoints. The concept seemed to function relatively well in the next six weeks or so, during which the *Jagdkommandos* carried out altogether 116 actions. The ever-growing tide of the Serbian insurgency had, however, rendered the concept obsolete. At the beginning of August, guerrilla attacks were largely carried out by groups of up to 40 men armed almost exclusively with rifles. Two months later, these groups were operating with 2-300 fighters apiece with enough MGs and ammunition. The hunting detachments had thus become death traps because of their small size; from now on, offensive operations would require at least a force of one reinforced battalion. This provision could hardly be met owing to the shortage of men, the 714th ID had already in August relinquished control of a sizable chunk of Eastern Serbia where no objects of military importance were located, and declared it a "restricted zone" (*Sperrgebiet*).[63]

The fact that only real front-line troops could salvage the situation in Serbia began to dawn on German decision-makers. In early September 1941, the WBSO granted Belgrade's pleas for reinforcements by dispatching the reinforced 125th IR from Greece. Shortly after that, Berlin ordered the 342nd ID, together with I/202nd Panzer Regiment (PzR)[64], from France to Serbia. Additional military measures included the strengthening of the gendarmerie to 5,000 men, as well as the creation of armed units from members of the clero-fascist political party "Zbor", and from the local White Russian émigré community. These formations would eventually become known as Serbian Volunteer Corps (*Serbisches Freiwilligenkorps*, SFK), and Russian Protective Corps (*Rusisches Schutzkorps Serbien*, RSK), respectively. The Germans also accepted the submission of Kosta Pećanac, the head of the pre-war Chetnik organization and the hero of the famous Toplica Uprising against the Bulgarians in 1917, and his armed followers (known as "Pećanac's" or "Government Chetniks"). All occupation and collaborationist forces in the country were now subordinated to the HQ of the XVIII Mountain Corps (MTC) and its commander, the Austrian-born General Franz Böhme, who was invested with dictatorial powers. The atmosphere he encountered in Belgrade was bleak: senior officers were suggesting further withdrawals, even proposing a complete abandonment of the territory lying southwest of the main railroad linking Belgrade and Skopje. Although this radical proposition was turned down, the new commander-in-chief knew that, for the time being, he could only play a firefighter's role, trying to stamp out the fires before they reached truly vital parts of the occupation edifice.[65]

The first order of business was to rid the agricultural surplus region of Mačva of guerrilla menace. On 28 September 1941, some 11,800 soldiers of the 342nd ID began crossing the

63 NARA/T314/1531/220 (749th IR, Report "Viktoria", 4.8.1941), 224-25 (704th ID to HKdo LXV, 9.8.1941); 232-35 (714th ID, Report "Kosmaj", 11.8.1941), 597 (HKdo LXV, Ia no. 500/41, 25.8.1941), 608 (BhS, Ia no. 384/41, 17.8.1941), 631-33 (HKdo LXV, Combat against communist bandits, 15.8.1941), 651 (HKdo LXV, Circular, 4.10.1941); NARA/T501/246, BhS, *Jagdkommandos* (10.10.1941); NARA/T315/2239/440-41, HKdo LXV, Enemy situation Serbia (15.10.1941); NARA/T315/2258/177, 714th ID/Oper., Activity report (1-31.8.1941).

64 The arrival of this unit with its 59 tanks brought the total number of armored vehicles in the occupied Serbia and NDH to 184; almost all were of obsolete French designs: NARA/T314/600, BhS to WBSO (2.10.1941).

65 Schmider, *Partisanenkrieg*, pp. 60, 64, 66, 69-70. The SFK and the RSK were given these designations in January 1943, and October 1942, respectively.

Sava River at Sremska Mitrovica and Šabac, marking the beginning of the German autumn operational cycle (dubbed the "First Enemy Offensive" by Yugoslav historiography). Advancing south with all three of its regiments abreast, the division had slashed and burned its way towards the northern slopes of Mount Cer within a week. The Partisans responded by withdrawing the units immediately facing the enemy (parts of the Mačva and Valjevo Detachments), while attacking the enemy supply lines between Obrenovac and Valjevo with their reserve (the Posavina Detachment).[66] The 125th IR, which had raised the blockade of Valjevo in mid-September by advancing from Belgrade, was now forced to re-trace its steps and clear the main road towards the capital instead of striking west as originally planned. The regiment had thus became unavailable for further offensive operations.

The second phase of the German onslaught involved striking through Mounts Cer and Iverak, across the Drina tributary, Jadar, and onto Krupanj. The Partisans fought back with road obstacles and well-placed demolitions: one German tank ended up in a ravine after trying to cross a seemingly intact bridge over the Jadar. On 6 October, however, they engaged in an open fight on the western slopes of the Cer, losing 14 KIA and 12 WIA to "Stukas" and heavy weapons. Despite this success, it would take the Germans another two weeks to clear the mountains and bring up supplies amidst worsening weather and road conditions. An attempt to capture Krupanj in a *coup-de-main* with two battalions failed when they ran into strong, prepared defenses along the Jadar River. The guerrillas would, however, not risk another costly frontal engagement and withdrew in haste before the major attack that finally carried the 342nd ID into Krupanj on 20 October. The last remaining task was to link the re-occupied area with Valjevo. Rotating its front 90 degrees, the division pushed through the defenses held by a pair of battalions belonging to the Valjevo Detachment in the Jadar Valley, and reached its objective two days later (23-25 October). After that, the 342nd went into cantonments around Valjevo from where it launched smaller anti-guerrilla sweeps into the surrounding countryside, at the same time preparing for the continuation of the offensive. At the cost of 10 KIA and 44 WIA, the 342nd ID had diffused the situation in northwestern Serbia, but its foe had not been dealt a decisive blow. The real guerrillas constituted only a small percentage of the estimated 3,500-4,000 "enemy dead" and executed "suspects", as witnessed by a relatively meager booty haul (342 pieces of small arms and two cannon until 14 October).[67]

The second flashpoint was located in the quadrangle Kraljevo–Kragujevac–Topola–Čačak. Kraljevo, with its 2,300-strong garrison, has been blockaded since early October, and depended on a small air bridge for supplies. In addition to the standard siege tactics (raiding sniping, etc.), the insurgents–4,500 men from the Partisan Kraljevo and Čačak and the Chetnik Jelica Detachments–also tried storming the place on at least three occasions. It was during these attacks that the Germans came to experience artillery fire and even armored assaults for the

66 NARA/T314/600, XVIII MC, Appendix 10 to war diary, Composition 342nd ID (21.9.1941). These three detachments, along with the Chetnik Jadar Detachment, had an estimated 6,000 men: Obrad Bjelica, "Nemačka ofanziva na slobodnu teritoriju Zapadne Srbije", in *Užička,* Vol. II, p. 217.

67 *Zbornik*/XII/2/1022-23, 1026-27, Ernst Wisshaupt, Quelling the uprising in the Southeast, Part I (undated); *Oslobodilački*, Vol. I, pp. 109-12; Dragoslav Parmaković, *Mačvanski partizanski odred* (Šabac: Fond narodnooslobodilačke borbe Podrinja iz Šapca, 1973), EPUB edition, Chapters "Borba kod Novog sela", Prodor kaznene ekspedicije u Jadar" and "Četrnaesti oktobar"; NARA/T501/250/1231, I/202nd PzR, Casualty return (18.11.1941); Schmider, *Partisanenkrieg*, p. 71; NARA/T315/2239/438, HKdo LXV, Enemy situation Serbia (15.10.1941).

first time in Yugoslavia. The guerrillas had four 75mm guns and enough ammunition from the stockpiles at Užice to keep up a lively fire against the town and the airstrip (e.g. 100 shell hits were recorded on 17 October 1941). The tanks were two "Hotchkiss" vehicles that were abandoned by the Germans on an earlier occasion, but found and repaired by the insurgents in the meantime. They caused a nasty surprise among their fomer owners during the final attack on the town on 1 November. In spite of all this, the odds stood on the German side, especially after one additional battalion succeeded in penetrating the blockade and reinforcing the garrison in mid-October. The decision to undertake frontal attacks–in direct contravention to the advice given by the SHQ–was inspired by the recent easy successes against enemy garrisons in the Western Morava Valley: everyone thought that, after Kraljevo, "Belgrade comes next!"[68] Other noteworthy actions fought in this period included the ambush by the 1st Šumadija Detachment on a column belonging to 521st Army Signals Regiment (*Armee-Nachrichten-Regiment)* outside Topola on 2 October, which resulted in a heavy loss of life on the German side (22 KIA, three WIA, 10 MIA). The III/749th IR spent the period 5-17 October marching and fighting along the roads linking Gornji Milanovac (which was burned down in reprisal), Rudnik, and Kragujevac; during the final leg of the journey alone, the battalion lost 10 KIA and 26 WIA.[69]

The Germans had been shooting and hanging all real or imagined enemies in droves since the beginning of the war, but the reprisals were often spontaneous, uneven in scope, and decided on a case-to-case basis. The losses incurred in the above-mentioned clashes in Šumadija, however, set in motion a new reprisal policy that called for execution of 50 hostages for each wounded soldier, and 100 for each dead (the infamous "Keitel's Order" of 16 September 1941). Spurred by simple arithmetic, mass executions dragged throughout what came to be known as "Bloody October", the worst atrocities being committed in Belgrade, Kraljevo, and Kragujevac. By the beginning of December, Böhme reported that his troops had executed close to 11,200 hostages, but the real figure is thought to be substantially higher. In addition to stronger military presence, mass murder was the second pillar of the German COIN efforts in the autumn of 1941. These measures were calculated to break the will of the insurgents and the civilian population, and this objective was achieved. Serbia was gripped by "deathly horror", wrote Milovan Đilas, and local commands were reporting a marked drop in morale and aggressiveness, and units being paralyzed by "psychosis" and "fear and restlessness."[70] Whereas the 714th ID recorded 47 guerrilla attacks and cases of sabotage in October, this number had dropped to only seven in November.

The Axis also scored significant victories against the Partisan forces in Eastern Serbia, including the effective destruction of the 1,200-strong Požarevac Detachment. This, and other units, had allowed themselves to get embroiled in frontal fighting against enemy tactical groups, which usually consisted of at least one Wehrmacht battalion and assorted quisling forces. By

68 NARA/T314/600, Major Jais, Report on trip to Kraljevo (6.10.1941); Milojica Pantelić, Radovan M. Marinković, Vladimir Nikšić, *Čačanski Narodnooslobodilački partizanski odred "Dr Dragiša Mišović"* (Čačak: self-pub., 1982), pp. 184-97; NARA/T315/2262/238, 717th ID, Daily report (17.10.1941); Jakšić, *Nad uspomenama*, Vol. I, pp. 158-59.

69 Walter Manoschek, *Serbien ist Judenfrei: Militärische Besatzungspolitik und Vernichtung der Juden in Serbien* (Munich: Oldenbourg Verlag, 1995), pp. 82, 158-60; NARA/T314/1531/518, HKdo LXV to 717th ID (10.10.1941).

70 Manoschek, *Serbien*, pp. 155-68; Djilas, *Wartime*, p. 94; *Zbornik*/I/1/199-200, II/Posavina Det., Activity report (1-20.10.1941).

the time the German operations ended in late November, only about 10 percent of the original 2,000 Partisans in this part of the country remained with the colors, others having deserted, surrendered, or been killed. The attempts by the 717th ID to eradicate the main NOP base in the area southwest of Niš in November and December had failed, however, and this was the only part of the country firmly in the Partisans' hands by the beginning of 1942. In addition to the active component (ca. 1,000 fighters in seven detachments), the army also had at least 1,500 auxiliary part-time soldiers organized in village squads.[71]

Böhme's last remaining objective was the NOP's main stronghold in the country, the so-called "Red Republic of Užice", and some 10,000 guerrillas estimated to be deployed there. The slow pace of the enemy autumn operations in Mačva and around Valjevo had led Tito to believe that an offensive against Užice would proceed in a similar manner. This would hopefully give the Partisans a chance to organize a successful defense. The abandoning of the liberated territory without a fight was apparently not contemplated: not only did the "republic" represent a solid base in the purely military sense, but it had also become a proving ground for the NOP's social experiment (see the next chapter). The single most important reason for the relative complacency that reigned in Užice was the almost complete lack of intelligence concerning the enemy plans. Had the Partisans known what their foe had in store for them, they would have probably thought twice about standing their ground. In strict secrecy, the HQ of the XVIII MTC issued the order for Operation "Western Morava Valley"/"Užice" on 18 November 1941. The 342nd ID would again carry the main burden of the fighting, advancing directly against the "red" capital from the north and northwest. Elements of the 714th ID plus collaborationist forces would attack from the northeast. The biggest surprise for the Partisans would come from the east and southeast in form of the 113th ID, which had just arrived from the Ukraine. Although the fighting on the Eastern Front had left it short of 4,000 men and all kinds of supplies (including socks), it was still a force to be reckoned with. The division, reinforced by parts of the 717th ID, was to advance concentrically from the direction of Kraljevo and Kragujevac to Čačak, and thence to Užice, destroying everything that might stand in its path.[72]

The time was just about right for a decisive offensive against the two guerrilla movements, for in the meantime they had gone from being unwilling allies to bitter enemies. Insurmountable ideological gap and entirely different concepts of resistance doomed the already half-hearted and insincere attempts at all levels (including the meeting between Tito and Mihailović on 26 October 1941) to forge a working partnership. Following a series of smaller incidents, the Chetniks attacked the Partisans on 1 November. The latter counterattacked and within a week or so brought the monarchists to the verge of collapse. Mihailović, who had already stood in contact with the Serbian collaborationist authorities through envoys, now decided to seek help from the Germans in person. Negotiating from the position of strength, the representatives of the Wehrmacht refused the colonel's pleas for ammunition and demanded his unconditional surrender instead (11 November). Mihailović withdrew from the talks and sued for a ceasefire

71 NARA/T315/2258/108, 41, 714th ID/Oper., Activity reports (1-31.10 and 1-30.11.1941, respectively); NARA/T501/246, BhS, Daily reports (12 and 13.11.1941); *Oslobodilački*, Vol. I, pp. 122-23; Milivoje Perović, *Srbija u narodnooslobodilačkoj borbi: Južna Srbija* (Belgrade: Nolit, 1961), pp. 121-31.

72 NARA/T314/600 [all XVIII MTC], War diary (28.10.1941), C-in-C visit to 113th ID (18-19.11.1941), and Operational order (18.11.1941); Schmider, *Partisanenkrieg*, pp. 77-79; Glišić, Miljanić, *Rukovođenje*, pp. 92-93.

with the Partisans; his request was granted, ostensibly in order not to bring the Soviet diplomacy into an awkward position *vis-a-vis* the British and their Yugoslav protégés. Although the newly-established mixed Chetnik-Partisan commission met several times in order to resolve disputes, the damage done to the morale of the majority of ordinary insurgents, who found the prospect of civil war deeply troubling, was irreparable.[73]

On 25 November 1941, the same day the German 4th Army erected pontoons on the Istra River some 40 km west of Moscow, two reinforced divisions of the XVIII MC launched their offensive against the heartland of the Serbian uprising. The sudden appearance of such a large and technically superior force, supported by at least 11 medium bombers, came as a shock to the Partisans. They immediately started a retreat in the general direction of Sandžak, but it soon became a rout. The Germans sliced through the liberated territory "like a knife through cheese", as Tito put it many years later.[74] The resistance was sporadic, at best, with the exception of the area Rudnik–Gornji Milanovac, where parts of two detachments were successfully holding off the Serbian collaborationist forces until they were reinforced by one battalion of the 714th ID with artillery and aircraft. Gornji Milanovac fell on 28 November, and the 113th ID entered Čačak on the same day.

In the meanwhile, the 342nd ID continued its advance towards Užice despite, "the heaviest use" of artificial obstacles by the enemy. By the 29th, the division's right-hand battle group, coming from the direction of the Drina Valley, had come within a striking distance of the town. At this critical moment, the SHQ ordered its only reliable reserve, Workers' Battalion of the Užice Detachment, to occupy the ultimate defensive position anchored on the hilltop known as Kadinjača. Noticing this, the Germans subjected the whole area to a lengthy artillery barrage prior to committing their tanks and infantry. When the smoke cleared, some 240 bodies were found on the scene, nearly the entire Partisan force; the division's own losses were only two KIA and two MIA. The sacrifice of Workers' Battalion was one of the founding myths of the Partisan saga, commemorated in monuments, books, and movies. Its last stand bought several hours for the evacuation of the SHQ and the wounded but could not save the capital: the 342nd's left-hand pincer arm entered Užice via Požega around 1430 hours on the 29th. The pursuit to the Uvac River continued for another five days, but the light-footed guerrillas ultimately managed to outrun their opponents and reach the relative safety of the Italian occupation zone.[75]

The Germans terminated Operation Užice on 4 December 1941 and turned their energies to mop-up activities and counting the booty. At the price of a mere 10 KIA and 22 WIA, the 342nd ID captured, among else, 2,723 rifles, 28 MGs, four cannon, one mortar, 23 motor vehicles, and 120 railway freight cars laden with various goods[76]; apart from that, the Germans retrieved over 3,000 tons of fuel they had left at Požega in September, and which the Partisans

73 Tomasevich, *Chetniks*, pp. 145-55; Trew, *Mihailović*, pp. 65-66, 75-76, 87-78.

74 Petranović, *Srbija*, p. 294.

75 Ernst Percy Schramm (ed.), *Kriegstagebuch des Oberkommando der Wehrmacht 1940-1945* (Herrsching: Manfred Pawlak Verlag, 1982), Vol. I, p. 776 (25.11.1941); Mikić, *Nemačka*, pp. 86-90; NARA/T315/2258/76-77, 714th ID, Enemy situation report (20.11-4.12.1941); NARA/T501/250/491, 342nd ID to BhS (28.11.1941); Slavko Odić, Slavko Komarica, *Partizanska obavještajna služba 1941-1942: šta se stvarno događalo* (Zagreb: Centar za informacije i publicitet, 1988), Volume II, pp. 125-32.

76 NARA/T314/1531/1121-23, 342nd ID, Report "Užice" (8.12.1941). These types of figures usually vary from report to report, and must therefore be taken only as approximate. For instance, one other document mentions 12 mortars and 80 freight cars, and puts the combined losses of the 342nd and

saved for the anticipated arrival of Soviet airplanes. Although content with the outcome of the campaign, the new Wehrmacht commander in Serbia, General Paul Bader, predicted that the uprising would flare up again in the spring. Knowing also that the front-line troops would soon be transferred to the main fronts (the HQ of the XVIII MC had already left, and the 113th ID was due to leave at the beginning of January 1942), the Germans sought to strengthen the occupation apparatus by relying on the locally available means. The Serbian collaborationist formations were to be strengthened from the current ca. 12,500 to 16,000 men. Furthermore, by the end of December, the Bulgarians agreed to set up their own occupation zone in Serbia proper stretching to Kraljevo in the west, Lapovo in the north, and Zaječar in the east, and man it with three infantry divisions.[77]

There could be no doubt that the Serbian partisans suffered a heavy blow. There were many reasons behind it, including the Axis numerical and material superiority, the fear of reprisals, the onset of winter, and the disillusionment caused by the civil war. It is not possible to make a precise breakdown of the Partisan losses owing to the chaotic circumstances of the retreat, and the German habit of lumping together all executed civilians and guerrilla prisoners under the category "enemy dead". Due to the fact that there were very few open engagements and that more than a half of all small arms captured by the Wehrmacht were not found on the battlefield (usually the best indicator of success in anti-guerrilla operations) but in magazines, it would be safe to assume that the Partisan detachments in Western Serbia had simply melted away before the enemy. What we do know is that the guerrilla force that was assembled around Nova Varoš during the first week of December 1941 had only about 1,500 men.

The NOP leadership held two meetings in order to discuss the recent events and determine future strategy. Following a round of criticism and self-criticism, Tito offered his resignation as the secretary-general of the KPJ. The other Politburo members present disagreed: it would look like admitting a mistake, and Moscow could again become suspicious that something is not quite right with the Party. Inexplicably, the situation in Serbia was described as being not that bad after all, and Tito opted to send some of the fighters back as soon as they were reorganized and rested. This decision was based on the assumption that the great Soviet winter counteroffensive "could develop at a lighting speed" and bring the Red Army to Yugoslav borders in a matter of weeks. The reorganization included the purge of all those who sinned against the cause: included were some leaders who failed to stop the looting during the retreat from Serbia, and a Party member who helped himself to the money from the Užice vaults. He and at least two other fighters were executed; "panic-mongers" and "malingerers" were only disarmed.[78] During the Užice period, a former major of the royal army, Branko Poljanac, served in unofficial capacity as Tito's chief of staff. The post was now formally created and entrusted to Arso Jovanović, the conscientious, but obstinate and prickly general staff officer of Montenegrin extraction.[79] Some

113th ID at six KIA and 34 WIA: NARA/T314/600, XVIII MC, Appendix 338 to war diary, Overall result "Užice" (2.12.1941).

77 Jovan R. Radovanović, *Požega u NOR i revoluciji* (Požega: SUBNOR, 1986), p. 97; NARA/T501/256/1171, BhS/Intel., Plan for buildup of Serbian government forces (1.12.1941); NARA/T314/1531/936, HKdo LXV, Situation map (31.12.1941); Wisshaupt, *Quelling*, pp. 1038-42, 1060.

78 *Zbornik*/II/1/92 (Ranković and Ivo-Lola Ribar to Tito, 10.12.1942), 124 (Djilas to Tito, 23.12.1941).

79 Due to the fact that both Poljanac and Jovanović opted for Stalin in 1948, the true extent of their contribution to the Partisan cause is still shrouded in controversy.

lessons from the past were still not learned, however. Acting on bad intelligence, the Partisans tried to take the regional center of Sjenica on 22 December, only to be beaten back by the local Muslim militia with the loss of at least 70 men.[80]

At the same time, an event of monumental importance for the course and outcome of the war was happening some 65 km to the northwest. The demise of the Užice Republic had amply illustrated the biggest shortcoming of the old detachments: they were organized on territorial principle, and their peasant rank-and-file would not fight too far away from their villages. This made them all but useless for anything other than local actions, to say nothing of the strategy on national level that the SHQ was trying to pursue. Judging that new opportunities could be found in the west, Tito decided in mid-December 1941 to take approximately one third of his entire force (which by now was composed of ca. 3,000 "refugees" from Serbia, newly-arrived Montenegrins, and fighters from Sandžak units) across the Lim River. These were the cadres for an entirely new type of unit: 1st Proletarian People's Liberation Assault Brigade was formed in the small town of Rudo on 21 December 1941 (*nota bene*, Stalin's birthday). Made up of highly motivated personnel (450 card-carrying KPJ members, 260 members of the SKOJ, the rest being sympathizers), the brigade was "to fight across [Yugoslavia] and go wherever sent". The brigade proved its battle worthiness already on the 22nd when it forced a company of the Italian 5th Alpine Division "Pusteria" to surrender after a brief but fierce engagement. At the price of nine KIA and 13 WIA, the Partisans captured 124 men, 12 MGs, five mortars, and a rich haul of much-needed supplies. At the head of his new elite unit, Tito headed west, deeper into war-ravished, desolate Bosnia, which would remain the main Partisan stronghold for the next two-and-a-half years..[81]

1.6 Uprising in Montenegro

Unlike the uprising in Serbia, which developed gradually, the so-called "July Uprising" in Montenegro had all the makings of the popular rebellions of the past: it was massive, came suddenly, and eventually subsided with equal rapidity. In the beginning, the Italian occupation of the province seemingly had all the ingredients of a success story: the population looked reconciled to the new scheme of things; the regime was light, the occupiers well-behaved, and food imports abundant. The mood began to change as economic situation deteriorated; rumors began circulating about the upcoming creation of a personal union with Italy, as well as plans for another round of territorial re-arrangements in the region, again at Montenegro's expense (the main benefactors would be the NDH and Greater Albania). All dissenters, including nationalists and members of pre-war elites, flocked to the Communists, the only people who appeared to know what they were doing. The KPJ's influence among the masses was strong, despite the fact that Montenegro was a deeply patriarchal society. It is estimated that the country had almost as many Party members as much more populous and urbanized Serbia (1,800 compared to 2,500 in 1941, candidates not included).

Even the Communists, however, were taken aback by the scale of the uprising that had broken out on 13 July 1941, only one day after the Italian-sponsored Montenegrin parliament

80 Glišić, Miljanić, *Rukovođenje*, pp. 93, 98-99; Petranović, *Srbija*, pp. 294-95; Djilas, *Wartime*, pp. 118-19; Schmider, *Partisanenkrieg*, p. 85.

81 Miloš Vuksanović, *Prva proleterska brigada* (Belgrade: Narodna knjiga, 1981), pp. 13-15, 23-24.

had proclaimed the country's independence under Rome's protection. It is widely estimated that the number of insurgents amounted to more than 30,000 (out of the total population of about 389,000).[82] The tidal wave of the rebellion swept away telephone masts, gendarmerie stations, and *Carabinieri* patrols in the countryside, and forced the startled soldiers of the "Messina" Division to seek refuge in urban places. The insurgents blockaded the bigger garrisons and proceeded to destroy the smaller ones. From 17 to 22 July, the Italian presence in the country was reduced to Podgorica, Cetinje, Pljevlja, Nikišić, and the coastal towns. All other strongpoints–including the battalion-sized garrisons at Berane and Danilovgrad–were forced to capitulate, some after having endured several days without water in the merciless July sun. Leaving the safety of fortified barracks, even in larger groups, was a highly risky proposition: on 15 July, a column consisting of one battalion each of border guards and Blackshirts (*Camicie Nere*, CCNN) ran into an ambush at the place called Košćele, just outside Cetinje. After three days of fighting in encirclement, the column was largely routed: the insurgents reported having captured, among else, 48 MGs, four cannon, and six mortars. Three days later, a similar fate befell the reinforced 108th CCNN Battalion outside Brajići, on the winding serpentine road leading from Budva to Cetinje. The Italians lost altogether 22 KIA, 37 WIA, and 169 MIA, together with their equipment, as well as 12 trucks and one tank. The losses would have been higher had the retreat not been covered by naval gunfire and armed seaplanes.[83]

After recovering from the initial shock, the Italians acted swiftly to quell the rebellion. Beginning already on 15 July 1941, major reinforcements were being released for the service in the troublesome highlander province. The XIV AC received the "Pusteria", "Cacciatori delle Alpi" (the 22nd ID), "Venezia" (the 19th Mountain Division, MTD), "Taro" (the 48th ID), and "Puglie" (the 38th MTD); with support and Albanian auxiliary units, the Montenegrin task force numbered about 70,000 men. According to the master plan, the former three divisions would advance from their base at Podgorica towards Danilovgrad, Mateševo, and Cetinje, respectively; the "Puglie" was to strike from Kosovo to Andrijevica and Berane. Instead of returning to Italy as originally planned, the "Taro" was transported by sea to the Montenegrin littoral; from there, the division was to strike simultaneously towards Cetinje and Vilusi. The task of these forces was simple: relieve surrounded garrisons and destroy their foe who was being described as "ready for anything and imbued with mystical fanaticism [...] those captured with arms go to their execution without blinking an eye."[84]

The guerrillas, for their part, were riding high on their recent, cheaply-bought victories: according to official statistics, the insurgents lost a total of 72 KIA and 53 WIA during the entire first phase of the fighting. Consequently, they felt confident they could stand up to the Italians in an open confrontation. Their optimism, at first, seemed well-placed: from 21 to 23 July, the

82 Tomasevich, *Occupation,* pp. 138-40; Venceslav Glišić, *Užička republika* (Belgrade: Nolit, 1986), p. 26; Federico Goddi, *Fronte Montenegro: Occupazione italiana e giustizia militare (1941-1943)* (Gorizia: Led edizioni Srl, 2016), pp. 28, 100.

83 *Hronologija Narodnooslobodilačkog rata* (Sarajevo: 27. juli, 1979), pp. 55-57 (13-18.7.1941); *Zbornik*/ XIII/1/147 (Armed Forces High Command [*Commando Supremo*, CoS], Notice for 18.7.1941), 163-64 (Prefect of Kotor to Governor of Dalmatia, 18.7.1941). These victories are still being commemorated in Montenegro today: http://www.cetinjskilist.com/index.php/drustvo/item/242-obiljezena-76-godisnjica-bitke-na-koscelama (accessed on 10.4.2018).

84 H. James Burgwyn, *Imperija na Jadranu: Musolinijevo osvajanje Jugoslavije 1941-1943* (Belgrade: Službeni glasnik, 2007), pp. 89-90.

local insurgents held at bay an Italian task force consisting of up to five battalions of infantry and two of artillery north of Podgorica, inflicting an estimated 170 casualties in the process. The pressure, however, kept growing not only at the front, but also behind it, and it was now guerrillas' turn to be shocked by their enemy's response. Unable to effectively engage the quick-moving Montenegrins, the units of the Italian Royal Air Force (*Regia Aeronautica*, RA) flying from the bases at Tirana and Shkodër, concentrated on suspect villages instead. Combined with deportations, hostage-taking, arson, and liberal application of death sentence, these measures had a devastating effect on the morale of the rebels: some surrendered themselves in return for amnesty, but the majority simply went home. By mid-August, the *Regio Esercito* had reoccupied practically the entire country against largely sporadic resistance. The Italian casualties during the July Uprising are estimated at 1,079 KIA and WIA.[85]

Given its vast experience with colonial warfare, the Italian Army was surprisingly ill-prepared for a COIN campaign. During the inter-war period, theory of irregular warfare was dealt with in two articles published in the official "Rivista Militare". In practice, it was something entirely new for both the officers and rank-and-file of the divisions deployed in Yugoslavia. The HQ of the "Taro" Division had therefore issued a set of brief guidelines in early August 1941. The document likened anti-guerrilla operations to hunting. First, the intelligence service must locate "the lair", which would then be encircled by strong and daring patrols supported by single mortars or pieces of artillery. Once "the cage" was shut, all rebels encountered within it, armed or otherwise, should be liquidated. Other tactics included ambushing the insurgents while they visit their homes for resupply, taking the relatives of guerrilla commanders hostage, and giving money in exchange for weapons. Offensive operations should be carried out by a force of at least one battalion of infantry and one battery of artillery, just as the Germans would soon be doing in Serbia. Prompted by the painful experiences from the past, the use of motor transport was prohibited: columns had to advance on foot, always throwing out flankers. Higher Italian commands, like the 2nd ITA and its V AC deployed in northwestern Croatia, were issuing their first guidelines as well. They all had the makings of a "beginner's guide to counterinsurgency", containing classic principles like the need to fight the guerrillas by using their own methods, be constantly alert and have a good intelligence service, erect all-round defenses, keep garrisons over-supplied, encircle the enemy whenever possible, and pursue him until he was utterly destroyed.[86]

Whether the units on the ground would be capable of following these seemingly simple rules remained to be seen. The Yugoslavs in general did not think much of the "New Romans'" martial qualities. One popular saying went like this: "What has feathers, but is not a bird? What runs away, but is not a rabbit? What carries a gun, but is not a soldier? A *Bersagliere*."

85 Mladenko Colić, *Pregled operacija na jugoslovenskom ratištu 1941-1945* (Belgrade: VII, 1988), pp. 38-41; *Zbornik*/XIII/1/185 (Pirzio Biroli to CoS, 22.7.141), 206-07 (51st IR to "Cacciatori delle Alpi", 26.7.1941); Vojislav V. Mikić, *Italijanska avijacija u Jugoslaviji 1941-1943. godine* (Belgrade: VII, 1998), pp. 28-30, 33; Burgwyn, *Empire*, p. 91.

86 Federica Saini Fasanotti, Basilio di Martino, Filippo Cappellano, Andrea Crescenzi, Alessandro Gionfrida, *L'esercito alla macchia: controguerriglia italiana, 1860-1943: l'esperienza italiana di controguerriglia dal brigantaggio alla Seconda Guerra mondiale* (Rome: Stato maggiore della difesa, 2015), pp. 209-10; *Zbornik*/III/4/401-02, "Taro", Operational order (21.7.1941); *Zbornik*/XIII/1/241-45 ("Taro", Combatting the insurgents, 1.8.1941), 448-55 (V AC, Guerrilla warfare, 20.10.1941), 461-63 (2nd ITA to V AC, 23.10.1941).

There were exceptions, of course: the prowess of Italian mortar crews, for instance, was widely acknowledged. In December 1941 one Italian unit scaled a 1,100 meter-high frozen hilltop outside Grahovo, thereby totally surprising the local Partisans (no small feat), and contributing to the subsequent relief of the town.[87]

Tito's misgivings as to the the viability of sudden, spontaneous uprisings and the Communists' ability to steer them, which he voiced to Đilas prior to the latter's departure for his home province in early July 1941, were seemingly confirmed. The Montenegrin leadership found itself stretched between adherence to the Party line and its own instincts. It first called upon the people to rise up, then turned them back for fear of going against the SHQ directives, only to realize that an avalanche, once triggered, cannot be stopped. Đilas was eventually sacked for his perceived errors and ordered to Užice; there he took up the post of the Politburo's main propagandist, a task much more suited to his nature.[88] The defeat of the uprising also made the leaders on the ground re-embrace the spirit of Tito's instructions by reverting to purely guerrilla actions. These included mining roads, felling telephone posts, and assassination attempts on collaborators and representatives of the occupation authorities; 13 such incidents were recorded in the last 20 days of November in the area of Kotor alone. However, it also included the classic ambush at Jelin Dub on 18 October, when the Partisans destroyed a column of about 40 vehicles and captured over 60 enemy soldiers, and the actions at Vilusi on 26 November (88 prisoners) and Podgorica four days later (60 prisoners).[89] The time between August and November was used to streamline the NOP's organization and strengthen its cohesion. The old "People's Army", a loose conglomerate of kin and clan companies, was slowly giving way to a Stolice-type field force with a firm chain of command and a core of dedicated fighters in each sub-unit. There were now four (soon to be reorganized into six) detachments with close to 4,500 armed men, not counting independent battalions and territorial units. Even if the post-war Yugoslav claim of altogether 20,000 armed Partisans at the end of 1941 seems vastly exaggerated (the MHQ Montenegro estimated its own effective strength at about 7,000 in January 1942), there can be no doubt that the uprising was going through a renaissance.[90]

This ambitious plan calling for the taking of Pljevlja, one of the largest urban centers in Sandžak, was illustrative of the newly-found confidence among the NOP's provincial leadership. The success would not only bring all the usual spoils (shelter, rare commodities, new recruits, as well as prestige), but would also enable a link-up with the Užice Republic and allow food imports into the shortage-plagued liberated territories in Montenegro. The country-wide campaign for volunteers that ran through most of November 1941 was met with an overwhelmingly positive response, although some HQs did not hesitate to brand those unwilling to serve away from their homes as deserters. By 26 November, all nine battalions of the special purpose command

87 Jakšić, *Nad uspomenama*, Vol. I, p. 228; Savo Orović, *Ratni dnevnik 1941-1945* (Belgrade: Hronometar, 1972), pp. 96, 122 (17.7 and 15.12.1941); *Zbornik*/III/4/84, Diary of Savo Orović (26.12.1941).

88 Djilas, *Wartime*, pp. 8, 23-25; *Zbornik*/III/4/12-32, Resolution of PK Montenegro (August 1941); *Zbornik*/III/1/68-69 (CK KPJ to PK Montenegro, 22.10.1941).

89 Ibid., pp. 71 (MHQ Montenegro, Proclamation no. 1, 26.10.1941), 262 (Zeta Det. to Lješko-Podgorica Btl., 3.11.1941); *Zbornik*/XIII/1/648-49, 664-65 (Police HQ Kotor, Situation reports 11-20.11, 20-30.11.1941), 773 (2nd ITA, List of incidents, 27.11.1941).

90 *Zbornik*/III/1/146-53 (Memorandum on leaders' summit, 15.11.1941), 325 (Lovćen Det. to MHQ Montenegro, 17.12.1941); Anić, Joksimović, Gutić, *Narodnooslobodilačka*, p. 76; *Zbornik*/III/4/96, MHQ Montenegro to SHQ (11.1.1942).

named People's Liberation Partisan Detachment of Montenegro assembled at the base of Mount Durmitor. Four days later, the detachment's 3,690 fighters (armed with light infantry weapons, one cannon, and six mortars) took up positions around Pljevlja, with the assault being scheduled to begin in the early morning hours of 1 December. From that moment on, everything went wrong: no attempt was made to infiltrate the town beforehand, and battalions went forward independently of one another. The state of enemy's defenses, and especially of his morale, was woefully underestimated: the garrison, consisting of some 2,000 men of the "Pusteria" Division put up a fierce resistance. The attackers were beaten back with the loss of 203 KIA and 269 WIA, making this one of the bloodiest single day's actions fought by the Partisans in the entire period prior to 1944. The loss of so many men "wrapped Montenegro in black" and compelled the MHQ to offer a public condolence to the entire country (which, in turn, earned it a rebuke from Tito who thought that such a gesture was un-military). Behind the scenes, a usual round of analysis, criticism and self-criticism, dominated the correspondence. The defeat had once again proved that the Partisan army, as it stood, still lacked the experience needed for more ambitious, frontal operations. Despite all efforts, *esprit-de-corps* was not sufficiently developed, as confirmed by the mass desertion in the aftermath of the battle; in the end, only some 700 fighters chose to stay in Sandžak.[91]

1.7 Country in Flames: Bosnia-Herzegovina

The uprising in Bosnia-Herzegovina was also a spontaneous affair, but it was caused by far more sinister reasons than hurt national pride. The new masters of the country, the Croatian ultra-nationalist Ustashe, blamed the Serbs for all the wrongdoings perpetrated in the inter-war period by the royal regime. Consequently, they viewed a full one-third of the NDH's population (close to two million people) as Belgrade's "Trojan Horse", and therefore the main obstacle to their dream of an ethnically homogeneous Croat state. Although the Ustasha leader, Ante Pavelić, was careful enough not to leave a paper trail, the gradual intensification of repression, was, if not always directly ordered, then definitely condoned and encouraged by Zagreb. Local Ustasha bands, consisting often of lowest dregs of society rallied around the movement's veterans, started murdering eminent Serbs (priests, officers, members of the intelligentsia) in their communities, or ship them off to recently opened death camps (such as Jadovno). Spurred by the rumors of the impending uprising, scheduled to begin on St. Vitus Day (anniversary of the Battle of Kosovo in 1389, and also of the assassination of the Austro-Hungarian crown prince in 1914), the anti-Serb hysteria had reached its zenith by June 1941. Not before long, entire villages were being massacred, often in a manner reminiscent of the Thirty Years War. Facing extermination, the Serbs took to arms and began to organize themselves into a self-defense force.[92]

91 *Zbornik*/III/1/193-94 (MHQ Montenegro to SHQ, 26.11.1941), 215 (Strength of Montenegro Det., November 1941), 370 (SHQ to MHQ Montenegro, 22.12.1941), 344-48 (MHQ Montenegro, About the Pljevlja raid, and Condolences, both 21.12.1941); *Zbornik*/II/1/288 (SHQ to MHQ Montenegro, 30.1.1942); *Zbornik*/III/4/67-72 (MHQ Montenegro to SHQ, 11.12.1941). The Italian garrison at Pljevlja also suffered heavily, altogether 74 KIA, 170 WIA, and eight MIA: ibid., pp. 449-54, "Pusteria", Report Pljevlja (10.12.1941).

92 For more on the Ustasha political program in theory and practice see Alexander Korb, *Im Schatten des Weltkriegs: Massengewalt der Ustaša gegen Serben, Juden, und Roma in Kroatien 1941-1945* (Hamburg: Hamburger Edition, 2013).

The first massive outburst of resistance took place in Eastern Herzegovina in June 1941. By the end of the month, the NDH presence in the area had been reduced to a couple of strongpoints, where the Ustashe and gendarmerie were barely holding out against thousands of armed insurgents. In an attempt to salvage the situation, Pavelić curbed Ustashe activities and tasked the army with pacifying the region. During the first week of July, the *Domobranstvo*, using altogether six battalions of infantry, a battery of howitzers, and some light aircraft (three of which were forced to land by enemy anti-aircraft [AA] fire) managed to relieve the besieged garrisons and restore control over road communications. Since the insurgents had also achieved their goal of keeping the NDH authorities out and far from their villages, an uneasy, informal ceasefire had set in.

So far, the Communists had little influence over the course of events: out of altogether 850 members the Party had in the provinces of Bosnia and Herzegovina, only some 130 were located in the latter. They did join the uprising after 22 June but were far from being the driving force behind it. During the lull in the fighting that lasted for the remainder of July and almost entire August, the Communists managed to place themselves at the head of the insurgents. Owing to the volatile and unpredictable nature of these masses, as well as the fact that the NOP's ideals were far from being universally popular, the Partisans neither insisted on their brand of discipline, nor dismantled the already existing military organization of the insurgents (system of village companies). On 26 and 31 August, the guerrillas celebrated their first major victories in the second phase of the uprising. In the type of incident that would keep occurring with alarming regularity until the end of the war, two battalions of Home Guards (the *Domobrani*; sing. *Domobran*) allowed themselves to be captured after only a brief firefight; most of them were set free after being stripped of their clothes and equipment. The garrison at Bileća was spared the same fate only through the timely intervention of the Italian "Marche" Division from Trebinje.[93]

Unlike the Germans who "knew only of either bombs or embraces" (Edmund Glaise-Horstenau) in the realm of foreign policy, the Italians were far more flexible. Using the turmoil as a pretext for further curbing the sovereignty of its renegade Croatian protégé, the fascist Italy re-occupied Herzegovina in early September 1941 with Zagreb's grudging consent. Everywhere they went, the Italians presented themselves as friends and saviors of the Serbs, expelling the Ustashe, restoring desecrated Orthodox churches, and handing out food to refugees. This cunning policy did not fail to produce the desired effect: the majority of the insurgents did not want to fight against the Italians. The uprising subsided again, and the ebb would last until December. The Partisans used the time to carry out yet another round of reorganization, which included the forming of battalions (ten by the end of the year, with about 3,500 men), and subordinating them to the HQ of the Herzegovina Detachment. In addition to smaller raids, the detachment also carried out several bigger actions in the last month of 1941. These included the thorough demolition of the railway installations linking the region with Dalmatia and the Bay of Kotor, an attack on a train laden with Italian soldiers (three KIA, five WIA, 40 MIA),

93 Davor Marijan, "Lipanjski ustanak u istočnoj Hercegovini 1941. godine", *Časopis za suvremenu povijest*, 35:2 (2003), pp. 545-76; Uglješa Danilović, "Ustanak u Hercegovini, jun 1941-jun 1942", in *Hercegovina u NOB* (Belgrade: Vojno delo, 1961), Vol. I, pp. 24-34; *Enciklopedija*, Vol. III, pp. 430-31; *Zbornik*/IV/35/21-22, Herzegovina Det., Cirular (26.9.1941); Anić, Joksimović, Gutić, *Narodnooslobodilačka*, pp. 47, 84-85.

ambushing supply columns outside Trebinje (six KIA, 29 MIA, seven trucks lost) and north of Mlini (two tanks disabled by mines). The Partisan presence was also felt in the northern part of the province, where the Konjic Battalion, formed around the core of KPJ members from Mostar, was launching attacks against the all-important Neretva Valley railroad.[94]

Officially, the start of Bosnia-Herzegovina uprising was 27 July 1941, when the Communist-led guerrillas liberated the town of Drvar in Western Bosnia. Just as in Eastern Herzegovina, locally organized groups of armed KPJ members and sympathizers who left the towns and "went into forest" (as the contemporary saying went) found a mass of determined, but only partially armed and leaderless insurgents. The successful storming of Drvar opened the floodgates, and the tide soon swept the entire region of Bosanska Krajina, destroying almost all semblance of the NDH authority in the countryside. In mid-August, the *Domobranstvo*, Ustashe, and gendarmerie launched a large-scale operation against the centers of the rebellion, Mounts Kozara and Grmeč, and the area around Drvar. The offensive, accompanied by widespread arson and massacres, lasted until the beginning of September and produced yet another proof of the total inability of the Zagreb regime to cope with the situation of its own making. Although some roads were (temporarily) opened and some garrisons relieved, the military potential of the guerrillas remained virtually untouched. Even when the insurgents fought from fixed positions, the NDH's armed forces could not deliver decisive results despite the involvement of comparatively strong forces (e.g. five battalions of infantry and three batteries of artillery north of Drvar in the last decade of August). Ultimately, the uprising would fall victim to an Italian intervention. This was not so much due to their military might, which was considerable (the "Bergamo" and "Sassari" Divisions of the VI AC), as to their skillful propaganda. Like their Herzegovinian kinsmen, the vast majority of the insurgents were more than willing to return to their homes provided they were guaranteed protection against the Ustashe. Consequently, when the Italians gave that promise and started their advance from the direction of Knin and Livno, guerrilla units were hit by mass desertions. Even so, the "Sassari" needed three full days to clear the die-hards from the 15 km stretch of road between its jump-off positions and Drvar, which was taken on 25 September. Three days later, the division made contact with the *Domobranstvo* forces north of the town, thus sealing the fate of the liberated territory.[95]

In addition to the treacherous monarchists (see below), the defeat was attributed to all the inherent weaknesses of insurgents' militias such as un-military bearing, loose coordination, and propensity to maintain defensive "fronts" around their villages. The ebb in the uprising caused by the Italian intervention was used by the NOP leadership to rectify some of these shortcomings. Out of approximately 6,000 rebels equipped with firearms in mid-August 1941, only about one-third chose to stay with the colors. These men were few in number, but willing to submit themselves to the Partisan discipline, making them militarily much more useful than a multitude of simple armed peasants. One of the first reforms was to abolish the system of "shifts", a compromise solution the Communists had to accept in order not to estrange themselves from the rank-and-file. The system allowed the insurgents to spend a certain period of time away

94 *Zbornik*/XIII/1/787, 823, 2nd ITA, List of Incidents (4, 19, 24.12.1941); *Zbornik*/IV/2/549-57, 6th HDB ID, Activity report (1-31.12.1941); *Hronologija*, p. 170 (18-19.12.1941); Enver Ćemalović, *Mostarski bataljon* (Mostar: City municipality, 1986), pp. 19-63.

95 *Oslobodilački*, Vol. I, pp. 79-83; NARA/T312/460, DGA, Situation report (28.8.1941); *Zbornik*/XIII/1/429-31, VI AC, Activity report (15-30.9.1941).

from the front line, so that they can tend to their private business. In October, all Partisan forces were reorganized into three Krajina Detachments, with the 1st being deployed between the Una and Sana, the 2nd was based on Mount Kozara, while the 3rd was spread from Kupres in the southwest to Doboj in the northeast. For almost two months, Drvar had been the heart of the NOP's action in this part of the country, a mini-version of the Užice Republic. An industrial center, the town was home to some 2,000 workers, making it an ideal recruiting ground. In addition, the presence of workshops even allowed for the production of hand grenades. After the Italian intervention, the Partisans moved their main base to the Kozara. Owing to the overwhelmingly favorable popular response to the NOP's program, this area was already a firm Partisan stronghold. This enabled the local command to cease holding fixed lines already in August, withdraw deeper into the forests, and concentrate on training.[96] The 2nd Detachment's aggressiveness and its proximity to the important Ljubija coal basin made it the target of regular Axis forays: the one from November involved four German (mostly from the 718th ID), and 10 NDH battalions. The result was disappointing: despite the fact that 860 "enemies" were reported killed, only two rifles and several revolvers were captured. This was not the first time Wehrmacht units were used in these parts. Two companies of the aforementioned division intervened on the Kozara in mid-August, losing two KIA; later the same month, the Germans helped their allies around Bosanska Kostajnica with three aircraft and an armored train.[97]

The uprising in Eastern Bosnia followed the same pattern as in the rest of the province: Ustasha massacres, followed by the arming and organizing of Serb village militias, followed by the dismantling of the NDH apparatus in the countryside. It shared several similarities with the insurrection in the neighboring Serbia as well, namely the existence of the Chetniks, and insurgents' propensity to engage in siege warfare. Zvornik, an important crossing point on the Drina River, was subjected to attack in late September 1941 after nearly all of the neighboring towns on both sides of the border had already been lost to the guerrillas. The garrison, consisting of one battalion of the 718th ID and some NDH troops, held its ground in semi-isolation for about two weeks until both the Chetniks and Partisans decided they had enough. Further south, the all-NDH garrison of Rogatica fought for 11 days before breaking out; the ferocity of the battle is evident from the high Partisan losses (40 KIA and 120 WIA). From there, the attackers proceeded to Višegrad, whose only life-line consisted of an occasional supply drop made by German and NDH airplanes. The planned assault, however, did not take place owing to the worsening situation in Serbia caused by Böhme's offensive. At the same time, the Partisans were successfully maintaining the defense of what could be described as their lines of circumvallation, thwarting all attempts by the Axis to re-open the ground communications between Sarajevo and the isolated garrisons in the Drina Valley. The Germans were forced to intervene already in the second half of August after their military bus had been ambushed near Mokro with the loss of six KIA.[98]

96 Dušan Lukač, *Ustanak u Bosanskoj Krajini* (Belgrade: VIZ, 1967), pp. 88, 159, 182, 206, 243-4, 250-5; Anić, Joksimović, Gutić, *Narodnooslobodilačka*, pp. 48, 83.

97 NARA/T315/2266/280-81 (718th ID to HKdo LXV), 284 (II HDB AC to 718th ID, both 1.12.1941); NARA/T315/2265/744-45, I/738th IR, Action report Puharska (14.8.1941); NARA/T312/460, DGA, Situation report (23.8.1941).

98 NARA/T312/460, XVIII MC, War diary (21.10.1941); NARA/T312/460, DGA, Situation report (21.8.9141); Arthur Strecker, "An der Drina", in Otto Weingartner (ed.), *Erinnerungen an die 118.*

The real crisis, however, came at the end of the same month in the part of the country that had been largely untouched by the rebellion until then. After a long period of preparations, on 23 August the KPJ organization on Mount Ozren launched an all-out assault against the Axis installations in the Bosna River Valley between Zavidovići and Doboj. The objective was twofold: capture the former Yugoslav army's ammo dumps located in the area, and demolish the Austro-Hungarian-built, narrow-gauge railway linking Dubrovnik and Slavonski Brod, the umbilical cord of Bosnia-Herzegovina. The operation was largely a success: the guerrillas had all but taken Doboj (the defenders held out in the medieval citadel), took some ammunition and blew up the rest, and inflicted light damage on railway installations (they lacked the expertise for more serious demolitions). The Wehrmacht rushed a battalion of infantry reinforced with tanks to the scene, forcing the insurgents to disperse and/or return to their mountain bases. The local Partisans would remain a thorn in their side, constantly launching smaller attacks against the train installations in the area. The NDH tried to eradicate this danger by launching its biggest operation yet, named "Ozren" (3-11 December), with an equivalent of 11 Home Guard and five Ustasha battalions. Despite the huge expenditure of ammunition (more than 6,700 shells and 373,000 rifle rounds) and human lives (the *Domobranstvo* alone lost 52 KIA, 202 WIA, and 12 MIA), the operation had merely succeeded in pushing the guerrillas deeper into the mountain.[99]

On paper, prospects appeared favorable for the Bosnian branch of the NOP at the end of 1941: six Stolice-type detachments with more than 5,600 fighters controlled most of the territory between Kalinovik in the south and Tuzla in the north. In reality, however, the momentum of the uprising had already begun to abate. The NDH military measures had little to do with it: the only success they achieved hitherto was the routing of the embryonic Majevica and Bijeljina Companies in early September, which had slowed down the development of the NOP in the northeastern corner of Bosnia. The real problem of the uprising lay in the fact that its leaders came from the two radically opposed political camps (Communists and the pre-war elites). The only thing precluding them from having a go at each other was the fear that the largely apolitical rebel masses would defect from whoever fired the first shot in a civil war.

The outbreak of the Chetnik-Partisan conflict in Serbia in early November heightened the tensions and hastened the process of differentiation among the Bosnian insurgents, but the guns remained silent. This would not change even after the Italians had relinquished control over the territory between the source of the Drina and Višegrad to the Serbian nationalists later the same month. The Chetnik leadership had opted for far more subtle, but nevertheless effective, methods of undermining the strength of its opponent. The arrangement with the Italians was presented not as an act of treason, but as a victory over the hated Ustasha state, and was also acknowledged as such by the majority of insurgents. Other propaganda slogans, like the one about the need to concentrate on domestic enemies rather than the occupation forces, or the one about the folly of following the "foreigners" and "adventurers" (i.e. the Communists)

Jäger-Division (frühere 718. Inf.Div.) (Klagenfurt: Self-pub., 1982), pp. 14-21; *Oslobodilački*, Vol. I, pp. 138-40.

99 NARA/T315/2265/837, 718th ID, Operations order no. 24 (25.8.1941); Todor Vujasinović, "Organizacija ustanka i važnije oružane akcije na Ozrenu", in *Ustanak naroda*, Vol. IV, pp. 543-50; Amir Obhođaš, Zvonimir Despot, Bojan Dimitrijević, Mario Werhas, *Ustaška vojnica: oružana sila Ustaškog pokreta u Nezavisnoj Državi Hrvatskoj 1941.-1945.* (Zagreb: Despot Infinitus, 2013), Vol. I, pp. 303-19. The Partisan losses on the Ozren amounted to at least 40 KIA and 80 WIA.

into a winter campaign, did not fail to have the desired effect. The military potential of the NOP units began to suffer as their men flocked to the Chetnik officers who were arriving from Serbia. Furthermore, their rear had now become insecure, and the reserves of ammunition had to be held back for the case of sudden eruption of hostilities against the "allies". The fate of the Kalinovik Detachment, which had nearly ceased to exist in December due to desertions, offers a case in point.[100]

1.8 Mixed Response: Croatia

Despite the presence of the largest single KPJ organization in Yugoslavia, numbering some 4,000 members, the uprising on the territory of today's Croatia did not get off to a universally good start. Right at the very beginning, the KPH witnessed one of the worst cases of breakdown in the chain of command, followed by one of the greatest tragedies in the history of the Party. The Ustashe held about 100 Communists in the detention camp at Kerestinec, which was being used as a hostage pool. Frustrated by the apparent lack of aggressiveness on the part of the local cadre, Josip Kopinič used his standing as the Comintern's agent and radio operator to take over control of the Zagreb Party organization. He then put in motion a hastily drawn plan calling for the rescue of the Kerestinec inmates. The latter did their part by disarming the guards and breaking out of the camp in the early morning of 14 July 1941, but there was practically no one to meet them on the outside and convey them to safety. The Ustashe immediately organized a pursuit, which lasted for the next several days. Out of 94 prisoners who made the escape, only 14 survived; 36 were killed during the manhunt, and 44 more were executed in Zagreb later on. The catastrophe prompted Tito to effectively put the entire Croatian leadership on probation and discipline all involved; this also applied to the unruly Soviet agents (Kopinič and one other), so as to assure that similar breaches of the Party discipline and hierarchy do not occur again in the future.[101]

Depending on factors such as ethnic composition, level of repression, and strength of local KPJ organizations, the events in the field followed two distinct patterns: one in those parts of the country lying south of the Sava River, and the other in the regions to the north of it. The distinction of being the oldest Partisan unit in Croatia belongs to the Sisak Detachment, which was formed already on 22 June 1941 from some 15 KPJ members who escaped from Sisak. The group–which had not been particularly active–survived two NDH attempts to destroy it (one in July and one in September), before leaving for Banija.[102] Being particularly heavily hit by the Ustasha terror, this ethnically mixed province, as well as the neighboring lands of Kordun, Lika, and northern parts of Dalmatia, became the hotbeds of armed rebellion in late July 1941. Northern Dalmatia, however, was out of the picture already in early August owing

100 *Oslobodilački*, Vol. I, pp. 86, 143-45; Tomasevich, *Chetniks*, p. 157; Anić, Joksimović, Gutić, *Narodnooslobodilačka*, pp. 83-84.

101 Ibid., p. 41; *SZH*/I/121-24 (Vladimir Popović to Tito, 17.7.1941), 126-28, 175-76 (CK KPJ to CK KPH, 17.7 and 10.8.1941, respectively), 179 (Tito to Comintern, 17.8.1941).

102 Adam Dupalo, *Banija i Sisak u NOP-u 1941. Događaji, svjedočanstva, dokumenti* (Zagreb: Savez antifašističkih boraca i antifašista Republike Hrvatske [hereinafter: SABARH], 2014), pp. 53-57, 79-81, 101.

to the dominant influence of the monarchists, who welcomed the Italians with open arms (the same thing would happen in the southern parts of Lika by the year's end).

The Communists managed to assert themselves as the leaders of the uprising in the remaining provinces, but the problem of how to organize, militarize, and lead the peasant masses remained. Moreover, weapons shortage here was far more acute than in Serbia or Montenegro. For instance, there were only about 1,000 rifles and 16 MGs available in the whole of Lika in late September. Around the same time, there were 28 detachments with altogether 668 men in Kordun, but only 260 rifles and some revolvers. Not even the commissars fared better: upon arriving to his unit from Zagreb, Ivan Šibl (whose war diary would become a bestseller) was handed an old sawed-off shotgun with a total of seven home-made cartridges. One exuberant local commander wrote that the capture of their first "Brno" LMG made the Partisans "feel more powerful than the [entire] NDH". Despite the shortage of arms, the NOP leadership decided to bind the people to the uprising by decreeing mobilization (which, the instructions went, should be limited "and politically well prepared"), and registering all able-bodied men on the territories it controlled. Following the traditional model, those between 20 and 40 years of age were liable for service with operational units; the men who were past their prime (between 40 and 60) were relegated to guard duties; finally, boys between 17 and 20 were assigned to youth details. The need for a reliable unit ready to serve wherever sent was recognized early on with the forming of the Flying or Assault Detachment numbering some 50 fighters. All the Partisan forces south of the Sava (including the separate HQs for Lika, Kordun and Banija, Gorski Kotar and Croatian Littoral) were subordinated to the MHQ Croatia, formed on 19 October. Operational Party Leadership [OPL] of the CK KPH would continue steering the war effort in Dalmatia and northern Croatia.[103]

The lack of arms had decisively influenced the size and scope of the Partisan actions in Croatia during 1941, which were never as large or ambitious as those carried out in the more easterly parts of Yugoslavia. With the exception of Donji Lapac, which fell right at the beginning of the revolt, the insurgents made no serious attempts against urban centers. Other armed actions remained modest in size and objectives were similar to those conducted by the Serbian Partisans during the first two months of the war. In other words, they consisted of ambushes against smaller NDH and Italian details, felling of telephone masts, railway sabotage, etc. In one notable action, the Partisans clashed with two battalions of *Bersaglieri* and Blackshirts south of Karlovac on 2-3 December, inflicting 11 KIA and 30 WIA. Less successful in material, but far more so in propaganda terms was the spectacular incursion into this Italian-occupied regional center two weeks earlier, when 24 Partisans dressed up as the *Domobrani* infiltrated the local hospital in order to rescue a wounded comrade. As the search ended with no result, the guerrillas took two recuperating Ustashe prisoner instead (they would be liquidated along the

103 Srećko Manola, "Skica za monografiju razvoja oružane borbe na Kordunu", in *Prva godina narodnooslobodilačkog rata na području Karlovca, Korduna, Gline, Like, Gorskog Kotara, Pokuplja i Žumberka* (Karlovac: Historijski arhiv Karlovac [hereinafter: HAK], 1971), pp. 211-18; Todor Radošević, "Stvaranje i organizacioni razvoj partizanskih odreda u Lici do jula godine 1942", in ibid., pp. 671-88; *Zbornik*/XIII/1/612; Ivan Šibl, *Ratni dnvenik* (Zagreb: Naprijed, 1960), EPUB edition, Chapter "Proboj Srijemskog fronta".

way), and very nearly succeeded in exiting Karlovac undetected. In a brief exchange of fire, the group killed three *Carabinieri*, and escaped the scene with the loss of one man.[104]

The going was harder in the coastal areas of Dalmatia, Croatian Littoral, and the rugged region located between Karlovac and Rijeka known as Gorski Kotar. Unlike the ethnically mixed provinces mentioned earlier, these lands were inhabited almost exclusively by Croats. The fact that Zagreb "sold them out" to Italy by signing the infamous Treaties of Rome from mid-May 1941, and that the Fascists immediately instigated a program of forceful Italianization, made the local population susceptible to the NOP's call to arms. Unlike Serbs, however, the people here did have a choice, and few took the decision to go to war lightly. As in the rest of the country, the first armed groups in Gorski Kotar and the littoral were formed already in July, but they would not go into action until the arrival of some experienced Party members in September. By the beginning of October, the local Partisans had carried out an estimated 49 actions, including the burning down of three sawmills. At the same time, they had set up their HQ in the town of Drežnica, which had been abandoned by the occupier. The Italians (elements of the "Lombardia" and some border guard units), led by local guides and well-informed on the position of enemy camps by their spies, returned suddenly at the end of the month and dispersed the guerrillas. Although not decisive, this sweep diminished the level of popular support for the Partisans, and compelled them to undertake an overhaul of their military organization, including setting up proper intelligence and early warning services. In mid-December, the NOP in this region had only 330 fighters on active duty; for comparison, Kordun and Banija had 1,715 and Lika 3,370.[105]

On 7 August 1941, two delegates of the CK KPH arrived at Split carrying instructions for the local Party leadership. Dalmatia, they said, was lagging far behind other provinces in terms of Partisan warfare. Waging an urban guerrilla campaign was not enough: detachments were to be formed and sent into the countryside within three days. Having been accused of "opportunism" in the past (a very serious offense in Communist eyes), the PK dutifully complied. The committee assembled six groups with about 350 armed men in Split and other towns in Central Dalmatia; their task was to establish contact with the insurgents around Knin and Bosnian border. The operation turned into a nightmare: some Party members refused to "go to slaughter" and some groups had no guides. Others have underestimated the difficulties of marching in the Dalmatian karst in the August sun: they went into circles, quickly exhausting their supplies of food and water. Croatian villages along the way thought that they were vengeful Chetniks and informed the NDH and Italian authorities of their whereabouts. In the end, seven or eight fighters reached Mount Dinara (they would later serve as the cadre of the Sinj Detachment), and 11 others managed to find their way to Drvar. All other groups fell victim to Axis pursuers, desertions, or were simply dissolved.

104 *Zbornik*/V/2/38-42 (HQ Banija and Kordun, Report Karlovac, 19.11.1941), 49-54 (CK KPH to CK KPJ, 25.11.1941); *Zbornik*/XIII/1/743, 755, 785-77, 2nd ITA, List of incidents (13, 18.11, 2 and 4.12.1941).

105 Antun Giron, *Zapadna Hrvatska u Drugom svjetskom ratu* (Rijeka: Adamić, 2004), pp. 68-70; *Zbornik*/V/2/117-27 (HQ Gorski Kotar and Croatian Littoral, Report no. 1, 6.12.1941), 147 (MHQ Croatia, Strength return, 13.12.1941); *Zbornik*/XIII/1/397-400 (V AC, Incidents September 1941), 642, 656 (V AC, Activity reports 1-15 and 15-30.11.1941).

Upon hearing the news of the disaster, the CK KPH issued a severe reprimand to the PK and instructed it to inform its membership of the punishment in an open letter. The PK, however, openly refused to do so before having the opportunity to present its side of the story. Surprisingly, the CK not only let such impertinence pass, but also showed willingness to discuss specific points raised in the reprimand. By the time the drawn-out correspondence on the matter had reached its end, the letter had lost all purpose and was never published. Not long after the issuance of the reprimand, the Croatian branch of the Party received another hard blow. Rade Končar, an electrical mechanic whose passion for the cause had earned him the position of secretary of the KPH and the member of the CK KPJ by the time he was 30, was ambushed and badly beaten by police agents in Split. All plans calling for a rescue action akin to the one involving Ranković came to naught; Končar was eventually tried and executed by the Italians in May 1942. He was the fourth member of the KPJ's highest caucus who had been killed while steering the uprising on the territory of the NDH since August 1941 (the others died in Dalmatia, Kordun, and Western Bosnia).[106]

Compared to the remainder of the country, the parts of the NDH lying to the north of the Sava River were relatively peaceful throughout 1941. The reasons for this were the absence of anti-Serb pogroms on the scale encountered elsewhere, weak resonance of the NOP propaganda among the Croat majority, and the poor work of the local KPJ organizations. Some armed groups decided to dissolve themselves and return to their home towns after having spent some time "in the woods" (the case of the Zagreb-Sesvete Detachment in mid-July), while some were dispersed by NDH security forces (e.g. the future Moslavina Detachment in early August). Some Party cells remained focused on sabotage and propaganda activities in urban centers well into December (e.g. Osijek and Vinkovci). The center of guerrilla activity in this part of the country were the Slavonian Mountains, and it would remain there until the very end of the war. After a long period of preparations, which included making propaganda tours through villages and establishing contact with small groups of Serbs who had fled persecution, the local Partisans went into action in October. By the end of the year, the NOP had up to 300 fighters in this region, half-decently armed with rifles and a handful of MGs captured from communal offices, village guards, and NDH patrols. They were subordinated to the single, recently-formed Slavonian HQ, which was supplied with experienced Spanish fighters and training manuals by the OPL. The total number of men serving with front-line units in Croatia in mid-December was estimated at 6,400.[107]

At this time, the MHQ Croatia also formulated its goals on operational and strategic levels. These included the elimination of a number of enemy garrisons that stood between the liberated territories in Lika, Kordun, and Banija, thus paving the way for the creation of a unified Partisan "republic". The MHQ also "declared war" against the all-important railway link between Zagreb and Belgrade by transferring Ivan Hariš (known as the "Thunderer") from Gorski Kotar to Banija. His propensity for self-aggrandizement was matched only by his great talent for demolition, which he had sharpened in the Iberia and the Italian occupation zone. The

106 Sibe Kvesić, *Dalmacija u Narodnooslobodilačkoj borbi* (Zagreb: Lykos, 1960), pp. 130-52, 163-70, 200-02.
107 *SZH*/I/181 (District Prigorje, Warrant, 20.8.1941), 237 (County Križevci to Supervisory department/Ministry of interior [MOI], 17.9.1941), 388-90 (Pavle Gregorić to OPL, 25.12.1941); *Zbornik*/V/2/139-40 (OPL to CK KPJ, second half of December 1941), 147-48 (MHQ Croatia, Strength return, 13.12.1941), 168-69 (OPL to MHQ Croatia, 15.12.1941).

insurgents had been targeting railway lines from very early on in the period 13 July–15 August, the Germans recorded 52 incidents in the entire NDH; the main line had been hit for the first time on 14 July. Hariš's job was to turn these largely uncoordinated and spontaneous attacks into a sustained campaign carried out by specially-trained sapper details.[108]

There was one other potential flashpoint in the north of the NDH, and that was Syrmia. The local Communists won the first round by staging a successful version of the Kerestinec action: 32 inmates escaped from the penitentiary at Sremska Mitrovica on the night 21-22 August 1941 through the tunnel of their own making. Two of them were later caught, several others were too old or too frail, but the remainder was ready to join the fight immediately. Most of them went to the occupied Serbia, while some served as the cadre for the Fruška Gora and Podunavski Detachments, both formed in September 1941. Those who stayed behind experienced the same frustrations as all their comrades fighting outside the heartlands of the insurrection. In addition to isolation, shortfall of funds and military professionals, the lack of arms was particularly acute: by the end of the year, there were only 26 active Partisans in the province, "badly" equipped with rifles, revolvers, and one unserviceable LMG. The shortage of weapons and ammunition not only kept the actions on a small scale, it also precluded the guerrillas from accepting peasants into their ranks. The best that they could do was to form village militias (the resonance among Serb peasants was apparently good despite the absence of large-scale Ustasha atrocities) and hope that the situation would improve with time.[109]

To conclude, a few words on the condition of the NDH armed forces and the experiences made during the first six months of the conflict. The main problem with the *Domobranstvo* was that it had hardly completed its formation before being thrust into a COIN campaign of vast scope and complexity. Nothing in the career paths of its senior officers (mostly re-activated veterans of the Austro-Hungarian armed forces, derisively nicknamed *naftalinci*, the "Mothballers"), could have prepared them for this kind of warfare. Those who understood that the key to all COIN efforts lay in winning over civilian population were often sidelined or frustrated in their efforts by the Ustashe, over whose polices they had no control. The junior officers, regardless of whether they had been drawn from civilian, or the ranks of the former royal army, were likewise out of their depth. The rank and file saw little point in dying for the new state, which was already tainted with massive crimes and almost unparalleled lawlessness. Their morale was further undermined by the non-existence of military mail service, caused by the authorities' refusal to acknowledge the fact that the *Domobranstvo* was fighting a real war at home. Moreover, the nascent army was suffering from all kinds of technical problems. Owing to the insurgency, supply lines were stretched to the breaking point, causing shortages of food and ammunition at the front. The units were lacking winter clothing, bandages, entrenching tools, and signal equipment. Worst of all, continuous deployment was making it impossible for the men to rest, wash up, or change clothes, which contributed to the alarming drop in combat worthiness (the Ustasha units, although better motivated and supplied, were suffering from the same problem).

108 Ibid., pp. 252 (MHQ Croatia to Kordun Det. (24.12.1941), 272-73 (MHQ Croatia to SHQ, 26.12.1941); *Zbornik*/XII/1/338-39, DGA/Trans. to German embassy Zagreb (26.8.1941).

109 *Zbornik*/I/6/7-13 (Letter of escaped prisoners to PK Serbia, 31.8.1941), 13-15 (Fruška Gora Det./Pol. to MHQ Serbia, September 1941), 25-6 (OK Srem to PK Vojvodina, 5.1.1942); *Zbornik*/I/17/9-10, NDH Gendarmerie General Headquarters [GHQ] to NDH Ministry of defense [MoD] (12.9.1941).

In late December 1941, the GHQ of the HDB estimated that its combat strength had shrunk to 30-35,000 exhausted men, adding that there was not "a single battalion in reserve". The GHQ concluded its gloomy report with the opinion that the salvation could only come from outside, in form of a decisive Italian and German intervention. If the protecting powers would agree to deploy a sizable contingent of their own troops, then HDB units could be pulled out of the front line and brought back to shape in time for the spring campaign (nothing came out of this unrealistic plan). Undeterred by the present difficult situation, the GHQ issued an official, 92-point guideline for anti-guerrilla warfare. In addition to a short summary of enemy tactics, as well as basic principles of one's own conduct, the document provided for the creation of *krstarski vodovi*, which can be roughly translated as "roving platoons". These small units, made up of 30-40 hand-picked, well-armed soldiers and gendarmes were to move swiftly through the countryside and make life miserable for the guerrillas by ambushing their details and destroying their hideouts. Whether the concept was borrowed from the German *Jagdkommandos* is not explicitly mentioned; in any case, it remained to be seen how it would work in the NDH.[110]

1.9 Slow Start: Slovenia

The insurgency in Slovenia was specific in many respects. It was the only Yugoslav province where the struggle against the invader was conducted within the framework of a popular front organization, here called Liberation Front of the Slovenian People (*Osvobodilna fronta slovenskega naroda*, abbreviated to OF). In addition to the Communists, the OF was composed of some Christian Socialists, left-wing intellectuals, and a group called National Democrats. This arrangement would last until the signing of the "Dolomite Statement" on 28 February 1943, when the non-communist factions relinquished their right to independent political activism and formally recognized the leading role of the KPS. While the OF had been created already in late April 1941, the start of the uprising had to be delayed until after the beginning of Operation Barbarossa. The MHQ Slovenia, formed in the capital on the 22 June, was responsible for the entire Slovene ethnic territory, regardless of the Axis arrangements in this respect. In the Italian occupation zone, there was a prompt and perceptible change in popular mood. One Blackshirt officer was "bitten on the hand" during the demonstrations on the outskirts of Ljubljana on 23 June. The city witnessed a far more tragic incident on the same day, when a young man was killed after firing three shots at a CCNN patrol. In the period 1-15 July, the Italian XI AC recorded nine more attacks with firearms, followed by 14 more incidents in the second half of the month. By mid-September, the number of sabotage acts against telephone and railway lines had tripled compared with July. These actions were carried out by armed resistance cells in urban centers, and by Partisan companies (usually counting up to several dozen men each) in the countryside.[111]

By this time, the danger they posed had become great enough to warrant a substantial intervention by the army: the "Granatieri di Sardegna" Division launched at least two sweeps, each involving 2-3,500 troops, in August and September. After weeks of combing the craggy,

110 *Zbornik*/V/2/377-85 (HDB GHQ, Revitalization measures, 12.12.1941), 392-407 (2nd HDB IR, Combat instructions, 16.12.1941); Obhođaš et al., *Ustaška*, Vol. I, p. 310.

111 In addition to active personnel, the Partisans also established People's Defense (*Narodna zaščita*) as a sort of second-tier/reserve formation.

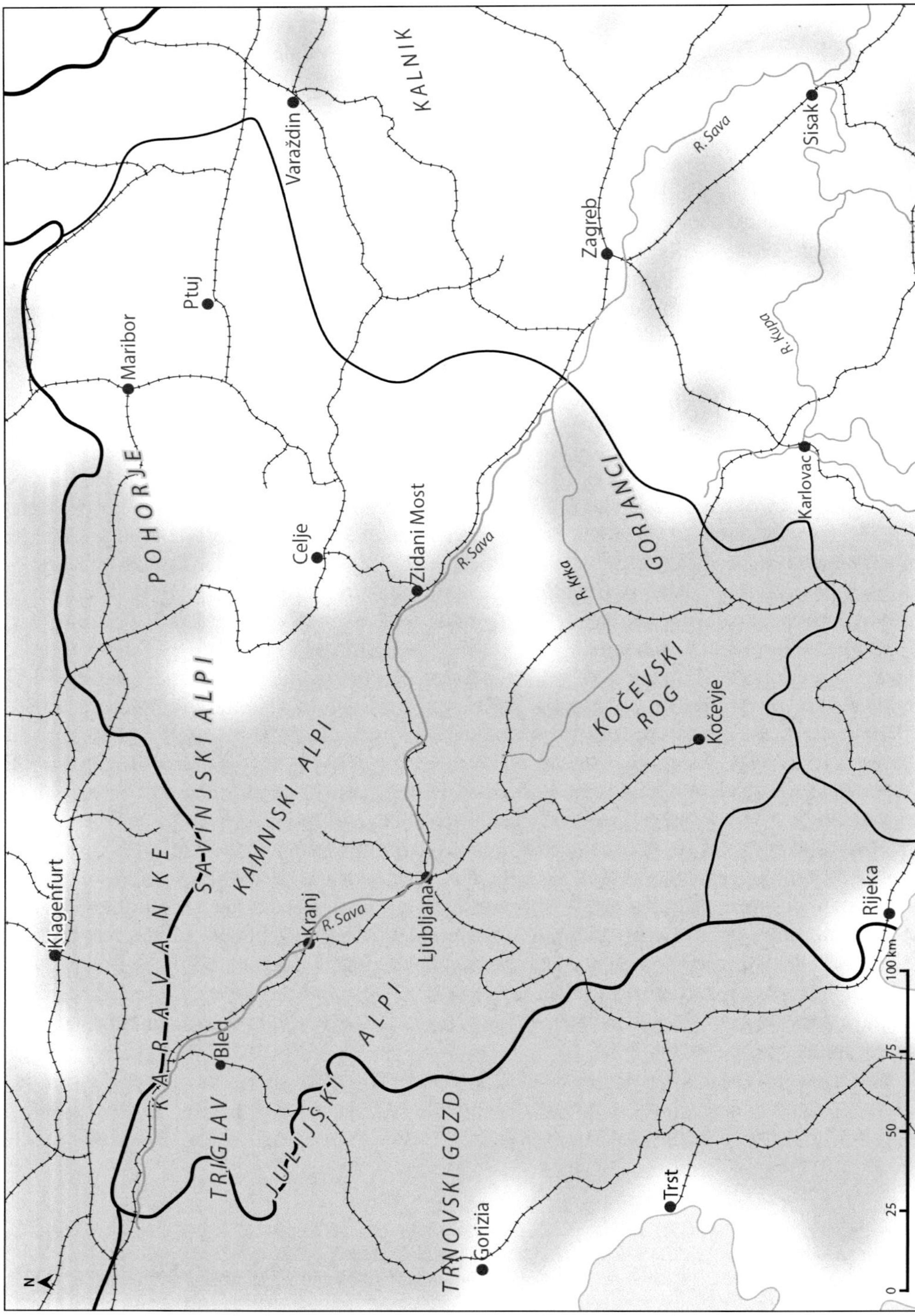

Map 4: Occupied Slovenia.

densely forested area south of the capital, the division had managed to surround the Partisan Krim Battalion in late October. This recently formed, 150-strong unit had just pulled off a twin attack on the smaller Italian border outposts at Lož and Bezuljak, killing three, wounding 23, and capturing seven enemy soldiers (the guerrillas lost one KIA and six WIA). Owing to the unrelenting enemy pressure and adverse weather conditions, the battalion had ceased to exist as an organized unit by the end of the month: some Partisans were killed, 44 were captured, and the rest dispersed. The only bright point in the entire story from the NOP's perspective was the daring return of some 20 former members of the battalion to Ljubljana by train, which passed unnoticed by the authorities. Only several days later (2 November), the Partisans were dealt another serious blow when elements of the "Isonzo" Division surprised the Bela Krajina Partisan Company at its camp, killing or capturing 19 out of its 27 men. These events marked the end of the first attempt at raising and operating classic guerrilla units in this part of Slovenia. The echo of the OF's call to arms remained weak outside the cities for several reasons: the Italians pursued a relatively mild occupation policy and were not rushing with the cultural assimilation. Furthermore, the traditionally dominant force in the countryside was the Catholic Church, and she was understandably not enthusiastic about the prospect of a Communist-run Slovenia.[112]

The uprising in the Nazi-administrative zone developed differently than in Ljubljana Province, and was shaped by two sets of factors. Probably the most important single detracting factor was fear. Unlike the Italians, the Germans made no attempts to make themselves loved, but punished every act of resistance with executions, burning down of villages, and sending of real or imagined suspects to concentration camps. The already mentioned uprooting of thousands of people and the brutal Germanization drive lent credence to the NOP's propaganda claims about the sinister nature of the occupation regime, which in turn facilitated recruitment. Moreover, the KPJ had a strong presence in this heavily industrialized part of the country: Štajerska was the home to one-half of the entire Slovene Party membership (ca. 1,000). During the earliest phase of the uprising–whose beginning was officially dated to 22 July–14 Partisan companies were formed in the German zone compared to only five in the Italian one. These companies at first acted alone, carrying out smaller actions in the vicinity of their camps, but soon began merging into battalions. Two such units were formed in early August in the Bled-Kranj area, the Storžič and the Gorenjska/"Ivan Cankar" Partisan Battalions. The appearance of these large "bandit" groups (the latter had 130 men with 45 rifles and one LMG), and the incoming intelligence about their plan to attack the Gestapo prison at Begunje, stirred the Germans into launching their first major anti-guerrilla sweep of the war. Beginning on 5 August, two

112 Klanjšček, *NOR u Sloveniji*, pp. 39-48, 79-82, 84; *Zbornik*/VI/1/243-4 (XI AC to 2nd ITA, 23.6.1941), 272, 282-3, 373 (XI AC, Intelligence bulletins nos. 16, 17, 23, 17 and 25.7, and 10.9.1941, respectively), 413-21, 431-441 (XI AC to 2nd ITA, 24.10. and 2.11.1941). Due to the fact that this paragraph closes the chapter on the operations of the Italian 2nd Army in 1941, this seems like a convenient place to cite some relevant facts and figures. The army recorded altogether 148 incidents during the last 25 days of September, 222 in the month of October, 165 in November, and 116 in December. The incidents include everything from scribbling anti-Italian graffiti on the walls of public lavatories to acts of sabotage and armed attacks. The (obviously incomplete) casualty returns speak of 27 WIA in September; 30 KIA and 78 WIA in October (soldiers only); 50 KIA and 128 WIA in November; 71 KIA, 125 WIA, and 136 MIA in December. One other document mentions 225 men still missing at the end of the year: *Zbornik*/XIII/1/476-608, 710-831 (2nd ITA, Lists of incidents, 5.9.-31.10., and 1.11-31.12.1941), 705 (2nd ITA, Meeting on 30.12.1941).

police, one *Luftwaffe*, and one SS battalion, reinforced by a company of mountain infantry (*Gebirgsjäger*), combed the suspect area, eventually succeeding in destroying the Storžič and dispersing the Gorenjska Battalion.[113]

A similar fate had befallen the Kamnik Battalion whose five companies went their separate ways in mid-August in hope of avoiding the Axis onslaught. During the next eight weeks, however, the Germans hunted down each one of these groups, either killing, or forcing their members to seek sanctuary in the Italian zone. In Štajerska, the main Partisan stronghold was located on Mount Pohorje just outside Maribor. On one occasion in mid-September, the local guerrillas forced a platoon of *Gebirgsjäger* to retreat from a hilltop after a brief firefight and then retreated themselves in order to evade retribution. Several weeks later, the same group joined hands with two other companies around Velenje and formed the Štajerska Battalion, counting ca. 50 fighters. On 7 October, the unit attacked the nearby town of Šoštanj, captured the main collaborationist office, burned the archives and the local sawmill, but ultimately failed to overpower the defenders. The battalion then took part on the abortive plan of the NOP leadership to stop the expulsion of Slovenes from the region adjacent to the Sava and Sutla by sending there all available companies from the German and Italian zones (five and seven, respectively). Just how this task was to be achieved with a couple of hundreds of fighters, at best, is unclear, but even a mere attempt was certain to produce a positive propaganda effect. In any case, the events from the final days of October and early November showed the Partisans were still too inexperienced for operations of such complexity. Some units were destroyed before they could move at all, others did not even leave their camps, and others still missed the rendezvous with their comrades and had to turn back; the deportations continued uninterrupted.[114]

It should also be noted that the Sava-Sutla operation took place after the Slovene delegates had returned from the conference at Stolice. Whereas Tito agreed to make an exception to the rule and leave in place the Slovene organizational system (company/battalion) for the time being, he did not hide his displeasure with the pace of the uprising. There were objective circumstances that precluded the northernmost Yugoslav province from ever becoming Serbia or Bosnia-Herzegovina in this respect. Slovenia had the most developed traffic infrastructure in the country, which meant that the occupying forces could intervene quickly wherever required. Furthermore, it was ethnically almost homogeneous, meaning that there were no ready-made insurgent armies composed of persecuted minorities who only needed leaders. Finally, the society lacked what used to be termed as "insurgents' traditions", developed over the centuries of Ottoman rule in Serbian and Montenegrin-populated areas. In spite of all this, both the SHQ and the leading Slovene Communists were of the opinion that more could and should be done, especially with regard to the creation of liberated territories and inciting a popular uprising.

113 NARA/T175/124, SS Reserve Infantry Btl. "Westland", Action report Bled (13.8.1941); NARA/T175/233, Sipo/SD, Event report USSR no. 48 (10.8.1941). Other anti-guerrilla measures taken by the Germans in this period included the imposition of curfew (28 July), establishing of special tribunals (29 July) and operational zones for police battalions (12 August), introduction of death penalty (16 August), and the creation of mixed police-gendarmerie mobile detachments (25 August): *Zbornik*/VI/1/285-87, 313-14, 317-18, 338.

114 Klanjšček, *NOR u Sloveniji*, pp. 61-66, 76-78, 82-85; NARA/T175/233, Sipo/SD, Event report USSR no. 89 (20.9.1941).

Consequently, a new plan was prepared which called for a winter campaign with the focal points in the area south of Ljubljana and in the western reaches of Gorenjska and Štajerska.[115]

The Partisans went into action in the first days of December 1941. In the Italian zone, the offensive had soon petered out despite having an auspicious beginning (the successful sabotage of the Prešerje railroad bridge). The incursion into Štajerska with the newly-formed 2nd Partisan Battalion was doomed to a failure the moment the Axis discovered the unit. Barely managing to evade the enemy concentrations on both sides of the border, the battalion ultimately retreated to a winter camp in the vicinity of the capital. In contrast, the developments in Gorenjska looked promising. Hitherto, the insurrection had been largely a Communist affair: for instance, of 356 Partisans registered in the province for the period 22 June-5 August, only five were peasants. Now, it was on its way to becoming a popular cause, not least because the opening of the Soviet counteroffensive around Moscow revived the belief in the quick end of the war. Among the 665 recruits who joined the ranks during the December Uprising, no less than 175 were peasants. About 350 of them joined the new "France Prešeren" Battalion, formed in mid-December beneath the towering 2,863-meter Triglav. The unit would prove to be short-lived, however: the enemy immediately organized a pursuit, causing most of the Partisans to desert; the last group of 23 survivors was dispersed in January 1942.

In the meanwhile, the Gorenjska Battalion had matured into a tightly-organized and effective guerrilla unit that dealt the Germans the first substantial blow of the war. On 12 December 1941, the Partisans ambushed a column of the 181st RPB, killing 45 men and capturing their equipment. This disaster, as well as the string of smaller attacks that had forced the gendarmerie to abandon a number of less important outposts, convinced the Nazi authorities that a decisive, large-scale action was needed in order to restore the situation. Under the auspices of specially-created army and police operational HQs, four reinforced RPBs (the 44th, 93rd, 171st, and 325th), along with the 322nd LSB, and the SS "Westland" Battalion, started their hunt on 25 December. After two weeks of marching in heavy snow and at least one sharp clash on the 27th (whereby the German police lost 13 KIA), the Partisans took up positions around the village of Dražgoše. The Gorenjska Battalion, now down to about 200 men after all those without weapons were allowed to leave, stood its ground for three days (9-11 January 1942) before escaping southwest. The Partisans lost nine KIA and 11 WIA during the battle itself, plus 12 KIA suffered when the Germans gave them a taste of their own medicine in an ambush on 13 January. After that, the guerrillas split into smaller groups and dispersed all over the province.[116]

The disbandment of the Gorenjska Battalion signified the end of the December Uprising. During the first six months of the war, a total of 1,924 people served in the Partisan units in Slovenia, while 134 Slovenes joined the guerrillas in other parts of Yugoslavia. Of these 2,058 fighters, 124 were killed in combat, 104 were tried and executed (additional 183 were captured), and 630 returned to their homes. If we add the fighters who were assigned to non-combat duties

115 Damijan Guštin, "Vprašanja oboroženega odpora 1941", *Prispevki za novejšo zgodovino*, 41:2 (2001), pp. 138-40.

116 Klanjšček, *NOR u Sloveniji*, pp. 97-103; Darko Cafuta, "Ugotavljanje števila padlih pripadnikov okupacijskih sil in partizanov", in Jože Dežman (ed.), *Nemci in partizani: Nemške izgube na Gorenjskem med miti in resnico* (Kranj: Gorenjski muzej, 2016), pp. 61–78; Tone Ferenc, "Množična vstaja na Gorenjskem decembra 1941.", *Borec*, 12 (1971), pp. 741-83.

(i.e. "political work") and those who departed for other provinces, the sum total of fighters who remained with the colors at the end of the year was 689.[117]

1.10 "Problem Children" of Uprising

As we have seen, the uprising and the NOP's military action developed differently from region to region, but there could be no doubt that, by the end of the first year of the war, it had taken root in the Yugoslav heartlands. On the other hand, there were areas where 1941 never happened, or where it came only after a long delay and amidst great difficulties. These "problem children" of the uprising were, for the most part, the border provinces, each with a set of unique characteristics that turned out to be detrimental to the Partisan cause.

The case of Macedonia had probably caused the most headaches for the NOP leadership. The biggest obstacle to the development of the uprising in this southernmost Yugoslav province lay neither in invader's policies, nor in population's disposition, but in the KPJ itself. In the spring of 1941, the head of the local PK and a known Bulgarophile, Metodi Šatorov-Šarlo, decided to recognize the new territorial arrangements in the region and submit himself and the organization he controlled to the authority of Bulgarian Communist Party (*Българска Комунистическа Партия*, BKP). As a consequence, he not only chose to disregard the KPJ's call to arms, but even instructed the membership (estimated at little over 1,000) to return hidden weapons. Tito requested Moscow's mediation, and by late August, the Comintern had decided to leave the Macedonian Communists under the auspices of the KPJ. The new provincial leadership, consisting of members with pro-Yugoslav sentiments, immediately introduced measures aimed at organizing a guerrilla war and an army to fight it. The first armed groups were formed between late August and mid-October. The Skopje Detachment (17 men) limited its activities to propaganda visits to the mountain villages north of the capital. Having received no instructions from the top, the group decided to disband itself and return home in early November, where many were arrested by the police. The Kumanovo Detachment, with 35 fighters in two companies, was formed on 12 October and destroyed only several days later. The Prilep Detachment (30 men) carried out the first notable action of the uprising, attacking the Bulgarian police station in its namesake town on 11 October. In early November, a stroke of bad luck had again checked the momentum of the uprising. The new head of the PK, Lazar Koliševski, had been arrested in early November, and the reigns of the provincial leadership were passed to another Bulgarophile, Bane Andrejev. Heavily influenced by the local representative of the BKP, Andrejev ordered the disbanding of the last remaining field unit (the Prilep Detachment), and called a halt to all armed actions so as to protect the cadres. From now on, the Communists would limit themselves to propaganda and other subversive activities including infiltration. For this purpose, they were even ordered to join the Bulgarian army if the authorities summoned them, a move which must have looked as blatant treason to the members of the "Yugoslav faction".[118]

117 Klanjšček, *NOR u Sloveniji*, pp. 104-05.

118 Banac, *Cominformist*, pp. 191-94; *NOB Makedonije: Publikacija fotografija, dokumenata i karata sa prigodnim tekstom o Narodnooslobodilačkoj borbi makedonskog naroda* (Skopje: Narodna zadruga, 1964), pp. 40, 49-55; *Enciklopedija*, Vol. VIII, p. 655 and Vol. IV, p. 763; *Zbornik*/VII/1/21 (Dragan Pavlović,

The Macedonian branch of the NOP remained passive until April-May 1942. By this time, the KPJ loyalists in the towns of Kruševo, Veles, and Bitola had decided to revive field units on their own accord. The PK sanctioned this action but kept the groups as small as possible in order to ensure secrecy and facilitate supply. Furthermore, it made sure that these bands were tightly controlled by the Party caucuses in their places of origin, and that they refrained from offensive activities. The change in their posture came only in June after the loyalists had seized power and formed a new provincial leadership; most of them would soon be arrested, but the timely arrival of a CK KPJ instructor ensured the continuity of the "Yugoslav" line. Macedonia received its own MHQ, and all Party organizations were instructed to form detachments and commence with a guerrilla campaign in the countryside. In addition to the already existing Kruševo and Veles groups, both Bitola and Prilep fielded their reconstituted units; named after the heroes of the struggle against the Ottomans ("Pitu Guli", "Pere Tošev", etc.), all these bands probably did not have more than a couple of hundreds of men.

In spite of their numerical weakness, the lively activity they developed in the period August-October, especially against municipal offices, soon forced the occupation authorities to instigate a full-blown COIN campaign. Among the measures adopted were the arming of loyal villages and the application of carrot-and-stick-policy towards the guerrillas and civilian population. The tactics included executions of captured Partisans, indiscriminate reprisals against whole villages, and cutting of food rations for the families of Partisan suspects; those NOP members who surrendered voluntarily, or those who chose to actively collaborate with the authorities, were spared or rewarded, respectively. In addition to the police, both infantry divisions deployed in the country (the 14th and 15th) now took active part in the operations and were even allotted two reconnaissance airplanes for this purpose. In November and December, these forces had foiled the plan of the Partisan MHQ to move the field units into winter quarters in the Macedonian-Serbian border area. Three out of five detachments were destroyed during this period, a blow which nullified much of the progress that had been made since summer. The campaign exposed many shortcomings of the NOP's armed wing, including the existence of parallel chains of command, inability to properly supply and direct the units in the field from urban centers, and adherence to the principle of least effort when it came to the choice of targets (concentrating on military instead on civilian targets would have yielded better results, both in propaganda and material terms). The process of mending these deficiencies would, however, not begin before the spring of 1943.[119]

In addition to previously mentioned Syrmia, the province of Vojvodina encompasses Bačka and Banat. Agriculturally probably the richest parts of Yugoslavia, these flatlands were hardly an ideal guerrilla country, the man-high corn fields being the only available cover for the insurgents during the summer months. The "corn war" (*Kukuruzenkrieg*), as the locals used to call it, began in mid-July 1941 with the standard repertory of arson attacks against the occupier's economic interests, assassination of collaborationists, and attacks on gendarmerie stations. The Germans responded by a sustained police action involving, among else, a flying squad of experienced

Report on Macedonia, 28.8.1941), 35-36 (PK Macedonia, Open letter, end of September 1941), 50-54 (CK BKP to PK Macedonia, 15.1.1942), 55-58 (PK Macedonia, Directives, January 1942).

119 *Oslobodilački*, Vol. I, pp. 222-23, 320-23; *Zbornik*/VII/1/444-45 (Skopje district directorate, Circular, 2.7.1942), 454-55, 481 (Bitola district director, Circulars, 22.8 and 1.9.1942), 482 (Bitola police director, Circular, 5.9.1942).

detectives armed to the teeth with MGs and hand grenades. Perhaps more importantly, they refrained from taking any steps that would antagonize the Serb minority as a whole: in Banat, the Serbs retained a firm, albeit second-class, position in the society, and were never exposed to such outrages as in the NDH. As a consequence of this policy (as well as the application of reprisals), the Partisans were deprived of the kind of popular support they needed. Already in August, ten original guerrilla groups were amalgamated into five bigger "detachments", but the move failed in its intention to create more potent battlefield formations. Once the crops had been harvested, they were denied cover and succumbed one by one to enemy countermeasures.

In October, the last remaining unit was destroyed while trying to reach the relative safety of Syrmia. All attempts to revive and expand military activities in the countryside during the following two-and-a-half-years failed. The Southern Banat Detachment was reconstituted in late 1942 with 33 men but had tremendous difficulties in maintaining itself in the field. Almost total isolation from the outside world and squalid living conditions in the dugouts built in sand dunes and swamps favored bickering and internal discord, which ultimately led to the execution of two of the detachment's commanders. The unit did carry out several attacks on the gendarmerie during 1943, but by early 1944, the Partisans' primary concern was avoiding pursuits organized by both the Germans and Romanians. The Northern Banat Detachment, formed anew in January 1943 around the core of some 60 fighters, held its ground until September of the same year, when it left for Syrmia.[120]

In Bačka, the Partisans were initially organized exclusively in squad-sized units, which were nonetheless very active. During the first four months of the uprising, these groups carried out 64, mostly smaller, attacks and acts of sabotage. The Hungarian occupation authorities retorted with arrests and executions: from mid-October to late November 1941, tribunals sentenced 96 out of 116 accused to death; 842 further suspects were either awaiting trial or were placed into custody. In early November, the NOP formed its first true field unit, the Šajkaška Detachment, with about 40 fighters. Armed with only 17 rifles, the unit could not withstand the massive enemy attack launched in the triangle between the Danube and the Tisa in the first days of January 1942. The Partisans dispersed, but the Hungarians followed up on the initial success by using some 2,000 members of the gendarmerie and the army. During a firefight on 5-6 January, the guerrillas killed two soldiers; the incident was used as the pretext for the notorious, semi-genocidal "Novi Sad Raid" or "Southern Bačka Raid" that cost the lives of close to 4,000 Serb and Jewish civilians. The savagery of the occupier's response had largely contributed to the stifling of NOP's military activities in this Yugoslav province; the things would not begin to change before mid-1944.[121]

The NOP was facing a particularly difficult situation in Kosovo. Only 20 out of 270 card-carrying Communists on the eve of the conflict were Albanians, who otherwise constituted the majority of the population. To make matters worse, the Party membership was soon halved on account of expulsions of those members of the Serb and Montenegrin minorities who had come to the province as colonists in the wake of the Great War. Consequently, the first armed groups

120 Zakić, *Germans*, pp. 156-57; Momčilović, *Banat*, pp. 229, 232, 234-35, 264-65, 320-21, 324, 327-30, 335, 363; *Enciklopedija*, Vol. I, p. 474.

121 Aleksandar Kasaš, *Mađari u Vojvodini 1941-1946* (Novi Sad: Filozofski fakultet, 1996), pp. 80-91; *Zbornik*/XV/1/197-207 (Gendarmerie Investigation Center to Minister of interior, 3.11.1941), 223 (Dr. Vilmos Dominich, Summary report on Communist action, 1.12.1941).

that were formed in mid-July 1941 failed to impress the masses by either their numbers or their ethnic composition, to say nothing of their all-Yugoslav political platform. The Serb employees of the Trepča mines who made up the Kopaonik Detachment conducted only one act of sabotage against their former place of work before leaving for the Ibar Valley in September. The following month saw the creation of another detachment in the southwestern part of Kosovo (known to the Serbs as Metohija), but this unit was more akin to the village sections organized in Southern Serbia than the Partisan detachment in the classic sense. It was a self-protection force with over 700 men, but none of them were active fighters. The NOP would continue assigning volunteers to the so-called auxiliary or "rear-area units" (*pozadinske jedinice*) in hope of recruiting them into field formations once the circumstances allowed it: by August 1942, they numbered about 2,000 men, only a third of whom were armed. The creation of the Temporary MHQ for Kosovo in November of the same year, and the division of the province into two operational zones [sing. *operativna zona*, OZ] in April 1943, were largely hollow moves, for active units proved to be almost impossible to maintain.

Partisan leaders themselves sometimes feared that armed actions could only result in the loss of the precious cadres. Guerrilla groups could not function without popular support, and not even the Serbs would continue to provide it in face of Axis reprisals. The Albanian population was, for the most part, decidedly hostile: whole villages would open fire on passing Partisan columns, and "every peasant and every herder" would inform the enemy on their movements. Active detachments had therefore remained small (up to 100 men) and served largely as a symbolic reminder of the NOP's existence; they would all be compelled to leave their native territories at one point in their careers. The "Zejnel Ajdini" Battalion carried out several smaller actions (including the ambush at Crnoljeva on 3 January 1943, which resulted in the killing of a *Carabinieri* captain and three soldiers) before being routed in the Bulgarian-held part of Kosovo two weeks later. Its remnants joined the "Emin Duraku" Battalion, but the latter also had to escape before Italian pursuers to Northern Macedonia in early May. The battalion joined up with the Šarplanina Detachment, which itself would experience a similar ordeal in late November. On this occasion, the detachment, together with some 40 escaped Soviet POWs, was dispersed by a mixed Albanian-Bulgarian-German force and would later be reconstituted for the fourth time. Finally, in February 1944, the Axis attacked the Malesija Detachment and the Temporary MHQ in their hideouts in what is today northeastern Albania and forced them underground.[122]

The "problem children" were to be found even in the hotbed of the Balkan insurgency, the NDH. Western Herzegovina was populated almost exclusively by Croats and dominated by the Catholic Church; furthermore, it was the home of many Ustasha veterans, who attracted a large following once they returned from exile as masters of the land. Until late 1943, those few individuals who opted for the NOP served mostly in Dalmatian units. In early 1944, a company made up of fighters from the Ljubuški area returned to their native soil and established the first permanent Partisan base. The choice of location was not accidental, for this was the only part

122 *Enciklopedija*, Vol. II, p. 681; Vol. IV, p. 658; Vol. IX, p. 484; Vol. X, 691; *Zbornik*/I/19/37 (Notes Boro Vukmirović, February 1942), 136-38 (OK Kosovo to CK KPJ, 21.8.1942), 171 (Temporary MHQ Kosovo, Proclamation, 1.11.1942), 205-08 ("Emin Duraku" Btl., Activity report, 17.4.1943), 209 (Tempo to Milija Kovačević, 27.4.1943), 257 (Miloš Glišić to OK Kosovo, 26.9.1943); *Zbornik*/XIII/3/16, High Command Albania to CoS (3.1.1943).

of the province in which the KPJ enjoyed a modicum of influence. The company (upgraded to a battalion in early July) carried out altogether 21 armed actions in Western Herzegovina and neighboring parts of Dalmatia over the course of the following six months. At the peak of its strength in early September, the local NOP branch, with its newly-formed Western Herzegovina Detachment, had only 137 fighters on active duty.[123]

The repeated inability of KPJ cells to operate in secrecy was the main reason for the almost total absence of armed activities in Međimurje, the Hungarian-annexed part of Croatia located between the Drava and Mura Rivers. The local Party organizations were successfully raided on at least three occasions, right after the beginning of the German-Soviet war, and once each in early and late 1942. Although there were no indiscriminate reprisals, and although even card-carrying Communists received only short prison sentences, the province came to be viewed as ill-suited for the type of guerrilla war being waged south of the Drava. Consequently, NOP's sympathizers began leaving Međimurje and heading for the neighboring Mount Kalnik, where they served in the local detachment. Exactly how many of them crossed into the NDH in this way until the end of the war is impossible to tell, but the figure was not inconsiderable: 709 of these "refugees" are known by name for 1944 alone. The cross-Drava traffic went in both directions. In addition to couriers, the Partisans would send experienced soldiers and political workers back into the province in order to serve as cadre for local units. One such outfit, numbering six armed and 12 unarmed members, operated in August 1943 in the eastern part of Međimurje. Raiding parties, consisting usually of the "refugees", would also visit from time to time, carry out their tasks, and then hurriedly return to the Kalnik. By late 1944, these raids could involve up to several companies, which usually went after the Hungarian gendarmerie posts and railway installations. Thanks to the improved supply situation, sabotage actions were becoming more and more ambitious: on a single occasion in June of the same year, the railway line between Čakovec and Kotoriba was blown in 98 places. Despite the fact that the Axis were irrevocably on the defensive, the Partisans would return to Međimurje for good only after the Bulgarian Army had entered the province in early April 1945.[124]

The course of events in Međimurje was in many ways similar to the one in the neighboring Slovene province of Prekmurje. Already in September 1941, the Hungarian police managed to arrest some 60 members of the OF, including all the leading KPJ members. These and other arrests, as well as subsequent trials in the city of Pécs, had effectively broken the back of the NOP in the province, with the surviving sympathizers fleeing across the Mura. Apart from the incursion of a single Partisan company from Štajerska in September 1944 (in what was effectively a propaganda tour), the province remained without guerrilla presence until the arrival of the Red Army in early April 1945. In addition to forming their own brigade, which would see action in the final battles on the Yugoslav soil, the Prekmurje Partisans also took part on the local reconnaissance raids on the Mura section of the Soviet-German front.[125]

123 Ivo Jerkić, "Učešće Zapadne Hercegovine u NOP", in *Hercegovina*, Vol. I, pp. 215-19; Jure Galić, "Zapadnohercegovački odred", in ibid., pp. 747-50.

124 Vladimir Kapun, "Međimurci na Kalniku", in *Sjeverozapadna Hrvatska u narodnooslobodilačkoj borbi i socijalističkoj revoluciji: zbornik* (Varaždin: zajednica općina, 1976), pp. 542-65; *SZH*/I/320-29, Public prosecutor Pécs, Indictment against Communists (8.11.1941).

125 Mitja Hribovšek, *Prekmurska brigada* (Ljubljana: Partizanska knjiga, 1975), pp. 11-42, 72-74, 84-85, 109-219; Central Archives of Ministry of Defense of Russian Federation, fond 956, opis 1, delo 313,

The ethnically mixed region known as Julian March (Julijska krajina/Venezia Giulia), represents a special case in the history of the NOP. The entire area had belonged to Austria-Hungary until 1918 when it was granted to Italy in recognition of its contribution to the Allied cause. As a result, it was the Italian Communist Party (*Partito Comunista Italiano*, PCI), rather than the KPJ, which called the shots here. Although divided and weakened after almost two decades of fascist persecution, the CPI was firmly opposed to the KPJ's agenda of the (Slavic) uprising and annexation of the Slovene and Croat-populated parts of Julian March to Yugoslavia. Without waiting for the Comintern's approval (which would arrive only in August 1942), the KPJ began building its own political and military organization in these parts. In September 1941, the MHQ Slovenia dispatched a group of nine men with the task of forming a military unit in the littoral (Primorska Company). The arrival of a further 19 fighters in March 1942 enabled the creation of another company. The string of smaller actions carried out by these units (including the killing of a *Carabinieri* commander at Postojna) had alerted the authorities to their presence. In April, the Italians came near to destroying both companies, which were forced to withdraw deeper into the interior with the loss of five killed and 11 missing men. By summer, the Partisan forces had been reorganized into two battalions, but neither played a significant military role. One was divided into small groups, which maintained the NOP's symbolic presence in the area between Istria and Slavia Friulana/Beneška Slovenija. The other one, numbering some 70 fighters, was routed in late July, its remnants forced to retreat to Ljubljana Province. Undeterred by this temporary setback, the Primorska men returned to their homeland in October, where they joined the recently formed Soča Detachment, whose HQ was responsible for all 300 or so Partisans in Julian March.[126]

The going was much slower in the Istrian Peninsula, not only because "20 years of servitude and [absence of KPJ's influence] had made the people averse to [...] organized fight", but also because local Croats were not entirely convinced of the sincerity of the NOP's agenda. By the time the first battalions had been formed in the Slovene Primorska in the summer of 1942, Istria was still without Partisan units. This is not to say that no progress had been made: the KPH had cells in all major urban centers, arms were being collected, and volunteers sent across the border into Croatian Littoral and Gorski Kotar. At the end of August, these men were combined into the "Vladimir Gortan" Company (named after the Istrian patriot executed in Rome in 1929), and sent back to their native province. As in other parts of the country untouched by the uprising, these Partisans initially devoted most of their energies to organizing, harnessing popular support, and establishing their authority by means of persecuting collaborators. Once they started targeting Italian interests (e.g. the railway sabotage at Jušić on 28 October 1942), authorities responded by launching anti-guerrilla sweeps. In early December, the "Vladimir Gortan" Company was surrounded in its base on Mount Planik; although the unit managed to avoid annihilation, it had to disperse and return to Croatia. Istria was again devoid of NOP's military units and would remain so until September 1943.[127]

list 118, 958th Rifle Regiment [RR]/299th Rifle Division [RD], War diary (8.4.1945) [hereinafter: TsAMO/fond/opis/delo/list].

126 Giron, *Zapadna Hrvatska*, pp. 89-91; Klanjšček, *NOR u Sloveniji*, pp. 80, 85-86, 110-11, 119, 138-40.

127 Giron, *Zapadna Hrvatska*, pp. 91-92; *Enciklopedija*, Vol. III, p. 688.

2

Uprising – Ebb (January – June 1942)

2.1 Political Backdrop of Campaign

In order to understand Partisan operations during the winter and spring of 1942 and beyond, it is necessary to take a closer look at the NOP's internal policies and political considerations of its leadership after the demise of the Užice Republic. As we have seen, in addition to fulfilling its "internationalist duty" towards the USSR with great fervor, the KPJ had shown itself to be a genuinely patriotic (and/or Yugoslav nationalist) force. At the same time, it was clearly pursuing a revolutionary agenda. Fighting against a foreign invader and fighting for a comprehensive social change were not two mutually exclusive tasks. On the contrary, the Communists saw them as being complementary: in order to carry out the revolution, one had to liberate the county first. In turn, this struggle could only be successful if the masses believed that their blood and toil would not only win them freedom, but also a better life in a more righteous society. Despite all the cautioning from Moscow to de-politicize their war agenda, the Yugoslavs found the temptation hard to resist; this was the opportunity they had been waiting for more than two decades. Already in the earliest days of the uprising, the leadership of the KPJ saw itself compelled to publicly refute the notion that its actions were motivated by narrow political interests; it also had to reign in some overzealous local committees that were proclaiming "the dawn of a new age". The initially widespread use of the red flag, as well as the word "revolutionary" in unit names, was discontinued for fears of alienating the people (the five-pointed star would remain, however, even despite Soviet objections). Warnings were issued about the danger of "sectarianism" and "leftist deviations" and about executing "kulaks" without a proof that they had actually committed some crime. Party documents also cautioned against the redistribution of land and sequestration of private property.[1]

Pragmatism, rather than conviction, stood behind these measures. Their main purpose was to a) deny the enemy propaganda the opportunity to scare the population with "haunting specter of Communism", and b) strengthen the inner-Party discipline. Nevertheless, the building of a new

1 *Zbornik*/I/1/37-38 and 63-66, PK Serbia to OK Šabac (12 and 20.8.1941); *Zbornik*/V/1/146 (CK KPH, Circular letter no. 3, 30.9.1941) and 210 (CK KPH to OK Karlovac, 19.10.1941); *Zbornik*/I/19/38, Notes Boro Vukmirović (February 1942); Glišić, Miljanić, *Rukovođenje*, pp. 31-33.

society went ahead hand-in-hand with the struggle against the occupier. A good example for the dual nature of Partisan efforts is the systematic destruction of municipal archives in Serbia. This was carried out primarily in order to disrupt the management and exploitation of the land by depriving the occupation authorities of such important data such as mobilization lists and tax records. The dismantling of the administrative system–which the Germans inherited from the *ancien régime* and which retained a distinctly traditional, monarchist outlook–was followed by the establishment of NOP's own bodies, People's Liberation Councils (sing. *Narodnooslobodilački odbor*, NOO). The main job of the NOOs was to facilitate the supply of Partisan units, but they also served as a visible sign of the movement's intention to be recognized as a political force capable of governing the country. The existence of a state-building agenda was further confirmed with the convening of Main NOO for Serbia in mid-November 1941. Nominally, this was an umbrella body responsible for coordinating the work of local councils on the territory of the Užice Republic, but in fact an embryo of a new government of Serbia, an alternative to both the Axis puppets in Belgrade, and the royal government-in-exile.[2]

Being in full control and with no need to compromise, the Partisans carried out a partial sovietization of the liberated area in Western Serbia. Industrial plants were nationalized; workers and youth were given preferential treatment and organized into separate councils and labor brigades; popular measures were introduced, such as the imposition of debt and rent moratorium, and opening of public kitchens for the unemployed. The "Red Republic" also had its internal security force: by late November 1941, around 100 persons had been executed in Užice and Čačak, most of them just prior to the evacuation of these places. It should be said that most of them were persons of modest means, implying they were not persecuted on the basis of class distinction, but because of their proven or suspected liaison with the enemy. The struggle against these so-called "fifth columnists" (*petokolonaši*) had been one of the main tasks of Partisan units across Yugoslavia from the day one of the war. In Serbia, this translated to the killing of 827 persons outside combat during the entire 1941 according to the collaborationist authorities. 167 of these were gendarmes and other government employees, while the rest were civilians of various professions and ethnic backgrounds. These included White Russian émigré priests (one "handed over a list of our comrades to the Germans", the other was "an active supporter of Ljotić"), a village teacher ("who served the Germans"), a station master ("a denouncer"), an older couple ("informed the Germans on Partisan movements"), and *Volksdeutsche* employees of a mine. Apart from the already mentioned executions at Užice, there was only one other case of mass killing involving more than 10 persons. Similarly, the official chroniclers in Belgrade registered a single instance of indiscriminate slaughter, whereby two children were murdered beside their parents.[3]

The events which transpired both at home and abroad in the last weeks of 1941 caused the NOP leadership to re-evaluate the movement's political line. The success of the Soviet counteroffensive at Moscow in early December rekindled the belief that the war would be won in a matter of months. Tito and the others reasoned that the victory over the Nazi Germany would signal the demise of the anti-Hitler coalition and return of old tensions, if not outright

2 Petranović, *Srbija*, pp. 240-41, 521-22; *Enciklopedija*, Vol. V, pp. 768-69.

3 Glišić, *Užička*, pp. 70-72, 155-56, 136-39; Milan Radanović, *Kazna i zločin: Snage kolaboracije u Srbiji: odgovornost za ratne zločine (1941-1944) i vojni gubici (1944-1945)* (Belgrade: Rosa Luxemburg Stiftung, 2015), pp. 69-76.

conflict, between the "capitalist-imperialist block" and the "first land of socialism". The creation of an unholy alliance of reactionaries on both sides of the fence, aimed solely at stopping the triumphant march of "progressive forces" gathered around the Communists, could already be observed in Yugoslavia. A sizable part of the pre-war bureaucratic caste in Serbia had readily offered its services to the invader; they had no qualms about working together with the fascists from the "Zbor" movement, or the treacherous White Russians who placed themselves at the Nazis' disposal despite all the suffering the latter inflicted on their old homeland. The officer corps professed anti-Axis feelings, but what they really feared was the prospect of a revolution. In order to secure the preconditions for the return of the monarchy after the war, the officers were willing to work with anyone, be it the above-mentioned collaborationists or the Wehrmacht itself. This was proved by the meeting at Divci and the subsequent "legalization" of Mihailović's units, which were simply accepted into the ranks of the "government Chetniks" with German blessing. The same could be observed in the lands west of the Drina, where Serbian elites were seeking closer ties with the Italians. Senior KPJ functionaries were certain that the plot was either instigated, or at least approved by that arch-reactionary power, the Great Britain. How else could it be explained that the Chetniks launched their attack on the Partisans only days after being visited by the first British mission to the country, and that they received the first delivery of weapons by the Royal Air Force (RAF) at the height of the Partisan counter-attack in early November? Adding insult to injury, British Broadcasting Corporation (BBC) was turning Mihailović into an all-Allied hero: in early December, the radio announced his promotion to brigadier-general, an unambiguous signal that the Yugoslav government-in-exile and its patrons in the Whitehall approved of his actions.[4]

Confronted with what appeared to be a vast ideological conspiracy, which was largely responsible for their bitter defeat in Serbia, the KPJ decided to "take up the gauntlet of class struggle thrown by the reaction". The new policy was formulated in a series of letters issued by the Politburo (i.e. Tito) during the course of December 1941, and on the conference of the provincial leadership for Bosnia-Herzegovina held in early January 1942 in the village of Ivančići. The Chetniks were now the main enemy, for both military and political reasons. Seen in the context of the liberation war, their mere existence was a mortal threat to the NOP, which was made up almost entirely of Serbs. With the main recruitment and economic base shattered by divided loyalties, the campaign against the occupier would be impossible to conduct. Seen in the context of the civil war–and this mattered the most at the time–the Chetniks were the main obstacle to a successful revolution. Unlike other anti-Communist factions that besmirched themselves through open collaboration, Mihailović and his followers were recognized by the Western Allies, making them the only serious contender for power in post-war Yugoslavia. Under these circumstances, the struggle against the "fifth column" gained new importance for the Partisans. True, the above-mentioned documents re-iterate the NOP's commitment to its original creed and continue to stress the need of maintaining a wide popular front against fascism opened to all sincere patriots. None of them explicitly link certain social categories with potentially hostile behavior or order the killing of anyone who owns more than one cow. The instructions do, however, link the rising tide of reaction with the "increased importance of class

4 Branko Petranović, *Istorija Jugoslavije 1918-1988* (Belgrade: Nolit, 1988), Vol. II, pp. 183-84; Elisabeth Barker, *British Policy in South-East Europe in the Second World War* (Serbo-Croatian edition; Zagreb: Globus, 1978), p. 11; Tomasevich, *Chetniks*, p. 160.

moment" and the presumption that the "second phase of the revolution" (i.e. open struggle for power) stood just around the corner. It was up to lower Party caucuses to decide on how to best carry out these ambiguous instructions in their respective home regions.[5]

As it turned out, the signals from the Politburo did not lead to the creation of a new, uniform Party line, but to the parallel existence of two lines. The regional leadership of Bosanska Krajina, for instance, decided in February 1942 that the "second phase" was still far off; consequently, the "intensification of class struggle" here remained largely limited to the realm of propaganda. The SHQ also continued practicing the old line, instituting a moderate rule in the newly-created liberated territory in Eastern Bosnia; religious activities here, for instance, were not only allowed, but actively sponsored by the NOP authorities. Only a several dozen kilometers to the south, in Eastern Herzegovina and Montenegro, the things looked entirely different. The Communists had long established themselves as undisputed civilian and military overlords of the countryside. Consequently, as Djilas put it, they considered all dissenters as rebels against legitimate authorities, and dealt with them accordingly. What made this showdown as ruthless as it was, was the hot-bloodedness and penchant for extremism commonly attributed to the members of these highland societies. The struggle against the "fifth column" soon degenerated into a classic example of "Red Terror": churches were desecrated and priests molested; well-to-do peasants were branded as "kulaks" and automatically suspected of harboring Chetnik sympathies, and a mere suspicion often meant death; sentences were carried out in secret but announced publicly, execution lists ending with a sinister "to be continued"; the Partisans were encouraged to inform on their family members and even partake on their execution. The precise death toll is impossible to establish, but it was substantial, especially when considering the relatively small size of the population living under the NOP rule in these parts. According to one internal KPJ report, some 500 "Chetniks" were liquidated by the beginning of spring 1942 in Herzegovina; in Montenegro, 99 persons found their deaths at the notorious mass execution site (the "Dog Cemetery") outside Kolašin alone.[6]

For the most part, the local Party cadre was convinced of the necessity of these measures. The steady rise of the Chetnik movement that was taking place precisely during this period was explained not by excessive repression, but rather by the lack thereof. Yugoslav historiography deliberately used the term "leftist deviations" so as to imply that these views were not shared by Tito, and that they represented a distortion of the Party line. The fact is, however, that the Partisan leadership condoned, and even encouraged, the application of the radical policy for as long as it contributed to the strengthening of the NOP's positions. "You should have treated the wreckers of the people's struggle more harshly. If you had shot a dozen or so, these things would not be happening", "Apply sternest reprisals against the Chetniks", "Reprisals must be applied"; phrases like this are often encountered in the documents of the SHQ throughout the winter and early spring of 1942. At the same time, the scope of repressive measures was widened: close relatives of hostile individuals could now be expelled from the liberated territories, their houses set on fire, and their belongings confiscated. Fearing that the things could go out of hand, the SHQ pointed out that targeted arson did not devolve into wanton destruction of whole

5 Rasim Hurem, *Kriza NOP-a u Bosni i Hercegovini krajem 1941. i početkom 1942.* (Sarajevo: Svjetlost, 1972), pp. 77-106.

6 Ibid., pp. 140-69, 174-78; Radanović, *Kazna*, p. 79; Interview with Milovan Đilas in TV-documentary "Jugoslavija u ratu", Episode 10 (RTV Beograd, 1992).

settlements and ordered that the culprits' families be allowed to keep a bare minimum of food. Units on the ground greeted the relaxation of the rules regarding living off the land and would regularly "visit" known enemy villages whenever they needed supplies. If the need was pressing, but only neutral[7] villages were in the vicinity, the Partisans would sometimes provoke a firefight in order to justify the requisitioning.[8]

Things began to change in late March and early April 1942, largely because the repressive policies were turning out to be counter-productive. In addition, the KPJ leadership had recently been severely criticized by Moscow for the pursuance of the revolutionary agenda. Tito shifted the blame on the subordinates: the top echelon of the Montenegrin PK–whom he described as being "dizzy with success", appropriately using Stalin's famous phrase–was accused of a series of errors and relieved. Since the situation in Herzegovina at that time still seemed in hand, the local military leadership was merely admonished. Its downfall would, however, come several months later, after the Chetnik tide had swept the NOP out of this region as well. The old habit of using brute force as universal remedy persisted for weeks after the policy had been officially changed: whole villages would still go up in flames, and some commanders continued setting fixed quotas of "wreckers" who were to be executed. The repentant ones, in turn, refrained from requisitioning even when their troops were starving, provided explanation for every case of excessive arson, and did not "even shoot a single captured Ustasha without investigation". The hunt for "fifth columnists" would continue until the end of the war, but with more moderation and never again within the context of class struggle: this proved to be detrimental to the war effort, but also to the prospects of a successful revolution in the long term.[9]

The break with the monarchists also prompted the KPJ to re-evaluate its nationalities policy. One of the core values of the NOP, encapsulated in the motto "Brotherhood and Unity", was that all Yugoslav ethnic and religious groups were equal; neither the movement nor the future common state would be dominated by any single one of them, as it had been the case with the Kingdom of Yugoslavia or the NDH. Right after the war began, however, circumstances on the ground compelled the Party to make compromises and "suspend" some of its ideals. The fact was that the majority of the population, overwhelmingly rural and conservative in nature, had little understanding for these elevated notions. For as long as one could remember, the "other" had been viewed with suspicion, if not outright hostility. The inter-ethnic divide became seemingly unbridgeable with the latest wave of lawlessness, terror, and genocide. This was especially true for the territory of the Ustasha state. There, a handful of KPJ members and sympathizers found themselves at the head of the army whose rank-and-file did not share their enthusiasm about

7 By early 1942 there was hardly a village in Montenegro or the NDH without some kind of self-defense force. Many settlements that, for whatever reason, received arms from the Axis still sought to avoid trouble with the guerrillas at all costs.

8 *Zbornik*/III/2/93 (Nikšić Det. to MHQ Montenegro 28.1.1942), 209 (MHQ Montenegro to Nikšić Det., 26.2.1942); *Zbornik*/II/2/341, 349, SHQ to Jahorina Det., and to MHQ Sandžak (13 and 20.2.42, respectively); *Zbornik*/II/3/21 and 24, and 126, SHQ to 2nd Proletarian Bde., and to Durmitor Det. (3.3. and 14.3.1942, respectively); Djilas, *Wartime*, p. 120; Jakšić, *Nad uspomenama*, Vol. I, p. 262.

9 Hurem, *Kriza*, pp. 258-59, 263, 267-68; *Zbornik*/II/3/251, Tito to Đilas (28.3.1942); *Zbornik*/II/4/400, SHQ, Order (23.6.1942); *Zbornik*/III/4/269 (Đilas to SHQ, 22.4.1942), 329 (MHQ Montenegro to Nikšić Det., 28.5.1942); *Zbornik*/III/3/384, MHQ Montenegro to Nikšić Det. (5.6.1942); *Zbornik*/ IV/5/11, Operational HQ [OHQ] Herzegovina to SHQ (3.5.1942); Interview with Milovan Đilas in TV-documentary "Jugoslavija u ratu", Episode 10 (RTV Beograd, 1992).

the idea of a multi-ethnic state. Commenting on the early days of the uprising, Tempo wrote: "Where communist influence was strong, there were leftist deviations [...] and where it was weak, the war was led not against the occupier and Ustashe but against the *balije* and 'Turks' [pejorative terms for Muslims]." Driven by the thirst for revenge, chauvinistic fervor, and plain greed, the insurgents had perpetrated several large-scale massacres of Croats and Muslims in Bosnia-Herzegovina. Those Communists who were serving with the perpetrators were not only unable to stop these tragic events but were often themselves in danger. In order to stay close to the masses, the KPJ had to bend its line: the Eastern Herzegovina leadership called a temporary halt to actions against the Axis fearing they would lead to further atrocities. After a couple of Muslims from Mostar had been murdered by those same insurgents they were supposed to join, volunteers were simply re-routed to the northern, safer, part of the province. Finally, non-Serbs often had to serve in their units under false, Serbian names. Paradoxically, the same Communists hardliners who had so ruthlessly sovietized the province proved surprisingly susceptible to ancient nationalist passions. The large-scale operation against the infamous Ustasha stronghold of Borač was carried out in the spirit of a crusade against the "Turks", and was marked by wholesale plunder, arson, and indiscriminate killings of able-bodied men.[10]

The policy of accommodation with Serbian nationalists went the farthest in Eastern Bosnia. The Partisans were unwilling to risk the power-sharing deal they had with the Chetniks and estrange themselves from the insurgents by upholding their proclaimed policy of equality at all costs. The arrangement may have appeared practical at the time but was in fact severely detrimental to the NOP's war effort in the long run, as it reduced the chances for a successful mobilization of non-Serbs. The latter became especially important as the movement's original recruitment base became severely reduced by the outbreak of hostilities against Mihailović. Although the arrival of units from Serbia and Montenegro to Eastern Bosnia in early 1942 put an end to the indiscriminate slaughter of Muslims, the old compromise was largely left in place. This reflected itself in the fact that the SHQ accepted thousands of former Chetniks into its fold under privileged terms of service. On the contrary, Muslim Battalion of the Romanija Detachment, formed in December 1941 and still being the only such unit in the army, was practically allowed to dissolve. Only the unfortunate events from the late spring of 1942 would finally convince the NOP's leadership that compromising on core values, no matter how opportune it may appear in a given moment, would invariably lead to the loss of political and military potential. Ultimately, the movement would be reduced to just another faction whose influence does not exceed the range of its rifles.[11]

What was the situation in other parts of the country? In Kosovo, the main task of the NOP was to survive in an extremely hostile environment. For that purpose, the Partisans went to great lengths to appease the majority. Here, the Serbs went around under assumed Muslim names (proving that this measure was not concocted by Serbian crypto-chauvinists within the KPJ with the aim of de-nationalizing Bosnian Muslims and belittling their contribution to the struggle, as sometimes claimed), and men would sometimes not wear the obligatory red star insignia for fear of producing a backlash. In late 1941, the local KPJ cells even considered it

10 *Zbornik*/IV/1/442-53, Uglješa Danilović to Tempo (17.9.1941); Tempo, *Revolucija*, Vol. I, pp. 217, 223-24; Marko Attila Hoare, *Genocide and Resistance in Hitler's Bosnia: The Partisans and the Chetniks 1941-1943* (Oxford: OUP, 2006), pp. 106-08, 222.

11 Ibid., pp. 113-17, 145-48, 169-70, 196-97.

opportune to take part on the Italian-sponsored nationalist celebrations, and completely avoided using the hated word "Yugoslavia" in some of their proclamations. Tito, always a pragmatist, condoned the policy of non-provocation towards Albanians: in late 1943 he advised that the NOP's propaganda avoid discussing the post-war fate of the province, and to simply invoke the conclusions of the Atlantic Charter instead.[12]

In the Kozara area, the Partisans enjoyed relatively good relations with the local Muslim population in early 1942, the result of the continuous involvement of the local Serbs with the NOP and the absence of radicalism propagated/tolerated by the SHQ at that time. Vladimir Bakarić, a keen intellectual and a former lawyer who served as the chief political officer of the MHQ Croatia, once famously observed that the "people's uprising" of 1941 in this province had been, in fact, a Serbian rebellion led by the Communists. Winning over the ethnic Croat majority had always been one of the main tasks of the NOP in these parts, but the going was hard for the same reasons as in Bosnia-Herzegovina. The prescribed punishment for notorious Ustashe individuals, consisting of physical liquidation and confiscation/destruction of property ("women and children [must] not [be harmed]"), would sometimes turn into indiscriminate burning and plunder of non-Serb villages. The perpetrators, however, would often manage to escape from custody with the help of other Partisans who did not feel that offenses like these warranted a capital punishment. In mid-June 1942, the 1st Battalion of the Banija Detachment attacked the Croat village of Prekopa. The battalion commander ordered the whole village burnt and all men above the age of 16 shot; much to their credit, his Serb fighters had largely refused to carry out the second part of the order. After much deliberation, the high command decided to make an example: the commander, who might have otherwise gotten away with a simple reprimand, was tried and publicly executed, and the sentence explained to the population in a special leaflet. Although incidents would continue to happen, they would remain isolated enough in order to convince the population that the Partisans were not simply Chetniks in disguise, as claimed by the Ustasha propaganda.[13]

This appears to be a convenient time for a brief discussion on the NOP's prisoner polices. The movement was faced with the perennial dilemma of all guerrilla armies, namely what to do with its captives. As mentioned earlier, releasing them was not uncommon in the early period of the war, for at least two reasons. One, the Partisans were still not brutalized by their war experience, and two, the question of prisoners was viewed in class terms. Ordinary German and Italian

12 *Zbornik*/I/19/28 (Town committee [*Mjesni komitet*, MK] Kosovska Mitrovica to OK Kosovo, November 1941), 43 (Notes Boro Vukmirović, February 1942), 196 (Conclusions from meeting of OK Kosovo, December 1942), 258 (OK Kosovo to 2nd Operational Zone [OZ], 26.9.1943); NARA/T313/196/7456964, PzAOK 2/Intel., Appendix to daily report (15.11.1943).

13 Hoare, *Genocide*, pp. 244, 249, 269; *Zbornik*/V/1/115, Minutes of conference of delegates from Kordun and Banija (19-20.9.1941); *Zbornik*/V/4/321, MHQ Croatia to SHQ (25.5.1942); *Zbornik*/V/5/124 (Banija Det. to 1st OZ, 19.6.1942), 167 and 250 (1st OZ to MHQ Croatia, 23.6.1942 and beginning of July 1942, respectively), 316-17 (1st OZ to Banija Det., 10.7.1942), 472 (1st OZ to MHQ Croatia, 28.7.1942). Joža Horvat, the Croat writer famous for his humorous war novel "Mačak pod šljemom" ("Tomcat under Helmet") and for circumnavigating the globe in a light sailing vessel in the mid-1960s, was at the time the battalion's *politkom*. The Prekopa affair left a lasting impression on him, as evident from the emotional interviews given almost 70 years after the event: https://www.youtube.com/watch?v=EzhdfXKPgCg (last accessed on 3.7.2018); see also Lordan Zafranović's documentary "Tito: posljednji svjedoci testamenta", Episode 5 (Kino dokument/Hrvatska radio-televizija [hereinafter: HRT], 2012).

soldiers were seen first and foremost as workers and peasants who were forced into this war by their reactionary superiors and members of fascist organizations. Consequently, the amnesty did not apply to German officers, members of the Nazi Party and "Gestapo" (blanket term for all intelligence and security services), and the Italian Blackshirts. Owing to this selective policy, hundreds of members of the *Regio Esercito* were released in Montenegro in the summer of 1941. The soldiers of the Wehrmacht captured in Western Serbia after August of the same year were not released any longer but were eventually brought to the main POW camp in Užice instead. No less than 316 of them were recovered by the advancing German troops in early December.

So far, the relatively good treatment accorded to Axis prisoners in general brought little real reward, except in symbolic terms: the guerrillas could now claim moral high ground, and the ability to keep prisoners reinforced their claim to the status of lawful belligerent. The change came after the fall of the Užice Republic. The Germans were showing neither the intention of improving the lot of the captured members of the NOP, nor the willingness to exchange them. The final straw was the massacre of more than 100 heavily wounded Partisans on Mount Zlatibor; after that, the guerrillas would as a rule execute all Germans who fell into their hands. On the other hand, the Partisans still had every incentive to maintain the old policy towards the Italians. They were not as universally hated as their Teutonic partners, and their commands did not shy away from entering direct negotiations or sending supplies for their men in captivity (which could then be "shared" with the captors). The SHQ had therefore encouraged units in the field to exchange prisoners, and this they did throughout 1942 and thereafter, with varying degree of success. What the SHQ could never fully achieve was the eradication of arbitrary killing of captured enemies. On one occasion in Montenegro, an Italian officer was shot merely because he led a spirited defense of his position. One of his colleagues who, along with two Blackshirts, was supposed to be offered in return for the KPH's chief secretary Rade Končar, were "lynched" by some Dalmatian Partisans who feared that the Italians, once released, would lead a punitive expedition to their villages. It was well within a guerrilla commander's prerogative to execute his captives if they became an unbearable burden or put his unit in danger, which is precisely what happened during the Partisan retreat from Montenegro in late spring of 1942.[14]

The same specific Partisan mix of pragmatism and ideology governed the treatment of domestic prisoners as well. As a rule, no quarter was given to the members of extreme-right parties such as the "Zbor" or the enemies of the Soviet state such as the White Russians. Owing both to its voluntary nature and massive crimes it committed in a very short time span, the entire Ustasha organization was viewed as no better than a club for dedicated sadists and mass murderers. Consequently, the Partisans announced early on that the membership alone warranted death penalty. This measure, it was hoped, would quench the thirst for revenge on the part of their base supporters (i.e. the Serbs), and prevent the insurgency from becoming a crusade against the Croats in general. There were very few exceptions to this policy during the

14 Gaj Trifković, "Making Deals with the Enemy: Partisan-German Contacts and Prisoner Exchanges in Yugoslavia, 1941-1945", *Global War Studies*, 10:2 (2013), pp. 10-15; Zoran Lakić, "Razmjena ratnih zarobljenika u Crnoj Gori u toku Narodnooslobodilačkog rata", *Vojnoistorijski glasnik* [hereinafter: *VIG*], 18:1 (1967), pp. 69-91; *Zbornik*/II/3/163, Ivo Ribar-Lola to Tito (17.3.1942); *Zbornik*/III/2/177, Cucko-Ceklićki Btl. to Lovćen Det. (19.2.1942); *Zbornik*/V/4/70-71, HQ of Dalmatia-Dinara Dets. to MHQ Croatia (16.4.1942); Djilas, *Wartime*, pp. 75-76, 154, 182.

war: an Ustasha would be spared or allowed to come over only for the purpose of exchange, or if someone would guarantee for him, respectively.[15]

The treatment of the NDH Home Guards was an entirely different matter. The Partisans quickly sensed that the army, with its unmotivated personnel, was the Achilles' heel of the satellite state. The ordinary *Domobrani* were therefore perceived less as enemy soldiers and more as potential recruits. Following the unit's surrender–and this often happened only after just a few shots–the soldiers would be offered to stay with the guerrillas; if they chose not to, they would leave behind everything of military value (including their uniforms) and then be set free. They would thus become the Partisans' best source of arms and their "walking leaflets". Their return refuted in the most effective way the official propaganda claims of how the insurgents were bent on killing every last Croat; it also undermined both the population's confidence in the NDH and the army's will to fight. The officers' case was not as clear-cut: they would sometimes be released, or kept for exchange, or forced to join the guerrillas. It should be noted that the treatment could be very different in the cases where Home Guards offered tougher resistance than usual. On one occasion in mid-1942, the 2nd Krajina Detachment defended its decision to shoot members of a German-trained unit captured after a hard fight by claiming that "there was nothing *Domobran*-like in their attitude."[16]

The treatment of Chetniks went along similar lines. Aware of how deeply unpopular the idea of a civil war was to the majority of Serbs, Tito issued a special order in early November 1941. In it, he effectively pledged that the Partisans would uphold the letter and spirit of international law in their struggle against the monarchists. The subsequent debacle in Western Serbia meant, however, that these provisions would be applied only selectively. By the time the SHQ had moved to Eastern Bosnia, all captured Chetniks who came over from Serbia (mostly former servicemen and gendarmes) were liable to be shot; the native royalists, minus their ringleaders, were to be spared and recruited into one's own ranks. The Partisans maintained this double-barreled policy for most of the war but did not hesitate to suspend it entirely if it suited their immediate needs. In order to strike fear into Chetniks' hearts and stop them from capitalizing on Italy's surrender in September 1943, the MHQ Croatia ordered that the monarchists were no longer to be taken alive. This, in turn, led to the massacre on Mali Lošinj later the same month; just how many of the 258 prisoners captured on this island were executed is unknown, but the affair was extraordinarily brutal (one of the rare contemporary Partisan documents mentions the use of "Ustasha methods" in dispatching of prisoners).[17]

15 *Zbornik*/IV/1/216, Bosnian-Herzegovinian Partisan Bde., Order (6.9.1941); *Zbornik*/V/4/67, OK Banija to CK KPH (16.4.1942); *Zbornik*/I/3/174-75, PK Serbia to Delegate for Požarevac (7.4.1942); *Коминтерн и вторая мировая война* (Moscow: Памятники исторической мысли, 1998), Vol. II, p. 399, Georgi Dimitrov to Tito (11.9.1943); Vojni arhiv Beograd, NOVJ Collection, box 119-1, folder 2, document 4, page 32-3, MHQ Croatia to all units (20.1.1944) [hereinafter: VAB/collection/box/folder/document/page (if available)].

16 *Zbornik*/IV/3/23 (Prisoners from Croatian Army, 1.1.1942), 213-5 (II HDB AC, Activity report 1-15.1.1942); *Zbornik*/IV/6/60, 2nd Krajina Det. to OHQ Bosanska Krajina (11.7.1942).

17 *Zbornik*/I/2/223-24, SHQ, Order (8.11.1941); *Zbornik*/II/2/243, SHQ to Montenegrin operational HQ [OHQ] (24.1.1942); *Zbornik*/IV/4/29, Kalinovik Det. to SHQ (22.1.1942); VAB/NOVJ/110/7/13, MHQ Croatia, Order (16.9.1943); Velimir Ivetić, "Slučaj partizanskih zločina u logoru na Malom Lošinju 1943. godine", *VIG*, 1-2 (2004), pp. 147-50.

2.2 Winter Operations in Eastern Bosnia

Four days after the 1st Proletarian Brigade had been formed (25 December 1941), Tito held a top-tier meeting in Rogatica to discuss how best to use this new tool of war. It was decided to head west, towards the industrial towns of Vareš and Breza, where the Partisan ranks would hopefully be swelled by reliable, class-conscious workers. By mid-January 1942, the task force around the SHQ had reached the area some 25 km north of the Bosnian capital. Hailed as heroes by the surviving Muslims, the Proletarians were acting chiefly as a police force, disarming unreliable units and holding drumhead trials of Chetnik suspects. It was here where the news of the new Axis offensive reached Tito. Operation "Southeast Croatia" (known in Yugoslavia as the "Second Enemy Offensive") was launched in an attempt to replicate the success achieved recently in Western Serbia and capitalize on the presence of the 342nd ID before it too was transferred to the Eastern Front. The first phase would take place in the area stretching roughly between Sarajevo, Tuzla, Višegrad, and Zvornik. The 718th ID would field one regimental battle group from each of the former two places, while the 342nd ID would advance from the latter two; the Italians were supposed to seal the demarcation line southeast of Sarajevo, and NDH forces were to block the Bosna River line. The objective of the Wehrmacht units was to advance concentrically towards the center of the aforementioned quadrilateral, neutralizing all insurgents encountered therein.

As soon as spearheads began to move out on the 15th, it was clear that the plan was overly optimistic. It failed to take into account that neither of the two divisions was experienced and equipped enough for a campaign in the middle of winter in an area as rugged as Eastern Bosnia. The Chetniks were under orders from their commander, Major Jezdimir Dangić, to avoid clashes with the Germans at all costs, even if it meant surrendering; the latter reciprocated by granting his men the coveted POW status. The Partisans, for their part, were instructed to yield ground in order to conserve strength. All of this meant that Bader's troops encountered very little resistance, the speed of their advance being limited only by winter and terrain conditions. The only noteworthy clash took place on 21 January, when the elements of the 342nd ID managed to surprise a battalion of the 1st Proletarian and some smaller local units at the place called Pjenovac (just west of Han Pijesak). The encounter resulted in one of the worst single-day losses on the Partisan side so far in the war; among the 59 dead was Slaviša Vajner-Čiča, the man whose great charisma and personal bravery had made him the undisputed leader of the Serb highlanders from Mount Romanija despite the fact that his background was so different from their own (Vajner, a construction engineer by profession, was born and raised in Croatia as the son of an Austro-Hungarian civil servant).[18]

Having combed all the terrain accessible to ordinary infantry, recaptured a string of smaller towns, and pushed the guerrillas away from lines of communication, the Germans terminated the first phase of the operation on 23 January 1942. Apart from the victory at Pjenovac and hundreds of Chetnik prisoners, the bag was largely empty; most of the insurgents simply disappeared into the woods. The SHQ exploited the fact that the Italians had failed to seal the demarcation line in a timely manner and crossed the Romanija and Jahorina with two

18 *Oslobodilački*, Vol. I, pp. 172-77; Jakšić, *Nad uspomenama*, Vol. I, p. 218; Schmider, *Partisanenkrieg*, pp. 108-10; NARA/T501/247, BhS, War diary (25.1.1942); Pavle Fukarek, Savo Pređa, "Slaviša Vajner Čiča", in *Sarajevo*, Vol. III, pp. 812-43.

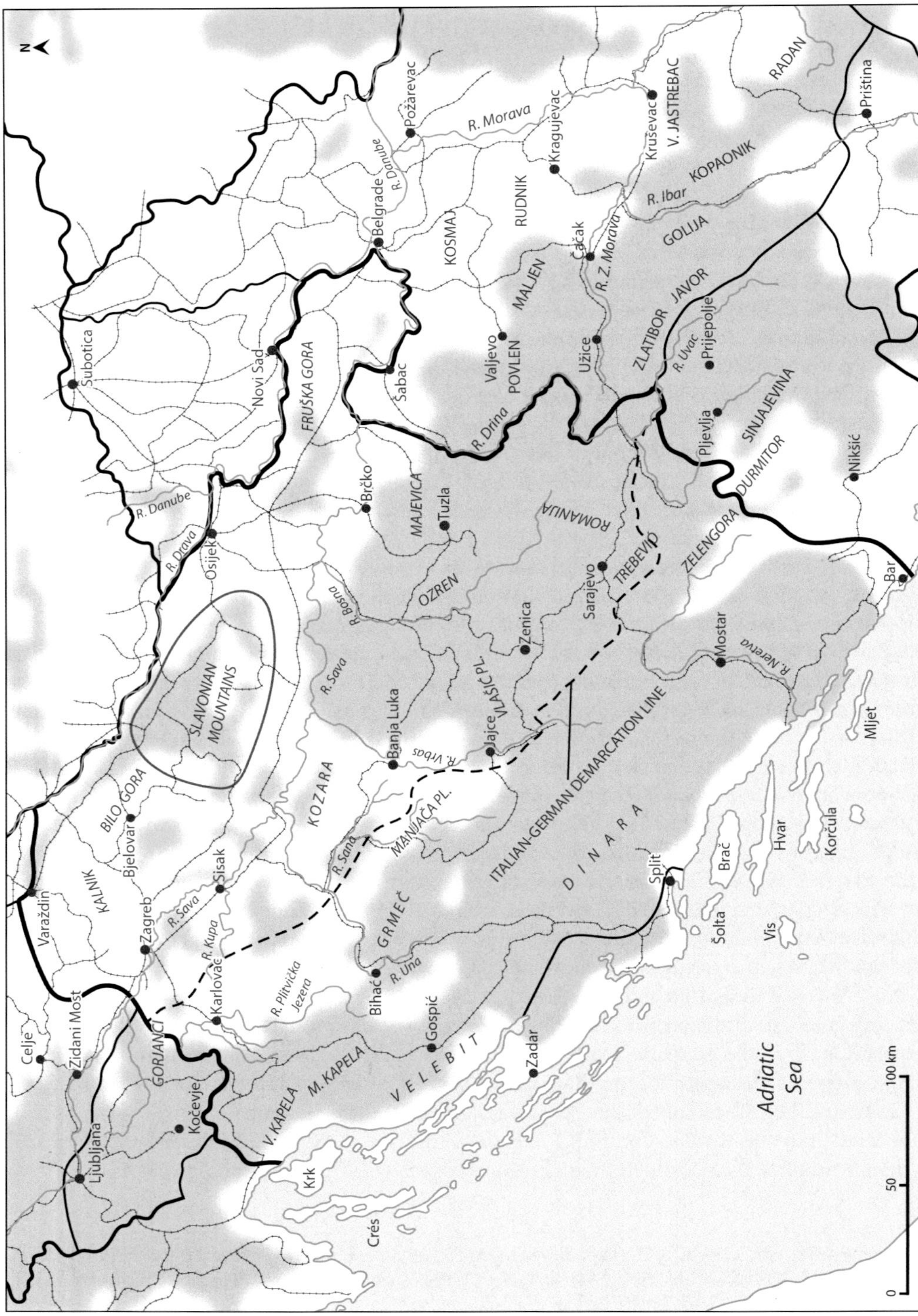

Map 5: Independent State of Croatia.

Proletarian battalions, reaching Foča on the 25th (the town had already been liberated by Montenegrin units). The remaining four battalions and the brigade HQ went in the opposite direction, hoping that the Axis would not be expecting them west of Sarajevo. This assumption turned out to be correct, but an encounter with the enemy would have probably been less costly than the encounter the brigade had with the forces of nature on the night 27-28 January. During the 18-hour long march across the frozen Mount Igman in temperatures of up to -30 degrees Celsius, the unit suffered almost 160 cases of frostbite. The wounded were transported, in part by a guerrilla-operated train, to a makeshift hospital in Foča. Over the course of the following weeks, the doctors managed to save most of them, albeit at a terrible price (236 toes were amputated, mostly without anesthetics).[19]

Meantime, the Germans had turned their attention to that old hornets' nest, the Ozren. Already on 9 January 1942, a mixed Axis force received a bloody nose while conducting a reconnaissance-in-force of the Partisan perimeter. By the 29th, Bader had concentrated both regiments of the 718th plus one from the 342nd ID on the southwestern and southeastern fringes of the massif. Divided into two battle groups of unequal size (one and two regiments, respectively), the Germans were to advance straight through the mountain in the general direction of Doboj; their objective was to destroy the rebels in their hideouts or push them towards the blocking lines along the Bosna, Krivaja, and Spreča Rivers held by 8-10 Home Guard and Ustasha battalions under the command of the 4th HDB ID. As soon as the fighting started, the guerrillas, together with the civilian population, withdrew deep into the mountain. The Germans were reluctant to follow in thigh-high snow and freezing weather and satisfied themselves with combing only the outer slopes. This second and final phase of Operation "Southeastern Croatia" was terminated on 4 February with the arrival of the attacking regiments to Doboj. As soon as the Wehrmacht spearheads had passed, the Partisan command decided to strike against the NDH troops from the second echelon. In a series of counterattacks lasting until 7 February, the Ozren Detachment managed to inflict substantial casualties and reclaim practically all of the territory lost during the enemy offensive.[20]

"The attempt to stamp out the hotbed of insurgency in Eastern Bosnia has failed", Bader concluded one of his reports from early February 1942. The Wehrmacht lost 25 KIA, 125 WIA, and one MIA in the first phase of the operation, and four KIA and 20 WIA in the second; the NDH casualties are estimated at 15 KIA, 35 WIA, five MIA, and 40 KIA, 42 WIA, and 141 MIA, respectively, a good indicator of the intensity of the fighting on the Ozren. Winter did not differentiate between the two sides and the Axis suffered just as heavily as the Partisans, having over 500 cases of frostbite. The losses of the insurgents in the Eastern Bosnian "quadrilateral" were computed at 1,471 prisoners with almost 1,000 pieces of infantry weapons and four cannon, those at Ozren at 489 prisoners but only 12 rifles (the Partisan estimates speak of 30-40 KIA and 80 heavily wounded). During the first phase, the Axis also recovered 104 Italian prisoners (most likely the same men who had been captured by the 1st Proletarian during its baptism of fire on 22 December), and 168 Home Guards.[21]

19 Vuksanović, *Prva*, pp. 31-41, 46-67.

20 Todor Vujasinović, *Ozrenski partizanski odred* (Sarajevo: Svjetlost, 1979), pp. 258-97; see also very detailed NDH documents in ibid., pp. 496-572.

21 NARA/T501/247, BhS to WBSO (30.1.1942); NARA/T314/1531/1219-20, HKdo LXV, Appraisal Operation Ozren (10.2.1942).

Things soon returned to "normalcy". The Germans spread their meager remaining forces to cover the most important objects and communications; the bulk of the Partisan army was firmly entrenched in the Foča-Goražde area, and to the north of it lay Dangić's large fiefdom centered on the town of Vlasenica. The latter soon became the focal point of all native factions. The Chetnik commander was relying on personal diplomacy to effect a transfer of authority over Eastern Bosnia to the Serbian collaborationist government of General Milan Nedić. Much to their disappointment, the German military authorities in Belgrade had to take back their consent in face of the stern opposition from Zagreb and Berlin. Despite this success, the Ustashe were concerned that as long as the monarchists were there in force, the possibility of such a settlement would remain present.

Before taking on Dangić, something had to be done about the besieged forward outpost at Rogatica. After the repeated attempts by the *Domobranstvo* to establish contact with the garrison had failed, Pavelić dispatched his top man, Lieutenant-Colonel Jure Francetić, to the scene. Deploying his crack force known as the "Black Legion" (due to the color of their uniforms), he fulfilled this task by mid-February. Acting in direct contravention to the orders from the 718th ID, which would have him continue his operations in southerly direction, Francetić turned northeast, striking from his base at Sokolac towards Han Pijesak with two battalions on the 26th. It took them eight days to reach their objective amidst heavy resistance by the local Chetniks augmented by Mihailović's officers and other volunteers from Serbia. So far, the only result of Francetić's sally was the emergence of a new Rogatica: the NDH forces now found themselves in an exposed position, practically cut off from their supplies. After launching an unsuccessful attack on the town on 10 March, the monarchists had ceased all their activities by the 16th due to the appearance of a large Partisan force in their rear. The Chetniks immediately suspected an anti-Serb conspiracy hatched by the Communists and Croatian fascists. The fact that this claim found its way into official Wehrmacht correspondence turned this episode into one of the most controversial ones of the entire war. Bader's reports from late March and early April mention repeatedly that the Partisans and Ustashe fought together against Dangić, and that the Communist-led guerrillas received ammunition from "the Croats" on at least two occasions. The Germans even made an inquiry with Francetić's aid, who denied any knowledge of the alleged collusion.[22]

The fact was that the incident caused as much commotion on the Partisan side as everywhere else. The decision to destroy the Chetniks as an organized force in the area Romanija–Višegrad–Žepa–Han Pijesak and subsequently use this territory as a springboard for an incursion into Serbia was made by the SHQ on 3 March 1942. The task was entrusted to a group of seven Proletarian battalions, including all four from the newly-formed 2nd Brigade, all in all about 1,500 men. Dangić had nominal authority over some 4,500 men, but they were spread across a wide area, and moreover had no desire to fight against their kinsmen.[23] The action would be steered by a joint council formed from the staffs of both brigades, with the senior officer present acting as *primus inter pares*. At first glance, the most communist of all Partisan units had a most unusual CO: frail-looking and un-military in appearance, Koča Popović was a scion of one of the richest families in Belgrade. In fact, this independent-minded and energetic commander

22 Tomasevich, *Chetniks*, pp. 206-09; Obhođaš et al., *Vojnica*, pp. 377-87; Schmider, *Partisanenkrieg*, pp. 124-25; NARA/T315/2268/618, Conversation Major Erhrich–Lt. Blasko (28.12.1942).

23 Vuksanović, *Prva*, p. 48; *Zbornik*/XIV/1/174, Radoslav Đurić to Mihailović (26.3.1942).

was also a veteran of Spain and the campaign in Serbia, where he successfully led the already mentioned Posavina Detachment. On 5 and 6 March, Popović received additional instructions: he was to extend his operations to the north and strike against Dangić's capital of Vlasenica, linking up with some local Partisan units there. After this objective had been completed on or about the 16th, the Proletarians were to move either against Han Pijesak, or towards Srebrenica and the Drina, depending on the situation. Tito's staff knew that the Ustashe were on the move but underestimated the speed of their advance. On the assumption they were still half-way between Sokolac and Han Pijesak, the SHQ ordered the task force not to attack the latter place because this would, among else, "give the appearance that we were paving the way for the Ustashe".

After liquidating the Chetnik base at Borike on the 9th, Popović moved a dozen or so kilometers to the west and spent the next four days trying to establish just what was happening on the Chetnik-Ustasha front before deciding on a course of action. Francetić was already in Han Pijesak, that much was now clear, and the local Chetniks were showing willingness to submit to the Partisans. Popović was in a tight spot. On the one hand, one of his main tasks was to isolate the monarchist rank-and-file from their commanders and bring them back to the NOP's fold; this could not be done by sitting idly while the Ustashe were burning down their villages. The Chetnik officers could not be attacked for "political reasons", i.e. as long as they were fighting Francetć. On the other hand, Popović was resolved not to commit his elite troops to purely defensive tasks and thus lose his operational freedom. Furthermore, opening of hostilities against the NDH battle group or its supply base at Sokolac would provoke an immediate reaction, effectively saving Mihailović's hard-pressed men.[24]

The dilemma was resolved on 13 March 1942 when a courier from Foča brought a copy of Tempo's letter to Tito, in which this high-ranking political worker suggests an immediate attack against Vlasenica "despite the presence of the Ustashe in Han Pijesak." Owing to the fact that the letter was forwarded by the SHQ with no comment, the combined staff of the Proletarian group assumed that it would be well within the limit of its authority to act on this suggestion. Facing no resistance along the way, the Partisans entered Dangić's capital on the 16th, and then turned east, trying unsuccessfully to stop him and the other officers from crossing into Serbia. In the meantime, the SHQ dispatched two letters to Popović on 13 and 15 March. In them, the SHQ re-affirmed that the combined staff indeed enjoyed full freedom of action, but at the same time advised against "an advance towards Vlasenica parallel with the Ustashe", mostly because of the negative impact this would have on the Serbian population. When the rumors of the alleged collusion reached Foča, the SHQ's tone changed completely: on the 16th, Popović and the others were accused of insubordination and reminded of the potentially "catastrophic political consequences" of their decisions. Never one to shy away from an argument, Popović firmly defended his actions before Tito and his staff, something he would have to repeat many times before the war was over. The Proletarian commander wrote that the final three sets of instructions from the SHQ had arrived with three to five days' delay, making it impossible to act on them. He also pointed out to the fact that the recently concluded operations ended in full success: the officers and their influence were removed, the local insurgents joined the Partisan

24 For the correspondence between the SHQ and the Proletarian task force see *Zbornik*/II/3/20-24, 38-42, 62-63 (3, 5, and 6.3.1942, respectively), and *Zbornik*/IV/35/100-04, and 108-13 (10 and 13.3.1942).

ranks, and a large booty was also made. The SHQ responded in a conciliatory tone but added that only a decisive attack on the Ustashe at Han Pijesak could help restore the NOP's tainted reputation (it should be noted that the insurgents' front around the town and along the supply road to Sokolac remained intact throughout this period; the Ustashe, for their part, stayed on the defensive).[25]

As far as the "Croat" shipments of ammunition are concerned, this had nothing to do with some clandestine arrangement with the Ustashe, but with the frantic attempts made by the Communist-led guerrillas to replenish their critically depleted stocks. The main effort was put into winning over the Home Guard officers in and around Sarajevo. During March 1942, the KPJ organization in the city had already acquired a small amount of ammunition in this way and sent it to the liberated territory. Later the same month, the Partisan units located in the area Mokro–Podromanija (i.e. in the operational area of the Proletarian task force) were instructed to establish contact with some sympathetic Home Guard officers who were willing to defect and who "had already given [us] some ammunition." The valuable commodity could be obtained in other ways too: one Muslim village not far from the Ozren was selling arms for money (a rifle with ammunition cost 800, a heavy MG 5-6,000 dinars). "The Croats" from Kalinovik and "possibly the Italians, too" were apparently not interested in money but in that other luxury item, tobacco: they were offering 100 bullets for each kilo. Thanks to the fact that the Proletarians had captured no less than 180 tons of it in Dangić's magazines, the SHQ gladly gave the green light for the swap (whether it ever came to fruition is unknown).[26]

In conclusion, it can be said that there is no firm evidence for the alleged Ustasha-Partisan collusion during the operations in Eastern Bosnia in March 1942. Bader's reports, the single "neutral" source for this claim, were in all probability based on the information obtained from the Chetniks and/or Nedić's men who took part in the fighting. Although he was dutifully applying the draconian reprisal policy (50 hostages for one German life), the German general was not ill-disposed towards the Axis-friendly Serbs and their political agenda. Like many of his colleagues, he was deeply unsympathetic towards the Ustashe, holding them responsible for the mess the Wehrmacht had found itself in. Bader's attempt to defuse the situation by negotiating a deal with Dangić was sabotaged by Zagreb. In response, he did not pass up the opportunity to portray the Ustashe in the worst possible light, i.e. as willing collaborators of the Communists.

The "temporary alliance" between the two could, in theory, be linked to the much-publicized ties they had back in the early 1930s, when their members were languishing together in royal penitentiaries. The fact remains, however, that both parties had underwent a drastic change during the intervening decade and now had practically nothing in common (the shared opposition to the Yugoslav idea had become a matter of the past). The view that the Communists of Croat origin were still ultimately Croats, and that at least some of them could somehow be reconciled to the new state, was not uncommon among the Ustashe. By contrast, the Communists coming over from Serbia (in this case the Proletarian task force) were considered as a mortal threat, a

25 Ibid., pp. 133-41, 145-49 (21 and 24.3.1942, respectively); *Zbornik*/IV/4/86-89 (16.3.1942); *Zbornik*/II/3/120, 130, 142-45, 258-59 (13, 15, 16, and 29.3.1942).

26 Ibid., pp. 34 and 157 (SHQ to MK Sarajevo, 3 and 16.3.1942, respectively), 303 (SHQ to Kraljevo Btl., 31.3.1942); *Zbornik*/IV/4/106-07 (MHQ Bosnia-Herzegovina to SHQ, 31.3.1942), 134 (Ozren Det./Pol. to OHQ Eastern Bosnia, 3.4.1942), 258 (SHQ to Kalinovik Det., 26.4.1942).

flipside of the same Greater Serbian coin that had Chetniks at the front. The KPJ membership, for its part, was not entirely bereft of the sense of ethnic belonging. This was especially true for those who had recently joined the party, but not only them. Milovan Đilas was so acutely aware of his heritage that he is considered a Montenegrin-Serb nationalist in some quarters. Moša Pijade, the oldest member of the CK (who was at that time waiting in vain for Soviet airplanes on a specially prepared airstrip on Mount Durmitor) famously styled himself as a "Serb of Moses' faith." Filip Kljajić-Fića, the premier *politkom* of the army in charge of the 1st Proletarian Brigade, would often repeat the saying "It is hard to be a Serb, but it is also beautiful." All said, the assumption that the members of Popović's task force were somehow suitable for, and capable of, forming an alliance with the arch-enemy of the Serbs simply because they called themselves "Proletarians" is erroneous and fails to grasp the complex and multifaceted nature of the KPJ and the NOP as a whole.[27]

2.3 Foča Reforms

The liberated territory centered on the Eastern Bosnian town of Foča (sometimes referred to as the "Foča Republic") existed from 20 January to 10 May 1942. The Partisan leadership used this unusually long period of relative quiet and stability to continue the work on the inner organization of the NOP. Much like the movement's political strategy during the same period, the development of the army also followed two parallel, but distinctive lines. On the one side, Tito's decision to win the allegiance of the insurgents in Eastern Bosnia by catering to their conservatism led to the creation of Volunteer Army of Yugoslavia (*Dobrovoljačka vojska Jugoslavije*, DVJ) in late January. The DVJ had no separate command and was in fact a blanket term for the Volunteer formations, all of which were subordinated directly to the SHQ. The basic unit, the detachment, was modeled after its Partisan equivalent; seven of these were formed from late January to late March (battalion-sized units existed as well). Their doors were open for all those who were still ready to fight against the NDH but were against leaving their home areas or choosing sides in the burgeoning inter-Serb civil war. Although they had a small cadre of veteran Partisan instructors in their midst, the Volunteers never fully adopted their values and principles, nor acquired their battlefield prowess. The new detachments were numerically strong, with about 1,000 armed men each, but were low on ammunition and military know-how; as such they were suited only for limited defensive tasks. Off the battlefield, they were a constant source of trouble, plundering, abusing, and even killing civilians and Home Guard prisoners. It is interesting to note that the Volunteer units were specific to Eastern Bosnia; everywhere else, local Partisan commands felt that the war aims could best be achieved within the already existing organizational frame.[28]

27 Tomasevich, *Occupation*, pp. 36-38; Ivetić, "Slučaj", p. 141; Hoare, *Genocide*, p. 218; Jovan Pavičević, "Ratni aerodrom na Njegovuđi", in *Durmitorska partizanska republika: materijali sa naučnog skupa održanog u Žabljaku 24, 25 i 26. avgusta 1977. godine* (Titograd: Istorijski institut SR CG, 1979), pp. 833-35; Rodoljub Čolaković, *Zapisi iz oslobodilačkog rata* (Sarajevo: Oslobođenje, 1985), Vol. II, p. 184.

28 Abdulah Sarajlić, "Stvaranje dobrovoljačkih jedinica u Istočnoj Bosni", in *Istočna Bosna u NOB-u: sjećanja učesnika* (Belgrade: VIZ, 1971), Vol. I, pp. 443-47; *Zbornik*/IX/1/170-73, OK Foča to CK KPJ (25.3.1942); *Zbornik*/II/3/192-93, SHQ to Rogatica Volunteer Det. (23.3.1942).

The emphasis on reorganization lay on creating more units in the mold of the 1st Proletarian. Although young, the brigade had already proven itself as versatile, robust, and–absolutely dependable. In light of the struggle against the monarchists and the expected "second phase of the revolution", political reliability came to be viewed as the main quality a unit could possess. Consequently, the 2nd Proletarian Brigade was formed in Foča on 1 March 1942 out of the 867 remaining fighters from Serbia. Although not authorized to create units of similar name and size yet, regional and provincial commands were given the green light to form smaller mobile units. According to the original plan, these outfits, made up of the best available personnel, were supposed to join the 1st Proletarian, ostensibly to give it an all-Yugoslav character. By the end of February, at the latest, Tito had changed his mind and left them with their parent HQs instead, to serve first as a security force, and then as the core of future brigades.[29]

The organizational process varied from place to place, subject to local circumstances. Proletarian Battalion of Bosanska Krajina was formed on 3 March 1942 from the already existing hand-picked units from various parts of the region (one company each from Podgrmeč and the Kozara, and a platoon from Drvar). Likewise, 1st Proletarian Battalion of Croatia, formed two months later, was composed of a company each from Gorski Kotar, Banija-Kordun, and Lika. Eastern Bosnia got its first two "Shock [*udarni*] Battalions" in March, with an additional one in April; in Herzegovina, the NOP felt confident enough to form eight of these units from late January to late May. In the beginning, the MHQ Montenegro believed that the destruction of the Chetniks was a necessary precondition for reorganizing the army, and not vice-versa. After repeated admonitions from Tito, the Montenegrins sought to redeem themselves by launching an ambitious program aimed at transforming their still largely tribal force into an army of shock battalions. No less than 25 of them were formed by the end of spring, but, as in Herzegovina, it turned out that the majority were elite in name only. In Slovenia, the first Proletarian Company was formed on 29 April, and the first battalion, named after the martyred organizational secretary of the KPS, Tone Tomšič, on 12 June. The local command in Štajerska did, in fact, form a "brigade" of about 300 fighters in early April, but the outfit was soon dissolved in pursuance of the SHQ instructions. The Partisans from Bosanska Krajina made a similar move in late May by forming, on their own accord, the 1st Krajina Shock Brigade; the unit corresponded fully to the prescribed standards, having close to 1,200 fighters with one MG per every 15 men. By the time the news reached Tito, the brigade had become firmly established as the backbone of the army, and the 1st Krajina was allowed to stay.[30]

Finally, in addition to the Proletarian and Shock units, the NOP leadership was placing additional emphasis on mobilizing the youth (defined as persons under 25 years of age). The youngsters would receive a standard two-week basic training, either in the so-called "reserve youth companies", or at the courses organized locally by the SKOJ and Party organizations, or field units. The curriculum–valid for the entire army–was divided into a military and a political part; the former was taught for four hours in the morning, the latter for four hours in the

29 Sredoje Urošević, *Druga proleterska brigada: ratovanje i ratnici* (Belgrade: Poslovna politika, 1988), pp. 39-40, 654; see Tito's orders to MHQs for Serbia and Bosnia-Herzegovina in *Zbornik*/II/2/191 (8.1.1942) and 394-95 (20.2.1942), respectively.

30 Anić, Joksimović, Gutić, *Narodnooslobodilačka*, pp. 128-58; Milorad Gončin, Stevo Rauš, *Prva krajiška udarna brigada* (Belgrade: VIZ, 1981), pp. 8-9; Jovo Popović (ed.), *Bihaćka republika: ratne uspomene Koste Nađa* (Zagreb: Spektar, 1982), p. 90.

afternoon. The topics covered everything from aiming a rifle and marching in single file to learning about the NOP's aims and ideals, the history of "the two imperialist wars" of the 20th Century, and "Stalin's Constitution" of 1936. Sometimes, a youth outfit would be paired with a Proletarian one, thus giving raw recruits a chance to learn directly from veterans. Probably the most famous youth unit was the all-teenager, 65-strong, ethnically mixed Foča Company, which was ultimately incorporated into the 1st Proletarian Brigade.[31]

There were changes in the command-and-control arrangements as well. The most important of these was the reorganization of mid-level commands. As of January 1942, the territory covered by the MHQ Bosnia-Herzegovina was divided into three areas, each under a separate OHQ (Eastern Bosnia, Bosanska Krajina, and Herzegovina; the latter included the entire area up to the Neretva Estuary). By mid-April, the MHQ Croatia would create altogether five OZs: the 1st covered the cradle of the insurgency, Lika, Kordun, and Banija; the 2nd–northern and northwestern Croatia; the 3rd–Slavonija and Syrmia; the 4th–Dalmatia and parts of western Bosnia and Herzegovina; the 5th–Gorski Kotar, Croatian Littoral, and Istria. The Slovenes, who had just introduced the Stolice structure (battalion–detachment), planned to divide their forces into four Groups of Detachments [sing. GoD], the 1st being responsible for Gorenjska and Koruška, the 2nd and 4th for Štajerska (the latter was never formed), and the 3rd for Ljubljana Province.[32]

As far as procurement of supplies is concerned, the civilian bodies, the NOOs, still played the dominant role. Immediately after establishing themselves in Foča, the Partisans proceeded with organizing elections for these committees on all levels. To be sure, voting was not done in secret, but it was open to all persons of both sexes over the age of 18. This was something unheard-of until then and did much to help win over two previously marginalized social groups, the youth and the women, for the NOP. As in Užice, the district NOO acted as a de-facto government for the entire liberated territory, responsible for both organizing the civilian life and catering to the needs of the army. More specifically this meant providing material help for the needy (e.g. opening of soup kitchens, allocating arable land), maintaining hygiene, organizing public events, operating road, rail, and telephone communications, opening workshops, and starting agricultural production. The food was obtained mainly through voluntary contributions or requisitioning; how much each household had to give was determined by its local NOO, but the main burden was to be carried by the "kulaks." As civil war intensified, confiscation was also increasingly applied: in this way, one NOO from the area northwest of Foča delivered 230 sheep, 50 goats, 38 horses, and 1,650 kg of potatoes. In the coming years, NOP executive bodies on local, provincial, and national levels would form special sections dedicated to handling economic matters (e.g. Central Economic Commission formed in August 1943 in Slovenia). Their main task was to ensure the food supply of the army and the population by organizing field works and regulating imports from the occupied territories. As we shall see, the onset of

31 *Zbornik*/III/3/413-18 (Durmitor Det., Class schedule, April 1942), 437 (Pijade to Tito, 25.4.1942); *Enciklopedija*, Vol. VI, p. 383.

32 *Zbornik*/IV/3/171-72, Tito to MHQ Bosnia-Herzegovina (8.2.1942); *Zbornik*/V/4/76, MHQ Croatia to SHQ (17.4.1942); *Zbornik*/VI/2/90-93, MHQ Slovenia to all units (4.4.1942).

harvesting season would always be a signal for all sides to step up their activities in order to protect the crop and, at the same time, deny it to the enemy[33]

Back to early 1942; whatever amount of food deemed necessary for the army would be handed over by the civilian authorities to the newly-created Quartermaster-General of the SHQ, which in turn would distribute it down the chain. Although the Partisans did have dedicated military-administrative bodies in the form of Place Commands (sing. *komanda mjesta*), they were (still) not responsible for supply matters. Their main task was to cooperate with the already existing executive arm of the NOOs, the People's or Village Guard (*seoska straža*) in maintaining law and order, issue identity papers, gather intelligence and stop the enemy from doing the same. In late April 1942, the SHQ created the first two Military Area Commands (sing. *komanda vojnog područja*), both located in northern Montenegro. Designed primarily to coordinate the work of two or more place commands and free operational units of all unnecessary burden, the area commands were also responsible for feeding all troops on their territory. Another novelty from the Foča period was the issuance of the daily food allowance table according to which each Partisan was entitled to 750 g of bread, 300-500 g of meat (depending on the sort), 500 g of potatoes or cabbage (or 150 g of beans), 200-250 g of preserved meat, 10 g of fat, and 10 cigarettes (alternatively, 10 g of tobacco). The authors of the document were certainly aware that it represented no more than a distant ideal, and that very few quartermasters in the country at that time were capable of meeting its requirements. The SHQ itself, along with everybody else in Foča, was for a while living off an "indescribably vile" bread made of barley and dried pears, large quantities of which were available locally.[34]

Apart from the addition of the post of quartermaster-general, the SHQ was widened so as to include 15 (later 19) distinguished commanders from across the country. Tito's staff also received a combat engineer section, and so did the Proletarian brigades. These sections were to be composed of suitable personnel (e.g. former miners), specially trained for only two tasks: demolition and negotiating water obstacles. The most important document regulating the inner life and structure of the Partisan units issued during the Foča Republic was "Statute of Proletarian Brigades." The statute outlined the nature and aims of mobile brigades ("a guarantee of success in the struggle against the occupier and his domestic lackeys as well as against national and economic oppression"), their discipline standards ("iron" but "conscious"; permanent three-member tribunals), composition (at least four battalions capable of operating independently, if needed), and insignia (red banner, red star with hammer and sickle). In addition to support services such as medical section and baggage train, each brigade had its own Culture Crew (*kulturna ekipa*, renamed after mid-1942 to *Agitprop*, portmanteau of "agitation" and "propaganda") whose task was to "[help raise] the ideological awareness of the fighters through political-propaganda means." Working closely with political commissars, the crews prepared proclamations and leaflets, organized rallies, gatherings, and theatrical sketches.

33 Luka Božović, "Narodna vlast u Foči u prvoj polovini 1942.", in *Istočna*, Vol. I, pp. 544-55; *Enciklopedija*, Vol. VIII, p. 11; *Zbornik*/IV/3/149, Birač Det. to MHQ Bosnia-Herzegovina (3.2.1942); *Zbornik*/II/2/354, Đilas to SHQ (14.2.1942). The organization and tasks of the NOOs were described in detail by Moša Pijade in the document called "Foča Regulations" (see ibid., pp. 411-20).

34 Ibid., pp. 237-41, SHQ to all units (January 1942); *Enciklopedija*, Vol. IV, pp. 430-31; Djilas, *Wartime*, p. 140.

In late June 1942, the SHQ added another tool to its propaganda arsenal by creating the post of Religious Advisors (sing. *vjerski referent*), i.e. military chaplains. Drafted from priests of all major denominations and appointed as required at brigade and battalion levels, the advisors were attached to medical sections where they kept death records and performed funeral rites. They were also responsible for "popularizing the People's Liberation Struggle" among the populace and performing all religious activities "free of charge." It should be noted that the appointment of chaplains did not come simply as the result of the repudiation of the "red terror". The Partisans, for the most part, had long been aware of the necessity to handle religious questions with care. This did not apply only in cases where the KPJ's influence was weak, like with the Volunteer Detachments, but also with veteran Partisan units. For instance, the 2nd Krajina Detachment celebrated Christmas and the Feast of St. Sava (the patron saint of Serbs) in addition to more worldly holidays like the New Year's Eve; important events from the history of the communist movement, such as the anniversary of Lenin's death, were also marked.[35]

2.4 Loss of Eastern Bosnia-Herzegovina and Montenegro

While the Partisans were hard at work organizing their army and the liberated territory, the Axis were busy making their own plans for the future. On 2-3 and 29-30 March 1942, the top German, Italian, and NDH brass met at the famous seaside resort of Abbazia (now: Opatija) and the Slovenian capital, respectively, to discuss joint spring operations. Everyone agreed that the main effort should be directed against the most dangerous flashpoint existing on the territory of the Croatian satellite state, Eastern Bosnia. Owing to the fact that they could contribute only one division (the 718th ID) to Italian three (in addition to the 1st Alpine Division "Taurinense", also the "Pusteria" and "Cacciatori delle Alpi"), the Germans were forced to relinquish the overall command to the HQ of the 2nd ITA; the NDH contribution would be limited to 8-10 infantry battalions. The operation, aptly named "Trio", should commence no later than 15 April, and was to be divided into two phases: the first phase would involve a concentric advance against the area Han Pijesak–Višegrad–Goražde–Sokolac, followed by a similar action in the triangle Han Pijesak–Zvornik–Bajina Bašta. The chances of success were seriously impaired by the behind the scenes struggle between the partners. Mario Roatta, the Roman-style politician-general and the recently-appointed head of the 2nd ITA, sought to expand the Italian influence beyond the demarcation line. He demanded and obtained the right to operate one division from the area of Sarajevo and proved unwilling to take firm action against the Chetniks in the zone of operations, something the NDH was insisting on.[36]

Fearing an additional loss of territory and prestige, Zagreb launched a pre-emptive strike. On 31 March 1942, for the second time in little over a month, Francetić launched an unauthorized attack against the insurgents around Han Pijesak.[37] Ever since its arrival, his forces had been

35 Anić, Joksimović, Gutić, *Narodnooslobodilačka*, pp. 173, 192, 196; *Zbornik*/II/3/194-97, Organization of pioneer units (March 1942); *Zbornik*/II/1/134-37, SHQ, Bulletin no. 14-15 (February-March 1942); *Zbornik*/IX/1/195, Jabuka Btl./Pol. to Jahorina Det. (6.4.1942); *Zbornik*/IV/3/120, 2nd Krajina Det., Activity report (30.12.-30.1.1942).

36 Burgwyn, *Empire*, pp. 130-35; Colić, *Pregled*, pp. 49-50.

37 Owing to the fact that the German sources keep mentioning "Dangić's Chetniks" as late as early April 1942–when they, in fact, had ceased to exist as an organized force already in mid-March following the flight of their leaders to Serbia–many authors, including Yugoslav ones, mix up Francetić's two raids

penned up in this desolate outpost, being supplied only by air or heavily guarded convoys. The storming of the town, although contemplated, had never been attempted by the guerrillas owing to the departure of Popović's task force to the area around Rogatica in the last week of March. Only one battalion was left behind to prop up the local Vlasenica Volunteer Detachment (two more Volunteer detachments and one Shock battalion were deployed facing the Drina). Having succeeded in getting reinforcements past the guerrilla ambushes along the contested road from Sokolac, Francetić now had three Ustasha and one Home Guard battalions, along with some artillery assets. This turned out to be more than enough: as soon as the attack began, all Volunteer units in the region began to disperse, forcing the remaining Partisans to retreat. As the result, Francetić captured Vlasenica already on the 1st; after taking a six-day pause to secure his rear, he continued towards the Drina, capturing Bratunac and Srebrenica before returning to Vlasenica on the 12th.[38]

Although carried out against their express orders, Francetić's brazen raid turned out to be very convenient for the Germans. What was planned to be the second phase of the "Trio" was now complete, and there was really no need for the *Regio Esercito* to push as far north as originally anticipated. Furthermore, the momentum created by the raid should be exploited immediately rather than wait for the painfully slow Italians who kept postponing the start of the operation. Repeating the same type of offense he accused Francetić of, Bader ordered his troops forward without consulting his Italian superior on 22 April 1942. The prospect of a successful encirclement was all but gone, but the Germans and their protégés cared only about occupying the demarcation line in force. The Partisans abandoned the siege of Rogatica (the half-hearted attempt to storm the town on the 7th had been repulsed by the Home Guard garrison), and withdrew in good order across the River Prača by the end of the month.[39]

What worried Tito now, however, was the growing Italian menace to his flanks and rear. On the same day Bader opened his attack, the "Pusteria" began its advance from Pljevlja to Goražde. Facing little opposition from the numerically much weaker and under-supplied troops of the MHQ Sandžak[40], the division entered the border town of Čajniče already on the 23 April 1942. In reaction, the SHQ sent the reinforced 2nd Proletarian to this sector with the task of protecting Foča from the northeast. Several days later, "Taurinense" finally started its own much belated march on Kalinovik from its temporary base at Sarajevo. Showing increasing maturity, the Partisans now refused to be drawn into pointless last-stand actions a la Kadinjača, and instead sought to stall the enemy by attacking his supply lines and demolishing roads (something the Kalinovik Detachment was especially proficient at). Moreover, in stark contrast to the situation in Western Serbia five month ago, the SHQ had been warned days in advance about the impending enemy offensive, which gave it ample time to prepare an evacuation.

and erroneously place his alleged "collusion" with the Partisans in the context of Operation "Trio": Vuksanović, *Prva*, pp. 49-50; Stevan K. Pavlowitch, *Hitlerov novi antiporedak: Drugi svetski rat u Jugoslaviji* (Belgrade: Clio, 2009), pp. 127-28.

38 NARA/T315/2268/643, Francetić to 718th ID (30.3.1942); *Zbornik*/IV/35/158-62, Popović to SHQ (28.3.1942); Obhođaš et al., *Vojnica*, Vol. I, pp. 420-30.

39 Ibid., pp. 436-38, 443; Schmider, *Partisanenkrieg*, pp. 126-28.

40 Sandžak, owing to its strategic position (located between Bosnia-Herzegovina, Serbia, Montenegro, and Kosovo) and specific inner situation (its ethnically mixed population included Serbs/Montenegrins, Muslims, and Albanians), became an autonomous military command already in October 1941: *Hronologija*, p. 129; *Petranović, Srbija*, p. 296.

On 4 May, the Axis forces began the final push–sometimes called "Operation Foča"–against the remnants of the liberated territory. Kalinovik fell on the 7th and the insurgents' capital followed three days later. Due to faulty planning and the unexpectedly strong resistance by the Herzegovinian Partisans (see below), the "Cacciatori delle Alpi" failed to seal the border area north of Gacko, which in turn enabled the bulk of the Partisan army to escape the encirclement together with the wounded and supplies. Being in no condition to continue the operations in this heavily rugged terrain, the Axis ended the pursuit on the 15th.[41]

Berlin, Rome, and Zagreb could be satisfied with the outcome of the spring campaign in the southeastern Bosnia-Herzegovina. For the price of 365 Italian, 34 NDH, and 21 German losses, this large and strategically important part of the Croatian satellite state was guerrilla-free again. According to Italian estimates, the Axis had inflicted at least 3,000 casualties, including 1,900 prisoners. The source, sadly, does not mention data on captured weapons; we know that during the "Trio I", the 718th ID and "Pusteria" took 1,161 prisoners but only 340 pieces of small arms between them.[42] In any case, it is safe to assume that most of the real guerrillas contained in this tally belonged to the Volunteer detachments, all of which disintegrated either as the consequence of the "Trio" or the so-called "coups" (sing. *puč*). The latter were, in effect, decapitation strikes staged by pro-Chetnik elements and aimed against the Communists, after which their units would either dissolve or simply change colors. The rank-and-file of the "real" Partisan units proved just as susceptible to this kind of subversive activity as their Volunteer counterparts. From the once numerous and aggressive Kalinovik Detachment, only 50 men chose to go on; ultimately, of all the detachments in Eastern Bosnia, only the one from Šekovići (the traditional NOP stronghold located just north of Vlasenica) survived the spring.[43]

Upon entering Herzegovina for the first time in late May 1942, the fighters of the 1st Proletarian were taken aback when a group of bare-handed Serb women assaulted them and tried to grab their guns. The ringleader, who was subsequently tried and executed, had been a wife of none other than a local *politkom*.[44] Where was this extraordinary hostility coming from in a supposedly friendly province? At the beginning of the year, the things looked entirely different. Being firmly in control of the countryside, and with the few remaining Chetnik chieftains on the run, the Partisans were free to concentrate all their assets against the occupier. The Italians, for their part, ventured out of their fortified bases practically only when a distant strongpoint needed a re-supply, and only in heavily armed convoys. From mid-January to late March, the 2nd ITA recorded nine major incidents, in which its units lost at least 79 KIA, 216 WIA, and 262 MIA. The Herzegovinians were also responsible for inflicting the single biggest defeat on the Germans in the NDH so far: on 10 March, they ambushed a column of trucks ferrying tobacco outside of Stolac, killing, wounding, or capturing almost 80 soldiers. April saw only one serious ambush, carried out on the 21st mid-way between Nevesinje and Gacko (60 Italians captured). The main focus of the Partisan activities at that time was directed at the already-mentioned Ustasha bastion of Borač, which was attacked on 17-18 April by a joint

41 *Zbornik*/I/16/40-41, MHQ Sandžak to SHQ (26.4.1942); Urošević, *Druga*, pp. 56-66; *Zbornik*/XIII/2/378, 2nd ITA, Bulletin no. 4 (6.5.1942); Colić, *Pregled*, pp. 51-52.

42 Fasanotti et. al., *L'esercito*, p. 249; NARA/T501/250/937-39, Battle Group [*Kampfgruppe*, KG] "Bader", Report Rogatica-Foča (4.5.1942). The losses of the "Taurinense" Division are not included in the total.

43 Hurem, *Kriza*, pp. 230-33; Borivoje Tepavčević, "Kalinovički NOP odred", in *Sarajevo*, Vol. III, p. 163.

44 Jakšić, *Nad uspomenama*, Vol. I, pp. 234-35.

force of some 2,000 fighters from Herzegovina, Bosnia, and Montenegro. The intensity of the fighting is evident from the fact that the attackers lost 46 KIA and 89 WIA; for comparison, the combined Partisan losses incurred in the ambushes on 10 March and 21 April amounted to nine KIA and 21 WIA.

After Borač, the local OHQ decided to launch raids into the lower Neretva valley and the Dubrovnik area, not least in order to draw away the enemy attention from the liberated territory around Foča. The move succeeded in disrupting the railway line between Mostar and Dubrovnik and bringing in a large number of livestock from Ustasha villages, but the Italians refused to take the bait. During the first three weeks of May, the OHQ Herzegovina was seemingly still on top of things. Its optimistic reports spoke of the increasing popularity of the NOP among the Serb masses, and of plans to expand the liberated territory beyond the Neretva River; on the battlefield, its battalions were successfully keeping in check a large enemy force around Gacko and repulsed several attacks near Čapljina. They also ambushed four enemy columns in as many days on the outskirts of Nevesinje.[45]

General Paride Negri, the commander of the newly-arrived 154th ID "Murge", was wounded on one of these occasions. His name was thus added to the ever-growing list of Axis dignitaries who came to experience first-hand the perils of insurgency. General Giovanni Battista Oxilia was ambushed in mid-March 1942 by the Slovenian Partisans while on his way from Zagreb, where he was serving as the head of the Italian military mission. Whereas Oxilia escaped unharmed, Vezio Orazi, the prefect of Zadar and former midfielder of the "Lazio" football team, was killed in late May. Other top brass who narrowly avoided death or injury during the first six months of 1942 included the notorious chief of the Ustasha secret police, Eugen Kvaternik, the commander of the German 718th ID, General Johannes Fortner, and the chief of the armed branch of the Ethnic German organization in the NDH, Lieutenant-Colonel Jakob Lichtenberger. All these persons just happened to be at the wrong place at the wrong time, although the Partisans were known to have set ambushes for particularly troublesome enemy commanders, such as the NDH Colonel Ivan Mrak. [46]

The Partisan situation in Herzegovina took a sudden and rapid turn for the worse in the last ten days of May 1942. The Chetnik leaders who had managed to get away with their lives sought refuge in Italian garrisons. The Italians, glad to have finally found a useful ally in this country, provided them with light infantry weapons and sufficient amounts of ammunition. The monarchists also received large quantities of food for the near-starving population and were granted distribution rights. Throughout late winter and most of spring, they bode their time, stepped up their propaganda and approached all those on both sides of the front lines who were unhappy with the Partisan rule. By the time the occupying forces had decided to stage a *reconquista* of the province, the number of armed Chetniks had swollen to about 1,800.

45 *Zbornik*/XIII/2/159, 181, 195, 209, 213, 243, 249, 293, 329, 2nd ITA, List of incidents (14 and 25.1; 3, 8, 9, 14, 26 and 28.2; 19 and 27.3.142); "Borbe protiv okupatora, ustaša i četnika", in *Hercegovina*, Vol. I, pp. 220-34; NARA/T501/266/146, DGA to OKW (17.3.1942); *Zbornik*/IV/5/9-12, 18-19, 26-31, 49-53, 99-105, OHQ Herzegovina to SHQ (3, 9, 12, 15, and 22.5.1942, respectively).

46 Ibid., p. 371, HDB GHQ, Daily report (15.5.1942); *Zbornik*/VI/2/391-92, XI AC, Daily report (13.3.1942); *Zbornik*/V/4/502, Governor of Dalmatia to VI AC (26.5.1942); *Zbornik*/IV/3/591, 4th NDH Gendarmerie Rgt., Activity report (11-26.3.1942); *Zbornik*/IV/3/518, II HDB AC, Activity report (16-28.2.1942); TsAMO/500/12450/616/258, German Ethnic Group in Croatia [GEGC], Situation report (1.4-30.6.1942); *Zbornik*/V/5/244, 1st OZ to MHQ Croatia (3.7.1942).

The first order of business was to rout the South Herzegovina Detachment and reestablish the communications leading to the coast. Although the bulk of the "Cacciatori delle Alpi" was made available for this task, the main brunt of the fighting would be carried by these native troops, supported by Italian heavy weapons. With their excellent knowledge of terrain and cross-country mobility, the monarchists could go where their partners could only dream of going. After several attempts by the local Shock units and two battalions of the 1st Proletarian to restore the situation had failed, the above-mentioned detachment simply imploded. By 4 June, the entire area south of the line Mostar–Nevesinje–Bileća was practically Partisan-free; according to incomplete reports, at least 350 Partisans defected and 150 were captured.

Seven days later, combined Chetnik forces stood poised to attack the last remaining NOP foothold in Herzegovina, located to the east of Gacko. The SHQ feared that the monarchists, if not checked, would cross the border and hit the heavily-engaged Montenegrin units in the back. Consequently, the HQ of the 1st Proletarian received the order to clear the enemy from the key position in the area, the hilltop known as Gat. Popović had at his disposal altogether fifteen battalions from both Proletarian brigades, as well as Montenegrin and Herzegovinian detachments. The relatively large number of units involved tells only half of the story. All Proletarian battalions were utterly exhausted, and the combined strength of the four Herzegovinian ones amounted to only 250, a potent reminder of the devastating effect of the "leftist deviations." What is more, the attackers lacked reliable guides, went into action piecemeal, and underestimated their opponents. The ensuing battle (12 June) demonstrated the vast potential for slaughter inherent to any civil war: the Partisans lost about 80 men, at least half of which were KIA; the Chetniks were hit at least as hard but managed to retain their positions. What followed was another round of recriminations between Popović and the SHQ, but all agreed that the retreat into the mountains along the border between Herzegovina and Montenegro was the only option left.[47]

The NOP downfall in Montenegro followed the same pattern as in Herzegovina but was a much more gradual process. The local anti-communists began their action already in early September 1941 by forming the clandestine "officer's organizations". By mid-October, Mihailović had appointed his representatives, and by mid-November, there were attempts to form People's Army, a right-wing alternative to the Communist-led detachments. Already in January 1942, Captain Pavle Đurišić, a veteran of the July Uprising and now the Chetnik commander in the northeastern part of the country, opened hostilities against the NOP. A month later, Colonel Bajo Stanišić followed his example by breaking away from the Partisans in the Zeta River Valley. The Italians maintained contact with both and sent them some weapons, but abstained from making formal commitments before the monarchists could prove themselves on the field of battle. By the beginning of spring, there could be no doubt as to their potential usefulness: according to their enemy's reports, Đurišić's men fought "like mad" and proved well-led on

47 *Zbornik*/XIV/1/288-91 (Report on liberation of Herzegovina, May 1942), 307-10 (Southeastern Herzegovina Chetnik Det. to National Committee Mostar, 7.6.1942), 397-403 (Dobroslav Jevđević to Ilija Trifunović-Birčanin, June 1942); Vuksanović, *Prva*, pp. 57-62; Miloš Vuksanović (ed.), *Koča Popović: beleške uz ratovanje* (Belgrade: BIGZ, 1988), pp. 44-48.

tactical level. Consequently, the *Regio Esercito* began supplying them with food, money, and large quantities of arms and ammunition, including some mortars and light artillery pieces.[48]

By the second half of January 1942, the Chetniks had cleared the entire Berane district and advanced into the upper reaches of the Tara River, destroying a battalion's worth of enemy troops from the Komski Detachment in the process. The Partisan Montenegrin HQ reacted by dispatching an ad-hoc brigade-sized formation to the scene with the orders to form a front facing east between Mojkovac, Kolašin, and Mateševo. Beginning in late February, the whole area erupted in fierce, seesaw fighting, which lasted for four weeks. Đurišić ultimately managed to wrestle control of all these places from the enemy (who was by now operating with over 2,000 men) but had no strength to continue his westward advance. At the same time, owing to the general demoralization caused by the increased Italian-Chetnik pressure, the Partisan Zeta Detachment, located around Podgorica, had imploded. Its remnants were merged with what was left of the "Bijeli Pavle" Detachment, which had in the meantime been pushed away from the communications in the Zeta Valley northwest of Danilovgrad. By the beginning of April, the Lovćen Detachment also stood on the brink of collapse, having suffered heavy casualties in the protracted fighting around Čevo. Only the Nikšić Detachment was still holding its own, repulsing all enemy attempts to get closer to the NOP's heartland centered on the town of Žabljak.[49]

These successes notwithstanding, the newly-created Italian Troop Command Montenegro (the XIV AC) was still not willing to commit the bulk of its forces to an all-out offensive, although it now had well over 70,000 men at its disposal. As in Herzegovina, the main effort was directed at re-establishing supply routes to isolated garrisons such as Nikšić and Grahovo. For as long as their rear was free of internal enemies, the Partisans could counter these moves. The Lovćen Detachment, for instance, had eight clashes with the Italians during the first three weeks of February. These included the taking of a hilltop position defended by 60 soldiers, and the sinking of the passenger steamship "Skanderbeg" on the Lake Skadar. As the year progressed, however, the Italians were increasingly making use of the "protective bubble" provided by the Chetniks and Montenegrin nationalists. Their presence made the invader's convoys and strongpoints practically off-limits to the Partisans. The most heavily engaged units of the *Regio Esercito* were the artillery and heavy weapons details that were working in close cooperation with the native infantry.[50]

As April 1942 came to a close, there were still about 4,000 Partisans in Montenegro. They were reasonably well armed with light weapons but were short on food and ammunition (on average, 40 rounds per rifle and 150 per LMG). In spite of their numerical weakness–Đurišić alone had half as many men on active service–the Partisans decided to go over to the attack in

48 Radoje Pajović, *Kontrarevolucija u Crnoj Gori: četnički i federalistički pokret 1941-1945* (Cetinje: Obod, 1977), pp. 127-37, 188-97; Milutin Živković, "Uspostavljanje saradnje komandanta Limsko-sandžačkih četničkih odreda Pavla Đurišića i italijanskih vlasti u Crnoj Gori početkom 1942.", *IDV*, 2:34 (2016), pp. 27-44; *Zbornik*/III/9/127, Montenegro-Sandžak Det. to SHQ (12.2.1942); *Zbornik*/III/3/161 (Lovćen Det. to MHQ Montenegro, 7.5.1942), 338 (Durmitor command to MHQ Montenegro, 28.5.1942).

49 *Oslobodilački*, Vol. I, pp. 184-91.

50 Schmider, *Partisanenkrieg*, p. 587; *Zbornik*/III/2/153-54, 179-81, Lovćen Det. to MHQ Montenegro (undated and 20.2.1942, respectively); *Zbornik*/III/3/229, 274-77, MHQ Montenegro to SHQ (14.5.1942), and to Đilas (19.5.1942), respectively.

the Tara Valley. During the fighting that lasted between 9 and 16 May, they succeeded in taking Mojkovac, but the real prize, Kolašin, remained out of their reach owing to exhaustion and bad coordination. The failed offensive turned out to be the "swan's song" of the NOP: on the 19th, the Chetniks counter-attacked, crossed the Sinjajevina range, and took Žabljak seven days later. The Italians and the collaborationists were on the march in other sectors as well. By mid-May, the Chetniks, supported by the elements of the "Taro" Division, had forced the remnants of the Lovćen Detachment to evacuate the extreme southwestern corner of the country and withdraw towards Mount Golija. At the same time, the "Ferrara" and monarchists were steadily pushing the Nikšić and Durmitor Detachments from the south; by the end of May they had taken Šavnik and established contact with Đurišić. In Sandžak, battle groups from the "Pusteria" and "Venezia" Divisions, reinforced by both the local and the monarchists who came over from Serbia, compelled the Partisan forces (the Bijelo Polje and Prijepolje Detachments, plus three independent battalions) to evacuate the province and retreat to the northeastern slopes of the Durmitor.[51]

All that remained of the once-mighty Partisan host from the southeastern parts of Bosnia-Herzegovina, Sandžak, and Montenegro, was now concentrated in the wilderness of the Piva River Canyon and the surrounding mountains. Their enemies had effectively canceled the pursuit; a few half-hearted Chetnik attempts to penetrate deeper into the defensive perimeter were thwarted by the recently-arrived Proletarian battalions. Although some commanders took the incident as a signal for a general counter-offensive that would lead to the restoration of the Partisan realm, the movement's leadership did not share their optimism. The fighters were so critically low on ammunition that the Chetniks derisively nicknamed them "Five-Bulleteers" (*petmetkovići*); the elite outfits were down to 25 rounds per rifle, the reserve ones had even less than that. Non-Proletarian units were decimated by mass desertions (including even Party members) and there was at least one case of open mutiny. Their numbers were also reduced by discharging of personnel, and by the decision to send small groups of reliable fighters and Party agitators into the enemy rear with orders to conduct a guerrilla campaign. The people who ran away were tired, homesick, disillusioned, but they were mostly hungry: by mid-June, the bread ration dropped to only 200 g per day. Thanks to the availability of a relatively large livestock reserve, quartermasters could partially offset the shortages by increasing the meat ration to one kg. This, however, was only a temporary solution, for the army could not subsist for long on such a low-carb diet.[52]

Tito and his small band of followers had to look for another base, but where to go? Serbian fighters were itching to return to their homeland, but for all practical purposes, it was a desert with a wary population, a multitude of enemies, and no secure foothold. Furthermore–and this was the main reason–the Soviet debacle at the Second Battle of Kharkov convinced Tito that

51 Ibid., pp. 134-35 (Milutinović to SHQ, 30.4.1942), 200 (MHQ Montenegro to OHQ Herzegovina, 12.5.1942); *Oslobodilački*, Vol. I, pp. 205-07.

52 Djilas, *Wartime*, p. 160; Vuksanović, *Prva*, p. 67; *Zbornik*/III/4/330, Krstac command to SHQ (29.5.1942); see also the documents of the Nikšić Detachment in *Zbornik*/III/9/307-08, 316, 323 (21, 29, 31.5.1942, respectively); ibid., pp. 334-36, Velimir Terzić to MHQ Montenegro (6.6.1942); *Zbornik*/III/3/311, 352 (correspondence MHQ Montenegro–Durmitor Det., 25 and 29.5.1942), 343 (Durmitor sector to MHQ Montenegro, 28.5.1942), 356 (MHQ Montenegro to SHQ, 30.5.1942); *Zbornik*/II/4/197-99 (SHQ/QM report, 26.5.1942), 267-69 (Pijade to Tito, 3.6.1942), 352 (Tito to II/2nd Proletarian Bde., 10.6.1942).

it would be years before the Red Army appeared on Serbia's eastern borders. Ultimately, after having considered other options, the leadership settled for Bosanska Krajina. In addition to the fact that this region was agriculturally far better-off than their present base, it was also full of NDH garrisons and busy communications that were ripe for taking; moreover, it was the home to numerous and well-organized local Partisans. In preparation for the "great march west", all Sandžak and Montenegrin units around the SHQ were reorganized into the 3rd, 4th, and 5th Proletarian Brigades. With four or five of these formations marching abreast, Tito remarked with confidence, "no force on earth could stand in our way."[53]

2.5 Developments in Western Bosnia: Battle of Kozara

As the winter of 1942 drew to a close, practically the entire area between the rivers Una and Vrbas (and, to a lesser extent, the territory between the Vrbas and the Bosna) was considered as hostile territory by the Axis. Towns and cities were in their hands, but the Krajina Partisans were the masters of the intervening countryside. Instead of the original three, there were now five (later six) detachments, with at least 6,700 armed fighters. Except for one, all of them operated either entirely or partially in the Italian occupation zone. Like their colleagues in Herzegovina and Montenegro, the Italian units deployed here (parts of the "Bergamo", "Sassari", and of the multi-regiment force called Zara Troops Command) had only two tasks, to hold their strongpoints and get a supply convoy through every once in a while. This allowed the two western-most detachments, the 1st and 5th, to develop a very lively activity over the course of the first five months of 1942. In addition to dozens of smaller actions, the Partisans had at least seven bigger clashes with the *Regio Esercito*, six of which took place on the road linking Drvar, Bosanski Petrovac, and Ključ. In these engagements, the guerrillas inflicted up to 230 casualties and even captured four artillery pieces. According to the contemporary Yugoslav sources, their own losses were negligible, only several killed and wounded fighters. Even if we assume that the Partisans lost more than they were willing to admit, ambush had once again proved its worth as a tactical tool. If, however, an ambush was not properly laid, the hunters would become the hunted. This is precisely what happened on one occasion in late May outside of Grahovo, when a Partisan company lost nine KIA and five WIA while retreating over open ground. The biggest success achieved against the NDH armed forces was the storming of Budimlić Japra (7 March), an important crossroads halfway between Sanski Most and Bosanska Krupa, which had been under siege since early winter. For the price of four KIA and several WIA, the Partisans captured 174 enemy personnel, together with 200 rifles.[54]

Until early February 1942, the 3rd Krajina Detachment was responsible for the large part of Bosnia stretching roughly between the Sana and Bosna. Then, in order to facilitate command-and-control, units operating to the east of the Vrbas were subordinated to a separate staff,

53 Djilas, *Wartime*, pp. 182-83; Petranović, *Srbija*, pp. 237-38; *Zbornik*/III/3/356, Tito to Ranković (31.5.1942).

54 *Zbornik*/IV/3/281-91, OHQ Bosanska Krajina to MHQ Bosnia-Herzegovina (5.3.1942); *Zbornik*/XIII/2/81-92, 2nd ITA, Dispositions (10.2.1942); ibid., pp. 175-77, 217, 241, 253, 279, 2nd ITA, List of incidents (27, 28.1; 19, 26.2; 2, 15.3.1942); *Zbornik*/IV/5/54, 65, 81, Activity reports of the 1st and 5th Krajina Dets. (mid-May 1942); Branko J. Bokan, *Prvi Krajiški NOP odred* (Belgrade: VINC, 1988), pp. 311-27, 339-47.

namely the 4th Krajina Detachment. During the first two months of the year, all of these formations were engaged in typical guerrilla activities, with varying degree of success. When caught out in the open, the NDH armed forces (primarily the Home Guards, but also the gendarmerie, and even the Ustashe) would usually buckle under pressure, as evident from a series of incidents which took place along the Vrbas in February. They could, however, prove steadfast when defending fortified places such as Kotor Varoš, whose garrison repulsed a major attack on the 19th, capturing eight Partisans and 40 rifles in the process.

Whereas this defeat had no wider consequences, the failure to take the Italian-held Varcar Vakuf (alternatively: Mrkonjić Grad) several days later marked the beginning of the inter-Serb civil war in this part of the country. The defection of a battalion commanded by a schoolteacher named Uroš Drenović sent a signal to all Mihailović sympathizers to start preparing coups. The speed with which they organized themselves can be partially attributed to the numerical weakness of the local branch of the KPJ: for instance, only about one-half of the commanders and political commissars in the 3rd Krajina Detachment were Party members. The OHQ for Bosanska Krajina used its "fire brigade", the recently-formed Proletarian Battalion, to rush from one flashpoint to another and nip seditious activity in the bud. The first clash with the Chetniks southeast of Banja Luka, in which the unit suffered 13 KIA and 12 WIA, showed that this would not be an easy task. Even more keenly felt was the death of the charismatic Dr. Mladen Stojanović, one of the authentic "people's tribunes" who had led the uprising against the Ustashe on the Kozara. As time progressed, the Krajina leadership was forced to order all its remaining mobile units into the fray: it is estimated that no less than 1,200 of its best fighters were involved in the operations against the Chetniks at one point. Ironically, the Partisans were now facing the same problem as Axis commands. Their enemy would fight only on his own terms: once the things became rough, he would simply disperse. Lacking the manpower and political influence needed for a permanent "occupation" of the area, the Partisans could not prevent the Chetniks from rallying as soon as they turned their backs on them. In the end, the 3rd Krajina Detachment lost control of the entire left bank of the Vrbas between Banja Luka and Jajce, and the 4th Krajina had practically ceased to exist. Additional blow came in mid-June, when numerically superior monarchist forces attacked and nearly destroyed the Proletarian Battalion on Mount Motajica; the outfit, down to less than 50 percent of its original effectives, had to seek refuge across the Sava River.[55]

In their struggle against the NOP, the Chetniks in Western and Central Bosnia found a most unlikely ally, none other than the NDH itself. Prompted by the apparently unstoppable growth of the uprising, Pavelić introduced a new policy towards the Serbs in spring of 1942, restoring some of their civil rights and allowing the creation of Croatian Orthodox Church. He also sought to capitalize on the Chetnik-Partisan split by offering non-aggression and cooperation treaties to the monarchists, provided they nominally recognized the NDH. Joint struggle against the NOP lay at the heart of the proposition: in exchange for active participation in military operations, the Chetniks would receive arms, ammunition and medical aid, none of which they

55 *Zbornik*/IV/3/213-14, OK Jajce to PK Bosnia-Herzegovina (20.2.1942); see reports of OHQ Bosanska Krajina to MHQ Bosnia-Herzegovina (ibid., pp. 288-89, 5.3.1942), and to SHQ (*Zbornik*/IV/5/211-22, 11.6.1942); *Zbornik*/IV/4/311-12, HDB GHQ, Daily report (5.4.1942); *Zbornik*/IV/6/365, HDB Banja Luka Bde., Activity report (June 1942); Savo Trikić, Dušan Repaić, *Proleterski bataljon Bosanske krajine* (Belgrade: VIZ, 1982), pp. 139-59.

could procure from other sources. The least common denominator, anti-communism, had proved stronger than the visceral hatred that reigned between the ultra-nationalists on both sides. One by one, the Chetnik groups in the western and central parts of Bosnia took up the offer from Zagreb. These included the Chetnik Ozren Detachment, composed of former members of the vaunted Partisan unit of the same name, which proved impervious to Axis offensives, but not to the monarchist subversion. The same goes for the Zenica Chetnik Detachment, which was led, ironically, by a former KPJ member.[56]

In the meantime, the 2nd Krajina Detachment was living up to its reputation of being the most active and reliable of all Partisan formations west of the Bosna. The detachment carried out more than five dozen actions in January 1942 alone, largely against the NDH targets in the area. The most spectacular exploit was the hijacking of an armored train by a group of Partisans dressed up as Home Guards. February and March, however, saw another clash with the Germans, who again had to intervene with their own forces. The operation was basically a rescue mission. The 923rd LSB had been deployed to Prijedor for some time in order to protect the local mines. Since the railway lines used to export the ore were in a state of permanent breakdown, Bader decided to pull out the badly exposed garrison. A regiment-sized relief force belonging to the 718th ID started moving south from its base at Bosanska Dubica on 17 February. The column was bound to a single road, and despite the presence of several hundred civilians armed with shovels, the thigh-high snow made the going extremely slow. The fear that the Partisans, who were opening sudden and murderous fire from well-concealed positions, would cut the road prompted the Germans to secure it by bringing in another battle group of a similar size, which also included one battalion of Ustashe from the nearby concentration camp at Jasenovac. It took the Germans ten days to cover the 30-odd km to their objective and another 12 to prepare the evacuation. By the time Operation "Prijedor" was completed (10 March), the Wehrmacht had lost 34 KIA, 48 WIA, and 15 MIA (the Partisans suffered altogether about 30 casualties).[57]

The Partisans had their sights on Prijedor at least since Tito had suggested the storming of the town in late March 1942. This would not only boost the NOP's prestige and fill its magazines but would also enable the linking of the territories controlled by the 1st and 2nd Detachments; moreover, this source of iron ore for German foundries would be shut down for good. By the evening of 15 May, everything was in place: roughly one half of the effectives (estimated at 2-2,500 men) would be used to secure the outer approaches to the objective, while the remainder did the storming itself. As was customary, assault details were led by the "hand grenade-throwers" (*bombaši*). Sometimes called the "Partisan Artillery", they were specially chosen youths[58] whose task was to soften-up enemy defenses in preparation for a charge. Along

56 Hurem, *Kriza*, pp. 206-18, 230-31.

57 For reports of the 2nd Krajina see *Zbornik*/IV/3/269-72, 319 (4.3 and mid-March 1942, respectively); for reports by the 718th ID and its regiments see NARA/T315/2267/1052-54, 1058-75, and 1109-12 (17, 15.3, and 4.4.1942, respectively).

58 Boško Buha, probably the most famous *bombaš* of the war, was expelled with his family from their native village near Virovitica, Croatia, by the Ustashe in summer of 1941. As a refugee in Serbia, he joined the Partisans when he was only 15 years old and died two years later in a Chetnik ambush. Buha was made into a role model for the Yugoslav youth, with many schools, kindergartens and a children's theater named after him: Danijela Lugarić Vukas, "Boško Buha i Pavlik Morozov: novi (jugoslavenski/sovjetski) čovjek u tijelu malenoga dječaka", *Narodna umjetnost*, 51:2 (2014), pp. 135-44.

with the "light machine-gunners" (*puškomitraljesci*), individuals deemed strong and reliable enough to be entrusted with the few precious automatic weapons the guerrillas owned, the *bombaši* had by now come to be regarded as the army's elite. The fighting began after midnight and lasted until late afternoon when the last NDH strongpoint in Prijedor fell; one day later (17 May) the mining town of Ljubija was taken as well. By all accounts, the NOP had won a truly major victory; for the price of about 30 KIA and 60 WIA, the Partisans had killed or captured some 1,300 enemy soldiers (one-sixth of whom were Ustashe and gendarmes), plus large quantities of arms, ammunition, supplies and money.[59]

Adding insult to injury, the Partisans were now attacking from the skies as well. On 23 May 1942, two NDH air crews defected to the 2nd Krajina Detachment together with their aircraft. Operating from makeshift airstrips, they flew altogether six combat sorties, dropping improvised bombs and leaflets, and causing much confusion on the enemy side. The NDH air force created a special search-and-destroy detail, and maintained air patrols around Zagreb, lest the rogue fliers tried to stage a propaganda coup by showing themselves over the capital. The first chapter in the history of the Partisan air force did not last for long, however: one of the planes was lost already on its first mission in early June, and its pilot, Rudi Čajevec, killed. The other remained operational for another four weeks before being discovered and destroyed on the ground by one of its German counterparts. The pilot, Franjo Kluz, would live to fly British "Spitfires" with Yugoslav markings, but lost his life on a mission over Dalmatia in September 1944.[60]

The fall of Prijedor compelled the Axis to revive the old plans calling for a radical cleansing of the Kozara; for as long as there were any guerrillas or hostile civilians remaining, this part of the NDH will never be pacified. By the end of May 1942, the WBSO had given green light for the creation of the battle group "Western Bosnia", under General Friedrich Stahl. A typical German ad-hoc formation, the group was composed of four infantry battalions, three-and-a-half batteries of artillery and three tank companies, all from the 714th (Stahl's own outfit) and 718th IDs, *Landesschützen* contingent, and the 202nd PzR. Together with support elements, the group numbered about 4,800 men. They were to serve as the core of a much larger force including the 1st MTD of the NDH Home Guard. This recently formed command represented the first concrete result of the efforts to reorganize the regular armed forces of the Croatian satellite state. Instead of the old, unwieldy infantry divisions, the army was to be reorganized into four mountain and four light infantry brigades, all of them trained in Austria and properly equipped. By the time the operation began, three of these units were ready to take the field. Another novelty in the Axis COIN efforts to the west of the Drina was the increased use of air power. Most of the flying would be done by the NDH's "Group Cenić": named after its commander, the group had between 20 and 28 aircraft and operated from the nearby Banja Luka air base. The Germans participated with only three machines but got to steer the entire

59 See the orders and reports of the OHQ Bosanska Krajina in *Zbornik*/IV/5/38-47 (14.5.1942), 110-12 (23.5.1942), 218 (11.6.1942); ibid., p. 396, II HDB AC, Activity report (16-31.5.1942).

60 Božo Lazarević, *Vazduhoplovstvo u Narodnooslobodilačkom ratu 1941-1945* (Belgrade: VIZ, 1972), pp. 40-46; Vojislav V. Mikić, *Zrakoplovstvo Nezavisne države Hrvatske 1941-1945* (Belgrade: VII, 2000), pp. 39-40.

effort through a specially appointed officer on Stahl's staff.[61] However, the most "exotic" units to take part on the operation were five gunboats belonging to the Hungarian Danube Flotilla; their task was to patrol the Sava and provide artillery support to the ground units. The overall strength of the Axis contingent in late June is estimated at 30-35,000 men.[62]

The Axis plan called for the creation of a tight ring around the Kozara, along the roads linking Prijedor, Banja Luka, Bosanska Gradiška, and Bosanska Dubica. The ring would then be gradually compressed, the guerrillas destroyed (either in combat or after it) and the entire civilian population shipped off to concentration camps. In marked difference to earlier operations, the timetable was generous and allowed for nearly five weeks for the completion of the task (10 June–15 July 1942). The Partisans' actions during this period were decisively influenced by several factors. First of all, owing to the total breakdown in intelligence gathering, their staffs knew nothing about the impending offensive. By this time, the guerrillas had also become complacent: for example, they had entirely neglected to demolish the main road from Banja Luka, which enabled the Germans to capture Prijedor already on the first day of the offensive. There were no breakout attempts during the first three weeks of fighting. The local Partisan commands were all in agreement that the abandoning of the friendly population to its fate would be both ethically wrong and detrimental to the war effort. Furthermore, having repulsed major enemy attacks on at least two occasions in the past, they did not believe that things would be any different this time. Rather than breaking out, the Partisans sought to reinforce their defenses by bringing in the 1st Krajina Brigade from the south. The period 11-16 June saw the first clashes with the "new model" Home Guards. Despite suffering heavy casualties, the 3rd Mountain Brigade (MTB) passed the test and maintained the integrity of its lines around Piskavica with some help from the Germans. Badly bruised (over 50 KIA) and in danger of being encircled, the Partisan brigade decided to try its luck on the western side of the perimeter.[63]

This leads to what was probably the biggest problem facing the Partisans, the complete lack of coordination between the units in and outside the cauldron. It was caused by the fact that there was not a single functioning W/T set between them, and that couriers had enormous difficulties getting through the densely-occupied Axis lines. Totally in the dark as to the plans of the 2nd

61 The NDH air force (*Zrakoplovstvo*) was equipped by a mixture of former Yugoslav and aircraft delivered by its patron powers. Although hopelessly outdated and suffering from all kinds of shortages, the *Zrakoplovstvo* performed a valuable service by flying supplies to blockaded garrisons, and by carrying out reconnaissance and fire support missions. By the end of 1942, there were altogether 14 squadrons with 185 machines, including 30 bombers and 40 fighters, which operated from three major air bases (Zagreb, Sarajevo, and Banja Luka). The insurgents shot down eight aircraft in 1941, and 16 in 1942: Ibid., pp. 24-25, 41, 61-66, 147.

62 NARA/T501/266/73-74, Minutes of conference in Thessaloniki (20.5.1942); Antun Miletić, "Neke mere i dejstva Vermahta na Kozari 1941-1942. godine", in Zdravko Antonić, Joco Marjanović (eds.), *Kozara u narodnooslobodilačkoj borbi i socijalističkoj revoluciji (1941-1945)* (Prijedor: Nacionalni park Kozara, 1980), pp. 201-02; Boško Baškot, "Epopeja Kozare u udžbenicima i u enciklopediji Leksikografskog zavoda SFRJ", in ibid., p. 284.

63 This, and the following paragraph are based on: Obren-Obrad Stišović, "Frontalne borbe i proboj obruča za vreme ofanzive na Kozaru u leto 1942. godine", in ibid., pp. 227-53; Mladen-Mlađo Marin, "O borbama prve krajiške udarne brigade u toku neprijateljske ofanzive na Kozaru 1942. godine", in ibid., pp. 262-65; Popović (ed.), *Uspomene Koste Nađa*, pp. 135-50; Schmider, *Partisanenkrieg*, pp. 148-51.

Krajina Detachment, the OHQ for Bosanska Krajina tried to ease the enemy pressure in two ways. One involved the attacks on four enemy-held towns in the Una and Sana valleys between 19 June and 4 July. Although the Partisans captured two out of four objectives together with over 300 prisoners, Axis commands refused to be distracted. The other involved another direct assault against the encirclement ring (22-28 June). In the end, only one battalion of the 1st Krajina Brigade managed to reach the friendly positions on the far side of the Bosanska Dubica-Prijedor road. Three battalions of the 2nd Krajina had actually pierced the ring in that same sector several days earlier (18-20 June), routing large parts of the 1st and 2nd MTBs in the process; the opportunity to escape, however, was not taken. By the time the detachment HQ had finally decided to break out (2 July), the western side of the perimeter had been reinforced by four German battalions of the 704th ID (the KG "Borowski") from Serbia. In the climatic charge which took place on the night 3-4 July, the guerrillas managed to overrun enemy positions and keep the breach open for several hours. This allowed some 800 of their own and ca. 10,000 civilians to escape to the west. The closing of the breach had also symbolically sealed the fate of the remainder of the 2nd Krajina Detachment: during the following weeks (the operation was not entirely over until 3 August), the Axis methodically combed the mountain, bringing in civilians and rooting out the remaining pockets of resistance.

Thus ended the "Epic of Kozara"; measured by human suffering, the battle had little parallel in the annals of the Yugoslav insurgency. It is estimated that the Axis captured and deported over 68,000 men, women, and children from this region. Thousands were shipped off to Germany and far-away Norway as forced laborers; untold number perished of disease or were murdered in camps like Jasenovac and Sajmište (known to the Germans as *Anhaltelager Semlin*). It turned out, however, that even such radical measures could not put an end to guerrilla activity (see below); for this reason, the Axis never tried applying them again on this scale. The Partisan losses were very heavy; depending on the source, the 2nd Krajina lost anywhere between 1,700 and 1,900 killed (including 3-400 wounded who had been executed after capture), which represented more than a half of its original strength. Whereas the German casualties were not unreasonably high for an operation of such length and intensity (63 KIA, 144 WIA, seven MIA), the NDH losses–426 KIA and 447 MIA–illustrate the inherent weakness of the Home Guard despite the "face-lifting" it had recently received.[64]

2.6 Connecting Dots: Croatia and Syrmia

During the first quarter of 1942, all eyes were focused on Lika. According to the plan conceived by the MHQ Croatia and subsequently approved by the SHQ, the Lika Partisans had the task of effecting a link-up with the liberated territories in Kordun and Bosanska Krajina by storming the Axis garrisons in the eastern part of the region. Although Donji Lapac was the original target of choice, it was decided to concentrate on the small town of Korenica instead, which was defended by three companies of the "Re" Division. As soon as the Italians spotted the guerrilla concentrations, they sent in a battalion-sized relief force. On 1 January 1942, the Partisans ambushed and routed this column, capturing at least 150 soldiers in the process. The worst, however, was yet to come. Three weeks later, the V AC launched a much bigger action involving

64 Miletić, *Mere*, p. 210; Drago Karasijević, "Ustanak i borbe na Kozari do oktobra 1942. godine", in Antonić, Marjanović (eds.), *Kozara*, p. 155; NARA/T501/351, BhS, Activity report (11-20.7.1942).

a two-pronged advance on Korenica from the northwest and southwest. The main column, consisting of four battalions (two from the "Lombardia" and two CCNN from corps' reserve) reinforced, among else, with a company of flame-thrower tanks, was met by fierce resistance by the "Marko Orešković" Battalion, and forced to turn back. The auxiliary column, composed of two infantry battalions from the "Re", ran into an expertly-laid ambush manned by less than 200 Partisans from the 1st Lika Detachment and was virtually decimated. "It was a black day, the blackest since the beginning of the war with Yugoslavia", noted a high-ranking staff officer in the HQ of the 2nd ITA; the auxiliary column alone lost 136 KIA, two tanks, four cannon, and hundreds of rifles.[65]

The guerrillas won a stunning victory, but this did not bring them any closer to their objectives. At first, the MHQ criticized the Lika command for allowing itself to be drawn into a formal siege; by early March, the capture of Korenica had become both a matter of prestige and military necessity (a success would free the besieging troops for other tasks). In the meantime, the guerrillas launched at least two direct attacks, both of which ended in failure. Their efforts were frustrated by the lack of heavy weapons, but also by some leftover habits from the early days of the insurgency. For example, the MHQ once had to send its representative with an armed escort in order to persuade a local commander to relinquish the control over his jealously guarded howitzer, which was sorely needed at Korenica. The Partisans also tried to weaken the garrison by–reinforcing it. Over 240 enlisted men (almost a third of whom were Blackshirts) captured in the recent fighting were released and sent to the besieged town. It was hoped that, with so many new mouths to feed, the garrison would quickly run out of food.[66] Thanks, however, to improved weather conditions, the *Regia Aeronautica* managed to keep the defenders' heads above the water with regular air-drops. The Italian command also tried to lift the siege by indirect means. During prisoner exchange negotiations, the Italians inquired about the possible terms under which the guerrillas would be willing to allow the garrison to withdraw. After being told that they could do so only in return for all of their weapons and equipment, the matter was dropped. On 24 March 1942, the V AC launched Operation "K" with parts of the "Re", "Lombardia", and a small battle group leased by the "Taurinense". Probably much to everyone's surprise, the units now faced only desultory resistance, as the Partisans realized that Korenica was not worth risking a major confrontation. Consequently, the garrison could be successfully evacuated by the end of the month.[67]

In the remainder of the province, the Partisans managed to capture Donji Lapac on 27 February 1942, but failed to dislodge one obstinate Blackshirt battalion from Srb during the siege that lasted from late January to late March (the defenders were ultimately relieved by a regiment of the "Sassari"). The link-up with Kordun was finally achieved in late April with the taking of Prijeboj and the Plitvice Lakes. The attempts to widen the liberated territory into

65 Stevan Opsenica, "Borbe oko Korenice (decembar 1941-mart 1942)", in *Kotar Korenica i kotar Udbina u Narodnooslobodilačkom ratu i socijalističkoj izgradnji* (Karlovac: HAK, 1979), pp. 733-45; Loi, *Operazioni*, p. 201; *Zbornik*/XIII/2/179, 267, 2nd ITA, List of Incidents (23.1, 10.3.1942).

66 During this period, the guerrillas released up to 200 additional prisoners (again, including members of the CCNN units) at various places in Lika and Kordun: ibid., pp. 185, 245, 261 (28.1, 28.2, 5.3.1942).

67 Loi, *Operazioni*, pp. 201-02; *Zbornik*/V/3/37 (Ivo Rukavina to CK KPH, 4.1.1942), 135 (Bakarić to CK KPH, 6.2.1942), 265 (MHQ, Circular, 12.3.1942), 221-22 and 276 (Lika GoD to MHQ Croatia, 2 and 12.3.1942, respectively). The Partisan losses around Korenica in January were estimated at 15 KIA, 28 WIA, and two MIA: ibid., p. 179 (MHQ Croatia to SHQ, 19.2.1942).

western Lika by attacking Podlapac and Udbina in late May and early June had, however, failed. The assault on Udbina is best remembered for the use of two captured Italian tankettes, which had to be pulled by oxen to the jump-off area due to the shortage of gasoline. By this time, the Partisan movement had entered a temporary stagnation and could not do much more at its present strength and level of organization. This was best evident from the events surrounding the Italian evacuation of Bihać in late June. The move came as a total surprise; the Partisans were stirred into action only after the NDH forces, which were tasked with paving the way west for their senior partner, had retaken Prijeboj and the Plitvice Lakes. Although the Lika command mustered over 1,200 fighters for a counter-attack, only one-sixth of this number actually came to blows with the enemy owing to poor planning and coordination. The opportunity to replicate the success achieved around Korenica in January, only on a much bigger scale, was thus lost.[68]

The 1942 Kordun campaign was off to an auspicious start. On 12 January, the Partisans captured the entire NDH garrison of Vojnić, consisting of over 400 Home Guards and gendarmes, as it tried to slip through the guerrilla blockade. Smaller outposts followed suite, and by early March, the two Kordun detachments had significantly widened their liberated territory, which now stretched approximately between Karlovac, Ogulin, and Vrginmost. In response to this threat, the NDH Utinja Brigade–one of the newly-introduced composite tactical formations responsible for pacifying a certain geographical area–launched its first offensive against the guerrilla stronghold on Mount Petrova Gora (18 March-5 April). The 1st Kordun Detachment suffered some 35 KIA, but ultimately managed to evade destruction. Most of the casualties were incurred in one night action when some 700 Partisan reserve troops, nicknamed *roguljaši* after their main and only weapon (*rogulje* = pitchfork), suddenly panicked and alerted the enemy to the approaching attackers. The second offensive, which began on 18 April and lasted, with short breaks, for almost a month, came very close to achieving its objective. In what was a miniature version of the Battle of Kozara, some 750 guerrillas, together with 10,000 civilians, found themselves surrounded by a much larger NDH force. Luckily for them, here there were no Germans who could reinforce the encirclement ring, and they ultimately managed to break out to the north and west. The Ustasha authorities estimated the number of enemy dead at 650-700 during the final phase of the offensive alone (9-15 May), but how many actual fighters perished is unknown; we do know that the 1st Kordun lost at least 67 KIA in this entire period.[69]

All the while, the Partisans received next to no help from the outside, highlighting one of the main deficiencies of the Kordun command, namely its relative passivity. Already in late March 1942, the MHQ complained of the fact that the local Partisans had become complacent and spent most of the time defending the "borders" of their much-cherished little "republic". In order to deflect criticism from above, they called this arrangement "permanent ambushes", "light blockade", or "pressure", all of which, in fact, referred to holding fixed defenses facing enemy garrisons. Apart from smaller actions, the first noteworthy attack operation came only in early June, as elements of both detachments tried to open the way to Banija by taking Topusko (the attack failed due to the rapid intervention of the NDH forces from Petrinja).[70]

68 *Oslobodilački*, Vol. I, pp. 238-39, 243-45; *Zbornik*/V/5/34, Tank Platoon to 1st OZ (5 June 1942).
69 Dušan Korać, *Kordun i Banija u Narodnooslobodilačkom ratu i socijalističkoj revoluciji* (Zagreb: Školska knjiga, 1986), pp. 244-50, 254-81; *Zbornik*/V/3/452-55, HDB District Command Karlovac, Report Vojnić (16.1.1942); *Zbornik*/V/32/265, HDB Utinja Bde., Report (15.5.1942).
70 *Zbornik*/V/3/420, MHQ Croatia/Pol. to SHQ (30.3.1942); *Oslobodilački*, Vol. I, pp. 245-46.

In Banija, the local detachment had grown to four battalions and a Proletarian company by early spring of 1942, but its activity remained limited to raiding Ustasha villages, smaller ambushes, and such. The initiative was largely in the hands of the NDH Petrinja Brigade, which kept its enemy occupied by aggressive patrolling and counter-raids. On one such occasion in late April, the NDH forces managed to surprise and kill Vasilije Gaćeša, a former farmer and NCO who had been one of the leaders of the 1941-uprising in the region. The brigade also launched two major operations against the Partisan-held territory. The first, lasting from 21 to 30 January, failed to achieve much except for widespread arson of Serb villages. The second offensive, named by the Partisans after the brigade's notorious commander Colonel Mrak (*mrak* conveniently meaning "darkness"), took place in mid-April. Informed of its impending start, the Banija Detachment decided not to allow itself to get trapped within the confines of Mount Šamarica, but to seek refuge on the far bank of the Una River. Their subsequent departure meant that the attacker's "bag" ended up empty, but it also allowed him to reestablish/strengthen his presence in a large part of the countryside. Fearing political backlash, the MHQ Croatia roundly criticized the maneuver and ordered the unit back to its native territory by the end of the month. The detachment's routine would be interrupted again in mid-June, as the elements of the 1st HDB MTD moved through the region on their way to Western Bosnia. The Banija Partisans tried to help the defenders of the Kozara by launching diversionary cross-border attacks, but the enemy refused to take the bait.[71]

In the far northwestern corner of Croatia, Primorsko-goranski Detachment was slowly recovering from the Italian autumn offensive. By June 1942, the Partisans had largely secured the mountainous area between the main roads linking Senj, Ogulin, Delnice, and Rijeka, eliminating several smaller NDH outposts in the process. The attempt to link up the liberated territory with the one in Lika by attacking Jezerane (16 April) had, however, failed with the loss of eight KIA and 16 WIA. The capture of Krivi Put (22 June), the ancestral home of Ante Pavelić, along with 20-30 "real hand-picked Ustashe", was greeted as a major symbolic victory. Of much greater significance was the establishment of firm ties with the Slovene Partisans following the capture of the NDH border post Brod na Kupi. A lively co-operation in the fight against the Italians would soon develop on both sides of the Kupa River. The Croats marveled at the "iron discipline" among their comrades from the north; the Slovenes, for their part, wanted to know more about the organization of liberated territories and took an instant liking to the specific, three-pronged cap worn by the Croatian Partisans that reminded them of Mount Triglav, their national symbol (the design actually came from Spain). The Italians would have probably left the guerrillas to dwell in peace in their mountain hideouts, but the increasing number of attacks against the railway line linking Rijeka with Karlovac forced the V AC to mount a punitive expedition. Elements of three divisions (the "Re", "Lombardia", and "Eugenio di Savoia") swooped down on the northern part of the liberated territory, capturing the Partisan strongholds of Mrkopalj and Ravna Gora and burning down scores of suspect villages (18-25 May). The enemy, however, had yet again managed to escape almost unscathed, and the action did little to stem the growth of the Communist-led movement in these parts. Thanks to the

71 Ljuban Đurić, *Banijski partizanski odredi 41-45* (Belgrade: VINC, 1988), pp. 96-158.

steady influx of new recruits, the 5th OZ could reorganize the Primorsko-goranski Detachment into two separate units on 30 May.[72]

Farther down the coast, in Dalmatia, the NOP was struggling to get back on its feet. At the beginning of 1942, the Partisans had launched yet another attempt to form new units in the countryside and establish secure communications between them. The going was slow: until the creation of the 4th OZ in late March, the HQ of Dalmatian Partisan Detachments was nominally responsible for the entire region, but in reality its authority did not spread beyond the Split-Knin area. The first months of the year were spent in organizing and launching smaller actions so as to acquire arms, experience, and prestige. On 3 January, the guerrillas staged a comeback by ambushing an Italian vehicle on the outskirts of Sinj, killing a lieutenant-colonel, veteran of the Abyssinian campaign (this event would later be celebrated in a very popular song). Three months later, the Partisans sawed off over 100 telegraph poles in the same area and then set a trap for repair crews. The Italians duly obliged by dispatching an entire CCNN battalion to the scene, which ultimately resulted in the death of 13 of its members. The Communist-led resistance was also beginning to make its presence known in previously quiet parts of Dalmatia. On 24 January, the Partisans attacked the small town of Gradac on what is today Makarska Riviera but could not dislodge the obstinate NDH gendarmes from their fortified barracks; on 3 May, they sank three dredgers in the Neretva Estuary, and on the 6th ambushed an Italian motorized column in the same area, capturing 18 soldiers.[73]

Unlike their comrades in Banija and Kordun, the Partisans in Dalmatia had one other, particularly menacing threat to tackle: the Chetniks. By early spring, the monarchists in the area of Knin and adjoining parts of Western Bosnia had organized themselves into Dinara Chetnik Division (*Dinarska četnička divizija*, DČD) with Italian blessing. The MHQ Croatia reacted almost in the same way as its Montenegrin counterpart, i.e. by creating an ad-hoc tactical formation called Combined Detachment. In addition to one Dalmatian battalion, it also included three of the best battalions from Lika and MHQ reserve, indicating the importance of its mission. The ca. 1,000-strong detachment spent the second half of May chasing in vain the elusive Chetniks and wrestling with Italian reinforcements; the main secondary task, the destruction of the scenic Bender railway viaduct, remained unfulfilled due to heavy enemy resistance.

Although Combined Detachment was disbanded soon thereafter, the command of the Italian XVIII AC[74] continued monitoring the growth of the hostile guerrilla movement in Dalmatia with apprehension. By now, the local branch of the NOP already had two detachments and three independent battalions, the most dangerous of which were located in central and northern parts of the province. The final week of June saw heavy clashes between these units and the

72 *Enciklopedija*, Vol. VII, p. 244; *Zbornik*/V/4/112, 5th OZ to MHQ Croatia (22.4.1942); *Zbornik*/V/5/161 (5th OZ to MHQ Croatia, 22.6.1942), 600-03 (Great County of Modruš, Situation report, 29.6.1942); Stevo Sunajko, *Sodelovanje slovenskih in hrvaških narodnoosvobodilnih enot 1941-1945* (Ljubljana: Partizanska knjiga, 1971), pp. 64-74.

73 Kvesić, *Dalmacija*, pp. 235-80; 89th CCNN Legion, War diary (7-10.4.1942), available at http://www.97legione.siena.it/Diario_Storico_97_Aprile_1942.html; see also the casualty list at http://www.97legione.siena.it/albo_onore.html (last accessed on 26.8.2018).

74 Having moved from Italy to Split in mid-February, the corps HQ had under its command the infantry divisions "Sassari", "Bergamo", and "Perugia", as well as the separate Zara Troops Command: *Dalmacija*/II/553-72, XVIII AC to 2nd ITA (20.2.1942).

Chetniks, logistically supported by the *Regio Esercito*. Two Partisan battalions that had been attacked on Mount Kozjak (several km southeast of Knin) managed to withdraw to Mount Dinara for the price of 15 KIA and 11 WIA. Ironically, the battalion that had been sent from beyond the Krka River as a relief force was itself encircled in the area southwest of the town. The unit lost 28 KIA during the initial breakthrough on 30 June, one of the worst single losses of life on the Partisan side so far. Worst still, many fighters deserted during the subsequent pursuit, and one high-ranking officer even defected to the Italians. Ultimately, the survivors were compelled to split into smaller groups in order to avoid a wholesale destruction.[75]

From the NOP's point of view, the northern and eastern parts of Croatia still represented the greatest challenges. The proverbial fish was rotting from the head down. Due to the failure to establish and maintain proper channels of communication and a unified chain of command, both the military (MHQ Croatia) and the political leadership (Organizational Secretariat of the CK KPJ for Occupied Territories) created its own HQ of the 2nd OZ; these separate bodies would not be combined before late August 1942. An "unhealthy atmosphere" developed as the result of this awkward arrangement, with a lot of personal rivalry and petty squabbles. The local Partisans were still by-and-large Serbs. No amount of proclamations or leaflets could convince the ordinary Croat peasant, as solid a supporter of Maček as ever, to leave the relative security of his home and throw in his lot with the "forest people". The NDH authorities, for their part, were careful not to antagonize the population (the majority of whom were first-class citizens after all) but would react massively whenever the guerrilla threat become palpable. In mid-April 1942, the 1st HDB ID mobilized up to 2,500 *Domobrani*, Ustashe, gendarmes, and village militiamen in order to hunt down some 60 members of the Kalnik Detachment. The detachment managed to avoid the enemy blow but had nevertheless ceased to exist when its members decided to split up into smaller groups. A little while later, a similar operation was launched against the Zagorje Company, which had grown to almost 150 armed men. This time, the NDH forces succeeded in killing 13 and capturing 14 guerrillas; most of the others ran away except for one platoon that switched its base to Samobor Hills. These two defeats would largely stifle the NOP's activities in the field for the next several months.[76]

The NOP in Slavonia was also facing an uphill struggle, but it enjoyed several advantages over the 2nd OZ. The local countryside was full of Serb fugitives eager to avoid either being sent to Germany as laborers or being drafted to the Home Guard's labor battalions (not just rights, but obligations as well were restored as a part of Pavelić's new internal policies).[77] Not being able to provide all volunteers with weapons, the local Partisans sometimes sent them away, which in turn earned them a sharp rebuke from the MHQ. Apart from reprimands, the Croatian command also sought to help the fledgling Slavonian units by sending them some "professionals". In late May 1942, a company of hand-picked fighters from Banija came to

75 Ibid., pp. 364, 368 (4th OZ to MHQ Croatia, 1.7.1942), 1148-50 (DČD, Report June 1942); Kvesić, *Dalmacija*, pp. 320-25, 343-49.

76 Marko Belinić, "O Drugoj operativnoj zoni Narodnooslobodilačke vojske i partizanskih odreda Hrvatske", in *Sjeverozapadna*, pp. 123-26; *SZH*/II/378, 2nd OZ to MHQ Croatia (1.6.1942); Žarko Miličević, *Kalnički partizanski odred* (Varaždin: TIVA, 2010), pp. 52-67; Filip Škiljan, *Hrvatsko Zagorje u Drugom svjetskom ratu 1941.-1945.: opredjeljivanja, borbe, žrtve* (Zagreb: Plejada, 2012), pp. 59-73.

77 Nikica Barić, "Položaj Srba u Domobranstvu Nezavisne države Hrvatske, 1941.-1945.", *Polemos*, 5 (2002), pp. 164-70.

Slavonia via Western Bosnia, where they had taken part on the storming of Prijedor (Lika helped Dalmatia and Kordun northern Croatia in a similar manner; not before long, Slavonia itself would be aiding its neighbors). An officer of the MHQ arrived with the company in order to help set the HQ of the 3rd OZ. Prior to his arrival, the staff of the Slavonian Detachment, which had been formed two months earlier, was in charge of the entire region. Its authority, however, was largely nominal: subordinated units, scattered and isolated as they were, were waging their own small wars against the Axis. Although they did not progress pass the initial stage of the armed struggle (liquidation of individual collaborators, ambushes on gendarmerie patrols, holding rallies, etc.), their mere presence in the agriculturally richest part of the country earned them an unwelcome attention from the NDH authorities. From late December 1941 to late April 1942, security forces carried out two major sweeps in the Slavonian Mountains, but with little result: by the middle of the spring, the (1st) Slavonian Detachment had grown to three battalions. In addition to the fighters from Banija, the 3rd OZ now had one other veteran unit at its disposal: after its defeat at the hands of the Bosnian Chetniks, Proletarian Battalion of Bosanska Krajina had found refuge in Slavonia. With these forces, the HQ decided to eliminate enemy presence in the mountains and finally establish a viable liberated territory. On 21 June, the local Partisans celebrated their first sizable victory with the taking of the fortified village of Bučko Kamensko (today: Kamenska), where they captured around 60 Home Guards and over 100 rifles. The attempt to replicate the success at Đulovac eight days later failed, however, due to heavy resistance of its Croat and ethnic German defenders, as well as the rapid intervention of the NDH armed forces from Virovitica. Nevertheless, it was now clear that the full-blown, Bosnian-style insurgency had reached Slavonia.[78]

The Syrmian partisans delivered the opening salvo of the 1942-campaign by capturing the gendarmerie station at Martinci on 26 February. Nominally, the Fruška Gora Detachment was responsible for the area to the west of the road Ruma–Sremska Kamenica, and the Podunavski Detachment for the territory to the east of it. In reality, they both preferred to operate in the vicinity of the Fruška Gora, the province's only mountain, which stretched 60 km parallel to the Danube. By the beginning of summer, the detachments carried out at least 90, mostly smaller actions; among the few notable exceptions was the disarming of an entire Home Guard company outside Petrovaradin on the last day of June. The NDH authorities reacted in the same manner as elsewhere, by forming composite formations and conducting massive sweeps involving up to 2,000 armed personnel in late March and mid-April. Officers on both sides were not happy with the performance of their men, none of whom were prepared for this kind of warfare. In order to rectify this, the HQ of Syrmian Detachments issued a special manual on guerrilla warfare and at least one critical analysis of the Partisans' shortcomings on the battlefield. The most notable of these was the tendency to panic, which led to heavy loss of life in the past (nine KIA and five MIA on one occasion). In early June, one company of the "Brandenburg" special forces division arrived to the province. Following the death of two NCOs in a firefight with the

78 *Zbornik*/V/4/332-33 (MHQ Croatia/Pol. to SHQ, 25.5.1942), 443-45 (II HDB AC, Propaganda speeches to population, 15.5.1942); *Zbornik*/V/5/93, MHQ Croatia to SHQ (15.6.1942); *Oslobodilački*, Vol. I, pp. 251-53; Trikić, Repaić, *Proleterski* pp. 191-92

enemy, the unit shot 257 inhabitants of the village of Grgurevci. The event, which caused much controversy among the Germans themselves, was ominous of what was yet to come.[79]

As with the formations under its command, the MHQ Croatia was undergoing a constant change. At the end of 1941, this body had only three members. Similar to the MHQ Serbia in its early days, these persons had no fixed posts, but spent their time visiting units and solving problems on-site. The growing size of the command[80] and increasing complexity of operations led to the expansion of the staff. In April 1942, it received five new members, each with a clearly defined set of duties (chief of administration, intelligence officer, liaison officer, etc.). The greatest novelty was the establishment of Officer School of the MHQ Croatia, which opened its doors to the first 52 candidates (including one woman) on 20 February. The main purpose of this institution was to provide the promising field officers and political leaders on platoon and company levels a 30-day crash course in the basics of military trade (a battalion-level course would be introduced later). The instructors were former junior officers and NCOs of the royal army; the curriculum was based on pre-war manuals, but also on contemporary documents and reports supplied by the MHQ. Mindful of the fact that the army was (still) fighting a guerrilla war, a special accent was put on topics such as battlefield reconnaissance, movement, security, ambush, defense of liberated territories, and demolition. The "leading subject" was, however, political education. Early morning classes, "when the listeners were at their freshest", were reserved for the lectures on the role of the KPJ and the USSR in the struggle against fascism, on the NOOs and the Red Army. By early November 1942, some 360 participants had completed the courses and had either returned to their old units, or been sent to assist the needy commands such as the 3rd OZ.[81]

To conclude, a few words on the campaign against the Axis rail communications in the region. Already in early November 1941, the 2nd ITA requested more railway security troops, claiming that the 11,500 men already tasked with this duty could not effectively protect more than 800 km of tracks in the army's zone of responsibility. Six months later, owing to the increasing number of attacks between Rijeka and Split, the Italians were forced to introduce wireless communication between stations (telegraph & telephone poles were usually the first victims of sabotage), add empty flatcars in front of compositions in order to protect engines from mine blasts, and reinforce their crew compartments with 10mm of armor plating.[82] The Germans also began playing a more active role in November 1941, when they offered their help

79 *Zbornik*/I/6/58-69 and 79-103 (HQ of Syrmian Dets., Lessons from actions in Syrmia, and Guerrilla warfare; May, and June 1942, respectively), 179-202 (3rd Det./3rd OZ, List of actions, February-October 1942); *Zbornik*/I/17/58-59 and 62-63 (HDB Syrmian Bde. to II HDB AC, 31.3 and 1.5.1942, respectively), 90-91 (GEGC/East Syrmia, Note, 6.7.1942); NARA/T501/248, Bader to Siegfried Kasche (18.6.1942).

80 According to various reports dated between the last days of May and the first week of July 1942, the overall strength of the MHQ Croatia amounted to at least 11,300 fighters: 1st OZ–6,500; 2nd OZ–200, 3rd OZ (Slavonia and Syrmia)–1,100; 4th OZ–1,500; 5th OZ–1,700; 1st Proletarian Battalion–300; see *Zbornik*/V/4/353, *Zbornik*/V/5/10, 52, 58, 140-41, 306-07, and *Oslobodilački*, Vol. I, p. 220.

81 Dane Rajčević, "Glavni štab NOV i POH i oficirska škola u Donjem Lapcu", in *Donji Lapac*, pp. 628-41; see also MHQ Croatia's reports to SHQ in *Zbornik*/V/3/384-85 (28.3.1942), and *Zbornik*/V/5/228 (1.7.1942).

82 *Zbornik*/XIII/1/621-22, 2nd ITA to *Regio Esercito* General Staff [REGS] (8.11.1941; *Zbornik*/V/4/426-27, REGS/Trans., Railway Rijeka-Split (9.5.1942).

to the NDH authorities with the setting up of proper defenses. By early April 1942, they were pushing for a fast completion of the first 27 fortified watchtowers on the section of the main line between the NDH border with the occupied Slovenia and the major junction at Slavonski Brod. A little while later, the 718th ID was made responsible for the protection of the entire line right up to Zemun; all NDH units deployed along it, as well as three LSBs, were subordinated to the division. These measures coincided with the creation of the first dedicated guerrilla demolition group on Banija and its subsequent arrival to the wooded area south of Ivanić-grad, adjacent to the premier rail communication in the Balkans. In April, there were 71 acts of sabotage on the territory of the Ustasha state; in May there were 82, and 36 in the first half of June, the majority of them occurring in the Italian occupation zone. For comparison, the annual overview compiled by Directorate of Serbian State Railways mentions only five "major" violent incidents during the first six months of the year; according to the cables sent from individual stations, there were altogether fifteen. In any case, these low numbers testify to the success of the German pacification efforts in the biggest Yugoslav province.[83]

2.7 Spring Uprising in Slovenia

Following the defeat of the December Uprising, winter months in Slovenia passed in relative peace. While the Partisan rank-and-file were undergoing training in winter camps, the higher echelons were pondering their next move. It was decided to make another attempt at igniting a general uprising, this time in the Italian occupation zone. With a little luck, the Italians would be pushed back into nearby forts, and a large territory liberated, which could then be used as a springboard for an "invasion" of other parts of the country. The Slovene leadership was so confident that it determined the number and disposition of the units that were just being formed not by the prevailing conditions on the ground, but by the projected success of the upcoming action.[84]

Unbeknownst to the guerrillas, the Italians were preparing a large-scale undertaking of their own, aptly named "Primavera" ("Spring"). The operation had its roots in one of the last memoranda which Roatta signed as the chief of army general staff, just prior to being made the CO of the 2nd ITA[85] in late January 1942. In short, he proposed three ways of fighting the insurgency: one, by launching major sweeps in coordination with the Axis partners (e.g. "Trio"), and two, by evacuating entire occupation zones (see the next chapter) in order to concentrate on defending the most important strategic objectives in this part of the Balkans. The third option, the one the general chose to apply immediately, basically represented a diluted version of the

83 NARA/T501/250/1378-79 (BhS, Protection of railway line Dobova-Zagreb-Zemun, 18.4.1942), 1381-83 (DGA/Trans. to DGA, 4.4.1942), 1391-97 (BhS/Eng. to BhS, 27.11.1941); Ljubomir Bošnjak, *Diverzantska dejstva u Narodnooslobodilačkom ratu 1941-1945* (Belgrade: VII, 1983), p. 132; see also bi-weekly reports by DGA/Trans. in *Zbornik*/XII/2/435-39 (20.5.1942), 464-72 and 503-10 (5 and 20.6.1942, respectively); Archives of Railway Museum Belgrade, Serbian State Railways, Folder 3 (1942), document 158, List of major incidents 1942 [hereinafter: ARMB/SSR/folder-year/document]; see also short summaries of cables pertaining to the first half of 1942 compiled by Tomislav Nikodijević, pp. 8-9 (hereinafter: Summaries year, page number). Copies courtesy of Miloš Bojanić.

84 Klanjšček, *Slovenija*, pp. 113-14.

85 In early May 1942, the 2nd Army would be renamed *Comando Superiore FF. AA. Slovenia–Dalmazia* (Higher Command of the Armed Forces Slovenia-Dalmatia), abbreviated to *Supersloda*.

second. Although in this case no region would be formally surrendered, the Italians would evacuate all isolated outposts and concentrate along the main communications and in a limited number of strong garrisons; from there they would actively control the surrounding countryside by means of motorized columns, "just as in some renegade colony". Future operations would be "colonial" affairs in one other respect as well, namely the unrestrained application of violence. Many Italian commanders envied the Germans and their methods of keeping Slovenes in line. By issuing the infamous set of COIN instructions known as *Circolare No. 3c* on 1 March, Roatta decided to introduce some of the Nazi practices to the daily routine of his army. Although it stopped short of prescribing death of 50 or 100 hostages for each dead soldier, the document ushered in a new and far bloodier phase of the Italian occupation.[86]

Both sides began to put plans into motion as soon as the worst of winter had passed. The "Primavera" was not conceived as a defensive plan; on the contrary, concentrating all forces in a handful of places (twelve to be more exact) was meant to facilitate offensive actions. Consequently, the Italians stepped up their usual COIN activities and launched local operations whenever they could pinpoint the location of enemy units. From 18 March to 20 May 1942, the XI AC carried out some 80 actions, with mixed results. For instance, the Partisans offered stiff resistance at Mounts Pugled and Mokrec but were surprised at Blatni Klanac and lost 12 men. The guerrillas responded with a wave of attacks across the width and breadth of the Ljubljana Province, reaching its culmination in the first half of May. On the 7th, the occupying forces suffered their worst defeat yet when the 2nd IR/"Granatieri di Sardegna" was ambushed near Logatec, losing 33 KIA (including its colonel) and 78 WIA. This episode epitomized the deep crisis the *Regio Esercito* was going through at the time. Despite having almost a year's worth of experience in anti-guerrilla warfare, one of the most venerable units in the entire army still allowed itself to walk into such a deadly trap. To make matter worse, the attackers were not Proletarians or even ordinary Partisans, but village militiamen belonging to the local branch of People's Protection, armed with only 15 rifles, two heavy and one light MGs. "Our troops do not fight, or at most, fight badly", complained the CO of the XI AC. Their officers were hardly any better, being prone to panic and laziness. This, in turn, led to all kinds of mistakes and shortcomings such as avoidance of night fighting, improper placing of artillery, and "disastrous" state of defensive works. By the end of May, at the latest, it was clear that not even the highest echelons were doing their job. The "Primavera" turned out to be a failure; it practically surrendered the initiative, along with the best part of the countryside, to the enemy, who was now more than able to tackle the sorties from the remaining garrisons. Both military and civilian authorities in the province were unanimous in describing the situation as very grave and requested reinforcements, even though the armed contingent already counted 40,000 men. The subsequent events seemed to confirm these bleak assessments. Both the "Isonzo" and "Granatieri" suffered a series of reversals during the fighting around Kočevje in the first half of June. The final "slap across the face" took place not far from Ljubljana on the 29th, when one battalion of the Pohorje Detachment liberated about 300 Slovenes from the train that was taking them to a concentration camp in Italy.[87]

86 *Zbornik*/XIII/2/35-38, Roatta to CoS (10.1.1942); Burgwyn, *Empire*, pp. 121-26.

87 *Zbornik*/VI/2/126-27 (MHQ Slovenia, Communiqué, 21.4.1942), 339-47 (XI AC, Plan "Primavera", 6.2.1942), 423-23 (Emilio Grazioli to Ministry of Foreign Affairs, 8.5.1942), 432-36 ("Granatieri di Sardegna" to XI AC, 10.5.1942), 448-51 and 454-61 (XI AC to *Supersloda*, 20 and 22.5.1942,

In stark contrast to the Italians, Partisan leaders were in an ebullient mood: "Honestly, I never thought Slovenes could fight like this", Kardelj wrote to Tito in late March 1942, adding that, with the exception of Montenegro, the conditions were nowhere near as favorable to the NOP as in Slovenia. Two months later, the same author spoke of a general uprising in Ljubljana Province that spread with startling rapidity. Practically the entire area between the NDH border along the Kupa River and southern outskirts of the capital was now in the hands of the Partisans. The OF had taken over the administration of the towns vacated by the Italians and introduced a series of popular measures like the sequestering and division of the property belonging to foreign and domestic enemies, granting right of use of forests and vacant land, etc. The number of active fighters swelled to 2,500;[88] militarily, the NOP had made great advances, but there was still much to be done. The core of the 3rd Group of Detachments was made up of reliable veterans of the winter camps. Newly arriving volunteers, on the contrary, were a mixed lot: a better part of those coming from Ljubljana were described as *lumpenproleteriat*. Despite the MHQ's repeated cautions against passivity, that "old sin of the Slovene Partisans", the units in the field were still somewhat ungainly and slow to seize an opportunity when one presented itself. This was largely caused by the troop commanders' lack of experience in leading operations which involved hundreds of men. Worse still, the nascent officer corps was also being plagued by "unhealthy practices". Some local commanders began to view themselves as absolute rulers in their home regions and were more interested in scheming against their neighbors then in inflicting damage to the enemy; they were nicknamed *vojvode* (sing. *vojvoda*) in derisive reference to provincial Chetnik warlords who routinely engaged in such behavior.

Speaking of native anti-communists, they started forming their armed groups in Slovenia in the spring of 1942. Although nowhere as numerous as the monarchists in Montenegro or Herzegovina, these groups, by their very existence, presented a major threat to the NOP. As a consequence, regular Partisan units and People's Protection had to devote their time and resources to hunting down these "White Guards" (*belogardejci*) and persecuting their sympathizers in the countryside. In addition, the OF's much-feared Intelligence and Security Service (*Varnostno-obveščevalna služba*, VOS) formed special workers' companies ready to nip even the smallest sign of subversive activity in the bud.[89]

What the Slovene leadership was really troubled by was the fact that the uprising was not spreading evenly throughout the country. Unlike in Ljubljana Province, the population in the German occupation zone was showing no enthusiasm for a rerun of the Gorenjska affair from last December. The Partisan activity had therefore remained limited to a handful of small-scale actions carried out by units not bigger than a platoon, or a weak company, at best. The strength of the 1st Štajerska Battalion, for example, peaked at about 90 men divided into three companies. Apart from the (partially successful) attacks on the Trbovlje mines on 28 April

respectively); *Zbornik*/XIII/2/443-46 (CCRR/XI AC to CCRR/*Supersloda*, 23.5.1942), 447-455 (XI AC, List of actions 15.9.1941-20.5.1942); Amedeo Osti Guerrazzi, *The Italian Army in Slovenia: Strategies of Antipartisan Repression, 1941-1943* (New York: Palgrave Macmillan, 2013), pp. 63-76; *Enciklopedija*, Vol. VII, pp. 26, 367.

88 The figure refers to Slovenia as a whole: *Zbornik*/VI/2/270, MHQ Slovenia to SHQ (ca. 25.5.1942).

89 DLRS/II/273-74, 277, Minutes of KPS conference (5-8.7.1942); *Zbornik*/VI/2/76 and 261-62 (Kardelj to Tito, 29.3 and 22.5.1942, respectively), 151 (3rd GoD, Order no. 5, 24.4.1942), 180 (MHQ Slovenia to SHQ, 1.5.1942); Tomasevich, *Occupation*, pp. 100-102.

1942 and the Ljubno gendarmerie station three weeks later, the battalion hardly ever operated as a single unit. The same is true for the 1st Group of Detachments operating in Gorenjska: the raid against three small enemy outposts around Škofja Loka on 26 June carried out by one of its battalions was an exception, rather than a rule. The security forces did not stand idly by but were actively seeking the guerrillas out. On 27 March, they succeeded in encircling and destroying a group of 18 Partisans in the vicinity of Kranj at the price of nine KIA and several WIA. The most dramatic engagement took place in the same area a little less than a month later, when a dozen or so Partisans of Kokrška Company sought refuge from a large police posse in the Okrogla Cave above the Sava River. It took a full day's fight, an AT gun, and satchel charges dropped by mountaineers while hanging over the cave on a piece of rope, to destroy the guerrillas (only two of them lived to tell the tale).[90]

The largest engagement during the spring also took place on the banks of the Sava, only further west, on the outskirts of the capital. It came as the result of the NOP's attempt to "export" the unrest from Ljubljana Province into Gorenjska. For this major effort, the MHQ Slovenia decided to commit its best unit, the 500-strong 2nd Group of Detachments. The operation started on 19 May 1942, as the Partisans crossed the demarcation line and headed for a river crossing near the village of Janče. Two days later, the Germans threw three police battalions against them. It took several hours of fierce fighting to dislodge the Slovenes from their hillside positions, but it was a hollow victory. Not only did the Germans lose more men than their enemy (at least 26 KIA compared to 11), but the guerrillas managed to pull off a nearly bloodless escape back to the Italian zone thanks to the copy of the German battle plan found on the body of a dead officer. Wars, however, are not won by successful retreats, and it was now clear to the NOP's leadership that an alternative route to Gorenjska had to be found.[91]

2.8 Serbia: Bleak Days

The withdrawal of the NOP's main force to Sandžak in early December 1941 did not signal the end of the Partisan presence in Western Serbia: two reinforced detachments, with an estimated 1,300 men, were still operating in the area of Valjevo. The SHQ steered their actions through written instructions and through its representative, Mirko Tomić, who effectively became the head of the MHQ Serbia. In short, the detachments were to hold out on their home terrains until spring, maintain contact with the peasantry, and conduct a campaign of small-size attacks against targets of choice. As it turned out, even such relatively modest objectives were beyond the guerrillas' capabilities at the time. The Wehrmacht was determined not to allow the uprising to flare up again, and collaborationist forces were equally eager to prove their worth on the battlefield.[92] Even before the Italians in Montenegro and Eastern Herzegovina, the Germans learned the critical importance of native formations for controlling the countryside. Wherever

90 Klanjšček, *Slovenija*, pp. 118-19; *Hronologija*, pp. 275, 293 (19.5, 26.6.1942); *Zbornik*/VI/2/205, MHQ Slovenia to 1st GoD (9.5.1942); Gendarmerie Safnitz, Report (28.3.1942) [copy in the possession of the author; original in Archives of Republic of Slovenia]; Günther Doebel, "Banditen in der Felsenhöhle", *Die deutsche Polizei*, 19 (1942), pp. 284-85.

91 Klanjšček, *Slovenija*, pp. 124-25; *Zbornik*/VI/2/464-65 (XI AC to *Supersloda*, 24.5.1942).

92 In the same period, some 1,200 Nedić's troops were conducting an offensive against the Partisans in Sandžak, capturing Nova Varoš on 6 February 1942: Milutin D. Živković, "Sandžak 1941-1943" (PhD thesis, University of Belgrade, 2017), pp. 545-51.

the Partisans went, they encountered hostile village militias who reported their every move to the authorities; large groups of Pećanac's Chetniks, gendarmes (now known as Serbian State Guard, *Serbische Staatswache* or SSW), and White Russian émigrés hounded them constantly despite the high snow and plummeting temperatures. The attempts to revive guerrilla activity in the valleys of Drina, Sava, Tamnava, and Kolubara by dispatching units there in late December 1941 and early January 1942 failed with considerable losses.[93]

Following a council of war held in the first week of February 1942, the guerrillas–now organized into a force of four detachments with close to 800 reliable men–decided to leave their mountain bases around Valjevo and head for Southern Serbia, where their comrades were rumored to be in control of a liberated territory. The march had barely started when dissenting voices, coming mostly from political workers who opposed the idea of leaving their native soil, had caused the leadership to reverse its decision and head back. Judging that smaller groups would have a better chance of evading the pursuers, the leadership then decided to split up the force and send individual detachments to their home regions. The ploy, however, did not work, and the Axis maintained the pressure. Due to constant skirmishing and shortages of food, ammunition, and winter clothing, the strength of the Partisan units dwindled rapidly. On 22 February, the Kosmaj Detachment was routed just southeast of its namesake mountain by the elements of the 714th ID reinforced by native auxiliaries. Incidentally, this was the only unit originally subordinated to the SHQ that had actually managed to cross over from Sandžak in mid-January (facing almost a total information blackout, Tito forbade sending any more men to Serbia soon thereafter). On 26 February, the same fate had befallen the Posavina-Tamnava Detachment in the area some 20 km north of Valjevo. On 18 March, after making another unsuccessful attempt to reach the Morava, the Suvobor Detachment was encircled and effectively destroyed southeast of the same place. Some 70 men of the Valjevo Detachment who managed to escape across the Drina in early March were among the few who survived the ordeal. The two heroes of Krupanj, the priest Zečević and Lieutenant Martinović, were among them, but countless others were lost, including Živorad Jovanović-Španac, the man who fired those first, fateful shots at Bela Crkva. Yugoslav historiography called the decision to stay in Western Serbia and split the force up a mistake. In truth, the local commanders simply dared not contravene the SHQ's outdated and unrealistic orders; several members of the Partisan staff would eventually be subjected to a Party investigation for their role in these events. The campaign left one lasting legacy: the iconic photograph of Stjepan Filipović, a battalion commander in the Valjevo Detachment, chanting Communist and patriotic slogans with his arms outstretched in a V just moments before being hanged on 22 May 1942. The photo came to symbolize not only the sacrifice of the Serbian Partisans that dreadful winter, but also that of the Yugoslav Partisans as a whole.[94]

In comparison to the rest of the country, Southern Serbia was still a guerrilla "El Dorado". To be sure, the local branch of the NOP had its share of internal problems. Based on the faulty

93 Glišić, Miljanić, *Rukovođenje*, pp. 108-11.

94 Dimitrijević, *Kosmajski*, Vol. I, pp. 279-344; Vladimir Dedijer, *Dnevnik* (Belgrade: Prosveta, 1969), Vol. I, p. 116 (18.3.1942); Bojić, *Posavski*, pp. 495-541; *Enciklopedija*, Vol. IX, p. 254; *Oslobodilački*, Vol. I, p. 214; *Zbornik*/I/3/254-59, Radivoje Jovanović-Bradonja to PK Serbia (June 1942); NARA/T315/2258/315-17, 425-28, 714th ID, Activity reports (16.1-7.2, and 8-28.2.1942, respectively); *NOS*, Vol. VIII, pp. 895-97, Higher SS and Police Leader Serbia [*Höhere SS und Polizeiführer Serbien*, HSSPF Serbien], Execution of Steva Filipović (2.6.1942).

interpretation of the CK KPJ's directive of 14 December 1941, which, among else, called for the creation of smaller, more maneuverable detachments of 50 men each, some HQs began releasing even reliable fighters home. Only the quick intervention of Party organs averted the potentially disastrous consequences of this measure. Ultimately, all seven detachments–ca. 1,000 active fighters–deployed in the mountains surrounding the valley of the Southern Morava and its tributaries could carry on with their activities. These units proved to be more than a match for Pećanac's Chetniks and Nedić's officials, but the things began to change with the arrival of up to 25,000 soldiers of the I Bulgarian Occupation Corps (BOC) in January 1942. Prodded by their senior Axis partner to finally put an end to guerrilla depredations, the corps began an active campaign in the middle of the winter. The behavior of Tsar Boris' army was unpredictable: in some places, its units would offer only scant resistance, and individual soldiers sometimes even defected to the Partisans. In other places, however, the Bulgarians were "worse than the Germans", fighting ferociously and carrying out mass reprisals. On 17 February 1942, the 17th BID massacred close to 500 civilians at the village of Bojnik in revenge for the killing of 12 and the wounding of 16 soldiers by the Jablanica Detachment. During the same sweep, the the Bulgarians recaptured the town of Prokuplje, which had served as the guerrilla capital in the south since October 1941. A little while later, a mixed force from the 1st, 17th, and 21st BIDs attacked the Babički and parts of the Svrljig-Nišava Detachments to the southeast of Niš and forced them to seek refuge at Mount Suha Planina. Probably the most dramatic event to occur during this period was the successful breakout of ca. 100 NOP sympathizers from the concentration camp at Niš on 12 February 1942. In addition to killing some 40 inmates during the incident itself, the Germans avenged the death of five of their guards by shooting another 850 persons, including all the remaining Jews and Gypsies.[95]

The imminent arrival of spring gave a new impetus to Axis efforts. By mid-March 1942, the Babički Detachment had practically ceased to exist, whereas the Svrljig-Nišava Detachment had to change its base of operations yet again by moving to the territory held by the Ozren Detachment north of Niš. The main objective of what was colloquially known as "March Offensive" was the destruction of the guerrillas who were operating in the area between the Toplica and Jablanica Rivers. The Bulgarians, reinforced by an assortment of Serbian collaborationist units, moved in from the direction of Leskovac and Lebane. Despite putting every available fighter to the firing line, including members of village militias, the Partisans found themselves encircled on the slopes of Mount Pasjača within a week from the beginning of the offensive. It was Western Serbia all over again: the hastily formed joint staff could at first not decide where to go, and then made the wrong choice. Instead of trying to reach the liberated territory on the far side of the Toplica, the Partisans decided to split into two columns and return to their old bases in the south. The results were disastrous: on 27 March, after two weeks of futile attempts to escape the pocket, the decimated Jablanica Detachment dissolved itself into smaller groups. Similarly, the Kukavica Detachment was effectively wiped out in the engagements fought on 19 and 26 March. During the mop-up actions, the guerrillas were dealt further heavy blows, like the destruction of an entire company of the Toplica Detachment on 12 April. In all, the units in

95 *Zbornik*/I/3/31 (OK Leskovac to PK Serbia, 23.1.1942), 145 and 188 (KPJ Commissioner Niš to PK Serbia, 16.3 and 21.4.1942, respectively), 354 (SSW report 26.2.1942); Glišić, Ristovski, *Bugarska*, pp. 40, 97-100; Venceslav Glišić, *Teror i zločini fašističke Nemačke u Srbiji 1941-1944.* (Belgrade: Rad, 1970), pp. 154-55.

Southern Serbia lost about 500 men until mid-May; of these, some 100 were Party members, including one detachment *politkom* and even one member of the CK KPJ. The NOP was hit especially hard in the Jablanica region and would need several months to get back on its feet.[96]

The last remaining major Partisan base in this part of Serbia was situated on the Jastrebac, the 1,500-meter high mountain nestled between the valleys of the Southern Morava, Toplica, and Rasina. The first Axis attempt to remove this threat to the nearby communications in late April 1942 turned out to be a total flop. Seeing through the enemy intentions in a timely manner, the Toplica (later renamed to Jastrebac) Detachment escaped west, to the relative safety of Mount Kopaonik. As a consequence, the Bulgarians and Nedić's troops crisscrossed the mountain without even seeing the guerrillas. Once the bulk of the enemy forces returned to its garrisons early the next month, the Partisans re-occupied their old bases and continued with their activities. Despite the fact that security forces were carrying out smaller sweeps almost on a daily basis, the situation was becoming progressively worse. By the beginning of summer, the I BOC had no alternative but to launch another major offensive. 3,000 men (not counting collaborationist troops) combed the Jastrebac for a whole week (15-23 June), but succeeded only in burning down dozens of houses and interning scores of villagers. Contrary to the suggestions of the civilian authorities, which recognized that the key to pacification lay in the permanent and visible presence of the army even in the most remote villages, the Bulgarians simply returned to their bases; this, in turn, allowed the Toplica and Rasina Detachments to do the same. Similarly, the operation that took place north of Niš from 25 to 30 June against the Nišava, Ozren, and Timok Detachments was described merely as "a grave instance of destruction of people and property". Although they were forced to split up and temporarily leave their home terrains, the guerrillas survived to fight another day.[97]

96 Perović, *Južna*, pp. 145-50, 165-66, 184-85; *Zbornik*/I/3/424-26, SSW, Activity report (31.3.1942).

97 Ibid., pp. 514-16 (Leskovac district, Bulgarian action in the field, 24.6.1942), 517-18 (SSW, Daily report, 29.6.1942); NARA/T501/248, BhS, Activity report (22.5., 10 and 20.6.1942); *Oslobodilački*, Vol. I, pp. 218-19. From February to 25 July 1942, the I BOC lost altogether 27 KIA and 34 WIA; for comparison, the Serbian quisling forces suffered 69 KIA and 13 WIA during March alone; see the already cited SSW activity report of 31.3.1942 and NARA/T501/351, BhS to WBSO/Pers. (26.7.1942).

3

Go West! (July – December 1942)

3.1 "March of Proletarian Brigades"

The Yugoslav version of the Chinese "Long March" commenced at dawn on 24 June 1942. According to the original plan, the march from Mount Zelengora to Bosanska Krajina would be carried out by the first four Proletarian brigades; the 5th, along with the remnants of Herzegovinian units, would remain behind in order to protect the hospital and maintain a foothold in the border area between Bosnia, Herzegovina, and Montenegro. Between them, the brigades belonging to the task force had close to 3,800 fighters equipped with light infantry weapons and a handful of mortars. At the first glance this does not seem much, but it should be remembered that practically all of these men and women were either card-carrying Communists or members of the affiliated organizations, dedicated veterans with nothing left to lose.[1]

In the meantime, representatives of the *Regio Esercito* and the Pavelić regime signed the Treaty of Zagreb on 19 June 1942. The agreement was the result of the long-standing desire of the Ustashe to re-establish their authority in the Italian occupation zone, which had been suspended in the course of the 2nd ITA's anti-guerrilla campaign the previous summer. They also wanted to ease the crushing economic burden caused by the presence of nearly 200,000 Italian soldiers in the country. Roatta and his peers, for their part, were seeking to indigenize the increasingly costly counterinsurgency to the greatest possible degree; to this effect, they had already ordered the evacuation of the entire Zone III and sizable reduction in troop levels in Zone II. Although the treaty prescribed a three-week period for the completion of the handover, the Italians proceeded with the withdrawal at such a breakneck speed that the NDH authorities simply did not have time to muster sufficient forces for securing the said areas. In practical terms, this meant that the entire south of the satellite state now lay exposed to the Proletarian brigades, which were just beginning to arrive from the east. It should be noted that Partisans leaders knew nothing about the NDH-Italian arrangement owing to the almost

1 Colić, *Pregled*, pp. 60-61.

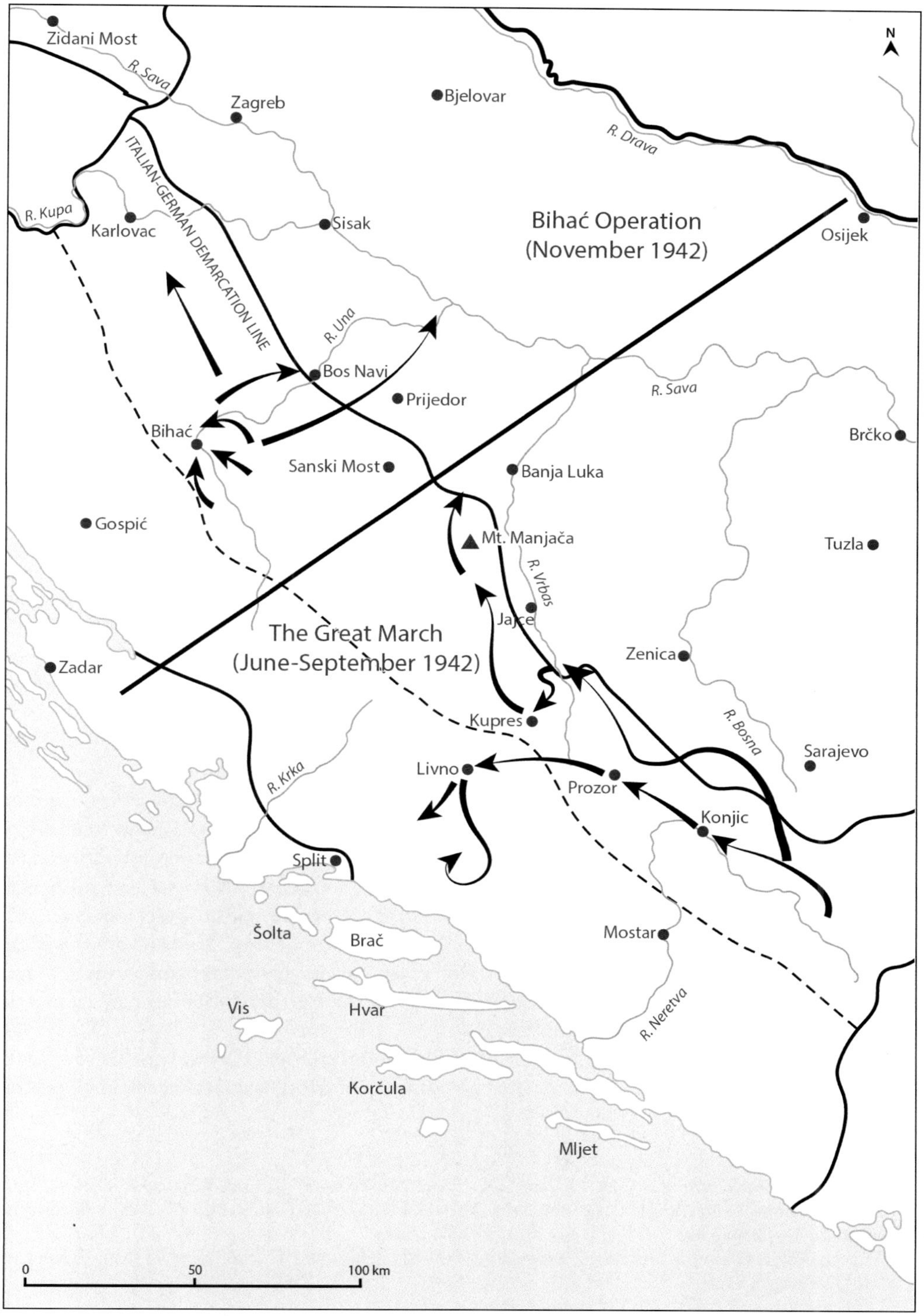

Map 6: March of Proletarian Brigades (June-November 1942).

total breakdown in communications with regional commands and intelligence centers on the occupied territory.[2]

The initial leg of the journey took the Partisans through the wilderness of Mounts Treskavica and Bjelašnica. The going was slow and exhausting due to near-winter weather and the fact that the entire task force had only one map of the area. By 3 July 1942, all four brigades–now divided into two groups of equal strength, the northern (the 2nd and 4th) and southern (the 1st and 3rd)–stood before their first objective, the railway line between Sarajevo and Konjic. The few NDH guard details deployed in this sector scattered almost immediately, allowing the guerrillas to thoroughly vandalize the railway installations during the next several days. Even though the lack of explosives and expertise precluded them from completely destroying the only link between Herzegovina and the remainder of the NDH, the line would not become fully operational until two months later. The demolition action was crowned by the storming of Konjic (7 July), defended by almost 600 local militiamen and Home Guard reservists. Still inexperienced in this type of warfare, the Partisans failed to close the encirclement ring, which allowed the bulk of the garrison to escape. Nevertheless, the battle did yield some political prestige and, more importantly, 50,000 rounds of ammunition; as the official chronicler of the 1st Proletarian put it, it was the booty one "could only dream of at that time".[3]

Leaving the wreckage behind, both brigade groups continued their westward movement. The northern one wandered briefly into the German occupation zone around Kreševo, provoking an immediate reaction by a regiment of the 718th ID. Having no intention of obliging their enemy with a pitched battle, the Partisans retreated hastily and proceeded to their next objective, the Vrbas River Valley. Gornji Vakuf fell almost without resistance on 12 July 1942, but it proved to be the group's last success in this sector. Owing largely to the inept handling and absence of a coherent plan, the brigades failed to launch a decisive attack on Donji Vakuf and suffered palpable losses in two futile attempts to seize Bugojno (16-17 and 20-21 July). Under the leadership of the singularly competent Home Guard Colonel Franjo Šimić, the NDH forces–including the freshly arrived elements of the "Black Legion"– mounted an energetic counterattack, forcing the Partisans to abandon their original plan and concentrate around Kupres instead. In the meantime, the southern group had crossed the Neretva and took Prozor by storm on 13 July. The nearby Franciscan monastery at Šćit could be taken only after a full day's fight with "a small group of fanatics", who inflicted more casualties (seven KIA and 10 WIA) on the 1st Proletarian than it had suffered since the beginning of the campaign. After that, the group continued its advance, taking Šujica and Duvno (today: Tomislavgrad) without much effort in the closing days of the month. Both places were abandoned almost immediately due to the Ustasha intervention from Kupres; luckily for the Partisans, their enemy lacked the strength to re-establish the road link to Livno.[4]

Far from being just another nondescript Bosnian provincial town, Livno was the seat of the "bauxite area", which reached all the way to the outskirts of Mostar and covered ca. 10 percent

2 Alberto Becherelli, *Italia e Stato Indipendente Croato (1941-1943)* (Rome: Edizioni Nuova Cultura, 2012), pp. 231-36; NARA/T501/268/291-93, 301-03, DGA to OKW (21 and 19.6.1942, respectively); Vuksanović, *Prva*, p. 80

3 Mišo Leković, *Ofanziva proleterskih brigada u leto 1942* (Belgrade: VII, 1965), pp. 43-134; Vuksanović (ed.), *Beleške*, p. 51.

4 Urošević, *Druga*, pp. 90-110; Vuksanović, *Prva*, pp. 95-106.

of Germany's needs in this precious ore (data from early 1943).[5] As such, the place and the surrounding villages were thoroughly fortified and held by an estimated 950 armed men. The SHQ therefore decided to commit the bulk of the 1st and 3rd Brigades; together with some local units, the task force numbered some 1,400 fighters. A well-coordinated assault started on the evening of 4 August, and by the following afternoon, the town was effectively under Partisan control. One Ustasha company and a group of German mining specialists (some of whom were decorated veterans of the Great War) refused to surrender and barricaded themselves in the fortress-like villa that served as the seat of the *Hansa Leichtmetall* Company. After a two-day siege, the guerrillas saw no alternative but to bring forward a field piece and pound the enemy into submission; this was a risky proposition for it was believed that the villa housed some three-and-a-half tons of industrial explosives (it later turned out it was six tons), enough to blow up half the town. Nevertheless, the gamble paid off and, after a few shots, the remaining defenders came out with their arms raised. The completeness of victory was a proof that the Communist-led army was learning the ropes quickly: unlike Konjic, Livno was properly sealed off, resulting in the capture of more than 650 enemy soldiers together with their weapons and a large haul of supplies of every kind.[6]

The "crazy and terrible" battle for Kupres, fought on 11-12 and 13-14 August 1942, differed from the storming of Livno in almost every respect. The importance of this small town of about 1,000 inhabitants lay in the fact that it controlled the strategic road linking Dalmatia and Herzegovina with Central Bosnia. The place was also a notorious Ustasha bastion, the taking of which would considerably bolster the Partisans' standing among Serbs. For this purpose, the SHQ reinforced the northern group with the recently arrived 1st (later renamed 10th) Herzegovina Brigade and some smaller units, and then with the 1st Krajina Brigade, boosting the guerrilla strength to 2,400 fighters. At the first glance, no NDH stronghold of this size could have been expected to withstand such a massive assault, but Kupres was no ordinary place. Well entrenched and provisioned, its garrison numbered 1,500 men, including one battalion of Francetić's veterans and almost 600 local Ustasha militiamen, determined to save their own skin and protect thousands of refugees from the surrounding countryside.

The first attempt against the town was a shambles. What was envisaged as a coordinated attack from all sides degenerated almost immediately into a series of skirmishes fought by individual battalions. Most of the fighting was done at the outlying villages, which absorbed the main shock of the guerrilla attack; once occupied, they were burned down and plundered, which served only to strengthen the Ustasha resolve. The second attempt was a far bloodier affair because the Partisans were now charging the town itself in pursuance a new, and much-flawed, battle plan.[7] Reprimanded for the lack of enthusiasm they had allegedly displayed during the first attempt, the Montenegrins of the 4th Proletarian now charged headlong across open terrain, only to be mowed down in droves by machine guns and mortars. One group of 10

5 NARA/T77/780/5507223, OKW, War diary (13.2.1943).

6 Žarko Vidović, *Treća proleterska brigada* (Belgrade: VIZ, 1972), pp. 64-70; NARA/T120/5787/301688-92, Hans Ott, Report Livno (15.8.1942); Slavko Odić, *Neostvareni planovi* (Zagreb: Naprijed, 1961), pp. 245, 254.

7 Although Yugoslav historiography blamed the failure in planing to the disgraced Arso Jovanović, the true extent of his culpability is debatable: Davor Marijan, *Borbe za Kupres: Pohod proleterskih brigade i borbe za Kupres u ljeto 1942. godine* (Zagreb: AGM, 1999), pp. 136-38.

Partisans held out for hours in the town house they had captured until the defenders killed all but two of them by direct cannon fire. Valor alone, however, was not sufficient. Colonel Šimić handled the battle with great dexterity, something that even the post-war historiography had to acknowledge. His reserves included a single armored car, which dominated the battlefield thanks to the fact that the Partisans had no AT weapons whatsoever. Even the few heavy weapons they did possess were not used properly: one field piece fired from a distance of no less than five km, effectively squandering what little ammunition was available.[8]

According to incomplete data, the Partisans lost 135 KIA and 224 WIA, and the NDH forces 54 KIA and 185 WIA around Kupres in the three weeks from 28 July to 20 August 1942. The 4th Brigade alone lost its deputy commander, three company *politkoms*, one battalion and two company deputy *politkoms* (all killed), while three battalion and two company commanders, as well as two battalion and one company commissars were wounded. Despite being their worst defeat suffered at the hands of the Ustashe yet, the battle had little impact on the course of the Partisans' summer campaign. With the seizing of the Livno area and establishing of fairly-well defined "front lines" towards the enemy–who, at the present, had neither the strength (the NDH) nor the inclination (the Italians) to intervene decisively–"the great march" came to an end. Tito and the core of his army had found a new and relatively secure base for future joint operations with the Dalmatian and Krajina units.[9]

The Herzegovina Brigade mentioned earlier was formed in early August 1942 from the Herzegovinian fighters who had just completed their own, rather dramatic trek from the Zelengora. On 22 July, the left-behind group of Proletarian units was suddenly attacked by the numerically superior Chetnik forces. Since its positions in the border area had clearly become untenable, the group's leadership decided to follow in the footsteps of the SHQ and head westward. It turned out to be the proverbial jump from the frying pan. While fighting a running battle with the monarchists, the Partisan column strayed into the same patch of German-held territory that had been "visited" earlier by the 2nd and 4th Brigades. Only through maximum exertion and non-stop marching did the guerrillas manage to escape the pursuit mounted by the alert and aggressive 738th IR (26-31 July). Even though the 5th Proletarian was far from being destroyed as claimed by the Germans, the march had been very costly: by the time the exhausted column reached the friendly positions outside of Prozor, nearly every fourth fighter–271 in all–had been killed, wounded, or missing. On a brighter side, the units retained their cohesion and their veteran core, and the hospital was saved; even a battalion that had been presumed lost during the march would eventually re-emerge and significantly reduce the overall loss figure.[10]

3.2 Expanding "Tito's State"

The Communist-led insurgency in Bosanska Krajina was showing no signs of abating in the summer of 1942. By early September, the local Partisans formed three more brigades and

8 Leković, *Ofanziva*, pp. 427-83.

9 Marijan, *Borbe*, p. 146; *Zbornik*/IV/6/246, 4th Proletarian Bde., Report Kupres (18.8.1942); *Zbornik*/II/5/142-43, Tito to 1st, 2nd, and 3rd Proletarian Bdes. (30.7.1942).

10 *Zbornik*/IV/6/191-97, 5th Proletarian Bde. and Herzegovina Det. to SHQ (4.8.1942); *Zbornik*/XIV/1/473-77, Vojislav Lukačević to Zaharije Ostojić (late July 1942); NARA/T315/2270/334-49, 738th IR, After-action report (3.8.1942).

reconstituted the 6th Detachment that had been subverted by the Chetniks only three weeks after its formation back in early May. Even the 2nd Detachment returned to the now-eerily quiet Mount Kozara and re-started its campaign of small-scale attacks against Axis military targets. The unit also helped put an end to the half-hearted attempts by Zagreb to settle the area with reliable Croat and Muslim "colonists". By the beginning of autumn, the detachment had grown into a full-fledged brigade, the 5th Krajina. These successes provoked a German reaction in the form of Operation "Kozara". From 19 to 27 October, one reinforced regiment of the 714th ID, augmented by a corresponding number of NDH troops, swept through the troublesome mountain, but managed only to temporarily banish the guerrillas.[11]

Nevertheless, the main point of guerrilla efforts was not on the Kozara, but in the area between the Sana and Vrbas Rivers. There were at least two reasons for this. First, securing the harvest in this agriculturally rich area was considered a task of paramount importance. Second, the influence of Chetnik leaders such as Uroš Drenović was still fairly strong here and had to be removed. The first steps were taken already in the second half of July 1942 as the units belonging to the OHQ for Bosanska Krajina took the town of Ključ and a number of hostile villages. The arrival of two Proletarian brigades one month later gave additional boost to the operations. Working together with a pair of local brigades, they took Drenović's main supply base, the NDH garrison at Varcar Vakuf, and continued to push north, towards Banja Luka. The fear of losing the second-largest city in Bosnia and the proposed new capital of the independent Croat state prompted its authorities to direct yet another salvo of SOS calls at their protectors. Preoccupied with other, more vital areas, the Germans agreed to dispatch but one reinforced battalion of the 714th ID to the scene. For the rest of the needed manpower, the Wehrmacht turned to the Serbian nationalists (who numbered ca. 2,400) and ordered the Home Guards to provide them with the needed materiel. The decision was probably based on the fact that the Chetniks had already fought under German direction during the spring, successfully interdicting the movements of Partisan reinforcements along the outer encirclement ring around the Kozara.[12]

The first round of fighting along the Varcar Vakuf–Banja Luka road lasted, with interruptions, for some three weeks. The aforementioned German battalion advanced to within 30 km from Varcar Vakuf before being stopped by the 2nd Krajina on 26 August 1942; the defenders, who also possessed a pair of AT guns, damaged several vehicles and even shot down two enemy planes. Taken aback by such staunch resistance, the Germans retreated to a defensive position at Kadine Vode. Eight days later, they again tried to break through towards the south; almost simultaneously, the 2nd Proletarian launched its own attack against the Chetniks on Mount Manjača. An awkward situation developed, whereby both sides were advancing parallel to each other, but in opposite directions. The Germans "blinked" first: with their flank disintegrating (the monarchists proved to be no match for the veteran brigade) and their rear exposed, they hurried back to the jump-off point. The Proletarians' attempt to outmaneuver this position failed owing to the bad coordination with the 1st and 2nd Krajina Brigades. All Axis troops–including two

11 *Oslobodilački*, Vol. I, pp. 269; *Enciklopedija*, Vol. IV, p. 689; Miletić, "Mere", pp. 211-12; Dragutin Ćurguz, Milorad Vignjević, *Drugi krajiški narodnooslobodilački partizanski (kozarski) odred "Mladen Stojanović"* (Prijedor: NP Kozara, 1982), pp. 791-800; Nikica Barić, "Kozara 1942.–sudbina zarobljenika, civila i djece", *Pilar*, 11:22 (2016), pp. 75-81.

12 Leković, *Ofanziva*, pp. 489-530; NARA/T501/248/289 and 554, BhS, Daily reports (13.6 and 27.8.1942, respectively).

NDH battalions of Colonel Mrak's feared Petrinja Brigade–were now placed under the HQ of the 721st IR and named *Kampfgruppe "Wedel"*. This battle group, amply supported by heavy weapons and combat aircraft, commenced its attack against the Manjača on the morning of 13 September. Despite the fact that they had captured a copy of the enemy battle plan several days earlier, the 1st Krajina and 2nd Proletarian were not able to withstand the pressure and pulled back south. The following day, however, brought a sudden and dramatic reversal of fortunes. Just when it seemed that the NDH troops would succeed in occupying the summit of the mountain, the Partisans used captured signal pistols to trick the enemy artillery into firing onto their own positions before making a charge. As a result, one NDH battalion was utterly routed, leaving behind 14 MGs and 130 rifles and a yawning gap in the center of the KG "Wedel". Mounting guerrilla pressure (the OHQ launched its own, admittedly disjointed, counteroffensive on the 18th), as well as "supply difficulties and lack of water", compelled the Germans to retreat to a defensive line centered on Kola, some 10 km southwest of Banja Luka.[13]

The SHQ was not content with the fact that a force of four brigades (including the lately-arrived 3rd Proletarian) was tied down in a protracted, high-cost, low-benefit type of contest, but this could not be avoided. The reason the Partisans offered battle in the first place was not in order to open their way to Banja Luka, but to provide flank protection for the real centerpiece of their September campaign, the storming of Jajce. The possession of this place, which was an economic and administrative center of one of altogether 22 counties of the Croatian satellite state, would provide both booty and a springboard for future operations in Central Bosnia. The Axis were likewise fully aware of its importance. "Jajce is more secure than Zagreb", some NDH officials remarked confidently, referring to the strength of the town's man-made defenses. In addition to the thick-walled medieval citadel, the last seat of Bosnian kings, all surrounding heights were covered in bunkers, trenches, and barbed-wire obstacles. The bulk of the garrison consisted of one battalion each of Ustashe and Home Guards. Many of these men had not been relieved for months, some for over a year; their combat readiness also suffered on account of the bad supply situation (little was coming in through the blockade) and the fact that the local guerrillas kept them up for nights on end by fire attacks.

The grand assault began at dusk of 24 September 1942. It followed the standard pattern with the exception that the eastern side of the town was intentionally left unoccupied in order to lure the fleeing defenders into the countryside, where they would be an easy prey. The main effort was directed against the northern and western sectors of the defensive ring. By the first light of the next day, three veteran brigades had broken through the defenses and entered the town itself. The fighting was heavy, with defenders launching frequent counterattacks and doggedly defending their many fortified points. This time, however, the Partisans used their two pieces of artillery and a handful of mortars with great effect, and the battle was over by 1700 hours. The garrison lost almost 350 KIA, WIA, and MIA (including 74 dead Ustashe), the guerrillas one-third of that number. The victory would have been even greater had the 4th Proletarian Brigade set up ambushes to the east of the town as originally planned.[14]

The loss of Jajce together with its chemical plant (owned by the industrial juggernaut "I.G. Farben", 90 percent of its production went straight to the Reich) had finally stirred the Germans

13 Leković, *Ofanziva*, pp. 531-603; NARA/T501/352/122, BhS, Daily report (19.9.1942).
14 Leković, *Ofanziva*, pp. 604-24.

into launching a long-overdue, large-scale operation in this part of the country. Bader's staff planned a concentric advance against the enemy forces in the triangle Banja Luka–Ključ–Jajce. For this purpose, the 718th ID would use two battle groups of five infantry battalions each (four of them German) to strike against Jajce from the direction of Donji Vakuf and Turbe. At the same time, the 714th ID's KG "Wedel" would attack south from its positions around Kola, hitting the guerrillas in the back. The operation, named after its main objective, started on 28 September 1942. The Partisans–"flushed with victory and a little complacent", as candidly observed by Kosta Nađ, the 31 year-old veteran of Spain and the head of the OHQ for Bosanska Krajina–were taken by surprise. Obviously facing an enemy of great strength, the SHQ decided to relinquish its recent gains in this region, and re-group in the traditional guerrilla stronghold of Janj, southwest of Jajce. On the northern front, the 3rd Proletarian and 3rd Krajina Brigades were conducting a fighting withdrawal to the south, leaving Ključ on the 30th, and Varcar Vakuf two days later. In the east, the 4th Proletarian fought a classic rear-guard action, combining stiff resistance from the front with attacks against the rear of the advancing Germans. The 718th ID entered the undefended Jajce on 4 October, effectively bringing Operation "Jajce I" to its end. The decision to immediately send the units back to their old quarters proved rash, however: both Ključ and Varcar Vakuf had to be retaken in mid-October by the 714th ID after the resurgent guerrillas had chased away their NDH defenders. The 718th was compelled to launch yet another operation ("Jajce II") in the area on 18 October, this time targeting Janj itself; the undertaking was canceled after two weeks of marching and some low-intensity skirmishing. The combined results of these operations were meager: for the price of nine KIA, 50 WIA, and one MIA (and a further 44 KIA, 82 WIA, and four MIA among the NDH troops), the 718th ID reported having captured only 145 pieces of small arms.[15]

The integrity of the "main" liberated territory was threatened not only by the Wehrmacht's operations described above, but also by the joint NDH-Italian-Chetnik efforts along its southeastern frontier. Already in the second week of September 1942, Colonel Šimić, acting on his own initiative, launched an attack from Kupres towards the south. The main purpose of the undertaking was not to re-take Livno, as feared by the Partisans, but simply to get one unruly and home-sick Ustasha battalion back to its native terrain around Imotski. Once this became obvious, the elements of the 1st Proletarian deployed here offered only a token resistance before retreating from Šujica and Duvno.

The real danger to Livno materialized one month later in the form of Operation "Dinara". Envisaged as a grand sweep of the entire Western Herzegovina, the operation was divided into two phases, "Alfa" and "Beta". The first phase, aimed at recapturing Prozor, lasted from 4 to 10 October 1942, and would be best remembered for the massacres of non-Serb civilians carried out by Voluntary Anti-communist Militia (*Milizia volontaria anticomunista* or MVAC). This was nothing but a recently introduced official Italian designation for the Chetniks in their service. Beside six of its own battalions, the VI AC had brought over some 3,500 monarchists from Eastern Herzegovina and Montenegro for the purpose of this operation. The arrangement

15 NARA/T314/1531/445, 718th ID, Report Jajce (15.11.1941); NARA/T315/2270/585-606, 722-30, 757, 718th ID, Reports Operation "Jajce I" and "II" (12.10 and 6.11.1942, respectively); NARA/T315/2258/891-92, 1024-25, 714th ID/Ia, Activity reports September and October 1942, respectively; Blažo Janković, *Četvrta proleterska crnogorska brigade* (Belgrade: VIZ, 1975), pp. 130-36; Vidović, *Treća*, pp. 92-108; Popović (ed.), *Uspomene Koste Nađa*, p. 207.

suited Chetnik leaders as well, who wanted to establish a firm link with their comrades-in-arms in Northern Dalmatia. The plan backfired: the atrocities they committed prompted the 2nd ITA to pull back nearly all Serbian auxiliaries from the area. Moreover, this ugly episode drove yet another wedge into the already strained Axis alliance, and only made the Communist-led guerrillas appear decent in the eyes of the population. Little was achieved in a purely military sense as well: the 10th Herzegovina Brigade managed to escape the blow, and joined the 5th Proletarian in the rugged area north of Prozor. Directed by a joint HQ since September, both units had been conducting a successful campaign of sabotage and small-scale attacks, reaching from the Lašva Valley in the north to the Neretva in the south. On one such occasion in early October, the guerrillas came very close to bereaving Pavelić of his top tactician, Šimić, when his truck was ambushed between Bugojno and Kupres (the colonel was only wounded, but eight Ustashe from his escort were killed).[16]

The "Beta" phase, which began on 20 October 1942, involved a concentric attack against Livno by three Italian columns of two battalions each (all belonging to the XVIII AC's "Bergamo" and "Sassari" Divisions) coming from Vrlika, Sinj, and Aržano; two Ustasha battalions were attached to the *Regio Esercito* units, and two more went forward independently from the line Kupres-Šujica. Despite the fact that their column was the weakest, the Ustashe stole the limelight. While the Italians were crawling forward, slowed down not only by elaborately demolished roads but also by heavy resistance (the Italians lost 11 KIA and 23 WIA in the fighting north of Aržano on the 23rd), one part of Francetić's men crossed Mount Cincar unobserved and entered the undefended Livno. Hit from the front, and now from the back, two battalions of the 1st Dalmatian Brigade had to disperse in order to escape the encirclement. The sole remaining Partisan unit in the area, a battalion belonging to the 3rd Dalmatian Detachment, also withdrew before the Italians and headed for the mountains southwest of the town. All in all, the guerrillas lost about 60 fighters in the brief struggle for Livno. The fear that the Axis would continue with the advance towards Glamoč caused the SHQ to recall the 4th Proletarian from the Janj sector. Fortunately for the Partisans, the fear proved unfounded: having reclaimed the bauxite area, the Italians were content to return to their garrisons.[17]

The string of Axis offensives curbed the expansion of the liberated territory in the eastern direction. The process of expansion in general, however, simply had to go on: the Partisans not only held the initiative, but also needed new lands in order to support their growing army. The SHQ therefore turned its gaze towards the west. The Italian base at Bosansko Grahovo had been a thorn in the Partisan side ever since the arrival of the Proletarian units to this part of the country. Manned by a full battalion of the "Sassari", the town served as a prop for the numerous local Chetniks; moreover, it stood directly between the guerrilla-held territories in Lika and Dalmatia and those in Western Bosnia. After it had become clear that the Croatian command was not in the position to provide additional troops for the attack, the SHQ decided to go in "with one boot off": the town would be invested only by the units from the Bosnian side of the border. For this purpose, the 1st and 2nd Proletarian, and the 4th Krajina Brigades were

16 Leković, *Ofanziva*, pp. 637-47; Tomasevich, *Chetniks*, pp. 232-33; Fasanotti et. al., *L'esercito*, pp. 257-58; *Zbornik*/IV/7/439, NDH Gendarmerie Bugojno to 5th Gendarmerie Rgt. (3.10.1942).

17 *Zbornik*/XIII/2/804-13, *Supersloda*, Diary (12-26.10.1942); *Zbornik*/V/9/54-57, 4th OZ to SHQ (5.11.1942); Mirko Novović, Stevan Petković, *Prva dalmatinska proleterska NOU brigada* (Belgrade: VIZ, 1986), pp. 111-15; Janković, *Četvrta*, p. 135.

brought under a provisional HQ, with Tito's delegate at its helm. For two consecutive nights (26 and 27 October 1942), the Partisans charged the enemy positions; the Italians, famously at their best when defending fortifications, beat them back both times, killing at least 14 and wounding 32. It was shown once again that courage alone could not offset bad planning and lack of equipment (only two cannon were available for the attack). The attackers vented their frustration on Chetnik villages: "The plain of Grahovo was put to the torch and plundered", wrote Đilas; ironically, the fire had nearly consumed the birthplace of the Partisans' role-model, Gavrilo Princip.[18]

Immediately following the fall of Jajce, the OHQ for Bosanska Krajina proposed the taking of Bihać and other Axis garrisons in the Una River Valley. If successful, the offensive would enable a link-up with the domains of the MHQ Croatia and provide the movement's leadership with a fitting capital (Bihać was a county seat like Jajce, only bigger). Tito agreed and authorized a major operation, one which should be brought to a victorious conclusion no later than 7 November 1942, the 25th anniversary of the October Revolution. According to the plan, which had been updated and revised several times in the intervening weeks, the place itself would be attacked by a force of four brigades, while four more would provide cover against outside intervention. Out of these eight formations, three came from Croatia (one each from the old guerrilla strongholds of Lika, Kordun, and Banija), and the remaining five from Bosanska Krajina. Between them, they had close to 9,000 fighters, making the upcoming operation the largest and most ambitious ever undertaken by the NOP. It was also marked with a couple of technical novelties. The first one was the introduction of German-made flamethrowers, a couple of which were captured in the field and repaired by the OHQ's workshop set up on Mount Grmeč. Another one was the mass use of artillery: in addition to four 37mm AT guns attached to the infantry, the OHQ also had at its disposal four 75mm mountain guns and three 100mm howitzers. Owing to the shortage of ammunition, the crews were allowed to use only 10 shells per gun for the initial preparation, which was nevertheless the first of its kind in this war. Facing this mighty guerrilla host stood the 4th Ustasha Active Brigade (UAB) and parts of the 2nd and 12th Home Guard Regiments with an estimated 4,300 men; half of them held the town, while the rest was deployed in its wider environs.[19]

Like nearly every urban center of any importance in the NDH, Bihać was prepared for all-round defense. The system however, had one serious flaw: the strongpoints it rested on were too wide apart, and the intervening space was not properly secured. As a consequence, the Partisans managed to infiltrate two battalions into the town already on the opening night of the assault (2 November 1942), thus entirely disrupting their adversary's defensive arrangements. By the following morning, the guerrillas were in possession of the right bank of the Una save one small pocket. The going was slower and a good deal bloodier on the opposite side of the river, where majority of the Ustashe were concentrated. Fierce house-to-house fighting lasted throughout that and most of the following day. Deserted by their commander and disheartened by the fact that the help from the outside would not go beyond a handful of air drops (neither

18 Rade Zorić, *Četvrta krajiška brigada* (Belgrade: VIZ, 1980), p. 25; Urošević, *Druga*, pp. 161-65; Vuksanović, *Prva*, 128-31; Djilas, *Wartime*, p. 207. The Italians lost 16 KIA and 59 WIA.

19 Colić, *Pregled*, pp. 72-75; Đorđe Bujak, "U bespuću je nikla nova radionica", in *Vojnotehnička radionica Vrhovnog štaba NOV i POJ u Grmeču* (Belgrade: Rad, 1979), p. 346; Miloš Pajević, *Artiljerija u NOR-u* (Belgrade: VIZ, 1970), pp. 39-41.

the Wehrmacht nor the *Domobranstvo* had any troops to spare), the remainder of the garrison finally withdrew north after a 42 hour-battle. Seeing the writing on the wall, all other NDH outposts in the area followed suite. In addition to Ličko Petrovo Selo, which they took by storm on 3 November, the Partisans entered Bosanska Krupa, Cazin, and Velika Kladuša without a fight; by the middle of the month, they stood on the outskirts of Karlovac and Glina. The spoils of victory were enormous: 870 prisoners, 1,500 rifles and SMGs, 102 MGs, eight artillery pieces, several thousand artillery shells, and no less than 1,000,000 rounds of rifle ammunition. The guerrillas also captured large stocks of all kinds of less glamorous, but critically important supplies. For instance, one brigade received 400 pairs of shoes from Bihać, a most welcome gift in the light of the approaching winter. The death toll among the attackers bears testament to the intensity of the fighting: according to incomplete data, there were 80 KIA, 180 WIA, and nine MIA in the town itself, plus an additional 20 KIA and 67 WIA in the countryside.[20]

Following the fall of Bihać, both sides turned their attention to the Sanski Most–Prijedor–Bosanski Novi triangle; among else, the area was the site of the strategically important Ljubija mines and the railroad used for the export of its high-quality iron ore. With the bulk of their army committed along the western frontier of the liberated territory, the Partisans kept only a token presence here. The 714th ID did launch two limited offensive actions in late October and early November 1942, but they served a decidedly defensive purpose: to push the guerrillas as far back from the Sana Valley as possible and shorten the length of Protective Line Southwest, the first line of field fortifications to be built in this war. Clearly anticipating a classic, frontal attack here, roughly 2,000 km behind the Wehrmacht's spearheads in Stalingrad, Axis engineers were working on a continuous belt of trenches and bunkers stretching from Bosanski Novi all the way to Sanski Most. By mid-November, these defenses–dubbed the "Maginot Line" by the Partisans–were occupied by an equivalent of three NDH regiments, with a reinforced regiment of German troops being stationed in reserve.[21]

Emboldened by their victory at Bihać, the HQ of the newly formed 1st Bosnian Corps had no doubt that the enemy defenses, no matter how strong, would crumble under a resolute attack by three veteran Krajina brigades. This presumption turned out to be correct. Acting as parts of the 4th Krajina Division, these units achieved a major breakthrough in the early morning hours of 18 November 1942, capturing an entire HDB battalion in the process. The Partisans spent the next three days demolishing the earthworks and clearing the surrounding area of the remaining enemy forces; Ljubija, however, remained out of their reach owing to the quick German intervention. Realizing that the continuation of operations here was not likely to achieve any further success, the 1st Bosnian Corps shifted its focus to Bosanski Novi. The aforementioned Partisan division, reinforced by one additional brigade, tried to storm this important railroad hub situated at the confluence of the Sana and Una Rivers on 26-27 and 28-29 November. Both times the guerrillas succeeded in getting into the town itself, but failed to dislodge the

20 Stevo Rauš, "Bihaćka operacija novembra 1942. godine", in *Bihaćka republika 4.XI 1942-29.I 1943* (Bihać: Muzej AVNOJ-a i Pounja, 1965), pp. 65-87; Ljubomir Borojević, Dušan Samardžija, Rade Bašić, *Peta kozaračka brigada* (Belgrade: Rad, 1973), p. 52; Colić, *Pregled*, p. 77; NARA/T315/2258/1214, 714th ID, Subordinated Croat units (11.11.1942).

21 NARA/T315/2258/1122 and 1139-40 (Orders operations "Sandmann" and "Ing", 25 and 31.10.1942, respectively), 1124-26 (Order "Protective line Southwest", 7.11.1942); Branko Damjanović, Savo Popović, *Šesta krajiška narodnooslobodilačka udarna brigada* (Belgrade: VIZ, 1985), pp. 76-84, 87.

German-NDH garrison. Still unwilling to throw in the towel, the Partisan command decided to try its luck against the single remaining sector of the defensive belt that had not yet been attacked, the one around Sanski Most. For this occasion, two brigades of the 4th Krajina would be supported by another two from its sister formation, the 5th Krajina, and by seven tubes from the corps' 1st Artillery Battalion. From 10 to 15 December, the Partisans made three frontal assaults against the town; as in Bosanski Novi, they managed to penetrate the outer defenses, but could not take the place itself. Eventually, the garrison survived thanks to the arrival of reinforcements from Prijedor and air drops, which kept it afloat during the subsequent blockade that lasted until the end of the month. Thus ended the autumn offensive of the 1st Bosnian Corps. The Yugoslavs proclaimed it a victory on grounds of the losses inflicted upon the enemy: more than 2,000 prisoners with their weapons, nine mortars, 10 pieces of ordnance, and another 1,000,000 rounds of ammunition. Although comparable to Bihać, these figures, however, could not hide the fact that the Partisans failed to capture any of their objectives apart from the fortified line, and that they themselves suffered heavy casualties (according to an incomplete tally, 180 KIA and MIA, as well as 528 WIA).[22]

Meantime, the divisions directly subordinated to the SHQ–the 1st and 2nd Proletarian, and the 3rd Assault–were hard at work expanding the liberated territory towards the east and southeast. The 2nd Proletarian spent the best part of November 1942 chasing the Chetnik and Ustashe militias in the Dalmatian hinterland. By the end of the month, the SHQ had come up with another task, one much more fitting for such a strong and experienced formation: the taking of Livno. The Proletarians would again cross swords with the "Black Legion" (or the 5th UAB, as it was now known), which immediately proved to be the same, dangerous opponent. A concentric assault on the town had to be postponed several times, chiefly because of the repeated enemy sorties: during one of them, the 2nd Proletarian Brigade even lost its standard. Spurred on by Tito's remark that this item "was not a rag" and his laconic and unequivocal order "Livno must fall!", the Partisans staged their grand attack on the evening of 14 December. The fighting was every bit as ferocious as all the earlier encounters between these deadly foes, but this time the Ustashe had no particular incentive to fight to the death. After they had spent most of their ammunition in 36 hours of fighting, and after it became clear that the relief columns from Bugojno and Duvno would not come through, the defenders began to pull out. Although the guerrillas had yet again failed to close all likely escape routes, they did manage to rake their fleeing foe with concentrated small-arms, mortar, and artillery fire. Out of the original 1,200-1,500 NDH personnel, 300 ended up being either killed or missing, with another 160 being wounded. The Partisans suffered 74 KIA and 210 WIA, yet had little to show for it in material terms. The battle's main effect was that it convinced the Ustashe to retreat from Šuica without a fight, and offer only a sporadic resistance at Duvno (18 December). Ten days later, however, they thwarted yet another, albeit tepid, enemy attempt to seize their *Alcázar*, Kupres. Since its drive had clearly lost the momentum, the 2nd Proletarian Division turned its energies to organizing and utilizing the recently acquired territory.[23]

22 Drago Karasijević, *Četvrta krajiška NOU divizija* (Belgrade: VINC, 1988), pp. 24-51; Milutin Morača, *Peta krajiška divizija* (Belgrade: VIZ, 1985), pp. 15-23.

23 Davor Marijan, "'Livno mora pasti': borbe dijelova V. ustaškog stajaćeg zdruga s II. proleterskom divizijom za Livno u prosincu 1942. godine", *ČSP*, 40:3 (2008), pp. 951-68; Tihomir Janjić, Đuro

The 1st Proletarian Division was enjoying some much-deserved R&R around Bosanski Petrovac in mid-November 1942 when it was ordered by the SHQ to make its way to Central Bosnia, clear the countryside of the Chetniks, and establish the NOP presence there. The road to the objective would take the division across the old battlefields of Sitnica, Mrkonjić Grad, and Jajce. On the 19th, the premier brigade of the army captured more than 30 Germans and 15 of their trucks at Sitnica (not to mention anywhere between 200 and 350 *Domobrani*), but lost 68 of its own men, including 22 KIA. Five days later, the entire division stood poised to storm Jajce from the north, while two brigades of the 3rd Assault would advance from the south. The presence of one company of the 718th ID had next to no effect on the outcome of the battle: by 26 November, the town was in the hands of the Partisans for the second time in as many months. Whereas the bulk of the garrison managed to escape after putting up a "desperate" fight, the Partisans succeeded in stopping the relief column coming from Donji Vakuf and forced it to turn back. The Axis losses amounted to 74 German and at least 126 NDH personnel, all of whom had either been killed or gone missing; the irrevocable losses on the Partisan side amounted to a tenth of this number, most of them from the 3rd Assault Division.[24]

This cheaply-bought victory paved the way for further advance into the hostile territory beyond the Vrbas. "In an unexpected thrust", the Germans noted, the 1st Proletarian Division (less one brigade) took Kotorišće (today: Kotor Varoš) on 4 December 1942, setting off alarm bells in Banja Luka. The 714th ID somehow managed to find a spare battalion, which then retook the town "with the help of the Orthodox volunteers [i.e. the Chetniks]", only to lose it again several days later. The Partisans had no more intention of advancing on the proposed capital of the NDH now than they had in September; the operations in this sector were conducted merely in order to secure the new liberated territory that was being steadily expanded towards the east and northeast. All the while, they were on the lookout for targets of opportunity, preferably those which would yield a rich booty without requiring too much time and blood in return. After briefly considering an attack on Prnjavor, the HQ of the 1st Proletarian finally settled for Teslić. This turned out to be a perfect choice. The attack, which began on New Year's Day 1943 and ended on 2 January, resulted in one of the biggest hauls in prisoners and arms taken in one place so far in the war: ca. 1,250 Home Guards, including one colonel and 38 officers, and corresponding quantities of equipment. What makes this particular victory even more remarkable is the fact that it was achieved with minimal losses (the guerrillas lost one dead and 10 wounded), which, in turn, speaks volumes about the state of morale in Zagreb's armed forces in this period.[25]

The 3rd Assault Division spent the last days of November 1942 preparing for the resumption of its advance towards the southeast. On the 30th, however, the scouts brought unnerving news about German concentrations around Donji Vakuf and Turbe. The 718th ID had, in fact, moved

Jovanović, Stevo Opačić-Plavanjac, "Borbena dejstva brigade do oslobođenja Imotskog", in *Druga dalmatinska proleterska brigada* (Split: IHRPD, 1982), pp. 47-72.

24 NARA/T315/2258/1179, 714th ID, Activity report (November 1942); NARA/T315/2266/882-87, 718th ID, Diary (25-26.11.1942); *Zbornik*/IV/35/362-66, 1st NOVJ Division [NOVJD] to SHQ (29.11.1942); Radovan Vukanović, *Ratni put Treće divizije* (Belgrade: VIZ, 1970), p. 40; *Oslobodilački*, Vol. I, p. 344; Vuksanović, *Prva*, p. 140.

25 NARA/T315/2258/1375, 714th ID, Enemy situation report no. 9 (11.12.1942); *Zbornik*/IV/35/447, 1st NOVJD to 1st Proletarian Bde., 22.12.1942; *Zbornik*/IV/9/39 (1st NOVJD to SHQ, 3.1.1943), 103 (1st NOVJD, Activity report 1-9.1.1943).

both its infantry regiments (plus six NDH battalions) to this sector with the aim of recapturing Jajce. The third Axis operation to bear the name of this Bosnian town began on 1 December. The objective was supposed to be reached in three days' time, but the timetable could not be met due to the skilled fighting withdrawal conducted by the Partisans. In addition to offering stout resistance from favorable natural positions, the guerrillas had also thoroughly demolished the road infrastructure in the area. By noon of 6 December, the Axis had finally entered Jajce. Apart from the place itself, they had little to show for 58 German and 23 NDH dead; not only did their enemy lost but a third of this number, but he also managed to evacuate or destroy everything of value. What was worse, the Axis showed no intention of pursuing the Partisans. As a consequence, the 3rd Assault was ready within a week or so to continue its eastward march. From 15 December onwards, the division operated from the mountains northwest of Zenica, destroying railway installations in the valleys of the Lašva and Bosna Rivers, and attacking smaller garrisons such as Turbe.[26]

From the Partisans' perspective, during the latter half of 1942, the entire area between the Bosna and the Drina represented a wasteland. The sole exception was their traditional stronghold at Šekovići, home of the 6th Eastern Bosnian Brigade, formed from the local Proletarian battalions on 2 August. These 600 or so fighters spent most of the summer marching up and down the northeastern corner of Bosnia trying to find the best way to help the cause. Still not being strong enough to tackle the local Chetniks, and unable to cross the Bosna, the Partisans finally opted for Syrmia. By the time the guerrillas returned from their one-month stay (5 October-5 November), they were reinforced, rested, and ready for a reckoning with their civil war foes. Three weeks later, the Partisans dealt a crushing blow to the united Chetnik forces on Mount Majevica, killing several of their top commanders and capturing 29 SMGs and 400 rifles. Despite monarchists' generally loyal attitude to the occupation authorities and their active participation in the struggle against the NOP, neither the NDH forces nor the Wehrmacht intervened. Although the 6th Brigade had exhibited only a limited activity against the Axis-held objectives during 1942, its very presence in this agriculturally rich and industrially developed area prompted the Germans to launch two major operations in five months. Named "S" (24-29 August) and "Tuzla II" (17-20 December), each of them involved five to six German and a similar number of NDH infantry battalions. Based as they were on the unimaginative concept of encirclement and concentric advance against a fixed objective (Šekovići and the Majevica, respectively), the Partisans succeeded in getting away on both occasions practically unscathed. The local anti-communist militias of all colors, on the whole, proved to be a much more dangerous opponent than Axis regulars. Since they fought in the same manner as the Partisans and knew the terrain well, they managed to surprise the 6th Brigade on several occasions, inflicting painful losses among the veteran fighters. These tactics, combined with a typhus epidemic, forced the brigade to cancel its "invasion" of the Chetnik realm on the Romanija in late December.[27]

26 *Zbornik*/IV/8/437-47, 3rd NOVJD to SHQ (2.1.143); NARA/T315/2270/897-901, 968, 995-1001 (718th ID, Operational order [30.11.1942], casualty list, and maps for Operation "Jajce III"), 938-44 (KG "Wüst", Report "Jajce III", 23.12.1942); Primorac, *Iskustva*, pp. 147-51.

27 Rudi Petovar, Savo Trikić, *Šesta proleterska istočno-bosanska brigada* (Belgrade: VIZ, 1982), pp. 129-64, 192-231; *Zbornik*/XIV/1/740, Trebava Det. to 4th HDB ID (3.12.1942); NARA/T315/2266/788-92, 718th ID, Diary (24-29.8.1942); NARA/T315/2270/381 (718th ID, OOB Operation "S", 17.8.1942),

3.3 New Army

By the time the Bihać operation was finished, Tito was the undisputed ruler of a unified liberated territory roughly 250 km long and up to 100 km wide. It was said that a guerrilla could walk from the Neretva to the Kupa without fear of running into the enemy; if he or she was willing to risk crossing a few thin strips of Axis-controlled territory (usually located along the main railway routes), then he or she could reach the outskirts of Zagreb, and even Slovenia. Th "long march" was envisaged not only as a military operation, but also as a campaign for hearts and minds of the population. Prior to the brigades' departure, Tito ordered sternest measures against indiscipline and made sure they were enforced. As a result, even the NDH authorities had to admit that the Catholics and Muslims were treated exceedingly well by the Serbian and Montenegrin fighters. As soon as they settled down in a particular area, the Partisans proceeded to organize the civilian life, drawing heavily on their experiences from Užice and Foča. The NOOs were elected, youth labor brigades formed, and markets regulated. Transportation was provided by a narrow-gauge train operating between Drvar and Mliništa, a distance of some 90 km. Entertainment was provided by Theater of People's Liberation, formed from a group of professional actors who had recently defected from Zagreb. The Wehrmacht commands were reporting on these orderly conditions with open envy, comparing them favorably with the perpetual chaos reigning on the territory of their troubled political fosterling. For all these reasons, the Germans dubbed the liberated territory "the Partisan Realm" or "Tito's State".[28]

The seat of the "Bihać Republic", as it was colloquially known among the Yugoslavs, soon acquired another trapping of a real capital. On 26 and 27 November 1942, the town hosted the first session of Anti-fascist Council of People's Liberation of Yugoslavia (*Antifašističko vijeće narodnog oslobođenja Jugoslavije*, AVNOJ). Tito toyed with the idea of creating KPJ-sponsored legislative and executive bodies on a national level on several occasions in the past eighteen months. Moscow, however, cautioned against it, and he duly obeyed. This time he went ahead with his plan, but amended it in the way his mentors would find acceptable. Consequently, the new provisional parliament did have its Executive Committee (i.e. a cabinet), but the two ministerial posts most commonly associated with a sovereign state, those of foreign affairs and defense, were conspicuously absent. Even though the Partisan overlord also refrained from taking overt and concrete measures against the monarchy, there could be no doubt that the Yugoslav government-in-exile now had a serious rival in the race for post-war power.[29]

The defense portfolio may have been non-existent, but the armed forces were certainly there. On 1 November 1942, the military wing of the NOP changed its name to "People's Liberation Army and Partisan Detachments of Yugoslavia" (*Narodnooslobodilačka vojska i partizanski odredi*

392-94 (Col. Faninger to 718th ID, 3.9.1942), 1022, 1072-73 (Commander of German Troops in Croatia [Befehlshaber der deutschen Truppen in Kroatien, BDTK], Operational order, and report on "Tuzla II", 10 and 28.12.1942, respectively).

28 NARA/T314/554/289, BDTK, Situation report (17-26.12.1942); NARA/T501/268/100, Horstenau to Löhr (16.11.1942); *Zbornik*/IV/6/403, NDH Gendarmerie Travnik to 5th Gendarmerie Rgt. (22.7.1942); Leković, *Ofanziva*, pp. 130, 275; Zora Popović-Smoljanović, "Sa Prvom omladinskom radnom brigadom na žetvi u Saničkoj dolini", in *Bihaćka*, Vol. I, pp. 372-74; Vjeko Afrić, "Sa Kazalištem narodnog oslobođenja u Bihaću", in ibid., pp. 500-17; Aleksandar Jelenković, *Saobraćaj u NOR-u Jugoslavije* (Belgrad: VINC, 1992), pp. 56-63.

29 Petranović, *Istorija*, Vol. II, pp. 220-21; Petranović, *Srbija*, pp. 521-22.

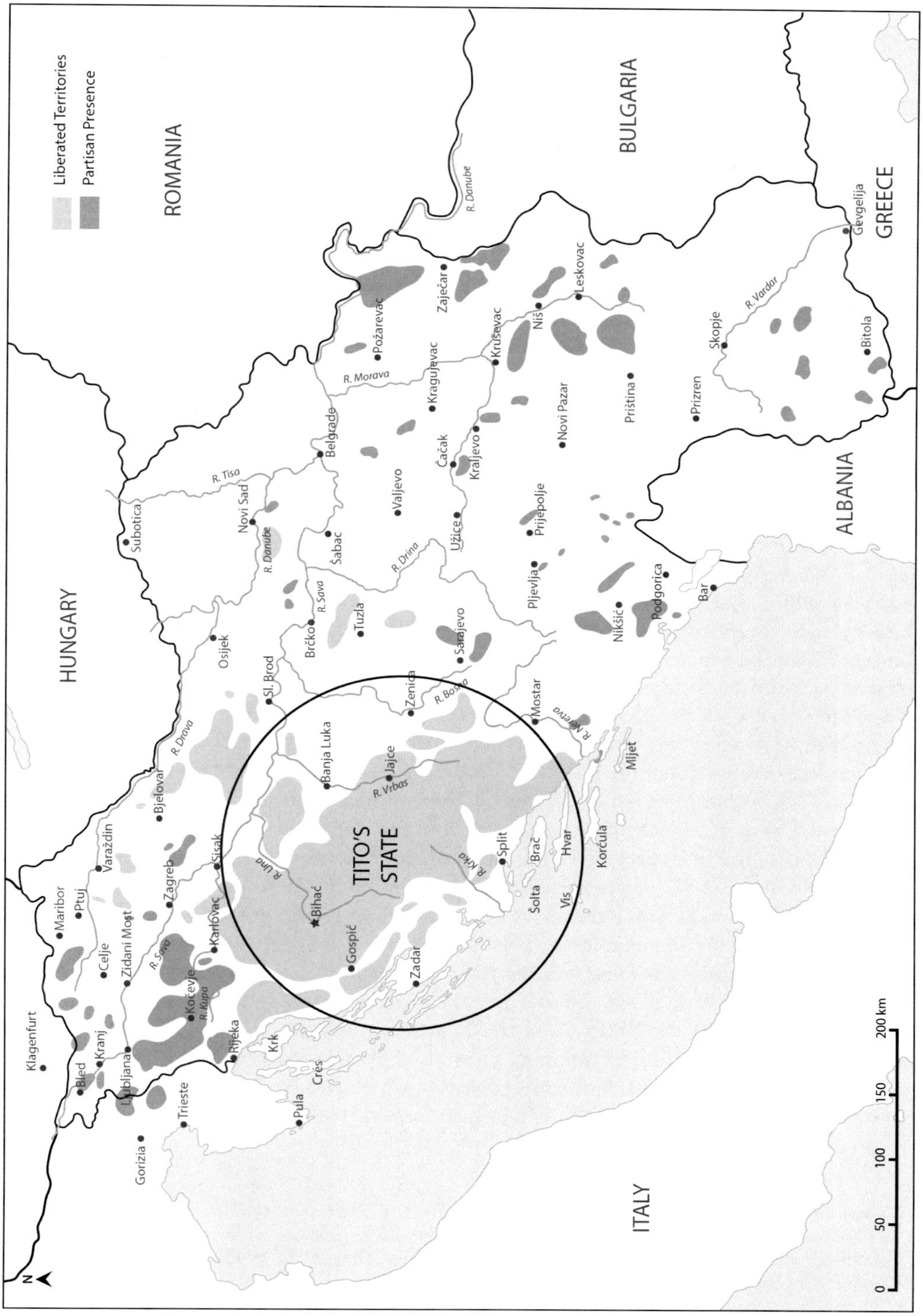

Map 7: Extent of Yugoslav Insurgency (November 1942).

Jugoslavije, most commonly abbreviated to NOVJ). The word "army" was not chosen only because it was an appropriate match for the terms like "state" or "republic", but also because it reflected the recent growth and changing nature of the guerrilla host. The second half of 1942 was marked by the ascendancy of the brigade system, with 31 such units being formed in the period July-December (18 in Croatia, nine in Bosnia-Herzegovina, and four in Slovenia). Although some of them actually had the prescribed strength of about 1,000 fighters, many of them had as few as 600. The Partisan leadership was obviously anxious to enlarge the pool of mobile formations, even if it meant that they had to operate with reduced capabilities for the time being; a sturdy and functional "skeleton" could later be easily coated with "flesh" (i.e. new recruits). Independent battalions, which came to be regarded as a stopgap measure and mere nuclei of future brigades, were being slowly phased out, their number dropping from 29 to 12. Although their number had also been reduced from 51 to 36 in the course of the year, the detachment maintained a secure position in the structure of the army. A brigade might be ordered away, but it was the detachment that stayed behind and safeguarded the NOP's interests in a given area. Despite the popularization of the large mobile formations through propaganda, many fighters still preferred to serve with the detachments, close to their hearths and homes; it was sometimes difficult to convince them to go to a different part of their own province, let alone the far side of the country. Some local commands also "sabotaged" the field army by withholding their best men and sending second-class recruits for the service with the brigades instead. Although the demise of Volunteer Army is usually dated with the fall of the Foča Republic, there is evidence that the SHQ tried to win over some Chetnik groups in Bosanska Krajina by granting them semi-autonomous status within the army during the course of summer 1942. The experiment was finally canceled towards the end of year when these units were made part of the line formations.[30]

The greatest novelty of the NOVJ's OOB was the introduction of divisions and corps. As we have seen, the ever-increasing complexity of battlefield tasks compelled the Partisans to group brigades under provisional commands ever since the operations in Eastern Bosnia in the late winter of 1942. Despite repeated pleas from high-ranking officers, the SHQ waited for the successful conclusion of the summer campaign before deciding to set up these headquarters on a permanent basis. The first three divisions–1st and 2nd Proletarian, and the 3rd Assault–were formed on 1 November 1942; out of the six more that followed by the end of the year, two were Bosnian (the 4th and 5th Krajina), and four Croatian (the 6th Lika, 7th Banija, 8th Kordun, and 12th Slavonian). Each division nominally consisted of three to four brigades (at least one of them being a veteran formation) plus some rudimentary support services, giving it an average nominal strength of 3,500–4,500 fighters. Apart from the Proletarian and Assault divisions (which remained subordinated to the SHQ), and the 12th Slavonian (which remained subordinated to the HQ of the 3rd OZ), all the remaining formations became a part of the newly-created 1st Bosnian and 1st Croatian Corps. Unlike the division, which had been conceived primarily as a tool of maneuver warfare, the early NOVJ corps were classic territorial commands, which came

30 Anić, Joksimović, Gutić, *Narodnooslobodilačka*, pp. 77-78, 179-80; *Zbornik*/II/5/268 and 318, Tito to OHQ Bosanska Krajina (12 and 16.8.1942, respectively); *Zbornik*/V/6/42, Lika GoD to MHQ Croatia (4.8.1942); *Zbornik*/V/10/253-54, 3rd OZ to 1st Slavonian Det. (21.12.1942); *Zbornik*/IX/2/499, 4th Bde/Pol. to CK KPH (end of December 1942); *Zbornik*/IV/35/287, 5th Proletarian Bde. to SHQ (17.8.1942).

into being by simply renaming the OHQ for Bosanska Krajina, and the HQ of the 1st OZ, respectively. The NOVJ's operational arm became fully developed with the creation of corps and divisions. The other two arms were a) "pure" guerrilla units like detachments and groups of detachments, and b) military rear area authorities, now consisting of fifteen commands scattered across Western Bosnia, Dalmatia, and Central Croatia.[31]

Unit composition remained largely unchanged, only now there were many more female Partisans (*partizanke*, sg. *partizanka*) in the front ranks. Already in February 1942, Tito responded to the popular demand and allowed women to serve in combat roles; by the time the brigades had reached Bosanska Krajina, they were literally swamped with volunteers of "fairer sex" demanding weapons. Axis sources contain numerous references to the permanent, all-female enemy field units, but they did not exist. The Lika command did form five such companies during the second half of 1942, but these were temporary training outfits whose members were subsequently transferred to brigades (one of them was the then-18-year-old Jovanka Budisavljević, who would eventually become Madame Tito). Coming from decidedly patriarchal milieus, the NOP's adversaries of every color were both terrified and fascinated by the *partizanka* phenomenon. Just like the French after their first encounters with the Dahomey Amazons, the Germans readily acknowledged their ferocity in battle, but were also quick to accuse them of being especially viscous towards prisoners. Despite their proven valor and the NOP's formal commitment to gender equality, the traditional prejudice shared by many of its male members, including card-carrying Communists, proved hard to overcome. They maintained that women were simply not fit for soldiering, that their presence was bad for morale, and that they were a propaganda liability (the enemy press usually mentioned them within the context of "free love" as a supposedly integral part of the communist ideology). Consequently, women had been quietly eased out of combat units by the early 1945 and relegated to "classic" jobs, like clerks, medical personnel, and political workers. Although the official figure of 100,000 female fighters who allegedly passed through the ranks of the NOVJ during the war is difficult to confirm, there can be no doubt that their number went into tens of thousands.[32]

Tito's own staff was also going through a period of change. By the end of the year, it boasted of seven departments–Operations, Intelligence, Economic, Military Justice, Rear Areas, Technical, and Medical, all of which were further subdivided into sections, and a separate Commission for Combatting Spies and Fifth Column (embryonic internal security service headed by Ranković).[33] The SHQ was the prime engine behind the expansion and reorganization of the army, steering the entire effort through a veritable flood of orders, instructions, and guidelines. Let us now take a look at a couple of examples:

1. The intelligence service was streamlined on the national level: both territorial commands (down to place level) and field units (down to battalion level) now

31 Anić, Joksimović, Gutić, *Narodnooslobodilačka*, pp. 201-23; *Zbornik*/IV/7/98, Vojislav Đokić to Sreten Žujović (18.9.1942).

32 Jelena Batinić, *Women and Yugoslav Partisans: History of WW2 Resistance* (New York: CUP, 2015), pp. 1-2, 124-66, 260; Desanka Stojić, *Prva ženska partizanska četa* (Karlovac: HAK, 1987), pp. 140-42; Edna G. Bay, *Wives of the Leopard: Gender, Politics, and Culture in the Kingdom of Dahomey* (London: The University Press of Virginia, 1998), pp. 231, 278, 296.

33 *Enciklopedija*, Vol. X, p. 624.

received their own intelligence organs, responsible for spying on the enemy and precluding him from doing the same. All these activities, including information analysis, were controlled by Main Intelligence Centers (sg. *Glavni obavještajni centar*, GOC), which were attached to provincial commands, and/or by the Intelligence Department of the SHQ. The pace of the reorganization differed from province to province, and was dictated by external events. The reform was much harder to complete in the divisions subordinated to Tito's staff, which were constantly in action, then in comparatively stable and well-organized commands such as the MHQs for Slovenia and Croatia.

2. Already in late September 1942, several dozen Partisan doctors gathered for a convention in the town of Bosanski Petrovac. Using the materials from the conference and drawing from his own considerable personal experience, the chief medical officer of the army, Dr. Gojko Nikoliš (who would gain additional fame almost half-a-century later by publicly opposing Slobodan Milošević) devised "Statute of Sanitary Service". The document outlined the structure and functions of the medical service of the field army; due to the highly varying conditions in different parts of the country, the regulations did not apply to medical arrangements in rear areas. Instead of only one, each company now had ten medical workers, and each brigade received its own mobile surgery team; divisions got one as well, plus a pharmacy, a field hospital, and a medical company consisting of 60 orderlies. Although the things have been improving lately thanks to the help of the friendly population and the existence of suitable infrastructure on the territory of the Bihać Republic, the NOVJ's medical corps was still facing immense difficulties, most notably a great shortage of doctors and trained auxiliary personnel, as well as medical supplies. Yet the disdain sometimes displayed by ordinary Partisans towards this branch of service was particularly hurtful. The medical workers were derisively nicknamed "undertakers", and the army's chief of staff himself was accused of "having no ear" for the service; some field officers at the battle of Livno insisted that nurses show the same courage under fire as combat troops, which led to unnecessary losses.[34]
3. Officer School of the MHQ Croatia became Military School of the SHQ in early November 1942 and moved to Bihać one month later. The living conditions there were much worse than in Donji Lapac, but the training for company and battalion leaders continued at full speed. By mid-January 1943, two such courses had been held, and a third was being prepared. In a marked difference to the earlier courses, the time devoted to the political education was cut back significantly in favor of purely military subjects. Apart from the officer school, the SHQ also organized specialist courses. The one for engineers was held in late October and early November and was attended by 80 candidates, mostly former miners from Lika. What the NOVJ really needed, however, were signals specialists. Until now, the main means of communication, both on the battlefield and in the rear, was the

34 Hajro Kulenović, "Nastanak i razvoj sanitetske službe od početka ustanka 1941. do prelaska Vrhovnog štaba NOV i POJ na Vis, juna 1944. godine", in *Sanitetska služba u Narodnooslobodilačkom ratu Jugoslavije 1941–1945* (Belgrade: VINC, 1989), Vol. I, pp. 109, 114-25; *Zbornik*/II/5/289-91, Nikoliš to Tito (12.8.1942).

courier; the guerrillas also used telephone whenever circumstances allowed. The radio, on the other hand, was scarcely ever used owing to the shortage of equipment, and, especially, of trained operators. Even the all-important link between the SHQ and Moscow was not maintained directly, but via the Comintern's own transmitter in Zagreb (ran by the controversial Kopinič, it would remain undetected throughout the war). The first attempt to establish a direct link in December 1941 had nearly led Tito's chief technician and the physicist of world renown, Pavle Savić, to commit suicide when he accidentally rendered the only suitable W/T set inoperable. Nevertheless, by mid-February 1942, the Partisan overlord had finally become able to send long "sausages" (cables) to Moscow on a daily basis. It would not be before October or November, however, before he would be able to communicate in a similar manner with any one of the provincial commands. By the end of the year, W/T sets, largely of Home Guard origin, were beginning to find their way to the HQs of major field formations, marking the beginning of a new era in the realm of command-and-control. Nearly all communication below the division level, however, would remain in the hands (or legs) of the runner for a long time thereafter. As a side note, the transmission of orders (and proliferation of propaganda) from the SHQ was greatly facilitated by the existence of Radio "Free Yugoslavia" (*Slobodna Jugoslavija*). Established in mid-November 1942 in the town of Ufa in the Urals and operated by Yugoslav Communists, the station broadcast news bulletins and coded instructions in Serbo-Croatian, Slovene, and (from mid-1944) Macedonian several times a day.[35]

4. There is a common perception–nourished by Yugoslav historiography–that the Partisan army was an all-volunteer force right up to late 1944, but the matter was not as straightforward. By the end of 1942, at the latest, the NOP had begun experimenting with conscription in some parts of the country. In Banija, most of the recruits were "called up", whereas only a few came forward of their own free will; in Slavonia, training camps were being prepared for the expected influx of conscripts. Given that local commands often pursued divergent policies in this highly sensitive matter, the MHQ Croatia felt compelled to issue a clarification. Forceful conscription could be applied only in order to deny recruits to the enemy, i.e. in all temporarily held towns and villages; in solidly pro-Partisan areas, a general mobilization could take place only if the population was prepared to go along with it. The creation of the Bihać Republic and the rapid expansion of the NOVJ prompted the movement's leadership to seriously consider conscripting all able-bodied males between the ages of 18 and 45. During the first half of January 1943, the SHQ had ordered the compiling of draft lists, but the course of events prevented all these

35 *Zbornik*/II/6/189-90 (Tito to 1st OZ, 6.10.1942), 334-41 [SHQ's orders pertaining to Military School, 4.11.1942], 472 (SHQ to 1st Bosnian NOVJ Corps [NOVJC], 27.11.1942); *Zbornik*/II/7/8-9 (SHQ to MHQ Croatia, 1.12.1942), 304 (SHQ/Rear. to MHQ Croatia et. al., 9.1.1943), 349-57 (Military School to SHQ, 12.1.1943); *Zbornik*/V/9/344, Franc Klainhapel to SHQ (27.11.1942); Mišo Leković, "Neki problemi rukovođenja Centralnog komiteta KPJ i Vrhovnog štaba NOPOJ u 1941. godini", in *Užička*, Vol. I, pp. 189-94; Mirko Ćetković, *Veze u Narodnooslobodilačkoj borbi* (Belgrade: VIZ, 1976), Vol. I, pp. 309-43.

> plans from materializing. This change in policy affected the treatment of captured Home Guards as well. For instance, at Teslić, only those soldiers who were born in this area were released after capture. Others, largely Slavonians, were retained with the units with the aim of "converting" them to the Partisan cause through political work, after which they would either join the 1st Proletarian Division, or be sent over to the 3rd OZ.[36]

The Germans did not fail to notice the change in their adversary's behavior. His "tightly organized" formations did not shy from a fight with superior regular forces as in the past, but stood their ground; during the operations in fall of 1942, they displayed tenacity and "a considerable level of military prowess".[37] Despite this obvious improvement, the Partisan army was still being plagued by various difficulties, both on and off the battlefield. Some of them are mentioned in the already cited letter sent to Žujović by Vojislav Đokić, the chief of staff of the 2nd Proletarian Brigade. This former active major of the royal army had noticed an unfortunate tendency to organize rallies and parades in liberated towns instead of pursuing and finishing off a beaten foe. Entrenching was commonly considered unmanly and not becoming of a soldier; NCOs and officers often equated leadership with reckless courage, which merely led to unnecessary losses. Once the shooting had started, the outcome rested solely in the hands of individual fighters; officers' ability to steer the course of battle was severely curtailed by their own inexperience, underdeveloped battlefield communications, and the very nature of the Partisan way of war (preference for night fighting, which is difficult to control even under the best of circumstances). The guerrilla heritage was increasingly becoming seen as a major obstacle on the path of building a modern field force. The sum of all negative tendencies in the army thus came to be subsumed under the term *partizanština*; this Russian loanword covered everything from faulty tactics to sloppy paperwork and improper addressing of superiors. The burning desire to look and act as a regular army also had its side effects. Many field commands, having for the first time a large number of men at their disposal, were now insisting on taking every objective "at all costs". The rise in losses prompted Tito to issue a special order against this disastrous habit in January 1943; he reiterated the need to conserve strength and reduce the butcher's bill through improved training and staff work. As we shall see, all the above-listed shortcomings would continue to haunt the armed wing of the NOP until the very end of the war.[38]

Internal discipline was beginning to suffer as the result of the NOVJ's rapid expansion. What used to be a conglomerate of small bands of idealists was now turning into a massive force counting tens of thousands of members from all walks of life. Unsurprisingly, it soon acquired

36 Rudolf Primorac, *Operativno-taktička iskustva iz prve polovine Narodnooslobodilačkog rata* (Belgrade: VINC, 1986), p. 41; *Enciklopedija*, Vol. VII, p. 178; *Zbornik*/V/10/100 (Banija Det. to MHQ Croatia, 8.12.1942), 172-73 (3rd OZ to MHQ Croatia, 17.12.1942), 247-48 (MHQ Croatia, Instructions, 21.12.1942); *Zbornik*/II/7/264, 267, SHQ, Orders (6 and 9.1.1943, respectively); *Zbornik*/IV/9/42, 1st NOVJD, Circular (3.1.1943).

37 NARA/T315/2243/1114, BhS, Activity report (10-19.12.1942); NARA/T314/554/264, BDTK, Activity report (15-25.11.1942).

38 *Zbornik*/IV/7/94, 98, Vojislav Đokić to Sreten Žujović (18.9.1942); *Zbornik*/V/10/276 (1st Croatian NOVJC/Pol., Circular, 22.12.1942), 315 (8th Bde. to 7th NOVJD, 26.12.1942); *Zbornik*/IX/2/272, 1st NOVJD/Pol., Circular (11.11.1942); *Zbornik*/II/8/277-83, Tito to 1st Bosnian NOVJC (8.1.1943); Leković, *Ofanziva*, pp. 272-73, 396, 475.

all those less-than-savory trappings commonly associated with "bourgeois" or "mercenary" armies. Rank-and-file proved very difficult to control during attacks on enemy strongholds, and reports often mentioned cases of "un-Partisanlike" behavior towards private property. The Proletarian formations enforced a strict teetotal policy until their arrival to Bosanska Krajina. There, following the local practice, they began issuing spirits in small doses as a way of augmenting the meager diet. By the year's end, however, the HQ of the 1st Brigade had to intervene against excessive consumption of alcohol. "Bureaucratism" (a very dirty word in the communist parlance) had also found its way into the army. By the time of the Battle of Kupres, the officers of the 2nd Proletarian Brigade ate better than their men, and had developed an obsession with riding horses. And then there was desertion: three smaller groups had left the aforementioned formation during the "long march", whereas the 3rd Brigade had lost an entire company in the same manner. Reasons for going AWOL were many, but usually had to do with the extremely harsh living conditions or homesickness; it was not unusual for a Partisan to take a few days off in order to visit his family and have a change of clothes before returning to his unit. Since no unified penal code existed, each command tackled the problem in its own way. For the first infraction (and provided he/she did not defect to the enemy), a fighter would usually get away with a reprimand; the third usually brought him in front of a firing squad. An overly liberal application of capital punishment in these cases was deemed counterproductive, as witnessed by the incident involving the shooting of seven deserters by the Kalnik Detachment in December 1942. The episode had such a negative resonance among the population that the Partisans were compelled to publicly explain their motives in the victims' native villages, and start combatting desertion with more subtle means.[39]

3.4 Operations in Croatia and Syrmia

The most important tasks standing before the MHQ Croatia during the latter half of 1942 included securing the harvest and denying it to the enemy, reorganization of the army, and spreading the fire of the uprising to all corners of the country. Ultimately, these efforts were facilitated by the stalemate that had set in along the "front lines" in Lika and Kordun. The lack of targets and the passivity of the Axis both compelled and allowed local Partisan commands to send their fighters to other provinces. The operations in Lika were basically limited to raiding enemy villages and lines of communication. For instance, the elements of the 1st and 2nd Lika Detachments took the NDH strongpoint at Podlapača on 3 July, capturing 160 rifles for the price of four KIA and 23 WIA. Soon thereafter, the 1st OZ's 1st Assault Brigade captured some 50 Italian soldiers and demolished railway installations between Vrhovine and Plaški. The Partisans did not forget about the Chetniks either: charging with the cries "Long live Comrade Stalin" and "Long live Red Army", the 9th Lika Brigade routed the "Karađorđe" Regiment (named after the founder of the reigning Serbian/Yugoslav royal dynasty) near Gračac on 24 October. Expecting another easy victory, the same brigade attacked the enemy stronghold at Velika Popina six days later. This time, the monarchists, fighting from fortified positions and

39 Urošević, *Druga*, pp. 91, 130, 137; Vidović, *Treća*, p. 63; *Zbornik*/IV/8/377-78, 1st Proletarian Bde./Pol., Circular (16.12.1942); *Zbornik*/IX/2/66-67 (2nd Krajina Bde., Political report, 5-16.9.1942), 408 (2nd Dalmatian Bde./Pol. to CK KPJ, 21.12.1942); *SZH*/III/772, Kalnik Det. to 3rd OZ/Pol. (21.12.1942); *Enciklopedija*, Vol. II, p. 426.

supported by Italian artillery, gave the Partisans a bloody nose: 12 KIA and 15 WIA, as well as 4,000 precious rounds of ammunition, were lost in vain that day. [40]

The *Regio Esercito* would intervene in strength only if the guerrilla encroachment in one area or another threatened to become more permanent. In mid-July 1942, the XVIII AC sent seven infantry battalions, plus the usual array of artillery, air support, and the Chetniks, against the 3rd Lika and Northern Dalmatia Detachments around Gračac. The operation, known as "Velebit", succeeded in pushing the Partisans to the northeast, towards Srb. The damage done to the guerrilla units was small, except for one Dalmatian battalion, which was at the end of its tethers after having been chased by the enemy for nearly a month without interruption. In late September and early October, the V AC used elements of the "Grantieri di Sardegna" and "Re", as well as the task force "Gianuzzi" of the XVIII AC (whose strength varied from three to seven battalions), to clear the stretch of territory between Gospić and the southern slopes of the Velika Kapela. The offensive succeeded in liquidating the recently-established Partisan "bridgehead" in Western Lika centered on the Kosinj Valley, but the 1st and 2nd Lika Brigades managed to extricate themselves without heavier losses. [41]

One episode deserves a special mention, the botched attempt to seize Udbina (22-24 August 1942), one of the last remaining NDH bastions in Eastern Lika. The task of storming this small, but powerful hilltop fortress controlling the southern end of the Krbava Field was entrusted to the 1st OZ's 2nd Brigade reinforced by two extra battalions, four pieces of ordnance, and two tanks. The clash itself bore uncanny resemblance to the Battle of Kupres fought only days earlier some 130-odd km to the southeast. The attacks were not properly coordinated, and the Partisans became disorganized and even smug after achieving some initial success. Their foes–largely Home Guards–were determined to fight to the last. They were effectively supported by the NDH air force which not only dropped food and ammunition, but also strafed and bombed the attackers, who unwisely chose to stay in their exposed positions during the daylight. By the time the 2nd Brigade decided to pull back, it had lost no less than 120 KIA and 180 WIA, which translated into a full third of its original strength. The only consolation lay in the knowledge that this young unit, formed only a couple of weeks earlier, took such a terrible beating without falling apart. The bloody episode at Udbina remained a footnote in Yugoslav historiography and is virtually unknown outside the borders of the former state, largely due to the fact that it did not belong to the glorified narrative about the "long march".[42]

As in Lika, the last six months of 1942 in Kordun were marked by fighting of low intensity. The Partisans concentrated their efforts against the railway line Glina–Karlovac–Ogulin and carried out a number of mostly unsuccessful attacks against smaller enemy garrisons and hostile villages (e.g. Slunj, Vrginmost, Sići, Batnoge). The NDH forces limited their activity to raids

40 *Zbornik*/V/5/374 (MHQ Croatia to SHQ, 15.7.1942), 407-11 (1st Bde. to 1st OZ, 20.7.1942); *Zbornik*/V/6/75 and 240, MHQ Croatia to SHQ (6 and 24.8.1942, respectively); *Zbornik*/V/7/190-92, 1st OZ to MHQ Croatia (20.9.1942); *Zbornik*/V/8/330-33, 367-70, 9th Lika Bde. to 1st OZ (25 and 30.10.1942, respectively).

41 Milan R. Drobac, "Razvoj partizanskih jedinica i njihove borbe u kotaru Gračac od aprila 1942. do januara 1943. godine", in *Kotar Gračac u narodnooslobodilačkom ratu 1941-1945.* (Karlovac: HAK, 1984), Vol. I, pp. 754-56; Đorđe J. Orlović, "Borbe u zapadnoj Lici (septembar—oktobar 1942.)", in *Kotar Gospić i kotar Perušić u Narodnooslobodilačkom ratu 1941—1945.* (Karlovac: HAK, 1989), pp. 586-606; *Zbornik*/V/5/455-63, Lika GoD to 1st OZ (27.7.1942).

42 Đorđe J. Orlović, *Druga lička proleterska brigada* (Belgrade: VIZ, 1983), pp. 18-41.

against the guerrilla-held territory, sometimes with the express purpose of disrupting the harvest works. The two most important events from this period both occurred within a single week in October. On the 24th, the 2nd Lika and 4th Kordun Brigades bagged more than 400 collaborationists in Tušilović, at the same time thwarting the relief effort launched from the nearby Karlovac, all for the price of 60 casualties.[43]

A week earlier, five battalions from these same formations ambushed the 14th Cavalry Regiment "Alessandria" of the "Eugenio de Savoia" Division, at the village called Donji Poloj, some 28 km south of the city. Popularly known in Italy as the "last charge of the Italian cavalry", the action is sometimes represented as a set-piece, dramatic ride of sabre-waving horsemen who eventually succeed in hacking their way through the vast multitude of hostiles and save their unit from utter destruction. Yugoslav sources tell a different story. The enemy column moved through the countryside without flankers, which enabled the attackers to achieve full surprise. After showering their target with a deluge of small-arms fire, the Partisans charged with the onset of darkness, almost immediately throwing the startled Italians into panic. What followed was a complete rout with "the cavalry galloping and infantry running" past and through the already disorganized Partisan battalions. Ultimately, the remnants of the column did manage to escape, but only thanks to the old weaknesses plaguing their foe, such as bad coordination, lack of reserves, and inability to mount an effective pursuit. Despite this, both sides agree that the Partisans had every reason to celebrate: between 30 and 50 prisoners, one tank, two guns, 11 motor vehicles, 155 pieces of small arms, and 300,000 rounds of ammunition were collected after the battle; the *Regio Esercito* suffered at least 70 KIA and 60 WIA. Italian sources usually claim that the Partisans enjoyed numerical superiority (2,500 fighters) and suffered more casualties (300) than the column, but neither is true. The strength of the five guerrilla battalions that took part in the action is estimated at about 1,500 fighters, but perhaps as much as one-third of them were unarmed. The cavalry regiment alone counted close to 800 men, but a full CCNN battalion and an armored company were also present, which practically evened the odds (not to mention their vastly superior firepower). Finally, the Partisans reported losing only four KIA and 15 WIA, some of them even from friendly fire, which basically confirms the Yugoslav claims regarding the nature of this engagement.[44]

The situation in Banija in July 1942 was similar to that in the neighboring Kordun, with each side trying to secure the harvest while keeping the other off-balance with small-scale actions. The following month, however, brought another major Axis onslaught against the liberated territory. The offensive lasted from 7 to 12 August and was carried out by the KG "Borowski" and the bulk of the 1st HDB MTD as a part of the mop-up operations following in wake of the Battle of Kozara. The history was repeating itself, much to the chagrin of the Partisan leadership in Croatia: for the second time in only four months, the Banija Detachment chose not to fight but to seek refuge in another part of the country. As a consequence, the enemy quickly pacified most of the province, in part also by adopting conciliatory attitude towards

43 *Hronologija*, pp. 303, 304, 305, 321, 323, 324, 341 (5.7, 10.7, 17.7, 1.8, 10.8, 13.9.1942, respectively); Korać, *Kordun i Banija*, pp. 301-08, 396.

44 Orlović, *Druga lička*, pp. 61-66; *Zbornik*/V/8/270 (4th Kordun Bde., Activity report 13-20.10.1942), 279-83 (2nd Lika Bde. to 1st OZ, 22.10.1942); Fasanotti et. al., *L'esercito*, pp. 256-57; for the casualty list (and a rather romanticized version of the battle), see Antonino Poma, *L'ultima carica della cavalleria italiana* (Buseto Palizzolo: Associazione di Lettere, Arti e Sport Dilettantistica Jò, 2007).

the Serbs. The Partisans would not re-establish their presence in the region before the middle of September, and would undertake their first and only major action only in late October. The newly-formed 7th and 8th Banija Brigades joined forces with the 1st Lika and 5th Kordun to form a temporary OHQ. The first order of business was to capture Glina, a sizable town notorious for the two large-scale massacres perpetrated by the Ustashe back in 1941. The assault took place on the night of the 22nd and carried the attackers into the town center, where they manage to free some prisoners from the local jail, but not to dislodge the obstinate defenders from their two remaining strongpoints. By the following morning, the Partisans had become so disorganized that their command had to order a general retreat, leaving behind 20 KIA, 40 KIA, and two MIA. After that, the Banija units carried out a number of smaller actions in the so-called "Banija Triangle", the easternmost part of the province located between the Sava and Una Rivers.[45]

In late November 1942, the 1st OZ had been reorganized into the 1st Croatian Corps with three divisions (each initially with only two brigades) and as many provincial detachments. While the latter pursued their old mission of guarding their native terrains and keeping the enemy off-balance through low-level, but constant activity, the mobile formations were used for offensive operations all along the Croatian section of the frontier of Tito's State. From 26 to 28 November, the 6th Lika and 7th Banija divisions aided 1st Bosnian Corps' operations against Bosanski Novi by attacking the neighboring Dvor na Uni. Despite maximum effort (over 300 casualties, including 85 KIA), the divisions proved incapable of either reducing the garrison or stopping the enemy relief column from coming through. Following the battle, the divisions parted way. The 7th stayed in Banija, where it interdicted rail traffic and stormed a number of smaller outposts. For instance, on 20 December, one of its brigades damaged and stopped a train near Blinjski Kut. Among the prisoners, there was an Ustasha lieutenant-colonel who subsequently managed to escape (which led to the public execution of the guilty Partisan sentry, the first incident of its sort in Banija), a young French woman who tried to charm the division commander into releasing her, and an Ethnic German medical student, self-confessed Nazi sympathizer who eventually perished as a Partisan doctor in Lika. A day later, the 7th Banija gave the newly-arrived German-Croatian 369th ID a bloody welcome to Yugoslavia when it killed 15 and wounded 16 members of the division's reconnaissance battalion and captured two brand new 50mm AT guns at Kostajnica.[46]

The remaining two divisions of 1st Croatian Corps were also back in their native provinces. From 8 to 16 December 1942, the 8th cleared all the remaining enemy outposts on the right bank of the Kupa west of Karlovac, thereby reducing the NDH presence in Kordun to the area of Topusko. The Partisans took some 350 prisoners during this round of fighting, at the same time losing 45 KIA and 107 MIA. In the meantime, the 6th Division was operating along the railway line Knin–Gospić in anticipation of the rumored withdrawal of the Italians from this

45 Đurić, *Banijski*, pp. 170-81, 195-98, 409-10; NARA/T501/248/444, 471 (BhS, Daily reports 8 and 13.8.1942, respectively), 63-64 (BhS to WBSO, 12.8.1942); *Zbornik*/V/6/255-58, 279-81, [correspondence Većeslav Holjevac–1st OZ] (26 and 28.8.1942, respectively); *Zbornik*/V/8/66-67 (MHQ Croatia to SHQ, 7.10.1942), 313-18 (OHQ, Report Glina, 25.10.1942).

46 Dušan Baić, *Četvrti korpus NOV Jugoslavije odnosno Prvi korpus NOV Hrvatske* (VINC: Belgrade, 1990), pp. 73-75, 81-84; Jakšić, *Nad uspomenama*, Vol. I, pp. 309-10; NARA/T315/2154/69-75, 369th ID, Diary (29-31.12.1942).

entire area. The rumor proved to be only partially true: a major reduction in troop presence in Lika was, in fact, planned for the early 1943, but for now the *Regio Esercito* merely withdrew its garrison from Gračac, leaving the much weaker Chetniks in charge. The Partisans, however, failed to take advantage of the opportunity and seize this important town. Adding insult to injury, the Italians and Ustashe managed to pull off a sudden and practically bloodless evacuation of Udbina. The 6th Lika finally got its act together in mid-December after an intervention from the MHQ Croatia, and launched two brigades against the part of the main provincial railway line between Lovinac and Raduč. Although Lovinac and most of the surrounding villages with NDH sympathies were quickly reduced, the move stirred a hornet's nest. After the first counterattack, carried out largely by the HDB and Ustasha forces, had failed, the "Re" sent two of its own battalions, plus parts of the "Sassari", to relieve the besieged Raduč and reopen the road between Gospić and Gračac. The Partisan division, exhausted by incessant marching and fighting over the past several months, decided not to brave the Italians in an open battle and retreated northeast on the 30th. Unlike its sister formations, the 6th Lika had little to show in terms of damage inflicted to the enemy. For the price of 35 KIA and 76 WIA, the division took only some 80 prisoners and 130 pieces of small arms, well below of what was usually expected in large-scale offensive operations.[47]

Unlike in Lika or Western Bosnia, the Italians had no intention of reducing their presence in Gorski Kotar and Croatian Littoral, the home territory of the 5th OZ. The fact that the local Partisans operated close to several objectives of strategic value–the city of Rijeka, the southern border of the Ljubljana Province, and the Karlovac–Sušak railway used for transporting the Romanian oil to Italy–brought them much unwelcome attention from the *Regio Esercito*. During the second half of July 1942, the V AC invaded the liberated territory centered on Mount Risnjak. At first, the 2nd Primorsko-goranski Detachment tried openly resisting its much better-armed foe, with predictable results: as casualties mounted (the unit commander was among them), the fighters began to lose heart and some 100-150 deserted. The remainder managed to escape, but the damage to the NOP's infrastructure was severe: civilians were interned or executed, friendly villages and forest bases razed to the ground, and crops burnt.

The same fate soon befell the main liberated territory on Mount Velika Kapela. Altogether eighteen infantry battalions, drawn for the most part from the divisions "Re", "Granatieri di Sardegna", and "Lombardia" advanced concentrically from the north, south, and east, hoping to catch the 5th OZ's 1st Detachment between them and crush it. This time, the Partisans refused to engage the attackers directly, and either escaped north and east, or sought refuge in the local, hard-to-reach hideouts. The operation was terminated after 13 days, on 30 September. Pressed by the need to send more reinforcements to other threatened sectors (e.g. Lika), the V AC could again spare no troops for the permanent occupation of this troublesome area. The attackers captured only 125 pieces of small arms, but this rather modest figure hides the fact that the NOP had been badly hurt by the systematic application of scorched earth policies that left the fighters and their remaining supporters on the brink of hunger.[48]

47 Baić, *Četvrti*, pp. 78-81; Đorđe J. Orlović, *Šesta lička proleterska divizija "Nikola Tesla"* (VINC: Belgrade, 1990), pp. 31-51.

48 *Zbornik*/V/6/97, 113, MHQ Croatia to SHQ (8.8.1942); *Zbornik*/V/7/310-11, 5th OZ to MHQ Croatia (7.9.1942); *Zbornik*/V/8/41-43, 5th OZ to MHQ Croatia (4.10.1942); *Zbornik*/XIII/2/927-35, V AC to *Supersloda* (15.12.1942).

It would be erroneous to conclude from the lapidary overview presented above that the Partisans in Gorski Kotar stayed passive throughout this period and thereafter. On the contrary, the region was very much alive with guerrilla activity, thanks largely to the presence of veteran units from the 1st OZ sent here on purpose by the MHQ Croatia. The 1st Proletarian Battalion, assisted by local fighters, ambushed a battery of the "Lombardia" on 18 July near Senj, a convoy carrying interned civilians on 2 August near Gerovo, and a supply column on 10 August near Delnice (15 KIA and 12 WIA Italians). The 1st Lika Brigade spent the time between mid-July and mid-September on the southeastern slopes of the Velika Kapela, from where it launched a number of attacks on collaborationist outpost along the border with Lika (e.g. Jezerane, Dabar). Having returned from Kordun, two assault battalions belonging to the 1st Primorsko-goranski Detachment overwhelmed a pair of platoons and one battery of the aforementioned Italian division on 28 September at Tisovac, killing 18 and wounding 17 soldiers. Only four days later, the resurgent 2nd Primorsko-goranski Detachment wiped out a full third of a 200-strong column belonging to the "Macerata" Division on the road leading from Delnice to the Slovene border.

In mid-October and late November, the best units of the 5th OZ were combined into the 6th and 14th Brigades. On 9 December, these formations stormed Gomirje, the westernmost Chetnik bastion in Croatia, capturing some 200 defenders in the process; a 47-mm gun, affectionately known as *Krnjo*, which had been given a hero's welcome in Drežnica upon its arrival from the MHQ a week or so earlier, played a decisive role in reducing monarchist bunkers. The Italians–who noted this was the first time the local guerrillas used heavier weapons–intervened on the same day with five companies but could not reach Gomirje before the morning of the 10th. The next Partisan target was the nearby Ustasha stronghold located in the village called, ironically enough, Ravna Gora. The defenders turned out not to be cut from the same cloth as their comrades at Kupres or Udbina; after a few shells, all 103 of them (not counting 20 gendarmes who had surrendered earlier) decided to accept the Partisan terms and lay down their arms on 17 December.[49]

Meantime, the already strong anti-Axis sentiment among the civilian population in Dalmatia had been further strengthened by the increasingly ruthless Italian COIN policies (keyword: *Circolare No. 3c*), and by the continuing decay of the Ustasha state, which, on top of everything else, had practically allied itself with the Serbian nationalists in the fight against other Croats. As a consequence, the NOP experienced a major revival during the summer and autumn months of 1942. The process was greatly aided by the arrival of the Proletarian brigades to the neighboring Western Bosnia. The ensuing cooperation between the SHQ and the 4th OZ is a good example of why the Partisan doctrine insisted on establishing firm physical links between liberated territories. The Dalmatian command had one war commodity in abundance, and that was manpower. From early August to late November, an estimated 3,500 new recruits had joined the Partisan ranks, but the trouble was that there were not enough weapons to equip them all. The problem was partially solved by sending some 2,000 of these men and women to

49 Ibid., pp. 395-96; 599, 635, 659 (*Supersloda*, List of incidents, 18.7, 2.8, 10.8.1942, respectively); *Zbornik*/V/9/359, 5th OZ to MHQ Croatia (28.11.1942); *Zbornik*/V/10/513-16, V AC to *Supersloda* (30.12.1942); Guerrazzi, *Slovenia*, p. 110; Jovo Popović, *Prva lička proleterska brigada (Marko Orešković)* (Belgrade: VINC, 1988), pp. 26-56; Vladimir-Dušan Matetić, *Četrnaesta Primorsko-goranska brigada* (Belgrade: VIZ, 1972), pp. 31-41.

replenish the depleted ranks of the Proletarian brigades. For their part, the SHQ and the OHQ for Bosanska Krajina provided the 4th OZ with some of the booty captured in Bosnia (the SHQ alone sent 1,000 rifles by the end of the year). They also dispatched experienced cadre needed for officering the rapidly expanding Dalmatian units, which now included three brigades. The recruits from Dalmatia would travel in groups of up to 200, mostly on foot, but also by truck and train; the food and lodgings along the way were provided by the local NOOs. All of this meant that the replacements reached their new units tired, but otherwise in good shape and without losses due to straggling or enemy action.[50]

Owing to the fact that it still lacked the knowledge, numbers, and equipment needed to assault larger NDH and Italian garrisons, the 4th OZ conducted a classic guerrilla campaign of raids and ambushes. On 22 July 1942, a company of the "Jozo Jurčević" Battalion attacked a small Italian convoy near Gradac, killing 12 soldiers; its own casualties consisted of three men who were injured when a Blackshirt, feigning to be dead, suddenly activated a hand grenade. One week later, the 1st Proletarian Battalion ambushed an Italian column outside Sinj; according to the NDH gendarmerie, the losses this time amounted to about 30 KIA and 50 WIA, along with six trucks. The 1st Dalmatian Brigade demolished the coal mine at Košute on 24 September and disarmed the 50-odd defenders of the NDH outposts at Otok two days later. On 13 October, the Mosor Company staged a major coup by derailing a passenger train between Split and Sinj, killing 21 members of the "Bergamo" Division. The first week of December saw two further incidents. In the ambushes laid by the 3rd Dalmatian Brigade and the Rogoznica Company outside of Split and Trogir, respectively, 33 Italian servicemen lost their lives and 20 were wounded; most of them were Blackshirts, but some belonged to the unfortunate "Alessandria" Regiment.[51]

The uprising spread to the Dalmatian islands as well. Although the KPJ had a network of cells there since before the war, their relative isolation precluded them from keeping pace with the rest of the country (some of these cells were still styling themselves "military-revolutionary committees" as late as August 1942). Prior to the second half of 1942, the main resistance activity consisted of getting the volunteers across to the mainland. The heavy-handedness displayed by occupation authorities made sure that there were always plenty of these. In late July, the *Carabinieri* rounded up ca. 60 youth from the island of Iž over the theft of some oil. During the transport, the prisoners killed their guards, seized the boat and went into hiding. A month or so later, the group, now close to 250 strong, fled to the liberated territory on the border between Dalmatia, Lika, and Bosnia. At the same time, the Partisans raided the local sardine factory on Hvar, handing out tons of fish oil and tens of thousands of tins to the population. In order to exchange two Party functionaries who were arrested shortly before the anniversary

50 See reports of 4th OZ to MHQ Croatia/Pol. in: *Dalmacija*/III/200-07 (1.9.1942) and *Zbornik*/V/9/297-306 (24.11.1942); *Zbornik*/II/7/166, SHQ to 4th OZ (25.11.1942); *Zbornik*/IV/35/388, 1st Bosnian NOVJC to SHQ (5.12.1942); Šime Vrančić, "Ne pucaj, žive hvataj!", in *Dalmatinci u Prvoj proleterskoj brigadi* (Split: IHRPD, 1982), pp. 140-41.

51 *Dalmacija*/II/822, *Supersloda*, Diary (23.7.1942); *Dalmacija*/III/25-26 ("Josip Jurčević" Btl. to 4th OZ, 2.8.1942), 33-34 (OHQ Central Dalmatia Dets. to 4th OZ, 3.8.1942), 344-45 (4th OZ to MHQ Croatia, 26.9.1942), 606-07 (6th NDH Gendarmerie Rgt., Activity report, 30.7-15.8.1942), 678-79 (Great county of Cetina, Situation report, 20-26.9.1942); *Zbornik*/V/8/439, Police HQ Split, Report (13.10.1942); *Zbornik*/V/10/384 (CCRR Trogir, Report, 6.12.1942), 392 (CCRR HQ Dalmatia to governor's office, 8.12.1942).

of the October Revolution, the guerrillas on Brač went on a prisoner hunt, capturing a high-ranking Italian officer and a dozen men of his escort. As the year drew to a close, the Korčula Partisans felt confident enough to stage bigger actions, like the one of 4 December, when nine Italian officials were killed and five more were injured.[52]

Guerrilla activities were not confined to the ground. The Partisans made their first assault on an enemy vessel ("Merkur") already on 24 January 1942 in the port of Gradac, followed by the capture of the motorsailer "Mira" near Podgora (23 May) and sinking of the steamer "Vis" in Živogošće (20 July). On 11 August, they scored their first victory on the open sea when they captured the motorsailer "Dux" with its cargo of olive oil off the coast of Korčula. Recognizing Dalmatia's huge potential in this respect, Tito authorized the creation of Navy Department (*Sekcija za ratnu mornaricu*) under the auspices of the 4th OZ on 18 December. The department's job was to organize all NOVJ activities in coastal waters including equipping and maintaining a fleet and mobilizing experienced seamen from the ranks of the former royal navy, but also those currently in the service of the NDH.[53] Thirteen days later, the nascent Partisan navy went into action from its newly-created station at Podgora. Two small boats carrying Coastal Platoon (*Primoski vod*), made up of fighters belonging to the Biokovo Detachment, captured a convoy of six vessels laden with food headed for the NDH garrison of Omiš. Taken aback with this brazen action, the *Maridalmazia* (Naval Command Dalmatia) dispatched five armed ships to shell Podgora and neighboring villages on 3 January 1943.[54]

As already stated, the Italians were responding to the spread of the uprising with heightened repression. Following the escape of the Partisan sympathizers from Iž, the *Carabinieri* had 361 members of their families interned in the notorious concentration camp at Molat. After two trucks carrying naval personnel had been ambushed outside Šibenik on 14 November (16 KIA, six WIA, and seven MIA), the army, navy, and air force shelled two and razed five more villages, and murdered an estimated 150 civilians. Just how easily the things could go out of control in such an acrimonious atmosphere is confirmed by a little-known episode from late September. Some overzealous officer from the XVIII AC authorized the use of 250 kg of mustard gas in order to contaminate a remote cave complex on Mount Mosor suspected of serving as a guerrilla hideout. This was too much even for Roatta, who demanded an immediate investigation and ordered the decontamination of the said area; the incident was logged as an exercise. It should be noted that, unlike in the NOP's "core provinces", reprisals still carried

52 Nikola Anić, *Dvanaesta dalmatinska udarna brigada (Prva otočka)* (Supetar: Domicil 12. dalmatinske NOU brigade, 1984), pp. 15-20; *Dalmacija*/III/56-58, Military-revolutionary committee Mali Iž to 4th OZ (5.8.1942); *Zbornik*/V/6/327-30, CCRR station Preko, Report, 9.8.1942); Drago Gizdić, *Dalmacija 1942: Prilozi historiji Narodnooslobodilačke borbe* (Zagreb: Savez boraca Hrvatske, 1959), pp. 399-400, 663; *Zbornik*/V/10/382, Police HQ Split, Report (5.12.1942).

53 Although Rome retained a firm grip over all aspects of life on the eastern coast of the Adriatic, and although it did its best to prevent the NDH from having its own navy, the HDB did possess a naval branch together with an admiralty, port authorities, training centers, and a handful of motorboats. After having completed training, the NDH sailors would continue to serve in one of the other branches of the armed forces: Ivan Košutić, *Hrvatsko domobranstvo u Drugom svjetskom ratu* (Zagreb: Matica Hrvatska, 1992), pp. 136-40.

54 *Zbornik*/VIII/1/13-15 (Tito to 4th OZ, 18.12.1942), 16-25 (4th OZ, [Correspondence regarding naval affairs], 25.12, 28.12.1942, 6.1.1943), 598 (*Maridalmazia*, Daily report, 12.8.1942), 601 and 608 (*Maridalmazia* to Supersloda, 3.1 and 6.1.1943).

some weight in Dalmatia. For example, Mosor Company decided to seek unequivocal approval from its superiors before putting the last few friendly villages at risk by staging attacks on the road between Split and Omiš. The failure of the 3rd Dalmatian Brigade to protect the civilians in the aftermath of its successful action outside Split (see above) caused the 4th OZ to issue a general order against such behavior.[55]

In addition to everyday anti-guerrilla activities, such as patrols, searches, and such (the CCRR's Dalmatian command alone conducted 156 of these actions in the period July-September 1942), the Italians also carried out several larger offensive undertakings. One involved an attempt by a task force consisting of five battalions from the "Sassari" and "Bergamo" to surround and destroy the main base of the 4th OZ on the eastern slopes of Mount Dinara. However, the operation (colloquially known as "Vještića Gora") had to be canceled after only three days (14 July 1942) owing to the unexpectedly strong resistance offered by three Partisan battalions. In the end, the attackers returned to their bases short of more than a hundred men, and had only 17 captured rifles to show for it.

The main target of Operation "Biokovo" (alternatively: "Albia") was the ca. 800-strong "Josip Jurčević" Battalion and its bases located on this rugged mountain. For this purpose, the *Supersloda* used elements of the "Bergamo" (XVIII AC) and "Messina" (VI AC), plus about 900 Chetniks of the Herzegovinian-Montenegrin contingent. The operation started on 12 August and lasted for three weeks. It was marked by atrocities committed by the Serbian nationalists, lots of hard marching through the karst, waterless terrain in the summer sun, and several sharp clashes with the guerrillas. In the end, the vast majority of them managed to escape towards Aržano. Roatta bragged about more than 1,000 enemy dead, but in reality, they were more like 14. The Italians also claimed they had captured 11 LMGs, 211 rifles, and 46 pistols; Yugoslav and NDH sources do not contain an explicit confirmation of this claim, but they do agree on the fact that the attackers had discovered several guerrilla magazines, where the majority of these arms probably originated from. The Italian losses amounted to 17 KIA and 41 WIA, the Chetnik ones to 38 KIA, 39 WIA, and 50 MIA.[56]

The 2nd OZ's three main centers of activity were Pokuplje and Žumberak, Moslavina, and the Kalnik. In early July 1942, the MHQ decided to combine all units in the area south of the Sava and north of the Kupa (two local, and two companies of fighters from Kordun) into the Žumberak-Pokuplje Detachment. Within a couple of months, the detachment had grown to two battalions operating on both sides of the Zagreb–Karlovac railway line. In late August, they were reinforced by the entire 4th Kordun Brigade, whose best known action from this period was the taking of Jastrebarsko, the site of the makeshift camp for children from the Kozara, notorious for its high mortality rates. On this occasion, the Partisans freed over 700 inmates, but could take less than half of them to the Žumberak Mountains. The rise in guerrilla activity

55 *Zbornik*/V/9/445-46, 454, PNF Šibenik to PNF Zadar (14.11. and 17.11.1942, respectively); *Dalmacija*/III/549-50, *Supersloda*, Notice, and Cable to XVIII AC (21.9.1942, respectively); *Zbornik*/V/8/195, Mosor Coy. to 4th OZ (14.10.1942); *Zbornik*/V/10/312, 4th OZ, Circular (25.12.1942).

56 *Zbornik*/XIII/2/579, 583, 587, 589, *Supersloda*, List of incidents (11.7, 13-14.7.1942, respectively); *Dalmacija*/II/416-18 (1st Assault Btl., Report, 12.7.1942), 813 (*Supersloda*, Daily report, 16.7.1942); *Zbornik*/V/9/477, CCRR Dalmatia, Three-monthly report (19.11.1942); Gizdić, *Dalmacija*, pp. 494-95; *Dalmacija*/III/263-84 (3rd Det. To 4th OZ, 8.9.1942), 502-03 (VI AC to *Supersloda*, 2.9.1942), 674 (Great county of Cetina, Situation report, 13-19.9.1942).

so close to their capital spurred the Ustashe into action. Two times they launched sweeps against enemy bases in the rugged area west of Samobor, and both times the Partisans sought refuge in the neighboring Ljubljana Province. The safety offered by the border was relative: during the second NDH sweep, which was conducted by a force of seven battalions from 14 to 18 September, one group of Ustashe crossed the border and captured a Slovene Partisan hospital, killing 15 inmates and members of the staff. Several weeks later, the 2nd OZ lost its commander, a farmer-turned-internationalist named Franjo Ogulinac-Seljo, in a firefight with the enemy. In the meantime, the 4th Kordun had left for home, taking the roundabout route through Slovenia (along the way, the brigade had effectively destroyed one company of the "Isonzo" near Tanča Gora on 22 September), and was replaced by the 1st Proletarian Battalion.

A period of low-level activity was cut short by the beginning of a major Axis undertaking called "Gorjanci" (the Slovenian name for the Žumberak), aimed at destroying the rebels on both sides of the border. Two-and-a-half reinforced divisions from the XI and V ACs made up the Italian contingent; the blocking line along the eastern and southeastern edge of the mountains was manned by four battalions of the UV. Sensing immediately that the main enemy blow was coming from Slovenia, the two battalions of the 2nd OZ that found themselves in the cauldron opted for a breakthrough towards the right bank of the Kupa. They breached the thin encirclement ring northwest of Jastrebarsko in a brief night action on 31 October and made good their escape almost without losses. As was the case with nearly all other operations of its kind, the "Gorjanci" failed to win the Axis anything but a short respite. Already on 14 November, the guerrillas were back from Kordun, now as a part of the 13th Assault Brigade "Josip Kraš" (later renamed to the 13th Proletarian Brigade "Rade Končar"). Setting itself up in its old bases, the brigade carried a number of attacks on smaller enemy outposts. Although largely successful, these ventures sometimes came with a heavy price: the storming of Novo Selo and Stojdraga, for instance, cost the brigade 13 KIA and 32 WIA.[57]

The Kalnik Detachment was "resurrected" on 10 October 1942 by using about 160 volunteers from Slavonian and Banija units. By early November, this number had doubled thanks, in part, to the arrival of one veteran company from the Žumberak after an exhausting 26-day journey. The fact that a guerrilla unit of this size was operating with impunity in this hitherto quiet, solidly Croat region, was bound to provoke a reaction from the NDH authorities. The reaction came in the form of Francetić and one of his black-clad battalions, who immediately started a pursuit. The casualties inflicted on the Partisans by late November amounted to only a handful of men, but the pressure had become unbearable. Consequently, the detachment decided to split up, with each of its three battalions going in a different direction. The 1st went to Mount Medvednica, on the very outskirts of the capital, where it raided a state convalescent home full of enemy personnel. The 2nd went to Mount Bilogora, where it disarmed a unit of 180 Home Guards; its commander, a Serb, was executed. The 3rd Battalion went as far as the River Sutla,

57 *Zbornik*/V/32/423, NDH MOI to NDH MOD (31.8.1942); Guerrazzi, *Slovenia*, p. 109; Boris Balaš, "Ustanak na Žumberku i u Pokuplju", in *Žumberak-Gorjanci (1941-1945)* (Novo Mesto: Dolenjski muzej, 2005), pp. 303-22; Bogdan Mamula, Rudi Bašić, Branko Vurdelja, Dušan Pekić, *Prvi proleterski bataljon Hrvatske* (Karlovac: HAK, 1983), pp. 241-61; Todor Radošević, *Trinaesta proleterska brigada "Rade Končar"* (Belgrade: VIZ, 1984), pp. 19-29; Marjan Južnič, "Sanitetska služba u Narodnooslobodilačkoj vojsci i partizanskim odredima Slovenije 1941-1945", in *Sanitetska*, Vol. III, p. 28.

crossed over into the Third Reich, and liberated five Soviet officers from captivity; treated almost as deities, they were immediately dispatched to the MHQ Croatia. By mid-December, the bulk of the detachment was again back on its namesake mountain, but would not stay there for long. According to the new plan, two if its battalions were to go to Slavonia, while a third would stay behind. After less than two weeks, however, even this small rearguard found it impossible to operate from the Kalnik, so it too headed east. The battalion would eventually manage to find its way to the Bilogora, but not without difficulties. While trying to cross the Križevci–Koprivnica railway line on 30 December, the Partisans ran into the elements of the newly-arrived German 187th Reserve Division (RD), losing seven killed and 10 wounded.[58]

The Moslavina uprising began to experience an upswing in late August 1942, when the local Partisan battalion was joined by three battalions each from Banija and Slavonia. Such an unprecedented concentration of forces did not happen by accident. For some time now, the HQs of the 2nd and 3rd OZs had their sights set on the oil and gas fields at Gojilo, located several kilometers outside of Kutina. Being supplied with first-class intelligence on enemy dispositions, the Partisans, directed by a joint OHQ, launched an all-out assault on the morning of 6 September. The garrison, consisting of only one company of the *Domobrani* and a platoon of over-aged *Landesschützen*, managed to kill 14 and wound 20 attackers before surrendering. Despite the fact that the monthly output of the NDH's oil fields averaged only 823 metric tons, and that the extensive damage caused by the attack would soon be repaired, the whole affair was deeply embarrassing to Zagreb. The *Vojskovođa* (Field Marshal) Slavko Kvaternik, the commander-in-chief of the Home Guard and Pavelić's number-two man, saw himself compelled to write an explanatory letter to Hermann Göring, in which he–unsurprisingly–blamed the debacle on both Serbs in general, and the Serb workers at Gojilo in particular.[59]

The idea of creating a large ad-hoc formation had obviously paid off, and the OHQ remained in place for the next month or so. During this time, the Partisans stormed collaborationist strongholds of Velika Mlinska and Grubišno Polje, and raided the railway stations of Pitomača and Kloštar Podravski on the far side of Mount Bilogora. Yet the biggest action of them all was the assault on Španovica on 6 October 1942. The Slavonian pendant to Kupres and Fazlagića Kula, this large village became synonymous with the Ustasha terror in this part of the country. The punitive expedition–which was carried out by ca. 1,700 Partisans, most of whom were Serbs–had therefore inadvertently acquired crusading overtones. In purely material terms, the operation was only moderately successful: for a price of a dozen killed and four times as many wounded fighters, 44 Ustashe were captured, together with a 100 rifles and a handful of MGs. Politically, the capture and subsequent razing of the village were deemed a great success. After Španovica, the joint staff was dissolved, with individual battalions returning to their native provinces.

During the following months, the Moslavina contingent–now formed into a 400-men detachment–continued with its campaign, at the same time escaping two encirclement attempts made by the 1st HDB MTD. The Partisans' luck did not always hold, however. Acting on a tip promising a rich booty, they laid an ambush for a cargo composition northwest of Kutina in

58 Miličević, *Kalnički*, pp. 77-115; *SZH*/III/757, 776, Kalnik Det. to MHQ Croatia, and to 2nd OZ (17 and 21.12.1942, respectively).
59 Vukašin Karanović, *Moslavački partizanski odred 1941-1945.* (Kutina: SUBNOR, 1981), pp. 91-99; Tomasevich, *Occupation*, p. 641; NARA/T315/2258/1487-91, Attack on Gojilo on 6.9.1942.

the evening hours of 21 December. Not before the firing had started did the attackers realize that they were actually up against an armored train; the detachment not only ended up empty-handed, but also lost five of its fighters that night.[60]

In early October 1942, the MHQ Croatia received the first official dispatches from the 3rd OZ in four months. According to these, the NOP in Slavonia was on the march: the Partisans, who had in the meantime formed a second detachment, controlled about 100 villages scattered across the local mountains. From here, they were raiding enemy settlements, interdicting traffic, and sabotaging the harvest. The Germans tried to put an end to their depredations by launching Operation "Psunj" (15-22 August) with five of their own battalions under the ubiquitous General Heinrich Borowski, but the operation was a total flop (only 25 counted enemy dead). By mid-October, the local Partisan leadership felt confident enough to form its first semi-regular unit, the 1st (later renamed 12th) Slavonian Brigade. At the same time, they were careful not to neglect the more traditional fighting methods. In order to spread the uprising into the hitherto dormant eastern part of the province, small "guerrilla groups" were formed of dedicated fighters, whose task was to carry out acts of sabotage, assassinate collaborationists, hold rallies and disseminate propaganda material.[61]

In addition to the standard array of NDH forces, the Slavonian Partisans faced one other enemy: the Ethnic Germans. The vast majority of ca. 170,000 *Volksdeutsche* lived in the fertile lands between the Sava, Drava and Danube. As in Banat, they enjoyed a high degree of autonomy, including the right to raise their own units. Nominally a part of the UV, the *Einsatzstaffel der deutschen Mannschaft* (ESDM; roughly, Action Squad of German Militia) had one active and three reserve battalions, plus support units, giving it a total strength of about 3,600 men at the end of 1942. Up to 4,400 others served in the German units of the Home Guard (e.g. two *Jäger* battalions and one mountain battery), or were "leased" to the Wehrmacht, mostly as interpreters. The native German units were originally conceived as a self-defense force, and with good reason: the authorities recorded 81 cases of guerrilla attacks against the lives and property of the *Volksdeutsche* during the second half of the year in Slavonia alone.[62] By this time, however, most of the best recruits were serving far from their homes, being attached to the 714th and 718th IDs as sorely needed reinforcements.

On 28 October, the "Prinz Eugen" Battalion of the ESDM, supported by the II/741st IR and six aircraft, surprised the 1st Slavonian Brigade on the southern slopes of Mount Krndija. Demoralized by an intense aerial bombing, something most of the fighters had never experienced before, the brigade retreated pell-mell, losing 18 KIA and 28 WIA. Eight weeks later, the Partisans got a chance to return the favor. After disarming the HDB outposts at Voćin and Podravska Slatina, the brigade (more precisely its 4th Battalion) stormed the village of Orljavac.

60 *Zbornik*/V/8/112-21, 133-34 (3rd OZ, Report Španovica, and 3rd OZ to MHQ, 7 and 21.10.1942, respectively); Karanović, *Moslavački*, pp. 108-52.

61 NARA/T501/248/463-64 (BhS to WBSO, 12.8.1942), 483-84, 491-2, 505, 508, 518, 529 (BhS, Daily reports, 15-22.8.1942); *Zbornik*/V/8/72-76, MHQ Croatia to SHQ (7.10.1942); *Zbornik*/V/9/243, 3rd OZ to MHQ Croatia (20.11.1942).

62 Tomasevich, *Occupation*, pp. 283-86; TsAMO/500/12451/616/120-26, 203-10 (GEGC/Leader, List of bandit attacks, 1.10-30.12.1942, and 1.7-30.9.1942, respectively), 156 (Civilian losses, 1.1.1943). According to the latter document, in the period up to 31 December 1942 (the starting date unclear, probably 1 January 1942), 113 Ethnic German civilians were killed and 88 abducted by the guerrillas on the territory of the NDH.

More than 50 members of the aforementioned ESDM unit were killed or captured on this occasion, bringing the irrevocable losses suffered by the Ethnic German armed formations in 1942 to 222. Satisfied with the achieved level of regularization in the units of the 3rd OZ, the MHQ created two more brigades with one stroke of the pen and immediately made them a part of the new 4th (later 12th) Slavonian Division on 30 December 1942.[63]

The harvest question has been mentioned several times, but nowhere was it more pronounced than in the "breadbasket" of the NDH, Syrmia. According to German estimates, in the summer of 1942, Pavelić's regime could count on barely one half of the last year's crop yield. The Partisans, for their part, were determined to deny it even that. By early July, their attacks from the Fruška Gora "had become so frequent, that it is already superfluous to list every single one of them". The crops and the harvesting machinery were especially hard hit, but other targets were not neglected. Individual German soldiers were prohibited from traveling between Ruma and Klenak by train for fear of attack, and on 5 August, the guerrillas successfully raided the ammunition dump at Vrdnik. Even though the rumors about the quantities of destroyed wheat turned out to be largely unfounded, the Axis proceeded with their plans calling for a radical showdown with the guerrilla menace in these parts. The Ustashe used this as a pretext for carrying out an anti-Serb pogrom so massive and ugly that even the German top brass–some of whom had complained only a little while earlier that there were "too many arrests and too few executions in Syrmia"–felt compelled to demand the removal of key perpetrators.[64]

In military terms, the key to the pacification of the province lay in the thorough cleansing of the Fruška Gora. In stark contrast to the last sweep carried out in the area (10-17 July 1942), which involved modest forces (three NDH battalions), and ended with even more modest results (four Partisans killed, three captured, no weapons found), the upcoming operation would rightly be dubbed the "Great Offensive" by the locals. Borowski and his staff, fresh from the campaigns in Bosanska Krajina, Banija, and Slavonia, were chosen to lead a force of five German and five HDB infantry battalions, supported by Hungarian gunboats and the NDH air force. According to the plan, the guerrillas should first be denied maneuver space by expelling them from the eastern and western ends of the mountain; then, the Axis main attack, launched from the south, would press the enemy against the Danube and destroy him. When Operation "Fruška Gora" commenced on 24 August, the numerically much weaker Partisans (some 460 in all) could do little else but try to avoid the blow. The Podunavski Detachment succeeded in doing so almost immediately by finding refuge in the corn fields around Ruma. Its sister unit, named after the Syrmian mountain, was not quite as lucky: while the bulk of it managed to reach the safety of the Bosut Forrests, one of its companies perished in the cauldron, along with the provincial HQ. By 4 September, the sweep was largely over. For the price of 11 KIA and 14 WIA, the

63 Ibid., 157-59 (Deployment of units, 31.12.1942), 160 (Losses, 1.1.1943); TsAMO/500/12451/621/32-34 (ESDM Btl. "Prinz Eugen", Activity report, 25-30.10.1942), 67-74 (Report Orljavac, 29.12.1942); *Zbornik*/V/9/28, 1st Slavonian Bde. to 3rd OZ (2.11.1942); *Zbornik*/V/10/316, 12th Slavonian Bde. to 3rd OZ (28.12.1942); *Enciklopedija*, Vol. VII, p. 384 and Vol. VIII, p. 665.

64 2,180 bodies were exhumed on the main execution sites alone: Korb, *Massengewalt*, pp. 328-69. See also NARA/T501/351, NARA/T501/248/377, and NARA/T501/352/29, BhS, Diary (26.7, 3.8, and 27.9.1942, respectively); *Zbornik*/I/17/92 (GEGC/East Syrmia, Report, 6.7.1942), 143-44 (5th Coy./2nd ESDM Btl., Report, 5.8.1942), 148 (Vilko Begić, Situation in Syrmia, 6.8.1942).

units reported having killed 369 and captured further 1,333 "bandits"; the Partisans admitted to losing about 30 fighters.[65]

In the end, the terror and the offensive brought but a brief respite. Already on 20 September 1942, an Ustasha patrol was ambushed near the mountain's summit, losing the same number of men as had been lost during the recent operations. Three days later, the local civilian authorities requested military reinforcements, adding that the situation was "almost the same as before". The center of guerrilla activity moved to the swampy and heavily forested area between the Sava and Bosut Rivers, and the arrival of the 6th Eastern Bosnian Brigade just added fuel to the fire. On 14 October, the Bosnians and Syrmians ambushed a company (not a battalion as often claimed in Yugoslav historiography) of the 737th IR/717th ID, killing 23 and wounding 15 Germans, and capturing an ammunition wagon and a mobile kitchen. In the meantime, the three local Partisan detachments were reorganized into one named the 3rd Detachment of the 3rd OZ, which had grown to over 800 armed and further 100 unarmed fighters by the beginning of November. Feeling that the unit had become too big for its own good, and worried about the possibility of an enemy winter offensive, the Syrmian leadership decided to accompany the 6th Eastern Bosnian on its forthcoming expedition against the Majevica; out of four battalions, only one would remain in Syrmia. For the HQ of the 3rd OZ, this "opportunistic" and "gravely mistaken" decision was tantamount to taking a winter break in the middle of the war. By the time this ill-founded criticism had reached the Syrmians, however, they had already become a permanent feature of the Bosnian war landscape.[66]

The Partisan campaign against the railways had reached new heights in the summer and fall of 1942. During this period, the Germans recorded 284 acts of sabotage in their own occupation zone in the NDH, plus 181 more in the Italian one. In order to protect the heavily threatened main line between the Slovene border and Belgrade, the Germans upgraded the existing railway security section under the auspices of the 718th ID into an independent staff controlling five Wehrmacht battalions and all the NDH units deployed there with the same purpose. By late November, 29 fortified towers were in function, with additional 111 in various stages of construction or planning (for comparison, Serbia had 177 and 64, respectively). Despite all these precautionary measures, the guerrillas were finding their way to targets with alarming regularity. In addition to the already mentioned episodes, a couple of more examples should be mentioned, like the burning of 17 carriages on the Hercegovac station in Moslavina on 11 September, and, especially, the derailment of a large cargo composition at Ličke Jesenice on 25 August. On this occasion, the fighters of the 1st Lika Brigade found 700,000 cigarettes, some of which were sent to the rear area as gifts. The remaining spoils were divided up between the attackers, with families of killed fighters receiving their share as well.

Apart from these and similar attacks carried out by the NOVJ line formations as a part of their everyday activities, there were also those that were carried out by special demolition

65 Ibid., pp. 219-24 (HDB Srijem Bde., Report, 25.8.1942), 246 (Kasche to *Reichssicherheitshauptamt* [RSHA], 4.9.1942); NARA/T315/2241/1076-78, BhS to HQ Borowski (21.8.1942); *Oslobodilački*, Vol. I, pp. 317-18.

66 *Zbornik*/I/17/260-63 (NDH MoI to Poglavnik's HQ, 23.9.1942), 272 (HDB GHQ, Daily report, 21.9.1942); NARA/T315/2262/977, 717th ID, Daily report (15.10.1942); *Zbornik*/I/16/107 (3rd Det./3rd OZ, Strength return, 2.11.1942), 211-12 (3rd OZ to 3rd Det., 2.12.1942); Petovar, *Šesta*, pp. 175-92.

groups. Most of the Partisan sappers north of the Sava were trained *in situ* by Hariš "the Thunderer" in his capacity as the chief of Sabotage Section (*Diverzantska sekcija*) of the MHQ Croatia. After he had finished training 20 hand-picked men from the 3rd OZ in November, Hariš dispatched his deputy to Moslavina in order to do the same, while he himself went to Bosnia. By the end of the year, even territorial units like the 3rd Lika Detachment were starting to group particularly gifted "wreckers" into separate platoons. All these details worked primarily with explosives, which were a rare and prized commodity (unexploded ordnance and raided mining facilities were the main sources). For example, mines were used to great effect on 15 August (21 dead and 20 wounded passengers; contrary to Yugoslav claims, no German servicemen were among them), 30-31 August (three German armored trains derailed; the train No. 23 was heavily damaged, losing one KIA and 37 MIA), and 22 December (a carriage reserved for the Wehrmacht attached to a train composition was "crushed", resulting in at least 15 KIA and 20 WIA).[67]

3.5 Slovenia: Bloody Summer

Italian generals began discussing a general "cleansing" of Ljubljana Province already in early June 1942. Since the bitter experience had shown that half-measures led nowhere, this would be a maximum-effort operation. The XI AC would receive two additional divisions (the recently formed 153rd ID "Macerata" from Italy and the veteran "Cacciatori delle Alpi" from Herzegovina), six Blackshirt battalions, and a number of other units, bringing its total strength to ca. 65-70,000 personnel. This meant that there was now one Italian serviceman to every five inhabitants, probably the greatest density ever achieved by any army of occupation on the Yugoslav territory. General Mario Robotti, the CO of the XI AC, did not mince words when it came to the nature of the upcoming offensive: the Italian supremacy and prestige were to be restored "even if it meant the death of every Slovene and the destruction of whole Slovenia". The operation, subdivided into eleven phases, was scheduled to begin in mid-July and expected to last about two months, during which the entire province would be methodically combed. The main blow would be directed against the principal liberated territory located in the southeastern corner of the country; this was the home to the majority of the estimated 4-5,000 Partisans (largely from the 3rd and 5th Groups of Detachments) in the Italian occupation zone. The NOP leadership did expect some kind of enemy reaction to the movement's latest successes, but did not think it would come before August. Not even the massive *razzia* in Ljubljana from late June–during which the occupation authorities checked every fourth citizen (ca. 20,000) and detained almost 3,000 suspects, thus shattering the OF's underground organization–could convince them that something was afoot.[68]

67 NARA/T501/351, and NARA/T501/248/603, BhS, Activity report (11-20.7.1942, and 21-31.8.1942, respectively); NARA/T501/248/491, BhS, Daily report (17.8.1942); NARA/T501/264/982, DGIA to OKW (21.8.1942); *Zbornik*/V/6/284-86, 1st Assault Bde. to MHQ Croatia (28.8.1942); *Zbornik*/V/7/364-65, Police area Bjelovar, Report Hercegovac (18.9.1942); *Zbornik*/V/9/243, 3rd OZ to MHQ Croatia (20.11.1942); *Zbornik*/V/10/62 (3rd Lika Det. to MHQ Croatia, 6.12.1942), 487-88 (Police area Nova Gradiška to HDB GHQ, 22.12.1942); *Zbornik*/XII/2/842, WBSO, Situation appraisal (29.11.1942); Krizman, *Pavelić*, p. 468.

68 Tone Ferenc (ed.), *Fašisti brez krinke: dokumenti 1941-1942* (Maribor: Obzorja, 1987), pp. 87-88, 389-90, Memorandum command conference XI AC (26.6.1942); Dr. Ivo Juvančič, "Izvodi iz okupatorovih

The summer offensive–known to the Italians simply as *ciclo operativo 'Slovenia'* ("Operations Cycle 'Slovenia'"), and to the Yugoslavs as *Roška ofanziva* in reference to Kočevski Rog–began on 0900 hours on 16 July 1942 after an artillery and aerial preparation.[69] Having observed first-hand the debacle at Užice, Kardelj was determined "to be independent from liberated territory", i.e. not to get drawn into a pitched battle over a fixed objective, no matter how important it appeared at the moment. Instead, the MHQ instructed the units to avoid frontal combat, but stick close to the enemy and pester him with small-scale attacks against his flanks and rear. Although they looked fine on paper, these instructions could hardly be put into practice, for the psychosis of retreat, along with the shock caused by the massive terror unleashed by the occupation forces, had already set in. As a result, the guerrillas were trying to avoid all contact with the XI AC's steamroller as it passed over the massifs of Krim, Mokrec, and Velika Gora. By mid-August, the Italians had turned their attention to Kočevski Rog. They knew this densely forested area housed guerrilla bases, but they did not know that the entire leadership of the uprising, including the CK KPS, MHQ Slovenia, and OF's Executive Council, was also there. Ivan Maček-Matija, one of the escapees from Sremska Mitrovica and the then-head of the MHQ, observed candidly after the war that he and his colleagues became the victims of their own wishful thinking. They namely chose to believe the rumors–spread by the Italians themselves–that the enemy troop transports headed for Kočevski Rog were, in fact, destined for the Axis expedition against Suez, which was to be launched from the Turkish territory.

Now the Partisans found themselves surprised and surrounded by two full enemy divisions, reinforced by elements of another two. The liquidation of the cauldron lasted from 14 to 23 August; during this time, the bulk of the guerrilla fighting units managed to break out, but the leadership remind behind. Luckily for its members, the Italians had failed to discover their masterfully camouflaged hideouts, even though they meticulously combed the area. Although it would not be formally concluded until 4 November, the offensive was already beginning to lose steam. The upcoming (and already discussed) operations in Gorski Kotar compelled the *Supersloda* to transfer the "Granatieri di Sardegna" to the V AC. Nevertheless, the XI AC went ahead with the plan, first sweeping the area between Kočevje and the section of the demarcation line to the east of Ljubljana, and then turning southeast again. The cycle was ended with operations on both sides of the border with the NDH (the clash at Poloj, and the joint enterprise with Pavelić's forces against the Gorjanci/Žumberak marked its tenth and eleventh phases, respectively).[70]

What were the results of the *Regio Esercito*'s great summer offensive in Ljubljana Province? For the price of 47 KIA and 133 WIA, the Italians reported having killed 965 guerrillas in combat, a further 791 were executed, and 1,136 were captured between 16 July and 15 September; at

dokumenata", in *Ljubljana u borbi 1941-45: zbornik sjećanja* (Belgrade: VIZ, 1978), p. 330; Slavko Odić, Slavko Komarica, *Partizanska obavještajna služba 1941-1942: šta se stvarno događalo* (Zagreb: Centar za informacije i publicitet, 1988), Vol. II, pp. 184-85.

69 The XI AC was supported by four air squadrons (36 machines), which represented a half of the *Supersloda*'s total air effectives. Operating from the bases at Ljubljana and Ronchi, these aircraft carried out at least 322 sorties until early November. This, in turn, represented ca. 10 percent of the total number of sorties flown during this year. Altogether 11 airplanes were lost in 1942 in *Supersloda*'s operational area, three of them through AA fire: Mikić, *Italijanska*, pp. 56, 68, 137.

70 *DLRS*/II/320-22, Kardelj to Ivo-Lola Robar (14.7.1942); Odić and Komarica, *Partizanska*, Vol. II, pp. 186-88; Klanjšček, *Slovenija*, pp. 140-46, 152-54.

the same time, some 800 pieces of light infantry weapons were secured. Yugoslav sources speak of about 1,000 killed or captured Partisans, plus another 900 who returned to their homes; combined, this amounts to ca. 38 percent of the initial strength of the Partisan army. "In material sense, we took quite a beating in this fight", Kardelj admitted, especially lamenting the loss of the forest bases together with "a beautiful hospital, fitted with the most modern equipment that cost [us] millions". Painful as these losses were, they were not as damaging to the OF as was the loss of influence among the population. Demoralized by the reprisals, the people began to turn to the local anti-communists, who included the monarchists, members of the People's Party (the Slovene equivalent of the Croatian HSS), and right-wing members of the "Sokol" gymnastics movement. Backed by the influential Catholic Church and profiting from the recent Italian decision to expand their native auxiliary corps in occupied Yugoslavia, these groups became the core of the Slovenian MVAC. By the end of the year, the collaborationist forces were divided into three battalions (colloquially known as "Legion of Death", *Legija smrti*), plus dozens of smaller detachments of the so-called "Village Guards" (*Vaške straže*) scattered across the countryside, for a total of ca. 4,500 men.[71]

Spurred on by recent offensive experience and the rise of a domestic foe, the Slovene leadership hastened the process of regularization. Groups of detachments were dissolved; the number of detachments was reduced to eight, and that of independent battalions to five. The "Tone Tomšič" Brigade (the 1st Slovenian) was reconstituted already in mid-July 1942, followed by three more (the 2nd "Matija Gubec", the 3rd "Ivan Cankar", and the 4th "Ljubo Šercer") in the period late August-early October. In addition to the fact that they all bore honorary names, the Slovene brigades also differed from their counterparts in other Yugoslav provinces by their smaller size (on average, less than 500 fighters apiece). Despite their low strength and lack of heavy weapons, these formations were expected to carry out more complicated battlefield tasks, the most important of which was the storming of MVAC outposts. The main problem, however, was the lack of experienced officers on all levels. In the already cited letter from 20 September, Kardelj asked Tito to spare a handful of veterans for service in Slovenia. In response, the Partisan supreme commander sent him his chief of staff, Jovanović, along with a dozen junior officers (mostly of Serbian and Montenegrin origin) from the Proletarian brigades. By early December, Jovanović helped organize four OZs, with the 1st covering Dolenjska, the 2nd Notranjska, and the 4th Štajerska; the 3rd OZ, covering Primorska and the western part of Gorenjska, was known as the "Alpine" zone. Despite his difficult personality and meddling in political matters, this professional soldier made a valuable contribution towards further development of the Slovene Partisan army. The same can be said for the men who came with him. Being initially deployed as deputy commanders or chiefs of staff until they learned the language and acclimatized themselves to the new environment, these *grognards* could share the extensive knowledge they gathered during the first eighteen months of the war with their comrades from the north.[72]

71 Ibid., p. 154; Guerazzi, *Slovenia*, p. 92; Tomasevich, *Occupation*, pp. 106-09; *DLRS*/X/34-35, Kardelj to Ivo-Lola Robar (12.8.1942); *DLRS*/III/207-08, Kardelj to Tito (20.9.1942).

72 Anić, Joksimović, Gutić, *Narodnooslobodilačka*, pp. 157-58, 224-25; *Zbornik*/II/6/380, Tito to 2nd NOVJD (9.11.1942); *Zbornik*/II/7/321-24, Kardelj to Tito (12.1.1943); *DLRS*/VII/77, OF/Executive, Situation report (8.5.1943).

The Slovenes also profited from the fact that they shared the liberated territory along the Kupa with the MHQ Croatia. This allowed the Croatian units not only to seek refuge in Slovenia in times of need, but also to lend a hand when necessary. For instance, the task of storming the fortified MVAC outpost at Suhor on 26 November 1942 was entrusted to a battalion of the 13th Assault Brigade, while the 3rd Slovenian (minus one company that was attached to the Croats) stood ready to repel any possible relief attempt from the outside. The loss of Suhor with its garrison of about 120 men compelled the Italians to abandon a number of other, smaller outposts in the area. The partnership between the two brigades continued well into December, with one Slovene battalion participating in the taking of Krašić in Croatia. By this time, the Slovene brigades–in this particular case, the "Tone Tomšič" and "Matija Gubec"–were already capable of reducing smaller targets by themselves, as shown by the example of Ajdovec (taken on 12 December, 70 White Guards captured) and the castle of Dob (27 December, 19 Blackshirts killed or executed). In addition to attacking enemy garrisons, these Partisan formations were also beginning to target lines of communication, tearing up tracks on the sections of the railway line Trebnje–Sevnica and Ljubljana–Novo Mesto. Heinrich Himmler concluded his scathing report on the conditions in Ljubljana Province, submitted to Adolf Hitler in December 1942, by stating that the "initial improvement" caused by the great Italian offensive was all but gone, and that the guerrillas, who were already "more numerous" and "better equipped and led" than before, were behaving as if the Italian administration and their "four-and-a-half divisions [sic] [...] did not exist at all."[73]

What the *Reichsführer SS* (RFSS) was really concerned about was the possibility of the uprising spilling over into the German zone. The failed attempt of the 2nd Group of Detachments to cross the Sava at Janče and reach Štajerska in late May 1942 was already discussed. One month later, the same Partisan unit tried its luck along the section of the demarcation line west of Ljubljana. The move coincided with the "thorough cleansing" of the occupied Slovene lands (Action "Enzian") that was ordered by Himmler himself on 25 June. As a consequence, the number of mobile police battalions in Gorenjska rose to six by mid-summer, half of them belonging to the newly-created and superbly equipped 18th SS Mountain Police Regiment (PR). From early July through early September, the Partisans tried to get past this thick protective screen and, at the same time, avoid encirclement in the mountains northwest of Škofja Loka. Ultimately they succeeded, but at a heavy price: two battalions had to turn back, while the remaining two reached their objective only after weeks of grueling forced marches over separate routes. Out of the original 541 men who embarked on the mission, only about 120 remained. With the departure of the 2nd Group of Detachments, the Germans turned their sights on its sister unit, Gorenjska's own 1st Group of Detachments. Within one week (9-15 September), this formation lost its commander and the former Spanish fighter Jože Gregorčič (its *politkom* would be killed several weeks later) along with at least 75 fighters, more than two-thirds of whom were KIA, and the rest captured.[74]

73 Lado Ambrožič-Novljan, *Cankarjeva brigada* (Ljubljana: Partizanska knjiga, 1975), pp. 61-72; Franci Strle, *Tomšičeva brigada* (Ljubljana: Partizanska knjiga, 1986), Vol. II, pp. 378-85; NARA/T175/124, Himmler to Hitler (14.1.1943).

74 *Enciklopedija*, Vol. III, pp. 326-27; Vol. IV, pp. 301 and 399; Vol. VII, pp. 26-27; Marcus Schreiner Božič, "Enzian–August bis Oktober 1942 in Gorenjska", in Dežman (ed.), *Nemci*, pp. 79-94; Vinko Demšar, "Pregled NOB na Škofjeloškem", *Loški razgledi*, 19:1 (1972), pp. 86-87.

The situation in Štajerska was far from rosy. Although the provincial 1st Battalion had in the meantime begun to act as a single unit again, its activities during the early and mid-summer 1942 were limited to the attacks on the mines at Huda Jama and Liboje, as well as a handful of other, smaller actions. In addition to this battalion, there were also independent companies at the Kozjansko and Slovenske Gorice, but they were both routed during August; the same goes for a group of native fighters, sent by the MHQ, who tried to infiltrate the province from the south. Having now more than 100 extra veterans at its disposal allowed the 2nd Group of Detachments to reorganize all the forces in Štajerska into four battalions. As a result, the Germans immediately noticed an increase in guerrilla activity. For example, from 20 October to 4 November, the Savinjski Battalion assassinated a pair of Nazi officials and ambushed two buses belonging to the *Reichspost*, killing 11 guards and wounding 16. The authorities launched three operations against this troublesome Partisan unit from late September to mid-November, involving at first three, then five, and finally eight battalions of troops. After the Savinjski Battalion had been routed with the loss of 24 KIA and WIA, the center of guerrilla activity moved to the Pohorje Mountains. The local battalion was credited with no less than 105 actions, including six acts of serious sabotage. Most of these took part before the beginning of December, when the Partisans started preparing winter quarters, hoping to spend the next several months in relative peace; this hope, as we shall see, will remain unfulfilled.[75]

Before moving onto the next sub-chapter, a few words on the German COIN practices in Slovenia. First, the trend of increasing utilization of local resources for anti-Partisan struggle found its expression in the creation of *Wehrmannschaftsbataillon Süd*. Formed in April1 1942, the unit originally consisted of volunteers chosen from the ranks of the paramilitary wing of *Steierischer Heimatsbund* (the roof organization encompassing practically the entire population of Štajerska apart from those considered unfit for Germanization). By July, the steadily deteriorating security situation compelled the authorities to call up 500 conscripts and plan the strengthening of the militia's nine companies to 2,500 men. Although well equipped with light infantry weapons, these *vermani* (sing. *verman*) proved to be ill-suited for active campaigning. For this reason, the battalion was disbanded in mid-November, its personnel being transferred to the newly-created Self-protection Force (*Selbstschutz*), or employed as police auxiliaries.

Unlike the "Janissaries"–as the members of the *Wehrmannschaft* were sometimes derisively called in reference to the fact that the majority of them were Slovenes–Anti-guerrilla Bands or *Gegenbanden* were seemingly precisely what the occupation forces needed. In pursuance of the old, yet hard to achieve concept of fighting the guerrillas the guerrilla way, the Gestapo in Škofja Loka formed a small unit composed of 40 hand-picked policemen plus 28 Slovenes (including some renegade Partisans), probably sometime in the early summer of 1942. Wearing NOP insignia and dressed in shabby civilian clothes (which would earn them the nickname *raztrganci* or "Ragamuffins"), these men were expected to look, talk, and most importantly, fight like the guerrillas. The first results looked promising, especially compared to the classic military operations taking place in Gorenjska at that time. A regular force of about 5,000 men could boast of only 14 dead and 17 captured Partisans at the end of one such undertaking; the original

75 Tomaž Teropšič, *Štajerska v plamenih. Taktika, orožje in oprema štirih vojsk na Štajerskem v drugi svetovni vojni.* (Brežice: Posavski muzej, 2012), pp. 60-61, 188-91; Tone Ferenc, "Wehrmannschaft v boju proti narodnoosvobodilni vojski na Štajerskem", *Letopis Muzeja narodne osvoboditve LRS v Ljubljani*, 2 (1958), pp. 98-104.

Gegenbande took only half a day to kill eight and capture five enemies. By the end of the year, the Gestapo had set up a special training course in Krško for ca. 350-400 suitable candidates, whose units were scheduled to become operational in the early 1943.[76]

3.6 Serbia: Aćimović's Offensive

The second half of 1942 was probably the most difficult period of the war for the NOP in Serbia. The fear of reprisals kept most of the population away from the Partisans, which made recruitment and procurement of supplies a difficult task. The number of active fighters in the I BOC's area of responsibility in the late summer and fall was estimated at between 280 and 450, which is probably not far from the truth. Requisitioning of foodstuffs and burning of municipal archives were their main activities; only one case in five involved demolition or exchange of fire with Axis forces. The number of sabotage acts also dropped sharply: there were only 11 Partisan attacks against mining or industrial installations during the last six months of 1942 in whole of Serbia, which is comparable to the figure recorded in August 1941 in the area of 714th ID alone. The statistics on railway sabotage compiled by various Axis agencies differ, but they all tend to support the conclusion that it was a relatively peaceful period, especially when compared with the NDH. The documents of Serbian State Railways speak of anywhere between 29 and 39 cases of sabotage, whilst Bader's staff recorded 26 incidents between late August and mid-November alone. It should be noted that Mihailović's resurgent organization was responsible for at least a part of these incidents, a result of the Allied-sponsored, but ultimately failed campaign against the Axis supply lines for the African theater of operations.[77]

Historiography of the socialist period makes much of the so-called "Black *Troikas*" (*crne trojke*), special Chetnik execution teams that gained notoriety by slitting throats of all real and imagined enemies. The fact remains, however, that the Partisans employed similar tactics, the only difference being that their own groups, usually consisting of three to five reliable fighters, were prohibited from using "sadistic methods" in dispatching their targets. In early November 1942, the MHQ Serbia admonished the southern detachments for making these executions their staple activity, and warned them of losing their distinct Partisan character and becoming "brigands". The size of the few open skirmishes that took place in Serbia during this period paled in comparison to what was happening to the west of the Drina. The Suvobor Detachment ambushed a SFK detail near Valjevo on 26 September, causing seven KIA and one WIA. The clashes between the Jablanica-Pasjača and Jastrebac Detachments and the SSW outside of Prokuplje and Lebane on 15 November and 10 December, respectively, resulted in seven KIA, one WIA, and seven MIA among the gendarmes. The 1st Šumadija Detachment tried storming the small town of Sopot on 12 December, with no result. Attacks on the Germans were few and far between; for all their wartime bravado and the embellished post-war image as

76 Ibid., pp. 81-109; *NOS*, Vol. III, 262-63, 332-33; NARA/T175/140, Chief of Security Police and Security Service [*Chef der Sicherheitspolizei und des SD*, SiPO/SD], Combat against bandits in Upper Carniola (18.8.1942).

77 *Zbornik*/I/4/294-303, I BOC/Intel., Situation reports July-November 1942; *Zbornik*/I/21/298-304, 316-22, 322-29, 330-37, 346-50, 355-61, SSW, Enemy activity report (July-December 1942); ARMB/SSR/3-1942/156, List of major incidents 1942; see also Summaries 1942, pp. 9-12; Trew, *Mihailović*, pp. 147-61.

uncompromising fighters, the Partisans thought it wiser not to provoke the savage reprisals. On one occasion in early October, they even acquiesced to the pleas of terrified peasants to spare and release a German serviceman whom they had just wounded (similar incidents were known to have happened during 1943 as well).[78]

The situation in various parts of the country was as follows: In what used to be the cradle of the insurgency, the western and central regions of Serbia, the NOP now had only one permanent detachment, the 1st Šumadija. The decision to reform the Čačak and Suvobor Detachments in late summer and early fall of 1942 proved rash, as the Partisans themselves acknowledged. The former had to be disbanded only days after it had been created, while the latter was routed by the Serbian collaborationist forces outside Valjevo in late October. The 1st Šumadija itself could not operate as a single unit; each of its three companies (ca. 80 fighters in all) acted independently of one another in their respective home areas. The same was true for the Požarevac Detachment, which lost one of its companies in early December to a sudden collaborationist attack; this reduced the unit's overall strength to only about 40 men. Direct enemy action was not the only danger facing these small bands of guerrillas. The constant fear of capture or death combined with protracted periods of seclusion and spells of frantic marching could have disastrous consequences for the inner cohesion of a unit, as exemplified by the tragic events in Eastern Serbia in late 1942. Having succumbed to maniacal paranoia after experiencing first-hand the recent Axis offensive around Niš (see below), one Party functionary began arresting fighters on trumped-up charges of espionage. He went on to execute altogether 16 people– one-fourth of his detachment–before the local OK could intervene and sentence him to death as an enemy agent in turn.[79]

By early summer 1942, Southern Serbia was still a thorn in the Axis side. The already mentioned Bulgarian undertaking around Niš in the last week of June was not yet over when Nedić started lobbying for another major sweep of the same area. The I BOC could not be involved this time because two of its divisions were being rotated back to Bulgaria. After some deliberation, Bader's staff allowed the Serbian collaborationist forces to organize and carry out the operation by themselves, and granted them close to 1,000,000 rounds of rifle ammunition for this purpose. The undertaking, known colloquially as "Aćimović's Offensive" (after the minister of interior, Milan Aćimović), involved a mobile force of about 2,000 men plus another 2,000 deployed on guard duties. Considering the numerical weakness of the NOP in these parts, this was a sizable figure indeed; yet it was not the numbers that made this offensive dangerous, but rather the way in which it was carried out. Unlike the heavy-handed tactics preferred by the Bulgarians, Aćimović opted for a far more subtle approach. The guerrilla ranks would be shattered by an offer of amnesty; their base would be eliminated by the permanent occupation of the villages that harbored them. This, in turn, would enable the peasants to

78 *Zbornik*/I/4/45 (MHQ Serbia to PK Serbia, end of July 1942), 132 (Leskovac Det. to OK Leskovac, 12.10.1942), 177-82 and 224-27 (1st Šumadija Det. to MHQ Serbia, 20.11 and 16.12.1942, respectively), 221 (MHQ Serbia, Circular, 5.12.1942), 373 (SSW, Intel bulletin, 26.9.1942), 402 and 412-13 (Nedić MoI, Daily report, 19.11 and 12.12.1942, respectively); *Zbornik*/I/20/256-57, PK Serbia, Circular (5.11.1942); *Zbornik*/IX/2/251, OK Aranđelovac to PK Serbia (7.11.1942); *Zbornik*/I/5/141, OK Mladenovac to OK Aranđelovac (1.5.1943).

79 Slobodan Bosiljčić, *Srbija u narodnooslobodilačkoj borbi: Istočna Srbija* (Belgrade: Nolit, 1963), pp. 63-88; Vitorović, *Centralna*, pp. 382-406; *Enciklopedija*, Vol. IX, p. 254; Pantelić, Marinković, and Nikšić, *Čačanski*, pp. 318-22.

overcome their fear of the Partisans and join the government-sponsored village guards. Using these volunteers and deserters as guides, troops would then seek out the remaining guerrillas in their hideouts, at the same time making sure that all the wells and sources of food in the vicinity were properly secured. The first phase of the offensive, targeting the Nišava and Ozren Detachments (ca. 160 active fighters) located to the north and northeast of Niš, started on 12 July and lasted for four weeks.

The novel approach did not fail to produce results, as even NDH observers had to admit: during this period, some 460 suspects were brought in, together with 17 MGs and large quantities of other weapons and supplies. Many of them were former Partisans who defected, and some had even killed or captured their officers before doing so. As a result, these two detachments had practically ceased to exist as fighting formations. From 11 August onwards, Nedić's forces turned their attention to the old guerrilla stronghold of Jastrebac. Informed beforehand that a major enemy action was in the offing, the leaders of the Jastrebac and Rasina Detachments (at least ca. 150 active members) decide to divide their commands into companies: some of them would maneuver on their home terrains, while the others would try to draw some of the enemy's attention by moving to the valleys of the South Morava and Rasina Rivers. The tactic worked: after three weeks of searching, the collaborationist troops could produce only the bodies of nine Partisans who, surrounded in a dugout with no chance of escape, committed suicide rather than be taken alive.[80]

By mid-autumn 1942, the NOP presence in the mountains around Leskovac had become a matter of growing concern for the Axis. This was not solely due to their everyday activities, but also because of the ability to export unrest to neighboring regions. For instance, in late September, the Babički Detachment sent 36 volunteers to the mountains north of Skopje with the aim of joining the local Partisans. The Vranje Detachment, as this group was called, was ambushed on 8 October by the Bulgarians (who, apparently, acted on a tip from the Albanian population), losing a third of its strength in the process. The remainder continued with the mission, demolishing the mine at Lojane in Macedonia before eventually returning home. Three weeks after the ambush, the Axis commanders in Niš agreed on a joint action against the Leskovac Detachment on Mount Kukavica. Codenamed "Rudolf", the offensive opened on 2 November and ended three days later. Although up to 5,000 personnel (including one German police battalion) were involved in one capacity or another, the net result was disappointing: 35 suspects were shot and 10 rifles found. After that, the Axis turned their sights on the Babički Detachment, which lost practically all of its political officers in a clash with the Bulgarians on 12 November, but otherwise remained intact. Finally, the I BOC and the SSW encircled and swept the Radan and Pasjača during the second half of November trying to catch the Jablanica-Pasjača Detachment. For once, low numerical strength turned to be an asset, rather than a liability: this entire Partisan unit thus went into hiding in a village not far from the major enemy garrison at Lebane, and stayed there until the danger had passed.[81]

80 NARA/T501/351, BhS, Diary (7 and 11.7.1942), and BhS, Daily report (22.7.1942); Borković, *Kvislinška*, Vol. I, pp. 323-24; *Zbornik*/I/21/304, and 308-15 (NDH Gendarmerie GHQ to NDH MoD, 12.8.1942); *Zbornik*/I/4/288-91, I BOC/Intel., Situation report (15.7-15.8.1942); Nikolić, *Jugoistočna*, pp. 203-15.

81 Ibid., pp. 235-54; Glišić, *Rukovođenje*, pp. 135-37; NARA/T501/352/469, 475, 487, BhS, Daily report (2, 4, 6.11.1942).

4

Greatest Trials (January – August 1943)

4.1 Operation "Weiss I": Storming of Bihać Republic

By early December 1942, the general war situation of the Axis powers had taken a sharp turn for the worse: the German 6th Army was surrounded at Stalingrad, and the Allies had landed in French North Africa. If the African continent were lost, the United Nations could be expected to strike their next blow against Southeastern Europe, probably Greece; hence, in the words of Colonel-General Alfred Jodl, "the Balkans had to pacified and secured"[1] before this threat could materialize. In a series of top-level meetings held in the second half of December 1942 and early January 1943 the Germans and Italians agreed on a massive operation with the ambitious aim of eliminating the guerrilla menace to the Adriatic coastline and the communications leading to the interior. The first phase of the undertaking, which was christened "Weiss", would target the core territories of the Bihać Republic, while the second would be aimed against the Drvar–Livno area; the third phase–which, as we shall see, never materialized–involved the disarming of the Chetniks in Herzegovina and Montenegro. Although nominally a joint venture, the "Weiss" would not be steered from a single center; instead, each Axis partner would conduct his own, separate set of sub-operations while working towards the common objective. In numerical terms, the winter campaign of 1943 dwarfed all its predecessors. Commander of German Troops in Croatia–a post created in November 1942 in order to facilitate the handling of the steadily growing Wehrmacht contingent on the territories west of the Drina–had three-and-a-half divisions deployed in the first line (with one more in reserve), one reinforced armored battalion, and three air squadrons. The 2nd ITA provided three divisions of the V AC, plus the usual MVAC contingent, as well as seven squadrons. The NDH contributed eight battalions of infantry (five to the Germans, three to the Italians), and four squadrons (subordinated to the Luftwaffe). In all, the Axis powers mustered up to 90,000 soldiers and about 150 serviceable aircraft for what was hopefully the final reckoning with Tito.[2]

1 Walter Warlimont, *Im Hauptquartier der deutschen Wehrmacht 1939-1945* (Frankfurt am Main: Bernard &Graefe Verlag für Wehrwesen, 1962), p. 295.
2 Schmider, *Partisanenkrieg*, pp. 175, 206-07; Mikić, *Nemačka*, pp. 105-06; NARA/T315/2154/546, OOB chart "Weiss" (9.1.1943); *Zbornik*/V/11/396-400, V AC, Winter operations (15.1.1943).

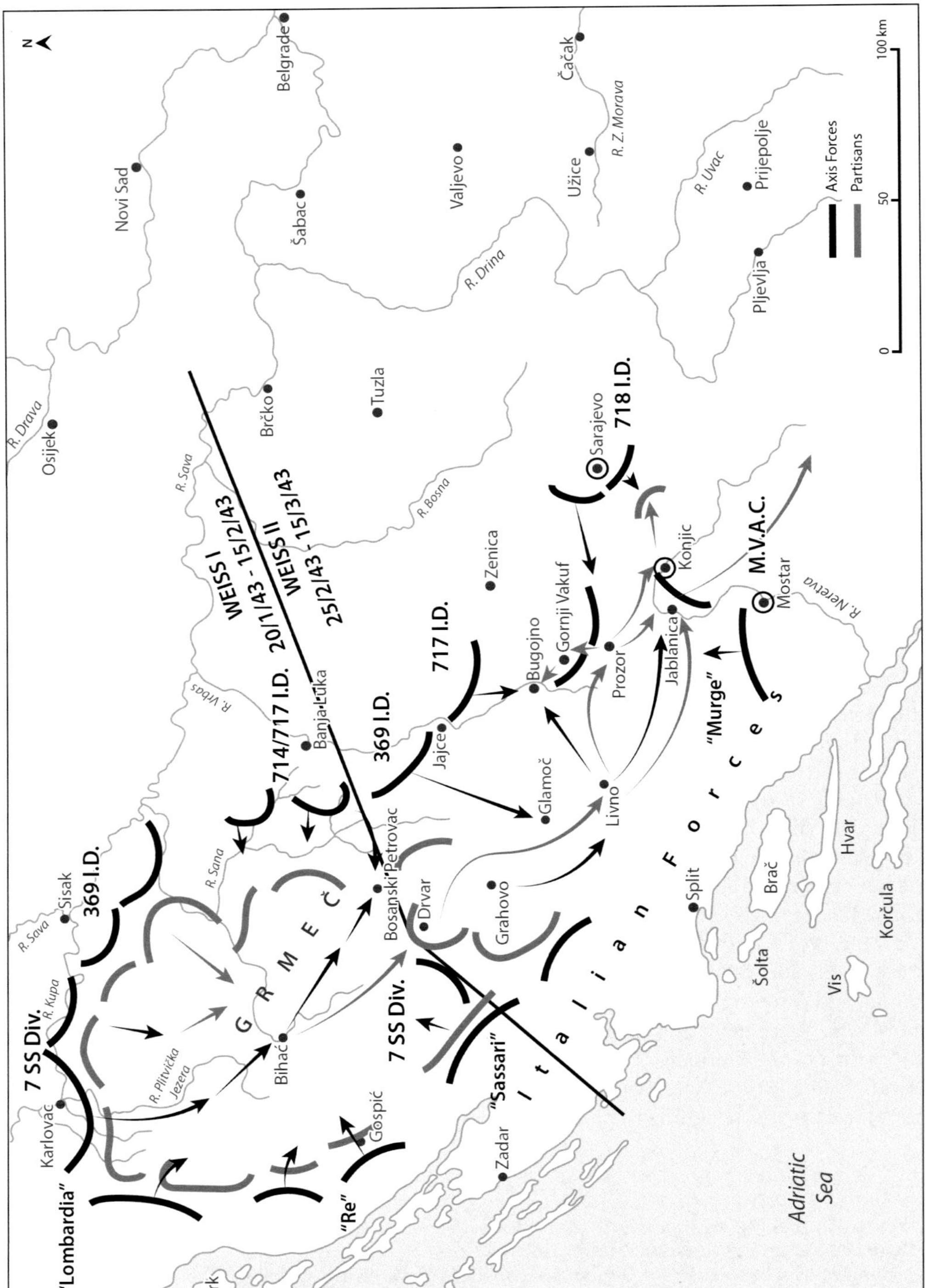

Map 8: Operation "Weiss" (January–March 1943).

Operation "Weiss I" began on the morning of 20 January 1943 with concerted attacks all along the edge of the main liberated territory, in Lika, Kordun, Banija, and Bosanska Krajina. While the units were conducting a slow, fighting withdrawal, the NOVJ's supreme commander and his advisors pondered on their next step. Even though the preparations for the evacuation of the wounded and supplies began immediately, the SHQ was reluctant to order a general retreat before making absolutely certain that the Bihać Republic could not be held. By the 26th, this much had become clear, and Tito put in motion a plan calling for a strategic advance towards the southeast. According to this plan (the basic concept of which had allegedly been outlined already in autumn of 1942), three of the NOVJ's best divisions (the 1st and 2nd Proletarian, and 3rd Assault) would execute another "long march", this time towards Southern Serbia, Macedonia, and Kosovo, where conditions were deemed ripe for a general uprising. In order to buy these forces time to concentrate and protect their rear while they make their way through the enemy-infested Herzegovina, the 1st Croatian and 1st Bosnian Corps were tasked with stalling the Axis spearheads for as long as possible.[3]

In early January 1943, the 1st Croatian Corps had about 16,000 men. Its three divisions and three detachments were, for the most part, operating in their respective native provinces. The 7th Banija Division staged another grand coup against enemy rail transport, derailing an ammo train outside of Blinjski Kut on the 5th. The 8th Kordun reduced the Chetnik stronghold in Lička Jesenica six days later, capturing some 200 enemy fighters. The attempt of the 6th Lika to take Gračac by storm on 15 January failed, however, owing to tough enemy resistance and torrential rains that turned the countryside in a sea of mud; two fighters drowned, 40 were KIA, 67 WIA, and 57 MIA. Despite the fact that the MHQ Croatia had been receiving intelligence on Axis concentrations throughout January, the units in the field were not ready for a major enemy attack. For instance, the HQ of the 6th Lika had even granted a large number of its fighters a short furlough on the very eve of the battle, and one of its brigades was still a good 80 km away from its designated sector on the day the "Weiss I" began.[4]

The 8th Kordun, deployed in the center of the corps lineup, had the most difficult task, that of protecting the northern approaches to Bihać. Arrayed against it stood the mammoth, 20,000-strong 7th SS Volunteer Mountain Division "Prinz Eugen", recently transferred from Serbia to the area of Karlovac. The enemy's vast numerical superiority was offset to some extent by adverse weather and ground conditions, but there could be no doubt as to the outcome of such an unequal contest. Nevertheless, it took the Germans nine days to reach the now-abandoned Partisan capital; the 8th Kordun withdrew to the eastern slopes of Mount Plješevica. Although their battle plan did not involve crossing the Una in this sector, the Germans launched a strong diversionary attack around the hamlet of Drenovača on 6 February with the aim of aiding the Italian operations taking place on the opposite side of the mountain. The attack foundered on the unexpectedly strong resistance by the elements of the 5th Kordun Brigade fighting from entrenched positions. Among else, the Partisans captured a "Panzer II" tank, which was subsequently repaired and went on to serve in the NOVJ until the end of the war (the vehicle can still be seen today on Belgrade's Kalemegdan Fortress). The events on the sector held by the 8th Kordun had direct impact on its right-hand neighbor. The 7th Banija was largely holding

3 Gojko Nikoliš, *Korijen, stablo, pavetina: memoari* (Zagreb: Liber, 1981), pp. 467-68; *SD*/XIV/315-16.
4 Baić, *Četvrti*, pp. 86-98; Orlović, *Šesta*, pp. 89-94; NARA/T315/2154/95, 369th ID, Diary (5.1.1943).

its own against the 369th ID, and even succeeded in routing one of its battalions in a surprise morning attack against Balinac on 23 January. The steadily deteriorating situation in Kordun and Cazinska Krajina, however, forced this Partisan division first to shift forces to its exposed left flank, and then to abandon its home region altogether by the 29th. After crossing the Una, the 7th was subordinated to the SHQ and made responsible for guarding the rear of the main Partisan *trek*.[5]

Meanwhile, the 6th Lika, reinforced by two brigades of the 5th OZ, was holding its 100 km-wide front against the Italians. The V AC fielded five battle groups, one each from the divisions "Lombardia" and "Sassari" (deployed on the left and right flank of the corps, respectively), and three from the "Re" (deployed in the center). Each of them had, on average, four Italian infantry battalions, plus auxiliary troops (including both the Ustashe and Chetniks), and support units. Their task was to assail the Bihać Republic from the line Gračac–Lovinac–Gospić–Otočac–Ogulin. Luckily for the Partisans, heavy snow compelled their enemy to direct his attacks exclusively along the few existing roads. Furthermore, the Italian commanders had little faith in the "Weiss" and were reluctant to change the leisurely pace of their operations at the time when the Germans themselves were inching forward. As a result, none of the battle groups of the V AC, with the partial exception of the northern-most one, had made any noticeable progress during the first five days of the offensive. The imminent fall of the NOP capital and the appearance of Wehrmacht spearheads on the eastern border of Lika changed all this. The *Supersloda* finally gave in to constant German prodding and instructed the V AC to protect the ever-lengthening right flank of the "Prinz Eugen" by launching a decisive action in its sector. In pursuance of this order, all three divisions doubled their efforts and pushed the Partisans out of Prijeboj, Korenica, Udbina, and Mazin by the first days of February 1943. From the NOVJ's point of view, the crisis had reached its zenith. Mount Plješevica, home to the 1st Croatian Corps' HQ, its magazines and hospitals, was now nearly completely surrounded; it was logical to assume that it would soon come under direct attack. To everyone's astonishment, nothing happened. Rather than starting a major battle of attrition in the middle of the winter, the Italians halted in their present positions and began small-scale mop-up operations in the reconquered areas.

At the same time, the high command–motivated by reasons of prestige more than operational necessity–ordered the "Sassari" to make preparations for an advance to Kulen Vakuf; there, the division was supposed to meet the German spearheads coming from the northwest. Mistaking the lull in the fighting for a sign of an impending withdrawal of Italian units to their starting positions, the HQ of the 6th Lika decided to weaken its defenses in the Lapac Valley in favor of strengthening its presence in the enemy rear. As a result, only seven out of the division's sixteen battalions were manning the front line when the "Sassari" opened its assault on 11 February. The latter had therefore little difficulty in reaching its objective after only three days of fighting. As far as the *Supersloda* was concerned, the "Weiss I" was now officially over, and the troops could return to their garrisons. It turned out that the above-mentioned mistaken decision on the part of the Partisan command was, in fact, a blessing in disguise: its enemy was now no longer

5 Baić, *Četvrti*, pp. 99-108, 111; Simo Mikašinović, "Od Saborskog do Drenovače", in *Osma kordunaška udarna divizija* (Karlovac: HAK, 1977), pp. 321-26; Boško Ranitović, "Pobjeda Pete brigade na Drenovači (6. februar 1943. godine)", in ibid., pp. 327-35; NARA/T315/2154/157-58, 174, 369th ID, Diary (23 and 26.1.1943).

concentrated, but stretched out along a single, 25 km-long mountain road, an ideal ambush terrain. The guerrillas started interdicting the traffic on the same day Kulen Vakuf fell, but the main attack was made between 18 and 21 February with an equivalent of three full brigades. The "Sassari" took a terrible beating on this occasion, and only the intervention by a hurriedly redeployed regiment of the "Re", saved the division from an even worse fate.[6]

The opening of the Axis offensive found the 1st Bosnian Corps (ca. 11,000 men) spread over a large part of Bosanska Krajina. The 4th Krajina Division had two brigades on the Kozara, and one each west of Sanski Most and at Bosanski Novi; two brigades of the 5th were deployed north of Ključ, while the parts of the third covered the old Manjača battlefield. The German 717th ID launched a two-pronged attack from its base at Sanski Most towards Bosanska Krupa and Bosanski Petrovac, where it was supposed to meet the spearheads of the 369th ID and 7th SS MTD coming from the north and northwest, respectively. The objective was to encircle Mount Grmeč, the suspected center of the entire NOP effort in this part of the country. However, the 717th ID's timetable was upset almost immediately by fierce enemy resistance and harsh winter weather that made off-road advance almost impossible. Seven days into the offensive, the division's regiments covered only some 35 km. The main column (the 749th IR) was stopped short of Ključ; a lieutenant-colonel, the commander of the I/202nd PzR, was among those killed along the way. The secondary column (the 737th IR) kept pushing on until it reached the hamlet of Benakovac. By now, the two brigades from Kozara, which had in the meantime been recalled to this sector, began taking up positions around the Germans. From 28 January to 4 February, the 737th IR was completely surrounded; it suffered heavy casualties and was kept alive only thanks to the sustained effort by the *Luftwaffe*. In spite of the spirited defense put up by the Partisans, the "Weiss" was moving inexorably forward. The 369th ID, reinforced with one regiment of the 187th RD, closed the ring around the Grmeč from the west and northwest, relieving the 737th IR in the process. At the same time, the 7th SS MTD brushed aside elements of the already weakened 7th Banija southeast of Bihać and made contact with the 749th IR east of Bosanski Petrovac on 9 February 1943.[7]

The Grmeč had no strategic value for the NOVJ in the present situation. In the opinion of the SHQ, holding it meant inviting "a second Kozara"[8] at the time when every available fighter was needed to cover the rear of the main force while it made its way towards the Neretva. The HQ of the 1st Bosnian Corps, however, failed to order the timely evacuation of the 4th Krajina; the local commanders held the view that the army could not simply abandon this solidly pro-NOP region and the thousands of refugees who were hiding in the mountain's thick forests. Unlike the Italians at the Plješevica, the Germans were undeterred by the heavy snow and the ruggedness of the terrain; they proceeded immediately with an all-out attack against the main guerrilla base at Trovrh. It took the 369th ID three days of heavy fighting (5-8 February 1943) to dislodge the obstinate defenders. Satisfied with their first clear-cut, if dearly paid, victory, the Germans failed to press on with the attack that might have finished off the 4th Krajina. By this stage,

6 Dušan Batinica, "Četvrta neprijateljska ofanziva i njen tok na području kotara Donji Lapac", in *Kotar Donji Lapac u Narodnooslobodilačkom ratu 1941—1945.* (Karlovac: HAK, 1985), pp. 325-92.

7 Branko Perović, *Borbe Prvog hrvatskog i Prvog bosanskog korpusa NOV I POJ u januaru i februaru 1943.: nemačka operacija "Vajs I"* (Belgrade: VIZ, 1977), pp. 60, 100-14, 143-54; NARA/T315/2263/734, 717th ID to BDTK (1.2.1943); NARA/T314/554/358, Air supply (22.2.1943).

8 *Zbornik*/II/8/30-32, Ranković et. al to Tito (5.2.1943).

the division's HQ had lost contact with all four of its exhausted brigades, which were acting independently of one another. Luckily for them, their enemy was also at the end of his tethers and failed to properly secure the encirclement perimeter. By 12 February, all Partisan units and the majority of refugees were out of harm's way. Most of the fighting men escaped north, across the Sanski Most–Bosanska Krupa road, while only a comparatively small number went south to reinforce the bulk of the 1st Bosnian Corps. The Germans spent the next few days combing the area and burning down the captured magazines and hospitals before officially declaring the "Weiss I" over on the 15th.[9]

4.2 Operation "Weiss II": Battle on Neretva

The situation of the mobile formations subordinated directly to the SHQ in the weeks immediately preceding the enemy offensive was as follows. Despite the loss of Teslić to a German counterattack in the first week of January 1943, the 1st Proletarian remained on the offensive, taking Tešanj, disarming one full HDB battalion at Prnjavor, and attacking the main Bosnian railway line in the area of Doboj and Derventa. The 3rd Assault entered Novi Šeher and Žepče and carried out numerous raids in the Lašva Valley. The 2nd Proletarian had once again launched a raid into the wider area around Knin (Kninska krajina), destroying the Chetnik stronghold at Strmica in the process. By the end of the month, all three divisions received orders to concentrate with all possible speed in the Duvno–Prozor–Gornji Vakuf area. Tito discussed the upcoming incursion into the Neretva Valley with his top commanders on 8 February. According to the plan, the 1st Proletarian would protect the army's northern flank by posting itself between Konjic and the Ivan Pass; its sister formation was made responsible for the southern flank, which was to be anchored on the village of Drežnica. The 3rd Assault was tasked with clearing the Rama River Valley and advancing towards Konjic. In addition to these divisions and the 7th Banija, the SHQ also assumed control of the 9th Dalmatian Division, which was just being formed on Mount Biokovo around the HQ of the now-defunct 4th OZ. In Yugoslav historiography, these five divisions were usually referred to as "Main Operational Group" (*Glavna operativna grupa*, GOG).[10]

As chance would have it that senior representatives of the two major Axis powers held a conference in Belgrade on the same day as their Partisan counterparts. They agreed to launch the "Weiss II" in two weeks' time using three German divisions (the 7th SS MTD, and the 369th and 717th IDs), which would advance concentrically against Livno via Bosansko Grahovo, Glamoč, and Kupres, respectively. The Italians would provide flank protection with the "Bergamo" Division (XVIII AC), but more importantly, make sure that the blocking line along the Neretva (VI AC) remained intact. On the same conference, the Germans reluctantly agreed to postpone the disarming of the Chetniks until after the bulk of the NOVJ had been destroyed. Although still wary of the royalists' true allegiance and intentions, the simple fact was that the Wehrmacht had no strength to open hostilities on this front as well. In the field, the divisions readily availed themselves of their services and used them mostly for scouting. Finally, in early March 1943, Army Group E (*Heeresgruppe E*, HGE)–as the WBSO/AOK 12 came to be known in late 1942–capitulated to reality and formally allowed those Chetnik groups

9 Perović, *Borbe*, pp. 154-57; NARA/T315/2154/656, 369th ID, Activity Report (9.1-15.2.1943).
10 *Oslobodilački*, Vol. I, pp. 346, 361, 374-75; Janković, *Četvrta*, pp. 159-63.

whose loyalty and usefulness were beyond doubt to retain their weapons. The Italians, for their part, planned to use every available member of the MVAC from Herzegovina and Montenegro for the forthcoming clash with the GOG. This suited Mihailović just fine, for he had been contemplating such a showdown for a long time. For this purpose he made sure the MVAC was reinforced by the Chetnik units from Sandžak and Eastern Bosnia and entrusted the handling of day-to-day operations to one of his closest subordinates, Major Zaharije Ostojić. The Italian HQs were to be cajoled, coaxed, or threatened into accepting the Chetnik battle plans.[11]

The opening shots of the second phase of the winter campaign of 1943 were fired by Howitzer Battalion of the SHQ in the evening hours of 15 February. The target was the heavily fortified *presidio* (garrison) of Prozor, held by a full infantry battalion from the "Murge" Division, reinforced by a battery of field cannon and a company of tanks. After the short (and not particularly effective) artillery preparation was over, three brigades of the 3rd Assault Division rushed forward across the open terrain surrounding the town. The attack, however, was repulsed in blood; the Partisans themselves later admitted that they were "dumbfounded" by the intensity and accuracy of the defenders' fire. The assault would be repeated the next evening under the slogan "Prozor must fall tonight!" Variously attributed to Tito and the commander of the 3rd Assault and known to every schoolchild in Socialist Yugoslavia, the phrase captured the spirit of determination to open the way to the Neretva for the thousands of refugees and army non-combatants who were retreating from the territory of the Bihać Republic. The night of 16 February was very dark and rainy, all of which reduced the effectiveness of enemy fire. Aided by a single howitzer deployed in a direct support role, the 5th Proletarian Brigade broke into the town, which fell by 0400 hours the following day. Đilas remembered that the Partisans, inspired by the Soviet example at Stalingrad, sent an ultimatum before the battle, threatening the garrison with annihilation if it did not lay down its arms. Since the Italians refused, the guerrillas went on to fulfill their ghastly promise and executed almost all of their captives. The official after-action report of the 3rd Assault makes no mention of the ultimatum; it states only that the enemy suffered 800 dead, and rather ominously omits any mention of the wounded or prisoners. In the meantime, the 2nd Proletarian had liberated Posušje and Imotski (9-10 February), subdued the Italian garrison at Drežnica, and routed a battalion-strong motorized column of the "Murge" heading north from Mostar (17 February). The 4th Proletarian Brigade then advanced upstream and stormed the town of Jablanica on the 21st, capturing an equivalent of yet another Italian battalion in the process. By this time, the entire 40km-stretch of the Neretva between the confluence with the Drežanka River in the south and Konjic in the north was free of Axis troops.[12]

At first glance, the Partisan campaign was proceeding smoothly: the *Regio Esercito* was dealt a series of exceptionally heavy blows, and the GOG's precarious supply situation was transformed practically overnight thanks to the vast quantities of captured stores. All this, however, will have

11 NARA/T315/2271/757-9, BDTK, Order "Weiss II" (12.2.1943); NARA/T315/2264/11, 717th ID, Diary (19.2.1943); NARA/T315/2154/687, 369th ID/Intel., Activity report (22.2-4.3.1943); Schmider, *Partisanenkrieg*, p. 271; Tomasevich, *Chetniks*, pp. 233-34, 240; *Zbornik*/XIV/2/255, Ilija Trifunović to Mihailović (24.2.1943).

12 Djilas, *Wartime*, pp. 219-20; *Zbornik*/IV/10/200, 3rd NOVJD, Report Prozor (18.2.1943); Rudolf Primorac, "Treća udarna divizija", in *Neretva: zbornik radova* (Belgrade: VIZ, 1965), Vol. I, pp. 184-96; Jovo Vukotić, "Druga proleterska divizija", in ibid., pp. 126-49.

been for naught if Konjic remained in enemy hands, for this small town controlled the only half-decent road leading to Eastern Herzegovina. The only unit within the striking distance of the town was the 1st Proletarian Brigade of the 1st Proletarian Division; its two sister formations had to remain around Gornji Vakuf and Bugojno due to the delayed arrival of the 7th Banija Division from the north. After having cleared all Axis outposts along the railway line Konjic–Tarčin by 21 February 1943, the brigade split into two groups of two battalions each. While the one remained guarding the brigade's original objective, the strategic Ivan Pass ("the gates to Herzegovina"), the other staged a surprise attack on Konjic. This ill-conceived plan, designed in anticipation of yet another easy victory over the Italians, backfired tremendously: neither could the town be taken, nor the pass defended with the forces at hand. As a result, one German and one NDH battalion from Sarajevo could reinforce the beleaguered garrison in the nick of time. The NOVJ forces, now under the HQ of the 3rd Assault Division, launched three full-scale attacks on the nights of 22, 24, and 25 February, all of which failed; not even the presence of six tankettes captured at Prozor could turn the tide of battle in the Partisans' favor (three of them were ultimately lost to enemy fire). On 26 February, the heterogeneous garrison–which consisted of the NDH Home Guard, Ustasha, Gendarmerie, Wehrmacht, and *Regio Esercito* units–was relieved "with the help of the brave Chetniks", as high-ranking German officers noted with gratitude. These were the first of an estimated 14,000 royalists who were approaching the battlefield from the south and east.

At this juncture, the SHQ decided on a radical change of plan. With the road to Eastern Herzegovina now seemingly blocked by masses of Chetniks and the unforgiving Prenj Massif, the GOG would have to break out elsewhere. Consequently, the divisions were given new tasks. The 1st Proletarian, which had thwarted all attempts by the regiment-sized KG "Annacker" to reach Konjic from the north during the preceding week, was sent northwest; the 3rd Assault took up a defensive position along the Neretvica. All NOVJ forces were withdrawn to the right bank of the Neretva, and on the 28th Tito ordered the five remaining bridges blown up. This task was entrusted to Vladmir-Volođa Smirnov, the Russian-born chief of Engineer Section of the SHQ, who would become famous for being played by Yul Brynner in the 1969-Yugoslav war epic "The Battle of the Neretva". While wiring the last two remaining bridges for demolition, the engineers were overflown by a lone "Savoia-Marchetti" bomber, which, however, did not shoot at them; Smirnov believed that the Italian air crew must have been dumbfounded by the sight of the "crazy" Partisans "shutting themselves up entirely in this dreadful canyon."[13]

Until the very end of the Socialist era, official historiography maintained that the destruction of the bridges was, in fact, a clever ruse devised by the NOVJ's supreme commander in order to confuse the enemy as to the real direction of the Partisan breakthrough. In reality, it was a near-disastrous decision resulting from the lack of intelligence on the Chetnik strength and dispositions, and the rashness on Tito's part. It only served to aggravate the already critical operational situation. On 25 February 1943, the 7th SS MTD and the 369th ID commenced their advance towards Glamoč and Livno (Operation "Weiss II"). Weakened by the winter campaign and developing typhus epidemic, the 1st Bosnian Corps could do little to counter

13 Velimir Terzić, "Bitka na Neretvi", in ibid., pp. 36-37; Ljubivoje Pajović, "Prva proleterska divizija", in ibid., pp. 72-96; Vladimir Smirnov, "Surova škola: doživljaji inženjeraca na Neretvi", in ibid., pp. 363-72; Primorac, "Treća", p. 201; NARA/T311/175/544, HGE, Memorandum (1.3.1943); NARA/T315/2271/830-35, KG "Annacker", Report Konjic (26.3.1943); *Zbornik*/XIV/2/304.

the enemy spearheads. Demolishing or blocking ground communications were the guerrillas' most effective means of defense: for example, German engineers found no less than 230 felled trunks on one stretch of road only six km long. Luckily for the GOG, the two above-mentioned enemy divisions–which were the strongest in terms of numbers and equipment–were tasked with securing the all-important Mostar–Livno bauxite area rather than seeking a battle of annihilation on the banks of the Neretva. Even so, the advance of the weakest German formation, the 717th ID, from Gornji Vakuf towards Prozor was considered a mortal threat, for just beyond the town, in the Rama River Valley, stood Central Hospital of the SHQ.

With the exception of "the long march", when it was temporarily dissolved, this institution had been providing medical care for the sick and wounded from the units around the SHQ since November 1941. In late February 1943, the hospital had some 3,800 patients (in addition to 700 more who were cared for by their units). The presence of such a large number of incapacitated fighters, many of whom were stretcher-ridden, had a decisive influence on plans and actions of the GOG. The bitter experience had taught the Partisans never to leave behind their wounded comrades; by early 1943, this had become an integral part of their credo and greatly contributed to the strengthening of the NOVJ's *esprit-de-corps*. The downside was that it bereaved the army of its greatest forte, the superior mobility: the pace of operations was now determined by the movement speed of the cumbersome hospital. The fate of the wounded weighted heavily on Tito: searching frantically for the best option, he changed his mind concerning the direction of their evacuation two times in three days. Before the evacuation could take place, however, the Germans had to be dealt with.[14]

The plan for a major counter-attack in the area of Gornji Vakuf was put in motion on the same day that the bridges over the Neretva were ordered demolished. Although Yugoslav historians maintained that it had been conceived as a mere feint, the operation was, in all probability, a maximum effort undertaking aimed at opening the way to Central Bosnia for the GOG. By using interior lines and captured vehicles, the SHQ managed to concentrate nine (out of altogether twelve available) brigades against six (later eight) infantry battalions from the 717th and 718th IDs, reinforced by the bulk of the I/202 PzR. The initial clash occurred on 2 March at the place called Vilića Gumno, when the 4th Proletarian Brigade arrived just in time to save the Central Hospital from the encroaching Germans. The main battle began two days later: stunned by the ferocity of the Partisan attack and the barrage of "unprecedented intensity" from heavy weapons found in Prozor and elsewhere[15], the Wehrmacht units began to yield ground. By the morning of the 5th, the threat of encirclement had compelled them to evacuate Gornji Vakuf and take positions some three km northwest of the town. With the greatest danger to the hospital thus removed, the SHQ decided to change the direction of the breakthrough. Braving the Chetniks and Mount Prenj was deemed preferable to a drawn-out slogging match against

14 Karasijević, *Četvrta krajiška*, pp. 98-99; Gaj Trifković, "A Case of Failed Counter-Insurgency: Anti-Partisan Operations in Yugoslavia 1943", *The Journal of Slavic Military Studies* [hereinafter: JSMS], 24:2 (2011), pp. 318-19; NARA/T315/2154/332, 369th ID, Diary (27.2.1943); *Enciklopedija*, Vol. II, p. 151; *SD*/XIV/102-03, 112, 122 (Tito's messages to 1st Bosnian Corps, 9th, and 1st NOVJDs, 2-5.3.1943), 331.

15 NARA/T315/2271/1108, 750th JR, Report Operation "Mostar" (6.4.1943). On being told that the huge stocks of howitzer ammunition in his captors' possession hailed from the *Regio Esercito*, one German major exclaimed ironically: "Oh, [our] dear Italians!": Dedijer, *Dnevnik*, Vol. II, p. 130 (5.3.1943).

the Germans, whose reserves (the 369th ID) were already being rushed to the battlefield. On 7 March, the 2nd Proletarian Division retook Jablanica and established a small bridgehead on the left bank of the Neretva; four days later, its lead elements already stood at Boračko Lake, after having completely routed the royalists. In the meantime, Smirnov and his pioneers erected a shabby pontoon, affixed to the skeleton of the railway bridge they had blown up only days earlier. It took a full week to get the Central Hospital and the bulk of the GOG across (the 3rd Assault Division made an independent crossing upriver from Jablanica). On 15 March, the last rear guards of the 1st Proletarian Division, which had conducted a slow, fighting withdrawal all the way from Gornji Vakuf, crossed into safety, burning the venerable edifice behind them. The "Weiss II" was officially concluded on the 17th: "There was no booty, no prisoners; not a single wounded [...] was found" (Colonel-General Löhr).[16]

Outwardly, the Germans appeared well-satisfied with the outcome of their winter campaign. Tito's State, which had stood so menacingly close to Zagreb, was destroyed and his best formations were forced to seek refuge on the fringes of the NDH; according to the much-publicized official tally, the Partisans lost no fewer than 12,500 KIA and 2,500 prisoners (not counting the losses inflicted by the Italians). In reality, the "Weiss" was anything but an unqualified success. The bulk of the NOVJ may have been chased away, but the 1st Bosnian and 1st Croatian Corps remained on their home terrains and could be expected to renew their activities soon; long-term pacification of these parts was out of the question owing to the inherently volatile nature of the Ustasha regime. Although the Partisans suffered an estimated 4,000 irrevocable losses (mostly from illness and exposure), they were far from being a spent force: the Germans captured only about 650 pieces of small arms, eight cannon, and one tank. Tito still had some 20,000 able-bodied fighters under his command, albeit without heavy weapons, which had to be dumped into the Neretva. Finally, Axis forces paid a heavy price for this largely hollow victory. The NDH formations operating under the Wehrmacht, which saw comparatively little action, had 126 KIA, 258 WIA, and 218 MIA. The German units reported having 536 KIA, 1,348 WIA, and 164 MIA; the 717th ID was the hardest-hit of them all, losing almost 13 percent of its original strength. The biggest losers, however, were the Italians: the "Sassari" lost about 1,000 KIA, WIA, and MIA, the "Re" and "Lombardia" about 600 each. The "Murge" was effectively decimated: official sources speak of 2,000 KIA and 1,300 MIA with all the appertaining arms and equipment.[17]

4.3 From Neretva to Lim

Although the GOG was safe from the Germans for the time being,[18] the main Chetnik force, largely intact, was still barring the way to the Montenegrin border. Both sides had offensive

16 Colić, *Pregled*, pp. 102-04; NARA/T315/2264/376-412, 717th ID, Diary (1-15.3.1943); Hrvatski državni arhiv (Croatian State Archives), HR HDA 1689, Document no. 97, Statment of Alexander Löhr (1947), p. 15.

17 Đuro Kladarin, *Slom Četvrte i Pete okupatorsko-kvislinške ofenzive* (Zagreb: Kultura, 1956), pp. 272-73; Mišo Leković, *Martovski pregovori 1943*, (Belgrade: Narodna knjiga, 1985), pp. 63-64; Loi, *Operazioni*, p. 213; Becherelli, *Italia*, p. 296; NARA/T314/554/377-78, Lüters to Vilko Begić (31.3.1943); NARA/T78/332/6290064, OBSO, Situation estimate March 1943 (1.4.1943).

18 The German decision not to pursue the Partisans deeper into Herzegovina was the result of internal considerations and strained relations with the Italians, and not, as sometimes claimed, of

intentions. After taking Glavatičevo on 19 March 1943, the Partisans (six brigades) continued their march on a wide front, aiming for Kalinovik, Ulog, and Nevesinje. The royalist command sought to push them back towards the Prenj and the canyon of the upper Neretva as soon as the reinforcements from Montenegro, Mostar, and elsewhere arrived. What resulted was the greatest confrontation of the two guerrilla armies so far in the war. The Battle of Kalinovik was fought for three consecutive days (20-22 March) between the veterans of the 1st and 2nd Proletarian Divisions and some 2,300 men under the command of their old foe, Pavle Đurišić; a senior Partisan commander remembered that the clash "was so intense that, once the guns fell silent, one could not tell who won".[19] The Chetniks abandoned their positions and retreated east only after being outflanked by the 2nd Proletarian Brigade coming from the direction of Ulog. In the meantime, the 3rd Assault Division took Nevesinje on the 22nd (killing, wounding, or capturing 239 soldiers of the "Marche" Division and seizing a large supply of much-needed food), lost it four days later to some 3,500 royalists coming from Mostar, and retook it again on the 29th with the help of the 9th Dalmatian Division. The most prominent Partisan casualty of this round of fighting was Petar Ćetković, a former captain of the royal army and now the commander of the 3rd Assault, who would, ironically, be best remembered for the photos from his own funeral procession that was led by an Orthodox priest. Although the JVuO/MVAC would continue harassing the Partisan rear guards in the coming weeks, Mihailović's army had effectively ceased to be a serious factor after the battles of Kalinovik and Nevesinje. Owing to the chaotic circumstances, it is impossible to provide a precise computation of the losses suffered on the banks of the Neretva and in Eastern Herzegovina; top Chetnik officers spoke of 800-1,000 KIA, although these figures were most probably inflated in order to impress the Italians. The majority of casualties were almost certainly incurred through desertion that took on alarming proportions despite the radical measures (shootings, floggings) employed to curb it.[20]

With the VI AC left entirely without reserves, and the Germans unwilling to heed the *Supersloda*'s calls for help, the GOG could continue its eastward offensive without fear for the safety of its rear. In the last days of March 1943, the SHQ ordered the 1st and 2nd Divisions to ford the Drina on both sides of Foča, eliminate this enemy garrison, and proceed into Sandžak and northern Montenegro; further south, the 3rd Division was to advance towards Nikšić via Gacko. The two weakest formations, the 7th Banija and 9th Dalmatian, were tasked with protecting the Central Hospital and establishing "people's authority" in the newly-liberated areas. Crossing the swollen Drina in small, hastily assembled rafts would have been a daunting task even in peacetime circumstances; now, two battalions of the *Alpini* from the "Taurinense" Division were waiting for the attackers in prepared hilltop positions on the opposite bank. The 1st Proletarian Division managed to gain a foothold at Ustikolina amidst fierce enemy resistance. With great difficulty, the Partisans assembled enough men for a series of desperate

Tito's controversial truce offer. For more information on these co-called "March Negotiations" see Gaj Trifković, *Parleying with the Devil: Prisoner Exchange in Yugoslavia 1941-1945* (Lexington, KY: University Press of Kentucky/Andarta Books, 2020), Chapter Three.

19 Vukmanović, *Razgovori*, p. 67.

20 *Oslobodilački*, Vol. I, pp. 395-401; *Zbornik*/IV/11/477, 520, 557, VI AC to *Supersloda* (16, 21, 25.3.1943, respectively); *Zbornik*/IV/12/400, 579, Lieutenant Jelinčić to VI AC (3 and 29.4.1943, respectively); *Zbornik*/XIV/485-87 (Borivoje Radulović to Ostojić, 18.3.1943), 535, 570 (Ostojić to Mihailović, 15.3 and 3.4.1943, respectively).

uphill charges which, combined with flanking attacks, finally carried the main Italian defensive line by the morning of 10 April. The entire next day passed in a seesaw struggle between two guerrilla brigades and t"Taurinense's" two reserve battalions, which ended in the latter's panicky retreat towards Čajniče. In all, the Italian division lost some 230 KIA, WIA, and MIA in these battles, including one battalion commander, as well as six mountain guns, nine mortars, and, on top of everything else, one regimental standard. In the meantime, the 2nd Proletarian Division, which happened to be opposed only by demoralized Chetniks, made a successful and largely painless crossing of the Drina and broke into the southern suburbs of Foča (6-9 April), but could not take the entire place. The town was then encircled and held under siege for about a month, but the planned and presumably very costly direct assault was repeatedly postponed and ultimately canceled.[21]

The 1st Proletarian Division spent the following three weeks in relative peace while holding the front towards Goražde. After that, the division resumed its march towards the Lim and Tara, reaching both by the middle of May 1943. The 1st Proletarian Brigade made its presence in the vicinity of Bijelo Polje known by ambushing a motorized column from the "Venezia" Division, capturing 70 soldiers and a rich haul of ammunition. After repulsing a strong attack by the resurgent Montenegrin royalists around Čelebić (15-19 April), the 2nd Proletarian Division spent some 10 days preparing for the resumption of advance towards the southeast. The first order of business was to secure the GOG's right flank, threatened by the presence of one battalion of the "Ferrara" Division and some MVAC units in the area north of Nikšić. In the early morning hours of 2 May, the 2nd Proletarian Brigade attacked the fortified enemy camp at the place called Javorak. At first it seemed that the defenders, supported from the air, would manage to hold their own. However, on being informed that two brigades from the 3rd Assault Division were poised to cut them off from Nikšić, the Italians started a precipitous retreat that soon turned into a wholesale rout. Almost 1,000 of them were killed, wounded, or captured that day with all their equipment, including seven tanks and four guns.

The ordeal of the "Ferrara" was not over yet, however. Just two weeks after the debacle at Javorak, the division's 383rd IR was called upon to assist the hard-pressed Chetniks just north of Podgorica. Their opponent was an ad-hoc NOVJ formation consisting of three Proletarian battalions and the resurrected Zeta Detachment, made up of about 160 local NOP sympathizers who emerged from their hideouts in the meantime. Thoroughly experienced by now in dealing with the *Regio Esercito* columns, the Partisans proceeded to divide and isolate the enemy (two battalions) before making an all-out attack. While the relief force coming from Podgorica–which had grown to four battalions by 17 May–remained stuck at a destroyed bridge, the guerrillas routed the encircled Italians at Bioče, inflicting about 750 casualties, including the colonel of the aforesaid regiment. With these victories, the road to the Kosovo border stood seemingly wide open. The Germans were showing no offensive intentions, the Italians had shut themselves up in their garrisons, and the royalists were on the verge of collapse. It even looked like the much-tormented wounded and sick might finally get some rest: on 6 May,

21 *Zbornik*/IV/11/525 (*Supersloda* to CoS, 22.3.1943); *Zbornik*/II/8/362-71, SHQ to 2nd, 3rd, 7th, and 9th NOVJDs (30.2.1943); *Zbornik*/IV/131/120-25, 2nd NOVJD to SHQ (9.5.1943); *Enciklopedija*, Vol. III, p. 544; *Zbornik*/XIII/3/349, Biroli to CoS (14.7.1943).

the confident Tito informed the Central Hospital that "there is no reason to fear an enemy offensive at this moment".[22]

4.4 Operation "Schwarz" I: Closing Ring

The Partisan supreme commander's optimistic appraisal of the situation from the first week of May 1943 could not have been farther from the truth. The Germans were, in fact, poised to launch what was one the biggest and most ambitious operations of the entire war, codenamed Operation "Schwarz". Ordered personally by Hitler in late March 1943, the undertaking was conceived as a showdown with both the Chetniks and Partisans, who could not be allowed to operate in such proximity to the potential landing beaches in the Adriatic. Secrecy was of paramount importance: neither the NDH authorities nor the Italians were apprised of the plans for fear that they would divulge the details with the guerrillas, inadvertently or otherwise. German planners benefited from the fact that their partner, after having suffered a series of humiliating blows at the hands of the NOVJ, was now actively seeking Wehrmacht's help. This enabled Lüters' troops to move closer to their targets under the guise of providing relief to the hard-pressed Italian garrisons in the valleys of the Drina, Tara and Lim. By mid-May, everything was in place: unlike in the winter offensive, large German formations stood on every side of the vast encirclement ring running roughly along the line Podgorica–Bileća–Foča–Pljevlja–Kolašin–Podgorica. With reinforcements that arrived later on, Berlin committed up to 100 combat aircraft, as well as ca. 60-65,000 soldiers in three complete (the 1st MTD, 7th SS MTD, 118th *Jäger* Division [JD]), one nearly-complete (the 369th ID), and parts of two other divisions (the 104th JD, and the "Brandenburg"). Fighting under the German command were also one Bulgarian infantry regiment (BIR) and the NDH 4th *Jäger* Brigade (JB). The upcoming battle was to be literally one of annihilation: "No able-bodied man is to leave the cauldron alive", read the standing order on the treatment of captured Partisans; the Chetniks, being Italian auxiliaries and anti-communists in their own right, were granted the privileged POW status.[23]

Operation "Schwarz" (or "Fifth Enemy Offensive" as it was known to the Yugoslavs) commenced on 15 May 1943 with the disarmament of all MVAC formations that failed to disperse in a timely manner. Within four days, the Germans had brought in over 2,900 royalists without noteworthy incidents (the figure would rise to over 3,500 by the end of the campaign). After protesting at first against such a brazen and unilateral action on the part of their ally, the Italians agreed to join in the operations against the Partisans with detachments from the "Ferrara", "Venezia", and "Taurinense" Divisions of the XIV AC. The chance would have it that the flower of the NOVJ had found itself in a similar situation on the same scrap of land for the second time in less than a year. The GOG now consisted of four divisions (the 1st, 2nd, 3rd, and the 7th; the 9th had been disbanded), along with the 6th Eastern Bosnian

22 Ibid., pp. 349-53; Vuksanović, *Prva*, pp. 207-16; Urošević, *Druga*, pp. 236-48; Jovan Kljajić, *Sedma krajiška brigada* (Belgrade: VINC, 1990), pp. 83-94; *Enciklopedija*, Vol. I, p. 614; *Zbornik*/III/5/366-73, VI AC, Daily reports (14-18.5.1943); *SD*/XV/83, Tito to Central hospital/Pol. (6.5.1943).

23 Gaj Trifković, *"Schwarz" auf "Weiss": 1943: Das Jahr der deutschen Großoperationen in Jugoslawien* (M.A. thesis, University of Graz, 2010), pp. 93-96; Mikić, *Nemačka*, p. 129; NARA/T315/2154/1410-16, BDTK, Order "Schwarz" (6.5.1943); NARA/T315/1302/286, BDTK to 118th JD (10.6.1943).

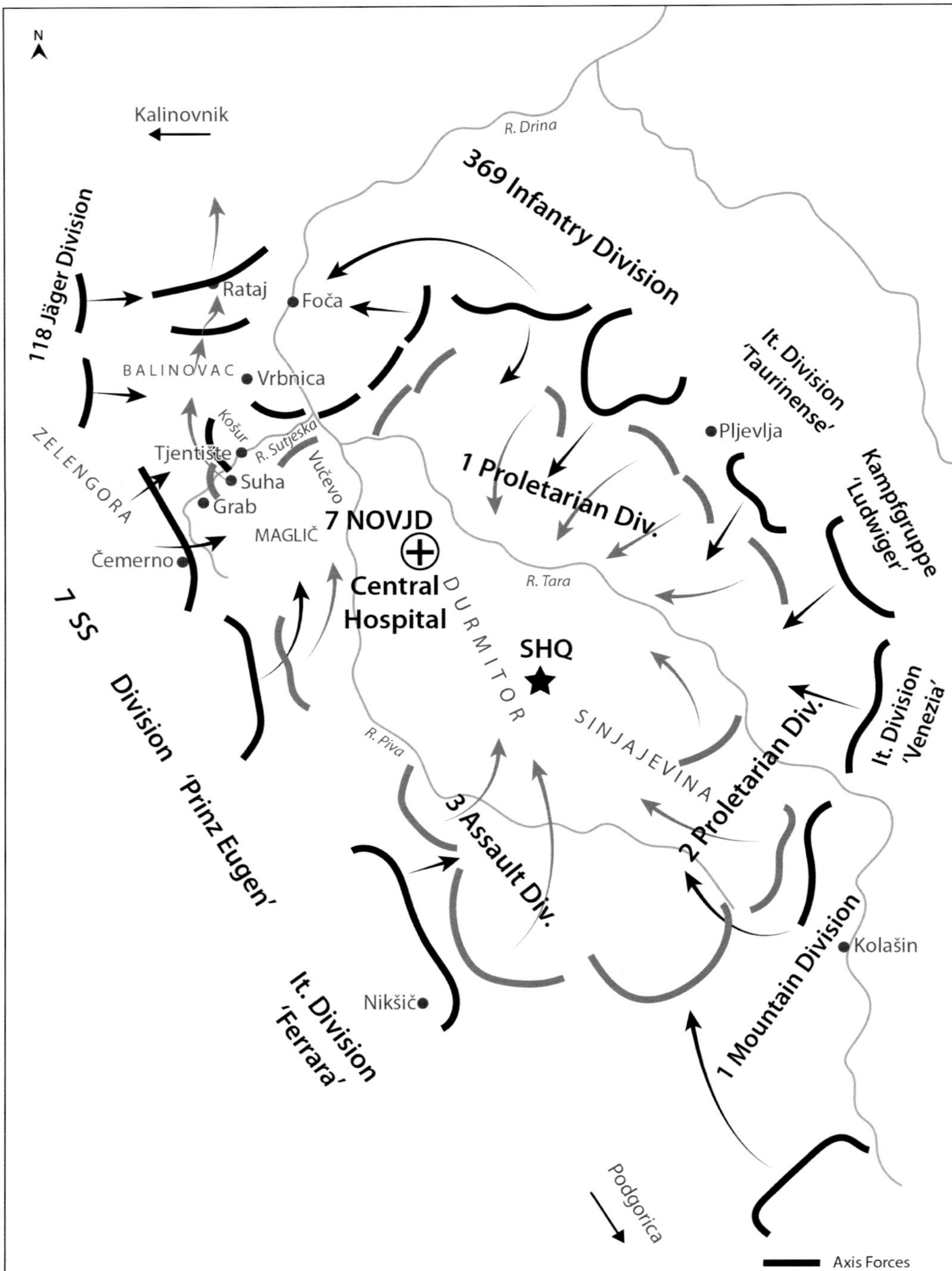

Map 9: Operation "Schwarz" (May-June 1943).

and Majevica Brigades (both of which arrived from the north in mid-April), for a total of ca. 18,000 able-bodied fighters. In addition, there were still about 3,500 wounded and sick in the Central Hospital. The GOG had evidently lost another several thousand men during its recent advance through Herzegovina and Montenegro. Although no precise breakdown exists, it can be assumed that comparatively few of them perished as the result of direct enemy action. For example: the 3rd Assault Division suffered altogether 110 casualties in the battle for Nevesinje, the 1st Proletarian Brigade lost 29 KIA and 79 WIA during the crossing of the Drina, and the great victory at Javorak was paid with "only" 10 KIA and 38 WIA. Exhaustion, hunger, and illness remained the biggest killers. Typhus epidemic had reached its height during this period, effectively putting the 7th Banija Division out of commission. Almost as worrying was the fact that the overall health situation of the army was not likely to improve in this remote and desolate area.[24] The uniqueness of the terrain on which the decisive battle of the war was about to be fought impressed even seasoned veterans of the elite 1st MTD of the Wehrmacht that had just arrived from the Caucasus:

> To the west of the upper Tara Valley stands the [...] plateau of Sinjajevina [2,277 meters], which consists of undulating, partly carstified and dry pastures. Further west, towering above all other peaks in the area, stands the highest mountain in Montenegro, the wild, high-alpine Durmitor [2,522 meters]. An undulating plateau spreads from there to the confluence of the Tara and the Piva. The canyons of these rivers are up to 1,000 meters deep with partially vertical cliffs; they can be crossed only at a handful of places, and therefore represent a major obstacle. Not even the deepest valley in the Alps is comparable with them in terms of depth and wilderness. [...] During the summer, the few existing streams dry out completely, which makes the entire area dependent on a few water holes.[25]

The Partisans thought that the initial German moves were aimed solely at saving the hard-pressed Italians, much like the relief of besieged Foča earlier the same month. By 18 May 1943, however, it was clear that another major enemy offensive was afoot. The SHQ consequently ordered the cessation of all offensive actions along the eastern and southeastern front and began shifting parts of the 1st and 2nd Proletarian Divisions towards the Šavnik and Foča sectors. The latter was especially important, as it controlled the most favorable exit route out of the encirclement ring; in addition, the Axis advance there was making serious progress and had to be checked. Consequently, three brigades of the temporary Drina Operational Group, reinforced by one (later two) brigades of the 1st Proletarian Division that had arrived from the Lim Valley after an exhausting forced march, went over to the attack on 21 May. The point of main effort was around Čelebići, on the left flank of the 118th JD's line stretching between the Drina and

24 Schmider, *Partisanenkrieg*, pp. 274-78; Trifković, *Schwarz*, p. 102; Vukanović, *Ratni*, pp. 106, 112; Vuksanović, *Prva*, p. 207; Viktor Kučan, *Borci Sutjeske* (Belgrade: Zavod za udžbenike i nastavna sredstva, 1996) p. 12; Pavle Jakšić, "Sedma divizija u IV i V neprijateljskoj ofanzivi", in *Sedma banijska divizija* (Belgrade: VIZ, 1967), pp. 188-89.

25 NARA/T78/332/6289987-88, 1st MTD, Report "Schwarz" (10.7.1943). No conventional map can convey how difficult must have been for any army to operate on such ground; the reader would therefore be well advised to use an online 3D mapping service while going through this chapter.

Ćehotina Rivers. One regiment of the 4th HDB JB deployed there was routed, which very nearly led to the collapse of the entire front. On the 24th and 25th, the Partisans carried out a series of frontal assaults against the hastily reinforced Germans and Home Guards some eight km southeast of Foča, but were repulsed each time with the help of massed artillery and air attacks. Realizing that no breakthrough could be achieved here, Koča Popović ordered his units to stand down. The SHQ, at first, did not take kindly to his decision, but the unfolding events confirmed its wisdom. Popović's positions had already effectively become untenable owing to the appearance of the 369th ID behind his back, in the area east of Čelebići. Although the Partisans managed to contain this German incursion over the Ćehotina, it was just a matter of time before Drina Operational Group would found itself crushed between the enemy pincers. Consequently, all units were ordered to withdraw south, and by 30 May there was not a single fighter left on the Tara's right bank.[26]

Meantime, the bulk of the 7th SS MTD was making its way from Eastern Herzegovina towards the wider area of Nikšić. A weak force of one battalion was tasked with occupying the strategic Piva crossing at Plužine. Sensing the opportunity, the Partisans encircled the lonely unit with two brigades (one of which arrived after completing a leg-breaking 80-km hike). In response to the crisis, Lüters sent in one additional battalion from the northwest and another one from the south; these measures helped restore the situation and enabled the resumption of the offensive. At this point (27 May 1943), the local NOVJ command decided to evacuate the bridgehead on the left bank of the Piva. This precipitous move could have had disastrous consequences, for it effectively opened the way to the remaining Piva crossings at GOG's disposal, at Mratinje and Gornje Kruševo. Luckily for the guerrillas, the Germans failed to act quickly and seize the opportunity; not knowing what lay ahead, they opted for a slow, careful advance north instead. The fear of ambush proved well-founded. Ordered by the SHQ to remedy their mistake, the Partisans (now reinforced to three brigades from the 2nd Proletarian and the 3rd Assault Division) executed a forced march north, re-crossed the river, and, on 31 May, attacked a battalion of the 118th JD that was inching its way towards the bridges. The old story repeated itself: the Germans took a beating and were forced to retreat, but the guerrillas had no strength to finish them off. After that, the Partisans established a thin defensive screen extending from the southeastern slopes of Mount Maglić to the bank of the Piva just south of Mratinje.[27]

As early as 22 May 1943, the SHQ ordered two battalions of the 2nd Proletarian Brigade to secure the Vučevo plateau and establish a bridgehead on the Sutjeska River, to be used as a kind of "reserve exit" in case the drive on Foča failed. Much to the guerrillas' surprise, the only enemy they encountered was a few scattered patrols. This was a direct result of the events described above. According to the original German plan, the Sutjeska Valley was supposed to be occupied by the entire 738th JR; from there, its three battalions were to strike east and occupy the Piva crossings. Enemy attacks around Foča and west of Plužine, however, compelled Lüters to use the *Jägers* to plug the gaps in these sectors instead. By the time the first Partisans had crossed the Sutjeska at Suha (25 May), there was not a single German soldier between Čemerno and Tjentište. Finally realizing its mistake, the Wehrmacht command now ordered all units still

26 *Bitka na Sutjesci* (n.p.: Yugoslav People's Army/Higher Military Academy, 1963), pp. 20-26, 32-33; Trifković, *Schwarz*, pp. 103-04.
27 Kljajić, *Sedma*, pp. 102-14; NARA/T314/560/816-20, 7th SS MTD, Report "Schwarz" (25.7.1943).

within striking distance of the Vučevo to take this critically important objective regardless of the cost. What followed was a series of vicious clashes along the northern and northwestern edges of the plateau on 29-31 May. One German battalion tried twice to fight its way to the summit, only to be thrown back–quite literary–by the Partisan reinforcements coming from the Piva (the 6th Eastern Bosnian and Majevica Brigades), with "many a man and beast of burden plunging to their deaths". In the end, the plateau and the approaches to the Sutjeska remained firmly in the NOVJ hands, but with one important exception: their foe managed to retain control over several lower hills on both sides of the river that dominated the Tjentište crossing.[28]

By the start of June 1943, it was clear to everyone that the battle would be decided along the banks of this small mountain river. The Germans therefore initiated a major troop redeployment. This included bringing the bulk of the 7th SS MTD to bear against the elongated enemy southern flank and concentrating the entire 118th JD in the Sutjeska-Drina sector; their places being taken over by the "Ferrara" Division and the 4th HDB JB, respectively. The Partisans, for their part, were seeking to expand the Sutjeska bridgehead with the help of the brigades arriving from the east: ten of them had crossed the Piva by 3 June 1943. Out of the remaining six units of this type that were at the SHQ's disposal at the time, the three belonging to the 7th Banija Division were deployed along the left bank of the lower Tara, where they would soon be facing the 369th ID and the "Taurinense". The three brigades subordinated to the 3rd Assault Division were holding a semi-circle extending from the Komarnica River, across the western slopes of the Durmitor, to the middle reaches of the Tara just north of Crno Jezero. These two NOVJ divisions were now in a very unenviable position. This applied in particular to the 3rd Assault, which not only faced a mighty Axis host–the 1st MTD plus parts of the "Venezia", "Ferrara", as well as the KG "Ludwiger" (the 724th JR/104th JD and 61st BIR)–but also stood far away from the proposed breakthrough area. Furthermore, they were responsible for the protection of the Central Hospital which, although reduced to about 2,000 patients thanks to the subsiding of the typhus epidemic, could not be expected to keep up with the fighting units in such rough terrain.[29]

4.5 Operation "Schwarz" II: Battle on Sutjeska

The period 1-9 June 1943 was marked by what was probably some of the most ferocious fighting of the entire war, during which both sides spared no cost to achieve their objectives. A force of five NOVJ brigades under the command of the 1st Proletarian Division tried to open the shortest route north by frontal attacks against the linchpins of the German defenses around Tjentište held by four battalions of the KG "Gertler". Hill 819 (called Borovno), located on the right bank of the Sutjeska, was taken, then lost, then taken again; the defenders, who resorted to hurling rocks due to lack of ammunition, were finally allowed to evacuate on the 5th. On the contrary, Hill 787–remembered by all involved simply as Košur–could not be taken despite a series of near-suicidal charges supported by what little artillery and mortars were still left.

28 Sredoje Urošević, "Druga proleterska", in *Sutjeska: zbornik radova* (Belgrade: VIZ, 1959), Vol. II, pp. 71-79; Rudi Petovar and Miloš Zekić, "Šesta istočnobosanska brigada u bici na Sutjesci", in ibid., Vol. I, pp. 217-221; Trifković, *Schwarz*, pp. 111-12.

29 Đuro Kladarin, *Bitka na Sutjesci* (Belgrade: VIZ, 1959), pp. 75, 160-64, 173-74, and Figures 9 and 10; Gojko Nikoliš, "Ranjenici u bici na Sutjesci", in *Sutjeska*, Vol. I, p. 285.

Although this otherwise unremarkable terrain feature must have appeared to the Partisans as being a sinister, impregnable Nazi bastion, the fact was that the Germans were holding out by the skin of their teeth: because of the mounting losses, even the heavily wounded had to stay on serving as MG assistants. On 6 June, the SHQ canceled all offensive operations in this sector, and changed the direction of the breakthrough towards Mount Zelengora.[30]

Two trails led from the river to the area of Lučke Kolibe, the GOG's immediate objective. The one going from Tjentište, then along the Hrčavka Creek, would be used by the 1st Proletarian Division. Its sister division was supposed to use the second trail, which led from the mouth of the Sutjeska Canyon at Suha through Bare. The latter route became the prime target of the KG "Anancker", which was attacking from the south and west with four infantry battalions. By now, the battlefield performance of the Partisans was beginning to suffer due to extreme physical and psychological exhaustion. It was caused by the incessant fighting and marching, enemy artillery and air bombardment, and especially by the lack of food: the reserves of bread were long gone, and some units were already slaughtering their horses. A battalion that was supposed to hold Bare until properly relieved left its positions without authorization in order to find something to eat. Coincidence would have it that the Germans were just completing their long climb from the Sutjeska Valley and taking positions short below the crest of Mount Tovarnica. Luckily for the GOG, the 2nd Dalmatian Brigade arrived in the nick of time and managed to thwart all enemy attempts to re-establish the front along the Sutjeska during five days of extraordinarily bitter fighting (5-9 June). Ultimately, however, the second trail could not be held, and the Partisans had to retreat via Tjentište and Hrčavka. The success of the 2nd Dalmatian came at a very heavy price. "We have lost two-thirds of our men", reported one of its officers, "but you can count on us as if we were at full strength".

Even more dramatic was the message sent from a battalion of the 4th Proletarian, one of whose companies was holding a mountain saddle known as Ljubin Grob that protected the NOVJ's bridgehead in the Zelengora from the west: "For as long as you can hear the shooting [...] the fascists will not pass; when you stop hearing it, you will know that there are no more Proletarians left alive [here]." The company managed to hold off a vastly superior enemy force for the better part of 9 June but was nearly wiped out in the process. The spirit of self-sacrifice displayed by the Dalmatians and Montenegrins at Bare and Ljubin Grob came to symbolize the mood of the entire army. As such, these clashes belonged to the best-known episodes of the "Sutjeska sage", so carefully woven over the decades of Socialist rule; they were commemorated by at least two monuments and a movie. That same 9 June is widely regarded as the most critical day of the battle as far as the NOVJ was concerned. In addition to the above-mentioned gains they made on the southern flank of the bridgehead, the Germans took the Milinklada ridge after a hard day's fighting, thus coming within inches of closing the Tjentište trail as well (their pincers now stood only about three km apart). Not far from here, in the early morning hours,

30 *Enicklopedija*, Vol. IX, p. 250; Ljubivoje Pajović, "Divizion Prve proleterske divizije", in *Sutjeska*, Vol. II, pp. 595-97; Hans Weise, "An der Sutjeska", in Otto Weingartner (ed.), *Erinnerungen an die 118. Jäger-Division (frühere 718. Inf.Div.)* (Klagenfurt: self-pub., 1982), p. 105; NARA/T315/1302/34, Group Weber to 118th JD (2.6.1943).

Tito and his entourage were caught in an air strike: while he escaped with only a flesh wound to his arm, the chief of the recently arrived British mission, Captain William Stuart, was killed.[31]

Instead of pushing north into the Zelengora without waiting for the enemy to tighten his grip, the 1st and 2nd Proletarian Divisions assumed defensive posture in the wider area of Lučke Kolibe, under orders to remain within striking distance of the Sutjeska for as long as possible. This hard-to-understand decision reflected the leadership crisis the SHQ–and the supreme commander in particular–were going through in this period. Same as during Operation "Weiss", the fate of the Central Hospital again lay at the heart of their dilemma. Initially, the hospital was supposed to follow the Proletarian units across the Vučevo and Sutjeska. However, after the repeated attacks from 31 May to 3 June had failed to breach the German lines around Tjentište, the SHQ was compelled to put the hospital, together with the 3rd Assault and the 7th Banija Divisions, under a separate HQ headed by the impulsive Đilas and a former jurist, now an experienced troop officer, Radovan Vukanović. Known simply as the "2nd Group" (the 1st and 2nd Proletarian Divisions being the "first"), this command was ordered to break through across the Tara into Sandžak. The plan immediately turned out to be impractical, as the 2nd Group had virtually no means of crossing the swollen river quickly enough. Consequently, Đilas and Vukanović requested, and were granted, the permission to head back and follow the rest of the army across the Vučevo. Only one day later (6 June), however, the SHQ rescinded its decision, citing the fragility of the Sutjeska bridgehead, which had just come under a heavy attack from the south. At the same time, the 7th Banija, which had already begun crossing the Piva over a makeshift bridge south of Gornje Kruševo, was allowed to proceed west.[32]

On 7 June 1943, however, the SHQ again had a change of heart: the 3rd Assault and the Central Hospital should definitely march towards the Sutjeska. The 7th Banija was ordered to make a halt and cover their crossing by forming a defensive line on the northeastern slopes of the Maglić. This heavily rugged area had seen some bitter fighting in the preceding days ("It's like Eastern Front here", a Partisan officer wrote in his diary), as three battalions of the "Prinz Eugen" pushed towards the Vučevo from the south. Despite the fact that their enemy's presence in this sector had been reduced from three to only one brigade (the 10th Herzegovina; the 4th Proletarian and the 7th Krajina had already left for the Sutjeska), the SS drive was only moderately successful. Mratinje was taken on 5 June, but the NOVJ still controlled the bridge in the vicinity of Gornje Kruševo. Two days later, the Germans scaled the summit of the towering Maglić (2,386 meters), and even managed to haul a mountain gun with them; from there, they took an occasional pot-shot at the guerrilla columns passing below. Although this feat had earned them the Partisans' respect, it was more of a publicity stunt than a worthwhile military mission. On the whole, the 7th SS MTD's advance was slow and overly cautious, which in turn enabled the Partisans to evacuate the Vučevo without interference. After the

31 Kladarin, *Bitka*, pp. 184-87, 190-93, 217; Obrad Egić, "Brigada u bici na Sutjesci", in *Druga dalmatinska proleterska brigada* (Split: IHRPD, 1982), pp. 129-69, 176; Janković, *Četvrta*, pp. 226-27; NARA/T315/1302/299-300, II/738th JR, Report Ljubin Grob (16.6.1943). Neither Stipe Delić's "The Battle on the Sutjeska" (1973), nor Zdravko Velimirović's "The Peaks of Zelengora" (1976) can be considered worthy successors to Veljko Bulajić's 1969-classic "The Battle of the Neretva". Despite lavish production and international cast–including Richard Burton as Tito–both films fail to capture the drama of these decisive moments of the war, and seek to substitute it with cheap pathos and propaganda clichés.

32 *Bitka na Sutjesci*, pp. 41-42, 49-54; *Enicklopedija*, Vol. X, p. 628.

HQ of the 2nd Group had informed the SHQ on the 8th that the 3rd Assault would try its luck on the Tara once more, this hotly contested plateau lost all operational value. Thereupon, the 7th Banija, together with some 600 walking wounded detached from the Central Hospital, executed a forced march towards the Sutjeska. They crossed the river during the night 9/10 June and managed to establish contact with the 1st Group's rearguards around the Hrčavka shortly before the German pincers met on the slopes of Mount Ozren in the early evening of the following day. The sudden appearance of this bloodied, but still combat-ready division bordered on miraculous, yet there was no time for rejoicing: the entire army was moving posthaste deeper into the Zelengora.[33]

Faced with the possibility that 118th JD would not be able to contain the Sutjeska bridgehead on its own, Lüters decided on 5 June 1943 to reinforce it with all available units of the 369th ID. By the 9th, an equivalent of a reinforced regiment was finishing deployment on the far right flank of the KG "Gertler", in the craggy and heavily forested area just west of Vrbnica. On the same day, the division had its first taste of real combat since Čelebić and it did not go well. Two battalions of the KG "Höhne" were forced off a dominant hilltop by a "stronger-than-expected" enemy (in fact, only three battalions), and had to retreat about two km to a clearing called Balinovac. The "enemy" was none other than the premier brigade of the NOVJ. Sensing the weakness in the German perimeter, Koča Popović immediately ordered his old command to continue the attack, at the same time sending the 3rd Krajina in support. The following morning, the Proletarians arrived at Balinovac undetected; with every man capable of holding a rifle deployed at the front, the entire brigade charged the unsuspecting legionnaires. The result was a wholesale rout, which the German officers and NCOs tried in vain to halt with drawn pistols and extra alcohol rations. For once, the guerrillas did not rest on laurels, but mounted a vigorous pursuit, and by the morning of the 11th, they stood before the German rear-area bases at Rataj and Jeleč. Tito's first reaction to Popović's unauthorized move was fury, for the 1st Group was still supposed to wait for the arrival of the 3rd Assault and Central Hospital. Luckily for Popović–and the Partisan cause in general–the supreme commander deferred to the advice of other senior officers, most notably the CO of the 2nd Proletarian Division, Peko Dapčević,[34] that the entire army should move through the breach at once. With the deliverance so palpably close, this mass of desperate men could not be stopped any more. Frantic German efforts to close the gap along the Kalinovik–Foča road on 12-13 June with two reserve battalions, all available aircraft, and a company of tanks failed. In a much-celebrated incident, gunners of the 2nd Proletarian Brigade knocked out a pair of *Panzers* by using an AT piece that they refused to bury along with the rest of their heavy weapons in direct contravention of the SHQ's orders. By the 14th, the 1st Group had completed the crossing of the road and reached the safety of the mountains beyond.[35]

33 Kladarin, *Bitka*, p. 154, and Figures 11 and 13; Rade Hamović, "Deseta hercegovačka", in *Sutjeska*, Vol. II, pp. 267-91; Pavle Jakšić, "Sećanja na borbeni put Sedme baniske divizije", in ibid., Vol. I, pp. 113-25; NARA/T314/560/821-22, 7th SS MTD, Report "Schwarz" (25.7.1943).

34 A British officer observed that "Dapčević had one special bond with Popović. They had both fought in Spain. It would be difficult to find any other personal characteristic which linked them, except a total indifference to physical danger.": F.W.D. Deakin, *The Embattled Mountain* (London: OUP, 1971), p. 104.

35 Vukasnović, *Prva*, pp. 236-46; Nenadović, *Razgovori*, pp. 79-87; Trifković, *Schwarz*, pp. 123-28.

The final act of the drama did not take place in the northern reaches of the Zelengora, but on the banks of the Sutjeska. After another failed attempt to cross the Tara, the HQ of the 2nd Group realized that they had no options left but to follow the path taken by the 7th Banija. All unnecessary equipment was discarded, archives buried, and the heavy wounded hidden in caves and other hard-to-reach locations. The 3rd Assault Division, followed by a long trail of patients from the Central Hospital who did not want to be left behind, crossed the Piva at Gornje Kruševo by mid-day of 10 June. The group's vanguard, the 1st Dalmatian Brigade, traversed the Vučevo without encountering the enemy, and took positions southeast of Tjentište after a full-day's march. The task of this brigade was to seize a foothold on the left bank of the Sutjeska and hold it until the remainder of the column was up and concentrated, which would take approximately another 24 hours. According to Partisan sources, the Germans were alerted to the Dalmatians' presence by a canine patrol. Realizing the game was up, the guerrillas charged across the river, capturing an enemy baggage train in the process. Preoccupied with the loot, the Partisans were ill-prepared to resist a German counterattack that pushed them towards the southwest. Even though the German sources for this day mention only a skirmish, one thing is clear: the 1st Dalmatian did cross the river, but failed to establish a bridgehead. On being asked after the war why that was so, the brigade commander answered candidly that he had lost control over his men, who would simply not stop once they were out of the cauldron. As this clash seemed to confirm that the bulk of the GOG was still located east of the Sutjeska, the Germans hurried to fortify the blocking line along the river. The last-ditch, desperate charge by the remaining two emaciated brigades (the 3rd and the 5th Proletarian) of the 3rd Assault came in the early morning hours of 13 June. The event came to be synonymous with the death of the division commander, Sava Kovačević. Already an epitome of fearless guerrilla warrior-hero, this Montenegrin peasant-turned-worker was adored by his men and ruthless to his enemies (something which was, unsurprisingly, never mentioned in official historiography). Kovačević, along with hundreds of others, were cut down by concentrated small-arms and artillery fire. The charge broke apart, and with it the 3rd Assault Division: small groups of survivors tried to find their way out of the encirclement, or went into hiding (Đilas' group found refuge in one of the last rainforests in Europe, the Perućica). With the battle practically over, the Germans and Italians proceeded with gruesome mopping-up actions on the Vučevo and Mount Pivska.[36]

Operation "Schwarz", in many ways *the* battle of the Yugoslav insurgency, was officially terminated on 16 June 1943. On operational level, it was a clear-cut Axis victory: the guerrilla threat to the littoral and eastern parts of the occupied Yugoslavia was removed, and Italian authority in Montenegro restored. Moreover, the NOVJ suffered truly staggering losses. According to the official, meticulously researched study on the subject, no less than 7,543 Partisans–every third member of the GOG–perished as the result of the battle.[37] Among them, there were an estimated 1,300 patients of the Central Hospital, at least 200 nurses, and 30 doctors, the majority of whom were executed after capture. The fallen fighters originated from

36 Ibid., pp. 129-30, 150-51; Novović and Petković, *Prva* pp. 183-99; Djilas, *Wartime*, pp. 152-54, 266-90, 300; https://www.vreme.com/cms/view.php?id=1100865 (last accessed on 24.6.2019).

37 For comparison, the U.S. forces suffered 6,812 KIA in the Battle of Iwo Jima, and the British and Commonwealth 4,600 in the Second Battle of El Alamein: Spencer C. Tucker (ed.), *Battles that Changed History: An Encyclopedia of World Conflict* (Santa Barbara, CA: ABC-CLIO, 2011), pp. 502, 543.

nearly every corner of the country, but the majority came from Dalmatia, nearly 30 percent of the total. Unlike in earlier sweeps, when high enemy death toll usually stood in stark contrast to quantities of secured weapons, the Germans could now boast of 16 captured cannon, 57 mortars, 220 MGs, and 3,608 rifles; the Italians took a further eight cannon, nine mortars, 52 MGs, and 2,577 rifles, and reclaimed those seven tanks ignominiously lost at Javorak. In addition, 650 Italian and three NDH soldiers were freed from captivity. Although these figures made sure that the "Schwarz" would be lauded in the Third Reich's armed forces official communiqué, the *Wehrmachtbericht*–incidentally, the first anti-guerrilla sweep carried out in Yugoslavia to be granted this honor–the fact remained that the operation failed to deliver strategic results. As we shall see, the main Partisan field force was far from being knocked out, and the news about its alleged destruction had very little impact on the levels of guerrilla activity in other provinces. Plus, the victory did not come cheap: the NDH forces had 40 KIA, 160 WIA, and 205 MIA, and the Wehrmacht had 583 KIA, 1,760 MIA, and 425 MIA. The following example speaks volumes about the ferocity of the recently concluded battle: the 718th ID/118th JD suffered about 400 KIA during the entire first two years of occupation; the death toll incurred on the Sutjeska amounted to 262.[38]

4.6 Bosnia: Return to "Normality"

The first six months of 1943 saw several notable NOVJ actions in Eastern Bosnia; neither the (ultimately unsuccessful) incursion of the Romanija Chetniks in early March, nor the departure of the 6th Eastern Bosnian and Majevica Brigades south a month later, affected the offensive capabilities of the local units. Until mid-June, the Syrmian detachments (soon to become the 1st, 2nd, and 3rd Vojvodina Brigades), working in cooperation with the fighters from Birač and Majevica, succeeded in disarming five *Domobran* battalions and taking Srebrenica. The arrival of the GOG signaled the end of the NDH authority in these parts. Acting in two separate division-sized battle groups, the Partisans had taken practically every town of any size between Sarajevo and Tuzla by 10 July, scattering a further five to six enemy battalions along the way. In what one impressed Vojvodina commissar described as "the Partisan *Blitzkrieg*", Popović's veterans stormed Zvornik (5-7 July). In a moment of supreme irony, scores of Ustashe defenders were cut down by guerrilla machine guns while trying to cross the bridge over the Drina and seek protection of the RSK's Orthodox White Russians on the Serbian soil.

The Germans could not sit idly while anywhere up to 20,000 NOVJ fighters were threatening the Tuzla industrial basin. After the unsuccessful attempt by the 369th ID to block the GOG's advance across the Sarajevo–Višegrad rail line, the division was hurriedly redeployed to the aforementioned region. The legionnaires then launched their own offensive aimed at catching the bulk of the enemy between themselves and a regiment-sized battle group belonging to the 7th SS MTD advancing from the southwest. This latest German move convinced Tito that a prolonged stay in Eastern Bosnia, as per original plan, was out of the question; there was nothing here valuable enough to risk another costly confrontation. Furthermore, the possible strategic implications of the recent Allied invasion of the Apennine Peninsula made

38 Kučan, *Borci*, pp. 33, 1209-12; Nikoliš, *Memoari*, pp. 536-37; *Zbornik*/XIII/3/378, Biroli to CoS (14.7.1943); NARA/T314/560/750-51, BDTK, Losses and booty report "Schwarz" (20.6.1943); NARA/T315/1301/493, 118th JD, Daily order no. 2 (1.5.1943).

the Italian occupation zone more important than ever before. Consequently, in the last week of July, the SHQ decided to dissolve the GOG after a six-month existence. The Partisan supreme commander would take the shortest route to Central Bosnia accompanied by the 7th Banija; the 1st Proletarian would head there as well by using a roundabout route via Sarajevo. The 2nd Proletarian was initially supposed to stay in Eastern Bosnia, but by 8 August, the SHQ had approved Dapčević's plan for a return to Montenegro. After the departure of these formations, the NOP's military and political interests would be safeguarded by the HQ of the 1st Bosnian Corps, which now controlled two newly-formed divisions, the 16th Vojvodina and 17th Eastern Bosnian. In addition to combatting the local Chetniks, the corps also staged successful attacks on NDH garrisons such as Bijeljina and Gračanica (13 and 30 August, respectively).[39]

The march towards Central Bosnia–or, more precisely, the area between the Vrbas, Vrbanja and Lašva Rivers–had been completed with little difficulty by mid-August 1943. The SHQ and the 1st Proletarian (the 7th Banija had been sent home in the meantime) were now "guests" of the 2nd Bosnian Corps, whose zone of responsibility stretched from the Bosna and Neretva in the east to the Una in the west, from the Sava in the north to the border with Dalmatia in the southwest. The already mentioned typhus epidemic, combat losses, and general exhaustion, all of which came as the result of Operation "Weiss", had forced the Krajina Partisans to limit the scope of their activities. Rather than staging ambitious operations against major enemy garrisons as in the previous year, they spent the spring and early summer of 1943 reorganizing, securing their rear against the monarchists, and carrying out guerrilla-style attacks. Among else, the reorganization included forming of new units: in addition to the 4th, 10th, and 12th (later 11th) Krajina Divisions, the corps had no less than ten detachments by mid-June. Operations against the Chetniks were both defensive and offensive in nature. In the last week of July, the 4th Division repulsed an attack made by three corps of the DČD in the area of Bosansko Grahovo. Nearly a month later, the same NOVJ formation launched its own assault against Drenović's forces on the Manjača. The Chetniks proved elusive as usual, and the pursuit had to be called off on the doorsteps of Banja Luka so as not to provoke a direct German intervention.

From the dozens of armed actions performed during this period, some deserve a special mention. For instance, on 25 April, a special assault detail consisting of 17 fighters broke into a makeshift holding facility outside Prijedor, killed the guards, and liberated 124 hostages. Ambush remained the preferred NOVJ tactic: from early March to early July, the 114th JD lost 76 KIA, 40 WIA, and 10 MIA, as well as 54 vehicles (half of them total loss) on the roads of Bosanska Krajina; this led the division's HQ to request a dozen armored personnel carriers for convoy protection duties. Other German formations deployed in the region had similar experiences. On 1 March, the 7th SS MTD lost a 40-strong salvage party that was on its way to the site of an earlier ambush; eleven days later, the same fate befell eight trucks carrying fuel. The 373rd ID was hit particularly hard on 24 August: one of its AT companies was effectively destroyed outside Prijedor, losing 66 men, 24 vehicles, and five cannon; a similar number of men

39 Colić, *Pregled*, pp. 126-30; *Enciklopedija*, Vol. III, p. 671; Mirko Tepavac, *Moj Drugi svetski rat i mir: o ratu i posle rata-autobiografski zapisi* (Zagreb: Razlog, 2013), pp. 108-09; Schmider, *Partisanenkrieg*, pp. 284-85; *SD*/XVI/83 (SHQ to 2nd NOVJD, 9.9.1943), 270, 272; *Zbornik*/IV/14/522-25, 551-53 (Reports of III HDB AC, June 1943); *Zbornik*/IV/16/151-58 (16th NOVJD, Activity report 3.7-19.8.1943), 342-44 (17th NOVJD, Diary, August 1943); NARA/T311/175/1247, OBSO, Daily report (7.7.1943).

was lost in similar circumstances just south of Kotor-Varoš. In marked contrast to its interdiction campaign, the 2nd Bosnian Corps' attempts at taking NDH strongholds more often than not ended in failure (e.g. Glamoč). The situation began to change only in mid-August, when the shortage of troops compelled the Axis to evacuate a number of less-important towns like Ključ, Jajce, Donji Vakuf, and Gornji Vakuf. The arrival of the battle-hardened NOVJ formations from the east also played an important role. The 1st Proletarian Division was thus instrumental in the successful storming of that old Ustasha bastion, Bugojno. The place fell after three days (22-25 August) of "truly tenacious" resistance offered by the members of the 5th UAB, many of whom preferred suicide to being taken alive. This battle symbolically sealed the birth of the "Jajce Republic", a compact liberated territory not unlike the one that existed in this part of the country in late 1942.[40]

In addition to the few industrial objects such as the Ljubija mines, the Germans' main interests in Bosanska Krajina were road and rail communications, especially those leading to the Italian occupation zone, where the Wehrmacht had established permanent presence in the wake of the winter and spring operations. The Germans sought to secure these objectives through active campaigning: from January through July 1943, the 714th ID/114th JD planned and/or executed at least 11 sweeps aimed against the Partisans, whereas the 373rd ID undertook three more between mid-April and mid-June. Owing to the paucity of forces, these operations involved, on average, only two infantry battalions (not counting the usually more numerous NDH units), and were aimed against individual, particularly troublesome enemy groups.[41]

No overview of events in Bosnia during this period would be complete without mentioning the journeys of the 5th Krajina Division. In response to Tito's repeated calls for more pressure against the outer side of the German encirclement ring in Eastern Herzegovina, the 1st Bosnian Corps dispatched the aforementioned formation there on 21 May 1943. Due to the great distances (Foča was almost 145 km away from the starting point of the march that was located halfway between Jajce and Donji Vakuf), adverse weather conditions (the swollen Bosna proved impossible to cross), and the fact that the 5th Krajina had no means of coordinating its efforts with the GOG, the division could be of no assistance to the GOG during the breakthrough from the Zelengora; the two would meet in Eastern Bosnia only at the beginning of July. A couple of weeks later, the division itself was threatened with encirclement and its HQ made an independent decision to return to Central Bosnia. The exfiltration went smoothly, and the outfit remained in its new operational area (the upper Vrbas Valley) until mid-September.

During this period, the 5th Krajina was responsible for some of the most effective Partisan actions of the entire war. These included the demolition of one of the biggest coal basins in the region, Kakanj, on 29 June (huge material damage), as well as the ambushes near Turbe on 12 June (41 killed, 17 wounded, and five missing pioneers from the 373rd ID) and Lepenica on 19

40 Karasijević, *Četvrta*, pp. 95-153; Drago Karasijević, *Peti korpus NOVJ* (Belgrade: VIZ, 1985), pp. 78-123; *Zbornik*/IV/16/270, 1st NOVJD to SHQ (28.8.1943); NARA/T314/554/406-07, 114th JD to BDTK (5.7.1943); NARA/T315/1294/229, 114th JD, Activity report (March 1943); NARA/T315/2171/248-49, 254, 373rd ID, Report on ambush (24.8.1943), and Daily report (25.8.1943), respectively; NARA/T314/559/493, XV MTC/Intel., Report August 1943.

41 For operational orders issued by the 714th ID/114th JD see NARA/T315/1294/52, 142, 236, 275, 294, 354, 530, 534, 537, 699, 708; NARA/T315/2170/126, 373rd ID, Situation report (14.6.1943); *Zbornik*/IV/16/355, BDTK, Daily report (1.8.1943).

July (47 KIA, five WIA, and one MIA from the 7th SS MTD's AT battalion; the Germans claimed they had been lured into the trap by a female agent, but the Partisan sources deny this). The most famous, however, was the storming of the Rajlovac airbase by the 1st Krajina Brigade on the night of 10 August. It was an impromptu action, caused by the nearly daily air raids the unit had to endure in recent weeks. Nevertheless, it was executed in a textbook manner: while two battalions blocked all approaches to the target and destroyed everything of military value within their reach, the third broke into the base and torched 12 NDH and five German aircraft. The combined Partisan losses in all the above-mentioned clashes were 18 KIA and 30 WIA. The stellar performance of the 5th Krajina and its 29-year-old commander, Milutin Morača, drew the attention of the SHQ and made sure that the division would be at the forefront of major operations in the future.[42]

The 10th Herzegovina Brigade was ordered to re-establish the NOVJ presence in its native region right after the breakthrough from the Zelengora. It was a daunting task: by early August 1943, there were less than 400 fighters who remained with the colors, and one-fourth of them came from dispersed Dalmatian units. There was a lot of straggling: the fighters of the crack Mostar Battalion, having lost all contact with higher commands in the aftermath of the last charge on the Sutjeska, decided to split into several groups and head for their respective home areas. More than 90 of them returned to occupied Mostar where some of them were arrested and executed later on. Moreover, the population in the countryside was wary of the Partisans' agenda and terrified of German reprisals, which were already taking place. Finally, the Chetniks were also hard at rebuilding their organization shattered by Operation "Schwarz". In the beginning, the brigade HQ thought it best if battalions acted independently of one another, for security and supply reasons. After several weeks of skirmishing with the Chetniks, the Partisans felt strong enough for more ambitious actions, like the ambush on a German troop train in Popovo Polje on 10 August. All this led to what was probably the last anti-guerrilla sweep of the war carried out jointly by the Wehrmacht and the *Regio Esercito*, Operation "Gama". Despite the fact that it involved three battalions from the "Prinz Eugen" and five from the "Messina" and "Marche" (plus three Chetnik brigades), the undertaking lasted only a couple of days before it became clear that the 10th Herzegovina had again out-marched its pursuers. That the brigade's retreat was merely tactical, and that the Partisans were, in fact, itching for a fight, was witnessed by the two clashes with the SS mountaineers on 24 and 28 August in the area between Gacko and Kalinovik. Whereas each side claimed victory in post-war publications (the Germans admitted to having 16 KIA and 19 WIA, while their opponents reported having captured 86 pieces of small arms), everyone agreed that the fighting was heavy; Eastern Herzegovina was again becoming a battlefield.[43]

42 Morača, *Peta*, pp. 53-82; NARA/T315/2170/91-92, 373rd ID to BDTK (21.6.1943); NARA/T311/175/1215, OBSO, Daily report (21.7.1943); NARA/T314/554/475-76, BDTK to OBSO (12.8.1943); *Zbornik*/IV/15/487-88, NDH Gendarmerie Zenica to 5th Gendarmerie Rgt. (6.7.1943).

43 Radomir Petković, "Borbe desete brigade u Hercegovini, juli-novembar 1943", in *Hercegovina*, Vol. I, pp. 672-75; Ćemalović, *Mostarski*, pp. 229-61; *Hronologija*, p. 526 (17.8.1943); Otto Kumm, *Vorwärts, Prinz Eugen! Geschichte der 7. SS-Freiwilligen-Division 'Prinz Eugen'* (Dresden: Winkelried Verlag, 2007), p. 94; NARA/T311/175/1169, OBSO, Daily report (11.8.1943).

4.7 Croatia and Syrmia: New Commands and New Offensives

Operation "Weiss" was barely over when the Italians put in motion the plan called "The 15th of January", originally proposed already in November 1942. Owing to the unfavorable course of events in Northern Africa and the assumption that the *Supersloda* would be compelled to relinquish a part of its effectives for service on other fronts (the "Sassari" and some smaller units had already departed for Italy), Roatta–who was now the Chief of General Staff and author of the plan–ordered his former command to concentrate in the coastal belt. Upon receiving the news of the impending Italian evacuation of Lika, Gorski Kotar, and Dalmatian hinterland, the 1st Croatian Corps immediately went over to the offensive with the 6th and 8th Divisions, despite the fact that both outfits were heavily hit by a typhus epidemic. The *Regio Esercito*'s main force, consisting of the reinforced "Re" Division, completed the movement to its new bases at Senj and Karlobag by mid-April without serious difficulties. The most notable clash occurred during the withdrawal from the Gacka Valley, when the Italians suffered at least 100 irrevocable losses and additional 70 wounded in the fighting against the Partisans supported by tanks and heavy weapons. The collaborationist forces that stayed behind were the ones who would feel the full weight of the NOVJ offensive. Having neither mobile reserves of their own, nor support from Roatta's regulars, they were forced to await their fate scattered in dozens of strongpoints. Not that the Partisan re-conquest of Lika was an easy task: it lasted from March throughout April, and saw some fierce fighting, for instance at the Chetnik bastion of Crna Vlast, or the NDH garrison of Široka Kula. Nevertheless, the campaign was a success: for a relatively modest price of 88 KIA and MIA, and 323 WIA, the 1st Croatian Corps inflicted substantial losses to the enemy, including 142 automatic weapons, 2,561 rifles, and 1,451 prisoners (note: the figures refer to April 1943 alone). Otočac became the center of this large new liberated territory and the NOP capital of Croatia and would remain so until February 1944. Only one thing stood between the guerrillas and a total triumph: Gospić.[44]

"Heaven save us from another Bihać!" noted one Ustasha captain, clearly worried about the very real possibility that the nightmare scenario from November 1942 would repeat itself in the town considered the cradle of the Croat fascist movement. Out of nine battalions originally subordinated to the NDH's Lika Operational Area Command (*Zapovjedništvo operativnog područja Lika, ZAPOLI*), only three were available for the direct defense of Gospić; together with local militia and gendarmerie, they numbered about 1,400 men. By the end of April 1943, the garrison found itself cut off from the outside world when their foe occupied the surrounding countryside and severed the main supply road leading to Karlobag."The boil has burst", wrote the same Ustasha officer in his diary for 9 May. Supported by four tanks and seven field guns, two brigades each from the 6th and 8th Divisions launched an all-out, concentric assault. Their target turned out to be not Bihać, but Udbina: well-fortified and motivated, the defenders fought back fiercely, stopping the guerrillas in their tracks. Partisan commanders had matured since Udbina, however: rather than pressing on with the attack, they canceled it as soon as it became clear that the cost would be too high (there were already 52 KIA and MIA, and 192 WIA).

44 *Zbornik*/XIII/3/185-213, *Supersloda*, Memorandum (26.4.1943); *Zbornik*/V/14/363-64 (1st Croatian NOVJC, Activity report, April 1943), 471 (V AC, Daily report, 15.4.1943); Dušan V. Baić, "Oslobođenje Gacke doline", in *Osma*, pp. 373-86.

Instead, they settled down for a formal siege. The great symbolic importance attached to the survival of the garrison is evident from the sustained supply-and-support campaign conducted by the air forces of all three Axis nations. The siege lasted for roughly one month before it was lifted by a joint Italian-NDH attack across the Velebit. By this time there was only one Partisan brigade left in the area, whose sole task was to watch over the Gospić garrison and defend the approaches to the liberated territory. The stalemate in this sector, punctuated by skirmishes, would last until early September. The greatest threat to the NOP's domain in Lika was coming in form of the Wehrmacht units that were making their way towards the coast from the east. This was the first time the local Partisans faced the Germans, and they proved to be just as vulnerable to ambushes as the Italians were. There was hardly a day in August without an incident on the Bihać–Kulen Vakuf road. The 114th JD lost two out of its three regimental commanders on the 18th, and a further 60 soldiers were killed 10 days later near Ripač by the 3rd Lika Brigade. Although effective, these small-scale actions alone could not stop the German advance, and by the last day of August, both Donji Lapac and Gornji Lapac were in their hands.[45]

Kordun and Cazinska Krajina were largely pacified as the result of Operation "Weiss". The things began to change only after the battle of Gospić, when the HQ of the 1st Croatian Corps decided to return the 8th Division to its home region. Its main tasks were to protect the harvesting and retake NDH garrisons in the region, thereby re-establishing the severed land connection between Lika and Banija. Between 16 and 21 June 1943, working in cooperation with Una Operational Group (roughly three brigades), the 8th managed to take Cetingrad and Slunj, but failed to finish off the obstinate defenders of Velika Kladuša. Having no desire to meet the intervening German and NDH forces (Operations "Clara", 20-22 June, and "Donnerschlag", 29-31 July), the Partisans surrendered their recently-won prizes and dispersed. The Kordun units then directed their attention to the Karlovac–Ogulin railway line, but reverted to targeting population centers as soon as their garrisons were reduced or withdrawn. Once in the open, HDB units were even more vulnerable than usual: 285 Home Guards were thus captured while retreating from Velika Kladuša. By mid-August, entire Kordun and the biggest part of Cazinska Krajina were liberated. The scope of the NOVJ's activities in the neighboring Banija was determined by the departure of the 7th Division with the GOG. This meant that there were no large-scale actions, but the local Partisans nevertheless remained very active. Among the numerous actions conducted during spring and summer, some deserved to be mentioned separately, like the "decapitation" of the I HDB AC on 29 May (the commanding general wounded, two senior staff officers captured), and the attack on a German ammunition convoy approximately one month later (13 KIA and MIA, two trucks destroyed).[46]

Very little was happening in Gorski Kotar during the first two months of 1943, but the Italians returned in March with their now-traditional incursion into the liberated territory

45 War diary of Josip Hübl (18.4 and 11.5.1943), available on http://www.cro-eu.com/forum/index.php?topic=1355.0 (last accessed on 20.7.2019); Đorđe Orlović, "Borbe na teritoriji Gospića i Perušića (april-maj 1943. godine)", in *Gospić*, pp. 844-78; Đoko Jovanić, "Šesta lička proleterska divizija 'Nikola Tesla' u trećoj godini rata (1.VII 1943-30.VI 1944)", in *Treća godina narodno-oslobodilačkog rata na području Karlovca, Korduna, Like, Pokuplja i Žumberka* (Karlovac: HAK, 1977), pp. 561-71; Mikić, *Zrakoplovstvo*, pp. 74-75; NARA/T315/1295/23-52, 114th JD, Diary appendices (August 1943).

46 Ibid., 19-21 (29-31.7.1943); NARA/T315/1294/674-75, 114th JD, Daily reports June 1943; Joco Tarabić, "Osma divizija u trećoj godini NOR-a", in *Treća*, pp. 149-55; Đurić, *Banijski*, pp. 230-60.

around Drežnica. The sweep, like all its predecessors, succeeded only in destroying the guerrilla infrastructure. There was little booty to be had: "No food was lost because we did not have any to begin with", lamented the local NOVJ command over the critical supply situation. At that time, neither of the two locally raised brigades, the 6th and 14th, were on their native terrain, but fighting in Lika. Upon their return in April, they were combined into the 13th Division (the 5th OZ was dissolved). After a month-long spell in the Ogulin-Karlovac area, both brigades were sent to the Brinje sector. The new task was unlike any they had had before: fortify the mountain passes outside Krivi Put and Žuta Lokva and secure the western approaches to Otočac. Their predecessors, the 1st Lika and 4th Kordun Brigades, had already repulsed one Italian sally from the direction of the coast. On 12 June, elements of the "Re" Division attacked again and succeeded in pushing the guerrillas to the western edges of the Gacka Valley. On the 23rd, the 6th and 14th Brigades counterattacked, inflicting over 60 casualties and knocking out two tanks (If this is true, they shoot better than us", commented one Italian officer). Unwilling to commit more resources to an operation of secondary importance, the V AC canceled the advance and retreated to a more defensible line on the slopes of the Velebit. Apart from patrol activity, this sector would remain quiet until early September. In the meantime, the newly-formed Primorsko-goranski Group of Detachments was conducting a classic guerrilla campaign, carrying out 19 actions in the period 25 July-22 August. Although enemy material and human assets were the main target, civilian casualties could sometimes not be avoided: on 30 August, an ambush on a woodcutting party outside Sušak left three soldiers and 17 workers dead.[47]

After 9th Division left to join the SHQ in late February 1943, the NOVJ presence in Dalmatia was reduced to about 700 men organized into three (later four detachments). By mid-April, this number had risen to ca. 1,500, two-thirds of whom were armed. This was not enough for more ambitious operations but sufficed for a purely guerrilla campaign. Among else, the Partisans successfully attacked Italian columns on several occasions (e.g. at Vodice on 15 February, Banjevci on 22 June, Kistanje on 28 August; among the killed were the commander of the "Alessandria" Regiment, and the chief of staff of the "Eugenio de Savoia" Division), blew up the hitherto unreachable Bender viaduct (15 March), and carried out three attacks on the Split–Solin railway in four days (3-7 June). The campaign was not confined to the mainland. Hardly a month passed without an "act of piracy" in the coastal waters. For instance, the NOVJ's Coastal Platoon captured three motor sailers between Split and Korčula in the period 22-25 February. The guerrilla actions on the islands culminated in the capture of Bol on 5 August. In order to lull the Italians and draw them out of the barracks, the local NOP branch organized a dance which they knew would be well-attended. The ruse worked, and the Yugoslavs had little trouble in disarming the entire garrison, capturing ca. 160 pieces of small arms. In response, the *Regio Esercito* launched a punitive expedition that razed six settlements on the island of Brač.[48]

47 Radoslav Kosanović Braco, "Šesta primorsko-goranska udarna brigada", in *Partizanska Drežnica* (Karlovac: HAK, 1982), pp. 202-04; Andrija Tus, "Četrnaesta primorsko-goranska brigada", in ibid., pp. 237-41; *Zbornik*/V/13/313-22 (5th OZ to MHQ Croatia, 23.3.1943), 572 (V AC, Daily report, 16.3.1943); *Zbornik*/V/16/504-08, V AC, Daily report (23.6.1943); *Zbornik*/V/18/336-38 (Primosko-goranski GoD to MHQ Croatia, 29.8.1943), 640 (V AC, Daily report, 31.8.1943).

48 *Zbornik*/V/14/212, Dalmatian GoD to MHQ Croatia (15.4.1943); *Zbornik*/V/16/523, and *Zbornik*/V/18/624-25, XVIII AC, Daily reports (25.6 and 29.8.1943, respectively); *Dalmacija*/V/273-74 (Dalmatian GoD to Svetislav Stefanović, 14.3.1943), 289 (OHQ Zrmanja to 1st Croatian NOVJC, 18.3.1943), 483-87 ("Eugenio di Savoia" to XVIII AC, 17.2.1943), 580-81 (*Maridalmazia*, Daily

In addition to reprisals, the VI and XVIII AC launched numerous actions of varying scope, usually in cooperation with the MVAC and, to a lesser degree, with the NDH armed forces. The joint operation of the "Zara" and "Eugenio di Savoia" in the area of Biograd na Moru, which started on 17 March 1943, was unusually successful, with "many" of the 119 enemy killed being Partisan sympathizers and KPJ members. Operation "Biokovo" (10 July-1 August), on the contrary, was a failure despite being probably the only genuine combined-arms anti-guerrilla undertaking of the war. With the force of fifteen Italian, one German, and two NDH battalions, supported by the *Regia Aeronautica* and *Regia Marina*, the *Supersloda* hoped to destroy the NOP bases on the Biokovo and Mosor once and for all. Having only about 550 men, the Biokovo Detachment had no alternative but to disperse, with two larger groups escaping to the area west of Imotski, and one to Hvar. Unaware of these events, the Cetina Detachment left the Mosor and headed for the Biokovo in an attempt to relieve their "cousins" there, but nearly lost one of its battalions to the enemy ambush at Lovreč on 22 July (42 KIA); bloodied, the Partisans retreated north. With no enemy left to fight, the Italians spent the next week or so destroying unregistered vessels, torching villages, and interning civilians.[49]

1943 began auspiciously for 2nd OZ. On 2 January, Krašić (incidentally, the home parish of the controversial Archbishop Alojzije Stepinac) fell to the 13th Proletarian and 4th Kordun Brigades after two days of bitter fighting. The battle will be best remembered for the nearly wholesale destruction of its ca. 600-strong garrison, and the mass execution of close to 200 captured Ustashe (the Partisan losses were 39 KIA and 63 WIA). This, and other depredations launched from the Žumberak, compelled the Italian XI AC to undertake a major sweep of the area. The action, which ultimately involved six reinforced battalions of infantry from the "Isonzo" and "Lombardia", lasted four days (29 January-2 February) and ended in the death or disappearance of almost 100 servicemen and wounding of another 160. The key to the NOVJ's success was the cooperation between the Croatian 2nd OZ and the Slovene 1st OZ, steered by a joint OHQ. In this way, three Slovenian brigades came just in time to hit the main enemy column in the back as it became heavily engaged against the Croatian units in the area west of Krašić. The Italians and NDH forces would launch at least three more expeditions against the Žumberak in the period March-August, but each would end in a similar way: their foe would first escape either to Slovenia, or across the Kupa, and then return to his old bases as soon as the pursuit was called off. The offensive from the second half of June presents an exception, as the need to protect the harvesting forced the 13th Proletarian to meet the attackers head-on (successfully, as it turned out). In the interim, the guerrillas went about their wrecking business, which would often take them to the gates of Zagreb. On the evening of 29 May, the aforementioned brigade staged a smaller version of the Rajlovac raid by capturing the HDB glider school at Sveta Nedelja without firing a shot; the base was destroyed (including two aircraft and all the gliders), and about 100 Home Guards led away into captivity.[50]

For the Kalnik and Moslavina Partisans, defeating enemy regulars in open battle, or storming battalion-sized strongpoints remained a distant wish. In these regions, the NOVJ's level of

report, 28.2.1943); Kvesić, *Dalmacija*, pp. 569-70; Miroslav Velić, Ante V. Petrić, and Mate Vuletić, *Mosorski partizanski odred* (Split: IHRPD, 1985), pp. 155-56.

49 Ibid., pp. 168-85; *Dalmacija*/V/522; Colić, *Pregled*, pp. 130-34; Fasanotti et. al., *L'esercito*, pp. 276, 290-91.

50 Radošević, *Trinaesta*, pp. 38-135; *SZH*/IV/54-57, 2nd OZ/Pol. to MHQ Croatia (8.1.1943).

organization remained largely where it had been in the second half of 1942. There were enough volunteers going around to transform the two local detachments into brigades, but the MHQ Croatia seemingly preferred to have these units serve as recruit depots for the 3rd OZ. In this way, during 1943, the Moslavina Detachment lost two, and its Kalnik counterpart three battalions, plus at least 500 additional replacements. Hence, bigger actions could only take place in conjunction with the mobile formations from Slavonia. These included the unsuccessful attack on Garešnica from 22 to 24 February and the successful taking of the notorious Lepoglava penitentiary on 13 July. The NOP propaganda made much out of the fact that the "Croatian Bastille" was stormed on the anniversary of the French Revolution. On this occasion, the Partisans liberated ca. 100-150 political prisoners; they made sure that the hardened felons remained locked up but released and/or recruited several hundred lighter criminals. This turned out to be a bad idea. Those who were taken into the army were undisciplined and prone to panic, and some of those who had been set free took up their old trade, sometimes posing as the Partisans. In any case, the continued existence of the Kalnik and Moslavina Detachments and their day-to-day activities–which, in the case of the former, included more than 60 attacks on settlements and gendarmerie or railway stations during the first eight months of 1943–drew much attention from their enemies. The five bigger Axis undertakings launched in this period were largely NDH affairs, involving, on average, an equivalent of up to two regiments of troops from the HDB's 1st ID and 1st MTD. They all ended disappointingly, even in those cases when the German 187th RD was available to lend a hand (e.g. Operation "Ivan", 4-6 July).[51]

In contrast to its westerly neighbor, the 3rd OZ was experiencing a major expansion. The envisaged conquest of the Požega and Daruvar basins had to be postponed due to Operation "Weiss". The 4th Division's attempt to disrupt German dispositions by staging a massive raid on the Zagreb–Belgrade railway line between Novska and Nova Gradiška in the last week of January 1943 had failed with 48 KIA and 69 WIA. After that, the bulk of NOVJ forces returned to the Slavonian Mountains and continued their operations as per the original plan. By mid-March, they had come so close to achieving their objectives that the situation could not be ignored any longer by the Wehrmacht. The time of half-measures was over: Operation "Braun", designed to be a battle of annihilation, would be carried out by an estimated 25-30,000 troops, including a sizable contingent from the 187th RD. During the first phase of the fighting (20-22 March), four Partisan brigades put up a heavy resistance on the Psunj and Papuk, but could not stop the Axis from closing a ring around them. Seeing no alternative, the Slavonians split up into three groups, each heading in a different direction. The Axis tried to pursue, but once the guerrillas decided that they had enough, it was very hard to catch them. The battle, including the small, inconsequential mop-up operation named "Virovitica", was largely over by 7 April; for the price of 40 German and 73 NDH irrevocable losses (the lowest estimate; according to one document, they were two to three times greater), 151 enemy "VIPs" and 262 pieces of small

51 Ibid., pp. 449-50, Moslavina Det. to 2nd OZ (13.3.1943); Vukašin Karanović, *Od Moslavačkih odreda do 33. divizije* (Čazma: Odbor za proslavu 35. godišnjice 33. divizije, 1978), p. 10; Miličević, *Kalnički*, pp. 116-68; SZH/V/499-500 (OK Varaždin, Announcement, 16.7.1943), 695 (12th Bde./Pol. to CK KPH, 1.8.1943), 704 (12th NOVJD to 2nd Croatian NOVJC, 2.8.1943), 717 (OK Varaždin to CK KPH, 3.8.1943); see entries for Operations "Moslavačka Gora", "Mirko", "Zagorje", "Ciril", "Ivan" in: https://www.axishistory.com/list-all-categories/135-campaigns-a-operations/anti-partisan-operations-in-croatia/1934-anti-partisan-operations-in-the-independent-state-of-croatia (last accessed 28.7.1943).

arms were reported captured. Although being celebrated as a major victory, the "Braun" was, in fact, a flop. This was amply proven on 16 April, when the 4th Division made an all-out assault on the HDB Slavonian Brigade near the place called Šušnjari and routed it completely, taking 500 prisoners. The huge amount of materiel captured on that day, combined with a steady influx of new recruits, helped make good the losses sustained during the past month-and-a-half (191 KIA, 309 WIA, and 137 MIA). In recognition of their martial qualities, the Slavonians would get their own corps one month later (re-designated 2nd Croatian Corps in late June; the 3rd OZ was dissolved at the same time), as well as another division, the 10th (later renamed 28th).[52]

By mid-June 1943, the Partisans had seized control of the entire Požega Basin except for the two biggest towns and were now seeking to expand their domains beyond the Slavonian Mountains; a couple of outlying posts around Daruvar and Virovitica had already fallen, and Našice itself was attacked. On learning that another major enemy operation was in the offing (codename "Antun"), the Partisans decided to de-concentrate before the blow could land. One brigade of the 10th Division would thus go to Banija, while the other would stay behind together with the local units. The NOVJ's main force, the 4th Division, would march west in order to spread the uprising to the Kalnik and Zagorje. The division became a high-priority target practically from the moment it started its journey on 27 June. The *Luftwaffe*, the *Zrakoplovstvo*, Pavelić's elite bodyguard units, plus the elements of the 1st HDB MTD, the 187th RD, and the recently arrived German 100th JD, all took part on the pursuit that lasted for four weeks. In these operations, nicknamed "Varaždin" and "Paula", the Germans captured some 455 pieces of small arms, five cannon, and 14 mortars. Even though the Partisans managed to avert disaster by constant maneuvering, it was clear that a sustainable "invasion" of Croatia's northwest would have to be postponed. By the beginning of August, the 1st Slavonian Corps was largely back where it had started, with one division on the Bilogora, and the other on the Papuk. Their posture was defensive: they rested and protected the harvest, which ultimately proved very bountiful. For now, offensive actions (including the demolition of agricultural machines on enemy territory) would remain the responsibility of the corps' six detachments.[53]

During the first quarter of 1943, the NOVJ presence in Syrmia consisted of one battalion of the 3rd Detachment/3rd OZ and the village guards. The latter were divided into two groups: while the "professionals" took over such tasks as ambushes, raids, and sabotage, the staple activity of the "amateurs" seemed to have been the killing of hostile individuals. The NOP's popularity was at an all-time high: by early spring, the detachment had grown to four battalions with close to 700 men. Hundreds of volunteers who could not be armed were sent as replacements to the

52 Colić, *Pregled*, pp. 108-13; *Građa za historiju Narodnooslobodilačkog pokreta u Slavoniji* (Slavonski Brod: Historijski institut Slavonije, 1960-1984), Vol. IV, p. 115, 4th NOVJD to Vlado Popović (25.1.1943) [hereinafter: *Slavonija*/volume/page]; *Slavonija*/V/145-49 (Statement Franjo Pavlek, 20.4.1943), 297-99 (1st Slavonian NOVJC, Orders, 17.5.1943); *Slavonija*/VI/224-25, 2nd Croatian NOVJC, Circular (20.6.1943); NARA/T315/1553/1087, 1168-69 (187th RD, Casualty return, and Report "Braun" and "Virovitica", 2.4 and 1.5.1943, respectively), 1303-04 (187th RD/Group "West", Situation report, 30.4.1943).

53 *Oslobodilački*, Vol. I, pp. 496-500; *Slavonija*/VI/465-66 (2nd Croatian NOVJC, Circular 20.7.1943), 488 (HQ Ustasha Transport Brigades to NDH MoD, 24.7.1943); *Zbornik*/V/16/434, II HDB AC, Daily report (15.6.1943); NARA/T315/1220/3-12, 100th JD/Intel., Activity report 1.6-27.7.1943; NARA/T314/559/353, BDTK/Intel., Situation report July 1943; *Zbornik*/XII/3/588, XV MTC/Admin., Quarterly report (July-September 1943).

Syrmian units fighting in Bosnia. In May, the province got its own Group of Assault Battalions, which became the 3rd Vojvodina Brigade in early June. Finally, on 2 July, the SHQ formally acknowledged Vojvodina as a separate sub-theater of war by dissolving the dysfunctional relationship with the Slavonian command and granting the province its own MHQ. By the end of the month, this staff controlled some 1,300 fighters. Inner consolidation and expansion went hand in hand with more ambitious undertakings. For instance, the storming of the gendarmerie station at Surduk (22 March), or the attack on an ESDM patrol near Grabovac (5 May), both of which resulted in the death or capture of up to 15 enemy personnel, were considered major actions at the time. By August, the Partisans already felt confident enough to take on bigger targets, like a pioneer company of the German 173rd RD (which was practically wiped out at Neštin on the 23rd with 63 KIA, three WIA, 23 MIA), and an HDB labor battalion at Bošnjaci on the 31st (227 prisoners, 180 rifles captured). However, the NOVJ units still lacked the know-how and heavy weaponry needed for taking fortified towns and villages, as witnessed by the twin repulse at Grgurevci and Irig on the 20th and 30th, respectively.[54]

4.8 Slovenia: Final Months of Italian Occupation

The focal point of guerrilla efforts in Slovenia during the first eight months of 1943 lay in Dolenjska and Notranjska, largely owing to the fact that the bulk of NOVJ's mobile formations was deployed there. In February and March, four brigades made a series of attacks on MVAC and Italian outposts (e.g. Pleterje, Ambrus, Hočevje), but failed to score a single clear-cut victory. In the process, however, they learned that they were quite capable of beating enemy relief columns in the open. On 26 March, the Slovenes celebrated their greatest success so far, routing a battalion of the "Macerata" at Jelenov Žleb, (at least 41 dead and 60 missing soldiers, over 200 pieces of small arms lost). Despite this success, the increasing pressure from the XI AC compelled the Partisans to de-concentrate, with one group of two brigades going towards Ljubljana, while the other headed back to the Gorjanci. During the next three months, the guerrillas–occasionally reinforced by their "cousins" from across the NDH border–limited their offensive actions to sabotage and raids, maneuvering constantly so as to avoid the increasingly active Italians.

As spring turned into summer, the SHQ decided that the Slovene branch of the army had matured enough to have its own divisions. Numbered 14th and 15th, these formations received their baptism of fire in late July in a major joint operation against the Blackshirt outpost at Žužemberk. Although the place itself was reduced with the help of two 47mm guns (the first such weapons in the Partisans' possession), the retreating defenders were ultimately saved by a rapid intervention from the neighboring garrisons. On this occasion, Italian gunners again proved their skill by destroying an enemy command post and killing the MHQ Slovenia's chief of staff, its deputy *politkom*, as well as the CO of the 15th Division. The fall of Mussolini in late July brought about another change in the NOVJ's plans. Augmented by mobile units

54 *Zbornik*/I/6/249, 262-64 (IV/3rd. Det., Activity report, 1.3.1943), 310 (3rd. Det./3rd OZ, Strength return, 14.5.1943), 319 (3rd. Det./3rd OZ, Activity report, April 1943), 358 (MHQ Vojvodina to SHQ, 27.7.1943), 409 (MHQ Vojvodina, Communique no. 6, 3.9.1943); *Zbornik*/I/17/398 (ESDM Btl. "General Laudon", Situation report 23.3.-1.4.1943), 481-83 (GEGC/East Syrmia, Report, 1.9.1943); NARA/T311/285/774, 173rd RD to OBSO (2.9.1943).

from across the country, the divisions were ordered to make preparations for the possibility of Italy's exit from the war. Instead of engaging in pitched battles, the Partisans were ordered to deploy along the major road and railway communications (most notably the line Karlovac–Novo Mesto–Ljubljana–Postojna–Trieste) and hinder the flow of Italian and German troops towards the Apennine Peninsula. Of the many incidents that occurred during August, the loss of three flatcars laden with motor vehicles belonging to the Wehrmacht's 24th Panzer Division (PzD) on the 24th deserves a special mention.[55]

After a lengthy period of stagnation, Primorska was experiencing a surge in guerrilla activity. Ironically, the Italians and their forceful conscription of ethnic Slovenes into the *Regio Esercito* were largely responsible for this state of affairs. The influx of draft-dodgers enabled the local branch of the NOVJ not only to send over 1,000 unarmed replacements to Notranjska and Dolenjska, but also to form a separate OZ in February and two additional brigades (the 5th and 6th) in April 1943. In pursuance of the well-established policy of exporting the uprising, these mobile formations were sent on an expedition to what was considered the far west of the Slovene ethnic territory. The undertaking, which took place during the first three weeks of May, produced mixed results. Its propaganda impact was considerable, not least because of the successful actions such as the ambush on the Kobarid–Bovec road on the 18th that resulted in the death or injury of over 20 enemy soldiers. On the other hand, the young brigades proved to be too weak, inexperienced, and under-equipped to maintain themselves for long so deep in the Italian metropolitan territory. Their foe–the XXIII, later also the XXIV AC, both from the 8th ITA–was constantly on their heels, and even managed to surprise and nearly destroy a large group of Partisans at Golobar on 26 April (altogether 43 KIA). Learning from these experiences, the brigades dispersed, each battalion conducting its own small campaign during late spring and early summer; the devastating attack on a CCRR bus outside Idrija on 23 June (15 KIA and five WIA) stands out in this respect. The already-mentioned master plan of the MHQ from early August had repercussions for Primorska OZ as well: the bulk of its fighters, now combined into a single (3rd Slovenian) brigade, were ordered to join the 14th Division on the outskirts of the capital.[56]

As in Primorska, the situation in the German-occupied parts of Slovenia during the early part of 1943 was further aggravated by the introduction of conscription. The ever-increasing needs of the Eastern Front "meat grinder" made the Nazis forget their racial theories and begin drafting ethnic Slovenes–ultimately, some 38,000 of them–into the armed forces. In response, the NOP launched its own recruitment drive, which was still voluntary in nature: the draftees should be made to feel "morally obligated" to join up through propaganda and political work. As a result, the strength of the Gorenjska Detachment grew from some 300 fighters in late 1942 to over 1,200 in June 1943; at the same time, the province received its own OZ (the 2nd) and a brigade

55 *Zbornik*/VI/5/278-328 (Actions of Slovene Brigades, 12.12.1942-3.5.1943), 650 ("Macerata" to XI AC, 27.3.1943), 653-69 (XI AC, Report Ribnica 22-29.3.1943); *Zbornik*/VI/6/23-27 (2nd OZ zo MHQ Croatia, 14.5.1943), 495 (Commander of Order Police [*Befehlshaber der Ordnungspolizei*, BdO] "Alpenland", Info bulletin no. 49 (25.8.1943); *Enciklopedija*/II/508-10 and VI/153; Lado Ambrožič-Novljan, *Petnajsta divizija* (Ljubljana: Borec, 1983), pp. 21-53; NARA/T315/806/15, 18, 24th PzD, Diary (25 and 28.8.1943, respectively).

56 *Enciklopedija*/VIII/715-16; Stanko Petelin, *Gradnikova brigada* (Ljubljana: Borec, 1983), pp. 22-109; *Zbornik*/VI/6/323, CCRR Gorizia to XI AC (23.6.1943); *Zbornik*/XIII/3/403-17, 8th ITA, Monthly report (July 1943).

(the 7th). On the downside, the units were so preoccupied with mobilizing, that they had little time for anything else, including fighting. The CK KPS admonished the Gorenjska Partisans in early summer for the "scandalous" fact that they "carried out practically no actions" in the recent period. While this was clearly an exaggeration, the guerrillas certainly limited both the scope and frequency of their operations. For instance, from 4 April to 17 July, the local detachment reported having carried out only 31 actions. The biggest of them was the successful attack on a gendarmerie patrol on 31 March (24 pieces of small arms captured); others included the execution of "a prostitute, who was a German informer" and the chasing off of the Bessarabian *Volksdeutsche*, who were re-settled here as a part of Himmler's Germanization policies. Unlike their comrades from Gorenjska, the Štajerska Partisans (the 4th OZ) were commended for their aggressiveness, even though they were operating in more difficult circumstances. According to the Styrian authorities, in February 1943 alone, the presence of the "bandits" was reported on 70 occasions. They were apparently mostly interested in foodstuffs and liquidation of hostile individuals. Armed confrontations were rare: from 8 January to 15 March, there were "only" 12 KIA and 90 WIA among the members of security forces. The capture of the gendarmerie station at Ihan, together with 27 rifles, on 6 March was probably the biggest NOVJ action from the period leading up to the capitulation of Italy.[57]

The conflict also reached the northern-most Slovene settlements, located in Carinthia. Dictated by necessity, the operations in the eastern part of the province were steered by the 4th OZ, whereas the Gorenjska Detachment controlled the west. In November 1942, the Štajerska command dispatched a group of 11 fighters to serve as the core of the Koruška Company. Reinforced by local volunteers and draft-dodgers, the unit (now upgraded to a battalion) successfully raided the small mining town of Mežica on 4 April 1943. In the meantime, the originally modest guerrilla presence in the area of Rosenthal–established already during last September–was being steadily reinforced by a trickle of volunteers from the south. By mid-May 1943, the Partisans felt strong enough to attack the town of Feistritz. In the process, they also liberated the local labor camp housing both the French and Soviet POWs. Appalled by the brutal treatment meted out to the Red Army prisoners and angered by the fact that the French were seemingly content with their present lot, the guerrillas put in practice the Marxist theory of "redistribution of wealth" by taking away food parcels from the latter and giving them to the former. Despite these successful undertakings, Koruška was still not important enough to warrant a permanent NOVJ "garrison". By early August, the majority of guerrillas had gone south in order to join the newly-created brigades, leaving behind only small groups of proven fighters and political workers.[58]

The low intensity of the Partisan campaign in the German zone was usually attributed to the combination of harsh winter, lack of weapons, as well as inexperience and inherent "passivity"

57 Tilen Klukovič, *Prisilne mobilizacije v Sloveniji v času 2. svetovne vojne–primerjava med nemško in partizansko vojsko* (M.A. thesis, University of Ljubljana, 2013), p. 45; *Enciklopedija*/III/236; *DLRS*/V/247-49 and VIII/104-05, CK KPS to PK Gorenjska (20.1 and 7.7.1943, respectively); *Zbornik*/VI/6/44-46 (Kamniško-Savinjski Det. to 4th OZ, 28.5.1943), 122-26 (Gorenjska Det., Activity report, undated); *Zbornik*/VI/5/561, 605 (Styrian Government, Staff conferences, 1 and 15.3.1943, respectively), 584-86 (Gendarmerie Kranj, Order, 9.3.1943).

58 *Enciklopedija*/IV/635-36; *Zbornik*/VI/5/233-43 (1st Koruška Btl. to 4th OZ, 10.4.1943) 237-41 (4th OZ to MHQ Slovenia, 12.4.1943); *Zbornik*/VI/6/29-34, Gorenjska Det. to PK Gorenjska (23.5.1943).

of the Slovene fighter. The most important factor, however, was the extraordinary effective anti-guerrilla campaign conducted by the security forces. Enjoying numerical superiority and having a highly developed intelligence service on all levels, the Germans were continuously in a position to thwart major enemy undertakings, or at least inflict heavy losses on him. On 7 January 1943, a 2,000-strong posse surrounded the fortified winter camp of the Pohorje Battalion, which had been wreaking havoc across eastern Štajerska for the past several months. In the ensuing firefight, all 70 Partisans, including the unit's all-female squad, were killed or executed (the German losses were 19 KIA and 31 WIA). That the OF leadership was still entertaining the idea of reinforcing the 4th OZ by the veterans from the Italian zone was first confirmed by the attacks on postal offices and gendarmerie stations around Mokronog in late April. The main assault came some five weeks later: the 1st and 2nd Brigades feinted against the demarcation line just east of the capital in hope of drawing the enemy attention, while the 3rd and 4th Brigades made the crossing of the Sava further downstream. The Germans, however, refused to take the bait, but quickly deployed two police regiments along the endangered section of the river, thus effectively crossing the Partisans' plan.

In August, the inter-Axis border came under pressure again, this time in the form of the 6th and 7th Brigades coming from the north. Formed in Štajerska and Gorenjska, respectively, these formations had 1,300 men between them, which represented roughly one-fourth of the NOVJ's total effectives in Slovenia. A considerable number of them were unarmed, but it was hoped that this problem could be solved in Ljubljana Province. The 6th Brigade managed to cross the Sava halfway between Ljubljana and Litija on 20-21 August, but nearly lost its rearguard (78 fighters) in the process. In the meantime, the Gestapo tricked the HQ of the 4th OZ into believing that some disenchanted members of this notorious Nazi organization were willing to procure no less than a thousand automatic weapons to the guerrillas. The 7th Brigade paid a heavy price for such hard-to-explain *naiveté*: while waiting for the promised delivery at Žirovski vrh (11 km northeast of Idrija), this formation was attacked and routed by the 19th SS PR on 2-3 August, losing 145 dead and captured. The remainder, minus the stragglers, managed to escape across the demarcation line. The occupation forces did not limit their efforts to large operations like the ones described above but remained active on local level as well. For instance, on 15 June, the 4th OZ's deputy *politkom* was killed and its commander wounded in a sudden attack, thus adding several more names to the ever-lengthening death toll among the KPJ's top cadres.[59]

4.9 Serbia and Macedonia: Small Steps Forward

The conditions in Serbia at the beginning of 1943 closely resembled those from the summer and fall of the previous year. Having only ca. 600-650 fighters on active duty[60], the NOP could do little to seriously disrupt the functioning of the occupation regime. Assassinations of

59 *Zbornik*/VI/5/386 (BdO "Alpenland", Situation report, 8.1.1943), 409-15 (Municipality of Oplotnica, Report, 10.1.1943); *Zbornik*/VI/6/190-93, MHQ Slovenia, Strength return (1.9.1943); *DLRS*/VII/537, Viktor Stopar to CK KPS (18.6.1943); See the following books by Lado Ambrožič-Novljan: *Gubčeva brigada* (Ljubljana: Borec, 1972), pp. 213-14, and *Cankarjeva*, pp. 185-91; Miroslav Stiplovšek, *Šlandrova brigada* (Ljubljana: Borec, 1971), pp. 43-77; Stanko Petelin, *Sedma NOU brigada "France Prešern"* (Belgrade: VIZ, 1973), pp. 8-27.

60 Nikolić, *Jugoistočna*, p. 272. Some authors claim the total was about 1,200, but this probably includes village guards, rear-area personnel, etc.: Petranović, *Srbija*, p. 339.

collaborationist officials and burning of municipal offices, combined with an occasional sabotage or ambush, were still the main forms of guerrilla activity. In the central parts of the country, these attacks only rarely (e.g. in mid-February) acquired the form of a sustained, purposeful campaign that would make the Germans contemplate a more serious intervention. The troops of the Serbian puppet state, propped by smaller Wehrmacht and police detachments, were still considered sufficient for the job, even though their performance in battle was far from balanced. For instance, the gendarmes managed to hold out in their fortified stations during the Partisan raids on Belanovica, Grocka, and Lazarevac. Early spring also saw clear-cut defeats at Kolare on 23 April, Azanja on 30 May, and Tesije on 3 June, all of which resulted in the death of at least 23 of Nedić's men (in addition to seven Germans). For their part, the Axis managed to inflict heavy losses on the guerrillas on several occasions, effectively destroying the new Čačak Detachment on 4 March, only three weeks after it had been re-formed (11 KIA), and routing one company of the 1st Šumadija Detachment at Lisović in mid-April (nine KIA). The heaviest blow to the NOP was landed in Eastern Serbia. The death of a colonel belonging to the 704th JD in an ambush outside Požarevac on 16 February served as the catalyst for a major anti-communist action that lasted for more than three months. During this period, the Požarevac Detachment, along with most of the underground organization in this region, practically ceased to exist: 36 fighters, including two members of the HQ, six company commanders, and seven commissars, were among the dead.[61]

Despite all the setbacks and the unfading fear of reprisals among the population that was still making wider recruitment impossible, the leadership of the NOP's Serbian branch decided to go ahead with the creation of mobile formations. In honor of its importance and revolutionary traditions, it was decided that Šumadija should be the birthplace of the first such unit. The 102-strong 1st Battalion of People's Liberation Army of Serbia was thus formed on 28 June 1943 and received its baptism of fire on the very same day (incidentally, the anniversary of the historic Battle of Kosovo). The raid on the nearby Aranđelovac was devised as a show of force and an opportunity to strike fear into the hearts of domestic enemies. After infiltrating the town and isolating the main enemy strongpoints, the Partisans proceeded to arrest, try, and execute ten notable citizens accused of collaboration and spying (two of them were confirmed German agents). Laden with loot and the much-needed cash taken from the local bank, the guerrillas left the town in the morning and headed back for their base on Mount Bukulja. During the ensuing firefight, they lost six KIA and two WIA, but managed to beat off the Axis pursuit, a small but psychologically important victory. During the following two months, the battalion devoted itself almost completely to combatting the resurgent JVuO. The Timok Battalion, formed already in mid-June in the east, followed a similar path. Well-armed with automatic weapons (every fourth of its ca. 100 fighters had one), the unit first routed a detachment of gendarmerie (at least three KIA and seven WIA), and then proceeded to demolish the coal mine at Bogovina. After spending July in fighting the Chetniks and disrupting the harvest, the Partisans raided the county seat of Knjaževac on 8-9 August. As in Aranđelovac, the defenders preferred to stay in their bunkers, effectively abandoning the town to the attackers. Content

61 Vitorović, *Centralna*, pp. 407-52; NARA/T501/249/29 (BhS, Situation report 21-28.2.1943), 339, 545, 585, 592 (BhS, Daily reports 25.4, 31.5, 2 and 5.6.1943); *Zbornik*/I/5/100-02, Čačak Det. to MHQ Serbia (March 1943).

with securing a large amount of medical supplies and setting fire to several public buildings, the Timok Battalion withdrew.[62]

Southern Serbia, the home of two-thirds of all the fighters in the country, remained the NOP's main stronghold. The local Partisans engaged in pretty much the same type of activity as their comrades in the north, only far more frequently; as a result, the situation in the region was nearly always described as "deeply worrying" by the Nedić's authorities. The biggest actions of the first eight weeks of 1943 were carried out by the Vranje Detachment. On 16 January, this unit demolished the mine at Momin Kamen, killing or capturing six members of the OT. On 3 February, the Partisans entered Crna Trava, liberated some of their members from the local jail, and held a rally; the Bulgarian company that was sent in pursuit was successfully ambushed at the village of Mlačište. Other Partisan units did not fare as well. The SSW and Pećanac's Chetniks surprised a group of 37 guerrillas from the Rasina Detachment while resting after days of hard marching; less than half of them emerged unscathed. In a similar incident, 10 out of altogether 12 members of the Ozren Detachment who had been dispatched with the task of "planting the flag" in the area of Aleksinac, were killed in an ambush.[63]

The next important step in the development of the Partisan army came in mid-February 1943, when Tito's old troubleshooter, Tempo, visited the region while on his way to Macedonia. He reorganized the Kukavica, Jastrebac, and Jablanica-Pasjača Detachments into the 1st South Morava, whilst the Vranje unit became the 2nd South Morava Detachment [SMD]. As for their new orders, the high envoy simply repeated the standing instructions from 1941: step up actions, recruit more men, extend NOP's influence in the hitherto "untouched" villages, and preclude the royalists from doing the same. The 1st SMD spent the next half year alternating between attacking targets of opportunity along the fringes of its domains and evading the inevitable Axis response. On one such occasion in mid-March, the guerrillas first raided the mine at Lece and then inflicted what was probably the biggest defeat on the Bulgarians since the skirmish at Bojnik thirteen months earlier, the killing and wounding of more than 30 soldiers at the village of Gajtan. The Rasina Detachment, which continued to exist in its earlier form, also remained active during the late winter and spring. On 17 June, the unit ambushed a German wheat requisitioning party, killing eight and wounding seven policemen. Ten days later, a group of fighters dressed in Wehrmacht uniforms entered the gendarmerie station at Gornji Stepoš and then shot all 15 of its occupants, accused of being Mihailović's sympathizers. Needless to say, nearly every attack on the members of the occupation regime, be they the Germans, Serbs, or Russians, was duly punished: for example, over 300 hostages were executed in Kruševac for the above-mentioned attack on the German police.[64]

By mid-summer 1943, the liberated territory around Jablanica came under threat from the Chetniks, who were now both strong and organized enough (2-3,000 men armed largely with British-delivered weapons) to launch a major attack. A pre-emptive strike, carried out jointly by the 1st SMD and the Rasina Detachment on 26 July around Retkocer, failed to disrupt the

62 Isidor Đuković, *Prva šumadijska brigada* (Belgrade: VIZ, 1978), pp. 61-142; Bosiljčić, *Istočna*, pp. 95-101; NARA/T501/249/691, 715, BhS, Daily reports (25 and 30.6.1943).

63 Ibid., 1188, BhS, Daily report (19.1.1943); for the monthly situation estimates compiled by Nedić's MoI in 1943 see *Zbornik*/I/21; Nikolić, *Jugoistočna*, pp. 276-89.

64 Ibid., pp. 304-12; NARA/T501/249/85, 87, BhS, Daily reports (14 and 15.3.1943); *Zbornik*/I/20/383, Rasina Det. to MHQ Serbia (13.7.1943); Glišić, *Teror*, pp. 171-91.

enemy plans. The JVuO then counterattacked (8 August), secured a foothold on Mount Radan, and threatened to push the Partisans into the Toplica Valley, where the Bulgarians were waiting for them. In this hour of supreme danger, the active units were reinforced to a strength of ca. 4-600 men by using all able-bodied sympathizers, as well as the KPJ and SKOJ members, a vivid proof of the maturing nature of the NOP organization in these parts. The decisive engagement took place on the 13th and ended in a Chetnik withdrawal from the Radan; by the end of the following week, they were forced to return to their jump-off positions for good. The intensity of the battle is evident from the fact that the Partisans lost at least 25 KIA, 30 WIA, and eight MIA, at the same time capturing 29 pieces of small arms.[65]

From the Bulgarian perspective, the 2nd SMD presented a particular threat owing to its proximity to both Bulgarian metropolitan and Macedonian territories, as well as the main railway line in the Grdelica Gorge. Acting in response to Tito's call for more pressure against the enemy rear during Operation "Weiss", the Partisans raided the Jerma mine, just 15 km north of the border town of Trn. Using the explosives found there, they blew up the strategically important bridge at Priboj on 17 March 1943. Five weeks later, a small Bulgarian garrison was expelled from Crna Trava; from then on, this large village, renowned for the skill of its construction workers, would serve as the main NOVJ base in this part of the country. Despite the fact that it had no more than 140 fighters and a vast territory to cover, the 2nd SMD embarked on an ambitious plan of southward expansion. From late May to late June, the Partisans succeeded in establishing themselves in the border region roughly between Mounts Kozjak and Dukat. In the process, they burned several municipal offices (e.g. Trgovište, Radovince), clashed with police at Duga Luka, and raided the minor chrome mine at Trnava. The Bulgarians responded by launching operations of varying size. For example, each of the two offensives from late July that targeted the liberated territories at Crna Trava and Kozjak involved elements from up to five infantry regiments, not counting smaller army and police units. Apart from reclaiming some villages and causing several high-profile deaths, including the CO of the 2nd SMD and one of its battalion commanders, these sweeps failed to achieve much; by the end of summer, the detachment already had 300 fighters.[66]

The arrival of the Serbian Partisans to the upper Pčinja Valley had a positive effect on the NOP in Northern Macedonia. On 20 August 1943, the Kumanovo Detachment was "resurrected" around the cadre of Macedonian Communists, some of whom came from the 2nd SMD; although only 17 strong, it was immediately sent in action south of the Kozjak. The new unit was made part of the 5th OZ, created several months earlier as part of the sweeping reorganization carried out by Tempo. Macedonia received its own, separate branch of the Communist Party (KPM) and a new MHQ. Field units would no longer be controlled by the Party committees situated in occupied towns and cities, but by dedicated military commands located in the countryside. The leadership also took decisive measures to instill aggressiveness and suppress Bulgarophile tendencies within the movement itself. The detachments were not to be disbanded under any circumstances if the going got tough, as was the practice earlier.

65 Perović, *Južna*, pp. 242-48; *Zbornik*/I/5/260-66, 1st SMD to MHQ Serbia (7.8.1943); Nikola Milovanović, *Kontrarevolucionarni pokret Draže Mihailovića: rasulo* (Belgrade: Slovo ljubve, 1983), p. 121.

66 NARA/T501/258/305, PzAOK 2, Important war economy installations (14.10.1943); Nikolić, *Jugoistočna*, pp. 299-304, 323-38.

By the end of August, the guerrilla army could boast of four OZ HQs, 11 detachments, and the "Mirče Acev" Battalion, the first "regular" unit formed in Macedonia. The center of the Partisan activity was located in the far southwestern corner of the country. In addition to the comparatively favorable conditions in what was then the Italian occupation zone, the proximity of the Greek and Albanian borders enabled the Macedonians to establish contact with guerrilla groups there and even operate together from time to time. Although the scale and intensity of the NOP's activites in general was imaginably low owing to its numerical weakness and lack of arms, the occupation authorities were keen on suppressing it altogether. In June, parts of the 14th and 15th BIDs tried to destroy two detachments in the area of Kavadarci, but succeeded only in chasing them away for a short period of time. The Bulgarians had more luck in the eastern parts of the country, where they wiped out the Bregalnica Detachment and shattered the NOP organization so thoroughly that it took almost a full year to recover.[67]

4.10 Opposing Armies in mid-1943

In organizational terms, the NOVJ changed little during the first two-thirds of 1943. The original structure seemed to have withstood the test of time, so it was merely expanded. The number of corps was doubled from two to four, that of divisions from nine to 18; the number of brigades rose from 37 to 54. As the NOP's influence spread, the detachment became more important than ever: by the beginning of September, there were 85 such units spread across Yugoslavia (compared with 37 eight months earlier). Furthermore, they were indispensable for keeping the mobile formations operational. The 15th Majevica Brigade returned to its native region after Operation "Schwarz" with only 200 fighters left; within days, this number rose to 700 thanks to the transfers from the local detachment. This unit, in turn, recovered its strength almost immediately by recruiting several hundred new fighters. An interesting phenomenon could now be observed, one closely connected with the developing *esprit-de-corps* of the "regular" branch of the Partisan army. As raw recruits, men were reluctant to leave their home detachments in order to join mobile formations; as veteran fighters, the same men perceived service in detachments as demotion, even when they were chosen for leadership positions. The opportunity to learn the military ropes in familiar surroundings of territorial units was deemed crucial for future successful service. The HQ of the 8th Kordun Division even suggested that no fighter should be allowed to join a brigade without completing this preparatory phase. As was customary, the training for rank-and-file was provided both in combat and in separate drill units; NCOs and officers received theirs through courses organized on all levels whenever the circumstances permitted. Casualties, frequent transfers, and youthfulness of the average Partisan meant that these measures were sorely needed. For example, 85 percent of the members of the Rasina Detachment never served in the army, and the unit had only one experienced NCO and one officer.[68]

Conscription in western and central parts of the country came into full swing during the first months of 1943. With the exception of Slovenia, it produced mixed results. The prospect of

67 Ibid., pp. 375-88; *Oslobodilački*, Vol. I, pp. 474-80; *NOB Makedonije*, pp. 82-88.

68 *Zbornik*/IV/15/339, 17th NOVJD, Diary (July 1943); *Zbornik*/V/17/70, 17th Bde. to 10th NOVJD (7 July 1943); *Zbornik*/IX/3/381, 8th NOVJD/Pol. to 1st Croatian NOVJC (31.3.1943); *Zbornik*/I/20/405, Rasina Det. to MHQ Serbia (18.9.1943); Anić, Joksimović, Gutić, *Narodnooslobodilačka*, p. 279.

facing the biggest Axis offensive of the war in the open, in the middle of the winter, dampened the spirits of all but the most fervent NOP sympathizers. Moreover, the army could still not provide enough officers, weapons, and basic necessities for any major influx of recruits. The fate of the 9th Dalmatian Division is a case in point. In early February, the provincial leadership proclaimed a general mobilization. The initial response was good, but it was soon clear that it would not be possible to get all the draftees to their designated units on account of Operation "Weiss". As a result, many of them had to be turned back, including a large number of islanders. Those who did make it to the area of Imotski were combined into the 2,100-strong division. The new formation was plagued by all sorts of problems: it was 600 rifles short,[69] had only 45 automatic weapons, and very little ammunition; the rank-and-file were largely unprepared for the harsh guerrilla life, and their leaders possessed little military knowledge. Being the youngest formation at the SHQ's disposal, the 9th was turned into a force of auxiliary stretcher-bearers, assisting the Central Hospital in the crossing of the Prenj in March. Raked by typhus, the division performed poorly around Nevesinje against the Chetniks, who correctly identified it as the GOG's weakest link, and exploited it accordingly. This was the final straw: on 12 April, Dalmatia's only capital unit was disbanded, with the remaining personnel being used to fill up other brigades. Although sometimes criticized as being unfair and politically inopportune, there is little to suggest that Tito's decision was motivated by anything other than purely military reasons. It was also a tacit recognition of the perils of a precipitous and overzealous mobilization.[70]

In order to widen its popular base, the NOP actively encouraged the establishment of minorities' units, where their members could serve under their own flag and use their own language. The first two such outfits, made up of Albanians, were formed on Kosovo in September 1942 and January 1943 (the already mentioned battalions/detachments "Zejnel Ajdini" and "Emil Duraku", respectively). The Czechs received their own battalion, named after the 15th-Century Hussite leader Jan Žižka, in early May, and the Hungarians followed three months later with the poet-revolutionary Sándor Petőfi. Both of these units would be eventually expanded into full brigades subordinated to the 6th Corps in Slavonia, their native province. The same region was the home of the "Ernst Thälmann" Company, created in mid-August in a last-ditch attempt to draw the *Volksdeutsche* to the Partisans' fold. The results were disappointing: the unit never grew past its original size, despite the fact that even people with mixed ethnic background and non-Germans came to serve in its ranks. The principle of forming "ethnic" outfits was not applied only to minorities. Just as Muslim Battalion of the Romanija Detachment in 1941, so

69 At that time, the Partisans in Serbia were facing precisely the opposite situation: the Požarevac Detachment alone had 427 functioning rifles and three MGs stacked in its magazines but lacked the necessary manpower: *Zbornik*/I/5/31, Požarevac Det. to MHQ Serbia (14.1.1943).

70 *Dalmacija*/V/155-57 (NOO Dalmatia, Circular No. 2, 7.2.1943), 179-81 (9th NOVJD to SHQ, 11.2.1943), 229 (NOO Dalmatia to NOO Hvar, Brač, and Vis, 5.3.1943), 259-60 (Split Area to OK North Dalmatia, 7.3.1943), 311-12 (Svetislav Stefanović to CK KPJ, 26.3.1943); *Zbornik*/IV/12/12-19, 9th NOVJD to SHQ (1.4.1943); *Zbornik*/II/9/57 (Terzić to Ranković, 9.4.1943), 83-85 (SHQ, Order, 12.4.1943); "Titov plan je bio pogrešan", *Danas*, 13.8.2012: https://www.danas.rs/drustvo/titov-plan-je-bio-pogresan/ (last accessed on 16.9.2019).

too was the "Matija Gubec" Battalion formed for the purpose of dispelling the rumors about the Greater Serbian nature of the NOP and facilitating recruitment of Croats in Lika in mid-1943.[71]

The Yugoslavs remained flexible when it came to command-and-control arrangements on the highest level. The Slovenian MHQ, which was still in process of being formed, received a post of Religious Officer, reflecting the special importance attached to this issue in Slovenia. In Serbia, the provincial Party leadership, rather than the MHQ, still had the last say in military matters, an anachronism dating to the first days of the uprising. Owing to the near-constant presence of the SHQ, as well as one, later two corps HQs, the Bosnian-Herzegovinian MHQ became redundant and was dissolved in April 1943. Provincial commands were also responsible for the training of officer candidates and specialists: Slovenia and Vojvodina had thus formed their own officer schools by middle of the summer. The 6th Slavonian Corps, being physically separated from the rest of the country, was allowed to set up its own institution of this kind. Reflecting the changing nature of the army, the MHQ Croatia opened a separate artillery school and also organized a course for signalers. New types of specialist units came into being; the 1st Sabotage Battalion, divided into five companies with altogether 132 sappers, was formed in Slavonia in mid-May; the second such unit followed three months later in Pokuplje. The armored vehicles used in the abortive attack on Gospić came from 1st Tank Company of the MHQ Croatia, created in March of the same year. The expansion of the army and liberated territories necessitated the establishment of internal security units. In Vojvodina, they were styled "People's Protection", in Central Croatia "Anti-Fifth-Column" (*Protiv pete kolone*, PPK). Fearing the Chetnik encroachment in Slavonia, the local corps formed the (short-lived) Anti-Chetnik Battalion, all of whose 100 heavily armed and reliable fighters "had to be Serb [volunteers]"; a similar unit, Flying Assault Battalion, was established in Western Bosnia.[72]

During the early phase of the war, the Partisan army had no ranks in the traditional sense, but used functional titles as "platoon leader", "company commander", etc. Finally, in May 1943, Tito announced the introduction of military ranks with the words that it represented "a logical consequence" of the NOVJ's growth. There were now four NCO (corporal, sergeant, sergeant 1st class, sergeant-major) and ten officer ranks (ensign, 2nd lieutenant, 1st lieutenant, captain, major, lieutenant-colonel, colonel, major-general, lieutenant-general, and colonel-general). Interestingly, the highest rank at that time (lieutenant-general) was not bestowed on a "Spaniard" or some other deserving revolutionary, but to the elderly colonel of the pre-war Yugoslav Army, Savo Orović. This was done not only in recognition of the fact that he was the most senior officer to join the Partisans in 1941, but also as an incentive to his former colleagues to come over and effectively continue their careers with the NOVJ. The rank insignia began to appear already in 1941 in various forms, and was streamlined by an order issued in early 1942 as a part of Foča Reforms. The five-pointed star and blood-red color, used extensively before, were conspicuously absent from the new pattern that accompanied the Supreme Commander's 1943-announcement. Instead, the NOP leadership opted for a more traditional combination of

71 *Enicklopedija*, Vol. V, p. 670; Nail Redžić, *Telmanovci: Zapisi o njemačkoj partizanskoj četi Ernst Telman* (Belgrade: Narodna armija, 1984); *Zbornik*/V/17/133-34, 6th NOVJD, Order (14.7.1943).

72 Anić, Joksimović, Gutić, *Narodnooslobodilačka*, pp. 237-76; Glišić, Miljanić, *Rukovođenje*, p. 153; *Zbornik*/I/6/275, IV/3rd. Det./3rd OZ, Intel report (7.3.1943); *Zbornik*/V/15/247, MHQ Croatia, Circular (26.5.51943); *Zbornik*/V/18/267, 2nd Croatian NOVJC, Circular (21.8.1943); *Zbornik*/IV/16/135-36, 2nd Bosnian NOVJC, Circular (19.8.1943).

gold-yellow and silver-white, and the six-pointed star, as if trying to shake off the image of a party army. In August, the NOVJ received its first decorations, the most coveted of which was Order of People's Hero. It was first awarded in February 1942 as an honorary title for acts of extreme valor or extraordinary contribution to the war effort (Tito would live long enough to become a three-time recipient).[73]

In regard to battlefield prowess, the classic Yugoslav Partisan army reached its peak on or about 15 March 1943. The GOG marched from Banija to Herzegovina in the middle of the winter encumbered with thousands of wounded and sick, fought off three different enemy armies, and made a near-miraculous escape across the Neretva with its combat potential intact. During Operation "Weiss", the guerrillas successfully combined their traditional fortes, like great mobility and ambush-laying (e.g. Drežnica) with regular army maneuvering and tactics (e.g. Gornji Vakuf) and showed a remarkable talent for improvisation (e.g. erection of makeshift pontoons across the Neretva, utilization of captured Italian hardware). The rising professionalism was not limited to the "core" divisions but could also be observed in their provincial counterparts. The best examples are offered by the defense of Lika by the 1st Croatian Corps, the encirclement of a German regiment at Sanski Most and defense of the Grmeč by the 1st Bosnian Corps, as well as the operations in Slavonia and Slovenia from the same period. The Partisans remained flexible in their choice of tactics. During the fighting around Sirač in early June, the 4th Slavonian Division tried to lure an enemy column into the open and destroy it in a massive ambush. The scheme failed, but the battle showed all the advantages of proper entrenching, as one company held its ground throughout the day in prepared positions without suffering any casualties. With the recent, bloody experiences in mind, Tito instructed Dapčević in early July to use guerrilla tactics only in his campaign in Northeastern Bosnia and even not to create a liberated territory in the classic sense, but stick to small, well-hidden bases.[74]

Yet, it was the sheer doggedness and determination displayed by the Partisans during the hellish Operation "Schwarz" that really won them the admiration of the Germans. The effusive praise that Lüters heaped on the NOVJ in his official after-action report made it to one of the most-cited documents in Yugoslav historiography. Among else, the recent fighting had shown that "the Communist forces under Tito were tightly organized, skillfully led, and had an astonishingly [high] morale [...] [The Partisans] proved to be fanatic, frugal, and tough fighters, entirely familiar with difficult mountainous terrain."[75] The last point was especially true: for one NOVJ division commander (and, undoubtedly, many of his comrades), this was the fifth time in the past twelve months that he marched and fought across this very same area.[76] Given the tremendous odds, the breakthrough from the Sutjeska cauldron would have probably been hailed as the NOVJ's best-fought battle. However, the overall "note" would have to be revised down due to the serious flaws displayed by the army's highest leadership and the truly terrible human losses suffered on this occasion. Tito bears the lion's share of the guilt. First of all, he allowed himself to be surprised by the enemy offensive. This came as the result

73 *Zbornik*/II/1/227-28, 255-56 and 271-72, 299-300 (SHQ Bulletins Nos. 23-27, 28, 29-31, December 1942-August 1943); *Enciklopedija*, Vol. VI, pp. 440, 446.

74 *Zbornik*/V/16/210-11, 4th NOVJD to 1st Slavonian NOVJC (16.6.1943); *Zbornik*/II/10/41, Tito to Dapčević (7.7.1943).

75 NARA/T314/560/746-47, BDTK, Report "Schwarz" (20.6.1943).

76 Jakšić, *Nad uspomenama*, Vol. I, p. 391.

of a critical failure in the functioning of the intelligence service on all levels (still the Achilles' heel of the army), but also of his own belief that he managed to passivize the Germans through the "March Negotiations". The battle-winning decision to secure the Vučevo and Sutjeska early on was nearly overshadowed by the frequent change of plans, as well as attempts to micro-manage the day-to-day operations through slow-moving courier and highly unreliable wireless. Whether the presence of his old chief of staff, Jovanović, would have brought more clarity and coherence, both here and on the Neretva, is open for debate. And then there was his temper: Tito was reportedly so angry with Popović's decision to attack north through the Zelengora that he decided to relieve him of command immediately after the battle. Luckily, he had changed his mind by then, but the old tension between the SHQ and the army's premier field officer continued to simmer (for his part, Popović voiced his displeasure with the conduct of operations on several occasions). Ultimately, the flower of the NOVJ survived the battle, but almost broke apart in its immediate aftermath when the mass of half-crazed, half-starved guerrillas began plundering every village along the way in search for food. In a lasting testimony to the success of the regularization efforts of the past two years, the discipline was restored and the army made combat-ready again in a matter of days.[77]

Even though the Partisans were devoting more and more of their resources to complex operations, their traditional campaign against railways continued unabated. As before, the vast majority of incidents (which included tearing or blowing up railway tracks, bridges and other objects, as well as telegraph-telephone lines) occurred on the territory of the NDH, over 2,000 in the period January-August 1943. For comparison, in Slovenia, the total amounted to 164 and in Serbia 82 (note: how many of these were carried out by the Chetniks is not clear). The attacks peaked in February during Operation "Weiss", and in the months leading to the Italian surrender. In early March, the Styrian authorities noted that a significant number of trains headed towards Italy had to be rerouted through their province; this was owing to the abysmal conditions in the Ustasha state, where traffic on some sections was interrupted by sabotage every few hours. The staff of one German corps traveled from Vienna to Slavonia in a state of full combat readiness, with extra ammunition and hand grenades being kept close at hand. This province, along with the remainder of what was then called "Northern Croatia" was the hotbed of guerrillas' wrecking activities. By May, an equivalent of a full HDB division (12,000 men) and a Wehrmacht regiment, subordinated to German Railway Security Staff Croatia (RSSC) were stationed here with the single purpose of guarding the railways. On 1 July, the Partisans first ambushed an oil transport outside Okučani, and then derailed the German Armored Train No. 64 that came to its rescue. Two weeks later, the same train had to intervene again when the Syrmian guerrillas attempted to unload the goods from the large freight composition that had been stopped several days earlier near the confluence of the Drina and Sava. Not far from there, on 27 August, a train carrying an artillery unit of the 173rd RD ran into an ambush, losing three KIA and 32 WIA. In order to counter the tidal wave of sabotage, the Germans were experimenting with a wide range of measures. In Serbia, a so-called "hostage carriage" was attached to transport compositions, whereas armored trains received special carriages containing all the necessary track-repair tools and materials; unarmed civilians from the nearby settlements were required to patrol their section of the railway and raise alarm if needed. Across

77 Vuksanović (ed.), *Beleške*, pp. 137-54, 59; Nenadović, *Razgovori*, pp. 79-87; Djilas, *Wartime*, pp. 300-01.

the border, a handful of German soldiers were attached to NDH outposts and watchtowers to serve as "corset bones [*Korsettstangen*]" and thus ensure at least a minimal participation of their unreliable allies in the struggle against the guerrilla menace.[78]

The Wehrmacht occupation contingent, in its original form, had shot its bolt by the beginning of 1943. This was plainly shown during Operation "Weiss", when inexperienced or ill-prepared units were required to fulfill grandiose, but entirely unrealistic plans drawn by staff officers who were clearly going through a creative crisis. The most blatant example is the case of the 7th SS, which was supposed to cover the distance of 70 km to Bihać in a single day. The generally poor performance of the 717th ID was partly caused by the near-total breakdown of its rear area services, which were struggling to cope with the protracted winter campaign. Its sister outfit, the 718th, fared a little better only because the nearly two years spent in Bosnia had taught its men to fend for themselves. For instance, the division improved its mobility by producing makeshift mountaineering boots and by copying some guerrilla methods. The need for a fully-capable, all-round force able to cope with a possible Allied landing, but also with the increasingly dangerous NOVJ, led to a complete overhaul of the Wehrmacht contingent in the Balkans. Beginning in early March and lasting well into June, the 700-formations were gradually transformed into the *Jäger* divisions, a cross between mountain and ordinary infantry units. They had around 13,000 soldiers apiece, mostly of younger age groups. The divisions were equipped with all the necessary war paraphernalia, including up to 4,800 horses and mules for better cross-country performance. The Slavonian and Kordun Partisans noticed the changes in their enemy's outlook and tactics as early as February. In late June, Tito warned subordinated commands that the Germans were now not only attacking frontally but were also laying ambushes and routinely occupying all dominant heights within their reach. Writing about Operation "Schwarz" after the war, Đuro Kladarin, the wartime chief of staff of the 7th Banija, observed that the enemy showed "unbelievable determination", sending whole units, together with cannons, to where only skilled mountaineers would normally dare to venture.[79]

Personnel changes within the Wehrmacht contingent did not only affect the over-aged rank-and-file: old commanders went home as well and were replaced with mountain warfare specialists. Despite the fact that he showed little aptitude for the peculiar type of conflict raging in Yugoslavia, Lüters stayed on until October 1943. By then, the command arrangements in this part of Europe had been thoroughly changed. In late August, the entire occupied Yugoslavia, with the exception of Slovenia, was placed under the newly-created HGF, whose head, Field Marshal Maximilian von Weichs, was also named Commander-in-Chief Southeast

78 Bošnjak, *Diverzantska*, pp. 184, 190; Glišić, *Teror*, p. 188; *Zbornik*/VI/5/529, Styrian Government, Staff conference (15.2.1943); NARA/T501/252, BhS to OBSO (13 and 20.7.1943); NARA/T501/264/523, Horstanau to Schuchardt (26.5.1943); NARA/T314/1544/9-11 (LXIX Reserve Corps [RC], Diary, 11-15.8.1943), 254-55 (Reserve Artillery Btl. 10 to 173rd RD, 31.8.1943); TsAMO/500/12451/457/31 (RSSC, Daily order no. 5, 31.7.1943), 32-33 (Armored train no. 64, Activity report July 1943); TsAMO/500/12451/518/407, Armored train no. 65, Experiences, 3.9.1943; ARMB/SSR/3-1943/226, 235, 246, Lists of major incidents (January-July 1943); see also Summaries for 1943, pp. 12-19.

79 Trifković, "Case", pp. 324-25, 330-32; NARA/T313/482/22, 118th JD, Personnel (22.11.1943); NARA/T315/1301/684, 118th JD, Horses (15.5.1943); *Zbornik*/V/12/22 (4th NOVJD, Circular, 3.2.1943), 141 (5th Bde. to 8th NOVJD, 12.2.1943); *SD*/XV/227, Tito to MHQ Croatia (27.6.1943); Kladarin, *Bitka*, p. 135.

(*Oberbefehlshaber Südost*, OBSO). From his seat in Belgrade, von Weichs controlled two major formations. The HQ of the 2nd Panzer Army (*Panzer-Armee-Oberkommando 2*, PzAOK 2), which had recently arrived from the Eastern Front together with its commander, General Lothar Rendulic, was made responsible for the NDH and the Adriatic coast from Istria to Greece. It had four corps commands, 10 divisions, three separate regiments, and one brigade, with at least 130,000 men (not counting smaller and support units)[80]; by the end of the year, this figure would almost double. The numbers alone, as imposing as they may appear, do not tell the whole story, however. The *Führerhauptquartier* was still reluctant to permanently commit high-grade troops to Yugoslavia, despite its increased strategic significance. Their place was taken by a mix of re-constituted East Front veterans (such as the 100th JD and 297th ID, both of which had originally been destroyed at Stalingrad), training formations with rotating personnel (the 173rd RD), and recently created outfits (the 11th SS Panzergrenadier Division [PzGD] "Nordland"). The Germans also began to rely even more on foreign nationals. The 373rd ID joined its older sister division (the 369th ID) already in spring, while a third legionnaire formation was undergoing drill in Austria. Another novelty was a mixed police force, under Himmler's own representative, with the planned strength of 20,000 (5,000 Germans and 15,000 Croats) divided into five regiments.[81]

Across the Drina, Bader's former post was renamed Military Commander Southeast (*Militärbefehlshaber Südost*, MBSO), and was now in the hands of General Hans-Gustav Felber; its operational responsibilities remained largely unchanged. The Wehrmacht presence hovered at about 15,000 throughout 1943, but the SS apparatus was expanded by adding three auxiliary police regiments composed of the *Volksdeutsche*, White Russian émigrés, and Soviet citizens. By the end of the year, the combined strength of all police forces was probably around 8,500. While those native formations deemed unreliable were either kept at the same size or disbanded (the SSW and Pećanac's Chetniks, respectively), those who proved their loyalty were expanded and rewarded. The RSK thus became fully integrated into the German armed forces in late 1942. In the meantime, it had grown to three regiments (6,000 men), with a fourth on its way: the replacements came in form of the White Russians from Romania, and Soviet POWs who "really gave a good account of themselves [in the past]". The SFK, which performed well against both the Chetniks and Partisans, had five battalions (later regiments), with ca. 5,000 men. These figures speak volumes about the German determination to keep Serbia quiet, and partly explain why the levels of guerrilla activity there could not nearly match those in the western parts of Yugoslavia.[82]

80 The strength returns (*Ist-Stärke*) for individual units come from: NARA/T313/482/150, 156 (the "Nordland", 369th and 373rd IDs), NARA/T314/1545/9 (the 173rd and 187th RDs), NARA/T315/1295/564 (the 114th JD). The strength of the 7th SS MTD is estimated at 20,000, that of the 100th JD and 297th ID at 12,000 apiece; regiments and brigades at 2,500 each.

81 NARA/T311/175/542, HGE, Memo (22.3.1943); NARA/T314/554/144, XV MTC, Army directory (undated); NARA/T313/189/7448665-70, PzAOK 2, OOB with timeline (31.12.1943); NARA/T501/264/523, Horstanau to Schuchardt (26.5.1943); Norbert Kannapin, Georg Tessin, Brün Meyer (eds.), *Waffen-SS und Ordnungspolizei im Kriegseinsatz 1939-1945: ein Überblick anhand der Feldpostübersicht* (Osnabrück: Biblio, 2000), pp. 601-03; Schmider, *Partisanenkrieg*, pp. 290-93, 587.

82 Ibid. and pp. 443, 448; Yad Vashem Archives, Record Group 0.51 (Ludwigsburg, USSR Collection), File no. 176.3, pages 305 (Official trip to Serbia, 15-25.6.143) and 376 (Meyszner to Himmer, 8.11.1943); *NOS*, Vol. IV, p. 657; Dmitri Petrovich Vertepov (ed.), *Русский Корпус на Балканах во время II*

Despite having more than 300,000 men in Yugoslavia, the *Regio Esercito* proved itself incapable of tackling the growing and increasingly sophisticated Communist-led insurgency. The fact that the defeats from the first half of 1943 took place throughout the entire breadth of the occupation zone, from southern Slovenia to central Montenegro, pointed to the existence of a deep structural crisis within the army. All the units that were on the receiving side of the guerrilla "stick" had at least nine months' worth of COIN experience, and some of them had been around since the day one of the war. The causes of the poor battlefield performance were manifold: unsuitable equipment or lack thereof (e.g. the notorious "Breda 30", few SMGs), bad supply situation, incompetent officers, unmotivated rank-and-file. All its shortcomings notwithstanding, the Italian Army was the first to theoretically formulate a novel tactical approach to combatting the guerrillas and put it into practice. Already in mid-1942, acting on instructions from Roatta, the 4th Blackshirt Border Militia Legion formed a special, 700-strong anti-Partisan unit in the Rijeka area, and set up a training course for NCOs. In October, the General Staff issued a manual on irregular warfare, *Circolare n. 36.000.* Among else, the document stipulated that enemy forces, rather than territory, must always be the main objective of operations in the field. Depending on the size of the target, these should be carried out by one or more logistically autonomous combined-arms groups; advancing simultaneously from multiple directions, they would seek out the enemy on his own terrain and pursue him as far and as long as possible. Although similar to the old German *Jagdkommando* concept, the Italian version used the battalion, rather than the platoon or company, as the basic unit for the new tactic.[83]

By early March 1943, the first Special Battalions–nicknamed *Arditi* (the "Daring Ones") in reference to the famous shock units of the First World War, also referred to by Robotti as the "Italian Chetniks"–were ready to go into action in Slovenia. Each of the division-sized formations of the XI AC ("Isonzo", "Cacciatori delle Alpi", and the CCNN Group "XXI Aprile") had its own unit of this type. They were fully motorized and lavishly equipped: for instance, one detail of 142 men had no less than 31 automatic weapons, two-thirds of them being the coveted "Beretta 38" SMGs. MVAC members were attached as guides and interpreters whenever practicable. By the end of summer, the Italians had decided to form three separate special units made up of Slovene personnel. Although called battalions, they had an average strength of only ca. 60 men. Special Battalions were apparently not formed outside of Slovenia, although both the "Bergamo" and "Sassari" of the XVIII AC, for instance, possessed *Arditi* companies. It should be borne in mind that the conditions in the XI AC's operational area favored the creation of such units. With the high troops-per-capita ratio, the corps HQ could take the required number of volunteers from the "front line" without fear of disrupting the day-to-day functioning of the occupation system. Other corps could probably not afford such luxury, and even if they could,

Великой Войны 1941–1945 г.г. (New York: Nashi Vesti, 1963), pp. 78, 114-16; NARA/T315/1242, HSSPF Serbien, Report on SSW (31.3.1943); NARA/T77/1423/1196, OKW, Memo (10.9.1943); NARA/T78/532/6404558, Felix Benzler to Foreign Ministry (30.7.1943); NARA/T501/352/850, MBSO, Memo (6.1.1944).

83 *Zbornik*/XIII/3/437, CoS, Situation report Balkans and Aegean fronts (1.8.1943); Fasanotti et. al., *L'esercito*, pp. 215-18, 336-44; see the divisional histories of the "Taurinense", "Sassari", "Re", "Ferrara", "Lombardia", "Macerata", and "Murge" in http://www.regioesercito.it/index.htm (last accessed 22.9.2019).

it is questionable if one special battalion per division would have made much difference against the NOVJ formations in the NDH, which were much more numerous and experienced than their Slovene counterparts.[84]

The presence of these highly-trained and heavily-armed units coincided with the period of unparalleled offensive activity on the part of the XI AC that would last right up until the end of the Italian occupation. Although the time of ambitious sweeps in the mold of the great summer offensive from 1942 had passed, the Italians hoped to paralyze the Partisans by constant, if smaller, attacks. These could include everything from multi-regiment operations to ambushes and even night raids (the latter were practically unheard-of until then). The *Arditi* battalions were used flexibly, either acting alone as "fire brigades" in their home sectors, in cooperation with their sister units in sectors of other divisions, or together with the ordinary line infantry. In late June 1943, the MHQ Slovenia reported with apprehension on the change in their enemy's tactics, on how he "meticulously prepares" every action and always seeks to encircle the Partisans. In what was described as "one of the fiercest battles ever" against the Italians, the brigades that had recently tried to cross the Sava into the German occupation zone were chased non-stop for two weeks before finally managing to break off contact in the vicinity of the Croatian border.[85]

The *Regia Aeronautica* never attempted a similar reform. Throughout 1943, it continued to operate in the traditional, decentralized way. Ground support missions were rarely carried out by more than one or two aircraft at the time, even at the height of major operations. Interdiction of the NOVJ columns crossing the Prenj was probably the most successful operation from this period, but its results are hard to quantify. The frugal use of air force by the *Supersloda* is evident from the fact that the army's aviation, whose strength averaged at about 90 machines (roughly one-fourth of them in Slovenia) at any given time, flew only 3,940 sorties. *Modus operandi* of the *Luftwaffe*, as well as the accomplished results, could not have been more different. In preparation for the winter campaign 1943, all available German and NDH units were subordinated to a single HQ, Air Commander "Weiss" (later renamed to Air Commander "Croatia", *Fliegerführer Kroatien* or FFK). This ensured great flexibility in handling of support requests from the ground units and enabled maximum concentration of force at critical points. In a stark contrast to the Italian practice, more rewarding targets were routinely engaged by up to a full squadron simultaneously. The 717th ID would have probably fared much worse during the NOVJ counterattack at Gornji Vakuf had it not been supported by every available aircraft. Similarly, all 64 combat sorties recorded for 9 June were flown over the small area around the Hrčavka in a desperate attempt to aid the sealing of the cauldron. Luckily for the Partisans, bad weather intervened in their favor on quite a few occasions during this period. In all, the

84 *Zbornik*/IV/11/362-65, Robotti, Conference in Rome (undated); *Zbornik*/IV/12/565, XVIII AC, Daily report (27.2.1943); *Zbornik*/VI/6/502, Special Btl. "Isonzo", Report (27.8.1943); Alexis Mehtidis, *Italian Army 8 September 1943-Regio Esercito 8 Settembre 1943, Part IX: 2nd Army–Slovenia–Croatia–Bosnia–Herzegovina* (unpublished manuscript), pp. 9, 13-14.

85 *Zbornik*/VI/5/601 ("Cacciatori delle Alpi" to XI AC, 12.3.1943), 637 ("XXI Aprile" to XI AC, 23.3.1943); *Zbornik*/VI/6/84 (MHQ Slovenia to Kardelj, 27.6.1943), 307 ("Cacciatori delle Alpi", Daily report, 15.6.1943), 343-44 (XI AC, Activity report, 15-30.6.1943), 497 (Special Btl. "XXI Aprile" to XI AC, 25.8.1943); for OOB details pertaining to some of the Italian operations from this period see ibid., pp. 231, 271, 371, 408, 479.

Luftwaffe, with approximately the same number[86] of machines, flew almost as many sorties during Operations "Weiss" and "Schwarz" (2,337 and 1,484, respectively) as the Italians did in their entire last year of the war.[87]

The Bulgarian forces in Serbia gained increasing importance beginning in late 1942 and early 1943, as more and more Wehrmacht effectives were drawn to the NDH and the Italian zone. In March 1943, the I BOC received an entirely new set of divisions, the 22nd, 24th, and 27th BIDs, all purposely formed for occupation duties. In July, the 25th BID was added to the contingent, making it ca. 28,000 strong. The strengthening of the corps was necessary, because its area of responsibility now encompassed nearly the entire country except for Belgrade and the Sava-Drina triangle. Although three motorized "hunting companies" and one "harassment company" had been established in August 1942 for use in offensive actions, the Bulgarian military developed a reputation for having a rather phlegmatic approach to the guerrilla problem. The Germans complained on several occasions of the fact that the I BOC was not reporting all enemy actions in its sector, and that its divisions were spending far too much time in their billets instead of chasing the Partisans.[88]

The situation in Macedonia was somewhat different. In addition to the 14th, 15th, and 17th BIDs of the 5th Army, the Bulgarians also had a comparatively strong and very active police contingent. In addition, unlike in Serbia, the occupation authorities could count on a certain level of support among the population. Already in summer 1942, one high police official suggested the forming of government guerrilla bands consisting of "patriotic" citizens, such as the former members of Internal Macedonian Revolutionary Organization (*Вътрешна Македонска Революционна Организация*, VMRO). Ironically, the idea occurred to him as he learned that Kingdom of Yugoslavia successfully used such units against Bulgarian *komitadjis* in the early inter-war period. It took until the following spring before the plan was put into practice. On 10 April 1943, the interior ministry decided to go ahead with the forming of *kontračete* (i.e. *Gegenbanden*, i.e. Anti-Guerrilla Bands). The bands did not have a fixed size but were formed according to circumstances around a core of specially chosen police officers augmented with (well-paid) volunteers. Subordinated to their home district authorities, they were supposed to actively patrol the countryside and look for any sign of guerrilla activity. By the first week of May, Skopje Police Area (one of the two in the country) had formed eight

86 There was some controversy regarding the *Luftwaffe*'s precise OOB during Operation "Schwarz", which can now be at least partially settled thanks to the "Ultra" decrypts. On 4 June, the following units were subordinated to the FFK: "Junkers 88" Group, 15./*Kampfgeschwader* 53 (with Croatian crews), "Stuka" Squadron, Harassment Squadron Southeast, Close Reconnaissance Squadron, and Liaison Flight, with altogether 91 aircraft, 73 of them serviceable. Five machines and two crews were lost during the fighting. The decrypts offer little evidence for the presence of a larger number of dive bombers over the battlefield, as earlier thought: Mikić, *Nemačka*, pp. 129-33; The National Archives of the UK, Collection DEFE 3, Folder 818, Cable ML3489, Units under GAF Croatia (5.6.1943) [hereinafter: TNA/collection/folder/cable]; TNA/DEFE3/822/ML5054, Losses and booty (24.6.1943).

87 Mikić, *Italijanska*, pp. 118, 125, 129-30, 134-36; NARA/T315/2264/635, BDTK to 717th ID (3.3.1943); Trifković, "Case", pp. 333-34.

88 V.N Krapchanski, D.D. Vazelov, G.R. Hristov, and I.K. Skachov, *Кратък обзор на бойния състав, организацията, попълването и мобилизацията на българската армия от 1878 до 1944г.* (Sofia: State military publishing, 1961), pp. 134-35 [copy courtesy of Dr. Bisser Petrov]; NARA/T501/248/409, BhS, Daily report (1.8.1942); NARA/T501/352/234, BhS, Diary (26.10.1942); NARA/T501/252, BhS to I BOC (3.7.1943).

kontračete, which "produced good results in the shortest period of time". On 23 July, 167 men were listed as serving with the bands; two weeks later there were already 259. One other "exotic" unit deserves a special mention here. Called Detachment "Biermann" after its commander (a lieutenant of the German Abwehr), this undercover outfit was initially composed of about 85 Germans and Bulgarians (Albanians and White Russians would join them later on). Its task was to protect the strategically important mines in Northern Macedonia and Southeastern Serbia by "systematically searching the area for the bandits and destroying them without mercy". The initial successes of the "Axis Partisans", much like those of the original *Gegenbanden* in Slovenia, could be attributed to the numerical and structural weakness of the NOVJ in these parts. The situation would soon change, however.[89]

The NDH armed forces remained both the strongest collaborationist army in Yugoslavia, and the weakest link in the occupation "chain". Building upon the moderately successful experiment with the HDB mountain brigades, the Germans decided to form four *Jäger* brigades in January 1943. Like their predecessors, these were, in fact, demi-divisions, 8,300-strong, with their own artillery, pioneer, and rear-area units. Each brigade would have its own "godfather" in the form of one of the 700-divisions that would provide the necessary guidance and support (this approach, too, was successfully tested earlier with individual HDB battalions). In practice, however, the new brigades were nothing more than the old *Domobranstvo* infantry regiments with different names. Instead of fresh, German-trained recruits, they were composed of the same unwilling reservists who had been dodging death for the past two years. Knowing this, the defeat suffered by the 4th JB during the Operation "Schwarz" does not come as a surprise. Berlin's increasing influence in all military matters pertaining to its Croatian satellite is evident from the following statistics. In late September, out of altogether 262,000 members of the NDH armed forces (including the UV and the Gendarmerie), 170,000 were being trained, commanded and/or supplied by the Third Reich, including nearly all front-line units.[90]

The combat performance of Pavelić's troops continued to deteriorate. Löhr estimated that the material losses sustained in June 1943 almost corresponded to the booty made by the Wehrmacht during the Battle of Sutjeska. From June to October, the new *Jäger* formations lost 4,100 men to desertion. The reasons for this sorry state of affairs remained the same, most notably the near-universal lack of support for the current regime. For instance, out of 9,500 persons called up for military service in Osijek, only 1,750 showed up. Zagreb sought to curb desertion and propensity for quick surrender by introducing stern disciplinary measures. In February 1943, court martial procedures were significantly simplified; eight months later, it was announced that family members of suspected "cowards" could be sent to a concentration camp or be denied financial support. To the Germans, these must have appeared as half-measures. Upon learning

89 Gjorgji Malkovski, *Профашистичките и колаборационистичките организации и групи во Македонија 1941–1944* (Skopje: INI, 1995), pp. 67-78; Björn Opfer, *Im Schatten des Krieges. Besatzung oder Anschluss. Befreiung oder Unterdrückung? Eine komparative Untersuchung über die bulgarische Herrschaft in Vardar-Makedonien 1915-1918 und 1941-1944.* (Münster: Verlag Lit, 2005), pp. 307, 318-19; *Zbornik*/VII/1/505, Bulgarian MoI, Circular (10.4.1943); see also reports of Asen Bogdanov to Director of Police in: ibid., p. 514 (3.5.1943), as well as in *Zbornik*/VII/4/346-50 and 351-80 (23.7 and 6.8.1943, respectively).

90 https://www.axishistory.com/list-all-categories/380-croatia-army/croatia-army-units/8333-introduction-to-the-jaeger-brigades-croatia (last accessed on 25.9.2019); Tomasevich, *Occupation*, p. 423.

that a Home Guard company refused to follow orders during the battle of Sanski Most in December 1942, Lüters decided to set an example by ordering a Roman-style decimation of the said unit. Of course, there were exceptions to the rule. The contribution of the 2nd HDB ID to the defense of Bosanski Novi was openly acknowledged by the Germans. The same goes for members of the specialist arms, like artillery or aircrews, who would often be lauded in after-action reports. The authors of the same did not hide the fact that the individual *Domobran* was sturdy and brave, and that he excelled in the role of scout (no wonder he also very often made a good Partisan). The lessons of the past two years of the war were not lost on NDH field commands, which fully understood the importance of having dedicated, mobile units, and maintaining constant activity. Lastly, the army was also not entirely devoid of reflective officers. In mid-April 1943–before any of his German colleagues–one lieutenant-colonel with the II HDB AC suggested replacing the obviously flawed concept of encirclement battle with the concept of free-ranging, self-sufficient group of battalions capable of engaging the enemy on his own terms. Although innovative, this idea could have hardly been put into practice owing to the chronic shortage of resources caused by the need to provide even the smallest settlement or object of any value with its own garrison. Unlike the Germans, who evacuated less-important parts of Serbia in the summer of 1941 when they could no longer hold them, the Zagreb regime could simply not afford any such thing for fear of losing what little prestige it still had left.[91]

Ustasha line units were usually considered a cut above the rest of the army, if for nothing else than the fact that they were compelled to fight to the end (mass surrenders such as Krašić remained a rarity). Even though they continued to enjoy privileged treatment compared to the rest of the armed forces, internal documents reveal the existence of severe material and personnel shortages, especially of trained officers and NCOs. The UV's great potential for anti-guerrilla warfare–it had motivated personnel with intimate knowledge of both the terrain and the enemy–remained largely untapped. Apart from the locally improvised *Jagdkommandos*, the militia remained a regular force; its best formation, Poglavnik's Bodyguard Brigade (*Poglavnikov tjelesni sdrug*, PTS), was being expanded into a full-blown heavy infantry division. Nevertheless, the Ustashe remained a dangerous opponent, as evident from the fighting around Gospić in the spring and summer of 1943. The siege of the town was effectively lifted when a column of approximately 600 local Ustashe crossed the Velebit in a night march and appeared suddenly behind the Partisan lines. In late June, the Ustashe surprised their enemy again by launching an attack across the Lika River under the cover of fog and darkness. Finally, on 28 August, the NDH forces effectively destroyed the NOVJ's Croatian Battalion "Matija Gubec", capturing 18 of its members and securing 52 pieces of small arms, as well as the unit's standard.[92]

91 Ibid., pp. 423-28; *Einsatzgruppe* [EG] "E", Daily report (31.8.1943), in: *Nationalsozialismus, Holocaust, Widerstand und Exil 1933-1945*. Online-Datenbank. De Gruyter: http://db.saur.de/DG20/basicFullCitationView.jsf?documentId=rk1443 (last accessed 25.9.2019); NARA/T315/1294/161, Poglavnik's HQ to DGA (7.2.1943); NARA/T313/487/997-98, Poglavnik's HQ, Order (1.10.1943); NARA/T315/2258/1390, 714th ID to BDTK (6.12.1942); see also reports by the 718th ID in NARA/T315/2270/993, and NARA/T315/2271/384-86 (14.12.1942, and 9.1.1943, respectively); NARA/T314/554/293 (BDTK to OBSO, 31.12.1942), 1392-95 (XV MTC to PzAOK 2, 27.8.1943); *Zbornik*/IV/9/485, II HDB AC, Activity report (January 1943); *Zbornik*/V/14/436-67, Battle group "South" to II HDB AC (10.4.1943).

92 Orlović, *Šesta*, pp. 200-14, 251-52; Obhođaš et al., *Vojnica*, Vol. I, pp. 162, 251-59, and Vol. II, pp. 170-79, 207.

5

Resurgence (September 1943 – February 1944)

5.1 Italian Surrender I: Slovenia and Northwestern Croatia

"Italy has fallen!" The news of the signing of Armistice of Cassibile on 8 September 1943 triggered a massive outpouring of joy among the Slavic-speaking population living in the Italian-controlled territories (the mood was powerfully captured by Lordan Zafranović's 1981-epic *Pad Italije*). The opposing commands were hardly surprised by this event; in fact, they had been preparing for it at least since the toppling of Mussolini some six weeks earlier. As we have seen, Tito moved his best divisions closer to the coast; furthermore, he released most of his Italian prisoners, and instructed lower commands to establish contact with their *Regio Esercito* counterparts. The Germans, for their part, put units on high alert and positioned them within striking distance of particularly important objectives still held by their wavering allies. In general, all sides were interested in two things: the Italian arms and Adriatic coast. As for the latter, both the Wehrmacht and the Partisans wanted to seize it before the British and Americans could contemplate a landing. For the NOP, it was a political matter of the highest order: under no circumstances were the Chetniks, or other Anglophile anti-communists, be allowed to establish contact with the Western armies. Consequently, the SHQ ordered its forces to avoid unnecessary clashes with the Germans and direct their energies to disarming the Italians, internal reorganization, and the fight against domestic enemies.[1]

In Slovenia, the Italian surrender transformed the Communist-led insurgency into a massive popular uprising; even though volunteers were pouring in from all quarters, the OF decided to proclaim a general mobilization. The ebullient Kardelj estimated the strength of the NOVJ at 30,000 men by the end of September 1943. For the first time during the war, weapons were not an issue, as the Partisans succeeded in disarming bigger or smaller parts of altogether eight divisions belonging to the V, XI, XXIII, and XXIV ACs.[2] The vastly outnumbered "Blue Guards", as Mihailović's followers were informally known, had little to hope for under these

1 *SD*/XVI/189, 195, Tito to MHQ Croatia, and to 2nd NOVJD (9 and 10.9.1943, respectively); Schmider, *Partisanenkrieg*, pp. 288-301.

2 Owing to the chaotic circumstances on the ground, it is impossible to ascertain which division surrendered to whom with absolute certainty: for the conflicting data, see ibid., pp. 302-03; Klanjšček, *Slovenija*, pp. 194-95; Agostino Bistarelli, *La Resistenza dei militari italiani all'estero. Jugoslavia centro*

circumstances: 200 of them were either killed or captured by the 2nd Slovenian Brigade at their fortified outpost at Grčarice already on the 9th. The "White Guards" (the former MVAC), abandoned by their masters, were facing a similar fate. Although numbering over 6,000 men, they were spread across the Ljubljana Province in dozens of detachments, which made them an easy prey. The exception was a group of some 700 anti-communists who managed to find refuge in and around the castle of Turjak, some 25 km south of the capital. After a five-day siege (14-19 September), the 7th Slovenian Brigade finally breached the thick medieval walls with captured heavy ordnance and forced the remaining defenders to surrender (up to one-third of them would be executed later on). The NOP in Istria, Croatian Littoral, and Gorski Kotar was also going through a renaissance. Istria now had two brigades and two detachments, and a multitude of smaller units, with a total of ca. 7,000 fighters; the 13th Primorsko-goranska Division received an estimated 8-10,000 new recruits. Tito's instructions concerning the royalists were carried out to the letter: on 13 September, a brigade of the 8th Kordun Division destroyed a group of about 700 Lika Chetniks who were trying to reach the coast; twelve days later, the Partisans carried out the already mentioned bloody operation against the island of Mali Lošinj.[3]

The NOVJ clearly held the initiative in the first two weeks following the Italian surrender. The German possessions were limited to the cities of Ljubljana, Trieste, and Gorizia, and the railroad lines between them. Further south, the 71st ID managed to secure Pula and Rijeka just before the guerrillas closed the ring around these places. Behind the horizon, however, the storm was already brewing. On 19 September 1943, Army Group B's II SS Panzer Corps (PzC) received orders to crush the guerrillas and restore the Third Reich's authority in these parts with any means necessary. "After this action", Hitler said, "the Slovene people will have ceased to present a threat to the German people". The first order of business was to reclaim the border area around Gorizia and thus open the gates to Slovenia. Here, the NOVJ's Primorska OZ held an elongated regular front, strengthened in places by the fortifications left over from the Great War. The Germans approached this problem in their standard manner, by launching flanking attacks from the north (elements of the 71st ID) and south (parts of the 1st SS PzD) on 25 September; simultaneously, battle groups of the 44th ID and the 24th PzD began their advance from the west, and the 901st Panzergrenadier Regiment (PzGR) from the northeast. The well-armed, but hastily raised Partisan units were not capable of withstanding this massive onslaught of the Eastern Front veterans. The 3rd Slovene Brigade was encircled on Mount Nanos and lost an estimated one-half of its original 900-1,000 fighters, mostly through straggling. In the meantime, the bulk of the guerrilla army found itself surrounded on the karst plateau of Trnovski gozd. Luckily for them, their foe had no intention of being drawn into a protracted cauldron battle. Content with having shattered the guerrilla organization, and opening of the

settentrionale, (Rome: MoD, 1996), pp. 81-82; Tone Ferenc, *Kapitulacija Italije in narodnoosvobodilna borba v Sloveniji jeseni 1943* (Maribor: Obzorja, 1967), p. 170.

3 Ibid., pp. 126-236; NARA/T313/196/7457139, PzAOK 2, Supplement to daily intelligence report [SDIR] (28.9.1943); Bernard Nežmah, "Turjak 60 let pozneje", *Mladina*, 3.10.2003 (https://www.mladina.si/96492/turjak-60-let-pozneje/ (last accessed on 10.10.2019); Giron, *Zapadna*, pp. 153-84; *Zbornik*/IX/4/294, 13th NOVJD to MHQ Croatia (20.9.1943).

Vipava Valley, the HQ of the SS corps terminated the first phase on 30 September and began making dispositions for the continuation of the offensive into Istria.[4]

The invasion of the heart-shaped peninsula began on 2 October 1943, and it was a real *Blitzkrieg*: within three days, the Germans had routed three Slovenian brigades, pushed to a point 25 km northeast of Pula, and erected a blocking line along the road Ilirska Bistrica–Rijeka. Startled by the speed and ferocity of the attack, the bulk of the Croatian Istrian units failed to evacuate in time and was routed in the Žejana Forrest. It was a crushing defeat: the number of KIA alone is estimated at about 2,000. Leaving the mop-up operations to the 1st SS PzD and 71st ID, the 44th ID and the 901st PzGR sliced through the thin front held by the 13th Primorsko-goranska Division around Sušak on 7 October and launched a two-pronged advance into Croatian Littoral and Gorski Kotar. By the 10th, the columns had reached Crikvenica, and established contact with the hard-pressed 14th SS PR at Ogulin. This unit had arrived to the area a full month ago as a part of the III SS PzC's drive to the coast, but could not make it pass the strong defenses of the 4th NOVJ Corps. In addition to daily raids against the regiment's only supply line leading to Karlovac, the Partisans also mounted a major (and ultimately unsuccessful) attack on 28-29 September using the reinforced 7th and 8th Divisions. The relief of Ogulin brought a temporary lull in the fighting: the Partisans concentrated on protecting the northern border of Lika and rebuilding their old bases in Gorski Kotar, while the Germans redeployed their troops north for the next round of fighting.[5]

In early autumn 1943, the main liberated territory in Slovenia encompassed nearly all of Notranjska and Dolenjska. From there, the newly-formed 7th Corps was not only launching small-scale attacks against the railroad between Ljubljana and Trieste, but also undertook more ambitious actions, such as the thrust towards the Sava between Litija and Brežice (11-18 October). The Germans decided to remove this dangerous "ulcer" threatening their border and the links to Italy and the Balkans in one fell swoop. Operation "Wolkenbruch" was devised as a classic, multiple-stage cauldron battle scheduled to take place in the quadrilateral Samobor–Ljubljana–Planina–Ilirska Bistrica–Ogulin over the course of several weeks. Although the NOVJ formations in this area were rated as "well-organized" (unlike those in Istria and Primorska), the Germans were certain the old tactics would work just as well. Apart from using fast-moving armored-mechanized columns for sealing escape routes, the units were instructed to use artificial smoke against the caves used as guerrilla hideouts. The biggest addition to the Axis OOB was the exotic 162nd "Turkoman" ID, largely made up of Soviet citizens, former members of the Wehrmacht's Eastern Legions.[6]

The "Wolkenbruch" began on 21 October and ended on 12 November 1943. The Partisans quickly realized the size of the force thrown against them and fought pitched battles only

4 Ferenc, *Kapitulacija*, pp. 288-99, 375-95; Petelin, *Gradnikova*, pp. 197-204. Although already Ferenc pointed out that the vaunted "Hermann Göring" Division was, in fact, facing the Western Allies at that time, the myth about its presence in Yugoslavia was perpetuated by many authors, including the otherwise reliable Colić. Also, the widespread claim that the German sweeps in Primorska and Istria carried the codename "Wolkenbruch" is incorrect; this name was reserved exclusively for the final phase of the II SS PzC's offensive (see below).

5 Giron, *Zapadna*, pp. 214-22; Miloš Šumonja, "Karlovačko-kordunsko područje u doba kapitulacije Italije (vojno-politička razmatranja)", in *Osma*, pp. 449-58.

6 Ambrožič, *Petnajsta*, pp. 99-114; NARA/T354/606/1267-72, II SS PzC, Order "Wolkenbruch" (11.10.1943).

when necessary. The brigades of the 15th and 18th Divisions either dispersed or made frantic evasion maneuvers, making good use of road demolitions to slow down their pursuers. The wounded were evacuated to safer areas (for instance, some 200 went to the Žumberak) or hidden in underground bunkers together with VIPs and non-combatants. The "Wolkenbruch" was followed by the largely uneventful landing on the Kvarner Archipelago (13 November), and by Operation "Traufe" (14-22 November), which targeted the two new NOVJ divisions (the 31st and 32nd) in the area between the capital and the Soča River. In the end, these offensives ended pretty much the same as most similar undertakings: some territory was reclaimed, and garrisons and traffic were (temporarily) restored. The Partisans' combat potential, however, remained largely intact despite the fact that the losses amounted to ca. 20 percent. The same can be said for the entire operational cycle carried out by the II SS PzC, with two important caveats: the Germans did succeed in securing the northern Adriatic coastline, and effectively paralyzed the Istrian branch of the NOVJ for months to come. Still, the autumn operations will best be remembered for the fact that they produced the single-largest haul of weapons and equipment of the war, 716 MGs and 12,427 other firearms. Moreover, the Germans captured 84 pieces of artillery and some 150 motor vehicles by 11 October alone, a vivid example of the impact the Italian surrender had on their guerrilla foe.[7]

5.2 Italian Surrender II: Dalmatia, Montenegro, and Herzegovina

Unlike in the northern parts of Yugoslavia, the Germans were in the position to start an all-out invasion of the Italian occupation zone in Dalmatia already on 9 September 1943. Dubrovnik and its surroundings were captured after some heavy fighting with the units of the *Regio Esercito*'s VI AC, which were ultimately forced to lay down their arms. On the opposite side of the province, the 114th JD had entered Zadar and Šibenik by the 13th, facing only sporadic resistance by the units of the NOVJ's Knin Sector. The main prize, however, eluded the Germans. Split, the seat of the XVIII AC and a major supply depot, was seized by the local NOP committee with the help of the population. The XV MTC responded by airlifting a reinforced battalion of the 7th SS MTD from Mostar to Sinj and sending it down the road to Split (10-13 September). This almost turned out to be a suicide mission. Upon reaching the village of Klis, the column was nearly overrun by the veteran 1st Dalmatian Brigade (which returned to its home region from Sutjeska in mid-August), reinforced by hundreds of volunteers from the city. The Germans sought refuge in the old fortress built by Venice as a bulwark against Ottoman invasions. The siege would last for 16 days, during which the defenders were subjected to daily bombardments from the guns of the "Bergamo" Division, and reduced to eating their pack animals.

In the meantime, both sides had thrown more forces into the fray. Apart from the local detachments and two brigades of the resurrected 9th Dalmatian Division, the SHQ released four brigades of the 1st Proletarian and 4th Krajina Divisions for service around Split. These forces encircled and almost annihilated another SS battalion that tried to reach Klis from Sinj, and stopped an enemy column from Imotski by using elaborate road obstacles. By the last week of September, however, the German pressure was becoming unbearable. Supported by

7 Ibid., 221-78 [all II SS PzC] (Diary, 21.10-22.11.1943), 420 (Strength return, 21.10.1943), 1275 (Enemy casualties so far, 11.10.1943); Klanjšček, *Slovenija*, pp. 233-41.

continuous "Stuka" raids, the newly-arrived 92nd PzGR[8] crossed the Cetina at Trilj, whilst the 114th JD advanced from Drniš. The Partisans therefore made the decision to abandon the Dalmatian capital as soon as the evacuation of the captured war materials (which had been going on practically since the first day) was completed. On the 26th, German advance guards reached the Klis Fortress, and one day later entered the deserted Split. It was an unusually costly battle: according even to moderate estimates, the 7th SS MTD lost more men on this occasion than during Operation "Schwarz" (176 vs. 150 KIA and MIA).[9]

With the fall of Split, nearly the entire Dalmatian coastline was again in Axis hands, but the fight was not over. The local Partisans, now under the auspices of the 8th Corps, reverted to their traditional tactics. The 19th Division was interdicting the enemy traffic in the Zadar–Knin–Lapac triangle. The 20th Division operated first from a bridgehead between Trogir and Šibenik, and then joined the 9th Division on the southern slopes of the Dinara. Their sister formation, the 26th, was raised from among the inhabitants of the Central and Southern Dalmatian Archipelagos, which were at that time firmly in the hands of the NOP. The division operated as far north as Imotski, blockaded the NDH garrisons at Omiš and Makarska, and maintained a foothold on the Pelješac Peninsula. The 114th JD and the fresh 264th ID carried out a series of smaller undertakings during October and November 1943 in the area between Zadar and Trogir (e.g. "Klein-Primošten", "Haifisch", "Delphin"), chasing the guerrillas from the outlying islands and opening sea lanes for coastal shipping.

In the meantime, the V SS MTC had launched a full-scale invasion of the liberated territory in Central Dalmatia with the 7th SS MTD and 118th JD. Attacked from the northwest, north, and southeast, the bulk of the 26th Dalmatian was forced into a fighting withdrawal towards the stretch of coast between Igrane and Podgora. After a failed breakthrough attempt towards the north, the division's HQ saw no other option but to attempt a sea evacuation to the islands of Brač and Hvar. The Yugoslav "mini-Dunkirk" succeeded contrary to all expectations: during 16-17 November, a fleet of small vessels belonging to the NOVJ Navy ferried some 3,500 fighters and 4,000 civilians to safety. As with all operations of this kind, the deliverance came at the price of abandoning all heavier equipment. The events on the mainland had a direct impact on the fighting on the Pelješac. Already on 23 October, the Germans carried out a sudden, combined land-sea attack on the green 13th Dalmatian Brigade (Operation "Herbstgewitter"). Threatened with encirclement, the Partisans hurriedly fell back to the isthmus at Janjina, where they were reinforced by the 1st Dalmatian Brigade. Although the arrival of this crack outfit did not fail to produce the desired effect, the dire situation faced by the rest of the division compelled the 8th Corps to authorize a retreat to Korčula on 10 November. The fighting on the Pelješac cost each side about 350 men.[10]

8 The unit was originally raised as *Grenadier-Regiment 92* but changed its name at least two times; for the sake of clarity, this abbreviation will be used throughout the text. The same goes for the 901st PzGR.

9 Kvesić, *Dalmacija*, pp. 605-32; Kumm, *Vorwärts,* pp. 95-114; Talpo, *Dalmazia*, Vol. III/3, pp. 1163-69; NARA/T314/554/19-29, [XV and MTC] (Diary, 9-27.9.1943), 955 (Daily report, 2.10.1943).

10 Nikola Anić, *Povijest Osmog korpusa NOVH 1943.-1945.* (Split: Udruga antifašističkih boraca i antifašista grada Splita [hereinafter: UABAGS], 2004), pp. 61-65; Milan Rako, Slavko Družijanić, *Jedanaesta dalmatinska udarna brigada* (Split: IHRPD, 1987), pp. 55-68; NARA/T315/2258/1518, 1542-44, 114th JD, Battle calendar (October-November 1943).

The news of the Italian surrender reached Dapčević's new command, the 2nd Assault Corps, around Foča. His units received the following tasks: the HQs of the 3rd Assault would take over the Bileća–Nikšić sector with two brigades (including the 10th Herzegovina). The HQ of the 2nd Proletarian Division, accompanied by a single brigade, was to establish contact with the 3rd Sandžak Birgade in the western part of this province. The remaining two brigades would advance towards Kolašin and Bijelo Polje. The corps was still numerically weak (ca. 4,000 fighters in total, including the local detachments), but it was hoped that this would be remedied by mobilizing on-site. In order to facilitate this process, the NOVJ units were warned not to seek indiscriminate vengeance against the Italians and beware of a potential resurgence of the "Red Terror". At the same time, they were also instructed to pursue an active campaign against enemy targets "regardless of the people's sentiments", for it often happened "that even those villages that were initially against the [open] struggle, would take up arms when the bullets started flying around their own houses."[11]

By the time the first NOVJ units entered Montenegro, the country was in total chaos. Two German divisions (the 7th SS and 118th JD) were racing towards the coast from the west and north, paying little attention to what was going on in their rear and flanks. With the chain of command disintegrating, each Italian unit fended for itself. Two divisions were interned by their erstwhile allies before they could embark on a sea voyage to Italy, while the remaining two assumed what might be termed as the posture of armed neutrality, waiting for the right opportunity to choose a side. The Chetniks were also doing everything to make the best out of the current situation, proclaiming a general mobilization and even attacking the German garrison at Prijepolje in front of British liaison officers (sing. BLO), whose mere presence enhanced their prestige in the eyes of both the population and besieged Italians. Prestige alone, however, could not win battles. In repetition of the events from March and April 1943, Dapčević's fighters dealt a series of blows to the royalists in the valleys of the Lim and Tara, pushing them to a small patch of territory near the Kosovo border west of Peć by mid-October. Despite the fact that it had supported the nationalists in the latest round of fighting, the "Venezia" Division now pledged itself to the NOP cause. Having in the meantime consolidated their hold over the southern part of the country, the Germans (the XXI MTC) felt the time was ripe for an incursion into the interior. The aim of Operation "Balkanschlucht" was to disperse or disarm the enemy in the Kolašin–Berane–Andrijevica area (the aforementioned Italian formation, plus the 2nd Proletarian Division) by striking from the south and east with the 118th JD and the 297th ID, respectively. On 22 October, after four days of seesaw fighting ("only by throwing the last man and weapon into the fray were we able to maintain [our] positions", read one German report), the attackers captured the towns, but it was a hollow victory. The enemy not only departed north in good order, but also demolished the roads and bridges so thoroughly that a pursuit was impossible. The impending return of the 297th ID to Albania and the transfer of the 118th JD to Dalmatia compelled the Wehrmacht command to relinquish its recent territorial gains and concentrate on the defense of the coastal strip.[12]

11 Radovan Vukanović, *Drugi udarni korpus* (Belgrade: VIZ, 1982), pp. 27-31; *Zbornik*/III/5/60-83, 2nd NOVJC, Circular (20.9.1943); *Zbornik*/II/10/315, SHQ to 2nd NOVJC (23.9.1943); *Zbornik*/III/6/130, 2nd NOVJC to MHQ Macedonia (9.11.1943).

12 Pajović, *Kontrarevolucija*, pp. 385-96, 402-07; NARA/T314/661/122-42, XXI MTC, Diary (18-23.10.1943).

After a brief halt in Herzegovina, the HQ of the 3rd Assault Division with the 5th Proletarian Brigade arrived to southwestern Montenegro in late September 1943. The capture of Grahovo from the hands of the demoralized Chetniks on 5 October allowed the brigade to establish contact with the "Taurinense" Division. This once-elite formation was on the verge of disintegration, as its officers and men could not agree on which side to take; individual units were even refusing to share food with one another. At about the same time, the ubiquitous 118th JD launched a concentric attack with four infantry battalions against the division and the Partisans from the direction of Risan and Nikšić. By the 10th, it was all over: more than 7,000 Italians were captured and hundreds killed, all for the price of about 100 casualties; less than 2,000 members of the "Taurinense" succeeded in escaping across the Nikšić–Grahovo road. Leaving the survivors to recuperate, the 5th Proletarian marched off to fight the Chetniks in the central parts of Montenegro. The crowning success came on 18 October, when the brigade destroyed the JVuO provincial high command after a four-day siege of the scenic Ostrog Monastery (contrary to the official version, Đilas maintains that the Chetnik officers were lured out by a promise of fair trial and then executed). Concurrently, the guerrillas had a number of clashes with the Germans who were trying to secure the communications in the Zeta River Valley. In these latest actions, the 5th Proletarian lost 35 KIA and WIA, including its commander.[13]

The 10th Herzegovina Brigade, whose ca. 600 fighters found themselves near the Sutjeska battlefield on 8 September 1943, was too far away to take any part in the disarming of Italian units. Instead, the formation first took Gacko and then proceeded to attack the Chetnik bastion of Bileća. Although the outer defenses had been breached by the 19th, the arrival of reinforcements from the "Prinz Eugen" Division caused a temporary postponement of the assault. The following two months saw much confused fighting, as the brigade played both the pursuer and the pursued across the entire southeastern part of the province. Ultimately, the departure of the Germans to Dalmatia enabled the Partisans to best the royalists and carve out a compact liberated territory reaching to the outskirts of Nevesinje, Stolac, and Trebinje. During this period, the 10th had become one of the strangest formations of its type, having eleven battalions divided into three tactical groups, plus a further seven detachments, with altogether 2,000 effectives. Finally, on 16 November, Tito formally approved the forming of the 29th Herzegovina Division, whose HQ would also serve as a separate territorial command under the auspices of the 2nd Assault Corps.[14]

5.3 Winter Operations 1943-44 I: Bosnia and Sandžak

On 1 November 1943, von Weichs submitted his now-famous situation estimate to the OKW. Even though the chances of an Allied landing were growing slimmer by the day, the enemy had, in fact, "already set foot on the Balkans". If something was not done about this threat to

13 Ibid, 819 ([all XXI MTC] Message to PzAOK 2, 4.10.1943), 851-54, 873, 931 (Daily reports, 9, 10, and 16.10.1943, respectively); Vukanović, *Drugi*, pp. 57-58, 67-70; Luciano Viazzi, *La Resistenza dei militari italiani all'estero. La Divisione "Garibaldi" in Montenegro–Sangiaccato–Bocche di Cataro* (Rome: MoD, 1991), pp. 288-93; Đilas, *Wartime*, p. 351.

14 Danilo Komnenović, Muharem Kreso, *Dvadesetdeveta hercegovačka divizija* (Belgrade: VIZ, 1979), pp. 67-90; NARA/T314/554/1328-29, 7th SS MTD, Monthly report (September 1943); NARA/T313/483/290, XV MTC, Daily report (18.9.1943).

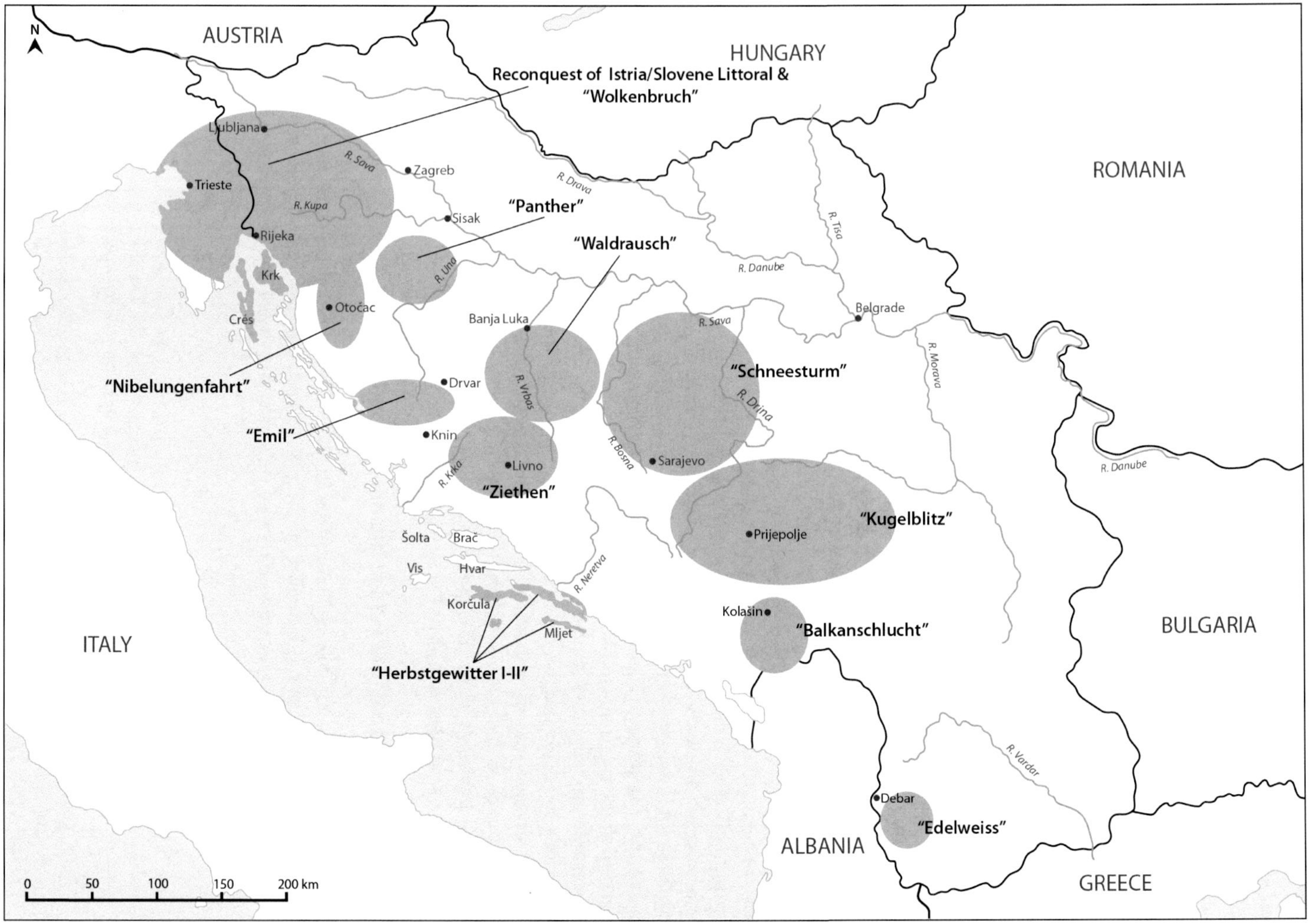

Map 10: Axis Operations (October 1943- February 1944).

the German rear, a possible Anglo-American invasion in the spring of the following year was certain to succeed. "The most dangerous foe is Tito", who was again in charge of a spacious "republic" and a well-organized army of 100,000 fighters.[15] In acknowledgment of the fact that the Communist-led insurgency had become too large in order to be defeated in a single set-piece battle à la "Schwarz", von Weichs proposed a series of limited operations in the southern and western parts of the NDH and northern Montenegro, each targeting a specific enemy concentration. The overall aim was to secure Serbia's borders, clear the communications leading to the Adriatic, capture the Dalmatian islands, and fortify the coastline. Berlin approved the plan and leased four more divisions to the PzAOK 2, including the crack 1st MTD.[16]

Owing to its geographic location between the NDH, occupied Serbia, Montenegro and Greater Albania, Sandžak had a huge strategic importance. This, along with its peculiar ethnic composition and history, made it eligible for a status of an autonomous provincial NOVJ command (MHQ), which existed from late 1941 to mid-1942. After the local Partisan units left to join the "great march" to Bosanska Krajina, the countryside relapsed into sectarian violence perpetrated by the Orthodox and Muslim militias. The revival of the NOP's fortunes began with the arrival of the 2nd Proletarian Division in early September 1943. Soon thereafter, the province received its own OHQ, a brigade, and a handful of detachments. The main purpose of these measures was to transform Sandžak into a solid base for operations towards Serbia. Time was of the essence, for it was rumored that the British would push for a partition of Yugoslavia into two separate operational areas, whereby the NOP would get the west and Mihailović the east. This meant that Serbia, with all its recruits and natural resources, would be effectively made off-limits to the Partisans. Moreover, the preparations for the second session of the AVNOJ were well under way, but how could this body be acknowledged as the legitimate representative of the entire country if its influence stopped on the Drina? Throughout October and November, Tito was personally orchestrating the shifting of troops towards the east: the 6th Lika Division was ordered to Bosnia, and the 5th Krajina Division, along with the bulk of the 3rd Corps, took up positions on the left flank of the 2nd Assault Corps.[17]

Dapčević's old command was the first to feel the full force of the German winter offensive 1943-44 (the popular designation "Sixth Enemy Offensive" was never endorsed by Yugoslav historiography). Its first phase, codenamed "Kugelblitz", started on 3 December with a daring action: a group of commandos from the 2nd "Brandenburg" Regiment entered Prijepolje dressed as Italians and Partisans, and seized the all-important bridge over the Lim intact. Simultaneously, the 1st MTD started its assault from the direction of Sjenica with the assistance of both Muslim militiamen and the local JVuO units, who had in the meantime agreed to a German-brokered truce. It was probably one of the worst-managed battles in the NOVJ history and would result in much recrimination and the sacking of the entire HQ of the 2nd Proletarian

15 Official historiography spoke of 320,000 fighters by the end of the 1943, but this figure seems excessive even with "activists of anti-fascist organizations" included: Vlado Strugar, *Jugoslavija 1941-1945* (Ljubljana: Partizanska knjiga, 1978), p. 144.

16 NARA/T313/189/7449011-24, OBSO, Situation estimate (October 1943); Schmider, *Partisanenkrieg*, pp. 319-22.

17 Čedo Drulović, *Tridesetsedma sandžačka divizija* (Belgrade: VIZ, 1983), pp. 9-66; Petranović, *Srbija*, pp. 605-06; *SD*/XVII/90-91, 184, Tito to 2nd and 3rd NOVJC, and MHQ Croatia (21.10, and 4.11.1943, respectively); NARA/T313/196/7457061, PzAOK 2, SDIR (21.10.1943).

Division. The Partisans, holding an overstretched front, were totally taken aback by the sudden attack. That they ultimately managed to evacuate their wounded from the town was solely due to the self-sacrifice of some encircled units belonging to the 1st Šumadija and 2nd Proletarian Brigades. Incapable of stopping the enemy onslaught, the 2nd Proletarian Division retreated to the south and west, while the 5th Krajina went north. The road to Eastern Bosnia now lay open for the Wehrmacht's mountaineers, who made contact with their colleagues from the "Prinz Eugen" in the area of Goražde on the fourth day of the offensive. In order to get here, the SS division had to make an arduous and costly march across the rugged northern Herzegovina; on 26 November, one its artillery companies was routed and one of its majors captured near Plana.

With the arrival to the designated area, the "Prinz Eugen" took its place on the southwestern side of the newly-created cauldron containing three guerrilla divisions. Blocking lines to the west (sector Pale–Vlasenica) were to be held by the elements of the 369th ID, 92nd PzGR, and 1st *Jäger* Reserve Regiment (JRR), those to the north (sector Vlasenica–Srebrenica) by the battle groups from the 187th RD and 901st PzGR, while the 24th BID occupied the right bank of the Drina. In pursuance of the SHQ's order calling for a dispersal of forces, the 17th Eastern Bosnian Division, along with the HQ of the 3rd Corps, exfiltrated the encirclement with little difficulty and marched northwest. Its sister unit, the 27th, crossed the thinly-held Vlasenica–Han Pijesak road with only a handful of casualties (including one of its brigade commanders) and reached the relative safety of the woods beyond. The 5th Krajina initially went southwest, but literally ran into the 7th SS in a heavy fog. Bloodied, it turned back and followed the path taken by the 27th, profiting from the fact that the Germans again failed to seal this exit route properly. The first phase of the Axis offensive (also called "Lim Operation" by Yugoslav historians) was officially terminated on 18 December.[18]

Without pause, the V SS MTC commenced another operation ("Schneesturm"/"Krivaja Operation") with the aim of pushing the three aforementioned NOVJ divisions into the heavily forested area between the Bosna and Krivaja and destroying them there. The 17th Division, divided into two groups, again succeeded in making a relatively painless escape, this time to Birač (one captured NDH general and three British servicemen got separated along the way and were found by the Germans). The remaining two formations went separate ways from their provisional camp north of Vareš. On Christmas Day 1943, the 5th Krajina routed a detail of the 1st MTD at Ribnica, forded the freezing Krivaja, first marched east and then veered south, towards the area of Sokolac. While moving south parallel to the river, the 27th Eastern Bosnian overran the command post of the 14th SS MTR at Romanovac on the 26th, capturing the enemy battle plans and throwing the entire regiment into confusion. By New Year's Eve, both NOVJ outfits were so far behind the enemy spearheads that the Germans had no other option but to cancel the operation.[19]

Thus ended the winter operations in Sandžak and Eastern Bosnia. The PzAOK 2 counted 4,176 enemy dead (plus a further ca. 5,600 killed or wounded that the guerrillas took with

18 Colić, *Pregled*, pp. 157-60; Ljubodrag Đurić, *Sećanja na ljude i događaje* (Belgrade: Rad, 1989), pp. 195-203; Komnenović and Kreso, *Dvadesetdeveta*, p. 125; Ahmet Džonlagić, *Dvadesetsedma divizija* (Belgrade: VIZ, 1983), pp. 78-79; Morača, *Peta*, pp. 113-15.

19 NARA/T313/487/261 (V SS MTC, Report, 27.12.1943), 285 (PzAOK 2, Daily report, 25.12.1943); Morača, *Peta*, pp. 116-29; Džonlagić, *Dvadesetsedma divizija*, pp. 83-99; Gligo Mandić, *Sedamnaesta istočnobosanska divizija* (Belgrade: VIZ, 1976), pp. 95-107.

them), and taking 3,390 prisoners along with 1,250 rifles, 131 MGs, 61 mortars, 24 cannon, and 105 motor vehicles. On the same occasion, the V SS MTC lost at least 142 irrevocable losses and 4-600 wounded. Even though these numbers suggested a major success, this was, in fact, not the case. Rendulic was already gaining notoriety for his widely inflated "body counts", and with good reason: according to the data published in the Yugoslav units' histories, the Partisans suffered some 680 KIA, 1,120 WIA, and 843 MIA. The booty was rather modest for an undertaking of this size, and the majority of the captives were either civilians or disillusioned Italians. The bottom line is that the "Kugelblitz" and "Schneesturm" failed to eliminate their main target, the NOVJ mobile formations that were threatening Serbia. Otherwise, the campaign remained in vivid memory of veterans on both sides due to the extreme conditions in which it was fought, with snow drifts of up to three meters and temperatures plummeting to 30 degrees below zero. The 369th ID reported at one point that the troops stood at the end of their tethers, while the 3rd Corps informed Tito that it suffered no less than 750 cases of frostbite–an equivalent of an entire brigade.[20]

The next objective of the V SS MTC was the main liberated territory in south-central and Western Bosnia. As already mentioned, the SHQ took up seat at Jajce in September 1943, from where it steered the operations of the newly-created 1st Proletarian Corps. This elite formation, consisting of the 1st Proletarian and 6th Lika Divisions under Popović, remained remarkably inactive during the last months of 1943. Apart from the half-hearted efforts to take the heavily defended Travnik, the corps served chiefly as a kind of operational reserve, aiding the neighboring sectors with individual brigades as required. The concept for Operation "Waldrausch" must have appeared elegant on a staff map: two mountain divisions would advance abreast from Bosna River towards the southwest, aiming for the upper Vrbas Valley, with the reinforced 369th ID closing in from the east and southeast. At the same time, two motorized regiments would race down from Banja Luka, take Jajce and close the western side of the ring together with the 114th JD.

Luckily for the Partisans, the plan was rendered unrealistic practically the moment it was drawn by an order from Berlin that called for an immediate transfer of the 114th JD and the 901st PzGR to other fronts. With dampened spirits, the PzAOK 2 gave a green light for the start of the operation on 4 January 1944. The Partisans offered stiff resistance, with mixed results: the Germans managed to surprise and inflict heavy losses on individual battalions of the 1st Lika and 5th Krajina Brigades on two occasions. At the same time, the 13th Proletarian Brigade gave a severe drubbing to a battalion of the 13th SS MTR outside Turbe. Three days into the offensive, the SHQ evacuated its seat and ordered the units to disengage. The 10th and 11th Krajina Divisions maneuvered on their respective home terrains, while the 6th Lika retreated towards Drvar. The 1st Proletarian Division, on the other hand, found itself surrounded between the now-deserted Jajce, Turbe, and Donji Vakuf. In what was to become a classic Partisan action, the division exfiltrated the cauldron by moving stealthily between the attacking pincers of the 1st MTD and ending up on Mount Vlašić. Adding injury to insult, the guerrillas

20 NARA/T313/190/7450122 (PzAOK 2, Report "Kugelblitz", 19.12.1943), 7450661 (PzAOK 2, Daily report, 30.12.1943); NARA/T78/331/6288020, OBSO to OKH (19.12.1943); NARA/T313/487/290 (V SS MTC, Report, 25.12.1943); NARA/T311/189/388, [N/A] Communist reports "Kugelblitz" (1.12.1943-15.1.1944); *Zbornik*/IV/21/375, 27th NOVJD, Diary (15.12.1943-15.1.1944); *SD*/XVIII/267.

then surrounded and inflicted heavy losses on three enemy companies near Travnik (11-12 January). Despite the fact that their enemy was out of reach by now, the Germans continued the operation until the 1st MTD joined hands with the 4th "Brandenburg" Regiment halfway between Bosansko Grahovo and Glamoč on 20 January. Apart from the 1,666 "counted" dead, the "Waldrausch" added only 333 prisoners and 618 pieces of small arms to the grand tally, a disappointing end to the V SS MTC's operational cycle.[21]

The winter of 1943-44 will also be remembered for two major NOVJ attack operations carried out in an attempt to alleviate some pressure from the units caught up in the German offensive. Both took place in Bosnia and represented the culmination of the campaign against enemy garrisons that the NOVJ had been waging with renewed intensity since the late summer. Exploiting the fact that the most Wehrmacht troops were on their way to the coast, the Partisans stormed Bijeljina on 24 September (ca. 300 *Domobrani* KIA, WIA, MIA), inflicted heavy damage on the industrial and mining installations in Zenica, Vareš, and Ljubija on 10, 15, and 22 October, respectively (bagging a further 700 NDH prisoners in the process), and captured Sanski Most with its ca. 1,100-strong HDB garrison on 21 October. Two months later, Tito gave the order to the 5th Corps to assault the city of Banja Luka and surrounding outposts. For this mission, the corps planned to use six brigades and five detachments, plus two brigades leased by the SHQ, or some 12,000 fighters in all. An operation of this size could not be kept secret for long: the garrison (two German and two NDH infantry battalions, plus staff and support units of the XV MTC and the 4th HDB JB) was placed on a full alert early on 31 December, just hours before the attack began. During the next two days, the Partisans took control of most of the city, but could not reduce the main enemy strongpoints, including the old Ottoman fortress of Kastel and the airfield at Zalužani. The failure to occupy the Sava crossing at Bosanska Gradiška doomed the operation. On 2 January 1944, Banja Luka was relieved from this direction by the 901st PzGR, which had been hurriedly dispatched to the scene from Eastern Bosna.

The NOVJ had an estimated 192 KIA and 503 WIA, the vast majority of whom fell in the ferocious street fighting. These heavy losses were partly offset by the liberation of some 200 political prisoners from the city's infamous jail, the "Black House". While the Germans got off relatively easy (59 KIA and MIA, 130 WIA), the NDH forces again took a heavy beating with 90 killed and over 700 missing soldiers.[22]

The second flashpoint in late 1943 and early 1944 was Tuzla. The 3rd Corps launched its first attack on this industrial city and its environs on 29 September and took it on 2 October 1943. That such a major prize was bought at a modest price of 51 KIA and 145 WIA could be partly attributed to the defection of an NDH colonel, who was instrumental in organizing the surrender of the ca. 2,000-strong garrison (he was rewarded with a ministerial post later on).

21 NARA/T311/285/639, PzAOK 2, Plan "Waldrausch" (6.1.1944); NARA/T78/331/6288132, 6288146, 6288152, 6288201, 6288207, OBSO, Daily reports (8, 11, 12, 20, and 21.1.1944, respectively); *Zbornik*/IV/22/82-92 (1st NOVJD, Monthly report, January 1944), 42-46 and 95-99 (9th and 7th Krajina Bde. to 10th NOVJD, 1 and 3.2.1944, respectively); Orlović, *Šesta*, pp. 301-27; Dušan Samardžija, *Jedanaesta krajiška NOU divizija* (Belgrade: VIZ, 1987), pp. 90-97.

22 *Zbornik*/IV/17/520, II HDB AC, Montly report (September 1943); *Zbornik*/IV/18/320 (3rd NOVJC to Birač Bde., 23.10.1943), 493-94 (5th NDH Gendarmerie Rgt. to Gendarmerie HQ, 14.10.1943); NARA/T314/558/805-18, XV MTC, Report Banja Luka (4 and 11.1.1944); Karasijević, *Četvrta*, pp. 175-81, 219-39.

The Partisans' new base turned out to be a veritable treasure trove. In addition to usual booty and supplies, the Partisans now controlled the local salt works, whose precious product they bartered "left, right, and center" for wheat and other foodstuffs. Finally, in early November, the LXIX RC scraped together an equivalent of a reinforced, mixed German-NDH regiment and launched a counterstroke (Operation "Ferkel"). The 3rd Corps refused to be drawn into a pitched battle and evacuated the city, accompanied by one-sixth of its 24,000 inhabitants. Two months later, Tuzla again became an object of interest for much the same reason as Banja Luka. On the evening of 16 January 1944, seven brigades of the 16th and 17th Divisions hurled themselves against the city's defenses. Much to everyone's surprise, the 3rd HDB JB, propped by a handful of recently arrived German reinforcements, withstood the four-day siege and inflicted 300 casualties on the attacker. Mines again proved to be a very effective weapon: in one brigade, 20 fighters lost either one or both legs in this way.[23]

5.4 Winter Operations 1943-1944 II: Croatia and Western Bosnia

The XV MTC started the winter campaign with Operation "Ziethen", aimed at recapturing Livno. The "gate to Dalmatia" had been lost for the Axis for the third time in early October 1943. Unlike on the previous two occasions, the town fell without a single bullet being fired when Francetić's old outfit (the 5th UAB), now under his former second-in-command, withdrew rather than risk battle with the well-equipped NOVJ formations returning from the coast. Livno became the anchor of the southern part of the Jajce Republic, stretching from the outskirts of Knin to the outskirts of Imotski. The Germans attacked on 4 December with five reinforced battalion-sized groups (largely from the 114th and 118th JDs) along the roads leading to the triangle Livno–Duvno–Šuica from the south, southeast, and west. The "Brandenburgers" and Chetniks took Bosansko Grahovo already on the 2nd. Two brigades of the 19th Dalmatian that were ordered to retake the place left the approaches to Livno unguarded, which enabled the attackers to enter the town on 6 December. This sudden coup totally disrupted the 8th Corps' defenses. The four brigades of the 9th and 20th Divisions that had been trying to stave off the attackers around Aržano and Posušje, now had to retreat and await the arrival of the reinforcements (altogether four brigades from the 1st Proletarian, 6th Lika, and 10th Krajina Divisions). From 15 to 17 December, the Partisans launched a series of badly organized and uncoordinated assaults, which the Germans repelled with little difficulty. Popović, who also arrived from the north, admitted to his diary that "we repeated [Arso Jovanović's] mistake from Bugojno last year".[24] Ultimately, the SHQ saw no alternative but to call off all further offensive actions in this sector. The "Ziethen" was an elegant and successful operation: for the price of 39 KIA and 173 WIA, the guerrillas were denied this important patch of territory, 215 prisoners and defectors were brought in, along with 502 pieces of small arms, and other supplies. The enemy's "so-called elite divisions", one German report read, did not avoid open fight this time; although they proved tenacious, their overall combat value could only be described as

23 Hoare, *Muslims*, pp. 133-35; *Zbornik*/IV/18/213, 3rd NOVJC to SHQ (16.10.1943); *Zbornik*/IV/19/516, NDH MoI to PTS (25.11.1943); NARA/T314/1544/467-74, LXIX RC, Report "Ferkel" (20.11.1943); Mandić, *Sedamnaesta*, pp. 109-21.

24 Vuksanović (ed.), *Beleške*, pp. 173-78.

"moderate". In repetition of the Prijepolje affair, Tito sacked the HQ of the 8th Corps for the poor performance of the Dalmatian units.[25]

Apart from low-level guerrilla activity, Banija and Kordun were relatively peaceful throughout October and the first half of November 1943. Then, on the 15th, the 7th Banija Division took Cazin together with ca. 300 members of the 2nd HDB JB and four cannon, but had to withdraw the same day due to the German pressure from Bihać. One week later, the division was back to its home region, making last preparations for an assault on Glina. From 23 to 25 November, the 7th tried in vain to overpower the garrison consisting of a battalion of Danes and *Volkdseutsche* from Romania, members of the 24th SS PzGR "Danmark"; in the process, the guerrillas lost 37 KIA and MIA, and 101 WIA, and two out of their three Italian-made tanks. In the meantime, the 8th Kordun Division, tasked with blocking the approaches to Glina, overran the SS company-sized outpost at Hrastovica. It was a small victory, but psychologically important: "Our fighters have realized that even the German soldier could be destroyed if one was tough and persistent enough."[26]

These events only reinforced Rendulic's intention to conduct a thorough sweep of Kordun and Banija, codenamed "Panther". As all other operations from late 1943, this one had limited aims: to ravage the old Partisan strongholds of Petrova Gora and Šamarica, confiscate or destroy everything of value, and seize all "suspicious" able-bodied males. The concept for the "Panther" could also hardly be described as novel. Coming east from Oštarije and Karlovac, the 371st ID (8-10 battalions), would hopefully drive the Partisans towards the battle groups of the 373rd ID (three battalions) and the 1st Cossack Cavalry Division [CCD] (six battalions), advancing from the direction of the Una and Sava Rivers, respectively. The Partisans responded in their usual way, by avoiding superior enemy forces and attacking his lines of communication instead; in this way, the 8th Kordun compelled the 371st ID to abandon one of its two supply roads. Moreover, the youthful soldiers of this Wehrmacht division (most of them were the class of 1925) had absolutely no knowledge of irregular warfare, and therefore suffered accordingly. On the fifth day of the offensive (12 December), the 371st ID left the Petrova Gora, largely empty-handed, in order to join the operations against the Šamarica. Realizing this strong enemy force might any day close the trap behind it, the 7th Banija, together with refugees and local units, retreated westward across the Klasnić–Žirovac road by the 18th. Unperturbed, the Germans continued according to the original plan for four more days, searching the terrain, burning down discovered guerrilla magazines and hideouts, and bringing in cattle. In exchange for 94 KIA and MIA, and 278 WIA, the XV MTC could show only 236 pieces of captured small arms and four cannon; apart from 212 prisoners, only 96 suspicious persons were found and evacuated (Yugoslav sources speak of altogether 400 casualties on their side). Compared with the figures from the "Ziethen", the "Panther" was clearly a failure. The same goes for the

25 Anić, *Osmi*, pp. 65-72; *Zbornik*/IV/18/464, 5th NDH Gendarmerie Rgt. Report (6.10.1943); NARA/T314/558/243 (XV MTC to PzAOK 2, 26.12.1943), 267-69 (V SS MTC, Plan "Ziethen", 2.12.1943).

26 NARA/T315/2171/348, 352-53, 373rd ID to XV MTC (17 and 16.11.1943); NARA/T314/557/449-50, III SS PzC to XV MTC (28.11.1943); *Zbornik*/V/21/541, 8th NOVJD to 4th NOVJC (28.11.1943); Tomislav Dulić, "Danish Waffen-SS Soldiers in Croatia, Autumn 1943: The Fighting at Glina and Hrastovica", *Journal of the Danish Commission for Military History*, (2016), pp. 76-94.

subsequent incursion into Pokuplje, Operation "Weihnachtsmann", which failed to catch the 28th Slavonian Division before its departure for its home region.[27]

The German invasion of the Central and Southern Dalmatian Archipelagos began on 22 December 1943 with the landing of three battalions (two from the 118th JD, plus the special Coastal *Jäger* outfit of the "Brandenburg" Division equipped with assault boats) on the northeastern tip of Korčula. Two inexperienced NOVJ brigades, the 13th Dalmatian and 1st Overseas, were outclassed in every aspect except overall numbers, and gave ground almost immediately. The arrival of a pair of battalions from the 1st Dalmatian helped stabilize the front roughly in the middle of the island, but then came another round of enemy landings, this time along the southwestern coast. What followed was a very hasty, almost panicky flight to Vis. Operation "Herbstgewitter II" lasted only four days and was an outstanding success: total NOVJ losses amounted to 1,150 men (including the commander of the 26th Division) with complete armament; the attackers lost less than one-tenth of this number. The investigation carried out by the army and Party bodies after the battle revealed many unpleasant truths, such as the cowardly conduct of some political officers, and the fact that armed escorts had to be placed on evacuation boats in order to ensure that they do not sail from Korčula only half-full. The episode had far-reaching consequences for the war in this part of Yugoslavia. After much deliberation, the Partisans decided to vacate all the remaining islands in favor of Vis, which was to be defended to the last man. As a result, the Germans had occupied Hvar, Mljet, and Šolta by mid-January 1944 without facing any resistance.[28]

October and first half of November 1943 in Lika were marked by the usual guerrilla activity against Axis traffic and other targets of opportunity, as well as the stalemate on the Gospić front. This situation changed with the departure of the 6th Division to Central Bosnia; in its stead, the provisional OHQ for Lika received two inexperienced brigades from the 13th Division. The *ZAPOLI* soon discovered about the transfer and decided to take advantage of it. After successfully probing the NOVJ defenses, the 4th UAB took the port of Karlobag in a surprising attack on 19-21 November. A further notable blow came on 14 December, when a Partisan battalion was routed southeast of Gospić. As far as the Wehrmacht was concerned, the region gained in importance only in early January 1944, when the 114th JD received its marching orders for Italy. On its way north, the division occupied the NOP's capital, Otočac, on which occasion the MHQ Croatia lost its chief intelligence officer (it is worthy of note that the town had been a scene of a sudden Ustasha raid a month earlier, resulting, among else, in the destruction of a huge quantity of captured Italian material). On 19 January, the 114th seized Senj, the last remaining port in Croatian Littoral still in NOVJ hands. After that, the division took part in the sweep of the Velika Kapela together with the 392nd ID (Operations "Nibelungenfahrt" and "Drežnica"). This Croatian legionnaire formation had only just arrived

27 NARA/T314/558/470-73, 479-85 (XV MTC, Plan and Report "Panther", 1.12.1943, and undated, respectively), 493-504 (371st ID, Report "Panther"); Uroš Krunić, "Sedma divizija u prvoj polovini 1944", in *Sedma banijska*, pp. 584-86 (see also ibid., p. 786); Marko Lučić, "Borbe Osme divizije u toku neprijateljske operacije 'Panter'", in *Osma*, pp. 492-99; Bogdan Bosiočić, *Dvadesetprva slavonska NOU brigada* (Belgrade: VIZ, 1981), p. 114.

28 *Dalmacija*/IX/913, PzAOK 2, Daily report (28.12.1943); NARA/T78/331/6288110, OBSO, Daily report (3.1.1944); *Dalmacija*/X/58-64, 351-56, (26th NOVJD's HQ, and Political section, Reports Korčula, 6 and 30.1.1944, respectively), 602-03, Special commission Korčula, Findings (15.2.1943).

to the country, and this was its first bigger action. Unlike the 8th Kordun Division, with which the 392nd already had "an unpleasant encounter" during its journey from Zagreb, the 13th Primorsko-goranska Division proved much less pugnacious, preferring obstacles and mines to open combat.[29]

Northern Dalmatia also saw its share of winter fighting, although it was not as bloody as elsewhere. After the fighting around Livno had subsided, the 19th Division was sent to the western side of the Dinara, suffering 100 cases of frostbite en route. On 24-25 January 1944, the Germans, supported by the Chetniks and Ustashe, carried out a small but successful operation called "Frühlingsgewitter" with the aim of clearing the road between Knin and Kistanje. With almost no losses to themselves, they captured 35 guerrillas "in English uniforms" and almost three times as many pieces of light infantry weapons. The XV MTC used the presence of the 1st MTD and 92nd PzGR, both of which were stationed to this area in the aftermath of the "Waldrausch", to get rid of the same troublesome guerrilla group. On 3 February, six German battalions opened Operation "Emil" by advancing from all sides against the Bukovica Plateau. Three days later, the Partisans–including the ill-fated 13th Brigade that had been shipped to the mainland just a short while ago from Vis–pierced the weak northern side of the ring, crossed the Knin–Gračac railway, and lost their pursuers. The HQ of the 1st MTD issued yet another of its famous self-serving after-action reports that praised the "heroic struggle" of the men, and mentioned 854 dead, wounded, or captured enemy fighters, as well as 162 pieces of small arms secured. The Partisans, however, admitted to losing less than one-tenth of that figure, adding that "the *Bura* [northern to northeastern wind typical of the Adriatic] and cold proved to be more dangerous than the enemy". Not to be outdone by the Germans, the HQ of the 19th claimed the enemy lost 200 KIA and 250 WIA, when, in fact, the real figures were nine, and 28, respectively. It should also be mentioned that a small Partisan force landed on the island of Ugljan, just across the bay from Zadar, on 20 January and claimed it after a brief firefight. The XV MTC responded ten days later by sending over a reinforced battalion, which restored the situation. As we shall see, this inconsequential action heralded the beginning of the second round of struggle for the possession of the Dalmatian archipelagos.[30]

5.5 Aftermath of German Offensives

The German offensive had petered out by mid-February 1944. After months of uninterrupted campaigning, even crack troops were beginning to show signs of physical and psychological decay. For instance, the combat effectiveness of the 13th SS MTR was eroded by exhaustion and losses to the point where senior commands considered disbanding the formation altogether.

29 Petar Kleut, "Borbe jedinica operativnog štaba za Liku oko Gospića i na teritoriji Perušića (oktobar 1943-januar 1944.)", in *Gospić*, pp. 879-908; *Zbornik*/V/19/672, *ZAPOLI*, Report (16.9.1943); NARA/T314/562/1017, XV MTC, Operational map (undated); Franz Schraml, *Kriegsschauplatz Kroatien: die deutsch-kroatischen Legions-Divisionen: 369., 373., 392. Inf.-Div. (kroat.) ihre Ausbildungs- und Ersatzformationen* (Neckargemünd: Kurt Vowinckel Verlag, 1962), pp. 231-39.

30 *Dalmacija*/X/284-86 (3rd Naval Coastal Sector [*Pomorski obalni sektor*, POS] to HQ NOVJ Navy, 25.1.1944), 1287-88 (264th ID to XV MTC, 25.1.1944), 1296 (XV MTC to PzAOK 2, 31.1.1944), 1343-49 (1st MTD, Report "Emil", 10.2.1944); NARA/T314/555/773-74, 114th JD, Situation report (5.12.1943); NARA/T314/562/1077, Operational map (undated); Dragutin Grgurević, *Devetnaesta dalmatinska divizija* (Zagreb: IHRP, 1964), pp. 85-121.

The undisciplined behavior of the 1st MTD, which reflected itself in widespread alcohol abuse, looting, and arson, provoked protests from the Wehrmacht units unfortunate enough to be tasked with policing the areas "pacified" by the division. Measured against their geographical and time scope, as well as the number of troops involved, the operational cycles from autumn and winter of 1943-44 were the biggest anti-guerrilla undertakings of the war. Measured against their limited objectives, they were also among the most successful ones. The bulk of the 2nd ITA was disarmed and interned; the eastern Adriatic coastline, communications to the interior, and the outlying islands were secured; the NOVJ was precluded from seizing the initiative and denied a period of peace needed to fully utilize the spoils of the Italian surrender. However, with the exception of Istria, the offensive failed to inflict any lasting damage to the Partisan army, which was certain to commence its own large-scale operations as soon as the general situation permitted.[31]

The former Ljubljana Province, together with the provinces of Friuli, Gorizia, Trieste, Istra, Rijeka, and Kvarner, were combined into Operational Zone Adriatic Coastland (*Operationszone Adriatisches Küstenland*, OZAK) already in mid-September 1943. The Germans immediately began to harness all locally available sources for their security apparatus: these included the former MVAC now known as the Slovene Home Guard (*Slowenische Heimwehr* or simply *Domobranci*), its sister formation in Primorska, Slovenian National Defense Corps (*Slovenski narodni varnostni zbor*, SNVZ) as well as the armed formations of Italian Social Republic (*Repubblica Sociale Italiana*, RSI). The strength of both the Slovene and Italian collaborationist units peaked at about 15,000 each. Unlike in the NDH, where the Wehrmacht's leading position in all matters pertaining to combatting the insurgency remained inviolable, the army and the SS had a power-sharing arrangement in Slovenia. The former were represented by Commander in the OZAK (renamed LXXXXVII Army Corps for Special Purposes in September 1944), and the latter by two HSSPFs, one in Trieste and the other one in Ljubljana.[32]

The withdrawal of German divisions that took part on Operation "Wolkenbruch" was the signal for the Slovene 7th Corps to re-commence offensive operations. On 13 November 1943, the 15th Division augmented by artillery launched an attack on Novo Mesto. Unlike in the past, the Partisans did not withdraw after the first attack was repulsed by the defenders (one battalion of the 19th SS PR), but launched another one, which ultimately ended the same way. Thereupon, the NOVJ command decided to start a blockade that would last until mid-January 1944. In the meantime, the 14th Division was involved in one of the sharpest engagements of the war, the siege of Kočevje. From 9 to 12 December, the Partisans tried in vain to open a breach through the thick walls of the town's medieval castle where one police and two companies of native auxiliaries found refuge. Ultimately, a reinforced regiment of the 162nd ID broke through the inadequately-held outer ring and relieved the remnants of the garrison. Among the 248 Partisan casualties was also the division's CO, Mirko Bračič (rumored to be shot in the back by one of his brigade commanders) and his Montenegrin chief of staff, who was heavily wounded. These battles symbolized the newly-found self-confidence and the increased staying power of

31 Kumm, *Vorwärts*, p. 156; Hermann Frank Meyer, *Blutiges Edelweiß. Die 1. Gebirgs-Division im Zweiten Weltkrieg* (Berlin: Ch. Links Verlag, 2008), pp. 561-62; Schmider, *Partisanenkrieg*, p. 336.

32 NARA/T175/126, Order of Führer (10.9.1943); Tomasevich, *Occupation*, pp. 121-25; Virgilio Ilari, "L'impiego delle forze armate della RSI in territorio nazionale", in *L'Italia in guerra–il quinto anno* (Rome: MoD, 1995), pp. 176-78.

the Slovene units, but also confirmed that the campaign in this part of the country entered a stalemate. In these circumstances, the MHQ authorized the sending of the 14th and 18th Divisions to Štajerska and Gorski Kotar, respectively.[33]

The onset of winter did not seem to have dampened the guerrillas' aggressive spirit: from 1 January to 15 February 1944, Commander in the OZAK counted 181 attacks on the military, resulting in the death or wounding of 503 servicemen. Out of the 16 major incidents listed in a report prepared in mid-March by Army Detachment "von Zangen" (responsible for the entire north of Italy, as well as the OZAK), 14 took place in the operating areas of the newly-created 9th NOVJ Corps. The attacks included the ambushes near Postojna and Komen on 28 January and 2 February, respectively (altogether 75 KIA), and the raid against the airbase at Ronchi on 5 February (three airplanes set on fire). When on defensive, the guerrillas were far less effective. That they still had a lot to learn about reconnaissance and battlefield security was confirmed on three separate occasions, at Pokljuka on 15 December (50-60 Partisan KIA and MIA), Javornik on the 23rd (38 KIA), and Cerkno on 27 January. The latter episode was especially painful: informed by defectors about the presence of a guerrilla NCO course, a company of heavily-armed *Gebirgsjäger* broke into town and killed 47 fighters for the price of only one of their own. The Germans also launched classic sweeps (e.g. Operations "Enzian" and "Edelweiss"), but the results were not as satisfying.[34]

Speaking of more ambitious undertakings, the Partisans launched only one, the 30th Division's expedition to Slavia Friulana. The operation, devised to popularize the OF and boost the morale of the local ethnic Slovenes, started on the last day of January 1944. During the next couple of weeks, three Partisan brigades crisscrossed the region, attacking the traffic between Tolmin and Kobarid, and the garrison at Faedis, less than 15 km from Udine. By this time, the enemy pressure had become unbearable. In addition to a force of about 5,000 soldiers bearing down upon them (Operation "Alpenrose"), the guerrillas were pounded from the air on a daily basis by a flight of "Heinkel" He-111 medium bombers. Ultimately, the NOVJ division managed to escape to the east, but not without difficulty: the crossing of the Soča was made by individual brigades, battalions, and even groups of fighters, who had to leave their heavy weapons behind. At the same time, the Partisans won a small, but psychologically important victory against the SS "Karstwehr" Battalion in a head-to-head clash on the slopes of the Kolovrat Range on 19 February, capturing 30 pieces of small arms. In the end, despite the loss of 102 KIA, 117 WIA, and 313 MIA (many of whom were just stragglers), and the failure to draw the local Slovenes into the NOP's fold, the expedition was deemed a success. The 30th Division was now a veteran formation and its exploits were allegedly "recounted across the entire Northern Italy with the greatest enthusiasm."[35]

33 Stanko Petelin, *Petnajsta divizija* (Ljubljana: Borec, 1983), pp. 149-89; Strle, *Tomšičeva*, Vol. III, pp. 583-615.

34 NARA/T77/787, Commander OZAK, Order no. 9 (22.21944); NARA/T312/1639/711, 736, 823, Commander OZAK, Daily reports (29 and 31.1, and 5.2.1944, respectively); NARA/T312/1640/946-47, "von Zangen"/Intel., Activity report (24.1.-29.2.1944); *Zbornik*/VI/9/268 (7th Bde. to 31st NOVJD, 22.12.1943), 322 (3rd Bde. to 26th NOVJD, 26.12.1943); *Zbornik*/VI/10/535-36, 2nd Coy./ Btl. "Heine", Report Cerkno (27.1.1944); *Zbornik*/VI/11/143-44, 9th Corps/Intel. to MHQ Slovenia (13.2.1944).

35 Boris Mlakar, *Pohod 30. divizije NOV i POJ v Beneško Slovenijo* (Ljubljana: Partizanska knjiga, 1984), pp. 18-102; NARA/T312/1639/895, 1015, Commander OZAK, Daily reports (10 and 19.2.1944,

Unlike in December 1942, when the rout of the "Vladimir Gortan" Battalion stifled all military activity for nine months, the defeat suffered in late 1943 did not mean the end of the NOVJ in Istria. However, everything had to be built from scratch. In the beginning, there were a dozen companies of 15-20 fighters set up by the OHQ for Istria across the peninsula. In the early 1944 they were combined into four, later five battalions. By March, the entire organization numbered a little less than 1,300 fighters. The type of activities they engaged in corresponded to the level of organization, i.e. ambushes on lone vehicles and patrols, cutting telephone lines, and occasional railway sabotage: 24 such actions were carried out in February alone. In the meantime, the Istrians, together with the 13th and 35th Divisions (the former OHQ for Lika), had become a part of the newly-formed 11th Corps. Apart from the always-active Gospić sector, its lines remained largely quiet throughout the remainder of the winter.[36]

All three divisions of the 4th Corps stood deployed in their home regions: the 7th in Banija, the 8th in Kordun, and the new 34th Division in Pokuplje and the Žumberak. After noticing that the 8th Division had spent almost four weeks without mounting any bigger offensive actions, the corps HQ ordered it forward again in early February 1944. Oddly enough, these instructions seemingly never reached the division, and it spent the remainder of the month in winter quarters. In the meantime, the Axis relinquished some territory (including Glina) and concentrated along the railway lines linking Zagreb with Ogulin, and with Bosanska Dubica via Sisak, respectively. Both sides limited themselves to skirmishing and raiding, with bigger clashes occurring at Gora (10 January), in the vicinity of Turopolje (10 February), and Krašić (17 February). In all, the 4th Corps lost 550 fighters during these two relatively quiet months.[37]

As soon as the "Kugelblitz" task force had passed through Sandžak, the Partisans and the local collaborationists resumed their daily skirmishing; the period of low-level activity would end only with the passing of winter. The remainder of Montenegro was effectively divided into two parts in the aftermath of the "Balkanschlucht". The Germans, now reduced to a single green division (the 181st ID), controlled only the urban centers south of the line Podgorica–Danilovgrad–Nikšić; everything to the north of it belonged to the realm of the 2nd Assault Corps. Parallel to the business of resting and reorganizing the troops (two more brigades were added to the roster by the end of the year), the corps engaged in a purely guerrilla-style campaign against enemy traffic and smaller targets. The only notable action was the one-month incursion of a brigade-sized group into the coastal sector. This resulted in several incidents, including the storming of Brčeli and subsequent execution of 49 Italian Blackshirts on 13 December, and the fighting along the Cetinje–Rijeka road on the 30-31 December (15 KIA and 19 WIA Germans).[38]

The brigades of 29th Division spent the winter months in constant movement and action in Eastern Herzegovina and southwestern Montenegro, attacking Bileća, Gacko, Avtovac, and

respectively).

36 See reports by the OHQ for Istria to 13th NOVJD and MHQ Croatia in *Zbornik*/V/21/363-64 (19.11.1943); *Zbornik*/V/22/84 (6.12.1943); *Zbornik*/V/23/138-47 (10.1.1944); *Zbornik*/V/24/454-61 (26.2.1944); Petar Kleut, *Jednaesti korpus NOVJ* (Belgrade: VINC, 1987), pp. 36-52, 58-66.

37 Baić, *Četvrti*, pp. 238-52; *Zbornik*/V/24/127-28 (4th NOVJC to 8th NOVJD, 9.2.1944), 534 (8th NOVJD, Monthly report, 29.2.1944).

38 NARA/T315/1544/1525, 1644 [all 181st ID], Daily report (31.12.1943), Message to OBSO/Prop. (13.12.1943); Vukanović, *Drugi*, pp. 79, 96-118.

Grahovo, but failing to keep any of them. One notable episode from this period involved the capture and execution of the highly-decorated *Luftwaffe* fighter ace Joachim Kirschner, who had been shot down by Allied planes; the same fate befell 28 men from the rescue party sent after him from Stolac (19 December). For as long as the large-scale operations in Bosnia lasted, the hard-pressed NDH and Chetnik forces in the region would have to fend for themselves. By late January 1944, however, units of the 7th SS had begun returning from the north. Not before long, the three partners embarked on a joint operation ("Falkenjagd") against the 10th Herzegovina Brigade that had in the meantime advanced as far south as the Trebišnjica River. From 9 to 17 February, the attackers tried to encircle their target, but the guerrillas' mobility saved them again. The brigade was nevertheless compelled to relinquish its recent territorial gains and join the rest of its parent division in the area between Bileća and Gacko.[39]

A chronic shortage of troops forced the Germans to sponsor an unprecedented expansion of the native auxiliary arm. The Chetniks in Herzegovina began offering cooperation already in August 1943, those in Montenegro in October, just in time to take part in the "Balkanschlucht". In addition to the royalists, there were also Montenegrin Gendarmerie and Militia (up to 3,000 and 1,500 men, respectively), Mussolini's Blackshirts (2,600 in March 1944), and the force officially known as SS Police Self-Protection Regiment Sandžak. Composed of 5-6,000 local Muslims of Slavic and Albanian extraction, this colorful formation was better known as "Krempler's Legion", after its creator, the potbellied, Austrian-born SS adventurer Karl von Krempler. Although a far cry from the 70,000 regular soldiers the Italian military governor used to have at his disposal, these collaborationist formations were instrumental in maintaining the Wehrmacht's tenuous hold over the region.[40]

5.6 Operations North of Sava

Like their comrades in Bosnia, the Partisans in Northwestern Croatia took full advantage of the demoralized state the *Domobranstvo* found itself in after the Italian capitulation, and the fact that the Germans had no troops to spare for this part of the country. In mid-September 1943, the 10th (later 28th Slavonian) Division was temporarily subordinated to the 2nd OZ. The division marched north and attacked Ludbreg on 3 October in cooperation with the local units, which had in the meantime effectively severed all direct links between Zagreb and Varaždin. While the Slavonians were fighting in the town, the locals managed to repel a relief force coming from the west but suffered terribly at the hands of enemy aircraft (42 KIA). In the end, the Partisans captured their objective with over 400 of its defenders. Emboldened by the success, the 2nd OZ went on to plan its most ambitious operation so far, the attack on Koprivnica. This mid-sized town of some importance was taken by a brigade of the 28th and the Kalnik Detachment on 7 November after a full-day's battle: the remnants of the garrison, less about 100 Kammerhofer's gendarmes and 350 Home Guards, managed to escape. "Our fighters have thus celebrated the anniversary of the Great October Revolution in a worthy manner", wrote a high Party official before listing the immense booty taken on this occasion. Beside 64 freight cars laden with

39 Ibid., pp. 127-47; Komenović and Kreso, *Dvadesetdeveta*, pp. 160-65; Trifković, *Parleying*, p. 204.

40 Pajović, *Kontrarevolucija*, pp. 406, 416-20; NARA/T314/663/12, XXI MTC to PzAOK 2 (1.3.1944); NARA/T313/483/1179, PzAOK 2, Situation sketch (21.9.1943); NARA/T313/484/270-72, von Krempler to V SS MTC (31.10.1943).

various goods, it included two fully functional printing presses, a gift from heaven for the local NOP propagandists.

Running out of viable targets in Podravina, Zagorje, and the area of Kalnik, the 2nd OZ directed the 28th Division south, towards Čazma. For a change, its two veteran brigades would now guard the outer perimeter, while the Moslavina Brigade dealt the target itself. The battle raged for three days in and out of the town with equal ferocity. By 2 December, it was all over: one battalion each of the German-Croatian police and the HDB were destroyed, an equivalent of a third lay dead or wounded along the roads leading to Čazma. In all, the Axis lost another ca. 1,000 men, the Partisans about five times as few. This last episode represented the high-water mark of the NOVJ's autumn campaign. The 2nd OZ went about organizing its liberated territory, which now stretched from the outskirts of Zagreb in the west to Virovitica in the east. Satisfied with the marked improvement in combat capabilities of the local formations, the SHQ authorized the creation of two smaller divisions (the 32nd and 33rd) in December, followed by the 10th "Zagreb" Corps in late January 1944. With this, the last vestiges of the old command-and-control arrangements based on operational zones were removed. In the meantime, the hard-hitting Slavonians left for Pokuplje, where they took part on the highly successful attack on the airbase at Velika Gorica on 19 December (12 KIA, 10 WIA, 18 MIA Germans, 149 missing NDH servicemen).[41]

Although the Germans considered these huge territorial losses unpleasant, the northwestern part of the NDH stood clearly on the bottom of their operational priorities. The Ustashe, on the contrary, had every reason to reclaim this ethnically compact Croat region as soon as possible. It took them until early January 1944 to muster sufficient forces for an offensive (at first, one reinforced regiment of the PTS, later also the 5th UAB). After some introductory fighting north of Zagreb, the first phase of Operation "Dubrovnik", aimed at re-establishing the road connection to Varaždin, started on the 21st. The 32nd Division offered only scant resistance and withdrew to the eastern part of the Kalnik. The second phase began on 8 February with a simultaneous drive towards Ludbreg and Koprivnica. Within two days, the Ustashe entered both these places, which marked the end of the three months-old Partisan "republic". The 32nd Division at first stayed behind and tried to re-take the initiative (e.g. by attacking Ludbreg on the 23rd), but the arrival of strong German forces, which were on their way to Hungary, compelled it to join its sister formation on the Bilogora. The "Dubrovnik" was an undoubted success, as it restored both the territory and some prestige to the NDH armed forces at a comparatively low price (14 KIA and 25 WIA). Although the losses suffered by the 10th Corps were not crippling (35 KIA, 49 WIA, and at least 39 MIA), the episode showed that this young formation suffered from all the usual teething troubles such as the non-functional intelligence service, lax battlefield security, and lack of inter-unit coordination.[42]

41 Belinić, "O Drugoj", pp. 134-36; Sekula Joksimović, "Osnivanje i razvoj oružanih jedinica Narodnooslobodilačke vojske severozapadne Hrvatske 1941—1945.", in *Sjeverozapadna*, pp. 154-56; see reports of the 2nd OZ to MHQ Croatia in *SZH*/VI/409-15, 561, and 637-38 (8, 17 and 28.10.1943, respectively), *SZH*/VII/92-100, 484-90 and 737-46 (6.11, 1 and 28.12.1943, respectively); NARA/T313/485/343, [all LXIX RC], Daily report (14.11.1943), and NARA/T314/1544/580-81, Losses Čazma (11.12.1943); NARA/T77/1421, LW Zagreb, Report Gorica (27.12.1943).

42 Obhođaš et al., *Vojnica*, Vol. II, pp. 273-311; *SZH*/VIII/561-63, 10th NOVJC, Circular (18.2.1944).

After 28th Division's departure for Podravina, the 2nd Croatian Corps (renamed to the 6th NOVJ Corps in early October 1943) was left with the 12th Division and the two newly-created groups of detachments, the Eastern and Western. Their main efforts was directed against traffic and smaller targets, like the Home Guard AA battery on the outskirts of Slavonski Brod (18 October), or the motorized column belonging to the 6th Regiment of National Socialist Motor Corps (*Nationalsozialistisches Kraftfahrkorps*, NSKK) that was nearly wiped out in an ambush laid down by the "Jan Žižka" Brigade at Sibinj on Christmas Day (36 lorries lost). The guerrillas also tried their luck against a number of Axis outposts, with varying degree of success. For example, the villages of Đulavec and Gašinci, each held, on average, by ca. 300-350 men (a mix of Home Guards, German militiamen, and gendarmes) were taken on 18 September, and 11 October, respectively. By contrast, the more substantial garrisons at Pakrac and Đakovo repelled the attacks made on 12 October and 14 December. The Virovitica affair deserves a special mention here. The reinforced 18th Slavonian Brigade broke into this important town on 6 November. With the help of their sympathizer, a *Domobran* lieutenant, they proceeded to disarm the entire 550-strong 2nd HDB Cavalry Group without a shot being fired. The remaining Germans and Ustashe barricaded themselves in the medieval citadel. As usual, the Partisans had no means of reducing the last pocket of resistance quickly enough and had to withdraw before the arrival of relief columns. As soon as the Axis reinforcements left, the 12th Division came back to finish what it started, but met with no success (12-14 November).

During the second half of December 1943 and the better part of January 1944, the Partisans switched back to guerrilla actions, primarily along the main railway line. The return of the veteran 28th Division from Pokuplje allowed the 6th Corps' HQ to plan another major action. This time, the target was not an urban center, but a cluster of villages at the eastern end of the Požega Basin that represented a threat to the NOVJ communications linking Mounts Dilj and Papuk. Whereas the attackers could not dislodge the *Volksdeutsche* defenders from some secondary objectives, they succeeded in wiping out three full companies of the 2nd UAB in Čaglin. The victory, however, was paid dearly, with the Partisans practically losing as many men here as in all the above-mentioned attacks combined (114 vs. 94 KIA, 227 vs. 324 WIA). Echoing a similar message sent to the OHQ for Bosanska Krajina a year earlier, the SHQ now had to caution the Slavonian command against making costly frontal assaults on fortified places.[43]

During this period, the Axis launched only one halfway serious undertaking against the units of the 6th Corps, the "Herbst I". The operation, carried out by the elements of the LXIX RC's 187th RD and two Ustasha battalions targeted the guerrilla bases on the southeastern slopes of the Slavonian Mountains. In four days of fighting (25-29 September 1943), the attackers managed to push back the Dilj Detachment and parts of the 12th Division and capture Paučje and Kutjevo, all at the price of ca. 100 casualties. In contrast to Slavonia, the Partisans in Syrmia

43 *Zbornik*/V/21/329-30, 12th NOVJD, Activity report (1-15.11.1943); NARA/T314/1544/169 [all LXIX RC] (Diary, 24.12.1943), 487 (Message to PzAOK 2, 25.11.1943); NARA/T314/1545/1064, 42nd JD, Division order (29.1.1944); *Slavonija*/X/397-430, 6th NOVJC, Activity report (January 1944); *SD*/XIX/30, SHQ to 6th NOVJC (9.2.1944); Rade Roksandić, Zdravko B. Cvetković, *Osamnaesta slavonska brigada* (Belgrade: VIZ, 1974), pp. 81-96; Nail Redžić, *Dvadesetpeta brodska brigada* (Belgrade: VIZ, 1976), pp. 28-89; Stevo Pravdić, Nail Redžić, *Šesnaesta slavonska omladinska NOU brigada "Jože Vlahović"* (Belgrade: VIZ, 1976), pp. 165-86.

had to endure nearly six weeks of constant enemy pressure. After the last brigade (the 3rd Vojvodina) had left for Bosnia in early September, the NOVJ presence in the province was again reduced to two local detachments. Nevertheless, the disruption they were causing on a daily basis made them a target of several large undertakings. Beginning on 15 September, Operation "Kammerhofer" first swept through the eastern part of the Fruška Gora, and then moved to the area between the main railway line and the Sava River. Since this police action failed to produce anything but scores of burnt-down villages, the LXIX RC decided to take the matters into its own hands. Operation "Arnim" (14-17 October) would be best remembered for the fact that the 1st CCD received its baptism of fire on this occasion. This colorful, 18,000-strong formation was composed of members of the Eastern Legions and those Soviet POWs who were desperate to escape the inhumane treatment in Nazi captivity. The "Circassians" (*Čerkezi*), as they were erroneously called in Yugoslavia, soon earned the reputation for brutality and rape. Although their officers (incidentally, many of whom came from the now-defunct cavalry arm of the Wehrmacht) tended to explain it in terms of "Bolshevik upbringing" and peculiarities of the "eastern" mentality, the fact remains that such behavior was really deemed problematic only when it occurred in friendly villages. When on enemy territory, the division acted no differently from any other German unit: during its first action, the 1st Cossack Cavalry Brigade (CCB) shot 206 males on the Fruška Gora, but captured only seven rifles.[44]

The real target of the offensive, the 1st Syrmian Detachment, managed to escape and join its sister formation in the old NOP bases located along the southern banks of the Bosut. In early October 1943, both detachments were again reduced to skeleton formations as their fighters filled the ranks of the new 4th Vojvodina Brigade. Together with the 2nd Brigade that came over from Bosnia in the meantime, the 4th took part in the 3rd Corps' unsuccessful operation against Brčko by attacking the northern end of the town's defensive perimeter. The mobile formations' stay in their native province was cut short by Operation "Wildsau" (26-29 October), designed to restore the railway line running from Vinkovci to the Bosnian border and throw the guerrillas into the Sava. Nearly the entire 1st CCD, reinforced by armor, artillery, and air assets, moved in from the north, east, and west. Faced with such long odds, the Partisans dispersed, the brigades going back to Bosnia, and the detachments to the Fruška Gora. The Cossack after-action report mentions 400 prisoners and 266 enemy dead, the majority of whom were "civilians suspected of spying", and the booty consisting of 38 pieces of small arms. This time, however, the attacker suffered 26 KIA and MIA plus 53 WIA, indicating that some combat had actually taken place.

Following the sweep, the Cossacks were redeployed to Banija and Pokuplje, just in time to take part in Operation "Panther". The Partisans, now numbering only ca. 600, resumed their usual activities, averaging some 50 actions a month in the period December 1943-February 1944. Most of these were small affairs, like assassinations and acts of sabotage; the biggest was the ambush at Obrež on 20 December, which resulted in the death of 55 NDH and German gendarmes. One other episode deserves a special mention. Much like the 30th Division's expedition to Slavia Friulana, the 1st Vojvodina Brigade return to Syrmia was motivated by the

44 *Slavonija*/VIII/84-86, 12th NOVJD to 2nd Croatian NOVJC (7.10.1943); NARA/T314/1544/55 [all LXIX RC], Diary (2.10.1943), and NARA/T314/1545/265-87, Daily reports (16.9-1.10.1943); NARA/T315/2281/123-34, [all 1st CCD], [Materials pertaining to "Arnim"] (12-18.10.1943), and NARA/T314/561/350-56, Report on discipline (23.1.1944).

need to raise the morale of the friendly population, shaken by the suffering caused by the recent enemy offensives. It was decided that this objective would be best served by taking Grgurevci, the staging point for raids into the liberated territory and the site of the notorious massacre from 1942. The attack began late on 22 November and ended on the afternoon of the 24th. Although the 1st Vojvodina was repulsed with the loss of some 125 men (one-fifth of them KIA), the Germans, who suffered even bigger losses, evacuated the village shortly thereafter.[45]

The situation in the original German occupation zone in Slovenia looked as follows. The western part of Gorenjska and Carinthia stood under the auspices of the Partisan 9th Corps. After recuperating from the aforementioned defeat at the Pokljuka, the 7th Brigade and the local detachment resumed their activities against smaller Axis targets in the valleys of the Selška and Poljanska Rivers. The campaign culminated in a twin-attack on the gendarmerie stations at Železniki and Selca on 22 January 1944. Due to negligence and bad coordination with the 31st Division, the 7th suffered yet another defeat, losing at least 20 KIA. The Gorenjska Partisans spent the rest of the winter reorganizing and securing/enforcing the recruitment drive. The West Koroška Detachment (formed already in late October 1943) was unable to establish a permanent base in its namesake province but could only send patrols across the pre-war Austrian border. The situation was much better in the east, where the Koroška Battalion (subordinated to the 4th OZ) carried out several high-profile actions on the territory of the Third Reich, including the raid on St. Veit im Jauntal on 3 November, and the attacks on the gendarmerie stations at Vellach on 6 November and Globasnitz two months later.[46]

Unlike the remainder of the country, the Italian surrender had a rather negative effect on the Partisan efforts in Štajerska. With most of the veteran fighters gone south, the re-constituted 4th OZ was back to "stage one"; by the end of September 1943, its effectives consisted of mere three green battalions. Two of them were incorporated into the reorganized 6th Brigade, giving this unit a total strength of only about 300. Despite their numerical weakness, the Partisans succeeded in killing 42 and wounding 86 Axis soldiers during October. Following in the footsteps of its famous predecessor, the battalion (later detachment) operating from the Pohorje Mountains was credited with 69 incidents in November alone. All things considered, it is no wonder that the Germans decided to embark on yet another "general cleansing" of the province. During the first phase, codenamed Operation "Schneegestöber" (6-10 December), eight reinforced battalions from the 14th and 19th SS PRs, as well as the Division No. 438[47], combed the Pohorje, but found no one: the guerrillas silently made their escape towards the northwest. The second phase, which took place in the area west of Kamnik from 16 to 24 December, ended in much the same way, with the 6th Brigade and the 4th OZ's HQ slipping away to Koroška.

45 NARA/T315/2281/142-43, 163-71, 1st CCD, [Materials pertaining to "Wildsau I"] (17.10-7.11.1943); *Zbornik*/I/6/481-93, [all MHQ Vojvodina] to SHQ (2.12.1943), and *Zbornik*/I/8/12-13, 52-53, 128, Monthly activity summaries (December 1943-February 1944); *Zbornik*/I/17/540, 544, HDB Syrmian Bde., Monthly reports (November and December 1943, respectively).

46 Petelin, *Prešernova*, pp. 77-98, 111-15; *Zbornik*/VI/8/29, 3rd OZ, Order (23.10.1943); see reports of 4th OZ to MHQ Slovenia in *Zbornik*/VI/10/220 (16.1.1944) and *Zbornik*/VI/9/39-43 (3.12.1943); see also ibid., pp. 372-73, 9th NOVJC, Monthly report (December 1943).

47 *Division Nr. 438* was formed on 1 November 1943 out of the 18th and 184th LSRs, with altogether seven territorial battalions and some smaller border guards units: Georg Tessin, *Verbände und Truppen der deutschen Wehrmacht und der Waffen-SS im Zweiten Weltkrieg 1939-1945* (Osnabrück: Biblio Verlag, 1978), Vol. X, p. 174.

At the same time, the Germans attacked the last remaining NOVJ bastion in the province, the Kozjansko, and forced the local guerrilla company to seek refuge in the Croatian Zagorje.[48]

All hopes for a peaceful winter were dashed in the first days of February 1944, when the security forces were alerted to the presence of a large guerrilla force on the southern border of Štajerska. The idea of a major incursion into the province was born in the MHQ Slovenia already in the closing weeks of 1943. The main aim of the operation was to bolster the NOVJ presence there and exploit the largely untapped reservoir of manpower that could provide an estimated 20,000 recruits. The oldest and most experienced division, the 14th, was selected for this task. Although its three brigades had only about 1,100 men and women, they were all physically fit and highly motivated. The march was prepared with the (stereo-) typical Slovene meticulousness: only the sturdiest pack-animals were chosen, Italian weapons were exchanged for the German ones, enough ammunition and medical supplies were brought along. Since the direct approaches to Štajerska were closely guarded, the Partisan planners opted for a wide detour through northern Croatia. This would hopefully allow the division to reach its objective unobserved, or at least not seriously opposed.[49]

The 14th Division expedition opened on 29 December 1943. During the following five weeks, the division crossed as many enemy-held railway lines, one major river (the Sava southeast of Zagreb), and one mountain (the Kalnik), lost one of its brigade commanders to an Ustasha ambush, and got wined and dined by the Croatian NOOs along the way (it turned out that the local, high-fat cuisine did not sit well with the guests). Finally, on 6 February, the Partisans crossed the Sutla into Štajerska not far from Tito's birthplace of Kumrovec. From then on, the division became a wandering cauldron: wherever it went, it ran into ambushes and blocking lines manned by the usual mix of soldiers, policemen, gendarmes, *vermani*, and even some grenadiers belonging to Himmler's own 18th SS PzGD, which happened to be in Ljubljana at that time. By the end of the month, the German OHQ that was specially formed to deal with the guerrilla incursion would have almost 3,200 men at its disposal. Braving the blizzards and heavy snow, the 14th first went westward, then turned north at Zidani Most and continued marching parallel with the Savinja until it reached Mount Konjiška. The attempted breakthrough towards the Pohorje on 17-18 February was only partially successful; an equivalent of two brigades with the division HQ and support units were still in mortal danger. Two days later, the Partisans forced their way across the Velenje–Slovenj-Gradec railway line at Paka, but were again surrounded on the ridges beyond. With all their officers in the firing line, the guerrillas charged with "desperate courage" and finally managed to pierce this last enemy ring northwest of Topolšica on 22 February, after which they split into three groups. The Germans continued with mop-up operations for several more days before proclaiming victory. In many respects, the campaign resembled both the Igman March and the Battle of Sutjeska, and it still holds great symbolic importance. It was a rite of passage for the Slovene branch of the NOVJ, one which showed that their brigades could survive privation and endless marching in the worst weather imaginable, and take heavy beating in an open fight, all without losing cohesion. The 14th Division suffered

48 Stiplovšek, *Šlandrova*, pp. 105-215; Mirko Fajdiga, *Zidanškova brigada* (Ljubljana: Borec, 1975), pp. 28-30; *Zbornik*/VI/8/424-25, SIPO/SD Maribor, Badnitry in Lower Styria (1.11.1943); *Zbornik*/VI/9/417-33, HSSPF Ljubljana, [Materials pertaining to "Schneegestöber"] (2.12.1943); *Zbornik*/VI/10/60-62, 4th OZ to MHQ Slovenia (6.1.1944).

49 Lado Ambrožič Novljan, *Pohod Četrnaeste* (Belgrade: VIZ, 1984), pp. 29-55.

terrible losses (367 KIA and MIA, and at least 261 WIA), but fulfilled its task and would eventually be ready to commence the spring campaign in its new operational area.[50]

5.7 Serbia and Macedonia: Finally Brigades

On 28 August 1943, "in light of developments both at home and abroad", Tito ordered the creation of brigades and divisions in Serbia. Since no couriers from Belgrade had reached the SHQ lately (a direct wireless link would be established only in late October), the Partisan overlord had no precise information on the NOVJ's strength and dispositions. He therefore could only give general advice and send a handful of veteran officers to Serbia, but the local leadership had to determine when and where these units were to be formed. Unsurprisingly, the choice again fell on Šumadija, where the so-called "Provisional Brigade", made up of the 1st Battalion and the local detachment, had been operating for some time. On 5 October, they were formally merged into the 1st Šumadija Brigade; the Kosmaj Detachment would provide the bulk of the fighters for the 3rd Battalion later on. Despite having only about 200 effectives at the beginning, the brigade proceeded aggressively, raiding the town of Lazarevac on 16 October, ambushing a German-SSW detail at Darosava on the 26th, defeating the Chetniks at Dučina and Baćevac on the 28th and 31st, respectively (altogether 56 prisoners), and demolishing the Junkovac mine on 13 November. Just as German daily reports began to resemble those from the height of the uprising two years earlier, the brigade received orders for the march to Sandžak. The controversial decision to "rob" the country of its best unit was rooted in the fear that the 1st Šumadija, being isolated and without a firm base, was running a very real risk of suffering the same tragic fate that befell the Serbian detachments in the winter 1941-42. Once properly trained and refitted on the liberated territory, the brigade could easily return in the spring. Chased by the Chetniks and elements of the 5th SS PR (Operation "Erich"), the 1st Šumadija finally reached the pickets of the 5th Krajina Division on the slopes of Mount Tara on 27 November. Ironically, this maneuver, which was supposed to remove the premier Serbian formation out of harm's way, nearly led to its destruction at Prijepolje less than a week later.[51]

The remaining NOVJ forces in Central Serbia, the Šumadija and Kosmaj Detachments, now had but one task, to survive in what had again become an extremely hostile environment. Their comrades from the eastern parts of the country were facing a similar situation. At first, it seemed that the things here were looking up as well. By the beginning of October 1943, the Timok Battalion had grown so large that it had to be upgraded into a full (Zaječar) detachment. Apart from the demolition of three mines located on the outskirts of its namesake town on 13 November, the best known action from this period involved the kidnapping of a train (25 October) and using it to disarm three Bulgarian station crews on the railway line to Prahovo. By mid-January 1944, however, the situation had taken turn for the worse; facing overwhelming odds and ammunition shortage, the Partisans decided to temporarily evacuate their home territory. After crossing the South Morava and defeating the Chetniks at Kulina on the 30th (70 rifles captured), the reinforced Zaječar Detachment continued to operate in the southern part of the country for the next several months. The ill-fated Požaervac Detachment, reconstituted

50 Ibid., pp. 56-296; *Zbornik*/VI/11/405, [German] OHQ, After-action Report (undated).
51 *SD*/XVI/134-36, Tito to MHQ Serbia (28.8.1943); *SD*/XVII/322; NARA/T501/266/756, 759, 786, MBSO, Daily reports (28, 26, and 14.11.1943, respectively); Đuković, *Prva*, pp. 143-244.

only in mid-October, attempted to perform a similar maneuver in order to join the NOVJ units around Mladenovac, but was practically wiped out in the process.[52]

The 1st South Morava Brigade was formed on 10 October 1943 from about 600 fighters belonging to the 1st SMD. The formation spent the next six weeks operating in the area southwest of Prokuplje and Leskovac. During this time, it had several successful clashes with the Bulgarians, Germans, and Nedić's forces, resulting, among else, in the death of one Bulgarian battalion commander and the capture of a least 16 soldiers. The royalists also received a severe drubbing at Šiljegovac on 16-18 November, losing 135 prisoners. Like its sister unit from Šumadija, the brigade received marching orders for Eastern Bosnia several days later. The march, punctuated with heavy fighting against the JVuO in the area of Lazarevac and Aranđelovac, lasted until 12 December, when the Partisans finally crossed the Drina. The brigade's departure did not produce a vacuum; a steady influx of new recruits allowed for the creation of three more South Morava Brigades (the 2nd-4th) by mid-January. The events on the battlefield confirmed the wisdom of fielding large mobile formations. They were instrumental in dealing the Chetniks the heavy blows at Stubla on 15 December, Grevci on 29 January, and Devča eighteen days later (over 150 pieces of small arms captured; the NOVJ lost one brigade commander, among others). Although they still lacked the strength and know-how to attack bigger garrisons, the guerrillas did raid several high-profile targets. These included the railroad car factory and the airstrip at Kruševac, as well as the Leskovac hospital (procurement of medical supplies being the main motive). The rising number of attacks on its members compelled the 27th BID to mount yet another sweep of Mount Radan and its surroundings in late January and the first week of February. The Partisans largely succeeded in escaping towards the Rasina: the majority of the reported 269 dead and 165 captured "bandits" were civilians. As already shown on several occasions in other parts of the country, exposure and "public relations" actions could incur more casualties than actual fighting. The 2nd Brigade was ordered to tour the villages on the far side of the South Morava and "demonstrate the strength of the people's army". By the time the two-week round trip was over in late February, the unit had suffered 65 cases of frostbite.[53]

The 2nd SMD (700 fighters) remained the NOVJ's principal unit on the right bank of the South Morava throughout late 1943. Its active campaigning provoked Bulgarian reaction several times, but without any result. Tired of half-measures, the occupation authorities launched a major operation (known to the Yugoslavs as "Total Offensive") against the Crna Trava liberated territory in the first days of 1944 using at least eight infantry battalions, one cavalry regiment, ten armored vehicles, plus police units. Despite the numbers and careful preparations, the offensive failed to close the net around the guerrillas, who escaped in the direction of the Kozjak. The attackers then proceeded with a Kozara-style action, interning every male they could lay their hands on. The Partisans responded by breaking into the holding camp at Kriva Palanka on 13 January and liberating some 2,000 internees, a major propaganda coup. The ultimate failure of

52 Vitorović, *Centralna*, pp. 532-82; Bosiljčić, *Istočna*, pp. 95-118.
53 *Zbornik*/I/21/608, Nedić MoI, Weekly report (4-10.2.1944); see also MBSO's daily reports in NARA/T501/266/850, 855, 861, 874, 885, (31, 30, 28, 24, and 19.10.1943, respectively) and NARA/T501/256/49 (9.2.1944); Perović, *Južna*, pp. 324-44.

the enemy winter offensive was symbolically celebrated by the creation of the new 5th and 6th Brigades outside Vranje and Vlasotince in early February and early March, respectively.[54]

The area of 2nd SMD was also the home of the "first" OHQ, created on 20 November 1943 for the purpose of steering the NOVJ war effort in Southeastern Serbia, northern parts of Macedonia and Kosovo, and even western Bulgaria. This meant in the first place combatting the Chetniks, whose organization was making progress here as well. The campaign was not off to a good start. By the early 1944, the JVuO managed to expel the Partisans from the Serbian-Macedonian border strip, effectively ending the "first" OHQ. The "second" OHQ, formed in the first days of February, was provided with extra arms and 450-500 men with which to launch a counterstroke. However, due to skirmishes with the Bulgarians and urgent side missions, such as escorting a large group of volunteers from Kosovo and preparing the ground for the arrival of the Macedonian MHQ, the showdown was postponed until 29th February (1944 was a leap year). On this day, the Chetnik Preševo Brigade attacked the main Partisan base at St. Prohor Pčinjski Monastery and got severely mauled in the process (97 prisoners). Three days later, the victory was sealed by the capture of another 30 Chetniks and the archives belonging to the JVuO's Vardar Corps.[55]

As in the remainder of Yugoslavia, the Italian capitulation proved to be a powerful catalyst for the growth of the NOVJ in Macedonia. Together with their comrades from Albania, the Partisans disarmed parts of the "Firenze" Division and carved out a large and well-organized liberated territory around Debar and Kičevo. The German XXI MTC, preoccupied with more important tasks on the coast, could at first spare no troops for this sector. What they could do was to send *Abwehr* operatives (including Reinhard Kopps, one of the organizers of the notorious post-war "Rat Channels" to South America) to the local Albanian chieftains and win them over with promises of arms and support. At least 3,000 militiamen from the area of Gostivar and Tetovo were the first to test the integrity of the NOVJ defenses in the first half of October. After some heavy fighting, the Albanians entered Kičevo, but could not progress any further. The Partisans, in their most ambitious action yet, brought up five battalions and retook the town on 1 November, capturing 14 Germans, including one lieutenant-colonel. The Albanians, however, re-formed unexpectedly quickly and pushed the Partisans out of Kičevo for good on the 5th. Determined to secure the lines of communication in this part of the country, the XXI MTC launched Operation "Edelweiss" with four battalions from the 297th ID, 100th JD, and the "Brandenburg" Division. On the second day of the offensive (17 November), the Germans took Debar and proceeded to link up with the spearheads coming from Struga and Kičevo. The operation lasted until 7 December, with shorter interruptions, and was proclaimed a success: 58 pieces of small arms, five cannon, and 18 vehicles were captured or destroyed. The fact was, however, that the bulk of the NOVJ forces–including the newly-formed, ca. 700-strong 1st Macedonian-Kosovo Brigade–managed to escape into the Bulgarian occupation zone.[56]

After the loss of the main base in the west, the MHQ Macedonia now had to decide where to go next. The choice fell on the 3rd OZ, operating from Mount Kožuf west of Đevđelija. Its better known actions included the capture of the Dudica mine on 2 October 1943 (10 Germans

54 Nikolić, *Jugoistočna*, pp. 417, 430-445, 461-63.
55 Ibid., pp. 445-51, 463-67.
56 Roberto Trajkovski, *Вермахтот и Македонија (1943-1944 година)* (Bitola: SBM, 2018), pp. 51-81; *Enciklopedija*, Vol. VII, p. 386.

shot, 80 miners recruited into own ranks), as well as the seizure of the Bulgarian border outposts at Lukar on 22 October (33 prisoners) and Konsko on 16 December (60 defectors; the second attack against the same place 10 days later was repulsed with a handful of losses on both sides). By the time the leadership had reached the Kožuf after a grueling two-week hike across the mountains of Northern Greece, there were enough fighters going around to form the 2nd Macedonian Brigade. The remaining three battalions were formed into a separate group. Having so many men in one place was certain to draw unwanted attention: in fact, the Axis started their operations (codenamed "Elefant" and "Wolf") against the guerrilla bases on the Kožuf already in the first week of January 1944. Consequently, the MHQ chose to split its forces into three brigade-sized groups and send them to different parts of the country. During this so-called "February Campaign", the 1st Brigade made an attempt to establish a new base in the central part of the country but was forced to turn back after reaching the area north of Prilep with the loss of 49 KIA. The 2nd Brigade tried assisting its older sister's efforts by making an incursion into the Vardar Valley downstream from Negotino, without much success. The 3rd Group of Battalions, with the Macedonian military and political leadership in tow, had the most difficult task of all: to reach the liberated territory southeast of Vranje by way of Northern Greece and the (entirely Partisan-free) eastern part of Macedonia. Apart from the great physical strain and winter weather, the 23-day, 440 km-long march proved remarkably uneventful; Tempo marveled at the tight-lipness of the Greek population that enabled the column to cross the Thessaloniki plain without even being noticed by the enemy. As we have seen, the Macedonians arrived to the Kozjak just in time to take part in the battle against the JVuO's Vardar Corps.[57]

5.8 NOVJ after the Italian Surrender

Probably the single most important event that occurred during the period covered in this chapter was the recognition of the NOP as a full-time member of the anti-Hitler coalition. It was a result of a complicated process that has been sufficiently explained elsewhere. Suffice it to say that Mihailović was the sole beneficiary of British support from the late 1941 to the spring 1943. There were several reasons why planners in London began to show interest for the other guerrilla movement. With the African campaign practically over, the Balkans became one of the possible choices for the next major amphibious operation. The Chetniks were not only besmirched with collaboration but have shown themselves to be of limited military value. Moreover, decrypted German cables revealed the massive scale and ferocity of the winter battles against the Partisans. The latter could also not be simply ignored any longer as a major factor on the Yugoslav political scene. Given that the Allies had no direct contact with the NOP since the days of the Foča Republic, it was decided to send liaison parties to Central Croatia and Northern Montenegro, both of which were suspected of holding large guerrilla concentrations. The first small group of British servicemen arrived to Tito's HQ on 28 May 1943, just in time to take part in the Sutjeska ordeal. As their original chief was killed during the bombing on 9 June, Captain William Deakin, an Oxford scholar and Churchill's personal acquaintance, took over.

57 *Zbornik*/VII/2/251-52 (3rd OZ to MHQ Macedonia, 20.11.1943), 383 (Skopje police, Activity report 1943); Roberto Trajkovski, *Вермахтот и Егејскиот дел на Македонија (1943-1944)* (Skopje: Sojuz na antifašsti-Antifa, 2019), pp. 122-33; Tempo, *Revolucija*, Vol. I, pp. 386-92; *Enciklopedija*, Vol. II, pp. 749-50.

His favorable impressions of the Partisans' fighting skills and level of organization seemed to confirm the intelligence obtained from other sources. Consequently, the prime minister decided to upgrade the status of the mission in September; this time, he sent over Brigadier Fitzroy Maclean, a Scottish-born warrior-politician who was no stranger to either Communists or life behind enemy lines. Finally, the Big Three announced their intention to give all possible support to the NOP on the Teheran Conference in early December. All this did not mean that the Whitehall was yet ready to renounce Mihailović (and especially not the Yugoslav government-in-exile), but he was effectively relegated to number two position.[58]

The KPJ membership had mixed feelings about their newly-found allies. On the one hand, they were glad that their sacrifices and contribution to the common cause were finally recognized. On the other hand, the British were still viewed with deep suspicion. Their plan to drop dozens of liaison and intelligence-gathering parties across the liberated territories was seen as a massive spy operation directed primarily against the NOP. Pragmatism, however, prevailed once more; in words of one US officer, Tito and his followers "were realists and horse-traders" who understood that the sorely needed material aid could only be obtained in this way. The first air drops, organized by Deakin, were small but had a major psychological impact even when they contained such unnecessary items such as anti-malaria drugs. By the end of the year, drop zones existed in almost every part of the country.[59] The Slovenes got some much needed AT weapons and explosives already in August, the Macedonians received light infantry weapons north of Struga in early November, and the 2nd SMD their first mortars around Crna Trava in December. Often overlooked, but probably just as important were other, less glamorous items such as food[60], medicine, and clothes. The Allied help was crucial in alleviating the effects of the chronic shortage of footwear plaguing the NOVJ. The 3rd Corps reported in early December that the need for shoes was great, but that they were hard to come by. Writing three months later, the same HQ noted that the situation approved markedly thanks to the "English" shipments. One document captured in Drvar reveals the extent of the aid program, listing hundreds of items received from the Allies in the period December 1943 to May 1944 on two single-spaced pages. In addition to 42,691 rifles, 8,778 MGs, 162 cannon, and 22 tons of explosives, there

58 Mark C. Wheeler, *Britain and the war for Yugoslavia, 1940-1943* (New York: Columbia University Press, 1980), pp. 234-38; F. H. Hinsley, *British Intelligence in the Second World War: its Influence on Strategy and Operations* (London: Her Majesty's Stationary Office, 1984), Vol. III/1, pp. 137-50; Dušan Biber (ed.), *Tito–Churchill: strogo tajno* (Zagreb: Globus, 1981), pp. XII-XVIII.

59 In the summer of 1944, the Germans launched Operation "Casanova", designed to trick enemy transport planes into dropping their cargo over false drop zones; the Partisans were also known to have employed captured enemy flags for similar purposes: Gaj Trifković, "Too Little, Too Late: Evolution in German Counter-insurgency Methods in Yugoslavia, 1943-1944" (appears in JSMS, 34:2, 2021), pp. 16-20; *Zbornik*/IV/12/275, 2nd NOVJD to SHQ (21.4.1943); *Zbornik*/IX/3/672, 16th Slavonian Bde./Pol. to CK KPH (20.5.1943).

60 One high-ranking British officer related the following anecdote about a shipment of dehydrated food that the Yugoslav cooks failed to prepare properly: "[It] had not been soaked but gulped down as it was. This was dry work, or so the Partisans thought, and so they washed it down with copious draughts of water from the neighbouring brook. Then, with disconcerting suddenness, the stuff began to swell inside them until it had reached several times its original dimensions. Their ensuing discomfort was considerable, though not so acute as that of another Partisan, who at about this time ate a stick of plastic high-explosive, mashing it up with milk, under the impression that it was some kind of maize porridge": Fitzroy Maclean, *The Eastern Approaches* (London: Jonathan Cape, 1949), pp. 436-37.

were also 97 W/T sets, 45,732 pairs of shoes, 26,113 blankets, 15,915 crates of hardtack, 5,319 crates of sugar and honey, and even 118 crates of matches.[61]

The majority of these supplies came into the county not by air, but by sea. The first such shipment was organized by the representative of the US Office of Strategic Services (OSS) in Bari, Major Louis Huot, on his own initiative, in mid-October 1943. By this time, the NOVJ was allowed to operate its own base on the outskirts of the city. Its main task was to organize the sending of supplies across the Adriatic, and handle all matters pertaining to the Yugoslav personnel in Italy. For this purpose, and with the Allied help, the NOVJ Navy maintained regular traffic between Bari and Vis with altogether 34 vessels by early January 1944. On their return trips, the vessels brought in the wounded, thousands of them. On 19 November, Dr. Nikoliš informed one of his British colleagues on the current state of the NOVJ medical branch, including the number of doctors (ca. 200) and patients (ca. 7,500, most of whom were injured in battle); three days later, the first group was already on its way to the hospitals in the West. In addition, the Allies took it upon themselves to arm and drill both infantry and specialist units made up of Yugoslav volunteers (with the exception of wireless operators and chyper clerks, whom Tito kindly refused to accept).[62]

The months following the capitulation of Italy saw a massive expansion and reorganization of the NOVJ. By 1 January 1944, the army had nine corps, 28 divisions, 103 brigades, and 105 detachments. In early October, the numeration of corps and divisions was streamlined on the national level: for example, the 1st Bosnian Corps became the 3rd Corps NOVJ, the 1st Croatian Corps became the 4th Corps NOVJ, etc. The composition and the range of tasks each of these unit classes was expected to perform remained largely the same, with one exception. The forming of the 1st Proletarian Corps in early October 1943 introduced the new type of corps that was not bound to a fixed geographical area, but expected to fight wherever sent. As regards command-and-control arrangements, the corps became the chief mid-level territorial command, replacing nearly all operational zones and even one MHQ (the one for Montenegro and Boka). The Corps HQ was reorganized into two departments: the Operational had operational, communications, intelligence, weapons, quartermaster, medical, and judiciary sections; Corps Military Area was divided into mobilization, transport, medical, security, and judiciary sections.

Chaotic conditions continued to mar the war effort in Serbia. The all-powerful head of the PK, Blagoje Nešković, finally joined the units in Šumadija after leaving his Belgrade hideout after almost two years. The hope that the political and military leadership would now act in unison proved vain. The secretary effectively "decapitated" the MHQ by transferring its most

61 *Zbornik*/II/10/362, Tito to Tempo (9.10.1943); Franklin D. Roosevelt Presidential Library and Museum, Safe Files, Box 4, OSS April 1944-45, Report of Major Weil on Yugoslavia, pp. 20-21 (probably spring 1944) [hereinafter: FDRL/collection/box/document]; Deakin, *Embattled*, p. 81; *Zbornik*/VI/6/172, MHQ Slovenia to SHQ (28.8.1943); *Zbornik*/VII/2/196, Kiril Krstevski to MHQ Macedonia (4.11.1943); *Zbornik*/I/7/40, 2nd SMD, Activity report (10.10.1943-7.1.1944); see reports of the 3rd NOVJC in *Zbornik*/IV/20/165 (10.12.1943) and *Zbornik*/IV/23/217 (8.3.1944); NARA/T314/565/814-15, Allied deliveries (4.6.1944).

62 Douglas Waller, *Wild Bill Donovan: The Spymaster Who Created the OSS and Modern American Espionage* (New York: Free Press, 2011), pp. 185-86; *SD*/XVII/349; *Enciklopedija*, Vol. I, p. 527; Kazimir Pribilović, *Četvrti pomorski obalni sektor Mornarice narodnooslobodilačke vojske Jugoslavije 1943–1945.* (Split: VINC, 1988), p. 188; *Zbornik*/II/11/99 (Tito to MHQ Croatia), 104-05 (Nikoliš to Mackenzie) [both 19.11.1943]; *SD*/XIX/38, Tito to MHQ Croatia (12.2.1944).

important cadres to the 1st Šumadija Brigade, and appointing a new commander instead, who was at that time lying sick in the capital. Nešković himself first traveled south, then accompanied the 1st South Morava Brigade on its journey to Eastern Bosnia, and then returned to Serbia in early 1944 without permission from the SHQ. Why Tito failed to intervene in such an important matter was never sufficiently explained by Yugoslav historiography. Owing to poor communications and a very sketchy picture of what was going on in Serbia, he probably felt that the local Party leaders knew best what needed to be done. By contrast, the Bosnian PK was expressly prohibited from meddling in military affairs in early October 1943, and the decision to demote the commander of the MHQ Croatia for his unsatisfactory performance during Operation "Weiss" was followed through despite the objections from the CK KPH.[63]

Playing on its own successes and the favorable international situation, the NOP was leading an all-out recruitment campaign throughout the latter half of 1943. For this purpose, the 3rd Corps formed the 16th Muslim and 18th Croat Brigades in the Tuzla area, hoping that the use of the special titles would make the service with the NOVJ more enticing to members of these two ethnic groups. The curious case of Huska Miljković deserves a special mention. Miljković was one of the rare pre-war KPJ members originating from Cazinska Krajina, a compact Muslim enclave in the far northwestern corner of Bosnia. Separated from his unit during Operation "Weiss", he returned home and started cobbling together his own private militia, which would number some 3,000 men by the end of the year. Unlike other Muslim formations that appeared in this period (most notably the "Green Cadre" of Nešad Topčić in Northeastern Bosnia), the militia was organized along military lines and had a real combat potential, no doubt a product of the know-how its founder had acquired in the NOVJ. As a result, all sides tried to woo him: his HQ was frequented by Ustasha functionaries, German officers, and Partisan commissars alike. Initially, he maintained hostile attitude towards his former comrades and took part on the defense of Velika Kladuša in late June, among else. The Partisans responded by sacking Cazin in early November and perpetrating some unwarranted executions, which drew the two sides even further apart. By late January 1944, Miljković had realized from where the wind was blowing and accepted the rank of colonel in the NOVJ, but it would take several more months before he cut his ties to the Axis for good (he was assassinated in late May by some pro-Ustasha relatives of his). Huska's units were reorganized into Una Operational Group with the 1st and 2nd Muslim Brigades, as well as the Krajina Detachment; they would end the war as a part of the 8th Kordun Division. The handling of the Huska affair exemplifies the war-winning pragmatism of the NOP leadership. The "Muslim" units included members of other faiths, but every effort was made to mollify the majority. This was done by appointing as many of their co-religionists as possible to command posts and ensuring that their most basic religious needs were met (e.g. only vegetable oil or tallow could be used for cooking).[64]

The NOVJ also had two Jewish units. The Rab Battalion was composed of 243 former internees of the Italian camp on the island of the same name (a further ca. 1,100 Jewish internees joined the NOP in other capacities). The unit's command, fearing that the inexperience and ethnicity

63 *SD*/XVI/53 and XIX/13-14, SHQ to MHQ Croatia (15.7.1943 and 6.2.1944, respectively); *SD*/XVII/11, SHQ to 1st Bosnian NOVJC (2.10.1943); Glišić, Miljanić, *Rukovođenje*, pp. 177-81, 192-99; Anić, Joksimović, Gutić, *Narodnooslobodilačka*, pp. 327-332.

64 Hoare, *Muslims*, pp. 118-20, 230-42; NARA/T314/566/665, BDTK to DGA (22.7.1943); VAB/NOVJ/128a/1/31, Commisar for People's Defense to MHQ Croatia [probably early 1945].

of the fighters would draw disproportionate and highly unwelcome attention from the enemy, suggested the disbanding of the battalion. The MHQ Croatia agreed, and on 3 October the bulk of the Jewish Partisans was transferred to the 7th Banija Division. The other unit was the Jewish Platoon of the 1st Overseas Brigade, made up of 20 Yugoslav and two Austrian citizens. Fifteen of them would get killed during the fighting on Korčula in December, after which this unit was also disbanded. The idea from early October 1944 to create a separate unit from the Jews liberated from Bor mines and those who had escaped from Hungary was not followed through.[65]

"Overseas Brigades" (*prekomorske brigade*) was the name given to the NOVJ units formed in metropolitan Italy from late 1943 to late 1944. They were composed of former Yugoslav POWs and civilian internees, as well as the Italian soldiers of Slovene (and, to a lesser extent, Croatian) origin who had been captured by the Allies. These units had very different war careers. After the end of the island campaign in early January 1944, the 1st and 2nd Brigades were sent to Western Bosnia and disbanded. In the SHQ's opinion, their well-armed but woefully inexperienced personnel could be better used for replenishing the ranks of the 1st Proletarian Corps. The 5th, and especially the 3rd Brigade, saw extensive action in 1944-45, whereas the 4th never left Italy and was used as a garrison/labor unit. In addition to infantry formations (incidentally, all of which were organized along the standard NOVJ pattern), the overseas contingent also provided air crews, sailors, and other specialists. In light of the rapid expansion the army was going through, the officers of the former royal army released from captivity were particularly welcome. They, however, had difficult time adapting to the Partisan way of war, which was entirely novel to them. For instance, one major was nearly lynched by his own men for suggesting surrender: "That is what I was taught in military schools–once surrounded, stack your rifles and hand yourself over."[66]

The first foreigner to join the Partisans was in all likelihood a former Austrian Communist who deserted from the garrison at Čačak in July 1941. The Slovene guerrillas could boast of having two Allied colonial soldiers of Arab origin in their midst, as well as a daredevil New Zealand corporal, John Denvir, who got wounded six times and eventually became a battalion commander. The Italian surrender and the psychological fallout it produced, as well as the increased presence of Axis legionnaire units, paved the way for the creation of entire units composed of non-Yugoslavs. The above-mentioned defectors from the Bulgarian border outposts were formed into the "Hristo Botev" Battalion. The 13th Proletarian and 1st Macedonian-Kosovo Brigades formed a separate company of former Red army soldiers. These much-feted representatives of the "first land of socialism" did not always measure up to the guerrillas' expectations. Unaccustomed to harsh living conditions, 32 Soviets attached to the Požarevac Detachment asked and received the permission to leave for Bulgaria or Romania; much to the Partisans' dismay, they went over to the Chetniks instead. In early 1945, all citizens of the

65 Jaša Romano, *Jevreji Jugoslavije 1941—1945. žrtve genocida i učesnici NOR* (Belgrade: Savez jevrejskih opština Jugoslavije, 1980), pp. 282-84; *Zbornik*/I/13/103, 25th NOVJD to 14th NOVJC (4.10.1944).

66 *Enciklopedija*, Vol. VII, p. 269; Srećko Vilhar, Albert Klun, *Prva in Druga prekomorska brigada* (Ljubljana: Borec, 1967), pp. 332-34; *Zbornik*/VI/7/73, MHQ Slovenia to SHQ (22.9.1943); Jakšić, *Nad uspomenama*, Vol. I, pp. 500-01.

USSR in Yugoslav service (420 of them with the Croatian units alone) were repatriated to their homeland.[67]

Italians constituted by far the largest contingent of foreign nationals within the NOP. They formed ten battalions of varying strength in the Italian-Slovene border region during September and October 1943. The Šušak-Kastav Detachment, the 1st Proletarian Brigade, the 1st Macedonian-Kosovo Brigade, all had a battalion or a company named after the revolutionary Giuseppe Garibaldi, easily the most popular figure among the new guerrillas. Other famous names included the author of the Italian anthem, Goffredo Mameli (a battalion composed of former members of the "Zara" Division and subordinated to the "Blue Adriatic" Detachment), and the martyred socialist Giacomo Matteotti (a battalion attached to the 3rd Krajina Brigade). The biggest number of Italians was to be found in Montenegro. On 2 December, the remnants of the "Taurinense" were merged with the bulk of the "Venezia" into the new "Garibaldi" Division, in all some 5,000 men in four brigades. A similar number of those Italians "who expressed the wish not to fight" were organized into a dozen-or-so labor battalions, while most of the specialists were divided between NOVJ units.

Despite its size, the "Garibaldi" had a limited combat value. The majority of the soldiers were neither physically nor psychologically prepared for the rigors of everyday guerrilla life. Probably unimpressed by their performance on the battlefield and chequered political past (i.e. the alliance with the Chetniks), the Partisans were reluctant to "squander" their meager sources on the Italians or entrust them with more complicated or sensitive tasks. To make matters worse, the liberated territory in Sandžak could barely feed its own population, let alone the thousands of members of the former, but still hated army of occupation. Spurred by reasons of prestige, Tito ordered Dapčević to provide the same rations to the Italians as to his own men or face the consequences, but threats alone were not enough. Finally, in mid-February 1944, the SHQ decided to disband one brigade, keep another with the 2nd Assault Corps, and send the rest (along a certain number of laborers) to Eastern Bosnia. In this way, the Italians could be both fed and managed more efficiently. Some Italian veterans and historians were not satisfied with this rather mundane explanation: according to them, the Communists actually did not want to share the honor of liberating the country with anyone else, and broke up the "Garibaldi" in order to indoctrinate its soldiers more easily.[68]

The NOVJ kept having troubles both on and off the battlefield. Information-gathering and dissemination remained deficient and disjointed: one area command in Syrmia had to remind its intelligence people to always add the current date to their reports. Even the most senior bodies

67 Heinz Kühnrich, Franz-Karl Hitze, *Deutsche bei Titos Partisanen: Kriegsschicksale auf dem Balkan in Augenzeugenberichten und Dokumenten* (Schkeuditz: GNN Verlag, 1997), p. 54; *Zbornik*/VI/1/89, PK Štajerska to CK KPS (September 1941); James Cafin, *Partisan* (Auckland: HarperCollinsPublishers, 2019), EPUB edition, Chapter One; Milan Guček, *Šercerjeva brigada* (Ljubljana: Borec, 1973), p. 290; *Zbornik*/VII/3/8 (Ljupče Arsov to Metodije Antevski, 2.1.1944), 251 (Cvetko Uzunovski to Dobrivoje Radosavljević, 28.6.1944); Radošević, *Trinaesta*, pp. 175-76; Vitorović, *Centralna*, pp. 541-42; VAB/NOVJ/119-4/2/2-5, MHQ Croatia to SHQ (13.3.1945).

68 Ferenc, *Kapitulacija*, pp. 241-42; Savo O. Trikić, *Treća krajiška proleterska brigada* (Belgrade: VINC, 1987), p. 215; Luciano Viazi, Leo Taddia, *La resistenza dei militari italiani all'estero: la divisione "Garibaldi" in Montenegro - Sangiaccato - Bosnia – Erzegovina* (Rome: MoD, 1994), pp. 198-203; *Zbornik*/V/19/176 and 494, *Zbornik*/V/20/261; *Zbornik*/VII/2/61; see also the cables from the SHQ to the 2nd and 3rd NOVJCs in *SD*/XVIII/7 (2.12.1943) and *SD*/XIX/46-47 (13-14.2.1944).

were making grave errors in this respect. The SHQ received advanced general warning of the Wehrmacht's winter offensive, but the corps and divisions entirely failed to identify the enemy preparations in the field. The Slovene leadership was convinced that "the German army was weak" and had no offensive intentions in late September 1943. As in Serbia two years earlier, the explosive growth of the movement in western Slovenia and Istria proved to be its undoing. There was simply not enough time or cadres to turn this enthusiastic, but otherwise totally unprepared mass into an effective fighting force. Vast number of volunteers was under the impression that, with Italy gone, the war was practically over. The speed and ferocity of the German riposte therefore came as a great shock: not even veteran fighters had seen so many armored vehicles in action in one place at the same time. This prompted the MHQ Croatia to issue special instructions on how to deal with enemy motorized columns. The same command also noticed serious shortcomings in staff and command work. The officers had become unimaginative, passive, and even downright sloppy; the concept of reserves was still not widely embraced, linear defenses were becoming more prevalent, and flanking attacks more seldom. The marked drop in mobility compelled the 5th Krajina Brigade to dissolve the company kitchens and reduce the size of headquarters; the post of "personal escort", who were in reality "common servants", was abolished. These were all the side-effects of the regularization. And then there was that whiff of chaos inherent to all things Balkan. The Lovćen Detachment reported that it had barely saved 50 vehicles that once belonged to the "Taurinense"; "a good part" of the captured materiel was taken home or rendered useless by peasants and Partisan guards alike. In Croatian Littoral, every unit was "supplying" itself on the spot, cars and trucks being a particularly coveted item; the evacuation of the vitally important booty to the interior suffered as the result.[69]

Despite the growing professionalism of the NOP's armed branch, local patriotism was still a factor to be reckoned with. This applied to newly-created and veteran units alike, as well as senior commands. A large number of fighters from the 26th Division who were reported missing at Korčula actually preferred hiding near their villages on the island rather than being evacuated to Vis. Upon hearing there was a local detachment in their native province who was accepting everyone "with no questions asked", at least 160 Lika fighters simply left the 19th Division. The rumor that the 7th Division was about to leave Banija and return to Bosnia–already a byword for suffering and death on both sides of the front[70]–caused "unrest and even demoralization" in its ranks at the height of Operation "Panther". Dalmatians had a reputation of not reacting well to officers from other parts of the country. In early February 1944, the CK KPJ went so far so as to accuse the province's top commissar (who, ironically, would author a book titled "The

69 Dželebdžić, *Obaveštajna*, pp. 219-20; *Zbornik*/I/6/521, Sremska Mitrovica area, Circular (22.12.43); *Zbornik*/V/20/357-61, 622-28, and *Zbornik*/V/24/259-62, MHQ Croatia, Circulars (17, 29.10.1943, and 14.2.1944, respectively); *Zbornik*/IV/14/241-43, 5th Krajina Brigade, Circular (19.9.1943); *Zbornik*/III/5/155, Lovćen Det. to MHQ Montenegro (end of September 1943); see also letters from the 13th NOVJD to MHQ Croatia (*Zbornik*/IX/4/293-96, 20.9.1943) and its 2nd Bde. (*Zbornik*/V/21/461, 26.11.1943).

70 In June 1942, a lieutenant of the German 714th ID wrote: "In Bosnia, the devil is abroad!"; Ben Shepherd, *Terror in the Balkans: German Armies and Partisan Warfare* (Cambridge, MA: Harvard University Press, 2012), p. 209.

Absurdities of Karl Marx" six decades later) of refusing to share the captured Italian arms and supplies with non-Dalmatian units. This problem would persist well into 1944.[71]

The introduction of compulsory service in many of the NOP's domains in late 1943, combined with the advent of winter and the realization that the Axis were far from beaten, caused a spike in desertion rates. In the past, a relatively small number of deserters went over to the enemy, because the Germans were in a habit of shooting anyone who tried to cross their lines, including some of their own undercover agents. However, after much deliberation, the Wehrmacht finally dropped its no-quarter policy towards the end of the year. The informal recognition of the NOVJ as belligerent side opened the way not only for the establishment of the prisoner exchange cartel in Croatia that would ultimately save at least ca. 2,000 men and women on both sides, but also for the creation of a defector program. The PzAOK 2 spared no effort in this regard, opening special "re-education" camps in Croatia and the Reich proper, publishing the propaganda monthly titled "Okupator", and encouraging individual units to issue target-tailored leaflets and enact other similar measures. As a result, the XV MTC alone reported 4,000 defectors in the period September 1943-May 1944. Zagreb's own campaign, aimed primarily at draft-dodgers, was also a success. In northern Croatia, an estimated 6,000 individuals chose to avail themselves of the 26th January amnesty by the middle of 1944.[72]

The novel, conciliatory attitude of the Axis also encouraged seditious tendencies within the NOVJ, which were especially strong in Banija. Already in May 1942, the Partisans discovered an Ustasha-sponsored plot, which resulted in the execution of seven alleged enemy agents. In the last days of August 1943, there was an outright mutiny in the one of the local battalions, caused by war-weariness. Most of the mutineers had a quick change of heart, which effectively sealed the fate of the dozen or so ringleaders. The discontent, however, continued to brew and finally spilled over four months later when some 200 armed fighters placed themselves under the Wehrmacht's protection in Kostajnica. With the German support, Self-Defense Force "Sunja" (*Selbstschutz "Sunja"*) would continue to operate in the so-called "Banija Triangle" (the area between the Una and Sava Rivers) until late 1944. A similar event occurred in April and May of the same year, when the commander of the Kordun Military Area, together with several high-ranking officers and scores of fighters defected to the Germans. Feeling oppressed by the alleged Croatian dominance within the NOP, they offered to form independent Serb anti-communist units. Due to the opposition of the radical Lika Ustashe, this proposal was only partially implemented. The Partisans responded by staging the much-publicized "Kordun Trial", followed by another round of executions. In any case, one thing is certain: had the Germans introduced this pragmatic policy earlier, it would have seriously undermined the NOP's war effort.[73]

71 *Dalmacija*/X/63-64, 26th NOVJD, Report Korčula (6.1.1944); *Zbornik*/V/23/99, 19th NOVJD to 8th NOVJC (9.1.1944); Krunić, "Sedma divizija", p. 585; *DCO*/XV/437-40, CK KPJ to PK Dalmatia (9.2.1944); *Zbornik*/IX/5/675, 8th NOVJC/Pol. To MHQ Croatia (25.3.1944).

72 Trifković, *Parleying*, pp. 196-306; Trifković, "Methods", pp. 16-20.

73 Đurić, *Banijski*, pp. 260-67; *NOS*, Vol. V, pp. 669-72; NARA/T315/2281/469, 1st CCD to XV MTC (29.12.1943); NARA/T314/566/44-52 [Correspondence XV MTC–PzAOK 2–392nd ID pertaining to anti-communists in Kordun] (7-18.6.1944); Milan Jaković, "Političko stanje na području okruga Karlovac između Drugog i Trećeg zasjedanja ZAVNOH-a", in: *Treća*, pp. 64-82; Svetozar Livada, *Kordunski rekvijem* (Zagreb: Euroknjiga, 2006), pp. 289-91.

Thanks to the availability of great quantities of Italian equipment, the Partisan army was becoming increasingly diversified. The 2nd Slovenian Brigade holds the distinction of becoming the NOVJ's first bigger (albeit temporary) motorized unit in September 1943. The 15th Division had a tank company that was kept in the field for as long as the spare parts and fuel lasted, after which the vehicles were hidden. The MHQ Croatia formed a separate Automobile, which by the end of the year had four companies with 80 vehicles. The two companies of the 1st Tank Battalion, with altogether 16 vehicles, took part in operations in Lika and Gorski Kotar. Artillery pieces of all types and calibers also became widely available: almost every division now had at least a battery of guns (either field pieces or AT, or both), whereas some (e.g. the 6th-8th) had both an artillery and a battalion of support weapons. There was also enough W/T sets and field telephones available in order to form signals units (usually company-sized) within corps, divisions, and even some brigades. In an attempt to remove the long-standing deficiencies in its information-gathering arm, the MHQ Croatia was the first to order the creation of dedicated reconnaissance units in late October. Each division should have a company, each brigade/detachment a platoon, and each battalion a squad of these handpicked fighters. Subordinated to the intelligence officer of their respective parent unit, they were tasked with conducting reconnaissance missions in depths of up to 50 km from their base. As qualified cadres were now in especially high demand, educational facilities on all levels were working around the clock. The re-opened Officer School of the SHQ (located first at Jajce, then at Drvar) organized courses for low and mid-level leadership positions, up to and including that of brigade commander. From September to November, 249 candidates successfully absolved the curriculum; the supreme commander personally handed them their diplomas, and also presented the best officers with an SMG.[74]

Even though the Partisans had been operating in coastal waters since the late 1942, the seizure of the Adriatic coast one year later marked the true birth of the NOVJ Navy. On 24 October 1943, all local naval commands from Trieste to Kotor were reorganized into Naval Coastal Sectors (sing. *Pomorski obalni sektor*, POS) and placed under the Navy HQ. Initially numbering six, their number would be reduced to four due to the loss of Istria and Boka Kotorska. The main tasks of the Yugoslav sailors were to maintain the links between the islands and the mainland, assist the land forces in amphibious operations (e.g. Mali Lošinj, Korčula), and interdict enemy coastal traffic. The small war now raging among hundreds of Dalmatian islands and inlets had all the attributes of the privateering campaigns of old; all loot, down to the last fountain pen, was divided as per detailed, centrally-issued instructions. According to the summary of activities and result achieved from December 1943 until April 1944, the Partisan raiders sank seven and captured five enemy vessels and brought in 136 German prisoners. Own losses were heavy (altogether 27 vessels), but not as debilitating as the generally low seaworthiness caused by the lack of spare parts, fuel, and regular maintenance. In numerical terms, only 52 out of 155 sailers and eight out of 15 steamboats were seaworthy (expressed in tonnage this reads as 14,150 out of 23,694). Combat vessels included four Armed Ships (sing. *naoružani brod*, NB) of up to 25 tons, and 27 Patrol Boats (sing. *patrolni čamac*, PČ) of up to five tons displacement.[75]

74 Ibid., pp. 318-25; Jelenković, *Saobraćaj*, p. 97.

75 *Zbornik*/VIII/1/127, Navy HQ to MHQ Croatia (24.10.1943); *Zbornik*/VIII/2/213-14, [n/A] Activity report (December 1943-April 1944); VAB/NOVJ/2023/2/4-1, Navy HQ to 1st POS (5.5.1944).

Already during September 1943, the Partisans in Slovenia and Croatia acquired several functional aircraft and used them for courier and training purposes. In mid-October, the SHQ created 1st Air Base of the NOVJ in Western Bosnia and ordered the concentration of all available specialists there. One month later, the base had ca. 80 men (including 20 pilots and seven observers) and two machines, both of which had once belonged to the NDH air force. Then the disaster struck: on 27 November, just as the Yugoslav "Dornier" Do-17 was preparing to take off from the Plain of Glamoč for Italy, a lone German "Henschel" Hs-126 appeared and showered its unsuspecting target with small bombs and MG fire. Among the killed were two British officers and Ivo-Lola Ribar, the charismatic head of the SKOJ. Although some Yugoslav historians blamed Catholic priest-spies for leading the attacker onto his target via radio, German sources give no indication that the affair was anything else but a "lucky kill" made on a routine reconnaissance mission. An even heavier blow was landed on 6 December, when the Germans suddenly broke into the seat of the 1st Air Base at Livno and killed 22 of its members; the sole remaining machine was set on fire by the Partisans themselves during the chaotic retreat from the area. After that, the remnants of the unit were evacuated to Italy and later to North Africa, where they continued their training under the Allied tutelage.[76]

As is customary at the close of a chapter, a few lines on the railway sabotage. The months after the Italian surrender saw a further expansion of the NOVJ's demolition arm. The 3rd Sabotage Battalion was formed in Moslavina in late November 1943 and subordinated to the HQ of the 2nd OZ (later 10th NOVJ Corps). The MHQ Vojvodina got its first such outfit, about 80 strong, during that same period. Independent companies were formed in Gorski Kotar (later relocated to Kordun), Istria (would become fully functional in the spring of 1944), and Međimurje. Detachments and brigades alike were instructed to send their handpicked candidates to the special courses held by Hariš and his "professionals". With their training done, the candidates were to return to their parent units and share the knowledge with the next batch of recruits, and at the same time organize actions in their home areas. The acute shortage of explosives could be partially offset by Allied airdrops and even some local production.

Although not a particular fun to read, statistics can give us a good idea of the size and scope of the NOVJ campaign against the Axis lifelines. The NDH authorities counted 2,369 attacks from September 1943 through February 1944 (compared to just over 2,000 in the first eight months of 1943). A much bigger increase was recorded in Slovenia, from 164 to 234 (note: the latter figure relates only to the last four months of 1943 and includes attacks on industrial objects). In Serbia, the grand total rose from 82 to 119 (again, the Chetniks were expressly named as culprits in only two incidents, but there were certainly more). Probably the most famous action of the Slovenian Partisans was the damaging of the Štampet Bridge on 14 October, which rendered the Ljubljana–Trieste line inoperable for two weeks. November was seemingly one of the worst months on record in the NDH. The single-tracked stretches of the main line were closed ca. 79 percent of the time, the double-tracked ones almost 23 percent; the Bosna Railway was closed nearly nine days. Six secondary lines, including those linking Zagreb with Varaždin, Sarajevo with Serbia, and Karlovac with Rijeka, were shut down throughout the month. Within a timespan of only eleven days, two German armored trains (Nos. 6 and 23)

76 Lazarević, *Vazduhoplovstvo*, pp. 54-59; NARA/T313/485/814, PzAOK 2/LW, Daily report (28.11.1943).

ran onto mines; one composition of 41 cars, more than half of which were laden with fuel, was ambushed and left to burn for a whole day; one passenger train was derailed in such a way that the bodies could be salvaged only with the help of blowtorches.[77]

As a part of the general reorganization of their southeastern command, the Germans placed all technical aspects of railway operations into the hands of General of Transport headquartered in Belgrade. By early December 1943, his command numbered ca. 18,000 railway personnel and foreign laborers. The security remained the responsibility of field commands, which were hard-pressed to find ways of countering the increasingly aggressive guerrillas. For instance, the Germans broke with the practice of occupying separate cars on civilian trains after noticing that the enemy concentrated all his fire there. Erecting of exclusion zones around railway lines proved to be impossible without causing severe disruptions in everyday civilian and economic life (evacuation of villages, excessive deforestation, etc.). The CO of the PzAOK 2, General Rendulic, believed sabotage could only be curbed through violence; he therefore introduced a harsh reprisals system to the NDH, not unlike the one being practiced in Serbia. Apart from endless suffering, this measure achieved little else: "The railroads are 'garnished' with hanged people", wrote Horstenau, but the guerrilla attacks became even more frequent. In the end, the NDH government suggested substituting hanging with pecuniary fines, believing they would have "a much greater effect".[78]

77 Bošnjak, *Diverzantska*, pp. 201-29; ARMB/SSR, Summaries for 1943 and 1944, pp. 19-20 and 1-10, respectively; NARA/T77/1421, OKW/Trans., Bandit activity (November 1943); see also TsAMO/500/12451/518/107 and 118-19 for November 1943 activity reports of Armored Trains Nos. 23 and 6, respectively.

78 NARA/T311/285, [all OBSO/Trans.], Activity report (1-10.12.1943), Railway security (2.12.1943), Organization of railways and transport in Southeast (12.8.1943); NARA/T314/1546/197, LXIX RC to PzAOK 2 (12.3.1944); NARA/T313/486/296, Inspector railway security Croatia to PzAOK 2 (3.12.1943); Peter Broucek (ed.), *Ein General im Zwielicht: Die Erinnerungen Edmund Glaises von Horstenau* (Vienna: Böhlau Verlag, 1988), Vol. III, p. 314.

6

Returning East (March – September 1944)

6.1 Chetniks

As the Chetnik movement will feature more prominently in this chapter than in any other, this seems like a convenient spot for a (somewhat belated) discussion on its organization. Here, we must differentiate between Serbia proper and the territories beyond the Drina and Uvac. After Operation "Weiss" and the subsequent battles, the JVuO in Croatia, Bosnia and Herzegovina, and Montenegro effectively ceased to be a major factor in a purely military sense. Löhr attributed the royalists' defeat to Mihailović's inept leadership, and he was not far off the mark. The Chetnik leader tried to steer the entire effort from his far-off base by issuing instructions to his plenipotentiary over the wireless. The latter, in turn, had an unenvious task of reconciling his superior's plans with those of the Italians, who controlled supply access. Thanks to the fact that in late March and early April 1943 they represented the only force that could, in theory at least, stop the Partisan advance into the Italian occupation zone, the Chetniks usually had their way. On the field of battle, the MVAC/JVuO turned out to be hopelessly inferior to its Communist-led foe. Although numerically large, the army was largely made up of reservists who had no desire to take part in what they still viewed as a fratricidal conflict between the Serbs. Their officers were clearly overwhelmed by the task at hand: the biggest operations they took part on hitherto involved, at best, several thousand men and a weak enemy (e.g. Operation "Alfa").[1]

Unlike the *Regio Esercito*, the Germans would not tolerate large Chetnik formations, nor had any inclination to enter a power-sharing deal with them. Pressed by manpower shortage, however, they were not eager to make new enemies and lose potentially useful auxiliaries at the same time. Not even major incidents–such the one at Mount Ozren in April 1943 when a bloody ambush provoked a mid-sized undertaking against the local Chetniks (Operation "Teufel")–led to permanent hostilities. Already in August 1943, when Berlin was still nominally insisting on their disarmament, the 7th SS MTD was pursuing "its own policy" towards the "Italian" Chetniks in Eastern Herzegovina. By the year's end, the monarchists had become one of the pillars of the occupation system in this province. The same goes for their comrades in Dalmatia,

1 Tomasevich, *Chetniks*, p. 250.

whom one German officer termed "the only ally we have in this accursed country". These Chetnik contingents, much like their counterparts from Bosnia, were allowed to retain their distinctive inner structure. Đujić's DČD was still the biggest formation in Croatia, while Eastern Bosnia and Herzegovina, and Western Bosnia, had their own separate commands. In December 1943, the Germans estimated the strength of the JVuO in these parts at ca. 12,000 men. It should be born in mind that this is only a rough estimate. For instance, the same document put the number of Chetniks in Dalmatia at 2-3,000, whereas it is known that the 264th ID provided for more than 4,400 auxiliaries in May 1944. At about the same time, the Germans began referring to them as Croatian Combat Community (*Kroatische Kampfgemeinschaft*, KKG), but even this cosmetic concession to Pavelić was limited to official correspondence only.[2]

Things were different in Montenegro. Đurišić, who had been captured by the Germans during Operation "Schwarz" and sent to a POW camp in occupied Poland, managed to escape and reach Belgrade in November 1943, where he was arrested again. Owing to the recent change in the German policies, he was not only released, but acknowledged as the leading auxiliary commander in the country. In the spring of the following year, Đurišić was made the head of the newly-created Montenegrin Volunteer Corps (*Montenegrinisches Freiwilligen-Korps*, MFK). Like its older "cousin", the SFK, the MFK consisted of two, later three small regiments with a total of 5,500 men equipped with infantry weapons (Note: the JVuO structure of the Montenegrin Chetniks continued to exist parallel to the MFK; in all, Đurišić could muster up to 10,000 men). The hopes that the staying power of the Chetniks would improve under German guidance and with regular supply were only partially met: although they now fought better than during the winter, they proved equally inept at handling bigger operations against the Partisans on their own (see below).[3]

The Chetniks could perhaps not win in a major open clash, but they still had much to offer in the realm of irregular tactics. By early 1943, at the latest, this had become a standard way of dealing with the NOVJ's mobile units. Ironically, the Partisans were now faced with the same problem as their Axis foes: how to force battle on an opponent who simply would not stand firm? Much like any modern army, the NOVJ first tried with the classic encirclement approach only to learn that it seldom led to any success. Having friendly civilians to warn them about the impending danger, the Chetniks would disperse in a timely manner and use their excellent knowledge of terrain to evade the pursuers. By the spring of 1944, the Partisans recognized the need to re-learn their traditional tactics, especially as many of the younger brigades had known nothing but attacks on fortified places and semi-frontal clashes with enemy regulars. It was found that the best way to catch the Chetniks was by using one's own equivalent of the *Jagdkommandos*, i.e. small, highly maneuverable, and well-armed units. Their sweeps would be combined with round-the-clock ambushes along all likely escape routes and sudden night raids against suspected enemy hideouts. If allowed to operate freely, the Serbian nationalist

2 NARA/T313/482/291, PzAOK 2, Memorandum (presumably October 1943); NARA/T311/189/262, [N/A] Presumed strength DM forces (December 1943); NARA/T314/565/823, XV MTC, KKG (10.5.1944); Schmider, *Partisanenkrieg*, pp. 373, 377-78; Edi Bokun, "Operacija 369. njemačke divizije protiv ozrenskih četnika (april 1943. godine)", *Gračanički glasnik*, 18:35 (2013), pp. 58-69.

3 Pajović, *Kontrarevolucija*, pp. 62-63, 471-81; NARA/T314/662/671-73, 769, 800-02 [all XXI MTC] (Diary, 3.3, 14.4, and 30.4.1944, respectively); NARA/T314/663/1118, Monthly report (11.5-11.6.1944); NARA/T314/664/497 (Situation report, 13.8.1944), 817 (Cable to HGE, 23.9.1944).

guerrillas could become quite a nuisance. This they proved on numerous occasions in the past while serving as MVAC auxiliaries, ambushing smaller, unsuspecting Partisans details in Dalmatia with little cost to themselves. Later on, their favorite targets in Bosnian-Croatian border regions were the mule caravans ferrying food and other supplies between the liberated territories. In Montenegro, frequent attacks on couriers, staffs, and members of rear services prompted the HQ of the 2nd Corps to order reprisals against the culprits and all those found guilty of supporting them.[4]

It was this particular set of skills that made the monarchists interesting to the Germans. They needed someone who knew how the Partisans thought and moved, someone who could provide flank protection for their exposed columns on narrow mountain roads. The monarchists rendered invaluable service as scouts, and the *Cetnik-Meldung* ("Chetnik report") became a ubiquitous phrase in Wehrmacht intelligence documents. Whenever possible, commanders in the field would avail themselves of the friendly guerrillas' help by attaching them to their battle groups. One example: for the purpose of a local undertaking around Bileća in mid-December 1943, a reinforced infantry company from the 181st ID was paired with some 250 Chetniks; these presumably came from the local brigade that was described as "reliable" and its fighting record as "good". The collaboration with the Germans brought many advantages. Those Chetniks who were wounded in joint operations were entitled to treatment in Axis hospitals; units from impoverished regions (e.g. Eastern Bosnia, Dalmatia) could count on being supplied with food. Although they agreed to work occasionally side-by-side with one another (usually on German insistence), the Serbian and Croatian nationalists were still very much at each other's throats. The former, however, now had a powerful protector: in early January 1944, the OBSO officially warned Zagreb that he would take drastic measures if Ustasha atrocities against loyal Serbs continued to take place. Despite all efforts to promote moderation, the Germans were forced to keep intervening in these matters until the end of the war.[5]

The greatest prize was ammunition. With prewar reserve stocks exhausted and the Italians gone, the Chetniks had no other choice but to turn to the Germans. Notwithstanding the shared anti-communist sentiment, the latter feared that the monarchists were stockpiling ammunition in order to use it against its former owners in the case of an Allied invasion (these considerations were not baseless). Consequently, they introduced stringent procedures regarding the issue of this critical war product. As a general rule, it would be handed out in carefully dosed quantities, and for immediate use only. For instance, the Chetnik Konjic Detachment received

4 *Zbornik*/V/13/412, 1st Croatian NOVJC to OHQ Zrmanja (29.3.1943); *Zbornik*/V/15/464 and *Zbornik*/V/16/513, XVIII AC, Daily reports (24.5 and 24.6.1943, respectively); *Zbornik*/IV/23/266 (Message to 1st Proletarian Bde. HQ, 13.3.1944), 443 (12th Bde. to 12th NOVJD, 20.3.1944); *Zbornik*/IV/25/61 (11th NOVJD to 5th NOVJC, 2.5.1944), 250-52 (3rd Bde. to 6th NOVJD, 15.5.1944); 571 (39th NOVJD, Monthly report, May 1944); *Zbornik*/IV/28/271, 21st Bde. to 27th NOVJD (13.8.1944); *Zbornik*/III/10/107-09, 2nd NOVJC to 37th NOVJD (20.4.1944).

5 NARA/T315/1294/146, 714th ID, Division Order Kotor Varoš (1.2.1943); NARA/T315/1544/1224 [all 181st ID] (Native units, 9.12.1943), 1279 (Message from 359th Grenadier Regiment [GR], 11.12.1943); NARA/T315/1295/816, 114th JD, Supply (2.12.1943); NARA/T314/566/241, OBSO to DGA (4.1.1944); NARA/T314/561/276, XV MTC, Daily report (24.1.1944); NARA/T175/20/2645891-97, 7th SS MTD to V SS MTC (6.7.1944); NARA/T3111/195/343, OBSO, Daily report (23.12.1944); NARA/T78/476/6459008, OBSO/Intel., Evening report (2.3.1945); *Zbornik*/IV/27/569.

altogether 3,803 rounds for the action in the sector Jezero–Kula–Čičevo from 15 to 18 April 1944. The Germans demanded written reports on a number and type of weapons in possession of a particular unit, as well as on the ammunition expenditure, without which they "would not give a single bullet". One Chetnik HQ complained that it was impossible to collect all the empty casings from the battlefield, which in turn made the replenishment out of the question. In some places, the Germans would give a special reward of 50 rounds for each dead Partisan.[6]

The development of the JVuO in Serbia took place in altogether different circumstances. With the Partisan threat negligible, the occupation authorities there could concentrate squarely on Mihailović; owing to their numerical superiority, the Axis also saw no need to negotiate or make compromises like in the NDH or Montenegro. As a result, the JVuO had to carry out its reorganization and expansion clandestinely. The basic structure of the army was laid down already in February 1942, with the company (nominally, three platoons with 40 men each) being the main building block. There were three types of companies: the youngest and the most fit recruits (20-30 years of age) were selected for active service, while the remaining two age groups (30-40 and 40-50 years) took care of rear-area tasks. Three to four companies would be formed into a battalion, and a similar number of battalions would constitute a brigade: each *srez* (mid-level administrative unit) was supposed to have at least one such unit. In early 1943, brigades were combined into corps, and these into groups of corps (late 1943-early 1944), which in turn were subordinated to regional HQs spanning the entire country (Central Serbia Command, Southern Serbia Command, etc.).

The defining feature of the JVuO was its militia-like character. The shortage of weapons, supply difficulties, and security concerns kept the strength of the active core at a low level. Roughly only a third of 9,625 men personally inspected by a U.S. officer in November 1943 were armed. An individual corps could have anywhere between several hundred and 3,000 combat-ready soldiers. Although most of them had completed the national service, their battlefield capabilities were severely curtailed by the lack of heavy weapons and shortage of ammunition (24-40 rounds per rifle, 150-200 per MG). The JVuO's weakest spot was its officer corps. Mihailović's lax leadership style, the decidedly territorial nature of the army, and the lack of activity contributed to the evolving of warlordism. Disputes were frequent and would sometimes end tragically: Colonel Jevrem Simić, one of the general's chief subordinates, was murdered while on inspection trip in early 1944. Each local commander ruled like "a sultan" or "a mountain *tsar*" over his fiefdom, which basically no one could enter without his permission, whether a private person or a friendly unit from the neighboring *srez* chasing after the Partisans. There were exceptions, of course: Dragutin Keserović (one of the few "who earned the Partisans' respect", wrote Đilas) and Radoslav Đurić managed to build a relatively efficient and disciplined fighting force in the south-central and southern parts of the country. By the end of 1943 and beginning of 1944, the JVuO in Serbia proper consisted of altogether 33 corps, with a combined strength of anywhere between 20 and 35,000 armed men (German vs. U.S. estimates).[7]

6 NARA/T315/2271/451, 718th ID to Chetnik commanders (17.1.1943); NARA/T315/2155/613, 369th ID, Diary (20.8.1943); NARA/T501/256/97, MBSO, Circular (23.2.1944); *Zbornik*/XIV/3/554-55, JVuO Konjic Detachment to German command (8.5.1944); *Zbornik*/XIV/4/302.

7 Tomasevich, *Chetniks*, pp. 177-85; FDRL/President's Secretary Files/154, Walter R. Mansfiled, Report on Mission to Mihailović (1.3.1944), pp. IV, 28-33, as well as Exhibits D and D-1; Živko Topalović,

The entire Chetnik military organization was built for one purpose only: to launch a general uprising as soon as the first Allied soldier landed in Yugoslavia. In the assumption that the long-awaited invasion would take place after the fall of Mussolini, Mihailović spurred his army into action. In Serbia, the JVuO's principle task remained the same, to cleanse the countryside of the NOP supporters; its anti-Axis campaign was therefore limited to a number of high-profile ambushes. The occupation authorities responded by mass executions of hostages and punitive expeditions (e.g. Operation "Maiskolben"). Mihailovć's main effort was taking place beyond the borders of the province, where the threat of reprisals was much smaller. As soon as the news of the Italian capitulation arrived, the Chetniks opened hostilities against the Germans in Sandžak, storming the garrison at Prijepolje on 12 September 1943. The second JVuO's thrust was directed against Eastern Bosnia. In early October, a large force composed of both the local and Serbian Chetniks captured the towns of Višegrad and Rogatica, inflicting heavy losses to the defenders (the 369th ID and HDB units) and massacring the Muslim population in the process. These events exacerbated the already difficult situation facing the Germans in this part of the NDH: it looked as Sarajevo would soon meet the same fate as Tuzla. Luckily for them, such a sizable Chetnik presence was bound to provoke a reaction from the NOVJ. Concerned by the loss of this strategically important region ("gates to Serbia") and the severing of communications between the 2nd Assault and 3rd Bosnian Corps, the SHQ dispatched the 5th Krajina, and 27th and 17th Eastern Bosnian Divisions to the scene. Within ten days (21-31 October), these forces recaptured all the territory between Sarajevo and Višegrad, chasing the Chetniks back east, and forcing the Ustashe to evacuate Sokolac.[8]

By the time the Partisan advance began, the JVuO offensive had already run its course. It was now certain that no invasion would take place until the following spring. Although the operation in Eastern Bosnia partially served to demonstrate the Chetnik commitment to the Allied cause (British and American officers witnessed the entire business), the Whitehall was not impressed. While demanding more actions against the enemy communications in Serbia, the Allies were clearly turning away from the monarchists, increasingly shifting material and propaganda aid (most notably the widely-listened BBC broadcasts) towards their Communist-led rivals. Mihailović reasoned that any continuation of hostilities against the occupier at the time when the NOVJ was preparing for a major incursion into Serbia would lead to the loss of his main base, and, therefore, of the war itself. Consequently, he turned to the only party whose agenda overlapped with his own, the Germans. Rapprochement with the Chetnik leader was made possible by the appointment of Hermann Neubacher as Hitler's special representative to Southeastern Europe in October 1943. This astute political operator sought to replace the crude and oppressive occupation system with the widest possible anti-communist front under the German leadership. What followed was a series of written, geographically and temporally limited agreements signed by Felber's and Mihailović's representatives. Conscious of the implications, the general himself kept to the shadows, but the rank and standing of the Chetnik signatories left no doubt that their action was sanctioned by the highest authority. These included Vojislav Lukačević (the commander of the JVuO forces in the southwest of the country), Jevrem Simić

Srbija pod Dražom (London: Budućnost, 1969), p. 92; Djilas, *Wartime*, p. 151; NARA/T501/256/907, MBSO to OBSO (19.1.1944).

8 Kosta Nikolić, *Istorija Ravnogorskog pokreta* (Belgrade: Srpska reč, 1999), Vol. I, pp. 393-413; Đonlagić, *Dvadesetsedma*, pp. 20-33; Morača, *Peta*, pp. 94-97.

and Nikola Kalabić (Inspector-General of the army, and the CO of the elite King's Mountain Guards, respectively, both in Central Serbia), and Ljuba Jovanović-Patak (the commander of Eastern Serbia). In practical terms, the agreements were similar to those signed by the Bosnian Chetniks with the NDH in 1942. In exchange for cessation of hostilities and the readiness to place themselves under Axis command during joint operations, the monarchists were promised protection, medical care, and a limited amount of that most prized item, ammunition. How well this uneasy alliance would work in the field would soon be seen.[9]

6.2 First NOVJ Incursion into Serbia

In early October 1943, with operations in the entire country proceeding favorably, Tito resurrected the plans for a return to the Yugoslav heartland. In his words, Mihailović was already politically defeated, but the "reactionary cliques abroad" will continue denying the NOP's claim to legitimacy for as long as the general was in control of the Serbian countryside. The initial phase of the operation involved reinforcing the old NOP stronghold in Southern Serbia with the 2nd Proletarian and 5th Krajina Divisions, which were united for this purpose into an ad-hoc formation known simply as the "Strike Group" (*udarna grupa*). The command was entrusted to the talented Milutin Morača, who presided over a war council consisting of the staffs of both divisions, plus Blagoje Nešković of the Serbian PK, and one other member of the SHQ; also present were a high-ranking member of the BKP and several Soviet officers who were on their way to Bulgaria. It was hoped that these six brigades with ca. 5,000 motivated veterans would help the Southern Morava Partisans turn the tables on all foreign and domestic enemies and enlarge their "republic", already positioned dangerously close to the Belgrade–Thessaloniki railroad. Further reinforcements, most notably from the 3rd Corps deployed in Eastern Bosnia, would be sent across the border as soon as they became available. The beginning of the operation was contingent on the improvement of weather conditions and the delivery of the much-needed river-fording equipment by the British.[10]

What could General Felber do to counter this imminent threat to his domain? By early 1944, German troop levels in Serbia had reached an all-time low. After the withdrawal of the last elements of the 173rd RD, mobile reserves were reduced to one armored and two motorized infantry battalions, as well as one motorized police regiment (as can be imagined, these units would be of little use in the predominantly hilly and forested terrain of Western and Central Serbia). Closely resembling European colonial armies of the past, this small core of "metropolitan" troops was augmented by a much larger force consisting of allies and native auxiliaries. These included Meyszner's ethnically mixed police force, the Bulgarians, the RSK, the SFK, the SSW, and the Chetniks. The recently concluded non-aggression and cooperation treaties between the occupation authorities and the JVuO were put to the test already in late December 1943 and early January 1944. In order to avoid Operation "Kugelblitz" raging in Sandžak and establish a springboard for future operations, the 2nd Proletarian Division crossed into Serbia and advanced as far as Ivanjica and very nearly took it on 9 January (the nearby Lisa antimony mine was inexplicably left untouched). The Partisan gains in this sector could be

9 Tomasevich, *Chetniks*, pp. 316-30.

10 Gaj Trifković, "The Key to the Balkans: The Battle for Serbia 1944", *JSMS*, 28:3 (2015), pp. 524-25, 528-29.

rolled back only with the help of the Chetniks. Munitioned and steered by the Wehrmacht town commandant of Užice, they took far heavier losses than the regiment-sized battle group from the 24th BID that was originally supposed to bear the brunt of the fighting.[11]

In addition to vast cohorts of native troops and highly-trained all-German units, Felber had one, truly genuine, ace up his sleeve. The Wehrmacht in the Balkans possessed an immensely powerful weapon whose existence was unknown to everyone except the thin upper echelon of commanders and their staff officers. Already in early 1942, a handful of cryptoanalysts in Belgrade began working on the Chetnik wireless traffic; by July 1943 they were reading 95 percent of the messages, including the top-secret communication between Mihailović and the Yugoslav government-in-exile. Owing to its near-absolute reliance on couriers, the NOVJ initially escaped the scrutiny of these enemy specialists. By contrast, individual German field units were in habit of setting up their own listening stations during operations: Popović's success on the Zelengora is commonly attributed to the fact that his W/T sets failed just before the beginning of the breakthrough. By the end of 1943, the vastly improved supply situation had led to a technical revolution within the NOVJ, which, inadvertently, laid the entire army bare. Weak ciphers and low quality of operators (in many cases, simply being literate made one a suitable candidate for the job) meant that the Germans could read nearly the entire traffic with impunity; only Tito's link with Moscow remained off-limits due to the usage of the one-time pad technique. All intelligence obtained in this manner was denoted with the phrase *sichere Quelle* (abbreviated to *s.Qu.*) meaning simply "safe source". In the course of the summer reorganization, the PzAOK 2 received a full signals' reconnaissance battalion with which to exploit this incredible opportunity.

In addition to the vast amount of intelligence on practically every aspect of the NOP's war effort (correspondence on politics and strategy, OOB data, strength and casualty returns, officers' personal information, details on supply situation, etc.), the radio surveillance program had a profound impact on the operations in the field. To cite only two examples that were already mentioned in the last chapter: the 1st Proletarian Corps' attack on Travnik in October 1943 had to be canceled even before it began due to the conspicuously well-timed arrival of enemy reinforcements. The bloody defeat of the 3rd Corps at Tuzla in mid-January 1944 was caused by the fact that the defenders had been informed of the attack days in advance. Although increasingly suspicious of the security of their wireless links, the Partisans had no other option but to continue using them, for the army had in the meantime become too large to be effectively steered by any other means. The Germans would retain the upper hand in this "signals' battle" until late 1944, when the NOVJ began introducing improved ciphers for high and mid-level communications with the help of Soviet advisors (low-end traffic would continue to be read until the end of the war). The radio surveillance would give Felber a distinctive edge in the upcoming struggle for Serbia, enabling him to maximally exploit his meager reserves and counter the superior mobility of his foe with timely movements of his own.[12]

11 Ibid., pp. 526-28; Ivo Javorčić, "Borbe u Crnoj Gori, Sandžaku i Zapadnoj Srbiji", in *Druga dalmatinska*, pp. 225-34; TsAMO/500/12460/43/68-92, District command [*Kreiskommandantur*, KK] 847, Appendices to diary (January 1944).

12 Gaj Trifković, "The German ‚Ultra': Signals Intelligence in Yugoslavia 1943-1944", *Journal of Intelligence History*, Vol. 17:2 (2018), pp. 104-120.

By mid-March 1944, Tito's patience had run out and he ordered Morača forward. The two divisions easily brushed aside the Chetnik pickets along the Lim and proceeded across the mountain ranges to the east. Two weeks later, the Partisans stood at their first immediate objective, the Ibar. The lack of rubber boats (these would arrive only in mid-April but without paddles, which was taken as another proof of British duplicity) compelled them to attempt a crossing at one of the bridge sites. With the second-most important railway line in the country running through it, the entire Ibar Valley was heavily defended. Although the Partisans managed to route one company of auxiliary police on the right bank, Axis reinforcements soon drove them back. Reconciled with the fact that the crossing could not be achieved under the present circumstances, Morača decided to establish a temporary base on the northern slopes of Mount Golija; this would give him a chance to rest and replenish his ranks while staying within the striking distance of his objective. The plan soon went awry. The fear of reprisals and the Partisans' heavy-handed policies caused the population to turn away from them. Even worse, the supposedly safe haven was rapidly turning into a deathtrap. The guerrilla incursion into the Ibar Valley triggered Operation "Kammerjäger". Unlike other maximum-effort enterprises, this one would go on without spatial and temporal limits until "Morača's Group", as the Germans called it, was totally annihilated.

Throughout the first three weeks of April, the Axis pressure was steadily growing. While the 5th Krajina was trying to stem the advance of the 25th BID in the Studenica sector (on this occasion, the Bulgarians confirmed their reputation of being ponderous in advance, yet obstinate in defense), the 2nd Proletarian sallied north to Dragačevo. There, it inflicted heavy losses to one JVuO corps, but could not establish a secondary base as originally planned. With the enemy closing fast from the west and southwest, Strike Group's HQ saw no alternative but to order a retreat towards the only potential source of help, the 3rd Corps. Each division would take a different route in order to confuse and split the pursuers. Informed of their itinerary, Felber rushed to erect blocking lines along the route, but the guerrillas again proved themselves unbeatable in the art of forced marching. On 26 April, the 2nd Proletarian announced its presence in the area east of Užice by ambushing a military train, after which it continued to the designated rendezvous point some 25 km southwest of Valjevo. The 5th Krajina had a much tougher going to the south and west of Užice, losing 50 KIA and 80 WIA before joining its sister unit on the 29th.[13]

The change of operational area did little good to Strike Group, for it turned out that the 3rd Corps was itself in need of assistance and therefore not able to cross the Drina. At the same time, Felber announced the beginning of the final battle "against the reds in Western Serbia", whom he sought to crush between his own forces coming from the south (five German battalions and ca. 1,000 Chetniks) and some 5,000 monarchists gathering on the slopes of the Povlen and Maljen. Seesaw fighting lasted throughout the entire first week of May 1944, after which the Partisans were forced to undertake yet another forced march, this time in the direction of Mount Tara. Wild, barren, and hemmed in between a major river and two roads, the Tara was the worst possible choice for a base. At this point, Morača convened a council of war, something he did whenever critically important decisions had to be made. Mostly on the insistence of Nešković, who was eager to reinforce the Serbian branch of the NOP at all costs, it

13 *DCO*/XVII/13, PK Serbia to CK KPJ (9.4.1944); Trifković, "Serbia", pp. 529-31.

was decided to send two brigades to Šumadija, while the remainder of the group, together with the hospital, would try to make it to Sandžak. Only three days later (11 May), this unrealistic plan was dropped in favor of a joint breakthrough. As a consequence, the bulk of the army had to make a costly stand on the Zlatibor against the Germans and seven JVuO corps until the two brigades could catch up (15 May). Four days later, the entire group stood before the last obstacle on the path to the liberated territory in Northern Montenegro, the Sjenica–Prijepolje road. The crossing, aided by one brigade from the 2nd Assault Corps, took place on 19-21 May against moderate resistance by the PzAOK 2's ethnically and confessionally mixed force that included the "Brandenburgers", German policemen, as well as Krempler's and Đurišić's men.[14]

The NOVJ's first attempt since early 1942 to re-claim operational initiative on the Serbian soil thus ended in a clear-cut defeat. Although Morača's veterans acquitted themselves admirably (the Germans wrote that they fought "fanatically" and "until the last bullet"), none of the objectives were attained and Strike Group lost one-fifth of its effectives in the process. The Axis propaganda had a field day, but there was, in fact, little cause for celebration. Despite being vastly outnumbered and outgunned, and with their radio communications fully compromised, two guerrilla divisions managed to operate in the heart of Serbia for eight weeks. As for the performance of Felber's troops, the SFK again received the most accolades and a green light to expand into a division-sized formation. The "Kammerjäger" was also a litmus test of the German-Chetnik battlefield alliance. For starters, no one could doubt the monarchists' commitment to the anti-communist cause: whereas the Germans suffered ca. 120 casualties, the Bulgarians 180, the SFK 358, the JVuO had 1,171, almost half of whom were KIA (this figure refers only to those units that fought together with the Germans; the losses of "independent" units were estimated to be just as heavy). These figures are indicative not only of the ferocity of the fighting, but also of grave deficiencies in the JVuO's organization and tactics. Hitherto, the biggest mobile unit was the "flying" or "assault" brigade, composed of the most motivated and best armed men in the corps. These units rarely exceeded the strength of several hundred men, which was sufficient for the cat-and-mouse game with the local Partisan groups, but not for clashes with the crack NOVJ divisions coming from across the Drina. In late May–apparently, on German suggestion–Mihailović authorized the creation of 4th Group of Assault Corps (GAC). Consisting of five corps, nominally with three brigades and 1,700 soldiers each, this powerful formation represented the JVuO's strategic reserve, ready to intervene wherever the Partisans chose to appear next. At the same time, the defenses in the most vulnerable sector, the border with Montenegro, were consolidated under the HQ of Southwestern Front.[15]

6.3 New German Tactics and Spring Stalemate in NDH

In the late winter of 1944, Rendulic faced the problem of keeping the gains won in the recent operations with the steadily dwindling forces at his disposal. As soon as the landing season was over, the OKW began redeploying troops from the Balkans to to main fronts. By early spring, the PzAOK 2 had been reduced to 10 divisions and two regiments, which made more ambitious operations nearly impossible. The Germans sought to compensate for the shortage of forces by maintaining a low-intensity, but constant pressure on their enemy. The ultimate aim was to

14 Ibid., pp. 531-33.
15 Ibid., pp. 533-37.

perpetuate the current stalemate for as long as possible by keeping the Partisans "on edge" and not allowing them to reclaim the initiative. Under the codename "Hasenjagd", each corps had to launch at least two regiment-sized operations, and each division had to do the same, only on battalion-level, by the end of March. Whether the action continued past this date under the same designation is uncertain; what is certain, is that it ushered an unprecedented level of activity in the field. By the end of September, over 100 operations were carried out, the vast majority of them bearing colorful names such as "Wechselbalg" ("Changling"), "Windrose" ("Wind Rose"), or "Himmelhund" ("Wretch"); some of them were quite small (e.g. "Blücher", conducted by a single company of the "Brandenburg" Division), others were substantial (e.g. "Blitz", carried out by two brigades of the 1st CCD, plus three other battalions).[16]

Throughout the early months of 1944, senior German commanders were debating how best to tackle the NOVJ peril under the present circumstances. Ernst von Leyser, the CO of the XV MTC, advocated a strategy of gradual rollback, whereby the German military and police forces would seek to hold a patch of guerrilla-infested territory long enough to allow the establishment of a functioning civilian administration. Rendulic preferred targeting particularly dangerous enemy concentrations when and where they appeared, and favored body count over territorial gains as a measurement of progress. In the end, Rendulic had his own way, but von Leyser's ideas were partially implemented in Northeastern Bosnia, which became a semi-autonomous fiefdom of the 13th SS MTD "Handschar". This, however, was more a result of Himmler's political considerations and his desire to appear as a champion of Muslim rights rather than a matter of military expediency. The "Handschar" was formed in mid-1943 around a core of Bosnian Muslim recruits reluctantly supplied by the NDH. Being the *Reichsführer*'s pet project, the division received the state-of-the-art equipment, but also traditional fez headgear that was once worn by the daredevil *Bosniaken* regiments of the Habsburg Empire. In spite of its troubled birth, marked by the famous mutiny in the French town of Villefranche-de-Roergue in September 1943, the 21,000-strong formation was shipped across the Sava in mid-March of the following year. Outnumbering the entire 3rd NOVJ Corps almost 3:1, the "Handschar" had comparatively little difficulty in establishing a firm hold over its security zone that would last until the early fall. Having for once enough troops to go around, the Germans could also provide a sizable contingent for active protection of Serbia's western border. The downside of the arrangement was that not even von Weichs dared deploy a single "Handschar" battalion to another part of the country without Himmler's express permission, which he was not in habit of giving easily.[17]

Operational practices were debated as well during this period. The proven ineffectiveness of the classic cauldron battle caused Hitler to make the following sardonic observation:

16 Trifković, "Methods". The basic information on the German operations in the NDH and Montenegro from this period that are mentioned in this chapter–including the dates and OOB details–comes from a list I compiled earlier using a variety of primary and secondary sources, most notably the daily reports and war diaries of the HGF and subordinated corps, unit monographs, etc.

17 Schmider, *Partisanenkrieg*, pp. 329-32; George Lepre, *Himmler's Bosnian Division: the Waffen-SS Handschar Division, 1943-1945* (Atglen, PA: Schiffer Military History, 2004), pp. 13-139, 164-86; *Zbornik*/IV/23/565, 3rd NOVJC, Cable (6.3.1944).

> Ha, I am going to listen to that old story again how we encircled six of Tito's divisions, but I already know how it will end: after a few days, there will be only three divisions, and then only one, and by the time we go into action, the only thing we find in the cauldron will be a handful of bare-footed and exhausted Italians, and a few sick donkeys.[18]

Unlike von Leyser, Rendulic, who was probably more realistic about his army's capabilities, maintained that it was the only way to force battle on the nimble guerrillas. Artur Phleps, the ruthless and capable mountain warfare specialist who had been "the father" of the "Prinz Eugen" and was now in charge of the V SS MTC, had other ideas. For a while now, he was working on what he called the "Free Hunt" (*freie Jagd*), basically a German version of the *Arditi* tactics employed in Ljubljana Province in the first half of 1943. In short, the concept involved the use of multiple attack columns advancing concentrically against a target without concern for their flanks or rear. If the guerrillas started retreating, one part of the force would follow hard on their heels, while the other would be hurriedly redeployed to a convenient spot along their presumed withdrawal route and re-engage them from there. Once started, the chase would continue without temporal or spatial restrictions until the enemy was destroyed or dispersed; the pursuers would stop only if utterly exhausted. Phleps maintained that the full utilization of the concept would require a force of two mountain divisions. With the 1st MTD leaving the Yugoslav theater in March 1944 and returning only five months later, and with the "Handschar" firmly bound to its security zone, this left only the "Prinz Eugen". Owing to other commitments, however, the division could devote an equivalent of only one regiment for "free hunt" operations.[19]

Another important change in the Wehrmacht's COIN approach involved putting more accent on small-unit tactics. The over-aged personnel and inexperienced officers of the original, pre-1943 occupation contingent were ill-suited for putting the *Jagdkommando* concept into practice. Not that they did not try to adapt and overcome. As already mentioned, the 718th ID replaced the unwieldy jackboots with self-made mountain shoes and instructed its men to carry their ammunition in bandoleers "in the Chetnik fashion"; the HQ of the 187th RD openly spoke of the need to "adjust our tactics to those of the rebels". The change, however, only came slowly: it took the PzAOK 2 until late March 1944 to establish sniper training courses with individual divisions (for comparison, the HQ of the 1st Proletarian Division set up sniper courses already in November 1942, in the first days of its existence). By this time, improved drill and the experience accumulated over two-and-half years of war finally allowed for a wider application of guerrilla-style methods. Raiding on company and platoon levels, aggressive patrolling, daytime and nighttime ambushes, all these became a standard repertoire of Rendulic's units. The results were promising: the 1st "Brandenburg" Regiment reported having severed the NOVJ supply lines in its area of responsibility in Dalmatia, and the 373rd ID registered only two cases of railway sabotage in four weeks; the 1st JRR operated with so much success between Karlovac and Zagreb that it considered switching to irregular tactics altogether.[20]

18 Hermann Neubacher, *Specijalni zadatak Balkan* (Belgrade: Službeni list, 2004), p. 170.
19 Trifković, "Methods", pp. 7-8.
20 Ibid., pp. 12-13; Todor Radošević, *Prva proleterska divizija* (Belgrade: Sekcija boraca Prve proleterske NOU brigade, 2010), Vol. I, pp. 35-36; NARA/T314/663/329, XXI MTC, Sniper training (5.4.1944).

In mid-summer 1943, the Wehrmacht also began forming their own *Gegenbanden*. Commonly called *Trupps* (abbreviated from *Bandenjägertrupps* or *Bandenvernichtungstrupps*), these all-volunteer, platoon-sized units were trained to operate behind enemy lines posing as the Partisans. Each division was supposed to have at least one of them. The training was initially done in a special course set up by the 114th JD at the Trappist monastery outside Banja Luka but would eventually become decentralized. For instance, the 181st ID ran its own course in Montenegro with the help of native instructors, and the 1st JRR was made responsible for all the candidates from the area of its parent corps. The *Trupps* were typical "black ops" units: their main task was to gather intelligence and spread terror. Their appearance caused much confusion and a quite a few losses on the NOP side. For example, the actions at Vrlika on 5 December 1943 and Otočac on 27 January 1944 produced ca. 30 dead or captured guerrillas with no loss to the attackers. Unit "Konrad", the Abwehr's own *Trupp* made up largely of Dalmatian monarchists of Catholic origin ("Croat Chetniks"), caused so much embarrassment by its bloody rampages that it had to be withdrawn from the NDH.[21]

The combination of all the above-mentioned measures did not fail to produce results, as evident from the NOVJ reports from across the NDH. These documents contain numerous references to the new, "brazen" enemy tactics, frequent incursions into guerrilla-held areas, ambushes, and such. At this time, the Partisan army was going through a sort of crisis, caused in the first place by months of interrupted campaigning. With the winter battles over, everyone from Tito down to the lowest company commander looked forward to a spell of peace. By now, senior leaders of the NOVJ had largely acquired the mindset of regular officers. In order to protect the liberated territories, without which neither rest nor preparations for the upcoming summer campaign could be contemplated, they opted for a purely defensive posture. As a result, a curious stalemate ensued along the "front lines" throughout Bosnia and Croatia, with the Partisans limiting their activities to the barest minimum. Just how static the NOVJ had become is best seen from the fact that Koča Popović's HQ remained in the same village outside Drvar for three full months. Higher commands understood the perils of inactivity and issued orders to this effect from time to time, but little was actually done; it seemed that everyone was content with the way the things were. The 5th Corps reportedly carried out close to 300 actions on battalion level from mid-February to mid-May, but only three attempts were made against Axis garrisons (Prijedor, Mrkonjić Grad, Kotor Varoš), none of them successful; during April 1944, this entire formation suffered less than 250 casualties.[22]

The 3rd Corps saw far more action, but nearly all of it was defensive in nature. The spring campaign began in mid-March 1944 with the invasion of Northeastern Bosnia by the 13th SS MTD, which then proceeded south in a slow and methodical fashion. After offering some stiff resistance on Mount Majevica in the initial phase of the contest, the 16th and 36th Vojvodina Divisions retreated to Birač. By this time (it was mid-April), 3rd Corps was finishing preparations for the crossing of the Drina with two divisions in an attempt to take some pressure off Morača's Strike Group. Informed of these designs through radio surveillance, the V SS MTC launched Operation "Maibaum" with the aim of sealing the border and crushing the guerrillas between the 13th SS MTD and one reinforced regiment of the 7th SS MTD coming

21 Trifković, "Methods"., pp. 14-16.
22 Ibid., pp. 4-5, 8-9; Karasijević, *Peti*, pp. 222-23; *Zbornik*/IV/26/56-57, 5th NOVJC, Monthly report (April 1944).

from the south. Having little knowledge of what was actually going on in Serbia and facing very long odds, the corps HQ decided to postpone the crossing. One of its divisions, the 17th Eastern Bosnian, broke through the encirclement southeast of Vlasenica after two days of bitter fighting (28-30 April), suffering an estimated 300 casualties in the process. The remaining three divisions (the 16th, 36th, and 38th) first tried going north, towards the Zvornik–Tuzla road, but then veered left towards Šekovići, where they managed to clear a bloody path through the "Handschar's" positions. Tito, infuriated by the unauthorized withdrawal, ordered the 3rd Corps to immediately help Morača according to the original plan. From 6 to 11 May, the well-informed Germans thwarted all attempts by two exhausted divisions to approach the Drina. Effectively admitting defeat, the SHQ sent the 16th to a new operational area between Tuzla and Doboj, while the 17th was ordered to Montenegro. The Axis now turned their attention to the Majevica, which was again becoming a hotbed of guerrilla activity. The Partisans' initial response was to send reinforcements in an attempt to hold this agriculturally rich area but were ultimately forced into a general retreat south after six days of disjointed fighting. In the period 8-21 May, the 3rd Corps suffered another 725 casualties.[23]

The extraordinarily active XV MTC managed to keep in check the NOVJ forces on the Dalmatian mainland, Lika, and Gorski Kotar. The Germans were aided in their efforts by a severe shortage of foodstuffs on the liberated territories, which led to a substantial reduction of their opponent's combat capabilities. The bulk of the 8th Corps spent the late winter and early spring months in training, interdicting Axis traffic, and attacking smaller Chetnik and Ustasha targets. To name a couple of examples: General Otto Lüdecke was severely wounded when his car hit a mine on 29 April 1944, only one day after he had taken over the 264th ID. Four weeks later, the 20th Division stormed Aržano and took 130 Ustashe prisoner, all but four of whom were executed thereafter (the incident had a negative propaganda fallout among the Croat population). At first glance, the official figures for May 1944 presented in the course of an inter-divisional contest seemed impressive, but the relatively light own losses (70 KIA, 177 WIA, 71 MIA; the 26th Division and Navy not included) and small number of prisoners (277) reveal the absence of a more ambitious offensive agenda. In Istria, the Partisans still largely fought in the traditional manner, but were already beginning to experiment with more complex actions, such as the (failed) attack on the collaborationist strongpoint at Lupoglav on 5 April. The steadily increasing strength of the NOVJ compelled the Germans to launch the first serious operation in these parts after the "Wolkenbruch". Despite the deployment of six battalions drawn from every available Wehrmacht, Waffen-SS, and police unit present, the undertaking was a flop; it will be best be remembered for the mass-murder of 263 civilians in the village of Lipa on 30 April, which still holds the preserved ruins of the old houses.[24]

23 Zdravko Antonić, Jeremija Perić, *Birač u Narodnooslobodilačkoj borbi* (Tuzla: Univerzal, 1982), pp. 310-21; Mandić, *Sedamnaesta*, pp. 149-70; Lepre, *Handschar*, pp. 151-69, 187-98.

24 *Zbornik*/V/26/79-89, *Zbornik*/V/27/33-45, and *Zbornik*/V/28/163-79, 8th NOVJC, Monthly and activity reports (March, April, and May-first half of June 1944, respectively); *Zbornik*/V/27/398 and 465, Messages to 11th NOVJC from the 35th, and 13th NOVJD, respectively (19 and 22.5.1944); Blanka Matković, Ivan Pažanin (eds.), *Zločin i teror u Dalmaciji 1943.-1948. počinjeni od pripadnika NOV, JA, OZN-e i UDB-e: dokumenti* (Zagreb, 2011), pp. 8-9, and 68-70 (8th NOVJC, Information bulletin May 1944); NARA/T314/560/1231, XV MTC, Diary (28-29.4.1944); NARA/T312/1640/1003, "von Zangen", Activity report (26.10-10.5.1944); Kleut, *Jedanaesti*, pp. 119-24.

Farther south, the bulk of the 11th Corps remained locked in a stalemate around Gospić and Otočac. In addition to the crack 4th UAB, the Partisans had a new opponent, the 392nd ID. In material respect, this youngest of the legionnaire outfits was treated "as if it were an SS division"; its equipment was modified for mountain warfare already during the training period in Austria. In the field, the officers and men of the 392nd proved remarkably tough and resourceful, quickly grasping the principles of anti-guerrilla tactics. Even with one of his two infantry regiments permanently deployed on coastal guard duties, the division's energetic commander Johannes Mickl (who once served under Rommel in Africa) maintained a hectic schedule of operations. During the first week of April, the Germans and Ustashe pushed back the 35th Lika Division away from Otočac and towards the Plitvice Lakes. Two weeks later, the Axis launched the traditional spring raid against the main NOVJ base in Gorski Kotar, Drežnica. Unlike similar operations launched by the *Regio Esercito* in the preceding years, this venture was a major success: among else, 30 tons of infantry and 15 tons of artillery ammunition of Italian origin were secured from numerous, overfilled magazines belonging to the 13th Primorsko-Goranska Division.

The routing of one Ustasha battalion at Ramljane and the appearance of the Partisans on the all-important road linking the two biggest garrisons in Lika (5-6 May) provoked a major reaction in the shape of Operation "Morgenstern". Axis planers had long toyed with the idea of securing the Krbava Field, which would not only deprive the guerrillas of a major source of food but would also facilitate the opening of one's own supply lanes to Western Bosnia. In addition to the 392nd ID's advance from the north, east, and west, the XV MTC intended to use one regimental battle group of the 373rd ID, plus the 92nd PzGR and some "Brandenburges", in order to seal the ring from the south. The "Morgenstern" lasted from 7 to 23 May, during which time the Axis captured nearly the entire liberated territory together with large quantities of supplies and equipment, including 502 rifles, 118 MGs, 21 cannon, 60 motor vehicles, and no less than 220 tons of ammunition. The units of the 11th Corps (altogether six brigades) lost some 250 men but managed to avoid destruction by dexterous maneuvering. The NOVJ's rear services passed this difficult test with flying colors, organizing the evacuation of more than 1,000 wounded and many more refugees to the massifs of Velebit, Plješevica, and even faraway Kordun. The Axis returned to their garrisons shortly thereafter, leaving behind ravaged fields and scores of razed settlements.[25]

The 4th Corps spent the late winter and early spring months in near-constant action along the extended borders of the liberated territories in Kordun, Banija, Žumberak, and the northwestern corner of Bosnia. Both sides operated largely in guerrilla manner, ambushing, raiding, and sabotaging each other with varying degree of success. Bigger undertakings were few and far between. On 9 April 1944, the 4th Corps launched an assault on Cazin with two brigades, while five more guarded the outer approaches to the town. In spite of their rich experience in taking fortified places, the NOVJ planners made two major mistakes: they failed to attach a sufficient number of veterans to the attacking force, and to ensure that the road communications leading to the target were properly demolished. Confronted with determined defenders and

25 Ibid, pp. 54-119, 124-63; Schraml, *Kriegsschauplatz*, pp. 239, 243-252; Adolf von Ernsthausen, *Die Wölfe der Lika: mit Legionären, Ustaschi, Domobranen und Tschetniks gegen Titos Partisanen: Erlebnisse in Kroatien 1944* (Neckargemünd: Kurt Vowinckel, 1959), pp. 23, 30-31; NARA/T314/563/243, XV MTC to PzAOK 2 (23.5.1944).

a strong relief force coming from Bihać, the Partisans withdrew after having suffered close to 200 casualties in two days. As a consolation, it turned out that the mighty Wehrmacht itself was still capable of making beginner's errors. By the last week of May, the LXIX RC was completing the preparations for Operation "Schach", an ambitious attempt to crush the 4th Corps in the area Bihać–Kostajnica–Sisak–Karlovac–Bihać. Then everything went awry. A regimental group of the 373rd ID, which commenced its advance one day ahead of schedule (23 May), was surrounded by three brigades of the 7th and 8th NOVJ Divisions northeast of Velika Kladuša and had to be relieved by the 1st CCD. At the same time, owing to other commitments, the PzAOK 2 withdrew the 92nd PzGR, effectively removing the left pincer arm of the operation. The "Schach" was thus downgraded to a tier-two operation limited to the area of Vojnić, lasting until the end of the month. Apart from the loss of about 250 men on each side, little else changed as a result.[26]

Unlike related older organizations, the youngest Croatian NOVJ corps, the 10th, managed to retain a modicum of initiative. After a long journey riddled with skirmishes, the 32nd Division returned to Zagorje via Mount Kalnik in the last week of March 1944. Reinforced with one brigade of the 33rd and local detachments, the division proceeded with the reduction of smaller enemy outposts along the edges of Mount Ivanščica. The high point of the campaign came on 22 April with the routing of a column belonging to Pavelić's bodyguard outfit at Kamena Gorica (30 killed, one intact medium tank and two AT guns captured). The Ustashe had their revenge six days later when they pushed back "The Radić Brothers" Brigade, capturing over 100 rifles in the process. This stemmed the guerrilla advance, but the situation was far from rosy: by mid-May, the NDH presence in the region was practically reduced to the garrisons at Lepoglava, Zlatar, and Novi Marof. Just as in the past, the Partisans now became the victims of their own success, for the regime could not afford to tolerate their presence so close to the capital. Effectively supported by the *Luftwaffe*, the reinforced 1st PTS Regiment launched Operation "Sarajevo" on the 15th and managed to surround the bulk of the already retreating enemy one day later. The Partisans broke through towards the southeast, but the Ustashe pursued them for four full days before finally making a halt before the western fringes of the Bilogora. Thus ended one of the most effective anti-guerrilla operations of the war: for the price of only six KIA and 18 WIA, the NDH forces reported capturing close to 300 pieces of small arms, five mortars, and three cannon. The Partisans were back to square one, their ranks shattered: the number of missing alone was estimated at 274, and the entire 32nd Division was reduced to less than 1,000 men.[27]

This was actually the second major defeat suffered by the 10th Corps since the opening of the spring campaign. The first one occurred on 29 March 1944 at Oborovo, where the 2nd Moslavina Brigade was waiting for a caravan with weapons from Banija. Alerted through the signals intelligence, the Cossacks mounted a surprise attack, effectively routing the enemy; according to the NOVJ sources, there were at least 37 KIA and 147 MIA. The Partisans could find some consolation in the fact that Günter Amelung, who had been awarded the famed Knight's Cross for his exploits in Russia, was among the dead on the German side. With Moslavina now effectively left without forces, the MHQ Croatia again called upon the 28th Division to save the

26 Baić, *Četvrti*, pp. 254-83; *Zbornik*/XII/4/266-67, 282-87, 310-12, PzAOK 2 and LXIX RC, [Materials pertaining to "Schach"] (19-25.5.1944); NARA/T314/1546/745, LXIX RC, Results "Schach" (undated).

27 Obhođaš et al., *Vojnica*, Vol. II, pp. 312-41.

situation. Arriving from Slavonia in mid-May, this formation attacked the enemy strongholds at Hercegovac, Narta, Kloštar Ivanić, and Veliko Trojstvo, but failed to take them. It is interesting to note that the old grudges between the Slavonian and "northwestern" officers (i.e. the former 2nd OZ) flared-up again and contributed to the unsatisfactory development of the situation in this sector.[28]

The German invasion of Hungary, Operation "Margarethe", had a direct impact on the situation in Slavonia. Roads and railway lines leading north were now clogged with troop transports, which the Partisans were doing their best to intercept. March and early April 1944 were therefore very busy, with the 6th Corps reporting more than 60 ambushes and attacks on various enemy targets, with good effect. The departure of Wehrmacht's mobile reserves also made bigger operations possible. The corps assigned both of its divisions for the planned incursion into Podravina, whose manpower potential, especially among the minorities, was still largely untapped. On 6 April, the Partisans took Podravska Slatina after a two-day fight, practically wiping out its battalion-sized Ustasha garrison in the process. Hastily assembled relief force (consisting largely of Kammerhofer's gendarmes) managed to retake the town, but the seesaw fighting here, and around Našice, lasted throughout the month.

With Admiral Horthy gone, the Germans could afford to transfer the bulk of the 42nd JD (the former 187th RD) back to its old operational area and plan an offensive of their own. Operation "Ungewitter" was to be just another one of those massive sweeps of the Slavonian Mountains that the Axis undertook at least once a year. On 26 April, four Wehrmacht infantry, five police, and five NDH battalions, supported by two armored companies and strong engineer, artillery, and air assets, started their concentric advance on Voćin from the south, northeast, and north; half as many battalions stood deployed in blocking lines in the west and east. The NOVJ units immediately commenced a fighting withdrawal towards the west. After an attempted breakthrough by both division around 1 May had failed, the 6th Corps decided to split its forces, with the 28th Division going to Moslavina, and the 12th staying behind. The Axis continued the search for 10 more days, then called the operation off (own losses included 87 members of the Wehrmacht and almost twice as many Croats or German policemen). In its after-action report, the Partisan command wrote that the "Ungewitter" differed from the similar operations in that the enemy was not targeting the NOVJ manpower as much as its infrastructure and economic base. Hundreds of objects, ranging from individual huts and workshops to large magazines, were burned down, their contents either carried away or destroyed. Despite this apparent change in the enemy's priorities, the uninterrupted campaigning was taking a heavy toll on the 6th Corps: ca. 1,250 fighters were lost in recent months, more than a third of whom were either killed or missing.[29]

28 *SZH*/IX/291-93, 33rd NOVJD, Activity report (20.3-5.4.1944); NARA/T78/331/6288533, OBSO, Daily report (31.3.1944); Radojica Nenezić, "Analiza borbenih dejstava u Moslavini i Bilogori od 8. maja do 24. juna 1944. godine", in *Dvadesetosma slavonska NO udarna divizija u Sjeverozapadnoj Hrvatskoj i u dvije borbe za oslobođenje Ludbrega* (Grubišno Polje: Centar za kulturu i informiranje, 1990), pp. 93-124.

29 See the reports by the 6th NOVJC in *Zbornik*/V/26/344-75 (18.4.1944), *Zbornik*/V/27/334-47 and 417 (17 and 20.5.1944, respectively), and *Zbornik*/V/28/214-38 (13.6.1944); NARA/T314/1548/182-85, 188-89, HSSPF Croatia, Monthly report (April 1944); TsAMO/500/12477/679/1-16, 42nd JD, Report "Ungewitter" (undated).

There was the one area of Yugoslavia where the Partisans held the initiative throughout the spring and most of the summer 1944: the Central and Southern Dalmatian Archipelagos. The center of the NOVJ activity was the now-heavily fortified island of Vis. By the beginning of May, the 26th Division had been reinforced by more than 2,000 British servicemen (and a company of Americans), most of whom were Commandos belonging to the 2nd Special Service Brigade. Furthermore, the Royal Navy operated a handful of small combat vessels and landing craft from the port of Komiža. Together, the allies sought to make life as miserable as possible for the Germans. During the first half of April, the British made six successful sorties, capturing three German boats and sinking two on the 11th alone. Although lacking the equipment and seafaring experience of their foreign comrades-at-arms, the Partisans went ahead with independent actions. On 1 June, NB-8 "Kornat" stood up to four enemy vessels at Blitvenica and prevailed. Nothing can be as deceitful as fortunes of war: only hours earlier, these same German boats, which were now limping back to their base, caught a small convoy with 77 Partisans, "two English parachutists", and a similar number of women and children abroad, all of whom were trying to flee from the mainland. The "Kornat" itself would run aground and be destroyed two months later. On 29 July, three NOVJ patrol boats captured a 120-ton armed merchantmen carrying food near Ist.

All this while, the Germans were debating as how best to tackle the growing threat to this part of the Adriatic. The army wanted to evacuate the exposed island garrisons altogether, while the navy objected, maintaining they were crucial for keeping the coastal supply lanes open. Everyone agreed that a successful invasion of Vis would solve most of the problems, but the project–codenamed "Freischütz"–had to be canceled owing to the insurmountable technical difficulties (e.g. lack of air cover). In the end, the Germans resorted to more blunt but proven methods: they forcibly evacuated up to 30,000 inhabitants from the islands. It should be said that a similar number of refugees ended up on Vis and in Italy, from whence they were transferred to the far-away El-Shatt on the Sinai. Here, they formed a self-administered Yugoslav community that had its own KPJ and SKOJ committees, NOP institutions, schools, etc.[30]

The main form of Allied activity in the archipelagos was amphibious raiding. Hvar was "visited" four times in the final eight weeks of winter 1944. On 22 March, elements of the 1st Dalmatian Brigade and Commandos gave a severe drubbing to a battalion of the 118th JD on the western part of the island, capturing 131 enemy soldiers. Precisely one month later, six Partisan battalions attacked Vela Luka and Blato on Korčula, taking both after three days of heavy fighting. It was a fitting payback for the defeat suffered on the island at the hands of these same Germans last Christmas: 549 prisoners and over 700 pieces of small arms were taken; an additional 46 prisoners were brought in from Mljet, which was raided concurrently. The fact that neither the surviving official documents nor post-war reminiscences of German veterans contain the exact casualty figure is indicative of the scale of the disaster (according to one brief–and obviously incomplete tally–the combined losses amounted to 450 men). After losing an entire company to enemy raiders in late March, the garrison at Šolta came close to

30 Anić, *Osmi*, pp. 77-80; Michael McConville, *A small war in the Balkans: British military involvement in wartime Yugoslavia 1941-1945* (London: Macmillan, 1986), pp. 169-78; Schmider, *Partisanenkrieg*, pp. 391-93; *DCO*/XVIII/467-68; *Zbornik*/VIII/2/352-56 (4th POS to NOVJ Navy HQ, 2.6.1944), 484-89 (2nd POS to NOVJ Navy HQ, 31.7.1944); NARA/T1022/3957, KM Admiral Adriatic, Diary (1-2.6.1944).

meeting the same fate again in mid-May. Thanks to a prior warning, however, the 264th ID was able to send reinforcements just in time to repel the two attacking Partisan battalions. The episode was marked by a tragic event. Although the German infantry refrained from firing on enemy wounded transports, which were carried out under the sign of the red cross, a *Kriegsmarine* vessel sank the NOVJ hospital ship "Marin II" with 60 patients on board near Vis. The Yugoslavs claimed she was properly marked, whereas the Germans mentioned nothing more than a sinking of a "large passenger ship".[31]

The biggest of the spring battles took place on Brač in the first days of June 1944, as the 8th Corps tried to draw some heat off the 1st Proletarian Corps, fighting for its life around Drvar at the time. Nearly the entire 26th Division was used for this purpose, as well as one battalion of the British special forces, and air and naval assets. After making a landfall at Bol, three attack groups proceeded inland against their objectives at Supetar, Nerežišće, and Sumartin. For two full days (2-4 June), the Allies hammered against the two fortified battalions of the 118th JD, with little result. Faced with the arrival of enemy reinforcements and the loss of the daredevil Commando leader, Lieutenant-Colonel Tom Churchill (who had been captured and taken to the mainland), the attackers withdrew. Although there is again some controversy concerning their own casualties (according to official reports, 41 KIA, 190 WIA, 51 MIA; according to the NOVJ, the number of enemy captured alone amounted to 220 along with the corresponding number of small-arms), the Germans celebrated a clear-cut victory, and the next three months would see no major amphibious raids.[32] The small-scale raiding, carried out by both regular forces from Vis and the local Partisans, continued unabated. Probably the most successful of these affairs took place on 13 August, when an entire German platoon was wiped out in a classic ambush on the Pelješac, without a single loss among the attackers. The Germans also carried out similar actions, using either ad-hoc amphibious *Jagdkommandos* (e.g. Unit "Dzaack" belonging to the 118th JD), or specially trained "Brandenburg" Coastal *Jägers*.[33]

6.4 "Where is Tito?": Raid on Drvar

It seems incredible, but it took the Germans until January 1943 to establish the true identity of the NOP's supreme commander, a lasting monument to the KPJ's culture of secrecy. Apart from the daily perils of guerrilla life (air raids, shelling, disease, etc.), Tito came close to being captured on several occasions. The Italians nearly got him at Nova Varoš in December 1941, and a similar incident occurred in June 1943, when he and his entourage incidentally crossed paths with a column of the 369th ID in the wilderness of the Zelengora. In fact, a special detail of

31 NARA/T1022/3956, KM Admiral Adriatic, Diary (11.5.1944).

32 The NOVJ losses in the major landings on Hvar, Korčula, Mljet, Šolta, and Brač were 184 KIA, 709 WIA, and 18 MIA: *Hronologija*, pp. 708 (22.3.1944), 733 (20-21 and 21-22.4.1944), 759 (10.5.1944), 789 (1.6.1944). For German losses see also NARA/T1022/3956, KM Admiral Adriatic, Diary (29.4.1944); NARA/T314/560/1181, XV MTC, Diary (20.3.1944); NARA/T314/565/638-39, XV MTC, Preliminary report Šolta (12.5.1944); NARA/T78/331/6288974, OBSO, Daily report (6.61944).

33 Anić, *Osmi*, pp. 80-86; Otto Weingartner, "Errinerungen an die Einheit Dzaack auf die Insel Brac", in Weingartner (ed.), *Errinerungen*, pp. 219-20; see also ibid., pp. 199, 206-18; Petar Kleut, *Partizanska taktika* (Belgrade: VIZ, 1983), pp. 249-51; see also OBSO's daily reports in NARA/T78/331/6288747 (27.5.1944), and 6289070-71 (23.6.1944); BA-MA/RH37/4835, 750th JR, Diary (1.7-1.9.1944).

German commandos dressed up as the Partisans was waiting for the opportunity to infiltrate the enemy army and assassinate its leader, but the "Schwarz" ended before the plan could be put into motion. As time passed and the NOVJ grew stronger, the Wehrmacht top brass were increasingly becoming in favor of hitting the head, rather than the body, of the insurgency. Throughout the late summer and fall of 1943, the Germans gathered intelligence and discussed ways of eliminating their high-profile target, including poison and a bomb wrapped as a present. The "Brandenburgers" were yet again called upon to provide suitable candidates for this mission. Owing to constant delays and inability to find a feasible solution, they ended up sabotaging the Partisan railways around Jajce instead, a telling example of just how completely the situation in Yugoslavia had gotten out of hand.[34]

In early May 1944, von Weichs decided to drop the idea of a classic *Attentat* in favor of a more ambitious plan that involved the use of paratroopers. These would not come from the ranks of the *Luftwaffe*'s famous "Green Devils", but from 500th SS Parachute Battalion (*SS-Fallschirmjäger-Bataillon 500*, SS FJB 500). Formed in late 1943 as a disciplinary outfit, it was transferred to the area of Kraljevo in order to complete its training. There, the battalion received its baptism of fire when it was briefly thrown into battle against Morača's fighters. The high losses among officers and NCOs suffered on this occasion prompted the PzAOK 2 to pull the unit out of the firing line. By mid-May the battalion got Himmler's blessing to take part on what went down in history as Operation "Rösselsprung". The centerpiece of this unique undertaking was the airborne raid against Tito's capital of Drvar, the cradle of the Bosnian insurgency. After a short but intensive air preparation, the SS FJB 500 would descend suddenly over its target and secure all important locations, including the SHQ's radio center and the seats of foreign military missions. The main prize, of course, were Tito's personal quarters (nicknamed the "Citadel") and their occupants; in the unlikely case the NOVJ's supreme commander allowed himself to be captured, a "Henschel" stood ready to flow him out under escort, just as it happened with Mussolini during the Gran Sasso Raid of September 1943. Concurrently, special battle groups (composed largely of crack reconnaissance and motorized units drawn from various field formations) would launch a concentric advance on Drvar from all directions with the aim of relieving the paratroopers and crushing the 1st Proletarian Corps in the process. In all, the XV MTC, which was entrusted with the conduct of the operation, had ca. 17,000 German troops at its disposal. The "Rösselsprung" proved to be the swan's song of the *Luftwaffe* in the Balkans: a massive force of 185 combat, 12 reconnaissance, and 40 transport airplanes, as well as 45 tugs with 60 gliders, was assembled in preparation for this assassination attempt of the highest order.[35]

All of their renowned meticulousness notwithstanding, the Germans failed to obtain one critical piece of intelligence: the exact location of the "Citadel". A part of the town called Šobića Glavica was originally identified as the most likely candidate, but in reality, it hosted only the

34 Trifković, *Parleying*, pp. 105-06, 274-79; Dedijer, *Dnevnik*, Vol. I, p. 68 (2.12.1941) and Vol. II, pp. 274-75 (14.6.1943); NARA/T315/1301/226, 118th JD, Diary (12.6.1943); NARA/T313/192/7452291-92, 7452963-66, "Brandenburg", Correspondence on action against Tito (28.10 and 12.11.1943, respectively); NARA/T313/190/7450661-7450662, PzAOK 2/Intel., Daily report (30.12.1943).

35 NARA/T501/256/634, MBSO, Daily report (29.4.1944); Slavko Odić, *Desant na Drvar* (Belgrade: VII, 1981), pp. 18-40; Georg Schlaug, "Der Luftwaffen-Einsatz beim 'Unternehmen Rösselsprung'", *Luftwaffe im Focus*, 2 (2003), pp. 37-43.

British mission (codename "London"). Unbeknownst to the Germans, the British relocated their seat on the very eve of the attack on account of the suspiciously repetitive flyovers by a lonely enemy scout. Thanks to the "Ultra" program, their superiors were informed of the preparations for some kind of a large-scale Axis offensive in the Balkans, but the target was not revealed until the very last moment. The Partisans were in general ill-prepared to deal with potential trouble: the only combat unit located in the town itself was the Escort Battalion, while the nearest reserves (the 6th Lika Division) were miles away. Aware of the possibility of an enemy airborne assault, Tito usually did not dwell in Drvar, but in the nearby village of Bastasi. Late on 24 May, however, he took up residence in his town HQ, located in a cave overlooking the Uvac River. There, in blissful ignorance, he hosted a private dinner for the senior members of the SHQ and foreign representatives and prepared for his own birthday celebrations scheduled to take place the next day.[36]

The "Rösselsprung" commenced in the early morning hours of 25 May 1944. The first wave of paratroopers met with fierce, if disjointed resistance by the NOVJ's rear area personnel, SKOJ functionaries, and candidates of the SHQ's Officer School. After two hours (0700-0900) of confused and costly fighting, the SS FJB 500 secured most of its original objectives, but Tito was nowhere to be found. Not before long, the attackers were alerted to a potential presence of a high-value target by an unusually dense enemy fire originating from the far side of the Uvac. The Partisan leader and his staff now found themselves pinned down in their hideout by concentrated small-arms fire, while the German assault details were getting ever closer. Thanks largely to the cool-headedness of associates like Žujović and Ranković, Tito agreed to be roped down a crevice to a spring bed bellow, from where he made his way to the plateau located above the cave. By 1200 hours, the entire party was out of harms' way and heading for the relative safety of Prekaje, some 15 km to the southeast.

It was now the paratroopers' turn to be on the receiving end. One by one, the battalions of the 3rd Lika Brigade were beginning to arrive to the town after completing a leg-breaking forced march from Trubar (10 km southwest of Drvar). Together with what was left of the original garrison, plus two additional battalions from the 1st Lika and 3rd Dalmatian Brigades, they began to push back the SS FJB 500, which was now complete, but bloodied and disorganized. By dusk, the Germans had chosen the elevated, walled cemetery at Šobića Glavica to serve as their last stand. Throughout that night, the Partisans launched repeated assaults, but the desperate defenders managed to hold them off. Fearing enemy air raids, the Partisans withdrew with the first light on 26 May 1944, enabling a column of the 373rd ID to enter the town from the west and relieve the exhausted paratroopers.[37]

This long-overdue relief force was supposed to be in Drvar already in the afternoon of the first day of the operation, but the schedule was totally upset by the masterfully conducted defense on the part of the 2nd Lika Brigade. The battle groups from Bihać (the 92nd PzGR), Knin (the 1st "Brandenburg" Regiment), Livno (the 105th SS Recon Battalion), and Banja Luka (the Assault

36 Odić, *Desant*, pp. 40-49; see the following contributions in *Za pobjedu i slobodu. Drvarska operacija: učesnici govore* (Belgrade: VINC, 1986): Dušan Biber, "Iza kulisa desanta na Drvar" (pp. 489-94); Slavko Odić, "Zašto je nemački plan desanta na Drvar bio pogrešan" (pp. 579-95) and "Savezničke vojne misije pri Vrhovnom štabu NOV i POJ u desantu na Drvar" (pp. 664-65).

37 Dragoljub Tmušić, "Hronologija", in Ibid., pp. 736-39; Djilas, *Wartime*, p. 394; Charles D. Manson, "Red Sun: A German Airborne Raid, May 1944", *JSMS*, 13:4 (2000), pp. 108-15.

Battalion of the PzAOK 2) made similar experiences in the fight against the elements of the 4th Krajina, 39th Central Bosnian, and 9th Dalmatian Divisions. Everywhere, the attackers encountered thoroughly mined and demolished roads covered by well-camouflaged weapons situated on the surrounding heights. For the NOVJ, the most dangerous enemy thrust was the one carried out by a reinforced regiment of the 7th SS MTD from the direction of Jajce and Mrkonjić Grad towards the wider area of Mlinište. The 1st Proletarian Division fought here with great obstinacy for nearly a week (26 May-2 June 1944) before retreating towards the southeast together with the SHQ. Realizing that the pocket around Prekaje was now empty (the 39th Division had in the meantime escaped north), the PzAOK 2 continued the pursuit into the Kupres Plain. It was too late: Tito was flown out in a Soviet plane to Italy on 3 June and thence to Vis, after which the 1st Proletarian broke off contact. As a consolation prize, the Germans hoped to catch the HQ of the 8th Corps and the bulk of the 9th Division in a pocket around Tičevo. These units had to endure two days of dramatic fighting before the Germans finally decided they had enough and began to return to their bases.[38]

Operation "Rösselsprung", known as "Seventh Enemy Offensive" to the Yugoslavs, represented the final German attempt to destroy the NOP leadership. Despite being a maximum-effort undertaking, it ended in a failure. Tito escaped, and so did the vast majority of his followers; the battle had hardly any influence on events in other parts of the country. The Germans had to settle for the Partisan leader's brand new uniform and a rich haul of booty, including, among else, the SHQ's radio center together with nearly all of its highly classified materials. According to the most reliable estimates available, the NOVJ lost 399 KIA (179 of them in Drvar itself) and 479 WIA during the entire operation; in addition, the Germans reported making 238 prisoners and 35 defectors. At the same time, they admitted to having lost 213 KIA, 881 WIA, and 57 MIA. Roughly one-fourth of them belonged to the SS FJB 500, which would soon be withdrawn from the country and never again used in an airborne role.[39]

6.5 Second and Third NOVJ Incursions into Serbia

Throughout the spring and summer 1944, the NOVJ's main operational areas in Serbia remained located in the central and southern parts of the country. In the former, the Partisans devoted most of their time and energies to the struggle against the JVuO, with varying degree of success. The first attempt to form a second brigade in Šumadija ended in a disaster on 12 May, when the young outfit lost nearly a half of its members (ca. 90) to a sudden Chetnik assault. The brigade was soon back on its feet, and by early September, it already had 500 fighters, the result of the NOP's steadily improving fortunes. The same could be said for that other venerable unit from this part of the country, the Kosmaj Detachment. In June, it had only 121 men; three months later, the number of armed fighters rose to 300, that of unarmed to almost 800. The influx of new recruits, many of whom came from Belgrade and even far-off Syrmia, enabled the creation of two more brigades. Their combat capabilities, however, remained very much on the level of territorial outfits, as witnessed by the failed attack on Aranđelovac on 5 September.[40]

38 Colić, *Pregled*, pp. 190-93.

39 NARA/T314/563/372-74 and 484-85, XV MTC, Results "Rösselsprung" (9 and 7.6.1944, respectively); Odić, *Desant*, pp. 271-78.

40 Vitorović, *Centralna*, pp. 583-637.

The most favorable situation was still in Southern Serbia. Operating from their main base at Crna Trava, the local Partisans were becoming ever more daring. On 12 April 1944, the attack on Kriva Feja netted over 300 captured policemen, a telling proof of the acute war-weariness among the Bulgarians. Another three successful clashes with the occupation forces followed over the course of the next eight days. This was the final straw for the general staff in Sofia. The last sweep of this area, carried out in March with a force of 14 battalions, was obviously not enough. This time, the 5th Army would have at its disposal two full divisions (the 14th and the 29th), plus an equivalent of three regiments. Known as the "May" or "Spring Offensive" to the Yugoslavs, the undertaking began on 30 April by simultaneous thrusts from the line Kumanovo–Vranje–Leskovac–Trn–Kriva Palanka–Kumanovo. After two weeks of confused fighting and frantic maneuvering, the guerrilla forces–in the meantime reorganized into five Serbian, one Macedonian, one Kosovo, and two Bulgarian brigades, plus the detachments and rear-area personnel–found themselves surrounded northeast of Crna Trava. As was customary in such circumstances, the Partisans split up, with one group heading back south along the Bulgarian border, eventually ending up in Northern Greece (see below). The other, containing the bulk of the Serbian units, broke through the thin Chetnik screen along the demarcation line and reached Suva Planina. Then, after couple of days of rest, the Partisans returned into the cauldron, interrupting the Bulgarian reprisal parties in their work. Owing to the unrelenting enemy pressure, a prolonged stay proved impossible: on 22 May, the guerrillas made good their escape by crossing the Southern Morava at Grdelica. Measured against the resources used, the offensive was a failure: even though no reliable statistics exist, it is certain that no NOVJ unit of any importance was destroyed. It did, however, succeed in pacifying this unruly area for weeks to come, and weakened the cohesion of these still-green guerrilla formations (straggling and desertion were seemingly widespread).[41]

During March and April 1944, the NOVJ forces on the left bank of the Southern Morava had a series of largely successful clashes with the Chetniks on the Radan, the RSK at Beli Kamen, and the Bulgarians around Lebane and Prokuplje. With the enemy on the defensive, the Partisans could plan more ambitious operations. In mid-May, one reinforced brigade returned to Eastern Serbia with the aim of re-establishing the NOP presence along the Timok. The move provoked a massive reaction by the JVuO and Nedić's authorities. Wherever they went, the Partisans ran into large, if under-equipped and inexperienced enemy formations. Although the Chetniks were badly beaten on the Bukovik on 8 June losing, among else, 150 prisoners, it was clear that the incursion of this kind would have to be carried out with a much larger force. Consequently, the attackers retreated to the Jastrebac a week later.

They returned to Eastern Serbia already on the 20th, this time as a part of the recently-formed 23rd NOVJ Division. Brushing aside the monarchists, the 1,500-strong outfit continued its northeasterly advance when it suddenly ran into a fortified battalion of the 22nd BID blocking the road to Knjaževac. Undeterred, the Partisans attacked. The battle lasted throughout the morning and early afternoon of 30 June; when the guns fell silent, the NOVJ celebrated one of the biggest victories over the Bulgarians yet. For the price of 15 KIA and 45 WIA, the enemy battalion was routed, with over 200 prisoners and 300 pieces of small arms captured. All these

41 Nikolić, *Jugoistočna*, pp. 484-513; NARA/T501/256/753, 772, MBSO, Daily reports (17 and 21.5.1944, respectively).

events did not fail to produce the desired propaganda effect in what otherwise used to be a solidly pro-Chetnik region. While resting in the vicinity of Sokobanja during the first week of July, 23rd Division received over 500 new recruits.[42]

The NOVJ operations in the area between the Southern Morava and Rasina were also proceeding favorably. The units left behind on the liberated territory of Jablanica and Pusta Reka (soon to be combined into the 24th Division) had chiefly defensive tasks, but they also engaged in offensive actions whenever the opportunity presented itself. For instance, the raid against the German airfield outside of Leskovac in late May resulted in three destroyed aircraft. The attack against the town itself, carried out jointly with the 22nd Division one month later, enjoyed only a limited success. In the meantime, the 21st and 22nd Divisions started their expedition against the Chetniks in the southwest. Unimpressed by the half-hearted Bulgarian attempts to intervene (two of their companies from Lebane, led by Communist sympathizers, even defected), the Partisans routed three JVuO corps at Oruglica on 27 and 28 May 1944, inflicting at least ca. 350 losses. It should be noted that the Chetnik ranks were already in disarray as the result of a mutiny against the head of the JVuO's southern command, Major Radoslav Đurić. His downfall was caused by his inactivity and infatuation with a young and beautiful double spy who increasingly meddled in the day-to-day running of the army. Whereas she could not escape her fate, Đurić defected to the Partisans, making him the highest-ranking Chetnik turncoat of the war (he continued on staff duties in the MHQ Serbia for a while, after which he was quietly sidelined). After this victory, the 22nd returned to its home base at Crna Trava, while its sister division continued operating against the JVuO in the area of Međeđa. Once its rear was secured, the 21st veered north in order to invade Keserović's fiefdom with the help of the 25th Division coming from the Jastrebac. The NOVJ onslaught that took place in the latter half of June forced the Axis to abandon the outposts at Blace and Brus and pushed the Chetniks out of Aleksandrovac.[43]

The "red invasion" of the Kopaonik and the poor performance of the Toplica-Rasina Group of Corps led the JVuO's Supreme Command to take drastic measures: the 4th GAC, which was on its way to Sandžak, was ordered to this area instead. The decision was made partly on the Germans' initiative, who had been contemplating a major operation against the main NOP bastion in the country for some time. They themselves could provide ammunition and reliable intelligence (obtained, as usual, through their decryption program), but little in terms of combat units. The Partisans spotted the enemy preparations and hastily withdrew south, abandoning even their forward base on the Jastrebac before the Axis occupied it in the first phase of their summer offensive (codenamed "Trumpf", 10-13 July 1944). In addition to eight Bulgarian, five SFK, and a single reinforced German police battalion, the Axis task force included anywhere between 10 and 14,000 Chetniks equipped with signal flags and white stripes for easier identification.

This massive host now turned to the main Partisan base in the Toplica-Jablanica area (Operations "Kehraus"). The MHQ Serbia–now headed by Koča Popović who had been flown

42 Bosiljčić, *Istočna*, pp. 195-216; Perović, *Južna*, pp. 344-49.

43 Ibid., pp. 396-401; Živojin Nikolić-Brka, *Dvadesetdruga srpska divizija* (Belgrade: Narodna knjiga, 1972), pp. 113-21, 134-43; Ljubinka Škodrić, "Vera Pešić i Radoslav Đurić. Jedna ratna epizoda na jugu Srbije", *Leskovački zbornik*, 59 (2019), pp. 361-79; *Zbornik*/I/21/699-700; NARA/T78/331/6288952, OBSO, Daily report (3.6.1944).

in with a group of veteran officers from the west–decided to launch a pre-emptive strike with the 21st Division against the extreme right flank of the entire enemy front. In spite of some initial success, the plan failed, and the lonely division soon found itself facing nearly the entire 4th GAC. With no alternative left, the NOVJ forces (the 21st, 24th, and 25th Divisions, plus smaller units and numerous camp followers) beat a general retreat towards the border of the Greater Albania. The prevailing assumption that the Albanians[44] would be "fairly easy meat", as one British observer put it, turned out to be dead wrong. Highly-motivated and well-versed in marksmanship and guerrilla tactics, the defenders not only stopped the Partisans, but sent their entire army reeling back in panic (26 July). The latest defeat marked the low ebb of the NOP fortunes so far in the campaign: with the road forward closed, and the vastly superior enemy approaching from the back, Popović's command once again stood on the brink of disaster. Help could come from only one direction: Montenegro.[45]

The 2nd Assault Corps agenda for spring 1944 revolved around interdicting enemy traffic, combatting the Chetniks, internal reorganization, and expansion of the liberated territory. A special, division-sized formation named Coastal Operational Group (*Primorska operativna grupa*, POG) was sent to the southwestern corner of Montenegro already in February. The nationalists responded later the same month by dispatching a 4,000+ strong force to the area north of Cetinje. Despite having much fewer men, the Partisans counterattacked and forced their foe into a panicky flight. In early April, Dapčević launched a major operation in the Zeta Valley, with a twofold purpose: to cut the most important traffic artery in the country (linking the capital with Nikšić) and tap into the still-intact human and economic resources of this region.

Just as the 3rd Assault Division was becoming heavily engaged along the northern side of the road and around Podgorica (the POG was attacking Danilovgrad), the news came that the Axis had launched a sudden offensive in the southern part of Sandžak. This undertaking (nicknamed "Frühlingserwachen") was also carried out largely by the collaborationists and on their own initiative; the Germans provided only some motorized infantry, and artillery support. In the beginning, the attackers made good progress, forcing back the overstretched 37th Sandžak Division to the left bank of the Tara, and taking Bijelo Polje, Berane, and Mojkovac (13-16 April). Since the first, half-hearted counterattack failed to improve the army's fortunes, the HQ of the 2nd Assault Corps brought over nearly the entire 3rd Division from the south. During the last week of April, the now-reinforced Partisans recovered all of the lost territory and compelled the Axis to cancel the operation and withdraw to Pljevlja and Prijepolje.[46]

The close of "Frühlinserwachen" ushered in a period of low-level activity in Montenegro that would last until mid-July 1944. With the Chetniks in disarray and with no reserves of

44 Same as elsewhere, the Germans relied heavily on native auxiliaries in Albania, Kosovo, Macedonia, and Montenegro. The Albanian armed forces in late spring 1944 consisted of the 1st and 4th *Jäger* Regiments (two battalions each), with the latter being posted to the northern part of Kosovo; in addition, there was also the gendarmerie and various militias. The overall strength of all these forces in April was between 10 and 13,500 men: NARA/T314/663/342 and 1066, [both XXI MTC], Memorandum (6.4.1944), and Message to PzAOK 2 (8.6.1944).

45 Trifković, "Serbia", pp. 537-38; *Zbornik*/XIV//3/813 (JVuO 3rd Assault Corps, Order, 9.7.1944), 833 (4th GAC, Order, 15.7.1944); NARA/T78/331/6289173, OBSO, Daily report (11.7.1944); TNA/WO202/196, Report by J.A. Earle (22.9.1944), pp. 4-5.

46 Mitar Đurišić, *Primorska operativna grupa* (Belgrade: VII, 1997), pp. 45-90; Čedo Drulović, *Tridesetsedma sandžačka NOU divizija* (Belgrade: VIZ, 1983), pp. 96-120.

their own, the Germans limited themselves to the defense of communications, patrolling, and local offensive actions. The supply road to Nikšić and its environs, especially the area of Čevo, remained the main flashpoint. Owing to its geographic position, Sandžak was placed under a separate command (the KG "Leeb", later renamed to Higher Command Montenegro), tasked with keeping the NOVJ at arms' length from the Serbian border by means of active defense. Operation "Endlich", for instance, involved a force of at least six German battalions and led to almost two weeks (18-23 June) of heavy–and ultimately successful–fighting against the 3rd Division along the Lim (the division lost more than 160 men).

As in other agriculturally passive regions, like Gorski Kotar or Dalmatia, the NOP's war efforts in Montenegro and Sandžak were seriously affected by the lack of food and fodder. Unlike the Italians in 1942, the Germans could not exploit the situation because they themselves could not even properly feed the population living in the occupied territories. The effects on the battlefield were unmistakable: heavy weapons had to be stored because of the lack of draught animals; the incursion into the area of Rožaje in mid-June, carried out by an equivalent of three brigades, was actually a large-scale foraging/requisitioning expedition. Under such conditions, Dapčević suggested in early July 1944 that the incursion into Serbia, where hunger was unknown, should take place as soon as possible. Tito agreed and released three divisions for this task: Morača's old outfits (the 2nd Proletarian and 5th Krajina), plus the 17th Eastern Bosnian, which had found refuge in Montenegro in the aftermath of Operation "Maibaum".[47]

Informed on these designs almost as soon as they were sent into the ether, the HGF and PzAOK 2 began planning countermeasures. Operation "Draufgänger" targeted the liberated territory on both sides of the Lim between Andrijevica and Berane, the main staging area and supply base of Dapčević's task force. The main thrust, coming from the direction of the Kosovo border, was carried out by one regiment of the 7th SS MTD, and the brigade-sized 21st SS MTD "Skanderbeg". Unlike the veterans of the "Prinz Eugen", who again proved their worth by piercing the NOVJ front and taking Andrijevica (19 July), the latest[48] addition to Himmler's Balkan legions proved to be a major disappointment. Raised from among (rather unwilling, as it turned out) ethnic Albanians in the spring of 1944, this was the units' first real battle. Much to their regret, they found themselves facing some of the toughest outfits in the Partisan army. Although under orders not to get involved into potentially costly battles before reaching the Serbian soil, Dapčević chose not to leave before restoring the situation in his rear. In a classic maneuver, the reinforced 5th Krajina first broke through the "Skanderbeg's" positions, took the Čakor Pass, and then joined hands with the 3rd Division advancing from the west three days later (26 July). In this way, the entire SS attack force was surrounded. Much to the Partisan general's regret, he could not finish the job. Concerned by the increasingly dramatic situation in

47 See the XXI MTC's monthly reports in NARA/T314/663/745-50 (12.5.1944), 1117-18, 1123, 1131 (13.6.1944), and NARA/T314/664/204, 209-10, 220 (13.7.1944); NARA/T314/663/679 [all XXI MTC] (Daily report, 5.5.1944), 1167 (Message to 21st SS MTD, 16.6.1944), 1366-67 (Diary, 12.7.1944); NARA/T78/331/6289048 and 6289112-13, OBSO, Daily report (18 and 30.6.1944, respectively); *Zbornik*/III/7/404 (2nd NOVJC to SHQ, 13.4.1944), 664-65 (2nd NOVJC to 2nd and 3rd NOVJDs, 17.6.1944); *Zbornik*/I/16/593-96, 37th NOVJD to 2nd NOVJC (17.7.1944); *SD*/XXI/96-97, 315, Tito to Dapčević (9.7.1944).

48 The "Skanderbeg" was followed by the 23rd SS MTD "Kama", which was formed in May-June 1944 around a core of veterans from the "Handschar". However, the experiment failed miserably, and the "division" was dissolved already in late October: Lepre, *Handschar*, pp. 228, 256-57, 266.

Southern Serbia, Tito sent him no less than five cables during the past week, urging immediate action and threatening punishment in the case of non-compliance. Leaving the 3rd Division to reduce the cauldron (which it failed to do), Dapčević took his command, dubbed Operational Group of Divisions (OGD), across Sandžak and towards the Ibar.[49]

The march was complete by 2 August 1944. Thanks to the wise decision to maintain strict radio silence, the Germans admittedly knew that the OGD was on the move but were in the dark concerning its strength or ultimate objectives. On the one hand, it was high summer and no boats were needed to cross the river this time; on the other, the Axis defenses were incomparably stronger now than in March. Rather than leaving it in Greece to watch over Napoleon Zervas or to serve as a reassurance against a possible Turkish invasion of Bulgaria, Berlin decided to use its strategic reserve, the 1st MTD, for another large-scale undertaking in Montenegro. As it happened, the bulk of the division was beginning to arrive to the Ibar just as the OGD was preparing to cross it. Surging forward in three divisional columns, the Partisans broke through across the railway line on 3-4 August, inflicting heavy losses to the defenders who barely had the opportunity to leave their trains and deploy for battle.

Inexplicably, the HQ of the Wehrmacht's premier mountain formation chose to declare victory, stating that only a handful of guerrillas made it to the right bank. The festive mood was spoiled by an intercepted cable from the MHQ Serbia reporting on the arrival of three full divisions to the Kopaonik. Felber then arranged for an intervention by the only reserve he still had left, the 4th GAC. Immediately ceasing all activities against Popović's hard-pressed command, the Chetniks rushed to meet the new peril from the west. The two forces clashed in the area of Brus on 7 August. After a full day's worth of fighting, most of it in thick fog, the Partisans ultimately managed to outflank their foe and send him into a headlong retreat. The surviving casualty figures are incomplete, but it is certain that the 4th GAC lost hundreds of men to desertion. Finally, on 11 August, the advanced guard of the OGD joined hands with the 21st Division south of Kuršumlija.[50]

Although important, Dapčević's incursion was but a part of Tito's master plan for the re-conquest of the Yugoslav heartland. The other major component involved getting as many divisions as possible from Bosnia to the western part of Serbia. The PzAOK 2 relied on signals intelligence and liberal application of the "free hunt" tactics in order to counter these moves. Ever since it reached Kupres in the aftermath of Drvar, the 1st Proletarian Division stood under constant pressure. In Operation "Amor" (12 June-1 July 1944), the V SS MTC threw eight battalions (a good half of them from the "Prinz Eugen") against it in the area between Bugojno and Konjic. The ferocity of the fighting reminded the Partisan veterans of the battles on the Neretva and Sutjeska, and Phleps noted in his diary that the foe was "very well led and trained, fights in a regular manner". In spite of the heavy losses–not crippling, as the Germans led themselves to believe–the 1st Proletarian managed to outmaneuver its pursuers, skirt Sarajevo from the south, and finally cross the Drina into Sandžak on 6 July. There, it

49 Trifković, "Serbia", pp. 539-40. The "Draufgänger" cost the NOVJ ca. 60 KIA and 200 WIA, and the Germans 100 KIA, 303 WIA, 454 MIA, the majority of them being Albanian recruits.

50 Ibid., pp. 540-42; NARA/T311/191/891-92, OBSO to OKW (11.7.1944); NARA/T311/192/833, OBSO, Diary (17.7.1944).

enjoyed a well-deserved five week's rest, during which it prepared for the continuation of the march to Serbia.[51]

Other divisions had an equally tough, if not tougher, time. Coming from the west, the 11th Krajina Division made two unsuccessful attempts to ford the Bosna at Begov Han on 29-30 July 1944. On the next day, the ubiquitous 7th SS, together with NDH units, counterattacked and nearly encircled the division on the left bank of the river (Operation "Feuerwehr"). Barely escaping destruction, the 11th moved north and made an unopposed crossing between Doboj and Derventa one week later. Once in Eastern Bosnia, the Krajina fighters became embroiled in constant fighting against the Germans, Chetniks, and Muslim militias. It took until mid-September before they could force their way through "Handschar's" dense security zone and move closer to the Drina.

In the meanwhile, the 6th Lika Division was fighting a running battle with the Germans practically since it started its journey from Glamoč on 17 July. After leaving all its wounded and sick in the care of the 8th Corps, the division went east, crossed the Bosna around Nemila on the 28th, and moved to the area northwest of Sokolac, where it met the units of the newly-formed 12th Vojvodina Corps (the 16th and 36th Divisions). Together, these three formations embarked on one of the most grueling marches in the annals of the Partisan war; by the time it was over, the Vojvodina units had crossed 800 km over some of the worst terrain in the entire Yugoslavia. Constantly harassed by the free-hunting SS mountain troops (Operation "Hackfleisch"), the corps very nearly imploded as the result of sickness, extreme fatigue, and hunger, all of which claimed dozens of lives and hundreds of stragglers. By the end of August, the exhausted Partisans had reached the blood-soaked battlefield of Sutjeska, where they hoped to find Allied aid and friendly units of the 2nd Corps waiting for them. Instead, it turned out that they merely jumped out of the proverbial frying pan and into the fire.[52]

"A general cleansing of Montenegro" by 1st MTD had been contemplated since the early summer 1944. After briefly considering sending the division after Dapčević, the Wehrmacht's Balkan command decided to stick to the original plan. It involved a concentric advance against the homeland of the 2nd Assault Corps from the east (the 1st MTD), northeast (the 14th SS MTR and 2nd "Brandenburg" Regiment) and south (the 363rd GR), in hope of catching the NOVJ units before they could set foot into Serbia. The stakes were so high that von Weichs called the upcoming battle (codename: "Rübezahl") "the most important operation since the beginning of the war". The Axis commenced their assault on 12 August. The Partisans, under orders to conserve strength, fought only when absolutely necessary, at the same time looking for weak spots in the encirclement ring. The 1st Proletarian thus skirted around the enemy garrison at Pljevlja, took the undefended Lim crossing at Priboj, and reached Mount Zlatibor by the 23rd; shortly thereafter, the 37th Division took positions on its right flank.

In the meanwhile, the 3rd Assault had to retreat under fire all the way from Berane to the eastern slopes of the Durmitor, with the 1st MTD in hot pursuit. For several days, it looked like another Sutjeska was in the offing: on the opposite side of the mountain, the 12th Corps and the 6th Division were barely holding their own against the 7th SS. The Partisans were, in

51 NARA/T78/331/6289022, OBSO, Daily report (14.6.1944); Radošević, *Prva*, Vol. II, pp. 197-251; Kumm, *Vorwärts*, pp. 225-37.

52 Samardžija, *Jedanaesta*, pp. 181-94; Orlović, *Šesta*, pp. 401-09; Paško Romac, *Kazivanje o Šesnaestoj vojvođanskoj diviziji* (Novi Sad: ISI, 1979), pp. 196-226.

fact, trading blood for time, protecting the massive airlift of their wounded and non-combat personnel from the airstrip at Gornja Brezna. As soon as the last Allied transport had left on 23 August, the guerrillas disengaged. The Vojvodina units marched across the waterless Golija, and the bone-strewn Zelengora, before finally crossing the Drina at Stari Brod two weeks later. The Lika division headed into the opposite direction, across the Tara, establishing contact with the 1st Proletarian by the end of August. While en route to the area of Kolašin, the 3rd Assault routed the 2nd "Iron" Regiment of the MFK at Krnovo on 25 August, netting some 300 prisoners (interestingly, German documents make no mention of this incident). The rest of the journey was largely uneventful, for the HGF had already canceled the "Rübezahl" and begun hastily redeploying the bulk of its troops to Eastern Serbia in response to the news of Romania's exit from the war.[53]

With Romania lost, everyone knew Bulgaria would soon follow. This placed Felber in a tight spot, for every second men of his ca. 65,000-strong command belonged to the I BOC. With the exception of the five regiments of the SFK and the all-German 5th SS PR, the remainder was practically useless for active operations. Faced with the ever-growing Partisan encroachment, the Reich's top military and political representatives in Serbia gave their support for Nedić's initiative for the creation of a united nationalist front. Mihailović could hardly refuse this offer and thousands of pieces of infantry weapons and ammunition that came with it. Although the actual deliveries were delayed by his clumsy proclamation of general mobilization on 1 September (which Berlin took as a hostile act), the alliance would largely remain in place for the remainder of the campaign.

The situation on the front definitely demanded it. Leaving the 37th Division on guard duties, the 1st Proletarian, soon to be joined by the 6th Lika, continued its advance across the Zlatibor. Apart from the bloody and entirely unjustified attack on a fortified Bulgarian battalion at Palisad, which claimed most of the 49 dead and 95 wounded fighters the 1st Proletarian had since crossing the Uvac, the march was completed without difficulties. By 3 September, both divisions–acting again as the 1st Proletarian Corps–had taken position along the line running from Mokra Gora to Arilje, where they planned to wait for the 12th Corps before resuming the offensive. Summoned several days earlier by the worried Mihailović, the 4th GAC was now beginning to arrive from Southern Serbia. On 5 September, Račić's men, together with one German police battalion, attacked the exposed right flank of the 1st Proletarian Corps, pushing the hard-pressed 6th Lika to the area south of Požega and re-establishing connection to Užice. At the same time, the other NOVJ division launched its own assault on the opposite side of the line, quickly reaching the area between Rogačica and Kosjerić. In reaction to this direct threat to his HQ at the nearby Ravna Gora, Mihailović ordered the entire 4th GAC to this area. Both sides set their sights on a low mountain called Jelova Gora. The attacking JVuO pitted five corps with ca. 12,000 men against altogether four Partisans brigades (the entire 1st Proletarian Corps may have had about 6,000 fighters). Although outnumbered, the latter enjoyed practically every other advantage: they were lavishly equipped with light weapons and even had a handful of

53 Drulović, *Tridesetsedma*, p. 152; Pajović, *Kontrarevolucija*, p. 92; Trifković, "Serbia", pp. 543-44. Both sides claimed to have killed more than 2,000 enemy soldiers during the "Rübezahl", but this can be safely ignored. The Germans reported destroying or capturing ca. 800 pieces of small arms and six cannon of various types: NARA/T311/193/864, OBSO to OKW (21.9.1944).

mountain guns, recently delivered to a forward airstrip; unlike many monarchists, who were forcefully mobilized after 1 September, the Partisans were largely veteran-volunteers.[54]

One of the last major clashes of the Chetnik-Partisan war began on 8 September 1944 with a series of all-out "brazen" frontal assaults against the NOVJ defenses. Although the lines held, the situation was dire enough to warrant the convening of a council of war, where some officers even proposed retiring to Sandžak. In the end, aggressive heads prevailed, and it was decided to go over to the counterattack with the aid of the freshly arrived 1st Proletarian Brigade. Aided by intense mortar fire that "tore apart" entire enemy units, the Partisans surged forward in the early hours of 9 September. By mid-morning, the Chetnik army was in full flight towards the north and northeast; its trail was allegedly marked by lumps of facial hair, as Mihailović's veterans tried to hide their past by shaving off their trademark beards. A final blow to their moral came on 12 September, as King Peter II called upon all his subjects to join the NOVJ (the speech was made over the BBC on Churchill's insistence). One day later, the 12th Corps reached the Jadar Valley, while the 1st Proletarian Corps arrived before the gates of Valjevo. In the subsequent attack, the Lika fighters broke into the town and surrounded the remnants of two German police battalions in the old army barracks. Their destruction was averted in the last moment by the arrival of an all-German relief column from the east. Neither side had the intention of getting bogged in a major clash over Valjevo. Consequently, on 17 September, the Germans loaded the wounded and survivors onto trucks and departed for Ub; the Partisans, for their part, pulled back to the southern bank of the Kolubara. Further west, the 11th Krajina Division had finally made it across the Drina and entered Krupanj, the scene of one of the insurgents' earliest triumphs from 1941. After having "extorted" more ammunition from the Germans, the reorganized 4th GAC, supported by some Majevica units, pushed the Partisans out of the town on 19 September. Victory proved to be short-lived, however. The 12th Corps counterattacked two days later, routed the Chetniks on Mount Cer and forced Mihailović to seek refuge in Bosnia; by the end of the month, the Vojvodina units stood before Šabac.[55]

According to the original plan, Dapčević's unit were supposed to stay in Southern Serbia no longer than a week or so before moving north but ended up staying almost a month. The reason for the delay lay in the tough resistance offered by the enemy and the fact that this ambitious timetable did not take into account the exhausted state of the OGD. The campaign had an auspicious opening: on 12 August 1944, the elements of the 2nd and 5th Divisions routed a battalion of the 122nd BIR coming from Kuršumlija, causing a loss of more than 300 men. The subsequent attack on the town itself, however, did not succeed. Apart from some desultory fighting on the western slopes of the Jastrebac and low-level guerrilla activity, the next two weeks passed peacefully. The Partisans used the pause to rest and reorganize; in exchange for the 2nd Proletarian, which was subordinated to the MHQ Serbia, the OGD received the best local division, the 21st. On 26 August, the peace was shattered by a sudden Chetnik offensive in Župa and the Rasina Valley. Within three days, the 17th Eastern Bosnian was pushed from Razbojna, Brus, and Aleksandrovac. Before Dapčević could put in motion his ambitious plan

54 Ibid., pp. 545-51; *Zbornik*/I/11/155, 1st NOVJD to SHQ (27.8.1944).

55 Trifković, "Serbia", pp. 551-53; Borivoje M. Karapandžić, *Građanski rat u Srbiji 1941-1945* (Valjevo: Novo videlo, 2010), p. 311; Samardžija, *Jedanaesta*, pp. 197-208. According to preliminary reports, the JVuO had around 400 bloody losses at Jelova Gora, the NOVJ's much less (the precise figures were never properly established).

calling for an encirclement battle, the 4th GAC and Toplica-Jablanica Group of Corps withdrew to the line Aleksandrovac–Trstenik; soon thereafter, Račić departed with his command towards Užice.

With the Chetniks out of the way, the OGD could start its own journey northwest. The first objective was to reach the upper reaches of the Western Morava and link up with the 1st Proletarian Corps. The march began on 6 September and lasted a week. Tito's instruction not to lose time and blood over insignificant targets went unheeded and Dapčević attacked Užice and Čačak, only to be repulsed by the newly-arrived 7th SS MTD. Leaving these places behind–which the Germans would evacuate shortly thereafter–the OGD continued its drive into Šumadija (it was the approach of these forces that caused the 1st Proletarian Corps to cease all activities in the Valjevo area and direct its efforts towards the southeast instead). The campaign culminated in the fierce twin-battle for Gornji Milanovac and Aranđelovac on 19-20 September, during which the Partisans captured nearly 1,000 Nedić's gendarmes, Ljotić's volunteers, and Chetniks. This episode is notable for the fact that the 5th Krajina attacked an enemy garrison during daylight for the first time in its history. The Partisans also managed to repel a German relief column, something that happened only rarely during the war. On this particular occasion, the 1st "Brandenburg" Regiment lost almost 100 men, which in turn led to the downsizing of Operation "Zirkus", an attempt to destroy the OGD in the Čačak–Topola–Lajkovac triangle using the reinforced "Prinz Eugen". By the end of the month, the Germans had succeeded in pushing the enemy away from the Belrgade–Niš road, but the rapidly deteriorating situation in the east forced them to effectively surrender this part of the country to the NOVJ.[56]

At the end, a few lines on the operations of the MHQ Serbia in the mid- and late summer of 1944. On 26 July, in wake of the ignominious defeat at the hands of Albanian auxiliaries, three NOVJ divisions prepared themselves for another breakthrough attempt. The 21st and 24th Divisions would try to reach their old bases in Toplica going via Mount Kukavica, while the 25th Division would strike east, towards the right bank of the Southern Morava. Whereas the 25th had little difficulties in reaching its objective, the 21st and 24th saw some heavy fighting on their way to the Radan. Their efforts were profoundly aided by Dapčević's breakthrough across the Ibar, which led to the cancellation of the "Kehraus" and departure of the 4th GAC for the Kopaonik (the 27th BID also returned to its garrisons).[57] Popović immediately went onto offensive, sending the 21st Division towards Kuršumlija, and ordering the 25th to link up with the 23rd in Eastern Serbia; the operational areas of the remaining two outfits remained the same. Following the end of the Chetnik offensive from late August, the 2nd Proletarian Division started its own campaign in the wider Rasina region. In addition to constant skirmishing around Kruševac, one NOVJ brigade crossed the Western Morava on 18 September. The incursion, however, met with unexpectedly heavy resistance by the Chetniks, and the Partisans were forced to withdraw after losing at least 60 prisoners and a substantial haul of equipment. Keserović retained the initiative, took Aleksandrovac and forced the 2nd Proletarian to retire to the right bank of the Rasina on the 26th. In order to bolster the division's

56 Morača, *Peta*, pp. 257-77; Mandić, *Sedamnaesta*, pp. 223-45; NARA/T311/193/847, OBSO, Daily report (21.9.1944); Trifković, "Serbia", pp. 553-54.

57 The Partisans suffered ca. 500 casualties during the "Trumpf"/"Kehraus"; the combined losses of all their enemies amounted to less than one-fifth of that number: Ibid., p. 539.

left flank, one brigade of the 24th NOVJD was dispatched from Prokuplje by train, something that had not been seen in Serbia since late 1941.[58]

The operations of the remaining Serbian divisions were greatly aided by Bulgaria's change of sides on 8 September 1944. Same as during the Italian capitulation exactly one year before, all sides vied for the weaponry and supplies of the I BOC, whose transfer out of the country had begun already in the last week of August. With the announcement of the news from Sofia, however, the withdrawal turned into a rout: discipline collapsed and soldiers marched home on their own, simply leaving all heavy equipment behind. Admittedly, most of it fell into German and Chetnik hands, but the Partisans got the territory and resources that went with it. Until mid-September, the entire southeastern part of the country, except for Niš, Leskovac, Vlasotince, and the strategically important mines at Mačkatica, was in the hands of the newly-formed 13th NOVJ Corps (the 22nd and 24th Divisions, plus no less than 18 detachments). The NOP was going through a renaissance in Eastern Serbia as well. The 23rd Division spent the entire July locked in a mortal struggle with the Chetniks. Just how important this fight was for the Chetniks is evident from the fact that their efforts were coordinated by none other than General Miroslav Trifunović, Mihailović's chief commander in Serbia. The decisive clash took place on the 24th halfway between Sokobanja and Paraćin. Despite being heavily outnumbered, two Partisan brigades made an uphill attack and pushed the Greater Morava Group of Corps from its fortified positions on Mount Bukovik. The intensity of the struggle is evident from the number and composition of the casualties: the NOVJ lost 43 KIA and 63 WIA, which puts this battle on pair with Jelova Gora or Brus; in addition to 160 prisoners and over 300 pieces of small arms, the aforementioned group of corps lost its commander and his entire staff to a well-placed mortar round. The propaganda effect could still be felt four days later, when two Chetnik battalions surrendered after only a brief firefight; the defection of some 100 monarchists on this occasion helped make up the losses suffered at the Bukovik.[59]

In order to aid the 23rd Division in its efforts and bolster the overall NOP presence in the region, the MHQ Serbia sent the 25th Division north in mid-August 1944. The division made a seven-day sweep of the Svrljig Mountains before continuing to the area of Sokobanja, where it established contact with its sister outfit. After much deliberation and a pointless trip to Niš, which was supposed to be "inherited" from the withdrawing Bulgarians, the two formations were ordered to advance towards the Timok. The road to the eastern state border had been opened already on 26-28 August, when the 25th defeated a mixed enemy force around Rtanj and Boljevac. The campaign culminated in the storming of Zaječar, which fell on 7 September after a day-and-a-half of bitter and costly fighting. Although a part of the garrison managed to escape in the direction of Bor, the Partisans took over 1,000 prisoners with their weapons; at least 600 of these were Germans from two auxiliary police battalions, which were subsequently stricken from the official roster. The 23rd Division, minus some 140 of its members who were

58 *Zbornik*/I/20/695-701, MHQ Serbia to General Anatoli P. Gorshkov (14.9.1944); Dobrivoje Jovanović, Dejan Tanić (eds.), *Izveštaji komande Srpske državne straže za Okrug moravski 1941-1944* (Jagodina: Istorijski arhiv Jagodina, 2001), p. 148 (entry 196/1944); *Zbornik*/I/12/505-31, MHQ Serbia, Diary (11-28.9.1944).

59 Mitrovski, Glišić, Ristovski, *Bugarska*, pp. 193-95; *Enciklopedija*, Vol. X, p. 131; *Zbornik*/I/11/338-41, 13th NOVJC, Circular (7.9.1944); Miladin Ivanović, *Dvadesettreća srpska divizija* (Belgrade: Savez udruženja boraca NOR-a [hereinafter: SUBNOR], 1994), pp. 75-95.

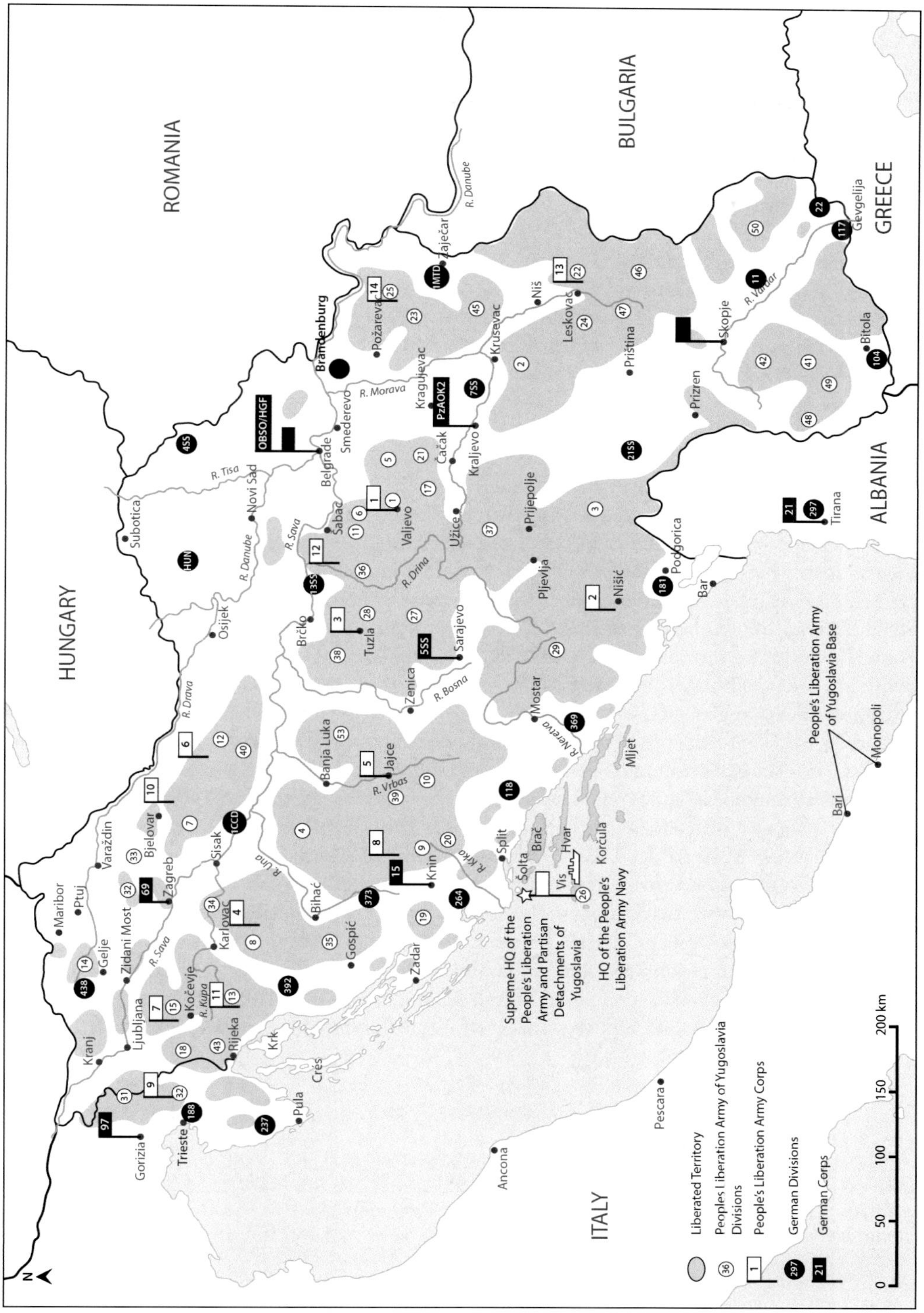

Map 11: Situation in Yugoslavia (September 1944).

either killed or wounded in the battle, had to leave the town only two days later owing to the arrival of the 1st MTD from Montenegro. Both sides were now racing towards the Danube, but it was ultimately the Germans who got to occupy its bank. The Serbian divisions, still too weak to face the best the Wehrmacht could offer in an open fight, withdrew to the interior and took positions along the narrow mountain roads leading west from Negotin and Bor.[60]

6.6 Summer 1944: Germans On Defensive

After the failure of the raid against Drvar, the Germans saw themselves compelled to go over to defensive in practically the entire country. The NOVJ, which was just beginning to come out of its winter torpor, could not take advantage of the situation immediately. One of its main tasks during the summer months of 1944 was to protect the harvest. In late March, Tito personally ordered the army to do its utmost to help the civilian authorities with agricultural works. Much to everyone's relief, the crop yield that year turned out to be unusually plentiful, which ensured both stability in the rear areas and functioning of the field units. There were several factors that favored taking the initiative. The practically uninterrupted string of defeats suffered by the Third Reich since the beginning of 1944 culminated in the disastrous Jassy-Kishinev affair, which led to the defection of Romania and Bulgaria, and brought he Red Army to the Danube. These events convinced all but a handful of the most ardent collaborationists that the German cause was lost. The NOP leadership chose the right moment to proclaim a general amnesty, guaranteeing life and rank to all members of native Axis formations (excluding the Ustashe) who defected until 15 September. In addition to the tidal wave of desertions from the NDH as well as its own legionnaire formations, the PzAOK 2 was confronted with the near-critical shortage of troops. In order to bolster the defenses on Serbia's eastern borders, the army had to surrender two "Brandenburg" regiments, as well as one regimental combat team each from the 118th JD, 181st and 264th IDs. This, in turn, would lead to the evacuation of a significant portion of the interior, and concentration in and around larger garrisons and main railway lines.[61]

From June through August 1944, the 5th NOVJ corps averaged close to 140 actions a month, but the vast majority of these were typical guerrilla attacks against enemy traffic and smaller targets. The capture of Kozarac, Teslić, Tešanj, and Gornji Vakuf between 7 and 29 July, which brought significant number of prisoners and booty, represent notable exceptions to the rule. No similar episodes took place during the following month, but the worsening situation in the enemy camp did not escape the Partisans. Consequently, they set themselves an ambitious agenda for September: to liberate the Vrbas and Sana Valleys in their entirety, and at least temporarily block the flow of enemy traffic along the Bosna River. The operation produced mixed results. The 4th Krajina Division successfully stormed Prijedor and Ljubija on the 7th; a

60 Ibid., pp. 95-148; Milojica Pantelić, *Dvadesetpeta srpska NOU divizija* (Belgrade: VIZ, 1977), pp. 51-68.

61 *Zbornik*/V/25/634-35, MHQ Croatia to 6th and 8th NOVJCs (21.3.1944); *Zbornik*/IV/26/325-26, 4th NOVJD, Circular (25.6.1944); *Zbornik*/V/31/178 and 234, 6th NOVJC to MHQ Croatia (10 and 16.8.1944, respectively); *SD*/XXII/270-71, To all misled lackeys of occupier (30.8.1944); Erich Schmidt-Richberg, *Der Endkampf auf dem Balkan: Die Operationen der Heeresgruppe E von Griechenland bis zu den Alpen* (Heidelberg: Kurt Vowinckel Verlag, 1955), pp. 27-28; NARA/T77/780/5506957, Army Detachment Serbia [*Armeeabteilung Serbien*, AAS], Campaign from August to October 1944 (4.11.1944).

large part of the garrison was caught in the open while trying to escape, and was either killed or taken prisoner. On that same day, an entire HDB regiment surrendered to the new Central Bosnian Division (later renamed the 53rd) in Derventa. The same NOVJ formation broke into Doboj, the third-most important urban center in the Bosna Valley, but failed to finish off the garrison before the arrival of a relief force. The 10th Krajina Division occupied the upper Vrbas Valley, which had been abandoned without a fight by the Axis, and advanced to the outskirts of Travnik.

The crowning achievement of the campaign was supposed to be the taking of Banja Luka. From 18 to 21 September, the Partisans (the bulk of the 4th, 39th, and the 53rd Divisions) reduced the heavily fortified city except for the Kastel, where several hundred men were still holding out. The 5th Corps also took nearly all strongpoints along the road to Bosanska Gradiška, including the fully provisioned Zalužani airfield. Prompted by desperate pleas from Zagreb (which, as always, feared a propaganda meltdown if Banja Luka fell), and the fate of its own surrounded men, the HGF reluctantly authorized a rescue mission, to be carried out by elements of the 1st CCD and the "von Rudno" Assault Brigade. With the battle now entering its ninth day, the Partisans decided they had enough and began pulling out; the exhausted defenders were relieved on the 27th. Despite its less-than-glamorous ending, the September campaign was an unqualified success for Slavko Rodić's command: 2,863 prisoners–including Karl von Dewitz-Krebs, the only German army general to be captured in Yugoslavia prior to May 1945–as well as 5,676 defectors were brought in. Among the huge haul of captured material, there were also eight serviceable airplanes; armed with improvised incendiary bombs, they were immediately used to bombard the Kastel. The victory did not come cheap: during the same period, the 5th Corps lost 330 KIA, 797 WIA, and 59 MIA.[62]

The Eastern Bosnian Partisans' greatest victory occurred at the very beginning, rather than the end, of the spring-summer campaign of 1944. In response to Tito's call for more heat in enemy rear during the Battle of Drvar, the 3rd NOVJ Corps decided to launch an incursion into the Majevica with three division-sized columns. The "Handschar" countered by launching Operation "Vollmond" with four battalions. The 16th Vojvodina routed one of them in a sudden night attack on Lopare (8-9 June), capturing an entire battery of 150mm cannon in the process. Less encouraging were the news, obtained from captured documents, that the entire corps was walking into a trap. Feeling they had done enough, the Partisans dispersed, with the Vojvodina units moving to the area between the Spreča and Krivaja Rivers, while the 38th Eastern Bosnian returned to Šekovići. The period from mid-June to mid-July passed in comparative peace. With the two Vojvodina divisions gone to the 12th Corps, the NOVJ's regional command was left with two divisions, which, however, had only three brigades between them.

The Germans launched two larger operations during the second half of July, one against the guerrilla airstrip at Osmaci, and the other against their supply bases in Šekovići. The latter undertaking ("Heidenrose") involved a force of five battalions from the "Handschar" and "Prinz Eugen", and was a huge success in material terms. Although the Partisans again made good their escape, the attackers seized 800 rifles and 500,000 rounds of ammunition. August was marked by fighting of low intensity, as confirmed by the rather modest casualty figures for

62 Karasijević, *Peti*, pp. 249-91; Lazarević, *Vazduhoplovstvo*, pp. 107-10; *Zbornik*/IV/30/426-27, 5th NOVJC, Monthly report (September 1944).

the 3rd Corps (40 KIA, 92 WIA). Among else, the 38th Division returned to Šekovići, the 11th was thwarted from reaching the Drina, and the 27th attacked the Ustashe stronghold at Srebrenica for the second time in as many months, without success. As in the rest of the country, the Partisans' efforts in September were greatly facilitated by the accelerating disintegration of Axis formations. The once-mighty 13th SS was especially hard-hit, having over 2,000 deserters, at least a third of whom opted to join the NOVJ. The Germans decided to surrender the bulk of the division's former security zone and withdraw to a bridgehead in the area Bijeljina–Brčko. With their main prop thus removed, native collaborationist units could not hope to withstand the "red flood" coming from the south. Kladanj fell on the 1st, followed by Zvornik on the 13th, Živinice and Kalesija on the 15th, Gračanica and Srebrenik on the 24th. The main prize, Tuzla, was captured after a brief fight already on the 17th, together with about 500 of its defenders. The NOVJ now had a firm and conveniently located platform for future operations, be it in the direction of the Serbian border, Sarajevo, or the valleys of Bosna and Sava.[63]

The focal point of the NOVJ activity on the Dalmatian mainland was still located in the northern parts of the province. Using the low karst plateau of Bukovica as its base, the 19th Division began operating towards Ravni Kotari in June 1944, reducing several collaborationist strongholds in the process. By July, the Partisans had rendered the road communications to and from Zadar nearly unusable, and, at the same time, opened up their own supply channel linking Vis with the interior. In response, the 264th ID carried out Operation "Pestbeule" (14-19 July), which succeed in temporarily removing the NOVJ presence in the coastal sector. During the next 10 days, the attackers succeeded in pushing the 19th Division to the northern bank of the Zrmanja. In order to help their hard-pressed comrades, the remaining two divisions of the 8th Corps, the 9th and 20th, launched a major assault in the upper Cetina Valley. After reducing the NDH strongpoint at Vrlika, both formations continued towards the main road to the south and north of Knin. An enemy intervention, however, forced the Partisans to withdraw to the Dinara.

By the end of August, the 19th was back at the Bukovica (the Germans had no strength to occupy it permanently), while its sister formations moved north in preparation for the storming of Gračac. The operation, which was supposed to achieve a link-up between the liberated territories in Dalmatia and Lika, ended in failure: the town and its mixed German-Chetnik garrison proved to be "a nut" too hard to crack. After the failure of both attacks on 28-29 August, the Partisans tried to blockade it (just like they did with the nearby Korenica in early 1942), but soon had to give up owing to the increasing Axis pressure from the direction of Gospić. September would pass in low-level activity with the exception of the storming of Benkovac on the 9th. According to the Germans, the town was lost due to the panicky flight of the Ustashe, who were apparently not immune to the news from the main fronts and increased enemy propaganda. On this occasion, the 19th Division managed to capture ca. 500 pieces of infantry weapons and liberate 75 NOP members from the local jail before being forced to leave the town on the next day. In the meanwhile, the flames of resistance in the remainder of Dalmatia were kept alive by territorial units, most notably the Southern Dalmatian GoD. Its attacks on traffic, infrastructure, patrols, etc., provoked the 118th JD and 369th ID into

63 See the 3rd NOVJC's monthly reports June-August 1944 (*Zbornik*/IV/27/202-208, *Zbornik*/IV/29/397-403 and 514-20), as well as its cables sent to the SHQ in September 1944 in ibid., pp. 537-53; Lepre, *Handschar*, pp. 213-75.

launching regiment-level sweeps once or even twice a month, usually without much success (e.g. "Morgenrot" at Makarska, "Schweissperle" at Vrgorac, "Wolfshöhle" on Pelješac, "Irrgarten" in the Neretva Delta).[64]

The Lika summer campaign consisted of a series of alternating thrusts by the 11th NOVJ Corps' 35th Division on the one, and the 4th UAB and 392nd ID on the other side, against each other's territories. In early July 1944, the Partisans broke through the Ustasha defenses just north of Gospić but were forced to retreat by an Axis counterattack in the direction of Korenica. Satisfied with having removed the immediate threat to the main supply road, the Germans and their auxiliaries paused for several weeks before resuming their eastward drive. The objective of the undertaking was evident from its rather ungainly Croatian name: "Operation on the Krbava Field for the Purpose of Capturing the Harvest". From 8 to 18 August, a force of five German, six NDH, and two Chetnik battalions ravaged the area of Korenica, capturing at least 400 tons of precious wheat before returning to their garrisons. The entire process was repeated again in early September, when the appearance of the Partisans south of Otočac provoked another Axis punitive expedition towards the western slopes of the Plješevica. In the meantime, the 13th NOVJ Division was operating against enemy targets in the triangle Rijeka–Ogulin–Senj. The Partisans withstood several enemy incursions into the Velika Kapela, most notably Operation "Florett" (30 June–4 July), and tried in vain to establish a foothold on the coast at Crikvenica. Their most successful action was the storming of Drežnica on 13 July, held by one company of the 392nd ID. Since a German-held outpost was never before taken in a direct attack, General Mickl decided to punish the responsible officers with several months in prison. August saw some heavy fighting in the areas of Vrbovsko and Fužine against Axis columns peddling between the sea and the interior. In late September, the 13th again tried moving its positions closer to the Adriatic by attacking the German outpost at Zlobin. The success of Drežnica was not repeated for two reasons: first, the Partisans failed to properly seal off the place; second, they overestimated the impact of Tito's amnesty and thought–erroneously, as it turned out–that the Croatian legionnaires would not fight. In all, between 20 June and 20 September, the 392nd ID lost 104 KIA, 410 WIA, and 55 MIA (the subordinated UV units lost 69/154/35, respectively); the majority of these were not incurred in the above-mentioned operations, but in the so-called "Canyon of Death", the stretch of road between Tounj and Generalski Stol, the guerrillas' favorite ambush spot.[65]

While all this was happening in Gorski Kotar, the NOP in Istria was experiencing one of its periodical upswings, caused this time by the transfer of a substantial part of German effectives (including the 278th ID) to the Italian front. During the spring and summer months, the guerrilla activity was primarily directed against the Trieste–Rijeka road and railway line, as well as against the Italian collaborationist outposts in the central and western part of the peninsula. Attacks on German-held places were seldom attempted, and with good reason: the Partisans lost 13 KIA and 29 WIA at Raša on 3 August with little to show for it. With landing season in full swing, Berlin could not afford to leave Istria's long shoreline undefended. The

64 See the South Dalmatian Group of Detachments' activity reports for June and August 1944 in *Zbornik*/V/29/245-58 and *Zbornik*/V/33/125-30, respectively; see also 8th NOVJ Corps' report for the period July through early September 1944 in ibid., pp. 313-63; NARA/T311/193/400, OBSO, Daily report (10.9.1944).

65 Schraml, *Kriegsschauplatz*, pp. 254-67; Kleut, *Jedanaesti*, pp. 185-234, 237-65, 274-89, 291-98.

arrival of the 237th ID signaled the end of the Partisan "revival", and they withdrew nearly all their forces to the rugged area of Klana. Despite this, the successful outcome of the campaign could not be doubted: the number of brigades went up from one to three, all of which became part of the new 43rd Istrian Division in late August. Facing supply shortages and a threat of encirclement, the divisional HQ requested and received the permission from the 11th Corps one month later to send the bulk of its units to Primorska and Gorski Kotar. As a consequence, the NOVJ troop presence in the peninsula again dropped to pre-summer levels (one brigade plus two detachments).[66]

The early summer weeks of 1944 was extraordinarily busy for the 4th NOVJ Corps. The main event in Banija was the storming of Komarevo by the reinforced 7th Division on 7 June. On this occasion, the Cossacks lost 24 KIA and 39 WIA, but the Partisan suffered roughly the same number of dead and almost three times as many wounded. During the same period, the Una OG was struggling to maintain the NOP's grip on Cazinska Krajina against increasingly refined enemy tactics. In Operation "Mausetot" (19-24 July 1944), the 373rd ID managed to incite a rebellion and subsequent defection of some 340 Muslims from Pećigrad through agents and propaganda (Yugoslav sources do not mention this incident). After making two failed attempts against some smaller Axis bastions in its native province, the 8th Kordun Division moved to Pokuplje in mid-June, where it met the bulk of the 34th Division. Together, they crossed into the Žumberak from where they planned to operate against enemy traffic on the main railway line.

This time, the Germans could not apply subversive methods, but they could and did use the crack 1st JgRR and some excellent Ustasha units, as well as two regiments of the 1st CCD and a couple of Kammerhofer's battalions. Operation "Dünkirchen" was fought from 27 June to 2 July, and again from 9 to 17 July 1944 in the area west of Krašić. In an unusual departure from their standard operating procedure, the Partisans chose to stand their ground. In the end, the Axis succeeded in clearing a scorched path through the mountains to Metlika, but had to retreat almost immediately, leaving the guerrillas in possession of the battlefield. "The term 'bandits' does not apply any longer", wrote a staff officer of the LXIX RC; the enemy was well-led, determined in defense, and used his reserves and heavy weapons with great skill. The regular style of fighting came at a price: the Partisans lost at least 116 KIA, 407 WIA, and 22 MIA, one-fourth of whom were Slovenians from the 15th NOVJ Division. As usual, the losses among officers were disproportionately high. In addition to one brigade *politkom* (Marijan Badel, whose family's famous liquor factory still carries his name) and the chief of staff of the 8th Division, killed or injured were also a pair each of brigade commanders, deputy brigade commissars, brigade chiefs of staff, and battalion commanders. After holding a series of rallies celebrating the victorious "fighting brotherhood" of Slovenes and Croats, the 8th and 34th Divisions returned to their respective home regions.[67]

August 1944 was unusually quiet, with the entire 4th Corps reporting only 30 KIA and 83 WIA. When not reconnoitering or raiding, the units spent time resting, reorganizing, and

66 Ibid., pp. 168-73, 234-37, 265-68.

67 Baić, *Četvrti*, pp. 283-301; NARA/T78/331/6289237 and 6289256, OBSO, Daily reports (21 and 24.7.1944, respectively); NARA/T314/1547/208, LXIX RC, Experiences "Dünkirchen" (23.7.1944); The LXIX RC reported losing 44 KIA and 221 WIA (not certain if these figures include the NDH units): ibid., 239 (17.7.1944).

securing agricultural works. As in the remainder of the country, the Partisans resumed large-scale operations in September. Apart from the demolition campaign against the railways, these included two multi-brigade undertakings against urban centers of some importance. Cazin fell on the morning of the 13th; more than a half of its 500-strong garrison ended up in captivity. Emboldened by this easy success, the Partisans launched a haphazard assault against the nearby Vaganac and were immediately repulsed. The corps HQ then decided to shift the point of main effort to Banija, or more precisely, to the town of Sunja and its surroundings. The battle was fought nearly concurrently with the siege of Banja Luka (26-27 September), and the two episodes ended in a similar manner. Even though it had six brigades and two detachments, plus the corps artillery and Tank Battalion of the MHQ Croatia, the NOVJ attack force failed to take the town in its entirety. It also proved unable to block the enemy relief force–composed, surprisingly enough, of the *Domobrani*–from reaching the defenders. The Partisans then placed Sunja under blockade and proceeded with the reduction of smaller outposts along the railway line while waiting for further instructions.[68]

In Northwestern Croatia, the NDH armed forces retained the initiative they had won during the early spring. The NOP presence to the north and west of the capital was reduced to a pair of detachments (some 600 men in all) after the new 1st Zagorje Brigade had been forced to leave in mid-June 1944. These local units kept on going as best as they could but could not seriously challenge the Ustasha supremacy. The lack of forces, combined with "political errors" (such as the arrest of a popular, but critical priest) and inability to ensure the orderly functioning of liberated villages, practically delivered Zagorje into enemy hands. The region became a kind of Axis safe zone, a rear area in the classic sense of the word where the recruits could be trained in peace and wounded nurtured back to health. Further east, the Partisans were having trouble in maintaining a foothold on the Kalnik and establishing one in Podravina. The 10th NOVJ corps decided in late June to attack Ludbreg with the 32nd and 28th Divisions. There could be no talk of surprise: the approach march was marked with heavy fighting, which, in turn, allowed the garrison to brace itself for the attack. In the ensuing battle (5-6 July), the Partisans were beaten back with heavy casualties: one battalion of the 17th Slavonian Brigade was practically wiped out, losing 78 KIA and MIA. Not satisfied with having merely repulsed the enemy, the Axis launched a vigorous pursuit, resulting in a temporary expulsion of the guerrillas from the western Bilogora 10 days later (Operation "Rouen").

The remaining division of the 10th Corps, the 33rd, also had a hectic summer. The campaign began in earnest on 24 June, when a failed attack on the NDH garrison at Čazma provoked response in the guise of Operation "Bienenhaus". On this occasion, two Cossack regiments and one HDB brigade forced the Partisans to seek refuge in the Bilogora. They returned to Moslavina in early August with the aim of establishing a permanent bridgehead on the Sava in order to facilitate the transshipment of grain from Slavonia to the impoverished provinces in the west (the plan could not be realized). Later the same month, the Partisans had to retreat north again because of Operation "Wildfang", a joint, multi-brigade Cossack-*Domobran*-Ustasha action targeting the wide area between Bjelovar, Ivanić Grad, Okučani, and Daruvar. The 33rd Division spent most of September in the vicinity of Križevci sabotaging the Zagreb–Koprivnica

68 Baić, *Četvrti*, pp. 311-17; NARA/T311/193/1102, OBSO, Daily report (28.9.1944).

railway, after which it departed north in order to take part in the renewed "invasion" of Podravina, this time with the full cooperation of the 6th NOVJ Corps.[69]

The Slavonian branch of the NOVJ responded to the raid on Drvar by stepping up its attacks against the Zagreb–Belgrade railroad and other enemy assets in its area of responsibility. In addition to the storming of Bizovac and an ambush on a column between Đakovo and Našice, the 12th Division celebrated a great victory on 20 June when it annihilated the German-Croat police outpost at Podgorač (100 prisoners, two AT guns and 650 rifles captured) for the price of only nine KIA and 29 WIA. An attempt to replicate the success five days later at Krndija failed, however, with six times as many irrevocable losses for the attacker. The Axis reacted to this apparent guerrilla invasion of Eastern Slavonia with a short counterstroke (Operation "Blitz"), which ended inconclusively in the first week of July. After that, both sides devoted all their energies to protecting the harvest works on their respective territories. The 6th Corps' only available division, the 12th (the 28th was with the 10th Corps at that time), was tasked with escorting the grain convoys to Banija.

It took almost a month before the Partisans could contemplate taking the initiative again. Since the enemy in Slavonia was showing no offensive intentions, the MHQ Croatia felt safe to send the bulk of the 6th Corps to the Daruvar Basin, whose "annexation" would bring additional economic and manpower resources. For most of August, three divisions (including the newly formed 40th) and three detachments operated around Daruvar, attacking outlying NDH bastions with mixed results. The *Domobrani* were thus forced to evacuate Grubišno Polje on 18 August with the loss of almost 200 prisoners, but stood their ground at Hercegovac two days later, inflicting almost 150 casualties on the startled attackers. The Partisans then turned their attention to the main railway line before resuming their campaign against the now-thoroughly demoralized NDH forces. The task was made easier by the fact that the German command had decided to concentrate whatever meager resources it had left around the most vital strategic objectives and effectively surrender the rest. The Axis defenders of Slavonska Požega thus managed to repulse an attack by the 12th Division on 5-6 September (the division's charismatic peasant-commander Nikola Demonja, one of the authentic heroes of the 1941 uprising in Banija, was among the dead), but nevertheless had to withdraw a week later. In the meantime, the 40th Division stormed Lipik, Pakrac, and Daruvar (13-16 September), after which the Axis evacuated the heavily contested Herecgovac. By the end of the month, the 6th Corps had started shifting its focus to Podravina and Eastern Slavonia. Between 25 and 27 September, the Partisans nearly wiped out the Ustasha battalion that defended Podravska Slatina and Čađavica (372 KIA, WIA, and MIA), after which they "reached the Hungarian border on a stretch of land 30 km wide". In all, September 1944 was the Slavonian Partisans' best month since the beginning of the war: the rich and populous Požega and Daruvar Basins were now firmly in their possession, and their ranks swelled with no less than 5,567 defectors from Pavelić's army.[70]

69 Škiljan, *Zagorje*, pp. 149-53; Obhođaš et al., *Vojnica*, Vol. II, pp. 343-78; Zdravko Krnić, *Tridesettreća divizija NOV Jugoslavije* (Zagreb: Spektar, 1981), pp. 158-206; *SZH*/X/663-73, Western GoD, Monthly reports (July 1944).

70 See the monthly reports by the 6th NOVJC in *Zbornik*/V/28/574-99 and *Zbornik*/V/29/259-62 (June 1944); ibid., pp. 631-51, *Zbornik*/V/30/179-80, and *Zbornik*/V/31/178-79 (July 1944); ibid., pp. 532-54, and *Zbornik*/V/33/139-41, 145-46 (August 1944); *Zbornik*/V/34/259-61 (September 1944); see also *Zbornik*/V/31/430 (40th NOVJD to 6th NOVJC, 25.8.1944), and 660; *Zbornik*/V/33/ 373;

The fortunes of war may have been turning against the Axis, but little of this could be felt in Syrmia. During the spring and summer of 1944 they repeatedly targeted Partisan concentrations in hope of destroying them, or at least, rendering them inoperable for some time. Already in mid-March, the 13th SS MTD launched a sweep of the Bosut Forrests as a part of the preparations for the crossing of the Sava. Colloquially known as "*Fesaroš* Offensive" (*fesaroš* meaning "the one who wears a fez"), this action failed to catch the guerrillas before they escaped to Eastern Bosnia but succeeded in killing hundreds of civilians. Barely a month later, the Germans (elements of the 42nd JD) had to go in again. Whether the choice for the name of the operation ("U-Boot", or "Submarine") had to do with the fact that the plan involved the use of artificial flooding in order to curb the Partisans' mobility, is not certain. What is certain, however, is that the offensive ended in the last week of April with very meager results (altogether four killed, 10 wounded, and one missing defender). During the first half of May, the 606th Security Regiment (SR) launched Operations "Maikäfer" and "Mira" against the enemy pockets on the Sava south of Ruma, but the Partisans managed to escape on both occasions.

Ultimately, none of these undertakings succeeded in curbing, let alone stopping, the growth of the NOP: from 30 May to 7 June, the Syrmian guerrillas carried out 16 actions, mostly against the Vinkovci–Zemun railway line. With the harvest season approaching, the Germans and NDH authorities decided on one last attempt to pacify the province, codenamed "Kornblume". For this purpose, the Axis brought up three police regiments, one Wehrmacht security regiment, one HDB garrison brigade, and other smaller units for a total of ca. 15,000 men. Although numerous, the low quality of these formations dictated the use of outdated tactics. Unlike the veteran Wehrmacht formations in other parts of the country that kept the Partisans on their toes through constant activity and application of semi-guerrilla tactics, the Axis in Syrmia had no alternative but to engage in large, set-piece encirclement battles, with predictable results.[71]

The "Kornblume I", aimed against the 1st Syrmian Detachment and 6th Vojvodina Brigade on the Fruška Gora, was compromised before it even began. The Partisan intelligence got wind of the upcoming attack, which in turn led to a general withdrawal to the Bosut. The Axis slowly combed the mountain during the latter half of June 1944, but caught only about 100 guerrillas, mostly unarmed new recruits and members of rear area services. While the Germans and NDH forces moved ahead with the second phase of the operation in the northeastern part of the province (which was, incidentally, entirely devoid of the NOVJ presence), the Partisans returned to their old bases from where they continued with their usual activities. Despite the ongoing enemy offensive, they attacked Čalma on 10 July, Nijemci on the 20th, and set fire to thousands of acres of ripening wheat. By mid-month, the Axis had turned back, invading the liberated territory in the Sava bend before making a thrust towards Crveni Čot, Fruška Gora's highest peak. Inexplicably, the guerrillas allowed themselves to be surprised and drawn into pitched battle, losing 24 KIA and 36 WIA. No such surprise could be achieved in the fourth and final phase of the summer offensive that targeted the well-known guerrilla bastion in the

Zbornik/V/34/674-75, NDH MoD, Daily report (16.10.1944); NARA/T314/1545/824, LXIX RC, Diary (20.6.1944).

71 Živan M. Ninković, *Šesta vojvođanska udarna brigada* (Belgrade: VIZ, 1973), pp. 37-70; Nikola Božić, *Sedma vojvođanska NOU brigada* (Belgrade: VIZ, 1984), p. 12; *Zbornik*/I/8/240-43, MHQ Vojvodina, Information bulletin no. 15 (10.6.1944); NARA/T78/331/6288653, OBSO, Daily report (20.4.1944).

Bosut area. In the early morning hours of 23 July, the Main HQ for Vojvodina, escorted by the 2nd Syrmian Detachment, quietly slipped through enemy blocking lines and reached the Fruška Gora shortly thereafter. In the meantime, the newly formed 7th Vojvodina Brigade, accompanied by a hospital, began its journey to Slavonia that would last almost 45 days and take the unit as far north as the Drava. The "Kornblume" was proclaimed over on 11 August: the self-congratulatory official reports spoke of more than 700 killed and 600 captured "guerrillas", but the upcoming events would clearly show that the offensive had, in fact, been a flop.[72]

Events occurring at home and abroad during late August and early September 1944 had an electrifying effect on the entire region. 115 officers and 2,500 other ranks from HDB garrisons in Syrmia chose to accept Tito's amnesty; the local NOP authorities were "concerned" (quotation marks in the original) by the fact that an estimated 10,000 volunteers had come forward even before a call to arms could be issued. In addition to four new brigades, the old ones were brought to full strength for the first time in their history. Operational zones were established in the long-dormant provinces of Bačka and Banat, each with a projected strength of three to five detachments; in line with the standard practice, a veteran battalion from Syrmia would serve as their core. The type of activities the guerrillas engaged in remained the same, but their battles were becoming longer and bloodier, a sign of increased staying power and cohesion. The combined losses in the attack on Manđelos on 22 August (17 KIA, 68 WIA) were bigger than in the recent clashes on the Fruška Gora. The storming of Ilok, the most ambitious Partisan operation in Syrmia so far, lasted one full day (29-30 September) and was marked by fierce fighting. Ultimately, the attackers could be expelled from the town (with altogether 88 casualties) only with the help of the river monitors armed with rapid-firing AA guns, as well as the Hungarian reinforcements from the opposite bank of the Danube.[73]

The 29th Herzegovina Division spent the spring and early summer of 1944 largely on the defensive. Apart from the standard ambush and demolition activities, as well as two brief, brigade-sized expeditions to the coast and the Neretva, there was little else to report. Having no artillery whatsoever, the Partisans could not even contemplate attacking enemy garrisons. The Axis were also active: in mid-July, the 369th ID (which had been deployed in the province since early March) launched Operation "Sonnenstich" against the main liberated territory. Despite the use of seven German battalions and five JVuO brigades, this last major Axis undertaking in this part of the country ended in a failure. As if stirred from a slumber, the 29th fought with great skill and determination, successfully alternating between regular and irregular tactics according to the situation. The Partisans were also aided by the fact that the plan of the operation had been found on the body of a dead German battalion commander already on the second day of the battle. After four weeks of fighting (13 July-10 August), the attackers returned to their garrisons; until 22 July, the 369th ID suffered 30 KIA, 154 WIA, and 54 MIA. The 29th suffered ca. 50 dead and close to 100 injured, as well as a similar number of missing, most of whom returned to their units later (for comparison: the Chetniks caused half as many fatalities during their sudden raid on a NOVJ hospital outside Konjic on 27 April; the alleged

72 Ninković, *Šesta*, pp. 71-84; Božić, *Sedma*, pp. 21-150; *Zbornik*/I/17/613, GEGC/East Syrmia, Burning of crops (27.7.1944); NARA/T311/192/636, OBSO, Daily report (19.8.1944).

73 Ninković, *Šesta*, pp. 94-98; Božić, *Sedma*, pp. 151-207; *Zbornik*/IX/7/108-09, PK Vojvodina to CK KPJ (20.9.1944); *Zbornik*/I/8/294-95 (Bačka-Baranja OZ, Circular, 23.8.1944), 451-53 (MHQ Vojvodina to Banat OZ, 28.9.1944).

shooting of another 22 "lightly wounded bandits" by the Ustashe in the same area five-and-a-half months later is not confirmed by the Yugoslav sources).[74]

The 2nd Assault Corps joined in the general NOVJ offensive in September 1944. As elsewhere, its efforts were significantly aided by the dropping German troop levels and demoralization among collaborationist forces. For instance, the Partisans entered the old NDH bastion of Fazlagića Kula without a fight and were even greeted by a handful of volunteers. With the Germans pent up in their remaining garrisons, the 29th Division turned its attention to the Chetniks. In late September, a group of senior commanders led by Lukačević deserted Mihailović and formed Independent Group of National Resistance with about 4,500 men. Expecting an imminent Allied landing, Lukačević tried to broker a truce with the NOVJ, opening the hostilities against the Axis at the same time. His plan misfired: although the Chetniks managed to surprise their former partners and capture some 350 legionnaires in the area of Trebinje, the attack on the town itself was repelled. On the 25th, the Germans intervened from the direction of Dubrovnik and lifted the siege. Worse still, instead of accepting the olive branch, the Partisans unfurled the black flag. Aided by some recently acquired cannon, two brigades of the 29th Division captured Lukačević's main stronghold of Bileća after several days of bitter fighting. Old Herzegovinian passions flared up again: dozens of prisoners, Chetniks and non-Chetniks alike, perished after the battle. In the meantime, the remaining formations of the 2nd Corps were expanding the liberated territory in Sandžak and Montengero. The XXI MTC's original plan to establish its northern front along the line Nikšić–Kolašin–Kosovo border and hold it with one regiment of the 181st ID and the nationalists, failed. In mid-September, the 3rd Assault Division re-took Kolašin, Berane, and Andrijevica after some hard fighting against the MFK, while the POG entered Nikšić. By the beginning of October, the Axis had taken up a defensive position in the Herceg-Novi–Danilovgrad–Podgorica area, where they still had to contend with guerrilla-style attacks on a daily basis.[75]

6.7 Slovenia: Demolition Campaigns and Assault Battalions

The 7th NOVJ Corps spent most of the winter 1943-44 on the defensive, maintaining a loose blockade of Novo Mesto with its single renaming division, the 15th. Its sister outfit, the 18th, returned from Gorski Kotar in mid-February, just in time to help repel the German spring offensive in Dolenjska. The offensive had limited aims: to strengthen the defenses of the main communications leading from Ljubljana to Novo Mesto and Kočevje by establishing a series of smaller fortified outposts along the route. The fighting intensified beginning in mid-March, with the Germans routing one battalion of the 5th Slovene Brigade at Javorovica, and the Partisans unsuccessfully attacking Ribnica. The main attack came on 23 April, as the bulk of the 14th SS PR started its southward drive from the direction of Ljubljana and Tržišče. Within several days, Trebnje, Mirna Peč, Žužemberk, Dobrava, and Dobrnič were captured and taken over by the

74 Komnenović and Kreso, *Dvadesetdeveta*, pp. 174-97; TsAMO/500/12483/82/9-18, and 25, 369th Signals Btl., Diary (13.7-10.8, and 13.9.1944, respectively).

75 Komnenović and Kreso, *Dvadesetdeveta*, pp. 333-48; Vukanović, *Treća*, pp. 352-70; Ferid Buturović, *Kuća mostarskog kadije: sjećanja skojevca, ilegalca, i partizana* (Sarajevo: self-pub., 2016), p. 152; NARA/T314/664/658 [all XXI MTC] (Securing Montenegro, 31.8.1944), 753, 778 and 792 (Daily reports, 13, 17 and 18.9.1944, respectively), 821 (Points for discussion 181st ID, 24.9.1944).

Domobranci. In response, the Partisans commenced an offensive of their own, recapturing these outposts one by one by the end of May. The struggle against the relief columns was as bitter as ever: the former two places changed hands four times each before the Germans finally decided they had enough. Ribnica, however, remained in the possession of its battalion-strong garrison despite the fact that the guerrillas used cannon and a pair of tanks in their final attack on 20 April. The Partisans then proceeded to symbolically seal the end of the campaign by launching an incursion across the old demarcation line and burning down the "Piatnik" factory at Radeče. Owing to bad organization, they could evacuate only eight tons of paper with which to satisfy the ever-growing needs of military and civilian bureaucracy behind the "front". The losses of the 7th Corps from 20 April to 3 June were 102 KIA, 212 WIA, and 79 MIA.[76]

As spring turned into summer, the 7th Corps reverted to a defensive, even passive, posture. The concern for the safety of the main liberated territory in Slovenia (still located in southeastern Dolenjska), lack of artillery ammunition, and aggressive small-scale campaigning practiced by the enemy were the main reasons for this. The only major action was the already mentioned joint defense of the Žumberak/Gorjanci together with the Croatian Partisans from late June to late July 1944. On the other hand, the sustained guerrilla-style offensive against Axis traffic continued unabated. For this purpose, the entire 15th Division took up positions along the Ljubljana–Trieste railroad. On 12 June, the Slovene Partisans used nearly a ton of explosives to put the famous Štampet Bridge out of commission, thereby causing a major disruption in the flow of goods between the Reich and Northern Italy. Even more successful was the expedition against the bridge at Litija on 20 September, which was immortalized in a series of photographs by *Life*'s correspondent John Phillips. The 18th Division's attempt to demolish the railroad tunnel at Šmarje in mid-August ended in a partial success and a costly battle with the Germans which left the division short of 43 KIA and 145 MIA. The same outfit pierced the improved defenses around Štampet Bridge and damaged it again in the last days of September.[77]

Having recuperated from the costly winter campaign by mid-March 1944, the 9th NOVJ Corps amassed the bulk of its forces (two divisions and three detachments) for an onslaught against the Axis positions between Logatec and Spodnja Idrija. The fighting, which lasted until early April, revealed that the local Partisans still had much to learn about complex operations of this sort: none of the three enemy outposts attacked on this occasion could be taken before the arrival of relief columns. In response, the 188th Reserve Mountain Division (RMTD) launched its own sweep in the same area (Operation "Wendelstein"), forcing the 30th Division to move south and west, while the 31st went east, to Gorenjska. Beginning in early June, the Partisans devoted most of their energies to traffic infrastructure. The entire section of the railway between Most na Soči and Podbrdo was put out of commission in a major action lasting from 29 June to 1 July. These disruptive activities, combined with the loss of the company-sized auxiliaries' stronghold at Hotavlje on the 19th (Rihenberk would follow three days later), forced the Wehrmacht into action. For the next three weeks, the Germans combed the area west of Idrija,

76 The main source for this sub-chapter are the monthly summaries sent by the MHQ Slovenia to SHQ, to be found in *Zbornik*/VI/14/7-14 (1.6.1944), *Zbornik*/VI/15/240-67 (31.7.1944), *Zbornik*/VI/16/156-81 and 459-92 (10 and 30.9.1944, respectively); the sources of additional information will be cited in separate footnotes. For this paragraph see Ambrožič, *Petnajsta*, pp. 226-73.

77 John Phillips, *Yugoslav Story* (Zagreb: Mladost, 1983), pp. 68-112; *Zbornik*/VI/15/612-20, 18th NOVJD to 7th NOVJC (20.8.1944).

but failed to inflict any serious damage. This, and smaller operations that followed (e.g. "Prien", "Zugspitz-Höllental", "Dachstein") failed to restore stability to the region. On 1 September, five NOVJ brigades stormed the SNVZ outpost at Črni Vrh and repulsed two relief columns coming from Idrija and Logatec, capturing 38 enemy soldiers and 66 pieces of small arms in the process. Emboldened by the success, the 31st Division then launched an incursion into the Dolomites, but turned back almost immediately after running into a well-prepared enemy. Its sister outfit again went south with the aim of creating a foothold in the Vipava Valley and beyond, but eventually had to withdraw across the Gorizia-Ajdovščina road.[78]

All this while, the NOVJ units in the western parts of the country remained extraordinary active in the classic guerrilla way. On 13 March 1944, the Briško-Beneški Detachment raided the Tricesimo auxiliary airstrip outside Udine, destroying three and damaging one more airplane. The bombings of a cinema and the local *Soldatenheim* in Trieste on 2 and 24 April, respectively, also deserve a special mention. Both attacks, which resulted in death or wounding of almost 100 German servicemen, were carried out by former Red Army soldiers, one of whom, Mehdi Huseynzade, would be posthumously rewarded with the title Hero of the Soviet Union. The Nazis responded by staging a macabre spectacle: they hanged 52 suspects from the balustrade of the internal staircase of Palazzo Rittmeyer, the site of the second attack. On 26 May, fighters of the Istrian Detachment ambushed a lone black staff car several km east of Trieste, killing the "Wild" Christian Wirth, one of the most repugnant figures from the ranks of Holocaust perpetrators. Although not as spectacular as above-mentioned actions, the sustained campaign targeting the railroads in Primorska in spring 1944 compelled the Axis civilian authorities to broach the possibility of a local truce. The police authorities in Gorenjska recorded 110 incidents in the period 1 June-30 August, the vast majority of which were carried out by the local Partisan detachment against the traffic infrastructure.[79]

After enjoying a brief period of rest after its epic winter march, the 14th Division went into action in mid-March 1944. The 4th OZ now had five brigades with which to wreak havoc on occupied Štajerska. The *Sicherheitsdienst* in Maribor recorded 36 acts of sabotage and arson in the period 1-25 April; 17 servicemen were killed and 20 wounded. By the first week of May, the guerrillas raided six industrial objects (including the major coal mines at Velenje) thus "jeopardizing the entire war economy effort in the province". In response, the Germans carried out several sweeps in the latter half of the month, with modest results: the biggest success was the capture of 36 pieces of small arms and 93 prisoners and defectors in the wider area of Šoštanj. Operating under the same instructions as their comrades in other parts of the country, the local Partisans devoted increased attention to enemy traffic during the late spring

78 See the 9th NOVJC's bi-weekly reports from March and early April 1944 in *Zbornik*/VI/12/131-45, 311-25, 442-61; Roland Kaltenegger, *Operationszone "Adriatisches Küstenland". Der Kampf um Triest, Istrien und Fiume 1944/45* (Graz: Leopold Stocker Verlag, 1993), pp. 76-87, 132-42.

79 Henry L. deZeng IV, *Luftwaffe Airfields 1935-45: Italy, Sicily and Sardinia* (n.p.: self-pub., 2015), p. 231; NARA/T312/1640/504 and 507, "von Zangen", Daily reports (3 and 25.4.1944, respectively); Marina Rossi, "Obešeni v Ulici Ghega", in *Po poteh nasilja v 20. stoletju v Tržaški pokrajini* (Trieste: Istituto regionale per la storia del movimento di liberazione nel Friuli Venezia Giulia, 2006), pp. 57-62; Petelin, *Gradnikova*, pp. 350-55; Maks Zadnik, *Istrski odred* (Nova Gorica: Partizanska knjiga, 1975), pp. 317-22; Trifković, *Parleying*, pp. 359-70; see also enemy activity reports compiled by Gendarmerie Kranj in *Zbornik*/VI/14/781-86 (1.6-15.7.1944) and *Zbornik*/VI/15/901-07 (18.7-30.8.1944).

and early summer months. In June alone, for instance, there were 26 acts of sabotage against trains (including an armored one) and other railway objects.[80]

The NOVJ's successes in the field, combined with the Third Reich's rapidly deteriorating position, had a profound physiological impact on the population. Instead of presenting themselves to the increasingly rapacious German recruitment commissions, ethnic Slovenes "went into the woods" in their thousands. Štajerska, still being the main reservoir of manpower in the country, gave over 6,600 new recruits to the NOP from May throughout July. Although the majority were "smuggled" over to the 7th Corps, the remainder was used to strengthen the local units and make them capable of more complex operations. The HQ of the 4th OZ already had a plan for the liberation of the Upper Savinja Valley. While other units were staging diversionary actions in their sectors, the 6th and 11th Brigades (acting under a separate OHQ) stormed Luče, Ljubno, and Šmartno ob Paki between 30 July and 1 August, capturing nearly 180 *Vermani* in the process. Even greater victory was achieved six weeks later when these same units took Letuš and Mozirje, bagging another 250+ prisoners. While the political workers and rear-area personnel were busy setting up NOOs and military facilities on what was the first "real" liberated territory in the province, the 14th Division advanced against the Pohorje. There, it managed to reduce four smaller enemy outposts in late August and early September, before the arrival of Wehrmacht reinforcements put a temporary halt to the NOVJ's expansion in this direction. The 4th OZ was also responsible for Koroška/Carinthia. In late April, the two local detachments were combined into a group of detachments. It operated relatively successfully until early September, when the MHQ decided to transfer most of its personnel south, reorganizing the remaining two companies north and four companies south of the Drava into a single detachment with about 500 men.[81]

Compared with the heady times of the Italian surrender, and the unusually busy winter 1943-44, the NOVJ's activity levels in Slovenia in spring and summer 1944 were rather stagnant. This refers primarily to more complex, "frontal" operations; the typical guerrilla activities had even increased and organizational efforts went on at an accelerated pace. In this respect, the local Partisans resembled their counterparts in Bosnia-Herzegovina and Croatia, who were also going through a period of passivity. The loss of initiative came as an inevitable result, a by-product, of the army's growth and regularization process. As late as August, the MHQ had to reiterate the importance of training, caution against "bureaucratism", and order the reduction in size of the ever-growing baggage trains and rear-area services. The introduction of new tactics by the Axis was also one of the major factors that contributed to such state of affairs. Already in early spring, the NOVJ commands noticed that the enemy was making increasing use of guerrilla methods, such as frequent raids and ambushes (also at night and in bad weather), which he combined with sudden, overwhelming attacks against exposed units. The influence from the nearby NDH is unmistakable: the Partisans even captured a set of the NDH Home Guard tactical guidelines. In late summer, the HSSPF in Ljubljana Province, SS General Erwin Rösener, authorized the establishing of an anti-guerrilla school on the grounds of the 12th-Century Stična Abbey.

80 See reports of SD Maribor in *Zbornik*/VI/13/698-99 (27.4.1944) and 721-26 (5.5.1944); *Zbornik*/VI/14/707 (Gendarmerie station Zagorje to SD Maribor, 2.6.1944), 710-14 (*Wehrmannschaft* Rgt. "Lower Styria", Monthly report, May 1944), 775-76 (18th LSR, Diary, 1.6-15.7.1944).

81 *Enciklopedija*, Vol. IX, p. 560, and Vol. IV, p. 636; *Zbornik*/VI/16/455-56, Koruška GoD to 4th OZ (29.9.1944).

There, particularly promising candidates from various armed services of the Third Reich would receive a one-month specialized training.[82]

Let us now examine a few episodes from the field examples. The "Heine" Battalion of the 188th RMTD gained notoriety and respect from its opponents for its deadly sorties launched from the base at Idrija (the battalion was originally tasked with guarding the local quicksilver mine, which was then the second-largest in the world). Mountain Regiment "Treeck" was formed in late July 1944 in Carinthia from various training units. The task of creating "a cohesive fighting formation" out of these raw recruits was entrusted to a small cadre of veterans led by a highly-decorated officer, Dr. Egon Treeck. In mid-September, the regiment was hurriedly redeployed to Štajerska in order to stem the 4th OZ's offensive. While the bulk of Treeck's assets were sent to the Upper Mislinja Valley, one battalion was left to "[hunt] freely in the bandit territory" around Podčetrtek. Interestingly enough, these second-line units with many forcibly conscripted ethnic Slovenes in their ranks gave a better account of themselves than some other formations with flashier titles or longer traditions. The training regiment of the "Brandenburg" Division, for example, left a rather undistinguished record from its period of service in Gorenjska in the latter half of 1944. The already mentioned SS "Karstwehr" Battalion was formed as a special mountain unit in mid-1942 around the core of geologists and natives of the rugged South Tyrol. By the summer of 1944, the battalion had been expanded into a small division (the 24th SS MTD), distinguished by the fact that 14 of its members were the only recipients of the Golden Bandit Warfare Badge (*Bandenkampfabzeichen in Gold*). However, the unit will probably be remembered for its crimes, rather than for military exploits. In mid-June 1944, its members decapitated two captured Partisans; the whole grizzly affair was photographed and duly mentioned in after-action reports.[83]

It was a Slovene phenomenon that collaborationist troops, rather than the Germans, became the foremost practitioners of the "free hunt" and other semi-irregular tactics. The Home Guard was initially divided into companies and "territorial" battalions with strictly defensive tasks. By the early spring of 1944, the *Domobranci* had earned enough trust to be allowed to form four battalions, informally called "assault". These units were composed of hand-picked personnel drawn from across Ljubljana Province and commanded by gifted officers from the former Yugoslav royal army; as some of them had also served in the MVAC, they were likely no strangers to the *Arditi* concept. Operating from their fortified bases at Rakek, Grosuplje, Stična, and Šentvid pri Stični, the battalions wreaked havoc on the liberated territory. Some of their most successful actions included the raid against Drašča Vas on 5 July (two NOVJ tanks destroyed and their crews killed; no own losses) and Žužemberk on 3 August (33 Partisan KIA), as well as ambushes at Dolenjska Vas on the 11th (17 Partisans captured; no own losses),

82 *Zbornik*/VI/12/270-77, 7th NOVJC, Circular (29.3.1944); *Zbornik*/VI/15/407-14, 422-26, and 430-34 (MHQ Slovenia, Orders and circulars, 9, 11, and 12.8.1944, respectively), 896-97 (HSSPF Ljubljana, Order, 30.8.1944).

83 Tomaž Štaut, "Elitne enote na območju današnje Slovenije med drugo svetovno vojno" (M.A. thesis, University of Ljubljana, 2008), pp. 63-70, 86-93; Milan Ževart, "Elaborat štaba Treeckove bojne skupine o narodnoosvobodilnem boju na Štajerskem," *Časopis za zgodovino i narodopisje*, 153:2 (1990), pp. 156-57; *Zbornik*/VI/16/931-32, Treeck to OHQ Ljubljana (13.9.1944); *Zbornik*/VI/14/731, Btl. "Heine" to 139th Reserve Mountain Regiment [RMTR] (12.6.1944); NARA/T312/1639/103, 188th RMTD to "von Zangen" (12.2.1944); Klemen Kocjančič, *Red mrtvaške glave pod Alpami: Enote in ustanove Waffen-SS na Slovenskem med drugo svetovno vojno* (Ljubljana: INZ, 2021), pp. 97-114.

Bloke on the 28th (seven members of a demolition detail captured; one own WIA), and Pikovnik on 5 September (14 Partisans KIA, 11 MIA; six own WIA). These results and their unwavering commitment to the anti-communist cause notwithstanding, the Germans never fully trusted the *Domobranci*, especially their officer corps. As a result, each of altogether six assault battalions received a German company and a German commander by the beginning of 1945. The sole exception was the 2nd Battalion that remained in the hands of the son of General Leon Rupnik, the head of the quisling administration (the "Slovene Nedić").[84]

6.8 Macedonia: From Spring Offensive to Bulgarian Capitulation

At the beginning of spring 1944, the things were looking up for the Macedonian branch of the NOVJ. After taking part in the battle against the Chetniks at Kozjak, the 3rd Macedonian Brigade (formed from the veterans who arrived from Greece) successfully raided the station at Ristovac on 28 March (24 prisoners, four loaded cargo trains destroyed) and the lead mine at Zletovo on 3 April (the Bulgarians had up to 50, the Germans less than half as many losses; the mine suffered minor damage) and seized the town of Kratovo on the 25th (170 prisoners). This very nearly turned out to be the last victory of the 3rd; due to the erroneous estimation of the size and scope of the Bulgarian "Spring Offensive", the unit was sent north, directly into the cauldron around Crna Trava. Thanks to luck and their own nimbleness, a group of 1,500 guerrillas managed to escape the trap and reach Mounts Kozjak and German (Герман) by mid-May. With the Bulgarians still after them, the Partisans decided to split-up. Some 500 of the fittest and best-motivated fighters–drawn from the 3rd Macedonian, 6th Southern Morava, and the Kosovo Brigades, as well as the Plačkovica Detachment–were formed into "Strike Group" and sent to Northern Greece.

The ten-day march through Eastern Macedonia (19-29 May) is illustrative of both the increasing military competence of the Partisans and the general decline of the Bulgarian Army. According to Yugoslav sources, in five clashes that occurred during this period (including one on the Greek territory), Strike Group captured 230 pieces of small arms, one cannon and two mortars, plus a large amount of much-needed supplies. Despite these successes, the expedition ended in a disappointment: instead of Greek Partisans welcoming them with open arms, the Yugoslavs found the villages on the western slopes of the Kroussia Mountains impoverished and devoid of friendlies (a sheep sold for eight British golden pounds). Seeing no alternative, they returned to Macedonia and headed for the right bank of the Vardar at Gradec but could not effect a crossing. Strike Group then turned north, repeating the *tour de force* from the previous month: in five encounters with the Bulgarians that took place from 11 to 19 June, the Partisans captured another 53 automatic weapons, 13 mortars, and two cannon; there were enough volunteers from the ranks of prisoners to form a new detachment. After completing its 950 km-trek, the 3rd Brigade remained the NOVJ's mainstay in the northeastern part of the country, launching occasional raids against targets of opportunity (e.g. the Lojane mine on 24 August, and Idrizovo

84 Boris Mlakar, *Slovensko domobranstvo 1943-1945: ustanovitev, organizacija, idejno ozadje* (Ljubljana: Matica slovenska, 2003), pp. 163-80, 213-35, 429; Štaut, "Elitne", pp. 109-12; *Zbornik*/VI/14/762, HSSPF Ljubljana, Daily report (6.7.1944); *Zbornik*/VI/15/393-98, 15th NOVJD to 7th NOVJC (8.8.1944). According to the above-cited monthly reports of the Slovene MHQ, the sum total of the NOVJ losses in June, July, and September is 644 KIA, 1098 WIA, 966 MIA.

prison on the 30th). These small affairs could be surprisingly costly: the outfit lost six KIA, 13 WIA, and 13 MIA at the railway station Tabanovci; for comparison, the recorded sum total incurred in all the clashes from late May amounted to 15 KIA and 34 MIA.[85]

In other parts of the country, the situation was as follows. The 2nd Macedonian Brigade was operating around Đevđelija, Tikveš, Azot, and Mariovo, and was most active during June and July 1944. Some of ca. 30 actions carried out in this period deserve special mention: the attack on a Bulgarian police *Jagdkommando* at Strmaševo on 12 June (18 pieces of small arms captured), the storming of an army outpost at Krnjevo on the 19th (13 prisoners), and the demolishing of the Drenovci mine on 16 July. In the meantime, the 1st Macedonian-Kosovo Brigade (soon to be split into the 1st Macedonian and 1st Kosovo Brigades) returned to Debarca with the aim of re-establishing the NOVJ's presence in this region for the first time since December 1943. The Partisans announced their arrival by ambushing a train near Kičevo on 6 May, killing eight and wounding 35 members of the German 297th ID. The Wehrmacht command could not tolerate this threat to its lines of communication to Albania. Consequently, the XXI MTC launched a series of operations in the period early May–late August ("Freiweg", "Einhorn", "Falkenauge", "Fritz", "Fuchsjagd"). The common denominator of all these undertakings was that they were small in size (the biggest involved an equivalent of five battalions of German infantry), cost little in blood, but also produce negligible results. Albanian auxiliaries took part on all of them, but their involvement proved to be a mixed blessing: in late June, 70 percent of them simply returned home in order to tend to their harvest. By early August, the Partisans had grown confident enough to launch "their first serious operation" in Western Macedonia, the attack on Debar. Acting in loose coordination with Enver Hohxa's Albanian Partisans, two NOVJ brigades broke into the town but proved incapable of reducing the last nests of enemy resistance before the relief columns appeared (1-5 August). Still, the Macedonians could be satisfied with the results, especially since their exploits were even mentioned in a "Reuters'" news bulletin.[86]

Owing to the arrival of the Red Army in the Balkans and Bulgaria's widely anticipated change of sides, Macedonia won immensely on strategic importance. For the Germans, the country represented the weakest spot in their eastern front, the "missing link" between Felber's Serbian command and the armies in Greece. As a consequence, they flooded the region with reinforcements. During the last week of August and beginning of September, the 4th SS PzGD secured the Vardar Valley, while the elements of the 297th ID and 21st SS MTD moved into the western parts of what was still known as "New Bulgaria". The Partisans also had great expectations for upcoming events. By this time, the local branch of the NOVJ had grown to a force of twelve brigades; the influx of volunteers was so great that the MHQ made plans for the creation of divisions and corps. The most pressing problem–the shortage of weapons–would hopefully be solved by "inheriting" the occupier's magazines. In spite of the repeated attempts to establish contact and agree cooperation with Bulgarian officers, the army remained

85 BA-MA/RW29/47, Mining Btl. "Southeast" to Mining HQ Southeast (7.4.1944) [copy courtesy of Dr. Roberto Trajkovski]; Kiril Mihailovski Grujica, *Treća Makedonska NOU brigada* (Belgrade: VIZ, 1976), pp. 24-247.

86 *Zbornik*/VII/4/7-11, 2nd Bde., Bulletin (June-July 1944); NARA/T314/663/1222, XXI MTC, Daily report (22.6.1944); Trajkovski, *Вермахтот*, pp. 153-202.

an implacable foe of the NOVJ until the very last moment, as witnessed by the heavy fighting around Stracin and Berovo in the first week of September.[87]

As soon as Bulgaria's declaration of war on the Third Reich was announced over the radio on the afternoon of 8 September, the Germans set in motion the plan, appropriately named "Judas", to disarm their erstwhile allies. Within days, the bulk of the Bulgarian 5th Army was either captured, fled east, or returned home (in the case of Macedonian-born recruits). The NOVJ disarmed an estimated 8,000 soldiers, while most of the army's heavy equipment fell into Axis hands. Only the garrison of Prilep (one infantry battalion and one artillery regiment) refused to surrender to the Germans, after which it was attacked and forced to seek refuge in the surrounding countryside. The Bulgarians then entered a partnership with the newly-formed 41st NOVJ Division; together, they counterattacked and re-took the town on 9 September, bringing in up to 200 prisoners in the process. The success proved to be short-lived. Not willing to leave the major road linking Florina and Bitola with Veles and Kavadarci in enemy possession, the Germans launched a two-pronged drive against Prilep on 16 September with a regiment-sized strike force. Fearing encirclement, the Allies retreated to the hills south and north of the road after three days of fighting during which they lost 45 artillery pieces of various types. After the loss of Prilep, the NOVJ in Western Macedonia continued with the reorganization and limited its battlefield activities to scouting, raiding, and ambushing the enemy columns moving north from Greece.[88]

Simultaneously, the HGE was also taking steps to establish its eastern front and secure the communications leading to it through the valleys of Strumica, Bregalnica, and Kriva Reka. On 17 September, one battalion of the Wehrmacht's 22nd ID entered the town of Strumica but was expelled four days later by the 4th Macedonian Brigade, which was soon reinforced by the elements of the 7th BID. Realizing the task would not be as easy as originally thought, the Germans returned on the 26th with a much larger force. Within next several days, the attackers reached the line Novo Selo–Pehčevo, pushing the Partisans into the mountains and the Bulgarians across the border (the latter lost another 50 artillery pieces and the same number of motor vehicles). In the meantime, the 11th *Luftwaffe* Field Division (LWFD) replaced the 4th SS PzGD in the central and northeastern parts of the country. On 16 September, one of its regiments was attacked by the 5th BID around Carevo Selo; despite the great numerical superiority, the Bulgarians advanced only four to five km before going over to defense. The 50th NOVJD tried to cut the Germans off by taking their supply bases at Štip and Kočane with two brigades, but both attacks were repulsed (21-24 September). The Allies' failure in the Bregalnica Valley allowed the Germans to shift their reserves to the northernmost sector, which stood under increasing pressure since the middle of the month. By the 24th, the Bulgarians (two regiments plus one of their own, newly-formed Partisan brigades) had finally managed to outmaneuver the main enemy position in the upper reaches of the Kriva Reka. Unfortunately, the flanking force that took Kratovo consisted of only one reinforced battalion, which could not hope to stand its ground against the German intervention from the south. Similarly, the two companies that occupied the hilltops north of Kriva Palanka were quickly chased away by the

87 Ibid., pp. 203-23; *NOB Makedonije*, pp. 156-58; Tempo, *Revolucija*, Vol. III, pp. 233-34; *Zbornik*/VII/4/68, MHQ Macedonia to SHQ (6.9.1944).

88 Ibid., pp. 79 (OHQ to MHQ Macedonia, 10.9.1944), 101 (Tempo to SHQ, 25.9.1944), 107-09 (2nd OZ to MHQ Macedonia, 27.9.1944); Trajkovski, *Вермахтот*, pp. 231-39.

town's garrison, signaling the less-than-glamorous end of the first phase of the Allied offensive in Western Macedonia.[89]

6.9 NOVJ in mid-1944: "British Honeymoon"

The basic structure of the NOVJ–or, more precisely, its main branch, which can already be styled "ground forces"–changed little during the spring and summer of 1944. The main accent was still placed on creating large field formations. Even though they were almost entirely relegated to a support role, the detachments could simply not be dispensed with. For instance, in June and July, the 2nd Assault Corps disbanded the Lovćen and Zeta Detachments, transferring their fittest fighters to the corps' new Reconnaissance Battalion, and the 8th Montenegrin Brigade, respectively. In early September, "due to needs on the ground", both detachments were reformed and three more created. In addition to the classic Partisan "infantry", in the course of 1944 the NOVJ received its first companies of Marines (one for each POS; their tasks: raiding the enemy-held islands and garrisoning one's own), as well as Cavalry Brigade (formed in Western Serbia in September, where it was initially used for security duties).

The reform of the internal security branch deserves a special mention. On 13 May, Tito created Department for the Protection of the People (*Odjeljenje za zaštitu naroda*, OZNA), streamlining the NOP's "secret police" on the national level. The service's executive arm initially consisted of the already available local forces, e.g. PPK Battalions in Croatia, People's Defense in Bosnia, and the Army of State Security–better known under its acronym VDV (*Vojska državne varnosti*)–in Slovenia. On 15 August, all of them became a part of Corps of People's Defense of Yugoslavia (*Korpus narodne odbrane Jugoslavije*, KNOJ). Each of the future federal republics would have at least one division; their strength and composition would be determined on case-to-case basis, depending on the circumstances on the ground. The cadre was composed of politically reliable veterans, whereas the rank-and-file came from various sources, including the detachments and newly-formed combat units. For instance, the 9th, 10th, and 13th Vojvodina Brigades became the 1st, 2nd, and 3rd Brigades of the 7th KNOJ Division. From a strictly military point of view, the creation of the KNOJ represented a palpable loss for the front, but the things were seldom that simple in Yugoslavia. First, the NOP's hold on liberated territories was never uncontested, and second, its revolutionary and state-building agenda could not do without such a force.[90]

On the whole, the army was becoming increasingly diversified, with the real change occurring in the realm of technical and support services. The idea of concentrating all artillery assets under a single HQ in a given operational area was first realized in Slovenia in May, where both the 7th and 9th Corps formed brigade-sized units (two to three battalions with dozen or so tubes in total). On 30 August, the recently-created Artillery Section of the SHQ issued a set of instructions on the further development of this arm. Each corps received a specialized staff section and an artillery battalion, and each division a battery; these units could later be

89 Ibid., pp. 239-54.

90 See the following orders of the 2nd Assault NOVJC in *Zbornik*/III/7/705-06 (28.6.1944); *Zbornik*/III/8/239 (9.9.1944); *Zbornik*/III/10/175-76 (19.7.1944); *Zbornik*/VIII/2/470-71, NOVJ Navy HQ, Circular (19.7.1944). The main source for the information on the organization of the NOVJ provided in this sub-chapter comes from Anić, Joksimović, Gutić, *Narodnooslobodilačka*, pp. 341-466; additional sources will be provided in separate footnotes.

expanded into "groups"/brigades and battalions, respectively. The use of cannon in the field remained flexible and dependent on the local circumstances: some units had no more than a couple of pieces, while others had a relatively impressive array. Apart from attacks on urban centers, there was still little opportunity or ammunition for a massive use of artillery; divisions would usually temporarily attach whatever assets they had to individual brigades for the solving of specific tasks.

The SHQ was a "trailblazer" for other branches of service as well. In mid-February 1944, Engineer Brigade was formed in Drvar. It was composed of four battalions, each with its own specialty. The 2nd Battalion would be used as a core of Railway Brigade, raised some seven months later in Serbia and made responsible for the maintenance of railways on the liberated territory. Nine more engineer brigades would be formed by the end of the war; they were usually attached to the largest field commands. On lower levels, each division received a battalion, and each brigade a company. In Croatia, Labor Battalions were composed of skilled laborers; in Slovenia, the designation referred to penal outfits tasked with repairing roads and other crude physical assignments. Combat engineers were spiritual successors to the *bombaši*. "There hardly exists a fortress that could stand up to them", boasted one report from Slavonia, where they were known as the *jurišni pioniri*, the direct translation of the German *Sturmpioniere*. Unlike their predecessors, who had little else apart from raw courage and some hand grenades, these elite sappers went into action with much-improved gear, including the "Partisan Sock", a fused charge wrapped in a piece of cloth. Their favorite weapon, however, was the British-made portable anti-tank launcher PIAT. In addition to its primary use, the guerrillas soon found out that the *Džonbul* (corruption of the English "John Bull", as the weapon was informally known) was an ideal tool for reducing bunkers and opening paths through walls in urban fighting, similar to the way the Soviet infantry used the "Panzerfaust". The growth and diversification of the army meant that the schools were working around the clock. In late August, the Croatian corps were ordered to inform the MHQ on the number and type of courses and graduates/candidates in attendance. The 6th reported having 70 medical NCO candidates, 11 cipher clerks, and 40 "technicians"; the 8th Corps: W/T operators–35, field officers–50, quartermaster–15, medical–60; the 10th Corps: field NCOs–324, medical NCOs–62, signalmen–116, saboteurs–240, technicians–40, nurses–18; the 11th Corps: officer candidates–21 (plus 117 graduates), reconnaissance troops–37 (24), saboteurs–(45), quartermasters–20 (20), veterinarians–22, interrogators–14, W/T operators–35.[91]

The development of the NOVJ and its battlefield successes from mid-1944 would have been unthinkable without material aid from abroad. Before we get down to specifics, we need to take a brief look at the political relations between the Partisans and the British, who still had the last word in determining the Western Allies' policy in the Balkans. While "The Big Three" were meeting in Tehran, the AVNOJ was holding its second plenary session in Jajce. On 29 November 1943–a date celebrated in Socialist Yugoslavia as The Day of Republic until 1990–the NOP's parliament proclaimed itself the sole legitimate representative of the Yugoslav peoples. It also forbade the king and government-in-exile from returning before the war was

91 *Zbornik*/V/25/361-62, MHQ Croatia to 8th NOVJC (21.3.1944); *Zbornik*/V/31/185 (6th NOVJC, Monthly report, July 1944) and 519-20; *Zbornik*/IV/26/388, 3rd Krajina Bde. to 1st NOVJD (28.6.1944); *Zbornik*/IV/30/429, 5th NOVJC, Monthly report (September 1944); *Zbornik*/VI/16/458, MHQ Slovenia, Instructions no. 1 (30.9.1944).

over. National Committee of Liberation of Yugoslavia (*Nacionalni komitet oslobođenja Jugoslavije*, NKOJ) with nineteen departments (ministries) was formed on the same occasion. Unlike in 1942, the Yugoslav Communists decided not to consult Moscow beforehand, and added the portfolios of foreign affairs and defense to this provisional government. The latter portfolio was held by Tito, who was also elected as the chairman of the NKOJ and awarded the honorary title Marshal of Yugoslavia.

Accepting reality, Churchill sought to improve the relations with, and extend de facto recognition to, the NKOJ. By doing this, and by dropping Mihailović, he hoped to secure Peter II and his supporters a place in the post-war political landscape of the country. The first step towards this goal would be the creation of a fusion government. The Partisan overlord was bound to at least consider this proposal on account that both the much-needed supplies and the all-important formal recognition of the NOP by the Western Allies depended on it. Consequently, after months of correspondence on the highest level and back-door maneuvering, he acquiesced to a meeting with the head of the new government-in-exile, the moderate Croatian politician Ivan Šubašić (Mihailović lost his ministerial seat, but remained the commander of the JVuO). For the Whitehall, this was the perfect time for talks. It was early June 1944, and the Yugoslav marshal had just been evacuated from Bosnia to Vis, where he was closely guarded by the Royal Navy and Air Force, as well as some 5,000 British servicemen ("I felt as if in a mousetrap", Tito observed later). An agreement was reached after several days of negotiations, thus paving the way for a joint Yugoslav war cabinet. The Anglo-Partisan rapprochement reached its culmination in a series of constructive, if not always easy, meetings between Churchill and Tito at Caserta and Naples in mid-August.[92]

Despite all of the prejudices and misgivings about each other's ultimate intentions, it seems that the British and Partisans established a good working relationship. Off the battlefield, the NOP's propaganda adopted a decidedly pro-Western stance. When the British, who feared retribution against their own men in captivity, protested about the killings of German prisoners by some Dalmatian units, Tito personally gave assurances that such accidents would not happen again. On the battlefield, the Partisans helped with the intelligence-gathering both in Yugoslavia and in the neighboring countries and aided the evacuation of the downed Allied aircrews; by the end of the war, an estimated 2,000 members of the United States Army Air Force (USAAF) would be saved in this manner.[93]

By mid-1944, practically the entire Yugoslavia was covered by a net of military missions; the BLOs could be found with the MHQs and corps command, and even some divisions. These men came from variety of backgrounds and reacted differently to the enormously complicated world they found themselves in. Their chief, Brigadier Maclean, was a firm, but not uncritical supporter of the NOP; the Yugoslavs held him in high regard and even allowed him to buy a house on the island of Korčula after the war, something normally not allowed to foreigners. Doctors like Lindsay Rogers and Collin Dafoe earned lasting respect for their tireless efforts in

92 Dušan Plenča, *Međunarodni odnosi Jugoslavije u toku Drugog svjetskog rata* (Belgrade: Institut društvenih nauka, 1962), pp. 209-84; Petranović, *Istorija*, p. 327.

93 See Tito's orders to all KPJ leaders, and to MHQ Serbia, respectively, in *SD*/XVIII/231-32 (30.1.1944), and *Zbornik*/II/12/58-59 (5.2.1944); Trifković, *Parleying*, pp. 293-95; Miloš Bojanić, "Evakuacija savezničkih avijatičara iz Jugoslavije tokom Drugog svetskog rata", *Zbornik radova Narodnog muzeja Čačak*, 49 (2019), p. 74; *Zbornik*/VI/14/387-88, MHQ Slovenia to Koruška GoD. (23.6.1944).

saving lives, working under the most difficult conditions in makeshift hospitals in Bosnia and Slovenia. Many of the BLOs "went native", identifying entirely with their hosts. For instance, one of the officers attached to the 1st Proletarian Corps wrote in the aftermath of the Battle of Jelova Gora that "we have hopes capturing Mihailovic [sic]", for which he was sharply rebuked by his superiors. Others, like the famous writer and devout Catholic, Evelyn Waugh, remained highly critical of the KPJ's aims and methods he had had the chance to observe in Croatia. A few other "celebrities" could be encountered in Yugoslavia. Randolph Churchill was parachuted into Bosnia and attached to the SHQ in early 1944, ostensibly as a token of thrust and appreciation the British prime minister had for the NOP. However, his lack of interest for anything but the bottle soon gave the impression that he had, in fact, been sent away so as not to cause further embarrassment to his father at home.[94]

Material aid stood at the heart of the Anglo-Partisan cooperation. Normally, orders would be sent up the ladder and all the way to the SHQ, which would then pass them on to the NOVJ's main base in Italy. In particularly urgent cases individual commands would file their requests with the BLOs, like in Serbia in September 1944, when Popović contacted Maclean personally. By this time, the administrative burden had become so heavy that the SHQ had to relax the rules to a certain extent and allow direct communication between field units and Bari. Once the order was received, it was the task of the Yugoslav personnel there to actually procure the necessary items from the British authorities. Doing so required patience and intricate knowledge of army bureaucracy. "The main thing is not to leave them in peace for a single moment and keep pestering them every day", wrote one NOVJ officer, adding that a few bottles of brandy or wine every now and then helped immensely in getting things done. Even if everything went smoothly in Italy, there were no guarantees as to what will actually be delivered to Yugoslavia, especially by air. The 4th Corps thus received 150 km of telephone cable, the 10th got 36, whereas the 6th and 11th did not get any at all. The 25th Serbian Division once received a consignment of 600 extremely small, and thus unusable, shoes. The emaciated fighters of the 12th Corps were startled to find that the planes dropped them heavy AT rifles at the height of the murderous running battle with the "Prinz Eugen" in the summer of 1944. "Enemy tanks were about the only thing we did not need fear at that time", observed one *politkom*, remembering that the rifles were defiantly thrown away in the presence of the BLOs.[95]

Red tape, bad organization, and carelessness were hardly a British specialty. The Yugoslavs were seemingly under the impression that the greatest empire the world had ever seen commanded practically unlimited resources. Consequently, no request for supplies of any kind was considered too exorbitant; Great Britain, a technical superpower, was also expected to deliver them on time and on spot regardless of circumstances. The NOVJ base at Bari pleaded with field

94 *SD*/XXI/182, Tito to MHQ Slovenia (18.7.1944); Brian Jeffrey Street, *The Parachute Ward: A Canadian Surgeon's Wartime Adventures in Yugoslavia* (1st electronic version: Edito Online Publishing, 1998), Chapter 19; Franklin Lindsay, *Beacons in the Night: With the OSS and Tito's Partisans in Wartime Yugoslavia* (Stanford: Stanford University Press, 1993), p. 270; Donat Gallagher, Carlos Villar Flor, *In the Picture: The Facts behind the Fiction in Evelyn Waugh's Sword of Honour* (Amsterdam: Rodopi, 2014), pp. 253-54; Djilas, *Wartime*, p. 369; Vuksanović (ed.), *Beleške*, pp. 203-04 (7.3.1944).

95 *Zbornik*/I/12/7-8, MHQ Serbia to Maclean (11.9.1944); *Zbornik*/I/9/177, 25th NOVJD to MHQ Serbia (5.8.1944); *Zbornik*/II/13/408-16 (Božo Borčić to SHQ/QM, 10.7.1944), 722-23 (Zlatko Kereković to MHQ Croatia/Sign., 15.8.1944), 726 (SHQ to MHQ Slovenia, 16.8.44); Tepavac, *Moj*, p. 151.

commands to state their needs as precisely as possible: how many tons of food for how many men, how many spare parts for what kind of trucks, etc. "Fancy" requests for hard-to-get items such as German-made medicine usually ended in a dustbin right away. The greatest problem was the often lengthy and unrealistic orders. These could originate not only from naive junior staffers in the province, but from the SHQ as well: in late August 1944, Economic Department placed an order for no less than 150-200,000 sets of winter clothes, to be delivered "as soon as possible". In mid-July, the SHQ gave the HQ of the 2nd Assault Corps a severe rubdown for failing to properly handle the received aid: "Peasants took a good part [of the supplies] with them. Individual units quarreled over distribution. The Allies saw an ugly picture [...] and are threatening to cancel further deliveries." The age-old custom of celebrating major victories by discharging weapons in the air proved impossible to eradicate. "It is absolutely forbidden to [celebrate] the fall of Odessa [in this manner]", read one order of the 1st Proletarian Brigade. In late October, the embarrassed Dapčević tried to justify one particularly massive outpouring of joy to a Western delegation, who was quick to remind him of all the difficulties the RAF went through to deliver the now-wasted ammunition in the first place. The misconceptions about the extent of the British resources and the functioning of the Anglo-Partisan partnership sometimes acquired bizarre overtones. The 3rd NOVJ Corps once requested from the SHQ "a flypast by three 'Spitfires'" on occasion of the NOP rally and swearing-in ceremony in Bašigovci, a hamlet five km southeast of the small town of Živinice in Eastern Bosnia.[96]

The impact of foreign aid on NOVJ operations cannot be overestimated. The commander of the "Skanderbeg" attributed the outcome of Operation "Draufgänger" to the fact that the guerrillas had more machine guns and ammunition than his own men. The 6th Corps reported in June 1944 that the "generous help from the Allies" solved the shortages of clothing, footwear, and ammunition. The landing of the bulk of the 26th Dalmatian Division–itself largely supplied and armed by the British–on the island of Brač was facilitated to a large degree by the presence of 1st and 2nd Landing Flotillas of the NOVJ Navy equipped with "imported", specialized landing craft. If the liberation of Serbia was paid for in Partisan blood, it was made possible by British hardware. From May to September 1944, the RAF delivered to Serbia enough weapons to arm 14,000 men; the deliveries included over 3,600 automatic weapons, 132 mortars, 10 light AT cannon, and an astonishing sum of more than 9,000,000 rounds of small-arms ammunition. The BLOs in the southern part of the country were particularly proud of the massive airlift of supplies that turned the raw, bare-handed and bear-footed 24th Serbian Division into a combat-ready formation within two weeks. The cannon used by the 1st Proletarian Corps on the Jelova Gora and the 29th Herzegovina Division at Bileća originated from British stocks. Although they came only as the result of Tito's personal intervention, the repeated airdrops of food, as well as the evacuation of over 1,000 sick and injured from the airstrip at Gornja Brezna, quite probably saved the 12th NOVJ Corps from destruction. This episode represented the culmination of the ongoing effort to get the Partisan wounded out of harm's way: 4,000 of them were flown out during July alone from nearly every corner of the country. This brought the total of Yugoslav patients in Italy to 6,500, where they were given "the best and most up-to

96 *Zbornik*/II/13/557-58 (Herbert Kraus, Ordering medical supplies, 26.7.1944), 877-88 (Mitar Vujović to SHQ, 30.8.1944); *SD*/XXI/119, SHQ to 2nd Assault NOVJC (12.7.1944); Charles Thayer, *Hands Across the Caviar* (London: Michael Joseph, 1953), pp. 46-47; *Zbornik*/IV/24/172, 1st Proletarian Bde., Circular (10.4.1944); *Zbornik*/IV/29/542, 3rd NOVJC to SHQ (13.9.1944).

date medical treatment by the British doctors". Non-combatants, including orphans from Eastern Bosnia and elderly Jews from Croatia, were also evacuated in this manner. The friendly aircraft did not only bring tools of war. In the area of the 3rd NOVJ Corps they brought both the agricultural seeds and highly-prized silk parachutes that could later be bartered for grain. Last but not the least, the psychological impact of the Allied aid on friend and foe alike was huge. On one occasion in August, the Kosmaj Detachment retrieved several containers that were presumably destined for the Warsaw resistance; although an accident, the episode had "an incredible effect" on the still-wary local population. The same effect was observed when the 3rd Macedonian Brigade received a prearranged drop on Mount Plačkovica while on its way back from Greece. The Bulgarian prisoners present were probably not so much impressed by the delivered automatic weapons as they were with chocolate, which "they had not seen in years".[97]

On 26 March 1944, the NOVJ Tank School opened its doors in Khatatba, Egypt. It was formed around the core of specialists from the Partisan bases in Italy and augmented by defectors from the rapidly-shrinking contingent of royal Yugoslav troops located in the Middle East. The instructors and all the necessary supplies and equipment were provided by the British. On the whole, the training went smoothly, with officers in charge being unanimously praised in commissars' reports for their dedication (some of the instructors, however, were heard saying "We train you today, but tomorrow you might turn against us", revealing the simmering political tensions beneath the Anglo-Partisan alliance). After completing two 35-day courses, the tankers were back to Italy, this time as a part of the 1st NOVJ Tank Brigade [TB]. By late July, the unit was 1,900 strong (most of them "overseas" Slovenes) and equipped with 56 "Stuart" light tanks and 18 armored cars. It continued honing its skills until September, when it was gradually assembled on Vis in preparation for its first combat assignment.[98]

On 12 March 1944, Tito and Maclean signed an agreement concerning the creation of the first "regular" Partisan air units. It was a curious amalgam: the units' official designations were 351st and 352nd Squadrons RAF, but the Yugoslavs called them the 2nd and 1st Squadrons NOVJ, respectively. They were made up of the members of the NOP, but also of the former royal servicemen who found refuge in Africa and the Middle East in 1941. The squadrons were a part of the RAF in every sense but flew under the Partisan insignia; they had no commissars, but the British did not interfere with their internal life and informal political structures. The training was done in Benghazi, Libya, between April and October, after which the squadrons were gradually moved to airbases in southern Italy and Vis. Equipped with the now-obsolete "Hurricane" and an older version of "Spitfire" (repeated Yugoslav requests for more modern types fell on deaf ears), the squadrons mostly flew ground-attack missions. These usually took

97 BA-MA/RS3-21/1, 21st SS MTD, Situation report (2.10.1944); *Zbornik*/V/29/37, 6th NOVJC, Monthly report (June 1944); *Enciklopedija*, Vol. II, pp. 405-06; TNA/WO202/196, John Henniker-Major, Report on Serbia (4.12.1944), p. 9, and Appendix "AA"; Pajević, *Artiljerija*, pp. 359, 364; Trifković, "Methods", p. 10; *SD*/XXII/313, Minutes meeting Henry Maitland Wilson–Tito (10.8.1944); *Zbornik*/II/13/295-98, Nikoliš to SHQ (19.6.1944); *Zbornik*/IV/27/216 and 556, 3rd NOVJC to SHQ (12 and 17.7.1944, respectively); *SD*/XXI/150, SHQ to MHQ Croatia (15.7.1944); *Zbornik*/I/20/685, OK Mladenovac to OK Požarevac (August 1944); Grujica, *Treća*, p. 196.

98 *Zbornik*/II/13/67-69; ibid., pp. 387-88 and 563 (Ranković to SHQ, 8 and 27.7.1944); *Zbornik*/II/14/105, Tito to Bari (14.9.1944); *Zbornik*/IX/6/582-84, 1st TB/Pol., Activity report (12.7.1944).

place according to the internal schedule of the 281st Wing of the Balkan Air Force (BAF)[99], but with two conditions: they had to be flown over Yugoslavia, and the needs of the NOVJ ground forces had to be taken into account. The latter placed their "orders" through the BLOs, which then forwarded them to air force authorities. Close air support was another "perk" that came with the British alliance. The German movements during Operation "Rösselsprung" were heavily interdicted from the air, with up to 160 vehicles being damaged or destroyed. Both Kastel in Banja Luka and the army barracks in Valjevo, the last bastions of German resistance during the September battles, were repeatedly strafed by rocket-firing "Beaufighters", undoubtedly to the absolute delight of the observing Partisans. By the beginning of August, the NOVJ Air Force had close to 2,500 members. Three months later, it would receive its own high command with an HQ and seven departments, including educational, technical, and meteorological.[100]

The Anglo-American air campaign over Yugoslavia started as soon as the first suitable bases in Southern Italy were captured in early fall 1943. The campaign included attacks by both tactical and strategic air forces on various military targets, most notably ground communications. The SHQ and other NOVJ commands were welcome to provide tips on especially rewarding targets, like troop concentrations, but whether one would act on them depended solely on internal considerations. Although Tito could not "order" raids on one city or another for political reasons as often claimed in revisionist circles in the post-Yugoslav societies, he was aware of the possible fallout: "It is on my head, so choose only important military objects", he used to tell his subordinates. Given that the USAAF considered a bombing accurate if 50 percent of the bombs landed withing a 600-meter radius of the target, his concerns were well-founded. Slavonski Brod, Maribor, and Belgrade, with their major bridges and marshaling yards, were repeatedly hit, receiving about 2,700 tons of high explosives each; Niš got 1,655 tons, Zagreb close to 1,400, Sarajevo and Podgorica ca. 1,000. The so-called "Easter Bombing" of the capital on 16-17 April 1944 claimed up to 800 civilian lives. An even greater tragedy befell Leskovac, which was literally flattened on 6 September by more than a hundred B-24 "Liberators"; an estimated 1,000 inhabitants died, whilst German losses were negligible ("Even the Partisans seemed subdued" by the ferocity of the bombing, wrote the equally shaken Maclean). Incidents such as these were considered unfortunate, but unavoidable. After the aircraft had mistakenly bombed the Partisan-held Bijelo Polje on 19 November, Tito's private secretary proposed the establishing of a special commission that would investigate such cases and determine indemnities. Air Vice Marshal William Elliot, the CO of the BAF, turned the idea down, saying that "allies do not interact in such manner". As a compromise, it was agreed that the aircraft should "bomb" the stricken town again, this time with food and medical supplies, as a token of apology.[101]

99 The BAF (official designation since June 1944) was a polyglot force composed of up to twenty combat squadrons of British, South African, Greek, Yugoslav, Italian, and, for a while, even Soviet aircraft. Until the end of the war, the BAF would lose 254 aircraft, mostly on account of German AA defenses: Jeff Jefford, "The Balkan Air Force", *Royal Air Force Historical Society Journal*, 46 (2009), pp. 63-80.

100 Lazarević, *Vazduhoplovstvo*, pp. 122-43; NARA/T314/563/372, XV MTC to PzAOK 2 (9.6.1944); Maclean, *Eastern*, p. 499; *Zbornik*/IV/29/565, 5th NOVJC to SHQ (27.9.1944); *Zbornik*/X/1/139 (NOVJ Air Force, Strength return, 1.8.1944), and 234 (SHQ, Order, 29.10.1944).

101 Miloš Bojanić, "Broj nastradalih civila u savezničkom bombardovanju Srbije 1943-44. godine: dostupni podaci, procene i analiza", in *Juhorsi zapis: tematski zbornik* (Kruševac: Istorijski arhiv, 2018), pp. 139-50; see also the map prepared by Dušan Dačić and Miloš Bojanić titled "Allied Bombing of Yugoslavia in World War 2 (1941-1945)" (courtesy of Miloš Bojanić); Kevin A. Mahoney, *Fifteenth Air Force*

By spring 1944, Anglo-American fighter-bombers (or *Jabos* as the Germans called them) had become a regular sight over railway lines in the Balkans. In April alone, they accounted for 68 locomotives and 955 railroad cars (compared with 32 and 170, respectively, destroyed by guerrillas); in August, 80 percent of locomotives in the NDH were put out of commission in this way. In the meantime, the Yugoslav Partisans went on with their wrecking activities with undiminished vigor. The authorities in Zagreb registered altogether 1,754 incidents in the period March-June. Some of them were quite serious: in the night 27-28 March, saboteurs detonated no less than 186 mines on the section of the main railway line between Slavonski Brod and Novska. While the number of attacks in Serbia remained relatively stable (ca. 100 incidents of various type from early March to late August, including robberies), the Germans had a new flashpoint on their hands, Macedonia. In August, the situation there took a rapid turn for the worse. The Partisans had practically closed the all-important "Eastern Line" between Skopje and Grdelica, and were slowly extending their attacks to the railway lines south of the capital. All this, combined with the shortages of rolling stock and personnel, as well as the alleged indolence of the Bulgarians (who refused to operate during the dark because of the sabotage and in the early morning hours because of the *Jabos*), made the link with the armies in Greece tenuous, at best.[102]

The idea of launching a joint ground and air offensive against enemy lines of communication was proposed by Wilson and accepted by Tito during one of their meetings in mid-August 1944. A special BLO was appointed to the SHQ with the task of coordinating the action, codenamed "Ratweek". In order to maintain secrecy, all instructions to the Partisan field commands were issued through courier, rather than wireless. It was a massive effort: eight NOVJ corps in Slovenia, Croatia, Bosnia and Herzegovina, one Serbian division, and four Macedonian brigades were ordered to hit targets in their respective operational areas. The "Ratweek" began as scheduled on 1 September and lasted for a whole week. The air force–which flew close to 2,000 sorties–attacked by day, the demolition teams by night. This, combined with the aforementioned large-scale military operations, made September 1944 probably the worst month of the entire war for the Axis transport system. A dozen railway bridges were damaged in Serbia during the "Ratweek", another 11 by the end of the month; three secondary lines in the east and the west of the country were put out of commission for good, while the main lines were operating were great difficulty. In addition to the line Skopje–Niš, the line leading from Edessa to the Macedonian capital was likewise cut. The lines between Zagreb and Novska had to be closed for the best part of September due to "a very large number" of air and ground attacks. The main lateral line in the NDH running through the Bosna and Neretva Valleys all the way to Dubrovnik was "damaged beyond repair in numerous places". As we shall see, the full impact of these actions on the operational situation in the Balkans will begin to show in earnest only the following month. For the NOVJ, the immediate result of the "Ratweek" was the decision to upgrade the already existing Demolition Battalions with the Croatian 4th, 6th,

against the Axis: Combat Missions over Europe during World War II (Lanham, MD: Scarecrow Press, 2015), p. 230; Maclean, *Eastern*, pp. 486-87; *SD/XX/8*, Tito to 2nd Assault NOVJC (19.4.1944); Biber (ed.), *Tajno*, p. 390, Minutes meeting Tito–Elliot–Maclean (7.12.9144).

102 NARA/T77/1421, OKW/Trans., Bandit activity (April 1944); ARMB/SSR, Summary for 1944, pp. 10-21; NARA/T78/331/6288525, OBSO, Daily report (29.3.1944); NARA/T311/188/440-42, OBSO/Trans., Monthly report (August 1944); Bošnjak, *Diverzantska*, p. 234.

and 10th Corps into full-blown detachments. Each of them had a permanent cadre of about 300 specialists, which could be augmented by auxiliary sappers in case of need.[103]

103 Ibid., pp. 277-80; Milovan Dželebdžić, "Dejstva na komunikacije u Jugoslaviji od 1. do 7. septembra 1944. godine—operacija 'Ratweek'", *VIG*, 3 (1970), pp. 7-61; NARA/T311/188/555-635, OBSO/Trans., Monthly report (September 1944).

7

Victory (October 1944 – May 1945)

7.1 Red Steamroller in Serbia: Belgrade Operation

On 6 September 1944, the first units of the Red Army reached the Danube in the vicinity of Iron Gates. At that time, the 2nd Ukrainian Front (UF) was under orders not to advance across the border into Yugoslavia, but this was soon to change. The Partisans, and the KPJ members in particular, were overjoyed at the news they had been waiting for the past three years. Sensing that the crucial moment of the war had arrived, Tito requested, and was granted, an audience in the Kremlin. To quote the enraged Churchill, the Yugoslav marshal "levanted" from Vis in total secrecy on the 19th, taking a Soviet airplane first to Craiova in Romania, and thence to Moscow. The details of the visit are still shrouded in mystery; what is known is that it lasted a week (21-28 September), and that Tito met with Stalin on at least two occasions. The first and foremost result of their talks was the Soviet decision to stage a limited offensive operation on the Yugoslav territory with the aim of liberating the capital and cutting the main enemy transport artery in the Greater Morava Valley. Tito also won a major concession in political and propaganda terms: it would be publicly announced that the intervention came at the official invitation of the NKOJ, which meant that the Western Allies could not land without obtaining one as well. Lastly, Stalin promised to sponsor a massive aid program aimed at transforming the NOVJ into a full-fledged modern army.[1]

When Tito asked for 80-100 tanks to spearhead the NOVJ operations against Belgrade, the Soviet *Vozhd* allegedly replied with a laconic remark "*Dvinem korpus!*" ("We'll give a corps!").[2] By the time the plans for the upcoming battle had been finalized, the attack force grew to two full armies, the 57th and 17th Air, reinforced with the 4th Guards Mechanized Corps (GMC), and a myriad of independent support units. In all, Serbia would be "invaded" by some 100,000 troops, 2,350 artillery pieces and mortars, 358 armored vehicles, and 1,300 aircraft; for Balkan conditions, it was an impressive host. Behind the front, a force of 18 NOVJ divisions stood ready

1 This subchapter is based on Trifković, "Amateurs", pp. 253-76. Additional sources will be mentioned separately; for this paragraph see Timofejev, *Rusi*, pp. 314-16; Maclean, *Eastern*, p. 498; Milan Radanović, *Oslobođenje: Beograd 20. oktobar 1944.* (Belgrade: Rosa Luxemburg Stiftung, 2014), pp. 67-69.

2 Djilas, *Wartime*, p. 406.

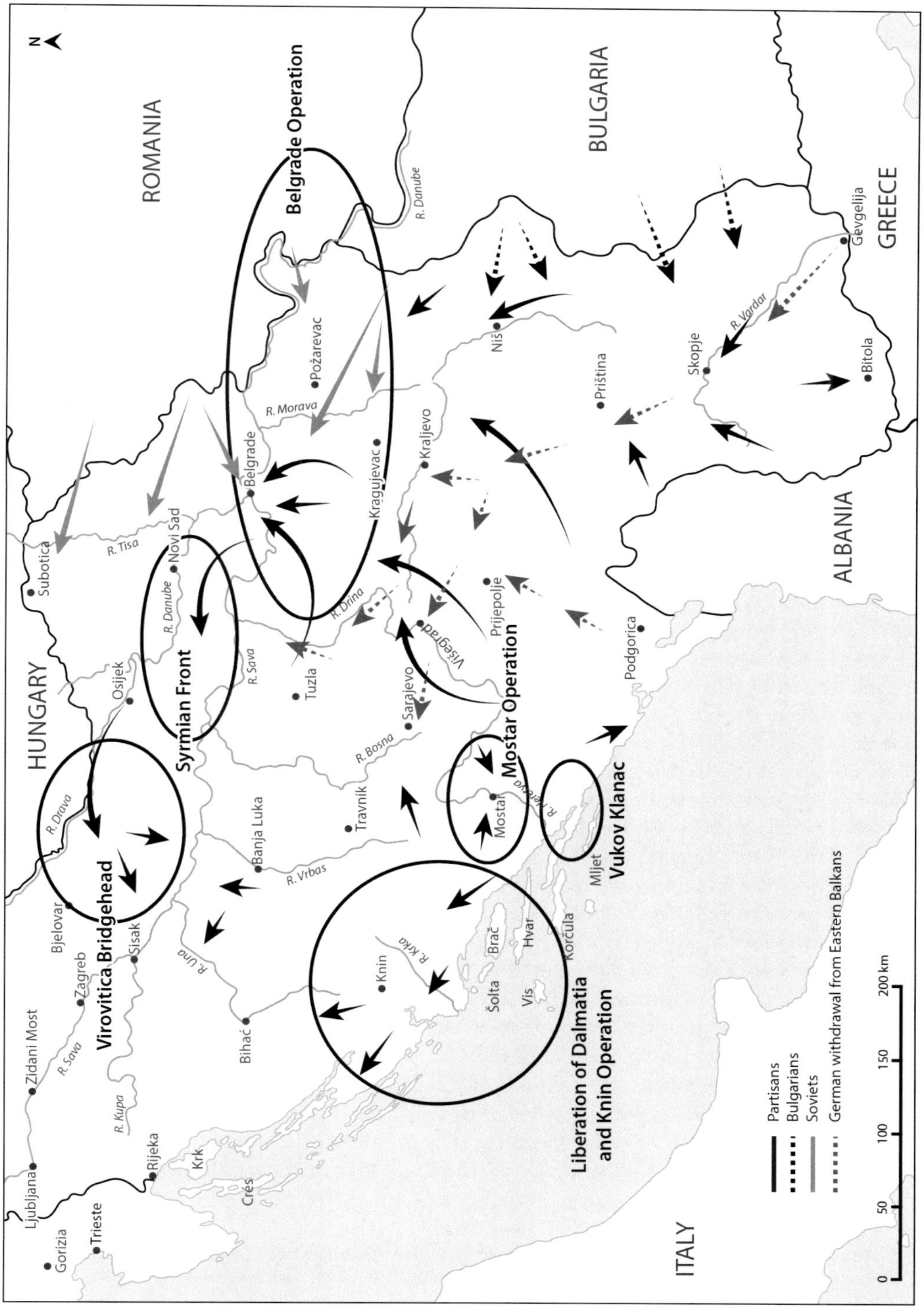

Map 12: Allied operations in Yugoslavia (1944-1945).

to disrupt the enemy rear and provide much needed infantry support for Soviet tanks and heavy weapons (by this stage of the war, the Red Army was experiencing a chronic shortage of plain riflemen). The strength of these divisions fluctuated greatly in the course of the campaign, but it can be assumed that each had about 3-4,000 lightly-armed fighters. The efforts of both armies would be coordinated by Marshal Fyodor Tolbuhin, the CO of the 3rd UF, and Tito, who established a temporary HQ in Craiova. On lower levels, individual NOVJ commands were instructed to seek out their nearest Soviet counterparts and work out a joint plan of action. In short, Tolbuhin intended to form a bridgehead in Eastern Serbia (roughly in the area Kladovo–Zaječar) and use it to launch a dash to the Greater Morava in the Lapovo–Velika Plana sector. Once there, his mobile units would veer northwest towards Belgrade; the secondary attack, aimed at securing the flank and the rear of the main strike force, would be directed at the wider area of Paraćin. Simultaneously, eight divisions of the 1st Proletarian and 12th Corps under Dapčević would move in on the objectives from the west; three divisions of the 14th Corps would first aid the Soviets in crossing the Danube, and then act according to the situation.

The defection of Bulgaria and Romania and the arrival of the Red Army to these countries represented a nightmare scenario for von Weichs. His entire eastern flank, which stretched from Timisoara in the north to Thessaloniki in the south, stood practically "in the air", widely exposed to a technically and numerically superior enemy. In addition to holding Serbia, the OBSO also had to secure the impending extraction of the HGE from Greece and help the neighboring HG "South" by surrendering its only mobile reserve of any importance (4th SS PzGD). Thanks to the persistent efforts of the Western Allies in the air and the NOVJ on the ground, moving troops around the peninsula became excruciatingly slow and tedious business. For example, it took three weeks to transport one-half of the 117th JD from Southern Greece to Belgrade (the other half never made it past Kraljevo before the lines were cut). A similar thing happened to the already mentioned regiment-sized battle groups dispatched from Albania, Montenegro, and the NDH, as well as the reinforcements coming from Macedonia. In the end, Felber's command (the AAS) could muster perhaps some 70,000 German troops with whom to brave the approaching storm. As we have seen in the preceding chapter, the "eastern front" along the Danube and Timok was hastily erected during September by using the 1st MTD, the bulk of the "Prinz Eugen", one "Brandenburg" regiment. These formations represented the best Felber had; the remainder of his command was largely made up of over-aged and under-equipped security battalions, Wehrmacht "refugees" from Romania and Bulgaria, and a couple of armored battalions equipped with obsolete Italian and French models. Collaborationist forces played a minor role in the campaign. The SFK, now reduced to ca. 4,000 men through fighting and desertion, was first withdrawn to Syrmia during the first half of October, and then moved to the OZAK; by contrast, all five regiments of the RSK stayed behind and shared the fate of the German commands they were attached to.[3]

In line with Soviet practice, two divisions of the 75th Rifle Corps (RC) began crossing the Danube at Kladovo on 22 September 1944 with the limited aim of securing the springboard for future operations on the Yugoslav territory. They immediately ran into heavy resistance and were subjected to a vicious counterattack on the 26th that very nearly drove them into the

3 NARA/T77/780/5506981-83, AAS, Operations August-October 1944 (4.11.1944); Vertepov (ed.), *Русский*, pp. 150-68; Bojan B. Dimitrijević, *Vojska Nedićeve Srbije: oružane snage Srpske vlade 1941-1945.* (Belgrade: Službeni glasnik, 2014), pp. 496-502, 520.

river. The critical situation the corps found itself in compelled the 57th Army to launch its own offensive two days earlier than planned. On 28 September, six rifle divisions (RDs) of the 64th and 68th RCs advanced across the Timok. By 3 October, the attackers had managed to take Bor and encircle Zaječar, thus splitting von Stettner's front into three parts. While the Soviet left wing laid siege to Zaječar (which would end five days later in the destruction of a better part of its regiment-sized garrison), the right wing pushed deeper into the mountains west of Bor encountering no resistance. Having found the weak spot in the enemy defenses, Tolbuhin decides to commit his mobile reserves. Using every available hand, including the guerrillas, civilians, and a multitude of recently freed laborers from the nearby copper mines, Soviet engineers managed to repair roads well enough to support the heavy equipment belonging to the 4th GMC. The Germans failed to notice any of this: as if out of the blue, the news reached them on the morning of the 9th that the Soviet T-34s had seized the bridge over the Greater Morava at Lapovo intact. The next several days were spent in frantic efforts to contain the breakthrough and muster enough troops for a decisive counterattack, but this proved to be an impossible task. Attacking from the west, Dapčević's three divisions (the 1st, 5th, and 17th) practically closed the Belgrade–Kragujevac road for enemy traffic and delayed the arrival of two German anti-tank battalions to the bridgehead. 11 October signified the end of the first phase of the battle; Felber ordered a general retreat to the right bank of the Greater Morava, and the elements of the 1st Proletarian Corps made contact with the 68th RC at Velika Plana. All eyes now turned to Belgrade.

Owing to its size, infrastructure, and geographical position, the capital of Yugoslavia undoubtedly represented a strategic object of the first order. The initial defensive measures were introduced in early September 1944, when the city was turned into a defensive zone and received a combat commandant (*Kampfkommandant*); all rear-area personnel were combined into an ad-hoc regiment. The work on the fortifications began at about the same time, but it was far from complete by the time the fighting had reached the city. This happened already in the first days of October as a direct result of the Red Army's advance into Vojvodina. Compared with the bitter fighting raging in Eastern Serbia, the 2nd UF's march through the Yugoslav part of the Banat seemed almost like a Sunday stroll. The Germans, having only six motorized infantry battalions and two batteries of assault guns (plus some other disorganized units), could not even hope to slow down, let alone stop, the advancing 46th Army with its nine rifle divisions. Within three days (1-3 October), the Soviets reached their first immediate objective, the Tisa River, inflicting heavy losses on the Germans in the process: the *Luftwaffe* alone lost 76 airplanes on the abandoned airfields at Alibunar and Ečka. While two rifle corps continued towards Subotica and Szeged, the 10th Guards RC headed to the area between Pančevo and the confluence of the Tisa and Danube.

According to official histories, the corps' subsequent actions were a cleverly conceived diversion, carried out with the aim of confusing the Germans and thus facilitating the main thrust carried out by the 57th Army. Primary sources, however, paint a different picture. Emboldened by the rapid collapse of the enemy defenses, the 46th Army genuinely believed it could take Belgrade on its own, without waiting for Tolbuhin. While the 49th Guards RD was engaged in the bloody siege of Pančevo, the last remaining German bastion on the northern bank of the Danube, its sister formation, the 109th, established a small foothold on the opposite bank at Ritopek. Placed astride the main supply road leading to Eastern Serbia, the Soviet bridgehead represented a mortal threat both to Belgrade and to von Stettner's front. After trying in vain for three days to throw the Soviets into the river with the force of four battalions, and after losing 25 percent of their effectives in the process, the Germans were compelled to go over to the defense. By this time (11 October), the OBSO had begun with the evacuation of the former Pančevo bridgehead (which succeeded admirably), and the 2nd UF decided to transfer the bulk of the 10th Guards RC to Hungary. This effectively meant that there would be no attack against Belgrade from the north; the pocket at Ritopek would remain intact until the end of the battle, but would play negligible role in the operations. It should be noted that the local NOVJ units were present in almost every major clash of the 46th Army, but that their overall contribution to the campaign was understandably small. Probably the most important action took place on 6 October, when the capture of a gendarmerie station southwest of Zemun by the 8th Vojvodina Brigade provoked the nervous Felber into rushing a full reinforced battalion to the spot, something he could ill-afford to do at the time.[4]

The main Yugo-Soviet offensive against Belgrade commenced on 12 October 1944 with the storming of Topola. The next day, two NOVJ divisions supported by one Soviet brigade took Mount Avala, the key topographical position before the capital. With this, the Allies found themselves on the edge of the city's inner defenses, and the enemy resistance stiffened accordingly. The attack could be renewed only on the evening of 14 October after the bulk of the 4th GMC had arrived from the south. The plan, worked out by the corps' CO General Vladimir Zhdanov and Dapčević, was relatively straightforward: frontal push in the direction of the Kalemegdan Fortress and the Sava Bridge with the the newly-arrived 12th NOVJ Corps on the left flank, three NOVJ and two Soviet rifle divisions in the center, and the Soviet motorized brigades on the right. It took the attackers, whose numbers were augmented by a large number of volunteers from the city itself, two days of bloody house-to-house fighting to reach their objectives. The final push, which everyone expected to be launched on the 16th, failed to materialize, however. The explanation for this sudden drop in the Allied pressure lay in the events transpiring just outside the city.[5]

We left the reinforced German 1st MTD locked in a mortal struggle with the 75th RC in Eastern Serbia. Although von Stettner managed to avoid encirclement on Mount Deli Jovan southeast of Majdanpek, his position was becoming more precarious by the hour. Already on 26 September, the sappers of the 14th NOVJ Corps effectively cut the main supply road leading from Petrovac. By the end of the first week of October, the Germans had practically run out of ammunition and the wounded could no longer be evacuated to the rear. The order for a general withdrawal to the Morava therefore came none too soon. In order to aid the breakthrough, Felber dispatched the KG "Witmann" (elements of the 117th JD and the "Brandenburg", as well as the remnants of the 92nd PzGR, which had recently been severely mauled by the Soviets in Romania) from Belgrade. By 16 October, von Stettner's provisional corps (estimated at 20,000 men and 1,500 vehicles) had managed to shake off the pursuers and cross the Morava at Smederevo. Being low on fuel, the Germans opted for a dash to the capital using the shortest route: it was the appearance of their advance guard at Mali Mokri Lug that caused the Allies to call a temporary halt to their offensive. On this day, the 21st Serbian Division was forced to

4 Gaj Trifković, "Operacije Crvene armije u sjevernoj Jugoslaviji 1944-1945. iz sovjetskih dokumenata", *VIG*, 2 (2017), pp. 205-15.
5 TsAMO/413/10372/511/112-17, 57th Army, Study Belgrade Operation (February 1946).

fall back on the Soviet positions in the suburbs, but the counterattack led by the reinforcements hastily redeployed from the city re-claimed the lost ground by the evening of the 17th.

Seeing no alternative, von Stettner decided to abandon all his wounded and heavy equipment, and use the roundabout route leading beneath the Avala. Again, the NOVJ lines south of the mountain buckled under pressure, and the deluge of desperate men poured into the open country beyond. Now all hell broke loose: in addition to concentrated small-arms fire and strafing runs by fighter-bombers, the Germans were subjected to murderous shrapnel fire from the Soviet howitzers, parked hub-to-hub along the retreat route. For the Partisans, it was the moment of supreme satisfaction, a day of reckoning with the hated 1st MTD that had been haunting them since 1943: veteran fighters concluded every attack order with the cry "Remember Sutjeska!" Nevertheless, just as they themselves had managed to escape from countless encirclements, the Germans did the same at Mount Avala, albeit at a terrible cost. An American officer who toured the field immediately after the battle remembered that "wherever you looked there were steaming, silent guns, sleeping Russians, dead Germans." The Yugoslavs, awestruck by the sheer scale of the carnage, were in no condition to mount an effective pursuit; moreover, Zhdanov would not commit any of his own troops for as long as the enemy was still holding out in Belgrade. As a consequence, up to 15,000 survivors of von Stettner's group (he himself was killed, the second Wehrmacht general to die in this area in the past week) reached the German bridgehead at Šabac, from whence they were evacuated to Syrmia. From Felber's perspective, maintaining a foothold on the right bank of the Sava now lost all purpose and he ordered the capital abandoned on the 19th. The process was successfully completed two days later, but not without problems. The Red Army and NOVJ, which resumed their attacks as soon as the external threat was removed, were determined to capture the main bridge intact. Eventually they succeeded thanks to a retired Belgrade schoolteacher who cut the demolition wires. In a dramatic ending of one of the most dramatic battles of the war, German engineers tried setting the bridge on fire and destroying it with an improvised truck bomb, to no avail: covered by artillery, a detail of Soviet infantry made a dash across the bridge and formed a defensive perimeter on the opposite side.[6]

Belgrade Strategic Offensive Operation, as the battle is known in Russia, was one of the smaller events of its kind, but was nonetheless very successful. At a relatively modest price of 2,370 KIA, 9,776 WIA, and 527 MIA, the 57th Army severed the main road and rail communications to Greece and shattered the main Wehrmacht force in the Balkans. The extent of the victory is evident from the official prisoner and booty tally: it included close to 14,300 prisoners (although probably less than half of them were German soldiers), 368 pieces of artillery, 121 tanks and armored cars, and more than 4,000 motor vehicles of various types. In addition to these immediate dividends, the liberation of the better part of Serbia solved the question of securing the Red Army's strategic left flank. This task would be overtaken by the NOVJ, which was now in control of a large and populous territory that could be easily supplied from the USSR. According to official sources, 2,953 of its members lost their lives during the operation, not counting the losses suffered by the 14th NOVJ Corps. Due to the fact that the Partisan units fought literally shoulder to shoulder with their Soviet counterparts, there was a

6 Dmitri A. Volkogonov and Sekula Joksimović (eds.), *Beogradska operacija: 20 oktobar 1944* (Belgrade: VII, 1989), pp. 303-04; Dedijer, *Dnevnik*, Vol. III, pp. 252-53 (19.10.1944); Thayer, *Hands*, pp. 36-37.

lot of double counting of captured enemy soldiers and equipment (a lot of both also changed hands, as we shall see later). Consequently, citing the NOVJ reports on this matter would do little good; suffice it to say that the battle helped temporary solve the shortages of small arms–and of uniforms–in Dapčević's command.[7]

7.2 Slaughterhouse: Syrmian Front (October 1944-March 1945)

Few episodes from the war are as controversial as the so-called "Syrmian Front", a series of exceedingly bloody battles fought in Syrmia and adjoining parts of Serbia, Croatia, and Bosnia in late 1944 and early 1945. The public opinion in contemporary Serbia widely regards the campaign as the prime example of the criminal callousness with which the Communists squandered the lives of Serbian youth, purportedly as a punishment for its lack of enthusiasm for the new order. Often heard is also the opinion that the campaign should not have been fought at all since the Germans were on their way out of the country anyhow. These simplistic and ideologically-colored explanations fail to take into account the *Zeitgeist* and ignore the complex military and political reasons actually dictating the course of the campaign.

To begin with, the front in Syrmia came into being as a natural consequence of the battle for Belgrade: the remainder of the German garrison retreated here, so the Allies had to follow. For the Yugoslavs, it was of paramount importance to add as much depth to the capital's defenses as possible: a sudden enemy jab in this direction, even if only temporarily successful, would have disastrous propaganda consequences. Third, the advance into the Sava-Danube interfluve was dictated by the dynamic of the Eastern Front. Guns had barely fallen silent in Belgrade when Tolbuhin began redeploying the 57th Army to Banat and Bačka, from where it should join the 3rd UF's main thrust into Southern Hungary. The Partisans, determined to cement the NOP's status as a full-fledged member of the anti-Hitler coalition, pledged to keep pace with the Red Army and keep its lengthening left flank secure. In the days immediately following the evacuation of Belgrade, German planers feared an enemy strike from across the Sava upstream from the capital, which would effectively trap Division "Böttcher" (combined parts of von Stettner's command plus the remanants of the Belgrade garrison) in Syrmia. Although Tito lobbied for precisely such a move, the Soviet command had no intention of altering the timetable of the invasion of Hungary. Apart from the temporary deployment of two rifle divisions in the easternmost part of Syrmia, the Red Army's involvement in the campaign would remain limited to a handful of artillery regiments tasked with supporting the Yugoslav infantry. As far as the Germans were concerned, that was about the only good news. The work on altogether six consecutive defensive lines stretching across the width of the province, which began in late summer, was not completed yet. The best the defenders could hope for was to stall the enemy advance until at least the main line, centered on the town of Šid, could be made ready.[8]

7 Ibid.; See also the following (all 57th Army): TsAMO/413/10372/400/59, Casaulty return (October 1944); TsAMO/243/2900/791/158, Results (1-15.10.1944); TsAMO/243/2900/839/139, Results (October 1944); Karl W. Böhme, *Die deutschen Kriegsgefangenen in Jugoslawien* (Munich: Verlag Ernst und Werner Gieseking, 1962), Vol. I/1, pp. 90-91.

8 This subchapter is based on Gaj Trifković, "Carnage in the Land of Three Rivers: The Syrmian Front 1944-1945", *Militärgeschichtliche Zeitschrift*, 75:1 (2016), pp. 94-122. Additional sources will be cited separately; in this case, see *SD*/XXIV/77, Tito to Tolbuhin (15.10.1944).

The Syrmian campaign commenced on 22 October 1944 with an attack by four divisions of the 1st Proletarian and 12th Vojvodina Corps from the bridgeheads at Belgrade and Obrenovac. General Karl Böttcher immediately began a fighting withdrawal, stiffening the resolve of his men with draconian measures: a *Luftwaffe* lieutenant-colonel who lost an important position on the second defensive line (named "Green") was tried and shot. Death sentences alone were not enough, however; a week into the fighting, the Partisans stood before the important town of Mitrovica. At this point, the Germans got the taste of Hitler's notorious interfering with day-to-day operations. Feeling that the main defensive lines were located too far to the west, he ordered the army to make a decisive stand here, on the "Yellow" line. The fighting lasted for three days (28-31 October), but the attackers failed to achieve a breakthrough. Despite having killed, wounded, or captured an equivalent of a guerrilla brigade, the Germans were compelled to continue the retrograde movement. On 7 November, they made a sudden about-face and counterattacked at the village of Manđelos with a pair of reinforced battalions, throwing the NOVJ's center into disarray and spoiling the celebrations of the anniversary of the October Revolution. Operation "Draufgänger", as this rear-guard action was officially known, bought the Germans two days needed for the orderly evacuation of the "Black" line.

By the middle of the month, the front had stabilized along the "Red" position. In addition to being reasonably well-fortified (although still not finished), its flanks were resting firmly on the Danube and Sava; all previous positions except for the first ("Brown", located just outside Inđija) invariably ended on the southern slopes of the Fruška Gora and were therefore easy to outflank. The SHQ recognized that the 12th Corps, in its present condition, could not carry the new enemy position. Its divisions had barely had a day's rest since they began their march to Serbia in July; the entire corps had only two artillery pieces and was generally short on ammunition. Belgrade therefore decided to call a temporary halt to the offensive. The 16th and 36th Vojvodina Divisions were transferred north of the Danube and replaced by the reminder of the 1st Proletarian Corps. In addition to bringing in "fresh blood", Tito finally managed to secure the full participation of the Red Army in the upcoming battle. One, later two, divisions of the 68th RC, together with support units, were brought over from Central Serbia, and took position on the far right of the Allied line. On the other side of the front, the veteran staff of the 118th JD had taken over, but this brought little concrete relief, as Syrmia was being constantly denuded of troops in favor of other sectors.[9]

In the early morning hours of 3 December 1944, the Allies started their "big push" on the Syrmian Front that was supposed to propel them to Vinkovci in only three days' time. The point of main effort was in the north, where the 52nd RD was attacking on a narrow front supported by nearly every available piece of artillery. To the south, the 1st Proletarian, 11th Krajina, and 21st Serbian Divisions simultaneously went forward in their sectors. By the end of the next day, the attackers had taken Ilok and Erdevik against very heavy resistance. This, combined with the landing of a mixed Soviet-Yugoslav force at Opovo, far to the rear of the front, spelled the end of the "Red" line. The German hope that the enemy could be stopped on the main defensive position in the province, named "Nibelungen", were dispersed on the very next day when the

9 NARA/T501/257/235, AAS, Daily report (26.10.1944); NARA/T311/194/708, OBSO to PzAOK 2 (28.10.1944); *Zbornik*/I/10/135-36, 12th NOVJC to 1st Proletarian NOVJC (13.11.1944); Ljubivoje Pajović, Dušan Uzelac, Milovan Dželebdžić, *Sremski front 1944–1945* (Belgrade: BIGZ, 1979), pp. 61, 66; NARA/T314/850/1258, Corps group "Kübler", Activity report (12.11-12.12.1944).

Partisans took Šid. Although the reserve trench belt held out for two more days, the Allies had cut the all-important Vinkovci-Brčko railway line at Otok by the 8th and were preparing to take on the final defensive line in Syrmia, codenamed "Green".

At this point, their offensive began to lose steam. The attempt to make another successful riverborne assault, this time at Sotin, failed and resulted in heavy losses to two Soviet battalions and one Vojvodina brigade. Undeterred, the Allies threw altogether four divisions against Vukovar on 14 December but were stopped in their tracks by the German reinforcements that were finally beginning to arrive from Bosnia. This was as far as Tolbuhin was willing to go: the precious Soviet troops were hurriedly transferred to the main front in Hungary and replaced by the 1st Bulgarian Army (BA). Although having a nominal strength of more than 100,000 men, its stay in Syrmia was brief and inglorious. On 22 December, two of its divisions tried to achieve a breakthrough in the northern sector but were repulsed with significant casualties. As the NOVJ units fared the same in their sectors, the offensive was canceled for good seven days later. Given that the Bulgarians had no desire to serve here in the first place, and that the Yugoslavs were equally eager to see them gone, the 3rd UF agreed to move the 1st BA to the Drava. By the beginning of 1945, the entire Syrmian Front was held exclusively by the Partisans: while three divisions stood between the Danube and Bosut, only one division was deployed in the large and heavily forested area between the Bosut and Sava.[10]

Having defeated the Allied December offensive, the HQ of the XXXIV AC (which had recently taken over from the 118th JD) began to contemplate a counterstroke. The first priority was to push the Partisans as far as possible from the railway line which lead to Bosnia. For this purpose, a task force consisting of one regiment each from the 297th ID and 11th LWFD and spearheaded by a battalion of veterans from the "Prinz Eugen" would assail the overstretched 21st Serbian Division around Otok. On 3 January 1945, white-painted tanks accompanied by white-clad infantry suddenly appeared on the Partisans' unprotected southern flank. The precipitous retreat towards the Bosut, which started almost instantaneously, nearly ended in a massacre when the Germans captured the main crossing site at Nijemci. The 21st was saved from destruction that day only by the fact that the river was frozen enough to support the weight of a man. The bulk of its Soviet-made heavy weapons–some of them still unpacked–had to be left behind on the western bank. Being low on artillery ammunition and not wanting to be drawn into a major engagement, the XXXIV AC stopped the attack on the 4th. The Germans had every reason to be well-satisfied with the results: an officer from the 7th SS even got a Knight's Cross, which was rarely awarded for actions in the Balkans. On the other side of the front, the mood was far from jubilant. Much like it did with the 2nd Proletarian Division after the disaster at Prijepolje some 13 months earlier, the SHQ now sacked the entire HQ of the 21st Serbian and disciplined the staffs of individual brigades.[11]

By the middle of the month, material preconditions for a much bigger undertaking were finally met. Operation "Wintergewitter" had two objectives: to re-gain the old "Nibelungen" line (which was far more favorable than the "Green") and destroy as many NOVJ formations as possible in the process. For this purpose, the 7th SS MTD and 117th JD would strike east and

10 TsAMO/243/2900/216, 68th RC, Map (3-7.12.1944); Pajović et al., *Sremski*, pp. 115-19; Nikola Mraović, *Peta vojvođanska brigada* (Novi Sad: ISI, 1985), pp. 324-39.

11 Milorad Gončin, *Četvrta srpska udarna brigada* (Belgrade: ISI, 1996), pp. 305-08; Stanimir Jovanović, Dragoljub Mirčetić, *Peta srpska NOU brigada* (Belgrade: VINC, 1989), pp. 241-43.

south from Sotin in hope of catching the bulk of the newly-created 1st Yugoslav Army between themselves and the 41st Fortress Division (later renamed "Infantry") advancing from the west. The Germans commenced the offensive on 17 January, only one day after Tito, blissfully ignorant of the gathering storm, had completed a tour of the front. The 1st Proletarian and 5th Krajina Divisions gave way almost immediately. For the "Italia" Brigade, which was a part of the army's premier outfit, it was a *gioranta maledetta* ("an accursed day"): hit from two sides simultaneously, the entire unit dissolved into a mass of panic-stricken stragglers. Tovarnik fell on the same day, forcing Dapčević to retreat to the line Šarengrad–Šid–Gradina. On the 18th, the Germans exerted the strongest pressure against the enemy center; the fighting was especially bitter in and around Šid, which was finally taken in the evening. Having already pushed beyond the original objectives, the XXXIV AC went over to the defensive.

The main task of the 7th SS and the 117th JD now was to buy enough time for the 41st Fortress Division to carry out the necessary works on the main defensive position. On 22 January, Dapčević launched an all-out counterattack with the help of the 2nd Proletarian Division, rushed to the front from Belgrade, and two Soviet air divisions. The Germans fought one of those clockwork-like rear-guard actions they became famous for; the Partisans had to take nearly every village by storm. After all attempts to breach the new enemy line centered on Tovarnik on the 23rd had ended in failure, the bloodied and utterly exhausted 1st Proletarian Corps was allowed to stand down. The events from the past several weeks convinced the Yugoslav planners that half-measures were not working and that the breakthrough could be achieved only by a thoroughly trained and equipped force. Syrmia ironically became one of the quietest parts of Yugoslavia during the following two-and-a-half months. Apart from the activities typical of trench warfare, such as patrolling, sniping, and shelling, there was little to report. Everyone knew, however, that all that would change in the spring.[12]

7.3 Ancillary Front on Drava (October 1944-March 1945)

Nearly all significant events that transpired in Podravina, Slavonia, and Baranja in late 1944 and early 1945 were in one way or the other connected to the Syrmian Front, hence the sobriquet "ancillary" in the title. Encountering practically no opposition, the Soviets and Partisans had liberated Bačka and reached the Danube in the area between its confluence with the Drava and the town of Baja by the end of October 1944. The next step towards the west will not be as easy, since the Axis were determined not to surrender this last major natural obstacle before Lake Balaton without a fight. The 57th Army, which had in the meantime taken its place on the extreme left flank of Tolbuhin's front, was again chosen to lead the attack. According to the original plan, the 75th RC, aided by the NOVJ's youngest division, the 51st Vojvodina, would first secure a bridgehead around Batina; then, mobile reserves (the 6th GRC) would be introduced into battle and race to Pécs and Nagykanizsa. The initial Allied landings on 7 November did not fail to achieve surprise, as the terrain here was considered particularly unfavorable for a major operation of this sort, with soft, swampy ground on the Serbian bank of the river, and a 200 meter-high ridge with vertical cliffs on the Croatian one. The Germans (the LXVIII AC of the PzAOK 2), however, quickly regained their composure and began a

12 Bistarelli, *Resistenza*, pp. 433-35; *SD*/XXVI/192; *Zbornik*/I/18/348.

series of counterattacks that very nearly drove the attackers into the Danube. Nevertheless, by 16 November, the Soviets and Partisans had managed to secure the village of Batina and the heavily contested Hill 169 nicknamed The Pyramid, or more tellingly, The Bloody Hill.

The contest, however, was far from over, as both sides threw ever more forces into the fray: the Soviets, their second-echelon 64th RC; the Germans, a host of smaller units (largely drawn from the Syrmian Front), as well as the 71st, and the 44th "Hoch-und-Deutschmeister" ID brought over from Italy. It was a battle of attrition, and the Wehrmacht had no chance of winning it: the entire LXVIII AC was beginning to "show signs of disintegration" as regiments melted into battalions, and battalions into companies. By the 29th, the Germans were in full retreat, with the Soviets in close pursuit; the 51st Vojvodina was ordered to occupy the section of the Drava overlooking Osijek and wait for the arrival of the 12th NOVJ Corps from Syrmia. For the Soviets, the Battle of Batina (a part of the wider Apatin-Kaposvár Advance Operation) was in many ways more important than the Belgrade Operation. For example, the losses in both campaigns were comparable (ca. 11,500 KIA, WIA, MIA) with the difference that 32 servicemen were awarded the title Hero of the Soviet Union for their actions at Batina, as opposed to only four in Serbia. The Soviet 17th Air Army averaged about 100 sorties a day in September-October compared with ca. 330 in November. For the young Vojvodina recruits, the battle represented a nightmarish baptism of fire: the 51st suffered an estimated 2,500 casualties, almost half of whom were KIA.[13]

By the time 12th NOVJ Corps had appeared on the Drava, a significant part of Podravina was already in the Partisan hands. As mentioned in the previous chapter, the 6th and 10th Corps with their five divisions began operating extensively in this direction already in September 1944. Using the northern slopes of the Bilogora as their base, they commenced their main offensive against the enemy garrisons located along the main provincial road in early October. On the 5th, the 12th Slavonian captured the important urban center Virovitica after a 40-hour fight against a mix of the HDB NCO candidates and Ustasha railway guards. Nearly simultaneously, the 32nd and 33rd Divisions took Pitomača and Kloštar Podravski; at the latter place, the last pocket of resistance had to be burned down together with its obstinate occupants. A week later, a similar fate befell Đurđevac, Virje, and Podravski Novigrad.

The survivors sought refuge in Koprivnica, the site of the major Partisan victory and seat of their local "republic" from late 1943 and early 1944. The staffs of the 6th and 10th Corps were now intent on replicating this success, but they failed to take into account the strength and determination of the defenders. It was thought that the objective was defended by only one full battalion, plus the remnants of the garrisons of the aforementioned outlying strongpoints, for a total of ca. 500 men. In fact, they numbered four times as many, divided into seven infantry, one mobile and one armored battalion. All of them belonged to the elite Ustasha outfits, the PTS and the 5th UAB; although they had taken a heavy beating in the recent days, their will to fight was far from broken. Consequently, when four Partisan brigades attacked in the early morning hours of 14 October, they encountered unexpectedly strong resistance. Lieutenant-Colonel

13 The main source for Yugo-Soviet cooperation on the Drava sector is Trifković, *Operacije*, pp. 215-25; additional sources for the Battle of Batina include NARA/T311/194/1064 (OBSO, Daily report, 22.11.1944) 1189 (OBSO to PzAOK 2, 29.11.1944); Sveta Savić, *Pedesetprva vojvođanska divizija* (Belgrade: VIZ, 1974), pp. 23-52; Timfejev, *Rusi*, pp. 326-27; Nikola Božović, *Rovovi i mostobrani: Osma vojvođanska brigada* (Novi Sad: ISI, 1989), pp. 295-99.

Rafael Boban, Francetić's old deputy and commander of the garrison, kept the spirit of his men high by having a music band play a mix of Croatian and Wagnerian martial music; he also had three of his own officers and a dozen men executed for unauthorized withdrawal. On the NOVJ side, nothing seemed to function except for the courage of the common fighter. There was little coordination between assault details; none of the 26 available cannon were used in direct support role but fired from afar with little effect. After repeated assaults with fresh reserves over the next couple of days failed to produce the desired effect, the Partisans withdrew, with the 10th Corps going to the Bilogora and the 6th to Slavonia. Both sides suffered heavily in the Podravina campaign. Among else, the Partisans captured ca. 650 pieces of small-arms in Virovitica, close to 200 in Kloštar Podravski (plus five tankettes), and 57 in the Đurđevac area (plus four tanks). Whereas the combined NOVJ casualties in these battles amounted to ca. 600, the losses at Koprivnica are estimated to have been around 1,000 men (compared to about 300 defenders), making it one of the costliest battles fought on Croatian soil.[14]

After enjoying some much-deserved R&R, the bulk of the 6th Corps went south in order to interdict the enemy traffic on the main railway line and roads leading towards the newly-established Syrmian Front. The twin-ambush carried out by the parts of the 40th Division on the outskirts of Okučani on 25-26 October 1944 deserves a special mention. Although the Partisans reported setting fire to altogether 51 motor vehicles and capturing a similar number of small arms, Axis sources are silent about this event. By mid-November, the corps had shifted the main point of effort to the eastern part of its native province; apart from one short intervention around Pleternica and Slavonska Požega in early December, it would stay there until early 1945. Its mission remained unchanged: to exert pressure on the rear of the enemy front in Syrmia by attacking the communications linking Osijek with Bosnia via Đakovo, as well as other targets of opportunity located on the edges of the Slavonian Mountains. The Partisans' main adversaries now were Kammerhofer's gendarmes, some 15,000 of whom were deployed in dozens of strongpoints of varying size scattered throughout this area. The series of encounters that followed confirmed that, in terms of combat potential, German-Croatian Police occupied the middle place between the *Domobrani* and the Ustashe. On 12 November, Osijek Brigade destroyed an entire battalion in the fortified village of Piškorevci; its own losses were 23 men, including its commander. "It is the second Podgorač", exclaimed the jubilant CO of the 12th Division, Milan Stanivuković, referring to the great victory over the policemen from June of the same year (Stanivuković, who replaced the late Nikola Demonja in early September, would himself be killed not far from Piškorevci along 30 of his comrades during one enemy attack in late December).

The NOVJ campaign culminated in the clash for Našice, styled "the biggest and fiercest battle in Slavonia yet". It lasted for over a week (17-25 November) and involved a force of 9,000 Partisans, who fired 750,000 rounds of ammunition. As it happened so often in the past, the attackers managed to take the town almost immediately, but failed to root out the defenders. What did change was the Partisans' ability to keep a relief force (including, in this case, two battalions and a handful of tanks dispatched from the Syrmian Front) at bay for days on end. In the end, it was a Pyrrhic victory for the Germans, whose irrevocable losses amounted to over

14 Zdravko B. Cvetković, *Osječka NOU brigada* (Belgrade: VIZ, 1981), pp. 105-12; Rade Bulat, *Deseti korpus 'Zagrebački' NOV i POJ* (Zagreb: Globus, 1985), pp. 146-85; Obhođaš et al., *Vojnica*, Vol. II, pp. 400-09.

400 men; the 6th Corps lost less than half as many and retired to the the mountains in good order.[15]

The Red Army established direct contact with the 6th and 10th NOVJ Corps in early December 1944. The latter had been operating against enemy communications in Moslavina, Zagorje, and around Bilogora since the Battle of Koprivnica. Now, it agreed to aid the Soviet advance by dispatching one of its divisions behind enemy lines in Southern Hungary. Ultimately, however, the plan was scrapped despite the fact that the "expeditionary force" had already crossed the Drava. Instead, the Soviets decided they needed as many troops as possible on the river's right bank in order to protect the 57th Army's advance towards the Balaton. For this purpose, the 233rd RD (up to 5,000 men) was tasked with erecting a defensive perimeter south of Barcs. From the OBSO's standpoint, what used to be an "ordinary" guerrilla-held territory in Slavonia and Podravina now turned into the Virovitica Bridgehead, a strategic threat of the first order. Although the Soviets had no offensive intentions here, the Germans could not ignore the possibility of a sudden thrust against the rear of their main front in the Balkans. Containing the bridgehead by using the reinforcements from Bosnia was impossible because Syrmia was "drawing troops like a magnet". For the time being, units of LXIX RC and NDH armed forces would have to do the job.

On 10 December, one Cossack brigade started frontally pushing the 10th Corps from Koprivnica. Soon, the elements of the PTS and recently-formed 1st Croatian Assault Division (*Hrvatska udarna divizija*, HUD) joined the fray by making a flanking attack through the Bilogora. The Partisans fell back to the fortified Soviet positions at Pitomača, which, however, proved unable to stop the Cossacks: on 26 December, the 233rd RD lost some seven percent of its manpower and nearly half of its artillery. The Axis onslaught finally ran out of steam just outside Virovitica 10 days later. They then tried approaching their objective from the south and southeast using one Cossack brigade and three NDH regiments (Operation "Bergpartie"). The offensive, met with a skillful defense by the 16th Vojvodina Division (which had come over together with the Soviets), petered out by the last week of January 1945 without having achieved any substantial success.[16]

In the meantime, the units of the 1st BA were beginning to arrive to the northern bank of the Drava from Syrmia, thus relieving the remainder of the 12th NOVJ Corps for service in Podravina. With these forces, General Nađ, the CO of the 3rd Yugoslav Army, now had seven divisions (the 12th, 16th, 32nd, 33rd, 40th, 36th, and 51st) with which to mount a limited offensive with the aim of aiding his colleague, Dapčević, who was being hard-pressed in Syrmia at that time (Operation "Wintergewitter"). The Partisans "went over the top" on 20 January 1945. The main point of effort was on the western side of the perimeter, where two Vojvodina divisions tried to capture Čađavica and the tactically important New Drava Canal. Although

15 *Zbornik*/V/35/29-31 (6th NOVJC, Activity report, October 1944), 62-64 (40th NOVJD to 6th NOVJC, 4.11.1944), 586-87; *Zbornik*/V/36/223-25, 6th NOVJC, Activity report (20.10-15.12.1944); NARA/T311/194/1003, OBSO to PzAOK 2 (17.11.1944); NARA/T311/191/366, 402, OBSO, Diary (21 and 26.11.1944, respectively); Cvetković, *Osječka*, pp. 128-29.

16 *Tridesetdruga divizija NOVJ* (Zagreb: Globus, 1988), pp. 169-76; NARA/T311/195/192, OBSO, Telephone conversations (14.12.1944); NARA/T311/191/481, 521, OBSO, Diary (10 and 22.12.1944, respectively); Colić, *Pregled*, pp. 298-300.

effectively supported by the Bulgarian artillery from across the river, none of the attacks came through. Consequently, Nađ called off the offensive on 1 February.[17]

The relative quiet would not last for long. With the Syrmian Front stabilized, the Germans could finally muster enough forces to deal with the Virovitica Bridgehead once and for all. Codenamed "Wehrwolf", it was to be one of the last, great anti-Partisan sweeps of the war involving parts of five German (the 1st CCD, 7th SS MTD, 11th LWFD, 297th ID, and Division For Special Employment "Stephan") and three NDH divisions (the 1st and 7th, and the PTS). The idea was simple: cut the base of the salient by simultaneous attacks from the east and west and destroy the enemy forces stranded on the southern bank of the Drava. By the beginning of the offensive on 4 February 1945, the bridgehead had lost its previous importance for the Allies: the Soviet contingent was withdrawn already in the second half of January. Four days into offensive, as it became clear that the positions could not be held for any length of time, Tito authorized the withdrawal of the 12th Corps to Hungary via the pontoon bridge at Barcs. The 6th and 10th Corps would stay behind and find their way out of the cauldron, just like in the old days. A cross-river evacuation under enemy pressure is one of the most difficult maneuvers known in the art of war; much to its credit, the 12th Corps now completed it with full success. By 10 February, the Germans had re-established a continuous front on the Drava.

While some outfits–such as the 297th ID, which had marched and fought all the way from Albania–finally got a chance for some rest, others were sent after the remaining Partisan forces, which were now concentrating on the southwestern slopes of the Bilogora and the adjacent parts of the Ravna Gora, Psunj, and Papuk. The second phase of the "Wehrwolf" ended in a partial success on or about 21 February. The 10th Corps was forced to leave the area of Daruvar and seek refuge in Moslavina. The 6th Corps managed to remain on its native terrain after having several sharp clashes with the enemy columns moving north-south over the mountain roads. Ultimately, the operation would be best remembered for the large quantities of food and other supplies captured or destroyed by the Axis. "At any rate, the Papuk remained a source of danger", noted the HGE's chief of staff. This was amply confirmed only days after the "Wehrwolf" ended, when the 12th and 40th NOVJ Divisions again gave a bloody nose to Kammerhofer's forces in the Zvečevo-Voćin area (one battalion lost half of its strength and most of its heavy weapons). However, the attacks on the police outposts at Stražeman and Velika on 21 March, as well as Vetovo on 10 April, ended up in costly defeats (45 KIA, 144 WIA, 36 MIA were lost at Stražeman and Velika alone).[18]

The re-capture of the Drava bank enabled OBSO's forces to take part in Operation "Frühlingserwachen", Hitler's last-ditch attempt to turn the tables on the Soviets in Hungary. The attack by the PzAOK 2[19] south of the Balaton was to be joined by two divisions of von Weichs' LXXXXI AC, which were to form a bridgehead in the area Harkány-Bolman and advance on Mohács from there. Operation "Waldteufel" opened on 6 March 1945: the 104th JD and 297th ID crossed the river at Donji Miholjac in the sector of the 1st BA, while the 11th LWFD struck at Valpovo against the startled 3rd Yugoslav Army (three Vojvodina divisions of

17 Ibid., pp. 301-02.

18 Pajović et al., *Sremski*, pp. 275-88; Schmidt-Richberg, *Endkampf*, pp. 96, 113-14; see also the 6th Corps' reports in *Zbornik*/V/39/31-54 (2.3.1945), 112 (16.3.1945), as well as the reports by the 40th Division to the 6th Corps in *Zbornik*/XI/3/122-29 (24.3.1945), 254-59 (13.4.1945).

19 The PzAOK 2 was subordinated to HG "South" in the aftermath of the Batina battle.

the 12th NOVJ Corps). After five days of fierce fighting, the two sides had fought each other to a standstill. Although they managed to contain the bridgehead, the Yugoslavs had no strength to liquidate it by themselves. Acknowledging the fact that a further advance was out of the question without reinforcements, the Germans dispatched the 1st CCD to the northern bank of the Drava on the 15th. Three days later, the division took Torjanci in what was the most serious attempt so far to affect a link-up with the western bridgehead (during this episode, a German officer was awarded the Knight's Cross, allegedly for leading a mounted saber charge against enemy artillery in the middle of the night). By this time, the main Axis offensive in Hungary had been defeated, and the order went out to evacuate the bridgeheads. Once the 104th JD and 297th ID were gone, the Soviet 133rd RC would be able to assist the Yugoslavs at Bolman. The Germans, however, again stole a march on the Allies by withdrawing in near-total secrecy on 20-22 March, leaving back nothing but mines and booby-traps. The 3rd Yugoslav Army re-occupied its old positions and began preparations for the upcoming spring offensive.[20]

7.4 Ancillary Front on Drina (October 1944-March 1945)

In terms of strategic importance, few regions in Yugoslavia could compete with Eastern Bosnia, particularly its border area along the Drina. During the first three years of the war, the Germans needed it in order to keep the Partisans away from Serbia (the Ustashe, of course, saw it as a buffer against "the Greater Serbian threat"). In fall 1944, however, the Partisans needed it to keep the Germans out of Bosnia. During this time, the region became the entry point for the hundreds of thousands of Wehrmacht soldiers and their camp followers coming from Greece, Albania, and eastern parts of Yugoslavia. Once they reached the Drina, usually in the Višegrad–Goražde area, the endless columns would continue to Sarajevo ("the promised land", as one veteran called it), which was turned into a major army transit camp. There, the soldiers were usually given a brief rest, together with a hot meal and winter uniforms, before continuing their journey north to Slavonia and beyond. This was the ideal case: combat outfits were more likely to be sent straight to the main front in Syrmia via the shortest possible route leading through Ljubovija and Bijeljina.[21]

Already on 9 October 1944, the SHQ made the interdiction of these enemy movements the primary task of the 3rd NOVJ Corps. Although having a large liberated territory to protect and few means to do it, the corps' HQ was determined to see this mission through. The 27th

20 Klaus Schmider, "The Yugoslavian Thatre of War (January 1943 to May 1945)", in *Germany and the Second World War, Vol. VIII: The Eastern Front 1943–1944: The War in the East and on the Neighbouring Fronts* (Oxford: Clarendon Press, 2017), p. 1064; VAB/German Collection [GC]/72/1/4/4, [Statment of] Hans Bauernstädter/11th LWFD (undated, but post-1945); VAB/GC/71/1/43/2, Hans Meinicke-Kleint/LXXXXI AC (13.7.1947); Heinrich-Detloff von Kalben, Constantin Wagner, "Zur Geschichte des XV. Kosaken-Kavallerie Korps", *Deutsches Soldatenjahrbuch*, 18 (1970), p. 110-11; see also the after-action reports of the 3rd Yugoslav Army in *Zbornik*/XI/3/27-34, 130-35 (11 and 26.3.1945, respectively).

21 NARA/T311/197/12, 14, HGE, Great Retrograde Movement in the Southeast (January 1945); NARA/T311/184, HGE/QM, Situation report (16.11.1944; Erich von Stering, *Jeder war ein Stück von uns: Leben und Kampf einer Kompanie auf ihrem Weg von Attika nach Sarajewo Herbst 1944* (Neckargemünd: Kurt Vowinckel Verlag, 1959), p. 238; Alois Beck, "Sarajevo—Slav. Brod—Donje Miholjac", in Alois Beck (ed.), *Bis Stalingrad...* (Ulm: Helmuth Abt Verlag, 1983), p. 290.

Division was therefore sent south to the new operational area between the Drina and Mount Romanija. In addition to attacking the traffic, the Partisans would also seek to reduce smaller NDH garrisons and spread the NOP influence in the area. The taking of Rogatica and Crvene Stijene in late October, however, provoked an immediate counterattack by the 1st UAB, which in turn led to the loss of over 40 men of the 19th Birač Brigade. There was also one other problem, the shortage of demolition tools. Luckily for the 27th, the alliance with the British, although troubled at the moment, was still functioning. Between 4 and 6 November, the division received a massive airdrop of supplies necessary for the completion of the main job. The Višegrad–Sokolac road became the scene of almost daily clashes with the passing Axis convoys. The Sjemeć Pass was a particularly dangerous spot for the latter: on 29 November, the Partisans ambushed a *Luftwaffe* column, destroying at least 30 vehicles and killing, wounding, or capturing over 100 men (NOVJ sources speak of much higher figures; OBSO's reports barely mention the incident).[22]

The northern half of the 3rd Corps' zone of responsibility remained comparatively peaceful during October and November 1944. The 38th Division and a handful of local detachments were guarding Tuzla, at the same time skirmishing with hostile militias. By the first week of December, however, alarming news were coming in from the Drina: the KG "Skanderbeg", marching from Sokolac and Vlasenica, joined hands at Zvornik with the 7th SS MTD and 11th LWFD arriving from the east. As there could be no doubt that the ultimate destination of this powerful enemy group was Syrmia, the SHQ ordered the blocking of the main northbound road with both divisions of the 3rd Corps; four divisions of the recently-formed Southern Operational Group (*Južna operativna grupa*, JOG) from Serbia were also thrown into the fray. In spite of these massive reinforcements, the Germans managed to fight their way through after two weeks of costly fighting (11-24 December). The 45th Serbian and 17th Eastern Bosnian Divisions suffered particularly heavy losses when they were caught in the open by the advancing "Prinz Eugen" around Bijeljina and Janja. The breakthrough had far-reaching consequences, enabling the XXXIV AC to stabilize its front in Syrmia and set up proper defenses on the Drava. For the Partisans, the only positive outcome of this episode was that the entire Drina Valley was now empty of enemy troops. Their forces in Eastern Bosnia now had a secure supply link to Western Serbia via the main crossing at Zvornik. The liberated territory became a favorable jump-off point for strategic offensives in several possible directions: to the north against the enemy positions guarding the right flank of the Syrmian Front; to the west against the all-important road and rail communications linking Sarajevo with Brod; and to the south against the HGE's bridgehead in the area Sarajevo–Višegrad.[23]

The German drive north along the Drina in mid-December 1944 was facilitated to a certain degree by the arrival of the main JVuO force from Serbia to Eastern Bosnia. In order to explain how it got there in the first place, we need to go back to the days of the Soviet offensive in

22 For the events in Eastern Bosnia from the NOVJ perspective see monthly reports by the 3rd NOVJ Corps in *Zbornik*/IV/30/495-503 (October 1944), *Zbornik*/IV/31/341-50 (November 1944), *Zbornik*/IV/32/403-12 (December 1944). See also: *Zbornik*/IV/30/493; *Devetnaesta birčanska brigada* (Belgrade: VINC, 1989), p. 244; TNA/HW5/625/HP8312, LW Greece to 4th Air Fleet (30.11.1944); NARA/T311/194/1184, OBSO, Daily report (29.11.1944).

23 *Zbornik*/IV/31/732-38, 14th NOVJC, Report Drina (31.12.1944); Mandić, *Sedamnaesta*, pp. 280-93; Kumm, *Vorwärts*, pp. 338-49.

Serbia. Ironically, Mihailović and his top commanders regarded the arrival of the Red Army as an opportunity to regain a degree of legitimacy in the eyes of the Big Three, and thus win some much-needed breathing space in the war against the NOP. Throughout September and October, several high-ranking Chetnik leaders offered their services to the Red Army, occasionally bringing in as a sweetener the Germans (including one corps' chief of staff) they had captured by surprise shortly before. Soviet troop commanders, having no knowledge of the intricacies of the war in Yugoslavia, were inclined to accept any helping hand regardless of its origin. The local Communists, who were otherwise deferential in the relations with their "older cousins", took an uncompromising stand on this issue. While higher commands filed protests with Tito's backing, officers on the ground would sometimes simply gun down any royalists they encountered in Soviet company. Eventually, Moscow intervened, prohibiting any further contact with Mihailović and ordering his men disarmed on sight. The general's plan had backfired spectacularly and the Chetniks were now literally alone. Lieutenant-Colonel Velimir Piletić, who crossed the Danube already in mid-September, was arrested in Romania. The same thing happened to some 2,000 Chetniks at Kruševac; their commander, Keserović, had barely escaped. The chaos that reigned in Serbia in those days is best shown on the example of Čačak. On 16-17 October, the 4th GAC attacked the German garrison there with the knowledge of the Soviet command. On hearing what happened at Kruševac, Račić and Neško Nedić contacted the town defenders, offering to lift the siege and return prisoners in exchange for ammunition "needed to fight Tito, who is backed by the Soviet occupier". Irony would have it that the 64th RC ordered one of its divisions to capture Čačak "in cooperation with the Chetniks" practically on the same day.[24]

Eventually, the Germans turned out to be the only ones willing to work with the royalists. By the beginning of November 1944, the ca. 15,000 remaining Chetniks from Serbia had retreated to the area Sjenica–Prijepolje. From there, they proceed slowly east, marching parallel with HGE columns. At this point, the relations between the two sides could be described as neutral; however, once the Chetniks designated Northeastern Bosnia as their ultimate destination (Mihailović himself was already there), Wehrmacht commanders again became interested in closer cooperation. In exchange for the release of their men from captivity, they agreed to "finance" the JVuO's advance on Tuzla with modest quantities of ammunition and other supplies. As far as Löhr was concerned, it was a win-win situation. The deal removed the unreliable royalists from his own lines of communication and was guaranteed to draw at least some enemy attention away from the 7th SS MTD and other units moving towards Bijeljina. The Chetniks, together with the remainder of the former SSW (now known under the grandiose name Serbian Assault Corps), opened their attack on 8 December. As predicted, the 3rd Corps took first one, than both of its divisions off the Drina sector and sent them against the JVuO.

24 *SD*/XXIII/105, Tito to MHQ Serbia (11.9.1944); *Zbornik*/XIV/4/402 (Mihailović to Wilson, 8.11.1944), 530 (Ostojić to Keserović, 22.10.1944), 578-79 (Račić to JVuO's forward HQ, 16-22.10.1944); NARA/T314/849/666, Corps Group "Müller", Telephone conversations (15.10.1944); Blažo Janković, "Oslobođenje Kruševca, Trstenika i Vrnjačke Banje i prodor ka Kraljevu", in Koča Jončić (ed.), *Borbe sa glavninom nemačke grupe armija E na ibarsko-zapadnomoravskom pravcu u oslobađanju zapadne Srbije 1944. godine* (Belgrade: VII, 1990), pp. 172-74 (see also pp. 573-76); TsAMO/956/1/142/5, 64th RC, Diary (14.10.1944); TsAMO/961/1/77/278, 93rd RD, Diary (22.10.1944); TsAMO/500/12460/43/31 (von Faninger to AAS, 17.10.1944), 33-40 [Correspondence 4th GAC–German command Čačak, 17-18.10.1944].

After three weeks of heavy fighting, however, the attackers stood on the Spreča, dangerously close to their objective; only thanks to the arrival of a third NOVJ division (the 23rd Serbian) could the offensive be defeated. Instead of spending the winter in the relative comfort of Tuzla, the exhausted royalists had to settle for impoverished mountain villages on the Ozren and Trebava.[25]

Barely had the Chetnik threat passed when the HQ of the newly-formed 2nd Yugoslav Army (CO: Koča Popović) received more bad news: the German 963rd Fortress Brigade (FB) had suddenly taken Vlasenica on New Year's Day 1945. The move represented the first step towards the re-occupation of the Drina Valley between Drinjača and Bijeljina. Probably under the impression of the NOVJ's poor performance during the "Prinz Eugen's" recent operations in the same area, the HGE came to believe that one reinforced division (the 22nd ID under Helmut Friebe) would suffice for the task. The preliminary fighting around Vlasenica, however, gave an ominous indication of what lay in store for the Germans in the weeks ahead. The town was soon surrounded by three Partisan divisions, and the garrison had to endure 10 days of constant shelling and direct attacks before being relieved on 18 January. The siege and the surprisingly tough resistance encountered by the 22nd ID along the road from Sokolac convinced its commander that the operation had lost the character of a march and became a breakthrough. After a brief pause, "the wandering cauldron" continued its movement towards Zvornik, which was reached on 3 February. Five days later, the Germans launched their main attack, at one point even making a temporary incursion onto the right bank of the Drina. During the counterattack which followed, the 17th and 27th Eastern Bosnian Divisions came within inches of splitting the cauldron in two but were eventually beaten back.

As it was now obvious that any prolonged stay in the Drina Valley would mean certain destruction, the original mission was aborted and Friebe allowed to take his entire command to Janja. A limited German-Chetnik attack northwest of Tuzla bought two days of relative peace for the 22nd ID, as the Partisans shuffled reserves to deal with this potential threat to their main base. By mid-February, however, the division found itself in a critical position. Its advance guard had reached the point just across the river from Loznica but could not progress any further owing to the lack of fuel. Moreover, the strength of the front-line units had eroded markedly after weeks of campaigning in freezing weather. At the same time, the Yugoslavs were preparing to administer a fatal blow with elements of the 17th, 22nd, 25th, 27th, and 38th Divisions, plus the 2nd Proletarian, which had been transferred from Belgrade especially for this occasion. The final act of the drama on the Drina took place between 14 and 18 February. The heaviest fighting took place at the northern end of the battlefield, where a German regiment tenaciously defended its hilltop positions at Šepak against enemy attacks supported by artillery and aircraft. Only through further contraction of the cauldron could Friebe secure enough reserves for the defense of these crucial heights. The help was already on the way from Janja in form of a supply convoy escorted by a battle group of the 104th JD. When the 28th Division south of the town gave way under German pressure, the 2nd Proletarian found itself between a hammer and an anvil and had to withdraw as well. On 19 February, the 22nd ID was finally relieved; during the next couple of days, the division slowly vacated the valley and took positions in its new area

25 Radanović, *Kazna*, pp. 379, 394-407; NARA/T311/184, HGE/Intel., Circular (10.12.1944), HGE/Intel. to OBSO/Intel. (16.12.1944).

of responsibility in the Drina-Sava triangle. Thus ended one of the toughest-fought battles of the war. Apart from causing massive suffering on both sides, it achieved little else: the Partisans were still firmly in control of the Eastern Bosnian "bulge" and supply links to Serbia.[26]

Things were soon back to normal in the operational area of the 2nd Yugoslav Army. Bijeljina, seen by both sides as the southern anchor of the Syrmian Front, had been under semi-blockade for the past couple of months. Constant small-scale fighting along the perimeter was interrupted by two major NOVJ assaults. The first battle took place in the second half of December 1944 and involved a force of two Partisan brigades. Not only did they fail to take their objective, but also suffered heavy casualties while defending their bridgehead on the Drina located on the town's outskirts. The second battle came as a direct consequence of the German winter offensive against the 1st Yugoslav Army. Already on 17 January 1945, the SHQ ordered Popović to step up activities all along his front with the aim of drawing enemy attention (and, hopefully, his reserves) away from Syrmia. In the ensuing two weeks, the 17th and 28th NOVJ Divisions lost up to 15 percent of their strength while trying to break the skillfully conducted defense of the KG "Skanderbeg". Much like the ill-fated attack on Udbina in August 1942, the bloody battle of Bijeljina remained merely a footnote in Yugoslav historiography.[27]

The going was also slow in the western sector, where the Partisans had to contend with a dense net of enemy strongpoints held by a mixture of the regular NDH forces, Muslim militias, and the Chetniks. The latter manned a buffer zone in front of the otherwise weak German garrisons at Doboj and Derventa (they were also present in lesser numbers at Brčko and Bijeljina), took part on joint operations with the Axis forces, and gathered intelligence for them. They could be counted on to keep doing this for as long as they were provided with ammunition, and for as long as enemy pressure remained within reasonable limits. Much to their discomfort, the pressure began rising already in late February 1945. With the threat to the Drina Valley removed, the 2nd Yugoslav Army was now free to concentrate on its primary strategic objective, the Bosna. In a preliminary move, three divisions of the 14th Corps were to clear the Ozren and Trebava and take Gradačac. Having no intention of sacrificing his army in defense of German interests, Mihailović retreated to Mount Vučjak northwest of Modriča at the first sign of trouble.

The XXXIV AC, on the other hand, reacted to this dangerous NOVJ encroachment by organizing a long-overdue offensive against Tuzla, without whose possession the front in this part of the country could obviously never be stabilized. The first phase, code-named "Nordwind", was aimed at encircling the exposed 25th Serbian Division in the newly-created Gradačac salient, to be followed by an attack against the city itself from the north and northeast (Operation "Rübezahl"; in Yugoslav works: "Maigewitter"). For this purpose, the Germans mustered nearly the entire 117th JD, two regiments from the 22nd ID, the regiment-sized KG "Geiger" from Doboj, plus the usual conglomerate of auxiliaries. The offensive began on 19 March. The Partisans, caught off-guard yet again, were forced into a precipitous and costly withdrawal; only

26 Milovan Dželebdžić, *Druga jugoslovenska armija* (Belgrade: VINC, 1989), pp. 99-111, 121-47, 168-202; Friedrich-August von Metzsch, *Die Geschichte der 22. Infanterie-Division 1939-1945* (Kiel: Verlag Hans-Henning Podzun, 1952), pp. 77-82; 22nd ID, Report on breakthrough from Sokolac and Vlasenica over Zvornik to Bijeljina [hereinafter: Report Drina] (28.2.1945), printed in: Karl Hnilicka, *Das Ende auf dem Balkan: Die militärische Räumung Jugoslawiens durch die deutsche Wehrmacht 1944/45* (Göttingen: Musterschmidt, 1970), pp. 325, 332.

27 Mandić, *Sedamnaesta*, pp. 286-93; 302-11; Dželebdžić, *Druga*, p. 167.

thanks to the intervention of one reserve division was the 14th Corps able to stabilize its lines just south of Gračanica and Srebrenik. The Germans renewed their offensive in earnest on the 28th, and for the next four days, the 2nd Yugoslav Army was barely managing to keep its front intact. Then, the chance intervened on its behalf. Owing to the rapidly worsening situation in Hungary, the HGE was forced to relinquish control over two of its divisions, including the 117th JD. This, in turn, led to the cancellation of the "Rübezahl" and the withdrawal of the XXXIV AC to a more defensible position Doboj–Srnice–Brčko; Bijeljina, the site of so much bloodletting in the winter, was surrendered without a fight on 2 April.[28]

7.5 Withdrawal of Army Group "E" From Eastern Yugoslavia (October-December 1944)

By the time Romania had left the Axis in late August 1944, the HGE had a supply strength of 308,000 men. Despite the rapidly worsening situation on the eastern flank of his Balkan armies, Hitler would still not give his blessing for a wholesale evacuation of Greece. For the time being, he would only agree to a reduction in size of the garrisons on the Mediterranean islands, and the gradual shifting of reserves towards the north, into Macedonia and beyond. By 3 October, however, even he had to bow to the reality and order a general retreat to the "Blue" line, running from Shkodër across Central Macedonia to Southeastern Serbia. The appearance of the Soviets at the Greater Morava one week later rendered this plan obsolete. The HGE would have to march all the way to the NDH using the only road still open to it, the one leading through Macedonia, Southwestern Serbia, Kosovo, and Sandžak. Luckily for the troops, Löhr and his staff had worked out a comprehensive plan of the withdrawal in complete secrecy while waiting for the belated, yet inevitable, green light from Berlin.

In addition to vast obstacles in terms of logistics, weather, and terrain, the Germans would be facing a multitude of hosts, whose aggregate numbers and operational position were vastly superior to their own. The basis of the joint Allied action in this part of the Balkans was laid on a meeting between Tito and Tolbuhin in Craiova on 5 October. On this occasion, the Partisan overlord agreed with the deployment of the troops of the Bulgarian Fatherland Front on the Yugoslav soil. Being the largest Allied contingent, they were expected to carry the brunt of the fighting. Three armies with 11 divisions would advance westward on a broad front between Pirot and the Bulgarian-Greek border with the aim of capturing the Vardar Valley and the Skopje–Kosovska Mitrovica railroad. The secondary thrust would be made by one Soviet corps towards Kragujevac and Kraljevo. All NOVJ forces were instructed to synchronize actions with the individual Allied commands in their respective sectors.[29]

28 Ibid., pp. 155-60, 202-06, 251-57, 259-71; von Metzsch, *Geschichte*, p. 83; TNA/DEFE3/516/BT7239, HGE, Report (13.3.1945); see also OBSO/Intel. reports from March 1945 in NARA/T78/476/6458835 (20.3), 6458892 (14.3), 6458943 (10.3), 6458970 (7.3), 6459053 (18.3), 6459060 (19.3), 6459066 (20.3), 6459157 (22.3), 6459172 (19.3), 6459185 (17.3).

29 This sub-chapter is based on the following two articles by Gaj Trifković: "'The German Anabasis': The Breakthrough of Army Group E from Eastern Yugoslavia 1944", *JSMS*, 30:4 (2017), pp. 602-629; "The Yugoslav Partisans' Lost Victories: Operations in Montenegro and Bosnia-Herzegovina 1944-1945", *Journal of Military History*, 82:1 (2018), pp. 95-124. Additional sources will be cited separately.

The outcome of the Eastern Macedonia campaign appeared to be a foregone conclusion: facing the 1st and 4th BAs in the valleys of the Kriva Reka, Bregalnica and Strumica stood only parts of the 11th LWFD and 22nd ID. To everyone's astonishment, the fighting took an entirely different course than predicted. The notorious ponderousness of Sofia's armies now came into play as never before: it took them between four and five weeks to cover the distance of ca. 60-90 km between their starting positions and the towns of Kumanovo and Štip. The Bulgarians would advance until running into a German blocking line, usually situated on the heights dominating the advance routes. They would then stop and begin preparations for a flanking movement against one or both enemy wings. Since the defenders lacked the manpower to extend their line, they would withdraw just before the main blow fell. The entire process would then be repeated several miles down the road. The most dramatic action took place during the first days of November 1944, when the Bulgarians, in a unusually daring move, established a bridgehead on the western bank of the Pčinja. By now, the German XXII MTC had received enough reinforcements from Greece to be able to launch a counterattack. Hit from two sides by as many regiments, the bridgehead crumbled with a heavy loss of life among its defenders. After this, the campaign reverted to its old, leisurely pace: the Germans evacuated Kumanovo on 10 November, and Skopje four days later; by the 16th, there were no more Wehrmacht soldiers in Macedonia.

The NOVJ took part in these operations with four divisions (the "Kumanovo", 42nd, 50th, and 51st). Although inexperienced and only lightly armed, they were far more aggressive than the Bulgarians. In addition to targeting German supply lines, they made direct assaults on the important traffic knots of Strumica (1-2 November 1944) and Veles (9 November), but were beaten back on both occasions. The Bulgarian division that was supposed to carry the main burden of the campaign in the Bregalnica Valley remained immobile on the border throughout October, and when it finally did advance, it received a bloody nose from the single enemy battalion it ran into. In the western part of Macedonia, the Partisans could snipe at the huge German columns passing day and night on their way north, could even attack or blockade urban centers such as Struga, but could not impede the progress of the withdrawal. All things considered, the Macedonian campaign was the first victory for the Germans: they completed the evacuation on schedule and with acceptable losses, leaving only scorched earth behind them. More importantly, no one followed them across the border: the 4th BA returned home, and the 1st would soon depart for Syrmia. The Macedonian Partisans stayed in their native province and began an intensive training program that would hopefully turn them into regular soldiers by the coming spring.[30]

The 2nd BA commenced its operations against the second-largest city in Serbia, Niš, on 8 October 1944. Two divisions attacked the German eastern defenses around Kalna and Bela Palanka, while another two went against the outlying garrisons of Vlasotince and Leskovac. The Bulgarians showed more aggressiveness here than in Macedonia, although it often came as the result of Soviet prodding. The lack of coordination with the 13th NOVJ Corps led to heavy losses among the Yugoslavs around Vlasotince. Nevertheless, the Germans (the 7th SS minus one regiment) were in full retreat by the 12th; two days later, they vacated Niš and crossed over to the western bank of the Morava. The only route left open to them led through Prokuplje, and

30 Trajkovski, *Вермахтот*, pp. 338-54.

the Partisans knew it: the 24th and 47th Divisions had already been re-deployed to this area. On 14 October, the head of a huge German column of about 800-1,000 motor vehicles arrived before the NOVJ blocking line at Jugbogdanovo. In a short but fierce fight, the advance guard managed to push its way through, but could not keep the road open for the remainder of the column, which already stood under attack from both flanks. In an irony of fate, the *coup de grâce* was delivered by the 1st Bulgarian Armored Brigade (BAB), whose state-of-the art equipment had been provided by the Germans themselves. This was the worst defeat suffered by the "Prinz Eugen" in its career: in addition to all heavy equipment, at least 1,000 of its members fell, were wounded or captured on this day. The losses could have been even higher had the Partisans mounted an all-out pursuit, which they failed to do for variety of reasons. This enabled the largest group of survivors (ca. 4,000 men) to reach the friendly garrison of Kraljevo after a week-long, grueling, guerrilla-like march through the mountains. With the last German formation of any size thus out of the way, the road to Priština/Prishtine seemed wide open.[31]

Kosovo remained a black spot on the NOP's maps throughout 1944. The Albanian-friendly policies introduced by Neubacher secured the loyalty of the majority of the population and kept the Serb-Montenegrin minority in check. In order to strengthen the unity of the anti-communist front, the Germans even outlawed the traditional blood feud, and sponsored a truce between the nationalists on both sides. As a result, there was only one active Partisan unit, the Malesija Detachment, which operated from the mountains southwest of Đakovica/Gjakova. In mid-September, the detachment made two successful ambushes on enemy columns coming from Albania. The approach of the Allied forces from the east one month later failed to weaken the popular pro-Axis sentiment, quite the contrary. Citing fears of the restoration of Yugoslavia and of "godless" Bulgarians, the local landowners managed to muster 5,000 volunteers for the defense of the area between Priština and Mitrovica/Mitrovicë alone. Although many of them probably came from the ranks of their own, rapidly dissolving "Skanderbeg" Division, the Germans were happy to provide them with light infantry weapons and supplies. These men would soon play an important part in the upcoming fighting by filling the gaps between the widely-spaced Wehrmacht battle groups.[32]

Following the rout of the 7th SS, the HQ of the 2nd BA was confident that its divisions would be in Podujevo/Besianë within two days of the start of the operation, scheduled for 15 October 1944. Much to everyone's surprise, the advance was stopped by a rag-tag collection of small German units, including Löhr's personal security detail, at the strategic passes at Prepolac/Përellacë and Merdare. While the Bulgarians were making preparations for another push, the 24th Serbian Division made an attempt to outflank the enemy line via the Kopaonik and Mitrovica. The attack ran into prepared defenses, however, and ended in a headlong retreat; the 24th was so badly trashed in the process that it had to be pulled back in reserve. In the meantime, the 2nd BA opened its offensive with three divisions on 25 October. Despite being supported by massed artillery, ground attack aircraft, and, ultimately, the tanks of the 1st

31 Trifković, "Amateurs", pp. 259-61.

32 NARA/T501/264/263, Final report Military administration Southeast (10.2.1945); NARA/T311/183/141-42, HGE, Diary (30.10.1944); BA-MA/N756/182/Estate Vopersaal-21 SS MTD, Sub-chapters "Organizational meassures" and "Situation in late September, early October 1944"; *Zbornik*/I/19/686 ([KPJ committee] Priština to PK Kosmet, 29.10.1944), 689 and 694 (Cables from OHQ Kosmet, 6 and 16.9.1944, respectively).

BAB, it took the Bulgarians nine days to pierce the enemy line at the Merdare Pass. Instead of exploiting the opportunity and going straight for the capital, the 2nd BA went over to the defense. The reason for this apparently inexplicable decision lay in the erroneous intelligence about the non-existent threat to the army's right flank. By the time the Bulgarians renewed their attack on 8 November, the Germans (now under the LXXXXI AC) had built solid defenses using the reinforcements from Macedonia. Fierce fighting here lasted for a full week, but, in the end, the lines remained largely unchanged. The secondary Allied drive, conducted by one Bulgarian cavalry division and the 47th Serbian Division in the area Vranje–Bujanovac, was equally unsuccessful. The 11th LWFD, ably supported by Albanian militias, conducted a slow fighting withdrawal, the pace of which was determined solely by the HGE's internal timetable. Bujanovac was thus evacuated on the 8th and Gnjilane on the 16th, right after the last soldiers of the former Skopje garrison had passed through it. By the 23rd, there were no more Axis troops in Kosovo. As in Macedonia, the Allies had won territory, but little else: three-quarters of the ca. 2,400 prisoners were Italian auxiliaries, and the Bulgarians captured a mere 110 motor vehicles. Probably the biggest single prize were the eight cannon the Germans had accidentally left on the right bank of the Ibar at Mitrovica.

The HGE columns passing Mitrovica would take either the northwesterly route into Sandžak (the "Green" Road), or would continue north, towards Kraljevo (the "Brown" Road). This town, the scene of the prolonged siege of 1941, was now the strategic linchpin of the Wehrmacht's position in this part of the Balkans. The so-called "Kraljevo Bridgehead" had its origins in the events that transpired in Serbia in mid-October 1944. At that time, the 64th RC (three divisions) and 14th NOVJ Corps (two divisions) were tasked with securing the flank and rear of the 57th Army by occupying the confluence of the Ibar with the Western Morava. As a bonus, this would also close the HGE's main withdrawal route. Facing them stood the "Friedrich-Wilhelm Müller" Corps (later renamed the XXXIV AC), which was, in fact, a division-sized formation composed of the remnants of the 1st MTD, 7th SS MTD, 117th JD, 181st and 297th IDs, and other survivors of the Red Army's initial onslaught.

From 16 to 20 October, the smallest of Müller's three battle groups completed a costly withdrawal from Kruševac to Kraljevo. The pursuing Allies (the 52nd RD and the 2nd Proletarian) were stopped on the line of hills just east of the town thanks, in part, to the arrival of the bedraggled veterans of the "Prinz Eugen" from Niš. On the opposite side of the front, the second German battle group was engaged in a desperate attempt to hold Kragujevac long enough to secure the evacuation of its precious magazines and hospitals (14-21 October). The garrison avoided utter destruction only thanks to the failure of the 93rd RD and the 17th Eastern Bosnian to cut the road and railway links to Kraljevo. By the end of the month, all Germans (including the remaining battle group form Jagodina) had withdrawn to Mount Kotlenik, the last natural obstacle before the Western Morava. While the fighting here went on, both sides were extending their lines towards Čačak. Fortunately for Müller, the trickle of reinforcements coming from the south was turning into a flood lately, finally enabling him to launch a major counterstroke on his left wing on 2 November. The main brunt of it fell on the 1st Yugoslav Brigade of the 23rd Serbian Division, which buckled under pressure and unhinged the entire Allied line. Now firmly in control of the low ridge shielding Čačak and the adjacent communications from the north, the Germans began to dig in; exhausted and bloodied, their foe did the same.

The relative peace lasted until the end of November 1944, when the Allies decided to launch simultaneous attacks on both ends of the bridgehead. Owing to their impending transfer to Syrmia, the Soviet divisions would play only a limited role; the NOVJ forces, now reinforced to five divisions, would have to do most of the fighting. On the 24th, the 2nd Proletarian appeared suddenly in the Ibar Valley, blocking the traffic there for the next two days. This potentially dangerous flanking move had next to no impact on the battle, for Kraljevo had already outrun its military usefulness. After seeing off the last convoy from Kosovo, the "Prinz Eugen's" rearguards withdrew from the town late on the 28th. While two of its sister divisions followed the enemy to Čačak, the 25th Serbian marched to Požega. The town had been the real flashpoint of the new Allied offensive since 20 November. For two weeks, the 23rd and 45th Divisions tried repeatedly to capture the key hilltop position of Loret from the 104th JD, with no success. The 25th now tried to perform a similar feat at Krstac Ridge southeast of town but was beaten back with heavy losses (3-11 December). By this time, the focus of the battle shifted north, to the area between Užice and Ljubovija, from where the 7th SS MTD and other units started their already-described drive towards Bijeljina and the Syrmian Front. Consequently, the 104th JD could vacate Požega on the 12th and retreat to the Višegrad–Dobrun area three days later with little enemy interference.

No depiction of the HGE's great withdrawal would be complete without mentioning the XXI MTC's dramatic breakthrough from Montenegro. According to the original plan, the designated main exit route led from Podgorica along the Zeta River to Nikšić, and thence to Grahovo and Trebinje (codename: the "Blue" Road); its ancillary connected Bar with Grahovo via the Bay of Kotor. The start of the withdrawal was to be synchronized with the movements of the bulk of the HGE, as well as the arrival of the 297th ID from Albania. The first setbacks occurred already in October 1944 as the result of the 2nd Assault Corps' autumn offensive. Stripped of its Chetnik protective screen, and with the morale of the Croatian conscripts at an all-time low, the 369th ID's battalion-sized strongpoint of Trebinje succumbed to a massive assault by the 29th Division on the 5th. Four weeks later, the entire province south of the line Široki Brijeg–Buna–Nevesinje was free of Axis troops. In the meantime, the POG took Grahovo after a five-day battle against its small, but stubborn Axis garrison (16-21 October). The Partisans then turned their attention to the coastal area, cutting the links between Cetinje and Kotor and laying down siege on Ledenice. The latter stands on a small plateau perched above the town of Risan and is surrounded by barren mountains of up to 1,300 meters in height. The defenders (one German and two Blackshirt battalions) were well-supplied and made good use of the old Austro-Hungarian border fortifications. Two NOVJ brigades, supported by two dozen artillery pieces, began systematically reducing the enemy positions bunker by bunker until the remnants of the garrison finally surrendered on 18 November. The remaining German forces blew up everything of military value and evacuated the bay area immediately thereafter.

German planners were not overly concerned by the permanent closing of the coastal road and by the increased NOVJ presence along the "Blue" one. Past experiences had shown that the guerrillas could rarely, if ever, stand up to a determined assault supported by heavy weapons. Consequently, the proposed drive from Danilovgrad to Nikšić went ahead as planned on 14 November 1944. Much to the Germans' surprise, the enemy stood his ground and fought tenaciously for every foot of it. Twelve days into the offensive, the lines moved only between two and four km into the NOVJ-held territory despite the fact that the attack force had grown to 10 infantry battalions. The battle culminated in a fierce Partisan counterattack on 25 November, in which two brigades of the POG routed a regiment of the 181st ID on the slopes of Mount Garač and killed its CO. The XXI MTC, with its ca. 50,000 men, was now effectively stranded on the small patch of land around Podgorica. With no alternative left, the corps decided to take the only route still open to it, the narrow mountain road leading north of the capital, through the Tara and Lim canyons, and into Sandžak. There, it was hoped, the corps would make contact with the remainder of the HGE coming from Kosovo.

The geostrategic importance of Sandžak was not lost to the SHQ. The 37th Division returned from Western Serbia already in late September 1944 with the task of defeating the remaining collaborationist forces and seizing control of its native province. Without the German support, the Chetniks and von Krempler's militia simply melted away, making the NOVJ the master of the area Sjenica–Pljevlja–Goražde–Višegrad by mid-October. As already noted, the secondary retreat route of the HGE passed precisely through this area, and Löhr took pains to secure it early on. While only a thin screen of troops was holding back the Bulgarians at Prepolac and Merdare, General Heinz Scheurlen was given command of a relatively strong, if motley, collection of battalions (including the remnants of the SSW, RSK, and *Luftwaffe* ground personnel) with which to secure the road to Višegrad.

Unlike their comrades in the Zeta Valley, the Sandžak Partisans opted to counter the enemy moves with more traditional tactics, especially the road demolition. The resistance stiffened only in the last days of October, after the Germans had reached the Lim in the area of Prijepolje. Scheurlen's attempt to open the road via the Jabuka Pass and Pljevlja to Čajniče was defeated by the spirited defense of the 3rd Sandžak Brigade (in addition to the Germans, the Partisans also had to contend with those same demoralized, but numerous JVuO units that had offered cooperation to the Red Army around Čačak). The other two brigades of the 37th took up positions along the eastern edge of the road Sjenica–Prijepolje– Priboj and interdicted the traffic by night ambushes and acts of sabotage, which many German troops experienced for the first time. On 14 November, Scheurlen's vanguard entered Višegrad and began building a pontoon over the Drina. Five days later, it met with a battalion of the 7th SS coming from Sarajevo halfway between Sokolac and Rogatica, signaling the beginning of the end of "the German *anabasis*". On the 22nd, Löhr instructed the LXXXXI AC (which had in the meantime taken over Sandžak) to aid the breakthrough of the isolated XXI MTC by dispatching Friebe's division towards the upper reaches of the Lim.[33]

On 22 November 1944, the elements of the 297th ID crossed the Morača at Bioče and began a slow ascent up the Vjeternik Plateau. The 3rd Assault Division had only two brigades and a pair of guns deployed in this sector, but their numerical inferiority was partially offset by the great natural strength of their defensive position. In a remarkable feat of soldiering, the Montenegrins managed to maintain the integrity of their line during almost two weeks of fierce fighting. They retreated slowly, using every opportunity to hit back: in a night counterattack on the 29th, they even pushed back a German battalion and killed its commander. By 5 December, the defenders were at the end of their tethers: in addition to combat losses, their ranks were decimated by frostbite (the Germans were suffering from the same problem, although on a smaller scale). The NOVJ command had no alternative but to order its men to stand down

33 Drulović, *Tridesetsedma*, pp. 171-204; Schmidt-Richberg, *Endkampf*, pp. 56-59; NARA/T311/183/95-96, HGE, Diary (21.10.1944); NARA/T314/1630/560 [LXXXXI AC] (Corps order no. 19, 6.12.1944), 608 (Enemy situation, 29.11.1944).

and limit their activities to fire attacks and ambushes against the passing enemy columns. In the north, the 22nd ID occupied the Lim Valley between Prijepolje and Bijelo Polje without encountering resistance. The Germans then launched a diversionary attack towards Berane, which drew whatever reserves the Partisans had left to this sector of the front. The bulk of the division then proceeded to capture Mojkovac on 8 December, but not before the enemy sappers had blown up the bridge across the Tara.

Unbeknownst to the Axis, the battle was now practically over; realizing the XXI MTC could not be stopped from leaving the country, the SHQ now wanted to make sure it did so as quickly as possible. From then on, the Germans' biggest foe were enemy aircraft (which had been pounding away incessantly since the beginning of the campaign) and weather conditions. The latter refers primarily to the the flood of near-Biblical proportions that swept away almost all the bridges in this part of the country. Finally, on 19 December, Friebe's men established contact with the 297th ID mid-way between Mojkovac and Kolašin; on the same day, the German rearguard left Podgorica. Except for skirmishing with the formations of the 2nd Assault Corps– which now included two divisions of Albanian Partisans sent by Enver Hohxa as a token of his internationalist commitment– the remainder of the journey to the Drina was largely uneventful. The HGE would maintain a foothold on its eastern bank until the last convoys had left for Sarajevo in mid-January 1945. After that, the 181st ID took up strong defensive positions on the Bosnian side of the river between Goražde and Višegrad.[34]

7.6 Yugoslav Offensive in Dalmatia and Lika (September-December 1944)

With the landing season drawing to a close, in early September 1944 the OBSO decided to take a calculated risk and begin a gradual evacuation of Dalmatia. At the same time, the NOVJ's first true regular formation, the 26th Dalmatian Division, received orders to capture the central and southern archipelagos as a prelude for the return to the mainland. On 12 September, two Partisan brigades landed on Brač and proceeded to attack the main enemy stronghold at Sumartin. Owing to conflicting orders and lack of coordination with the navy, the garrison (one battalion of the 118th JD) was not evacuated on time; it was forced to capitulate after five days of bitter fighting. The mistake was not repeated on Korčula and Hvar, which were surrendered without a fight before the arrival of the two remaining brigades of the 26th. The Partisans suffered the first setback at Ston, whose imposing medieval walls controlled the isthmus of the Pelješac Peninsula. Not being able to take the town by storm, they settled down for a formal siege.

The events that had transpired in the meantime in the eastern parts of the country were becoming increasingly felt in Dalmatia. On 7 October, the OBSO ordered a general withdrawal to the line Senj–Knin–Livno–Mostar–Gacko; it was hoped that the shortening of the line would enable the sending of two more divisions to Serbia. The SHQ, for its part, made sure everything was being done to prevent the enemy from leaving unscathed. On 16 October, one Dalmatian brigade landed at Neum with the aim of cutting the coastal road to Dubrovnik. Simultaneously, another brigade landed behind Ston and destroyed its battalion-sized garrison in a direct assault (among the German dead was August Landmesser, who is most commonly

34 TsAMO/500/12483/105/4-5, 11 [all 181st Recon Btl./181st ID] (Report 30.11-19.12.1944), 30 (Diary, 23-26.12.1944); Schmidt-Richberg, *Endkampf*, p. 87.

identified as the person who famously refused to give the Nazi salute in Hamburg in 1936). The landings came none too soon, for the Axis forces were already preparing to leave the seat of the historic Ragusan Republic. By 19 October, a long column consisting of elements of the 369th ID, *Kriegsmarine* personnel, and the Italian Fascist *Legione "San Marco"* (altogether between 3,000 and 4,500 men), reached the pass at Vukov Klanac. Ironically, the Germans had only themselves to blame for what happened next. Upon reaching the spot, the Partisans found–and detonated–a powerful explosive charge placed there by Wehrmacht sappers in anticipation of an Allied landing. The Germans spent the next three days trying to get the heavy equipment around the massive crater created by the explosion while suffering withering fire from the adjoining heights. On 22 October, the survivors straggled to Metković on foot, carrying nothing but personal weapons and and their wounded with them.[35]

On 26 October 1944, the 26th Dalmatian's second strike group (two brigades plus elements of the 1st TB that had just arrived from Italy) landed southeast of Split, entering it a couple of days later. All the remaining German forces from the coast–now formed into the KG "Allermann" (a reinforced regiment of the 264th ID plus "refugees" from other service branches)–were converging on Šibenik. The Partisans came just in time to engage the enemy while he was leaving for Drniš. Throughout 2 November, the Germans fought a desperate, running battle with the guerrillas, who were constantly trying to split the column and destroy it in detail. In the end, the members of the KG "Allermann" had more luck than their comrades in the south: they managed to reach their objective without losing cohesion but suffered heavy human and material losses in the process. The HQ of the 8th NOVJ Corps, emboldened by its recent successes and convinced the enemy was leaving the entire Dalmatia for good, thought that Knin could be taken from the move. This assumption, however, proved to be wrong: the attackers were met with dogged resistance from prepared positions, and even had to give ground in face of determined counterattacks. Realizing the Germans here could not be dislodged without serious preparations, the corps called off the offensive after eight days of fighting (7-15 November).

The dispositions of 8th NOVJ Corps on the eve of the Battle of Knin looked as follows. The 26th Division, reinforced with additional artillery and the 1st TB, would assail the southern, strongest, part of the defensive belt. The 19th and 20th Divisions had the orders to encircle the town from the west and east, respectively, while the 9th Division stood in reserve. At this stage, the German garrison consisted of roughly one half of 264th ID's artillery and infantry effectives, one battalion of naval infantry, and the bulk of one coastal artillery regiment (half of which was without guns). In addition, the bulk of the 373rd ID was also deployed to the area, augmented by an equivalent of one regiment of the 392nd in the closing phase of the battle. Considering them more as a liability than an asset, the XV MTC had the remaining NDH forces evacuated from the area in the days preceding the battle. Đujić's Chetniks were also preparing to leave, since the Germans could no longer provide them with supplies.[36]

35 This sub-chapter is based on my manuscript "The Long Way to Trieste: Operations in the Yugoslav Littoral 1944-1945" which will be published in 2021 by Brécourt Academic either as an article or a part of an edited volume. As already customary, the additional sources will be cited separately, in this case http://www.fasena.de/courage/deutsch/5a.htm and http://www.fasena.de/courage/deutsch/10.htm (last accessed 22.5.2020).

36 Gaj Triković, "'Katastrofa izbjegnuta za dlaku': njemački izvori o Kninskoj bitci 1944.", ČSP, 53:2 (2021), pp. 561-62.

The great Yugoslav offensive against HGE's key position in this part of the peninsula began on 25 November 1944. The Battle of Knin was a typical *Materialschlacht*, and the odds were not on the side of the Wehrmacht this time. In addition to being numerically stronger, the Partisans enjoyed a clear-cut superiority in terms of heavy weapons and ammunition. Thanks to Western Allied shipments, the 8th NOVJ Corps could now release an unprecedented volume of fire on enemy positions, including 21,000 mortar bombs and 31,000 75mm-shells (the intensity and continuity of the barrage features prominently in the reminiscences of German eyewitnesses). The fighting itself was as fierce as any seen during the war. Formally threatened with decimation and summary execution for cowardice, the soldiers of the 264th fought with desperate courage. This alone, however, was not enough to turn the tide. Over the course of eight days, the Dalmatian brigades pushed the enemy slowly, but inexorably, towards a small patch of land on the northwestern outskirts of the town. By the time the garrison was finally given permission to withdraw on 3 December, it was already too late: the 19th and 20th Divisions had closed the ring north of Knin, while the 26th entered it from the south. The desperate breakthrough attempts attempted by individual groups were largely unsuccessful: according to German estimates, the garrison was losing about 700 men a day at this stage of the battle. An especially tragic event occurred when a stray projectile ignited the ammunition stored in the Stara Straža railway tunnel that was also used as a shelter for hundreds of German wounded. By 5 December, the only thing remaining for the Partisans to do was to gather prisoners and secure massive quantities of equipment lying about the battlefield.[37]

The Knin catastrophe could not have come at a worse moment for the German high command: the enemy offensive in Syrmia was at its height, the Soviets had established presence in Podravina, and HGE's rearguards were heavily engaged in Western Serbia and Montenegro. Now, with the demise of the 264th ID, the road to Lika and Bihać also lay wide open. Already in October 1944, the MHQ Croatia decided to move the bulk of the 11th Corps closer to the border with Dalmatia and the advancing 8th Corps. The aim of the operation was to finally establish a secure link to the friendly ports and thus solve the long-standing problem of supply in Lika and Gorski Kotar. In the last days of November, the 13th and 35th Divisions were massing around Gračac, an important knot on the main, all-weather road leading north. Assuming that the garrison would soon receive evacuation orders, the units took up positions along the most likely escape routes. Although technically still part of what the Yugoslavs called Knin Operation, the 8th Corps' advance into Lika began already on 3 December, as the fresh 9th Division received orders to pursue the enemy as far as Velika Popina. By the 9th, the Partisans had broken through the legionnaires' thin defensive line at Otrić, triggering a general withdrawal towards Donji Lapac and Srb. In the course of the movement, a reinforced battalion of the 373rd ID that used to occupy Gračac ran into an ambush just as predicted and was annihilated.

Despite this auspicious opening, the SHQ would limit the further involvement of the 8th Corps in the Lika campaign to only one division and one artillery battalion (as we shall see later, this decision was made largely for political reasons). Nevertheless, the 11th Corps pressed on north, seeking to establish contact with the 4th Corps around Korenica. Around 15 December, the German situation had become so desperate that Löhr ordered the immediate transfer of the

37 TsAMO/500/12477/793/2-3 (264th ID, Diary, 3-4.12.1944), 19-31 [Eyewitness reports, January 1945], 35 (264th ID to XV MTC, 7.12.1944), 42 (264th ID/Pers., Activity report, December 1944).

last remaining available battalion of the 1st MTD to Bihać, to be followed shortly by the entire 104th JD. This, however, proved to be unnecessary, for the Partisans had clearly overestimated their capabilities. Even though they took Korenica, their attempt to push beyond Ličko Petrovo Selo and the road to Otočac failed due to a combination of exhaustion, bad weather, and a very skillful defense conducted by the Ustashe and elements of the 392nd ID. After two of its brigades were ambushed on 29 December, the 11th Corps decided to call off the offensive. The OBSO's chief of staff fittingly observed that the XV MTC–meaning the right flank of the entire German front in the Balkans–"avoided catastrophe by a hair's breadth".[38]

7.7 Internal Front I: NDH (October 1944-March 1945)

In addition to the newly-opened, "regular" front in the eastern parts of the country, the NOVJ still maintained a significant presence in what was now the German strategic rear area in the Balkans. Units of the 4th Corps largely spent the fall and winter of 1944-45 campaigning against enemy strongpoints and traffic in their respective home areas. The 34th Division, for instance, scored several easy successes, including the destruction of the police outpost at Mavračić on 24 October (ca. 100 pieces of small arms captured) and the garrison at Babići on 12 December (close to 380 dead or missing *Domobrani*). On the whole, these relatively small affairs were becoming increasingly bloody and each victory was dearly bought. During the ambush on a column of enemy vehicles on the road Dubica–Kostajnica on 12 November, the 7th Division lost one of its brigade commanders, who was KIA along with a dozen other fighters. The 8th Division and Una OG took Cazin two times in November and December, each time at a cost of more than 200 men; one-and-a-half times as many were killed or wounded during the storming of the battalion-sized Ustasha garrison at Vaganac on the New Year's Eve.

The Axis did not limit themselves to passive defense, but kept launching forays into the liberated territory whenever practicable. On 1 February 1945, the always-dangerous 1st JgRR surrounded an entire battalion of the Žumberak Brigade outside the neutral zone at Pisarovina and forced it to surrender. The incident was the last straw for higher commands, which were already inclined to explain the rising casualty and desertion rates in this part of the country as the work of enemy agents. In the resulting purge, the entire staff of the aforementioned brigade was sacked; three high-ranking members of the 34th Division HQ were accused of espionage, tried, and shot (the affair was never properly investigated by historians, not even in post-Yugoslav times). After the bulk of the 11th Corps had departed for southern Lika, the 43rd Division–now full assembled in Gorski Kotar–effectively came under direct command of the MHQ Croatia. Owing chiefly to the adverse supply situation, the division's activities were limited to raiding and sabotage. The two Partisan detachments that were still active in Istria could likewise not hope to achieve much against the vastly superior enemy forces deployed in this most important strategic spot of the Eastern Adriatic.[39]

38 Kleut, *Jedanaesti*, pp. 324-55; *Zbornik*/V/36/190-96, 9th NOVJD to 8th NOVJC (12.12.1944); Schraml, *Kriegsschauplatz*, pp. 210-12, 271-72; NARA/T311/195/206 (HGE to OBSO, 14.12.1944), 209 (OBSO to OKW, 15.12.1944), 243 (Telephone conversations, 17.12.1944).

39 Baić, *Četrvti*, pp. 317-83; Kleut, *Jedanaesti*, pp. 314-19, 361-63; *Zbornik*/IX/9/26-27, 34th NOVJD/Pol. to CK KPH (1.3.1945); Vladimir Hlaić, *Tridesetčetvrta udarna divizija NOV i PO Hrvatske* (Zagreb: SABARH, 2002), pp. 305-07.

Not long after the conclusion of the "Wehrwolf", the OBSO authorized another large-scale sweep, code-named "Bergwind". The objective was to push or destroy enemy field formations in Moslavina, eliminate his infrastructure and deny him the remaining recruits from that region. For this purpose, three NDH divisions of the so-called "Group Moškov" attacked from the line Bjelovar–Križ–Banova Jaruga on 8 March 1945. At this moment, the bulk of the 10th Corps was on its way to Podravina in order to help the hard-pressed 12th Corps by attacking the German bridgeheads on the Drava from the rear. The need to protect the evacuation of hospitals and magazines in Moslavina, however, compelled the Partisans to turn around and face Moškov. During the following week, the 32nd Division suffered heavy casualties while trying to hold off the enemy in a series of head-on clashes. The "Bergwind" was called off after the guerrillas had been pushed to the southern slopes of the Bilogora (20 March), but the fighting continued until the end of the month. In an ill-advised attempt to regain the initiative, the 33rd Division attacked Narta and Čazma, and was very nearly wiped out in the process. In all, it was one of the most successful months in the history of the NDH COIN efforts: "several hundred rifles", close to 230 automatic weapons and 31 mortars were captured, together with carloads of various supplies. Heavy losses suffered by the HDB and UV–over 900 KIA, WIA, and MIA–bear witness to the fact that the 10th NOVJ Corps had come a long way from its humble beginnings on the Kalnik in terms of military professionalism.[40]

The arrival of Löhr's armies to the Drina and the need to get them to the Pannonian Basin as quickly as possible gave an added importance to the Bosna Valley. Since the Axis had limited their activities in Western Bosnia to defending the Una Valley and the Banja Luka bulge, the 5th NOVJ Corps was free to concentrate most of its effectives in this direction. For all practical purposes, the campaign from the fall and winter 1944-45 can be viewed as a prolonged contest for the possession of Travnik. This venerable town, which had served as the capital of the Ottoman Bosnia throughout the 18th and the first half of the 19th Centuries, was now seen as an outward bastion of Zenica and the critically important road and railway communications in its vicinity. Travnik was attacked on (only) two occasions in the past, in October and November 1943, both times unsuccessfully. The first sign of the renewed Partisan interest came on the evening of 30 September 1944, when elements of the 10th Krajina Division tried in vain to force their way into the town. The latest failure convinced the HQ of the 5th Corps that the objective could be taken only in a major, multi-divisional operation. After three weeks of preparations, two brigades from the 4th and 10th Divisions went in again on 20 October, the same day the Germans were chased out of Belgrade. There were no Wehrmacht units in Travnik, but the defenders (one battalion each of the "Black Legion" and Ustasha refugees from Kupres and other places, as well as one battalion of the *Domobrani*) fought just as toughly. It took two days of bitter house-to-house fighting until the remnants of the garrison were finally forced to lay down their arms. At the same time, the Partisans repelled a relief force coming from Sarajevo consisting of the elements of the 1st UAB. Both sides suffered heavy losses: the 5th Corps's first operational officer, the deputy commander of the 4th Division, and the beloved commander of the corps' Tank Company were among the 100 or so NOVJ dead. Three of the highest-ranking

40 Bulat, *Deseti*, pp. 257-77; *Zbornik*/IV/34/1037, 1044, 1075, 1091, HDB GHQ, Daily reports (20, 22, 29.3, and 2.4.1945, respectively).

NDH officers present shared their fate, while the fourth was taken prisoner along with ca. 700 other defenders; the number of captured small arms alone amounted to nearly 1,400.[41]

With the capture of Travnik, the 5th NOVJ Corps gained access to the only remaining stretch of the Bosna Valley that had hitherto been off-limits. The 10th, 4th, and 53rd Divisions began with a sustained campaign against the enemy movements between Sarajevo and Bosanski Brod. Even under the best of conditions, the low-capacity, narrow-gauge railway could not have satisfied the needs of the HGE. Worn out after three years of war, repeatedly shattered by sabotage and air raids, the railway was now operating at the barest minimum. From 20 October to 7 November 1944 not a single train passed along it; in December, the line was closed for nearly 500 hours. The road traffic was much more difficult to stop thanks to the fact that there was hardly a spot along the ca. 200 km-long route that was not occupied by an enemy solider or a vehicle at any given time. Even though the heavily-armed convoys usually reached their destination, such situation was intolerable in the long run. Already on 9 December, a mixed German-RSK-Ustasha battle group attacked from Busovača towards Vitez but made little headway in face of adverse winter conditions and determined NOVJ resistance. Since the "Snowflake" ("Schneeflocke"), as the operation was christened, was obviously not powerful enough to dislodge the enemy, the HGE decided to turn it into the "Avalanche". On the 29th, the V SS MTC launched Operation "Lawine", this time with one regiment each from the 104th and 118th JDs, two regiments of the White Russians, plus some German support battalions. By the end of the following week, the attackers came to within five km from their objective, only to be stopped by an energetic counterattack. After this, the XXI MTC (which had taken over from the SS in the meantime) called for yet another pause and a round of "troop joggling", during which the remainder of the 104th JD was brought over from Eastern Bosnia. The "Lawine" was resumed on 19 January, more or less according to the original plan whereby the main strike came from the direction of Zenica, and the secondary along the Lašva. The enemy was now far too strong for the 4th Krajina Division, three of whose battalions were on a detached duty on the right bank of the Bosna. Consequently, the Partisans withdrew from Travnik four days into the battle.[42]

Over the next three weeks or so, the front lines in this part of the NDH remained stable. Behind the scenes, the 5th NOVJ Corps was hard at work preparing a new offensive of its own; for this purpose, the 4th Krajina was reinforced with two additional brigades, and artillery and armored assets. In contrast, the departure of the 104th JD to Northeastern Bosnia (see above) made the Axis positions more vulnerable than ever. The fighting opened on 15 February 1945 and ended two weeks later with the Partisans standing on the confluence of the Lašva and Bosna. The KG "Eberlein" (one German security and two RSK regiments) was soundly trashed in the process; among the prisoners was its elderly commander, a well-known nationalist figure from the period of the revolutionary upheaval in Germany. The RSK suffered particularly heavy losses: "Busovača will be remembered as one of the glorious places of the Russian military history as soon as God sees fit to restore the national Russia", wrote one veteran of the corps. Löhr again

41 Milan Inđić, *Borbe za Travnik* (Travnik: Borac, 1979), pp. 47-228.

42 NARA/T311/185, Cpt. Peter to HGE (17.11.1944); NARA/T311/188/871, OBSO/Trans., Monthly report (December 1944); *Zbornik*/IV/31/671-92 and *Zbornik*/IV/32/698-737, 4th NOVJD, Monthly reports (December 1944 and January 1945, respectively); Andrei Samtsevich, *Марш Смерти Русского охранного корпуса* (Moscow: Iuza, 2019), pp. 216-18.

had crisis on his hands, just days before the beginning of the critical spring offensive across the Drava. Since the transfer of one reinforced regiment of the 181st ID to Zenica had done little to stabilize the situation, the OKW authorized the use of the 7th SS MTD. The division arrived to the area Vranduk–Nemila from Slavonia by train in the first days of March, and immediately launched a thrust towards Vitez. Hit in the rear, the startled Partisans withdrew in great haste towards Travnik. The "Prinz Eugen's" short but effective intervention helped secure this sector for the next five, crucial weeks. In the remainder of the Bosna Valley, the Partisans would occasionally achieve a local success, but the existence of a dense net of enemy strongpoints on both sides of the river, which were well covered by reserves, would each time prevent them from establishing a permanent foothold.[43]

Demolition remained a staple activity of the NOVJ forces deployed behind the main German-Yugoslav front. For instance, 72 acts of sabotage were recorded on the main railway line linking the Third Reich's border with Zemun in October 1944. The Partisans would maintain the tempo of their sapping operations, hitting the same line 307 times during the first four months of 1945 (plus six more times in May). Despite the fact that Axis engineers succeeded in removing some 500 explosive charges from the Zagreb–Karlovac line during December, the guerrillas nevertheless rendered the line inoperable by cutting the tracks on more than 100 places in the course of a single night. The Slovene Partisans carried out 261 attacks on enemy targets during the last six months of the conflict, most of them in January and February 1945. The 9th Corps was responsible for four-fifths of the actions, followed by the 4th OZ, and the 7th Corps. Mines continued to exact a heavy toll on troop trains right until the end of the war. One of the worst incidents of this sort occurred on 19 March 1945 outside Ivanić-Grad, resulting in 27 dead, 58 heavily "and numerous" lightly wounded members of the Wehrmacht. By this time, the Yugoslavs were also seeking to spare the infrastructure they were about to inherit as much as possible: only light demolition works were allowed on the Bosna Valley railroad in April, while the border bridges on the Drava in Slovenia were to be blown only in case they were threatened with capture (mid-May).[44]

7.8 Internal Front II: Slovenia (October 1944-April 1945)

Unlike the rest of Yugoslavia, where the NOVJ was going through a period of unparalleled growth and success, Slovenia was threatening to become a black spot on SHQ's maps. In fact, the late 1944 and early 1945 is often described as being the most difficult period in the history of the local NOP branch. By now, war-weariness among the population had reached an all-time high: the prospect of joining the guerrillas with winter just around the corner was unappealing, to say the least. The Partisans lacked in everything, especially in artillery ammunition (experiments

43 Karasijević, *Četvrta*, pp. 384-97; Lev Bulgakov, "Череповски поход" in: Vertepov (ed.), *Русский*, p. 299; TNA/DEFE3/512/BT6230, TNA/DEFE3/514/BT6647, TNA/DEFE3/515/BT6895, TNA/DEFE3/516/BT7003, HGE, Situation reports (2.3, 25.2., the latter two 4.3.1945 respectively).

44 Bošnjak, *Diverzantska*, pp. 300-03; see also the following contribution by the same author: "Diverzantske jedinice u vrijeme formiranja armija i njihova uloga u završnim operacijama", in *Za pobjedu i slobodu. Armije u strategijskoj koncepciji NOR i revolucije: učesnici govore* (Belgrade: VINC, 1986), p. 466; NARA/T311/190/232, OBSO/QM, Monthly report (October 1944); NARA/T311/188/880, OBSO/Trans., Monthly report (December 1944); NARA/T78/476/6459174, OBSO, Daily report (19.3.1945); *Zbornik*/XI/2/261, 45th NOVJD, Order (10.4.1945).

with home-made shells resulted in several destroyed cannon), a vital ingredient in the "war of strongpoints" that was raging in a large part of the country. Moreover, Slovenia had effectively become a rear area to the Italian, Eastern–and later on–Yugoslav fronts. Now more than ever, the Germans needed to protect their interests in the country, and they intended to do so by relentless campaigning. For this purpose, Rösener and others could count on numerous units of all shapes and sizes that were withdrawing from, or moving through, this corner of occupied Europe.[45]

The Dolenjska campaign was largely being fought in the triangle Kočevje–Žužemberk–Novo Mesto and was almost static in nature. The Axis sought to keep the Partisans off-balance by launching frequent sallies against the liberated territory; the latter responded by attacking enemy strongpoints. The arrival of the OHQ (the 6th and 11th Brigades) from Štajerska in mid-October 1944 failed to break the deadlock: their attacks on Št. Vid, Jevnica, and Kresnice ended in failure. The assault on Litija and Šmartno in the Sava Valley together with the 14th Division had to be canceled when it became clear that the Western Allies could not provide air support as originally planned. On 13 November, the Germans launched Operation "Schneegestöber", a concentric advance from Kočevje and Novo Mesto against the NOP capital of Črnomelj. The attacking force (one German police and three Home Guard battalions) met with unexpectedly heavy resistance by the elements of the 15th and 18th Divisions and had to turn back after two days with close to 50 killed or missing. Seeking to exploit the confusion in the enemy ranks, the Partisans immediately moved against Kočevje. Despite the fact that they could now count on friendly fighter-bombers, the attackers made little headway against the town's strong defenses and had to withdraw on the third day of the battle (20 November).

Following a six-week lull, the fighting erupted again in the first week of January 1945. The Partisan attempt to take Občina provoked an Axis counterstroke that "sliced off" the part of the liberated territory lying north of the Krka. After a short pause, the Germans launched a thrust across the river with the aim of surrounding the guerrillas southeast of Žužemberk in cooperation with forces advancing from the west. On 21 January, the Partisans won their greatest victory over the *Domobranci* when the 9th Brigade ambushed the notorious 4th Battalion at Veliko Lipje and inflicted 54 losses. Incidentally, the battalion's original commander–a Bosnian Serb by birth, known as the foremost practitioner of the "free hunt" tactics–was killed a shortly before. This was the final straw for the attackers, who withdrew to their starting positions soon thereafter. The 7th Corps' attempt to capitalize on its defensive success by taking some smaller outpost around Žužemberk in mid-February had likewise failed. March saw two bigger actions, none of which helped change the overall situation. First, there was an expedition by two NOVJ brigades to the Sava, where they were supposed to aid the planned, but never realized, crossing of the units belonging to the 4th OZ. The Axis, for their part, launched another thrust into Suha Krajina, this time with an equivalent of two regiments. One of them was the recently-formed 1st SS Special Regiment "Waräger", made up of Russians loyal to that Soviet arch-renegade, General Andrei Vlassov. Whereas the combat prowess (or the lack thereof) of these legionnaires failed to impress the Partisans, the Home Guards were as pugnacious as ever. By the time the offensive–marked by "the fiercest fighting in months"–had petered out by mid-March, the

45 *Zbornik*/VI/16/583-85, MHQ Slovenia to SHQ (3.10.1944); *Zbornik*/VI/18/500, 9th NOVJC, Monthly report (January 1945).

lines remained largely unchained. On the whole, the only tangible result of the winter fighting was the loss of Notranjska to the NOP; after being surprised twice during January, the local detachment was in no condition to effectively patrol the province. For the time being, the Axis had little use for its rugged interior, but this would soon change.[46]

The operational area of the 7th NOVJ Corps won drastically on significance in early April 1945, primarily in the context of the Yugoslav Army's great spring offensive in the littoral (see below). On the one hand, the main liberated territory was seen as a ready-made bridgehead across the Kupa and springboard for future advance into central Slovenia; alternatively, it could be used for a roundabout march to Trieste. On the other hand, if not secured properly, the enemy could use the wider area of Kočevje to strike against the 4th Yugoslav Army's increasingly lengthening, and therefore vulnerable, right flank. This possibility was not lost on the Germans, who launched their biggest attack yet against the 15th and 18th Divisions on 8 April. A week later, the Serbian collaborationist forces (including three regiments of the SFK and two Chetnik brigades) launched a separate drive from Kočevje to the Kupa; if successful, the attack would pave the way for a deep penetration in the rear of the main Yugoslav front. Although the Axis made some initial gains, their plan failed to take into account the changing balance of forces and the much-improved supply situation of their adversary. The first, tentative link between the 7th Corps and the NOVJ bases in Northern Dalmatia was opened already in January; by this time, the Slovene Partisans had also become the main beneficiaries of the Western Allied air deliveries. As a result, not only could the men be clothed and fed, but the wounded could be transported out and reinforcements brought in. For instance, the large and well-armed 5th Overseas Brigade arrived in the nick of time to bolster the defenses of the 15th and 18th Divisions, whose combined strength had by now sunk to ca. 3,500 fighters. Moreover, their firepower was vastly increased thanks to the arrival of 20 pieces of light artillery with enough ammunition. With these forces at hand, the 7th Corps could not only stabilize the situation in its sector by the end of April, but also contemplate an offensive in the direction of Ljubljana.[47]

The 9th Corps' main tasks in late 1944 and early 1945 were to hold onto its possessions, pester the enemy with guerrilla-style actions, push back the collaborationists' sphere of influence, and acquire new sources of food. The latter meant bringing under control, or at least gaining access to, the Vipava Valley and the Kras Plateau, as well as the Gorenjska hinterland. For this purpose, the reinforced 31st Division carried out a series of assaults on strongpoints in the valleys of the Bača, Selška Sora, and Poljska Sora during October and November 1944. The Germans responded by reinforcing particularly endangered outposts (such as Hotedršica) and re-establishing those that had been lost to enemy attacks (e.g. Poljana, Gabrk). In the south, they went from aggressive patrolling and an occasional incursion into enemy-held territory to systematic expansion and strengthening of their hold over the Vipava Valley. Thanks to the

46 The operations of the 7th NOVJ Corps are reconstructed on the basis of its periodic activity reports published in *Zbornik*/VI/17/98-113 (26.10.1944), 367-91 (15.11.1944), 505-16 (21.11.1944), 552-64 (25.11.1944); *Zbornik*/VI/18/269-84 (9.1.1945), 543-60 (9.2.1945); *Zbornik*/VI/19/33-49 (1.3.1945), 116-20 (10.3.1945), 613-26 (27.4.1945), as well as *Zbornik*/XI/4/71-98 (April 1945). Additional sources will be cited separately; in this case see the following: *Zbornik*/VI/17/941-54 [after-action reports of individual battalions for "Schneegestöber", 16-20.11.1944]; Štaut, "Elitne", pp. 97-98; Klemen Kocjančič, "Between Vlasov and Himmler: Russian SS-Sonder-Regiment 1 'Waräger' in Slovenia, 1944–45", *JSMS*, 30:1 (2017), pp. 54-59.

47 Dimitrijević, *Vojska*, pp. 538-41.

presence of a veteran combat formation (the 71st ID) and the greatly increased number of strongpoints, the entire area became practically inaccessible to the units of the 30th Division. Then, in late November, the Germans left for Batina, allowing the Partisans to re-enter the now-undefended valley and replenish their ranks with supplies and recruits. This gift, which fell so suddenly in their lap, would not stay long in their possession, however. On 19 December, the Germans launched Operation "Adler" using five of their own and four foreign battalions, plus the elements of two RSI divisions. Advancing from Gorizia, Idrija, Postojna, and Dutovlje, the attackers managed to push the Partisans away from the valley and onto the Banjšice Plateau and Trnovski Gozd. This was the first major action of the elite *Divisione fanteria di marina Xª* (colloquially known as "Decima Mas") against the Yugoslav Partisans, and it did not bode well for the future. On the 22nd, its second-in-command was killed in an ambush; on the 23rd, the 19th Slovene Brigade attacked a column of the division in the Čepovan Valley and captured an AT gun in the process.

The biggest shock, however, came in late January 1945. In the aftermath of the offensive, the Axis established a number of new outposts including Trnovo, now occupied by ca. 200 members of the "Fulmine" Battalion. The HQ of the 9th Corps came to regard the village as the key to the Vipava Valley and decided to throw the entire reinforced 30th Division against it. As a result, the garrison was all but wiped-out in the ensuing assault (19-21 January); the battle is still commemorated by the Italian extreme right as a valiant stand against the "Slavic invasion" of Gorizia. The victory at Trnovo provided a major morale boost for the Partisans in this fourth winter of the war even though their own losses were far from negligible (31 KIA, 77 WIA, and 33 MIA). Otherwise, the first weeks of 1945 passed peacefully, except for the constant ambushing and raiding: the Partisans even complained that the enemy succeeded in making the procurement of food impossible in this way. In early February, the Germans decided to have another go at the main guerrilla bases at the Banjšice Plateau and Trnovski Gozd. Operation "Rübezahl"[48] had three phases and lasted, with interruptions, until early March. As with most other late-war anti-guerrilla sweeps, its main objective was enemy infrastructure rather than his army. Even these limited aims, however, could not be met with the meager forces employed (in this case, an equivalent of two regiments, only one of them being German). In the end, apart from several captured magazines, the 30th Division got off practically unscathed.[49]

As it turned out, the "Rübezahl" was but an overture for the biggest Axis offensive in Primorska since the autumn of 1943. Its aim: the destruction of the 9th Corps, which by now had ca. 10,000 men in two Yugoslav, and one Italian division; the latter, named "Garibaldi" had crossed the border and placed itself under the corps' command in December 1944. The

48 By now, German planners were clearly runnning out of ideas for the names of their operations: this "Rübezahl" should not be confused with the ones from Montenegro (August 1944) and Bosnia (March 1945).

49 The operations of the 9th NOVJ Corps are reconstructed on the basis of its periodic activity reports published in *Zbornik*/VI/16/900-10 (20.10.1944), *Zbornik*/VI/17/262-73, 486-96, 644-60 (3, 18 and 30.11.1944, respectively); *Zbornik*/VI/18/128-49, 223-34, 468-99 and 491-500, 803-30 (23.12.1944, 5.1, 31.1-1.2, 28.2.1945, respectively); *Zbornik*/VI/19/86-90 (9.3.1945); *Zbornik*/XI/4/624-41 (13.5.1945). For German documents on the "Rübezahl", see *Zbornik*/VI/18/941-43 and 946, as well as *Zbornik*/VI/19/809-14 (2 and 11.2, 2.3.1945, respectively); for Trnovo, see Ezio Ferrante, "Borghese e la Decima nella bufera (1943-1945)", *Bollettino d'Archivio dell'Ufficio Storico della Marina Militare*, 28 (2014), p. 98.

attack force consisted of ca. 40,000 soldiers drawn from nearly every military and paramilitary organization that owed allegiance to the Third Reich in one way or the other. In addition to four SS police regiments, also present were the Slovene *Domobranci*, Vlassov's Russians, Đujić's and Jevđević's Chetniks, Ljotić's Volunteers, and even some Greek collaborationists. The first phase of the operation, named "Frühlingsanfang", targeted the 31st Division and Italian Partisans in the Cerkno Hills. In the period 16-25 March, the Axis surrounded three guerrilla brigades, along with numerous members of territorial units and rear-area services, around Mount Porezen. Only about a half of these men and women (ca. 1,000) managed to escape north, towards Bohinj; the remainder was either killed, captured, or dispersed.

This success freed up additional forces for use in the ongoing Operation "Winterende" against the bulk of the 9th Corps in the south. By the last days of March, the Partisans had found themselves cornered, without food, on the southeastern slopes of the Trnovski Gozd. And, as always in such critical situations, they decided to split up and disperse. While the exfiltration towards the west and southeast succeeded almost without a fight, the north-bound group ran into heavy opposition and was barely able to reach its destination by 3 April. Mop-up operations continued for several more days, after which the attackers began returning to their old bases and the newly-erected strongpoints in the former liberated territory. The "Winterwende" inflicted at least another ca. 1,000 casualties to the NOVJ (most of them stragglers), but the overall success of the great spring offensive in Primorska is debatable. On the one hand, the 9th Corps was practically rendered inoperable until late April, by which time the Germans had no need for this part of the country anyway. On the other hand–as Yugoslav historians were always quick to point out–the result of the offensive was not commensurate with the resources used. Moreover, the local Partisans survived long enough to participate in the dramatic finale of the war (see below).[50]

The 4th OZ began the autumn campaign of 1944 by sending the OHQ with the 6th and 11th Brigades to the collaborationist-infected area of Kamnik. Before their presence could be seriously felt, however, both formations were ordered to join the 7th Corps. The 14th Division and smaller units that remained behind would face the full weight of the extraordinarily diversified and persistent German COIN efforts. The widespread fear of a hungry winter played well into the hands of the occupation authorities. One enterprising civil servant in the Mežica Valley took away the ration cards from the families of all those who "went into the woods"; as a result, the latter returned and "volunteered" for labor in the local lead mine. From mid-October to late November, Treeck's regiment carried out a systematic cleansing of the Pohorje, leaving behind re-established outposts and municipal offices, and taking every head of cattle and able-bodied man it could find. Lacko's Detachment was routed in the process, losing, among else, over 200 MIA.

The centerpiece of the German campaign, the *reconquista* of the Upper Savinja Valley, began already on 27 November with concentric attacks from the direction of Celje, Kamnik, and Solčava. Acting in accordance with the NOVJ doctrine, the 4th OZ surrendered the liberated territory in order to preserve its strength. While the 14th Division went east of the line Velenje–Celje–Zidani Most, rear-area and support units withdrew towards Moravče. The guerrillas fought back with mines, obstacles, raids and ambushes: on 15 December, a special assault detail

50 Colić, *Pregled*, pp. 335-40.

even managed to release 360 inmates from the Celje prison. The Partisans also tried to re-gain the initiative by bringing back the OHQ, but the plan failed to take into account the sorry state of this command upon its return from Dolenjska. By New Year's Day 1945, only 420 fighters remained with the colors; twenty days later, the number dropped to 140. Exhausted by the fighting south of the Sava, with no winter clothing or food, most men simply went home (a lot of them also went over to the enemy). As a result, the 6th and 11th Brigades spent the first three months of 1945 moving around the snow-covered mountains between Domžale and Vransko, and between the Sava and Dreta Rivers, desperately trying to find shelter and supplies. Despite freezing temperatures, the Axis hounded them constantly. In mid-March, the Partisans made a much-celebrated escape from the cauldron formed by the 14th SS Grenadier Division "Galizien" on Mount Menina. On an interesting note, the breakthrough is commemorated by the 2019-film "Preboj", which holds the distinction of being the first project of the Partisan genre made since the demise of Yugoslavia.[51]

Just prior to the Menina episode, the Partisans' daily struggle for survival was interrupted by the order of the SHQ calling for a retreat of all mobile formations from the hostile territory of Štajerska. Although the HQ of the 4th OZ considered the solution too drastic, it duly proceeded to concentrate its five brigades east of Litija. From late February to early April 1945, the Partisans made four attempts to cross the Sava with the help of pontoons, wooden peasant boats, and rubber dinghies provided by the Western Allies; all of them failed due to high water levels, treacherous rapids, and enemy action. The news of the arrival of the Red Army to the Mura put an end to these endeavors: the brigades would now be more useful wreaking havoc in the rear of the Eastern Front than in Dolenjska. The fact that the Germans threw nearly all available men against the Soviets practically opened the gates to the central parts of Štajerska. By the end of the month, the 14th Division was operating in guerrilla manner over a wide area reaching from Dravograd in the north to Trbovlje in the south, and almost as far east as Slovenska Bistrica. By this time, the morale of Axis soldiers on garrison duties had plummeted to an all-time low: on 24 April, the 2nd Slovene Brigade took Šentvid pri Zavodnju and captured 60 Ukrainian legionnaires of the 14th SS for the price of "only" one dead and three wounded fighters. One other incident from this period deserves a special mention. On 16 April, the Partisans captured Conrad Heidenreich, a famous pre-war architect who was now an OT *Einsatzleiter* (major-general) in charge of construction of defensive works in this corner of Europe. All hopes that he could be exchanged for some high-ranking NOP leaders were thwarted by his premature death under suspicious circumstances.[52]

51 See the 4th OZ's activity reports in *Zbornik*/VI/16/786-811 (15.10.1944), *Zbornik*/VI/17/200-33 (31.10.1944), 396-432 (15.11.1944), 672-731 (2.12.1944), 748-51 (4.12.1944); *Zbornik*/VI/18/30-57 (18.12.1944), 705-802 (16.12.1944-26.2.1945). For the actions of the 6th and 11th Brigades see ibid., pp. 464-67, OHQ to SHQ (28.1.1945), and Fajdiga, *Zidanškova*, pp. 602, 611, 628, 633, 637-41. For German countermeasures see *Zbornik*/VI/17/956 (Gendarmerie Prevalje, Bi-weekly report, 27.11.1944), 976-87 (Treeck to HSSPF Ljubljana, 10.12.1944).

52 For the actions of the 14th NOVJ Division in early 1945, see its diary in *Zbornik*/VI/18/879-89 (10-28.2.1945), *Zbornik*/VI/19/432-66 (1.3.-19.4.1945) and 711-33 (April 1945); see also the following articles by Klemen Kocjančič in *Studia Historica Slovenica*: "'Prvi general ujet od nas': zajetje in smrt Konrada Heidenreicha", 17:1 (2017), pp. 217-36; "Galicijski levi v bojih proti partizanom: 14. grenadirska divizija Waffen-SS (galicijska št. 1) na Slovenskem", 19:3 (2019), pp. 815-46.

7.9 Partisan Army in Final Stages of War

Understanding Yugoslav-Soviet relations is the key for understanding the final stages of the development of the Partisan army. Despite Tito's repeated pleas for an increased Soviet presence, the Kremlin decided to send its official representatives to the SHQ only after the Big Three had formally recognized the NOP on the Tehran Conference. The mission arrived to Bosanski Petrovac in the last week of February 1944. It was headed by an experienced officer, General Nikolai Korneev, who brought with him a mix of experts on guerrilla warfare, Spanish Civil War veterans, and intelligence operatives, together with a driver and a cook. In the course of the year, smaller Soviet missions would be established with provincial MHQs and some corps. The Partisans established their own mission to Moscow in April of the same year with General Velimir Terzić at its helm, a former royal officer and Jovanović's deputy. The Yugoslavs, and especially the Communists among them, were overjoyed at finally having members of the legendary Red Army in their midst. In a telling gesture, Tito entrusted the handling of his personal wireless communications to a Soviet expert; "Like a brother–he laughs like us, and talks about everything, and interests himself for everything", wrote Popović about a member of Korneev's entourage; a Partisan commander in Serbia said that "we were basically more saddened by the losses among Soviet warriors than we were by our own". As such, Red Army soldiers was allowed liberties no other allied force was permitted. For instance, they stripped Serbia bare of every motor vehicle they could find, although the Kremlin promised that the NOVJ could keep all the booty made in joint operations. The same goes for German prisoners, who were often "stolen" from the Partisans at gunpoint. Not even the numerous instances of looting, drunken behavior, and even rape and murder, that occurred during and after Belgrade Operation were allowed to spoil the "honeymoon". The Yugoslavs usually ground their teeth and looked the other way, except, ironically, for the chief KPJ ideologue, Đilas, whose loud protests eventually got him into trouble with Stalin himself.[53]

The Soviets, for the most part, treated the Yugoslavs with a mix of benevolent paternalism and outright contempt. The latter was especially palpable in officers, who, as most "regulars", tended to look down upon guerrilla fighters as little better than an armed mob. On the battlefield, however, the Soviets quickly recognized the advantages of having the Partisans on their side:

> "[They fought] marvelously [...] They're brave, shoot straight, know how to handle themselves and above all they never hesitate to put themselves under the command of any Russian who turns up, no matter what his rank [...] they're not as well trained professionally as our soldiers are, but they're damn good amateurs."[54]

Stavka planners probably felt the same; without the bellicose Yugoslavs, the long, rugged, strategic southern flank of the Eastern Front would require a permanent presence of at least one

53 This sub-chapter is largely based on the following works by Trifković: "Amateurs", pp. 260, 269-77; "Carnage", pp. 111-22; "Anabasis", pp. 615-16, 618-25; "Victories", pp. 115-20; "Trieste", pp. 16-23; "Operacije", pp. 219, 223. Additional sources will be cited seapartely; in this case Timofejev, *Rusi*, pp. 294-305, Vuksanović (ed.), *Beleške*, p. 201 (29.2.1944), *DCO*/XVIII/118-19, Đilas to Stalin (June 1944); Djilas, *Wartime*, pp. 420-21, 428-29.

54 Thayer, *Hands*, pp. 38-39.

Soviet rifle corps, perhaps even more. Its main task would be to serve as a prop for the Bulgarians, who would have to take over this entire sector despite their disappointing performance in the October-November 1944 campaign. The single redeeming trait of the Bulgarian army was its large size (287,000 front-line troops); practically everything else was a mess. First and foremost, the army had not faced a regular opponent since the Great War. The purge of "monarchist-fascist elements" that began with the takeover of power by Fatherland Front, removed the last notions of self-initiative and flexibility among the officer corps. As a result, the army's behavior on the battlefield became predictable to the extreme: the Germans knew, for example, that the Bulgarians never attacked at night and on Sundays. The majority of common Partisans held some sort of grievance against the Axis and had also been thoroughly indoctrinated by the finely-tuned propaganda. Their Bulgarian counterparts, on the contrary, found it difficult to shoot on their erstwhile allies. The functioning of rear-area services and quality of staff work left much to be desired: on one occasion in mid-October, instead of going to Kosovo, the 1st BAB famously traveled 30 km in the opposite direction. And then there were problems with discipline and in relations with their nominal Yugoslav allies. In many cases, the "new" Bulgarians were just as rapacious as the "old" ones, and the Serbs in particular found it difficult to work with the people against whom they fought four wars in the past 60 years. There were positive examples too: the 22nd and 46th Divisions, for instances, established good working relations with their partners during the Kosovo campaign. Nevertheless, it must be said that for all its shortcomings on and off the battlefield, the Bulgarian Army bore the heaviest brunt of the fighting in the southeastern parts of Yugoslavia: alone the campaigns in the Kriva Reka, and around Niš and Kosovo, cost over 7,000 KIA, WIA, and MIA.[55]

Prior to the liberation of Serbia, the Soviet material help to the NOP was symbolic. This was chiefly due to the immense technical difficulties involved in the transport of supplies from the USSR. From May to mid-June 1944, the grand total therefore amounted to only 132 tons. During July, the Soviet government took steps to increase the flow by sending a fully-loaded cargo ship (3,000 tons) from Iran to Bari, the new home base of a special Red Air Force transport squadron tasked with operating above Yugoslavia. The real breakthrough, however, came only in September with Tito's visit to Moscow. The aid package agreed on this occasion was truly massive: among else, it included the full complement of arms, equipment, and supplies for twelve rifle and two air divisions (336 aircraft), and two tank brigades (130 T-34/85s). The material would be accompanied by instructors, twelve for each rifle division. Out of 111 advisors present in February 1945, one-half was attached to the high command in Belgrade and staffs of the field armies, and the remainder to military schools and various technical and support services. Moreover, the USSR agreed to host and train over 2,600 particularly promising Yugoslav candidates from every branch of service. Moscow's magnanimity compared favorably to the perceived cynicism of the Western Allies, who were often accused of bartering their tins for Yugoslav blood and withholding modern weaponry for political reasons. The realization of the Soviet program, however, did not go without hiccups. The failure to deliver enough heavy artillery shells, high-octane gasoline, and summer-grade tank oil by the beginning of the spring

55 *Zbornik*/I/15/88, 114, Reports by 46th and 22nd NOVJDs to 13th NOVJC (17 and 19.11.1944, respectively).

campaign 1945 had severely curtailed the offensive capabilities of the Yugoslav Army and led to additional, heavy losses (see below).[56]

Of all the Soviet-trained formations, the air divisions were the most important. In order to make them operational as soon as possible, they would not be built form scratch, but "converted" from the already existing Red Air Force units. Chosen for this purpose were the 10th Guards Assault and 236th Fighter Divisions, combined into Group "Vitruk", named after its commanding general. Every Soviet unit down to the smallest maintenance detail had its Yugoslav "shadow": in case of fighting formations, these were the 42nd Assault and 11th Fighter Divisions, which were combined into Group of Air Divisions (*Grupa vazduhoplovnih divizija*, GVD). Group "Vitruk"/GVD was based in Vojvodina and flew support missions for the NOVJ and the Red Army using mixed Soviet-Yugoslav aircrews. As the training progressed, the younger partner was gradually entrusted with more responsibilities, and finally took over completely in April 1945. Vitruk's fliers rendered valuable help to the ground units in Syrmia, and along the Drava and Drina: according to Dapčević, the "Shturmoviks" were instrumental in slowing down the German winter offensive in his sector. In all, from mid-January to late May 1945, the GVD carried out 4,568 combat sorties.[57]

Two NOVJ ground combat units were formed on the Soviet territory. Four batches of hand-picked candidates left Bari for the USSR in mid-September and early October 1944 in order to serve as the core of a new tank brigade. By the end of the year, these ca. 650 men were joined by about 200 Yugoslav economic migrants from Iran and Iraq, who now volunteered for service in the home country. Despite Tito's requests for a speedy return of the unit, the Soviets refused to be rushed: the 2nd TB was officially created only on 8 March 1945 and sent to Yugoslavia early the next month. It had three armored battalions with altogether 65 T-34/85s, plus a motorized battalion that was added shortly before going into action. Attached to the 1st Yugoslav Army, the brigade played an important part in the initial phase of the great spring offensive; otherwise, it had an undistinguished wartime career, though not through any fault of its own.

The other unit formed in the USSR was a good deal more exotic and controversial. The 1st Yugoslav Brigade was formed on 1 June 1944 in Kolomna from the Yugoslav citizens who had been captured as members of various Axis armies. Most of them came from the 369th Reinforced IR (colloquially know as the "Croatian Legion"), an all-volunteer outfit formed with Pavelić's blessing in the summer of 1941 for the purpose of the "crusade against Bolshevism". Also present were Slovenes from the Wehrmacht, as well as Vojvodina Serbs forcibly conscripted by the Hungarians. The legion's last commander, a competent professional officer called Marko Mesić (not related to the second president of modern-day Republic of Croatia Stipe Mesić as often thought), was chosen to lead the new brigade. Trained and equipped in the Soviet fashion, but, awkwardly enough, clad in the uniforms of the old royal pattern, the brigade left for Serbia in October 1944. Attached to the 23rd Serbian Division, it received a devastating baptism of fire at Čačak; there, it bore a full brunt of the German November counterattack, losing over a third of its strength (ca. 500 men) in only three days of fighting. Already apprehensive of the unit's

56 Russian State Archive of Socio-Political History (RGASPI), fond 664, opis 1 and 2, contain Soviet documents from May 1944 to February 1945 dealing with aid for Yugoslavia. See also *Zbornik*/II/13/274, Terzić to Tito (13.6.1944), as well as *SD*/XXI/307.

57 *Zbornik*/X/1/366-67, 10th Guards Assault Air Division to Terzić (20.1.1945); Stevan Roglić, "Komandovanje i rukovođenje vazduhoplovnim jedinicama", in *Vazduhoplovstvo*, pp. 56-58.

composition ("riddled with hostile Ustasha elements", one report read), the Partisan leadership used the episode as a pretext to purge the brigade of "unreliables" and replace them with NOVJ veterans. Among others, Mesić was relieved and assigned to a staff position, even though the SHQ had been consulted by the Soviets regarding his original appointment.[58]

The arrival of Soviet arms removed one of the main obstacles on the NOVJ's path of becoming a full-fledged regular army. The other great hurdle, the shortage of manpower, would soon be solved as well. Before we go into details, a few introductory remarks would be in order. Already by late summer and early fall of 1944, the NOVJ had grown into a force of respectful size. Notwithstanding the fact that the Partisans were known to inflate strength figures in order to receive more material aid from the Western Allies, their army did, in fact, have between 250 and 300,000 men roughly distributed as follows:

- MHQ Slovenia: 29,462 (as of 1 October)
- MHQ Croatia: 125,580 (30 November)
- 5th Corps: 26,290 (1 October)
- 3rd Corps: 7,820 (29 November)
- 2nd Assault Corps: 11,311 (mid-August-to mid-December)
- OGD and MHQ Serbia: 50,000 (mid-October)
- MHQ Vojvodina: 15,000 (September)
- OHQ Kosovo: 1,850 (September)
- MHQ Macedonia: 17,500 (September)

Earlier the same year, Tito confirmed his public statement that he had 300,000 men under arms in a private conversation with Đilas. The number, namely, included rear-area personnel, resistance groups, village guards, etc., in other words, also some members of the non-military branches of the NOP. The figure of 350,000, found in Soviet intelligence documents from late September, can probably be explained by using the same logic.[59]

Even though the army's strength was impressive, especially considering its humble beginnings, it was still too weak to embark on the final great campaign of the war. The liberation of the eastern parts of the country, whose manpower potential was largely untapped, provided the solution. On 3 November 1944, the NKOJ proclaimed a general mobilization, which resulted in the drafting of some 280,000 persons in Serbia alone by next February. Most of the draftees were sent to the newly-established Replacement Battalions and Brigades, where they underwent

58 *DCO*/XVI/190, Dimitrov to CK KPJ (6.3.1944); *Zbornik*/II/13/231-32 and 458, Terzić to Tito (1.6 and 14.7.1944, respectively); *Zbornik*/II/14/346, Tito to Terzić (3.11.1944); *SD*/XXIV/58 (Tito to Terzić, 13.10.1944), and 249-50; *SD*/XXV/13, Tito to 1st Yugoslav Bde. (17.11.1944); *Zbornik*/I/14/519-24, 1st Yugoslav Bde. to SHQ (3.11.1944); Timofejev, *Rusi*, pp. 358-59.

59 The sources for the figures are as follows: MHQ Croatia–*Zbornik*/V/35/546-67; MHQ Slovenia–*Zbornik*/VI/16/504-05; 5th NOVJC–*Zbornik*/IV/30/566; 3rd NOVJC–ibid., pp. 728-30. For individual divisions of the 2nd NOVJC see Vukanović, *Treća*, p. 365, Drulović, *Tridesetsedma*, p. 218, Đurišić, *Primorska*, pp. 132-37, and *Zbornik*/IV/28/169. Owing to chaotic circumstances, the figures for Serbia proper, Vojvodina, Kosovo, and Macedonia can only be estimated; for the OGD and MHQ Serbia see Trifković, "Amateurs", p. 256; MHQ Vojvodina–*DCO*/XIX/448-49; OHQ Kosovo–*Enciklopedija*, Vol. IV, pp. 662-63; MHQ Macedonia–*Zbornik*/VII/3/67-68, 107. See also Djilas, *Wartime*, p. 375, and TsAMO/975/1/102/15, 3rd UF, Armies in the Balkans (28.9.1944).

a one- or two-month crash training program, depending on the branch of service. Upon completion, the recruits were allotted to combat units, usually with the 1st, 2nd, and the 3rd Yugoslav Armies, but also to the 2nd and 3rd Corps in Eastern Bosnia. Whilst the majority of them came forward because they had no other choice, the ideals of the NOP still appealed to many: General Friebe noted that the number of volunteers in enemy units facing him in the Drina Valley was "astoundingly high".

According to one notion that gained special popularity in the post-Socialist period, the Communist authorities sent these half-trained youths in headlong charges on the Syrmian Front in a deliberate attempt to punish the traditionalist Serbian society and break its will to oppose the new order. Although these claims lie in the realm of conspiracy theories, the almost-peacetime atmosphere encountered on the far side of the Drina must have provoked bitterness among the grizzled veterans coming from war-ravaged provinces such as Bosanska Krajina, Lika, or Slavonia. This sentiment was shared by U.S. Colonel Charles Thayer, who, like Maclean, had served as a diplomat in Moscow during the 1930s and was by no means sympathetic to communist ideology. While traveling through Valjevo in October 1944, he was amazed at a "great number of men, young and old, who lolled about in the shady streets". Belgrade nightclubs–which were still working despite all the dramatic events which took place in and around the city–were packed with "the golden youth", dancing and enjoying themselves."We knew their fun wouldn't last long", Thayer wrote gleefully; "sooner or later these fat young men would pay for the peaceful idleness they had enjoyed while the rest of their generation, all over the world, was fighting".[60]

In the western half of Yugoslavia, the shortage of manpower continued to represent a major problem for the NOVJ. It should be noted that the bulk of the population living in the liberated territories had by now recognized the NOP as the de-facto state authority. In Slavonia, the turnout was good despite the generally sullen atmosphere caused by the mobilization; in Dalmatia, a large number of draftees came forward on their own free will. On the whole, after three-and-a-half years of war, new recruits were imaginably difficult to find. For instance, the entire liberated territory of Tuzla gave only ca. 10,000 recruits between September 1944 and January 1945. Less than a half of them had actually ended up in combat formations, while the rest was needed in industry and rear-area services. By spring, draft commissions were scraping the bottom of the proverbial barrel: the old NOP strongholds of Banija and Kordun could provide only 926 recruits for the 4th Corps in February; in March, the 10th Corps authorized the drafting of 16 year-olds (the age limit was usually 17 or 18). By April, the Yugoslav units fighting in Croatian Littoral were increasingly being replenished by Kosovars, who had to make an arduous journey from their home province via Albania and Montenegro.[61]

With the most important technical prerequisites met, the Yugoslavs went ahead with the regularization efforts at a breakneck speed; the aim: transform the bulk of their semi-irregular army into a modern force capable of liberating the country by itself. This process ran parallel

60 *SD*/XXIV/167 and *SD*/XXV/145-47, Tito to MHQ Serbia, and to 2nd Yugoslav Army [YA] (2.11 and 25.12.1944, respectively); 22nd ID, Report Drina (28.2.1945), printed in: Hnilicka, *Balkan*, p. 361; Thayer, *Hands*, pp. 21, 71-73.

61 See the monthly reports of 3rd, 6th, 4th, and 10th NOVJC in *Zbornik*/IV/32/623 (January 1945), *Zbornik*/V/35/32 (October 1944), *Zbornik*/V/38/99 (January 1945), and *Zbornik*/V/39/320 (March 1945), respectively. See also *DCO*/XXI/263, OK Dalmatia to CK KPJ (8.12.1944).

to combat operations and would not be completed until the end of the war. Outwardly, the Partisans parted with another piece of their guerrilla heritage already in April 1944, when the clenched-fist salute in mobile formations was replaced with the common military salute. They also developed a taste for military pageantry of a distinctly un-revolutionary sort: all twenty hand-picked veteran brigades that had been awarded Order of People's Liberation in July had to have a special red banner made of silk or velvet with gold embroidery. The first NOVJ medals–Order of Partisan Star (in three classes), Order of Brotherhood and Unity, Order of Valor, and Medal for Bravery–were designed by the famous sculptor Augustin Augustinčić and produced in the USSR. They were awarded to individuals for the first time in November in the newly-liberated capital. Finally, on 1 March 1945, the NOVJ became Yugoslav Army (*Jugoslovenska armija*), and the SHQ changed its name to General Staff.[62]

In terms of the OOB, the main novelty was the introduction of armies as the highest field commands beginning in January 1945. As the front moved closer to the borders, the armies gradually absorbed "provincial" units, thus making the majority of corps HQs redundant. The MHQs remained in place but were practically relegated to administrative responsibilities. By the beginning of the spring offensive in late March, the Yugoslav Army had reached the zenith of its strength, with altogether 186 infantry, 28 internal security (KNOJ), 24 artillery, 12 training, seven engineer, two tank, two cavalry, one railway and one traffic brigades. At the same time, there were 36 detachments still in existence; incredibly, the last three of these relics of 1941 (two in Bosnia and one in Slovenia) would be disbanded only after the end of the war. Diversification of the army progressed at an accelerated pace: combat formations now received HQ Units (basically, the military police), mine clearance teams, ski reconnaissance platoons, and even courier dog details. Following the Soviet pattern, the regiment was introduced into the army: in addition to six air units of this type, there were also one each of AA, signals, and motor transport troops.[63]

The Soviet influence went far beyond the mere naming of units. In fact, the Partisan leaders did their best to sovietize the army as thoroughly as possible. This was not done solely for ideological reasons, but also because the course of the war had confirmed the soundness of the Red Army's methods and tactics. The trend was especially palpable in the realm of support and rear-area services. For example, in late 1944, all medical personnel within the division were reorganized into a separate battalion known under its original Red Army acronym MSB or *medsanbat* (Medical-Sanitary Battalion); the training curriculums for signals troops and engineers were based almost exclusively on imported manuals. Two units of a distinctly Soviet type found their way into combat formations. In late 1944, each company was ordered to form one platoon of soldiers armed exclusively with SMGs (*automatičari*) as a type of a shock/intervention unit. As we have seen, the institution of disciplinary outfit was known and employed by the Partisans at least since 1942, but it usually had the character of menial labor detail. Now, the "eastern" branch of the NOVJ received penal units in the mold of the notorious

62 For the sake of clarity, the abbreviation "SHQ" will be retained throughout the remainder of the text.

63 *SD*/XX/33 (SHQ, Order, 25.4.1944), 111 (Tito to Terzić, 18.5.1944); *SD*/XXI/244 and 251, Tito to 6th and 1st NOVJDs 25. and 26.7.1944, respectively); *Zbornik*/IV/32/210, 379-81, 385-87, 14th NOVJC, Orders (8, 13, and 16.1.1945); *Zbornik*/IV/31/181, 10th NOVJD to 5th NOVJC (7.12.1944); *Enciklopedija*, Vol. VI, p. 273; Anić, Joksimović, Gutić, *Narodnooslobodilačka*, pp. 470, 478-79, 490, 522-23.

shtrafbats, whose members were to "redeem their guilt with blood" on the field of battle. Finally, in the spring of 1945, it was decided to reorganize the then-standard 10,000-man divisions into 6,000-man "Rifle" formations, but the process would not be completed until after the war. It should be noted that the Yugoslav units deployed in the enemy rear and in the Adriatic littoral remained largely spared of these influences. In fact, the liaison with the Soviets had a positive impact here. The plan for the Yugoslav spring offensive was based on a lecture on Šiauliai Advance Operation from July-August 1944 given by a Red Army colonel before a select few officers of the MHQ Croatia. Admittedly, the ultimate success of the offensive was also due to the fact that the 4th Yugoslav Army could maneuver far more easily and was facing much weaker opposition than its sister formations.[64]

Whether the high losses suffered by the NOVJ during the last six months of the war were at least partially attributable to the Soviet teachings is debatable. The infantry training was, by and large, conducted according to old Yugoslav textbooks, usually by former officers and NCOs of either the royal or one of the Axis armies. Moreover, we have seen repeatedly (e.g. in Bosanska Krajina in late 1942, or in Slavonia in early 1944) how Partisan commanders tended to compensate for the lack of heavy weapons and ammunition by utilizing the only resource they had plenty of, and that was manpower. Compared to earlier times, an individual fighter was much better equipped in 1945, but this was still not enough for the novel, material-intensive type of warfare he was now forced to conduct. In the end, the idea of overwhelming the enemy with superior numbers still seemed as the most practical solution. This was true not only for all those who were eager to ape the Soviets, or those who were simply unimaginative, but also for more enlightened officers. Back in 1942, Popović criticized his superior, Jovanović, for being "insensitive to a man's physical condition"; in early 1945, however, he wrote: "Oversensitivity to losses is now out of place–it hampers proper work and [eventually] makes losses even higher". At the same time, he was painfully aware of the fact that the only advantage he had over the enemy was the numerical one. In response to an angry cable from Tito, in which the latter criticized the inability of the 2nd Yugoslav Army to crush Friebe's division in the Drina Valley despite its six-fold superiority, Popović responded that the army's actual fighting strength corresponded to "less than 10 percent" of its nominal strength owing to the immense objective difficulties plaguing the NOVJ at that time.[65]

"Calling the enemy 'bandits' and the war against him as 'guerrilla' has definitely shown itself to be wrong", wrote von Weichs in his situation appraisal from late September 1944, adding: "With the exception of the newly-formed units, the [enemy] is [...]dynamic, operationally and tactically well-led, enviably armed with heavy weapons, and of steadily growing strength".[66] It was indeed a flattering comment, but it can also be regarded as a kind of farewell address to the Partisan army of the old that had given so much headache to the Wehrmacht, primarily thanks to its uncanny ability to alternate between guerrilla and regular tactics. The fact is, the final period of the conflict saw a rapid decline in the NOVJ/Yugoslav Army's battlefield proficiency. The main reason for this was that the Partisans now had to practice a type of warfare their enemy excelled at, and they themselves had little experience with. A head-to-head encounter in

64 Ibid., pp. 489-90, 520; *Zbornik*/II/15/281-85, SHQ, Orders (25.3.1945); *Zbornik*/IV/32/262, 14th NOVJC, Order (13.1.1945).

65 *SD*/XXVI/72, Tito to Popović (8.2.1945); Dželebdžić, *Druga*, pp. 173-74.

66 NARA/T311/191/638, OBSO to OKW (20.9.1944).

the open or a defense of an important hilltop, both of which occurred fairly often in the past, could not compare with a protracted, intensive regular campaign that was now on the table. In order to play this kind of game, the army needed to grow, but the sudden and huge influx of recruits proved to be a mixed blessing. Units now became heavily "diluted": what little veterans were left were automatically promoted and sent to officer other, equally raw units of every shape and size that were now springing up like mushrooms all across the country. The army had become unwieldy, its famous maneuverability gone for good. Like any other regular force, it was now dependent on magazines and could march only as far as the supplies allowed. The Germans learned to exploit this to their advantage. In December 1944, the 22nd ID launched a diversionary attack towards the 2nd Assault Corps' main supply base at Berane with the purpose of drawing the enemy reserves away from the real objective, the Tara Valley (the radio surveillance soon confirmed that the Partisans had taken the bait).

No one on the NOVJ side was prepared for things like the trench warfare in Syrmia: not even the old fighters had ever faced such elaborate minefields or experienced shelling on this scale, let alone the conscripted youths with no experience of war whatsoever. Partisan troop officers, used to handling relatively small units, now found themselves in charge of thousands of soldiers. The shortage of heavy weapons and ammunition needed in order to achieve a breakthrough through fortified enemy defenses has already been mentioned; the same was true for simple but critically important items such as shovels and helmets. Moreover, the chaotic internal conditions meant that the country could barely support the army of this size, even with the Soviet aid pouring in. For example, the 22nd Serbian Division undertook an unauthorized withdrawal from its positions along the main German withdrawal route in Sandžak in December 1944 in order to find food and shelter for its starving and frost-bitten men. Even when the supplies were available, the problem of getting them to the front remained. Horses and oxen were hard to come by this late in the war, and motor transport was so rare that it acquired an almost mythical status. On 15 February 1945, Dapčević's entire army had only 289 trucks and 8,920 horses; for comparison: on 1 March, the "Prinz Eugen" alone had 317 and 3,937, respectively.[67]

In addition to these very real objective circumstances, the NOVJ's combat efficiency was further reduced by what may be termed subjective reasons. The Partisans' desire to complete the transformation into a regular army soon began to manifest itself in a dogmatic struggle against the *partizanština*. As stated in one of the earlier chapters, this hard-to-translate term originally referred to all the negative earmarks traditionally associated with the guerrilla army, such as familiarity, lax discipline, sloppy paperwork, and so on. The notion that the officer's first duty was to lead his men pistol in hand was considered one of the main symptoms of the *partizanština*. The efforts to eradicate this unfortunate leftover from the old days, which led to disproportionate losses among the leadership cadres, gave rise to the second adverse phenomenon called the *uštabljivanje*. Even more difficult to translate than the *partizanština*, the word referred to the propensity to conduct operations without leaving the headquarters (*štab*) at all. Reminder: the Slovene branch of the NOVJ was first to experience such behavior on the part of some of its commanders already in 1942 in the guise of the *vojvodstvo*. There were other old habits that proved difficult to root out. Heavy weaponry, an item that could, until recently, be obtained only through capture from the enemy, was jealously guarded and kept back even when

67 Jelenković, *Saobraćaj*, p. 233; NARA/T78/530/77, 7th SS MTD, Status report (1.3.1945).

its presence was critical for the success of an attack. The Partisans also persisted in refusing to acknowledge the importance of digging-in despite seeing the Soviets do it as a matter-of-course. It took a lot of time, effort, and unnecessary losses to convince them otherwise: by April 1945, Dapčević's men had dug some 600 km of trenches in Syrmia.[68]

The real trouble began when the sound and time-tested irregular tactics also came to be regarded as the *partizanština*. This view came into vogue at the time when the Axis were just beginning to perfect their "free hunt" approach and rely on constant small-unit activity in order to keep the burgeoning NOVJ danger in check. In an ironic twist, the Partisans became outmatched in their own original game and were compelled to re-learn its basics. The Slovenes, already deeply embroiled in positional warfare, were the first to act by forming "Storm" (*jurišne*) companies and battalions in mid-November 1944. Comprised of 40-60 hand-picked fighters, every third of whom was armed with an automatic weapon, these units were conceived as a direct response to the prowling Home Guard Assault Battalions. In late March 1945, the 3rd Assault Division formed an ad-hoc group of two battalions whose task was to operate in guerrilla fashion behind enemy lines south of Sarajevo; the units were to leave their heavy weapons behind, attack at night and rest during the day. At about the same time, the 3rd Corps refrained from creating large brigades as per the new regulations, feeling that the smaller and more nimble units of the original pattern (ca. 1,000 men each) would be much easier to handle and supply.[69]

Based on everything written above, the reader might get an impression that the Partisans had become a bunch of bungling amateurs. While undoubtedly true for some outfits, there were also those which earned praise for their battlefield performance. The course and outcome of the Battle of Knin made some Germans believe the rumors that the Yugoslavs were actually led by British officers; in any case, the offensive capabilities of the 8th Corps were described as "astonishing". Friebe noted that the foe he faced in the Drina Valley was "unanimously described as being well-equipped, well-trained, and well-led". The oldest and most venerable brigade of the Yugoslav Army, the 1st Proletarian, retained the reputation of being "a particularly problematic" adversary. In his after-action report for Operation "Lawine", General Hartwig von Ludwiger of the 104th JD wrote that, in terms of leadership and combat capabilities, the 5th Corps and 4th Krajina Division equaled "regular Russian troops".[70]

At the operational level, the Yugoslavs largely retained the mindset of guerrilla fighters despite all the efforts to act and think like regular soldiers. The war was viewed as a drawn-out struggle in which the foe is not brought to his knees in a few devastating battles but dies the proverbial death of a thousand cuts. On paper, plans almost invariably involved a clause about the destruction of enemy forces, but the Partisans would usually content themselves with the capture of a physical objective. Once a designated city or area were captured, they would, just like in the old days, make a lengthy pause in order to collect booty, organize rallies and parades, and round up hostile elements. Pursuit was either half-hearted or did not take place at all. "This is our weakest spot", wrote the HQ of the 6th Corps in October 1944, adding that it

68 *Zbornik*/IV/31/642, 38th NOVJD, Circular (29.12.1944); *Zbornik*/V/37/621, 51st NOVJD to 12th NOVJC (31.1.1945).

69 *Zbornik*/VI/17/392-95 (4th OZ to Kokrški Det., 15.11.1944), 586-87 (MHQ Slovenia to SHQ, 27.11.1944); *Zbornik*/IV/34/431-32, 3rd NOVJD, Circular (29.3.1945).

70 22nd ID, Report Drina (28.2.1945), printed in: Hnilicka, *Balkan*, p. 329; von Metzsch, *Geschichte*, p. 86; *Zbornik*/XII/4/816-17, 104th JD, Report "Lawine" (26.1.1945).

ordered thousands of copies of an "excellent" manual on this topic written by a former Austro-Hungarian/Yugoslav/NDH officer. With the partial exception of Knin, however, little was done in this respect: the battles of Belgrade, Mostar, and Sarajevo could have ended a good deal worse for the Axis had they been followed by an energetic pursuit.[71]

The NOVJ's rapid growth in late 1944 and early 1945 brought huge disciplinary problems with it. The vast majority of new recruits came either from the former occupied territories or from enemy formations, most notably the *Domobranstvo* and JVuO. Thanks to their training, members of units such as the "Handschar" or "Devil's Division" proved to be a valuable asset if they chose to stay. Unused to the rigors of the Partisan life, especially in wintertime, and indifferent to the NOP ideals, the majority of the newcomers could not be expected to perform as well as the "original" Partisans. To make matters worse, the political workers, whose job was to keep everyone in line, were overwhelmed by the human deluge that swamped their units: if a brigade commissar had once been responsible for 700-1,200 fighters, the number now rose to 2-3,000. The combination of all these factors produced a palpable loss of morale, spike in desertion rates, and even outright mutinies. Spurred by nationalism, some Macedonian Partisans refused to go to Syrmia in late 1944, demanding they be allowed to march on Thessaloniki instead. In Syrmia itself, the widespread looting and abuse of civilians led one high-ranking commissar to observe with indignation that the NOVJ had become "a professional [i.e. mercenary] army". In the old days, getting killed was often considered preferable to being wounded; now, it was the other way around. The rising number of cases of self-inflicted wounds led Tito to intervene personally into the matter in late December, ordering "harsh punishment" for all those found guilty of this crime. Despite punitive measures, incessant propaganda, and the fact that victory was now in sight, the soldiers kept deserting in droves until the very end of the war. "Save your head" was the motto even some veterans chose to live by: in April 1945, there was a group of deserters around Kutina led by a fighter who had taken up arms in the very first days of the uprising. In January 1945, the 4th Corps had 1,246 AWOL cases out of the total strength of 22,700. The 6th and 10th Corps also suffered heavily in this respect during and after the battles on the Virovitica Bridgehead, Slavonian Mountains, and Moslavina in late winter and early spring.[72]

Finally, a few words on the command-and-control arrangements in the final stages of the war. The military "brain" of the NOP reassembled in Belgrade in the weeks following the city's liberation. In March 1945, the SHQ was subordinated to the newly-established Ministry of Defense. By this time, it had operational, intelligence, organizational, training, cipher, historical, testing, and foreign liaison departments. In his capacity as Defense Commissioner of the NKOJ/Minister of Defense, Tito still firmly held all rains in his hand, issuing a steady stream of orders, regulations, and instructions on almost every aspect of the war effort. The level of Belgrade's involvement in the day-to-day operations of individual field commands depended on the perceived importance of a given operation. For example, Tito took an almost unhealthy interest in the Drina campaign of February 1945. He attempted to micromanage the battle by

71 *Zbornik*/V/34/257, 6ht NOVJC, Monthly report (September 1944).

72 *Zbornik*/II/14/442, SHQ, Circular (25.12.1944); *Zbornik*/IX/7/525-30, CK KPH, Circular (10.10.1944); *Zbornik*/IX/8/230, 14th Herzegovina Bde/Pol. to CK KPJ (16.1.1945); *Zbornik*/IX/9/49 (33rd NOVJD/Pol. to CK KPH, 2.3.1945), 69-70 (40th NOVJD/Pol. to CK KPH, 3.3.1945), 198 (12th NOVJD/Pol. to CK KPH, 8.3.1945); *Zbornik*/V/39/539, 10th NOVJC/Rear., Monthly report (April 1945).

wireless, no doubt an old habit from the days when he commanded a small group of guerrilla brigades. This brought about yet another of those periodic clashes with the headstrong Popović, who had enough troubles steering the battle as it was.

For the sake of truth, it must be said that the SHQ continued to give subordinated commands a fair share of latitude in planning and execution of operations. In early March, Belgrade allowed the 2nd Yugoslav Army to go ahead with the attack towards Gradačac but cautioned against advancing too far into the Bosna-Sava triangle. The advice was not heeded, which, in turn, led to the rout of the 25th Serbian Division in the opening days of Operation "Nordwind". Tito missed the start of the Yugoslav grand attack in Syrmia, being on a visit to the USSR (5-20 April), but came back just in time to coordinate the final phase of the offensive in the littoral. Owing to the sensitive nature of the entire enterprise, the most important directives could not be conveyed by wireless. Instead, the marshal dispatched the army's chief-of-staff as his personal delegate to the scene. Frustrated by the slow progress of the attack against Rijeka and acerbic as always, Jovanović accused the 26th Dalmatian Division of cowardice. The division's commander, who also happened to be a Montenegrin, regarded it as a personal insult, and the two nearly came to blows with potentially tragic consequences. The incident indicates that, despite the uniforms, medals, and all the other paraphernalia of a regular army, many Yugoslav officers were still living in the heroic past of their warrior-forefathers, or, perhaps, re-living their own early, idealistic days of the insurgency.[73]

7.10 Fighting Until End: Axis Forces in Final Months of War

In spite of all the heavy blows they received in late 1944, and in spite of the clearly hopeless situation of the Third Reich, the German armies in the Balkans were far from being a spent force.[74] First of all, they were numerous: on 1 November, the supply strength of the OBSO was about 660,000 men (and 80,000 horses). During the following six months, there were several major changes in the OOB, including the PzAOK 2's departure for Hungary following the Battle of Batina and the subordination of the LXXXXVII AC, as well as other military and police forces in Slovenia, in the closing weeks of the war. On 1 December, there were 448,595 persons who "ate from the German pot", as the popular phrase went; by 26 April 1945, this number had dropped to 396,000. A sturdy logistical system made sure that the pot was never empty. It is fair to say that an average German soldier was better clad and fed than his Yugoslav counterpart at all times. The HGE was entirely self-sufficient during its retreat from Greece and remained reasonably well-supplied until the end of the war: for example, in mid-April, Löhr still had 52 days' reserve of vegetables, 25 of preserved meat, 20 of fat, 15 of bread, and 17 of fodder. The situation with ammunition, especially for the rifle and MG, was not as favorable, but the Germans somehow managed to get by, as they always did. The HGE was also heavily armed: according to the incomplete returns from the same month, there were 164 serviceable AT platforms (tanks, self-propelled or towed guns of caliber 75mm or higher) and 307 tubes of field artillery (plus another 78 with the LXXXXVII AC). The number of AA guns amounted

73 Anić, Joksimović, Gutić, *Narodnooslobodilačka*, p. 530; *SD*/XXIII/8, SHQ to MHQ Serbia (1.9.1944); *SD*/XXVII/11, Tito to 2nd YA (6.3.1945); see also ibid., p. VIII.

74 This sub-chapter is based on the following articles by Trifković: "Anabasis", pp. 625-28, "Trieste", pp. 24-25, and "Victories", pp. 121-24. Additional sources will be cited seprately.

to 941 20mm (much feared among the Partisans, especially its quadruple-barreled version), 139 37mm, and 181 88mm.[75]

The *Luftwaffe* rendered a valuable service during the evacuation of Greece and eastern parts of Yugoslavia by flying out thousands of wounded (3,223 from Kraljevo alone) and flying in 31,690 servicemen (including the 22nd ID and Assault Regiment "Rhodos") from the Aegean islands to the mainland. Most of its combat effectives were eventually diverted to the Eastern Front: in late October 1944, only two squadrons remained available for operations in the NDH. After making its last significant appearance in November 1944 over Batina, German fighters and bombers almost vanished from the skies. By the end of the year, the HGE decided to utilize the presence of the air force soldiers arriving from Greece by forming Security Battalions, three each in Sarajevo and Slavonski Brod. Finally, in the closing weeks of the war, the *Luftwaffe* high command released thousands of members of the now-defunct units and rear-area personnel for service at the front.[76]

By the close of summer 1944, the *Kriegsmarine*'s permanent contingent in the Balkans had more than 55,000 men, three-fifths of whom were deployed in the far south. They took part on ground fighting during the great withdrawal, usually serving in separate battalions attached to various *Heer* formations: in early January 1945, there were still 13 such units, scattered from Prijepolje to the Drava. Although one often gets the impression that the sailors were more of a burden than a blessing owing to their inadequate training, there can be no doubt that the HGE was far better-off with than without them. Compared with the bulk of the Yugoslavs they were facing, all of them had, at the very least, completed the boot camp. Moreover, many had served on small combat vessels and now had the chance to prove their weapons expertise, as had happened during the siege of Bijeljina. Notwithstanding the fact that most of these men were eventually evacuated from Yugoslavia, some were "stuck" with ground units until the end of the war. By early 1945, the naval component, now operating exclusively from the bases in Istria and Croatian Littoral, had ca. 80 combat and 60 transport vessels; the ground component consisted merely of coastal batteries and some engineer units. The fact that the enemy now controlled a well-defined territory with accompanying infrastructure led the navy to launch its own "guerrilla" actions using saboteurs and fast attack boats. These included the raids on the Veliki Rat lighthouse and Split harbor in mid-February, and an attack against the Soviet and Yugoslav shipping on the Danube at Ilok and Novi Sad in late March 1945.[77]

75 NARA/T311/190/232, OBSO/QM, Report (15.11.1944); NARA/T77/1423/292, OKW, Supply strengths (1.12.1944); TsAMO/500/12450/183/60-62, OKW, Armor situation Southeast (1.4.1945); TsAMO/500/12450/226/34, OKW, Supply strengths (May 1945); TNA/DEFE3/567/KO662, OBSO, Artillery report (11.4.1945); TNA/DEFE3/568/KO840 (LXXXVII AC/QM, Report, 10.4.1945), KO841 (OBSO/QM, Report, 15.4.1945); Canadian Department of National Defence/ Directorate of History and Heritage, Roll T-2422, frame 339, LW/Chief of Staff, Flak ammo return (24.4.1945).

76 NARA/T311/186, HGE, [Island evacuation until 7.10.1944]; TNA/DEFE3/242/HP4321, LW North Balkans, Cable (21.10.1944); see the cables from LW Greece in TNA/DEFE3/319/HP9860 and TNA/DEFE3/316/HP9119 (9 and 10.12.1944, resepctively); TNA/DEFE3/565/WA587, LW/ Chief of Staff, Order (2.4.1945); TNA/DEFE3/567/WA835, LW Croatia, Report (9.4.1945); TNA/ DEFE3/569/KO1124, HGE, Report (16.4.1945).

77 Schmidt-Richberg, *Endkampf*, p. 24; NARA/T1022/3957, KM Admiral Adriatic, Strength return (1.9.1944); NARA/T1022/2585, KM Southern Command, Activity report (August 1944-January 1945); BA-MA/N756/182b/Estate Vopersal, Actions KG "Skanderbeg", pp. 4-5; Vladimir Isaić,

One of the greatest advantages the Germans held over the Partisans lay in the quality of the officer corps. By late 1944, the level of officers' proficiency had reached an all-time high. On the one hand, most of them had served in the Balkans long enough to learn the traditional ways of their adversary; at the same time, they were infinitely better prepared for the classic, frontal warfare that was just beginning to come to the fore. Von Weichs was still standing at the top, although he was described as "a tired old gentleman", and his staff (the HGF) was becoming increasingly redundant. Nevertheless, Hitler would keep the awkward arrangement of having two army groups deployed side by side in a such a small area until late March 1945. On the 25th, all German forces in the NDH were subordinated to the HGE, which had, in fact, been the main operational formation at least since December. Like Albert Kesselring, Löhr proved to be a capable and dynamic leader of ground troops despite the fact that he originally came from the air corps. He and his senior commanders believed in leading from the front: during the rush for Kosovo in mid-October, Löhr flew to Kosovska Mitrovica, which was at that time practically no-man's land. General Müller could literally see the front line from his command post at Kraljevo; for comparison, his Soviet and NOVJ counterparts attempted to steer the operations from the far-off Kragujevac. That the 104th JD retained high combat value even after the repulse suffered at the Drava bridgeheads was directly attributed to the popularity of its long-time commander. Despite the horrendous casualty rates, the war was producing so many veterans that some of them ultimately filtered down even to the lowliest units: the 1025th Security Battalion was largely led by old hands who saw action in France and the USSR. Naturally, the officer corps deployed to the southeastern theater could not have boasted of representing the flower of the Wehrmacht; the best candidates were, as always, reserved for the main fronts. Even so, thanks to the unified training, shared traditions, and singleness of purpose, they usually proved tactically superior to all their opponents, with the partial exception of the Soviets. In a telling anecdote, the exasperated Dapčević said that "one German mortar is more effective than two of my batteries" after he had lost a significant part of his artillery in the January 1945 battles in Syrmia (when Đilas asked Popović if the same thing could happen to him, the latter responded "Oh no! I'm keeping mine on the right bank of the Drina."). Professional pride, however, could sometimes turn into downright arrogance, with grave consequences. The decisions to hold the Knin bulge or the entire lower stretch of the Drina with an equivalent of only reinforced one division reveal that the German generals were having a hard time acknowledging the fact that the enemy they were now facing were not the poorly armed irregulars from the years 1941-42.[78]

Remarking on the spirit of self-sacrifice displayed by the Partisans during the Battle of Sutjeska, the veteran Communist Moše Pijade observed that any other army would have given up under such circumstances. Dapčević's brother Vlado (who would go on to become the most famous Stalinist dissident after the war) replied to the effect that many, if not most,

"Dejstva njemačkih pomorskih snaga na Jadranu protiv mornarice NOVJ", in *Za pobjedu i slobodu. Jugoslovenska mornarica u završnim operacijama za oslobođenje Jugoslavije. Učesnici govore* (Belgrade: VINC, 1986), p. 280; Nikola Anić, "Neka operativno-strategijska razmatranja njemačke odbrane na jadranskom vojištu 1944/45. godine", in ibid., pp. 293-97. For more on the KM small-unit actions see the following: TNA/DEFE3/683/ZTPGM100792, KM Spec. Ops. Unit 71, Report Operation "I" (15.2.1945); *Zbornik*/VIII/3/504, NOVJ Navy HQ, Monthly report (February 1945); NARA/T78/476/6459126, OBSO, Daily report (27.3.1945).

78 VAB/GC/71/1/43/3, Statement Heinz Meinicke-Kleint/LXXXXI AC (13.7.1947); TsAMO/500/12483/158/23, 1025th Sec. Btl., Status report (14.8.1944); Djilas, *Wartime*, p. 442.

of them fought until the last breath simply because they knew that captivity meant certain death. In late 1944, the same was true for the German soldiers on the Yugoslav soil. The fear of capture was all-pervasive: it was shared almost in equal measure by die-hard Nazis, forcibly conscripted Poles and Czechs, and everyone else in between. The biggest surprise in terms of morale and combat performance were the penal infantry battalions, distinguished by the number "999" in their designation. Of altogether 29 such units created by the Wehrmacht, 17 were subordinated to the HGE. Roughly 60-70% of their members were "criminals", the remainder political prisoners, mostly unrepentant leftists. By the time the occupation of Greece was coming to its end, there was a notable increase of common disciplinary infractions and at least one uncovered communist plot. As soon as the fighting in Macedonia had begun in earnest, however, the cohesion and will to fight were restored. These disgraced soldiers became practically indistinguishable from the "normal" units: "They fight like dogs", one Partisan report read, "[and] hold their positions almost until the last man." Unlike them, the Croat (see below) and non-Cossack "eastern" legionnaires had no desire of ending up on the wrong side and were becoming increasingly unreliable. An entire battalion composed of former Soviet citizens belonging to the 181st ID had to be disarmed after one of its companies had defected to the Partisans in late November 1944. The Italians, who were still present in large numbers within the OBSO's area of responsibility, were a mixed lot. The majority of them served as unarmed auxiliaries or in railway repair crews and surrendered gladly when given the opportunity; the remaining Blackshirts of the "San Marco" Legion, on the other hand, were still fighting in April 1945 and probably continued to do so until the end of the war.[79]

The HGE continued to receive a trickle of replacements from home depots well into April 1945, a remarkable fact considering the modest strategic importance of the Yugoslav theater of operations and chaotic internal conditions within Hitler's crumbling realm. For instance, a group of 15 officers reached the 369th ID on the outskirts of Sarajevo on the 5th after a two-week journey from Vienna. Some three weeks later, the XVIII Military District was ordered to send 2,000 men to the 104th JD, but how many actually arrived is not certain. As always with the Wehrmacht's Balkan contingent, self-help was the order of the day. In late January 1945, a separate combat outfit (the KG "Engelbrecht", later renamed to Assault Brigade "Southeast") was formed around the nucleus of former German instructors attached to NDH field units. Roughly a month later, the OBSO ordered a 10 percent reduction in the size of rear-area services in favor of the front. The best way to replenish combat divisions was by "cannibalizing" smaller units. This was done on a massive scale for the first time in the course of the December 1944-reorganization of the HGE, which had by then become a conglomerate of highly heterogeneous ad-hoc battle groups. Line formations could sometimes be subjected to this measure (e.g. the best part of the 264th ID's surviving regiment was incorporated into the 11th LWFD), but they mostly applied to the *Landeschützen*, security, and fortress infantry battalions. It was a sound solution, albeit one born out of necessity. These units, with their specific type of personnel (the average age of soldiers in the above-mentioned 1025th Security Battalion was 41, and 30 percent of them were invalids), could be reasonably used only for guard

79 VAB/GC/71/1/21/10–11, Hans Höffer–Karl Novotny/Fortress Battalions 999 (11.10.1948); NARA/T78/412/6380739-40, OKH, [OOB Italian forces] (February 1945); Danilo Komnenović, "U napadu za oslobođenje Sarajeva", in *Za pobjedu i slobodu. Sarajevska operacija: učesnici govore* (Belgrade: VINC, 1986), p. 221.

duties in the rear. However, when combined with younger, more active cadre, even these men could help raise the overall fighting potential of the outfit they were attached to.[80]

We will now examine individual German combat formations at the closing phase of the conflict. At the top of the list stood the 7th SS MTD, 22nd ID, and 104th JD by virtue of both their numerical strength (each had ca. 10-13,000) and fighting qualities. The former was probably the single best outfit at OBSO's disposal, equally apt at the "free hunt" offensive and regular defensive tactics. The normally critical staff officer Meinicke-Kleint wrote that the division's morale was "good" even in early May 1945. This probably had to do with the fact that the Ethnic Germans from Yugoslavia, Hungary, and Romania, who still constituted the absolute majority of the personnel, had by now lost their homeland and effectively become desperadoes. The 22nd ID counted among the most venerable units of the Wehrmacht, having fought in every major campaign from 1939 to 1942 including the siege of Sevastopol. The division had ample time and opportunity to hone its skills through extensive training during the subsequent two years of garrison duty on Crete. During the evacuation to the mainland, the 22nd had to leave all of its state-of-the-art heavy equipment behind. Luckily, the shortages could be temporarily bridged by utilizing the captured Bulgarian stocks. Speaking of "island" reinforcements, Assault Regiment "Rhodos" was also an elite outfit and would have been a welcome addition had it been transferred to the mainland in a more coherent fashion. In reality, groups of several hundred men would be flown each night to the airfields around Belgrade and immediately sent to the front, where they would be absorbed for good by various other units. The 104th JD had been deployed to the Balkans since its creation in May 1941 and had again shown its worth in recent engagements against the NOVJ and Bulgarians. As we have seen, Yugoslavia was repeatedly drained of troops in favor of the front in Hungary. In this way, the OBSO lost many of its best units in late 1944, including the 1st MTD, 118th JD, the "Brandenburg" Division, and so on. However, the withdrawals that took place on the eve of the Yugoslav spring offensive 1945 were especially damaging. The presence of the 297th ID, whose every second soldier was a veteran of the Russian campaign, would have certainly had a huge impact on the operations had it stayed in the country after Operation, "Waldteufel". The same goes for the 104th JD's sister division, the 117th, whose ca. 9,000 men and 120 artillery pieces were taken out of the trenches in Syrmia in early April and replaced by a single brigade of fortress troops.[81]

The middle tier was occupied by those divisions that performed adequately under the circumstances and managed to retain cohesion until the end. The 41st ID was originally welded together from penal and fortress battalions in January 1945 and saw its first major action during Operation "Wintergewitter". The division spent the entire winter and early spring training and

80 NARA/T311/195/385-88, OBSO to OKW (26.12.1944); NARA/T78/529/240, OKH to OBSO (30.1.1945); OBSO to OKH (29.3.1945) [copy in the possession of the author]; TNA/DEFE3/601/WA717, HGE, Cable (25.2.1945); TNA/DEFE3/572/KO1917 (OBSO, Report, 26.4.1945), WA880 (OKW to OBSO, 28.4.1945); *Zbornik*/XII/4/819, 104th JD, Report "Lawine" (26.1.1945). Schraml, *Kriegsschauplatz*, p. 131.

81 VAB/GC/72/2/1/9, August Schmidhuber/7th SS MD (19.8.1945); BA-MA/RH10/211, Assault Division "Rhodos", Status report (1.9.1944); NARA/T311/194/446 [all OBSO] (Circular, 14.10.1944), 246, 319, 349 (Movement reports, 7, 9-10.10.1944); TNA/DEFE3/309/HP7353, OBSO to OKH (12.11.1944); NARA/T78/305/6256936, XXXIV AC, 117th JD Status report (4.4.1945); VAB/GC/71/1/43/5, Heinz Meinicke-Kleint/LXXXXI AC (13.7.1947). The latter document contains several more references to other units that will be mentioned in the subsequent paragraphs.

manning the lines in Syrmia. These three months of comparative peace would stand it in good stead in the upcoming operations, as we shall see shortly. The 188th RMTD and 237th ID are usually presented as being the typical third-class formations the German generals in the Balkans were supposed to work miracles with, but the truth was somewhat different. While it is true that they had no experience with bigger operations, they were well-armed and rested, knew the terrain well (they had been deployed in the same area–Istria and Primorska–since their arrival), and had the advantage of fighting from heavily fortified positions. None of these divisions had suffered a serious setback before, but this is only because they were comparative newcomers or because they never met serious opposition. The 11th LWFD had a chequered career. Inadequate training and lack of experienced leaders led to heavy losses in Macedonia, but the division redeemed itself on the Valpovo Bridgehead, where it first bested the numerically much stronger 12th NOVJ Corps and then carried out a textbook cross-river withdrawal. The spring battles would again put the 11th to the test, but it would nevertheless keep fighting until the last day of the war. Following the same criteria, the Cossack formations also belong in this group. By early 1945, they had been reorganized into the XV SS Cossack Cavalry Corps (CCC) with the 1st and 2nd CCDs and a separate rifle brigade. Despite their reputation as being little better than a band of drunken marauders, the Cossacks were actually quite successful in their anti-guerrilla role and also showed themselves capable of tackling the Soviet and Bulgarian regulars.[82]

Had it not been for their ultimate fate, the 264th and 392nd IDs would have also been included into this group. Both suffered unjustly at the hands of critics, the first one being derisively called "the clerks' division" (*Beamtendivision*), the other simply being lumped together with other legionnaire outfits. The loss of one company on Šolta in March 1944 was about the worst single defeat suffered by the 264th in the entire period leading up to the Battle of Šibenik. Given that the division was not facing a few scattered detachments, but mid-tier NOVJ formations (e.g. the 19th and 20th Dalmatian Divisions), this was a fine result indeed. Despite being the youngest of the three "Croat" divisions, the 392nd ID had probably the best combat record. Together with the Ustashe, the division held in check the 11th and parts of the 4th NOVJ Corps throughout 1944 and early 1945 through constant small-unit activity and liberal application of semi-guerrilla tactics. As far as it is possible to ascertain, the biggest single loss of life (30 men) occurred in late winter 1944 around Plaški. In the end, both the 264th and 392nd had the bad luck of running into what was the best-led, trained, and equipped Partisan field force, the 8th NOVJ Corps/4th Yugoslav Army.[83]

At the bottom of the list stood one all-German division, the 181st, and both remaining legionnaire formations, the 369th and 373rd. As we have seen, in late 1944, the 181st was soundly defeated at Ledenice and the Zeta Valley. In 1945, it would conduct itself well during the withdrawal from Eastern Bosnia but would again suffer heavily in the fighting around Sarajevo. The 373rd never gained the notoriety of its older sister, nor the battlefield proficiency of the younger. It was probably the least remarkable of the Croat-manned divisions, except for the fact that the only Knight's Cross ever awarded to the members of these formations went to a

82 TNA/DEFE3/326/BT1707, HGE, Cable (6.1.1945); VAB/GC/73/1/4/4-6, Werner Honeck/41st ID (12.7.1947); NARA/T175/141/2669015-17, SS-Führungshauptamt, Order (4.11.1944); von Kalben and Wagner, "Zur Geschichte", p. 107.

83 Schraml, *Kriegsschauplatz*, pp. 242, 250, 262.

colonel of the 373rd for his actions at Knin. Ultimately, the division turned out to be hopelessly inferior to the new, well-equipped units of the Yugoslav Army that began taking the field in the last months of the war. The 369th never got over the teething troubles (and bad luck) that had been plaguing it from the very first day of its existence. From altogether 877 replacements sent to the division in mid-November 1944, about 300 deserted along the way. There were even more serious troubles than desertion: during the fighting on the Pelješac a month earlier, an entire company mutinied, killed its German officers and NCOs, and defected to the Partisans. The Germans responded by disbanding the entire battalion, decimating the suspects and sentencing the remainder to forced labor in the Third Reich; they also used black propaganda, showing sham NOVJ leaflets threatening all defectors with death sentence. Fritz Neidholdt, the division's first commander and former advisor to Chiang Kai-shek's government, was replaced as well. After the defeats in Herzegovina, the division was reorganized with a strengthened German cadre. All these measures, however, could not compensate for the fact that the division stood alone on the southern flank of the HGE facing the numerically and technically superior Yugoslavs. The 369th survived the next series of enemy blows more by luck then by design, ultimately reaching the Austrian border as a mere shadow of its former self.[84]

In addition to divisions, more than a dozen independent regiment/brigade-sized Army (963rd, 964th, 966th–969th, and 1017th Fortress Brigades, the 606th and 639th Security, 81st *Landesschützen*, and 20th *Jäger* Regiments, Assault Brigade "Southeast") and two purely German police formations (the 5th and 18th SS PRs) stood at OBSO's disposal in the early spring of 1945. Their quality and fate varied greatly. The documentary evidence is lacking, but it can be assumed that most of the fortress brigades ended up being absorbed by the divisions (e.g. the 1017th), while some continued to operate until the very end (e.g. the 963rd). On the other hand, the already mentioned Engelbrecht's outfit, as well as the 20th *Jäger*, were excellent combat units. The 20th (also known as "Hammerschmidt's Regiment") was formed out of the veteran 1st JRR; although it now had 16 and 17 year-old badly-armed levies in its ranks, the regiment would live up to its reputation and play a prominent part in the upcoming campaign.[85]

To conclude, a few words about the NDH armed forces during the final period of existence. The apparently impending implosion of the *Domobranstvo* and the exposure of the so-called "Voković–Lorković Affair" (a pro-Allied plot supported by the HSS sympathizers in the officer corps) gave Pavelić the immediate excuse to carry out the "Ustashizing" of the army. The increased importance of the NDH after Bulgaria's and Romania's defection, and the fact that he was making similar efforts in his own Wehrmacht in the wake of the 20th July assassination attempt, made Hitler susceptible to the idea. During the fourth and last meeting with Pavelić in mid-September 1944, the Nazi overlord pledged his support for the reorganization: in the following two months alone, the NDH was allotted ten AT guns, 125 mortars, 500 MGs, and 10,500 carbines, all German-made. The process itself started in early December, when Pavelić

84 Ibid., pp. 110-12, 212; NARA/T311/184, 369th ID to V SS MTC (14.11.1944); TNA/DEFE3/234/HP2481, V SS MTC, Cables (21 and 24.10.1944); TNA/DEFE3/302/HP5668, V SS MTC (21.10.1944).

85 OKH, Situation maps east (26.2, 18.3, 18.4.1945) (copies in the possession of the author); VAB/GC/71/1/43/3-6, Hans Meinicke-Kleint/LXXXXI AC (13.7.1947); TsAMO/500/12450/226/74-75, OOB OBSO (6.5.1945); TNA/DEFE3/572/KO1917, HGE, Cable (26.4.1945); Tessin, *Verbände*, Vol. XIII, pp. 166-69, 223; Schmidt-Richberg, *Endkampf*, pp. 113-14.

proclaimed himself the commander-in-chief, but it would never be entirely completed. In theory, the HDB and UV were to be merged into the unified Croatian Armed Forces (*Hrvatske oružane snage*, HOS). In reality, the army and Ustasha formations were simply lumped together into Croatian Divisions (sing. *Hrvatska divizija,* HD), without losing their individuality. The latter were still enjoying preferential treatment, not only in terms of arms and supplies, but also of recruits. At about this time, the service in the UV ceased to be voluntary in nature, and the main recruitment office made sure Ustasha brigades–whose number now equaled that of the regular army–got replenished first. The mere presence of the party militiamen would hopefully induce the Home Guards to stand and fight; if not, more proactive measures would be taken. 1944 saw several high-profile trials of officers suspected of espionage. The Ustashe were not above settling their disputes with real or imagined enemies out of court. One of the army's premier tacticians and defender of Kupres, General Franjo Šimić, was assassinated in Mostar in early August of the same year by "unknown" culprits. In the field, the punishment was swift and merciless: after two HDB battalions had gone over to the enemy southeast of Bihać in September, 43 defectors caught in pursuit were executed on the spot. Such incidents were not typical solely of the ground forces: on 15 December, the tiny NDH navy (eight boats) was caught in the attempt to leave Rijeka and reach a NOVJ-held port. The already dire situation facing the *Zrakoplovstvo* (only a half of 180 planes available in mid-September were serviceable) was further compounded by defections of individual pilots and crews, which grew more frequent as the war drew to a close.[86]

HDB and UV strength at the end of 1944-early 1945 is usually put at 70,000 and 76,000, respectively; these figures most probably do not include the air force, navy, and the gendarmerie, which would probably add up to ca. 30,000 men to the total. Roughly 90,000 Home Guards and Ustashe served in 16 infantry divisions (two more would be added by the end of the war). The divisions were nominally subordinated to three, later four corps, but most of them were actually controlled by German field commands. Although they were relatively numerous, the combat potential of the NDH forces was still limited by the same old factors, most notably the perennial lack of ammunition. The Germans may have provided their auxiliaries with weapons, but were unable to supply all the needed bullets at the time when their own units were experiencing shortages. In any case, the vast majority of senior Wehrmacht and Waffen-SS officers probably considered the entire business a waste of time and resources. As far as they were concerned, Pavelić's army was and remained beyond salvation. Artur Phleps, the CO of the V SS MTC, wrote a scathing critique of the interior conditions in the NDH in July 1944. Despite still being of the opinion that the "Balkanite [*Balkanmensch*] [...] needs to feel the whip", he described with dread the latest round of bloody misdeeds committed by the 1st UAB in Eastern Bosnia, at the same time calling its battle performance "feeble"; the *Domobrani* were "an undisciplined horde [entirely] devoid of the will to fight". In an overview of NDH combat formations prepared by the PzAOK 2 four months later, only the PTD, one out of 26 brigades, and five out of 19 battalions received decidedly positive notes; 14 brigades and three battalions were considered mediocre or suitable only for defense; 10 brigades and seven battalions were deemed unreliable or unusable (no data for the remaining one brigade and four battalions). In a telling move, the

86 Tomasevich, *Occupation*, pp. 430-31, 437-39, 456-65; Obdhođaš et. al, *Vojnica*, Vol. II, pp. 138-43; *Tko je tko*, p. 381; NARA/T78/412/6380827, OKH, OOB NDH Armed forces (1.2.1945); NARA/T311/192/120, OBSO/QM, Weekly report (10-16.12.1944); NARA/T311/193/317, OBSO, Daily report (8.9.1944); NARA/T311/184, HGE, Circular (15.12.1944); Mikić, "Neprijateljeva", p. 97.

XV MTC ordered the remaining 1,500 or so Croatian auxiliaries out of Knin before the battle began, obviously considering them a burden rather than an asset. The creation of divisions changed little in this respect. Writing at the beginning of April 1945, the official diarist of the OKW noted that there were altogether 12 NDH divisions deployed at the front, all of them "of little combat value".[87]

Truth be told, German professionals were prone to measuring the performance of native formations against their own, high standards, and would often pin the blame for defeats squarely on their shoulders. One of the most blatant cases of this "Croat-bashing" happened during and after the Battle of Knin, whereby the alleged poor performance of the legionnaire regiments was named as the single most important cause of the debacle. The inability of the 100 percent-German 264th ID to hold its heavily fortified positions, or the failure of the XV MTC to provide sufficient ammunition, were passed over in silence. Naturally, there were exceptions: one high-ranking staff officer remarked that "the Croats have recovered remarkably quickly", thus allowing an orderly withdrawal into Lika. General Schmidt-Richberg, the chief of staff of the HGE, was probably closest to the truth when he wrote that NDH units "occasionally fought bravely and provided good support to the German troops on a local level". They continued to serve as a "cushion" that helped absorb the enemy's first blow and leave him disorganized, thereby giving the German command the time and opportunity to initialize countermeasures.

The Ustashe contribution in particular cannot be ignored, since they were condemned men whose fate was inextricably tied to that of their foreign patron. The increasingly unruly behavior and brazen attitude the Croatian fascists began to display in their relations with the Wehrmacht in the second half of 1944 had no seditious overtures, as widely suspected at the time. They were most likely the combination of other factors, including Hitler's unconditional backing of Pavelić and the frustration caused by the German army's high-handedness, as well as its continued involvement with the Chetniks and other Serbian nationalists. In any case, Ustasha-related incidents must have appeared quite serious to the contemporaries. On 7 December, 36 members of the SFK who had survived the battles in Serbia were dragged out of a train in Zagreb and shot. Three weeks later, guards from the notorious death camp at Jasenovac freed some sentenced legionnaires of the 373rd ID from a German POW train. This period saw at least three cases of entire UV units refusing to carry out orders, either from their own officers or German HQs: the attempted mutiny at Vaganac had to be put down with the force of arms at the price of 11 KIA and 35 WIA.[88]

87 *Zbornik*/V/35/535, (MHQ Croatia to SHQ, 9.12.1944), 756 (HDB I AC, Monthly report, December 1944); *Zbornik*/V/38/671, 685, 2nd and 4th HD [respectively], Monthly reports (February 1945); Schmidt-Richberg, *Endkampf*, p. 117; NARA/T175/20/2645833-51, Phleps to Himmler (10.7.1944); NARA/T311/196/389-91, PzAOK 2 to OBSO (7.11.1944); *KTB OKW*, Vol. IV/2, p. 1224 (5.4.1945).

88 Schmidt-Richberg, *Endkampf*, p. 82; NARA/T311/195/115, OBSO, Telephone conversations (8.12.1944); NARA/T311/184, [all HGE] Cable to OBSO (7.12.1944), Circular (12.12.1944); NARA/T311/185, [all HGE], Daily report (21.12.1944), Cable to OBSO (23.12.1944); TNA/DEFE3/330/BT2697, HGE to OBSO (4.1.1945); TNA/DEFE3/331/BT2817, HGE, Cable (30.12.1944); *Zbornik*/V/36/643 and 715, HDB GHQ, Daily reports (7 and 25.12.1944, respectively).

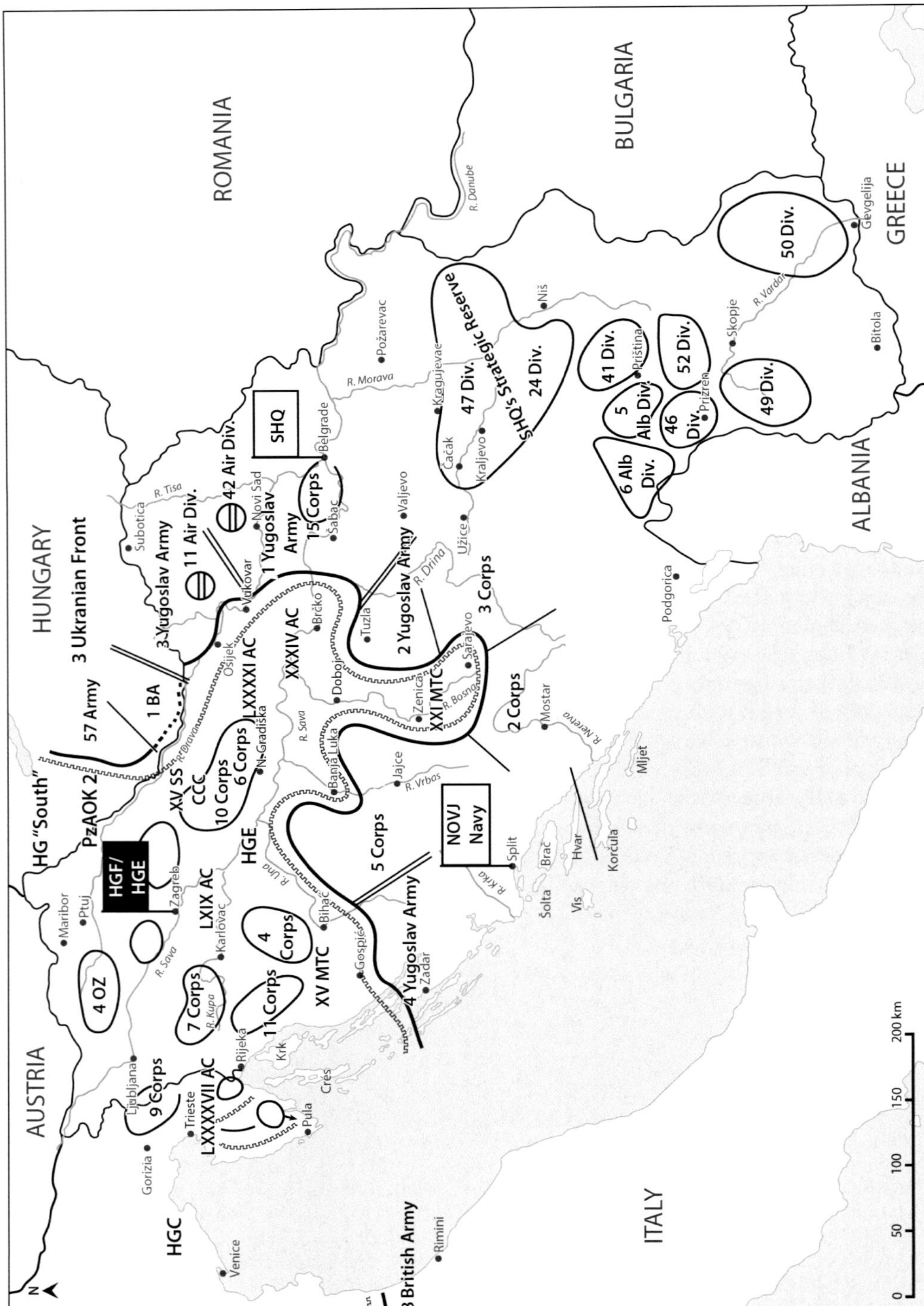

Map 13: Situation in Yugoslavia (March 1945).

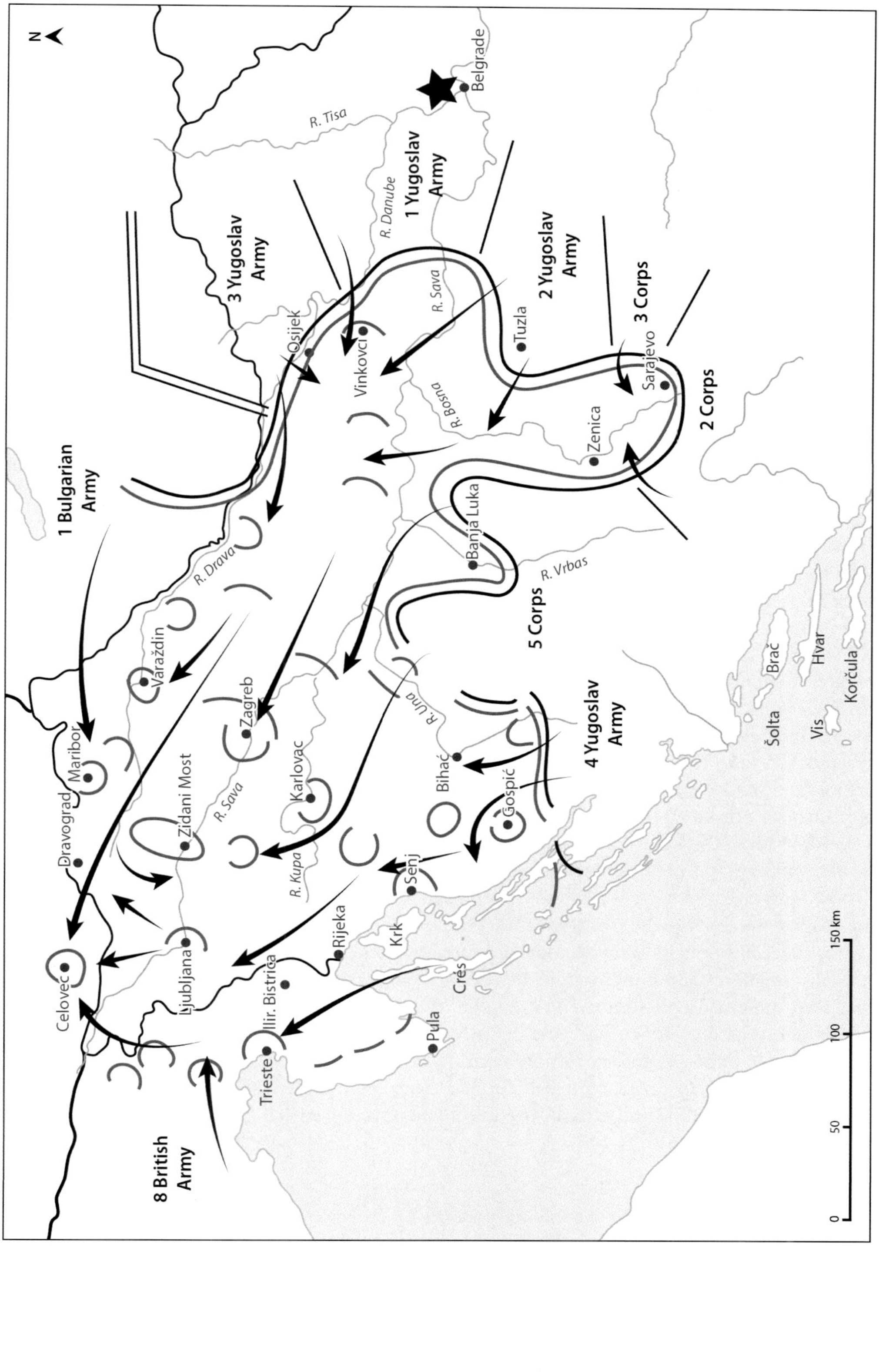

Map 14: Yugoslav Army final operations (March-May 1945).

7.11 Spring Offensive I: Plans and Dispositions

A general outline of the final Yugoslav offensive of the war was drawn on a series of meetings between Tito and his chief lieutenants in Belgrade in late February and early March 1945. The offensive had three main and complementary objectives: the liberation of the country, the expansion of its northwestern borders, and the destruction of all enemy forces. The first objective is self-explanatory, but the remaining two need some clarification. In the aftermath of the First World War, Italy and Austria were awarded several disputed regions inhabited by a large Slovene/Croat minority. In addition to Dalmatia, these included the southern part of Carinthia, and, most notably, the Julian March (Venezia Giulia/Julijska Krajina) with its four provinces, Istria, Rijeka, Trieste, and Gorizia. Kingdom of Serbs, Croats, and Slovenes fought for the possession of these lands both in the field and at the negotiating table and failed; it was now the Communists' turn and they were determined to succeed. The NOP owed much of its popularity in western parts of Yugoslavia to the promise that the "enslaved brethren" would soon return to the fold, together with their ancestral lands. The third objective was closely related to the issue of borders. The Germans could retreat only westward, i.e. towards the disputed areas. If they are not subdued quickly enough, they might still be in possession of a large chunk of the country when the war ends. In this case, all the collaborationist/anti-communist forces that depended on the Wehrmacht for their survival could seek the British and American protection and even present them with the ready-made bridgehead within Yugoslavia in case the latter decided to intervene militarily. Nipping this potential *Vendée* in the bud therefore represented a task of the highest order.[89]

Tito announced his views and intentions concerning the Julian March to the British already in October 1943, but with the Nazi menace still present, the issue was largely academic. One year later, with victory in sight, the question of post-war borders came to the fore and became an additional point of contention in the rapidly deteriorating inter-Allied relations. Little had been done on the merger of the royal government-in-exile and the NKOJ since the signing of the Vis Agreement in June 1944. Churchill was in haste to secure the place for Britain's proteges in the new political landscape before the arrival of the Soviets, and Tito procrastinated for the very same reason. Both knew that, with the Red Army in the country and supply lanes to the USSR open, the Whitehall's leverage on Yugoslav politics would be all but gone. By conditioning the flow of supplies on political concessions, and by withholding deliveries of heavier, more modern military hardware, the British cemented their reputation of being cynical imperialists who were quite willing to sabotage the struggle against the common enemy for their own narrow interests. In turn, the Communists were accused of lying about their real post-war agenda and of using the foreign-made supplies not to fight the Axis, but to further their political aims. The Western Allies were now becoming worried about the Yugoslav pretensions on parts of Italy (and, to lesser extent, Austria), which had been an ally since Armistice of Cassibile and already being considered as "a bulwark against communism" in this corner of Europe.

The Anglo-Partisan Cold War–which had been interrupted by the already mentioned "honeymoon" of late 1943 and early 1944–now flared up again with increased intensity. Members

89 This sub-chapter is based on the following articles by Trifković: "Trieste", pp. 28-34; "Carnage", pp. 53-55; "Victories", pp. 120-21. Additional sources will be cited separately.

of the Western Allied missions had always been closely observed: the OZNA in Slovenia, for instance, had a personal dossier on each one of them. Their already limited freedom of movement was further curtailed throughout the country in mid-September 1944, with the exception of Dalmatia (after all, the 8th NOVJ Corps was entirely dependent on foreign imports). It should be noted that the Partisans, who viewed themselves as the sole legitimate representatives of Yugoslavia, had always been very sensitive about the issue of sovereignty. A mixed Italian-British group that landed without the SHQ's authorization on the island of Lošinj in November 1943 was arrested and held under house arrest for weeks before the matter could be settled. The Partisans' mistrust of the British almost turned into paranoia after a series of incidents in late 1944 involving the accidental killing of the 8th Corps' commander Vlado Četković by the RAF, and the death of the CO of the MHQ Slovenia, Franc Rozman, who lost his life while testing a newly-delivered British-made mortar. The long arm of the dreaded *Intelidžens servis* (Intelligence Service) was detected even in far-away Slavonia, where the chief spy of the 6th Corps was assassinated by a bomb and 40 of its fighters poisoned by food (it was later established that the real culprits were, in fact, the Ustashe or German-trained saboteurs).[90]

In October 1944, Tito grudgingly approved of the landing of the so-called "Floydforce", originally composed of a regiment of Royal Artillery and a Royal Navy commando. From its base in Dubrovnik, Floydforce took part on operations in Montenegro, especially at Ledenice, Nikšić, and Podgorica. Despite providing valuable support and establishing good working relations with the local NOVJ commands, this battle group was never again allowed to take the field and was withdrawn in early 1945. The British insistence on deploying ground troops, ostensibly for protection of important harbors and airfields, was met with utmost apprehension: after all, what was the purpose of having a handful of battalions when the NOVJ already had tens of thousands of effectives deployed in the coastal area? It was widely suspected that these British "bridgeheads" were, in fact, established for no reason other than to serve as beacons for counter-revolutionary forces.

These fears were seemingly confirmed in early December 1944 with the British intervention in the Greek Civil War. Already during the controversial March Negotiations of 1943, the Partisan representatives stated to the Germans that they would oppose any unilateral Western Allied landing in the Adriatic with force of arms, if need be. This factor kept playing an important role in the NOVJ operational planning. In late October 1944, the 19th Dalmatian Division was ordered to destroy the British landing that was said to have taken place at Vodice (thankfully, the rumor soon turned out to be false). The decision to attack Knin, rather than make a wide flanking move towards Gračac as some proposed, was partly based on the need to interpose the 8th Corps between the German garrison and a suspicious group of British warships that had just spotted off the coast of Šibenik. Finally, the news from Greece were directly responsible for the fact that only the 20th Dalmatian Division continued the pursuit north after the fall of Knin; the bulk of the corps was ordered to take up defensive positions along the coast. As we have seen, the Axis front in Lika was very weak at the time and probably would not have withstood a major onslaught. Had this happened, the lines in the spring of 1945 would have been located far more to the northwest than they actually were. Similarly, the 2nd Assault Corps had to give up

90 *Zbornik*/IX/7/590; NARA/T313/196/7456955, MHQ Croatia to SHQ (7.11.1944); *Zbornik*/II/11/231, SHQ to MHQ Croatia (13.12.1943); *Zbornik*/II/14/354, SHQ to MHQ Slovenia (9.11.1944); *DCO*/XXI/22, Ranković to Ivan Krajačić (3.11.1944).

an equivalent of two brigades for securing Dubrovnik, Montenegrin coast, and the area around Podgorica, instead of sending them after the retreating XXI MTC.

That said, it is little wonder that the Yugoslavs kept the ultimate objective of their grand offensive a closely guarded secret. Outwardly, they pretended not to be overly concerned with a potential British landing in Istria or islands in Croatian Littoral that were discussed as a part of the "Ljubljana Gap" strategy so favored by Churchill. During a series of high-level bilateral meetings held in Belgrade in late February 1945, Tito promised to support the Western Allies' drive through northeastern Italy by launching an operation along the Eastern Adriatic coast, to be followed by a vaguely-defined "attack north of Bihać". The real target was the city of Trieste, but not even internal correspondence made any mention of it; all orders were transmitted verbally, usually through senior officers. Since the undertaking of this size would have been unthinkable without the foreign aid, Tito had again relaxed the relations with the British, even allowing them to station ca. 7,000 men in the area of Zadar.

The 4th Yugoslav Army, which was given the main role in the drive to Trieste, could not be reasonably expected to defeat the two German corps in its front, destroy collaborationist forces, and then secure the new border against a possible Western intervention. What the Yugoslavs had to do at all cost was to bring the remaining three armies to Slovenia as quickly as possible, and this meant piercing the Syrmian Front. Apart from opening the shortest and most favorable path to the west (good terrain, developed communications network), a victorious set-piece battle against their vaunted German foe would have a major physiological significance for the Partisans. It was considered a rite of passage for the army of the new Yugoslavia (the coalition government was finally formed on 7 March) and a fitting end to years of regularization efforts. Also, capturing an entire German army group would vastly improve the country's prestige and cement its status as the most important "junior" partner of the Big Three.

As already stated, one could often hear the argument in post-Socialist times that the bloodletting in Syrmia was in vain because the Germans were on their way out of the country anyhow. In fact, they had no intention of leaving practically until the last day of the war. According to the OKW directive from 10 February 1945, the OBSO was to halt at the line Senj–Bihać–Banja Luka–Doboj–Syrmian Front, and thus provide flank protection to the army groups in Italy and Hungary. Ever the politician, Hitler ordered the wider area of Sarajevo and the Bosna River Valley be held as long as possible out of consideration for Pavelić. The OBSO's argument that this task would be well-nigh impossible to fulfill without the divisions selected to stay in Hungary in the aftermath of the upcoming operations along the Drava, fell on deaf ears: Hitler's only concession was to leave the 7th SS MTD in Bosnia as a mobile reserve. In the closing days of March, the high command bowed to the inevitable and authorized the evacuation of the southern parts of the NDH and withdrawal of the main front from Syrmia to a line just east of Slavonski Brod and Donji Miholjac. Finally, in mid-April, Löhr was allowed to occupy the "Zvonimir Line", a defensive position running from the Drava to Sava east of Zagreb (although its construction had formally begun already in late 1944, it still existed largely on paper). No order calling for a general withdrawal towards Austria was issued while Hitler was alive. First decision in this direction came in the first days of May, when Löhr informed the new head of state, Grand Admiral Karl Dönitz, of his decision to prevent "the total bolshevization" of his old homeland with the help of his army group. He also expressed the hope that the

Western Allies would agree to use it as a kind of auxiliary police force, or, at the very least, accept its surrender.[91]

7.12 Spring Offensive II: From Gospić to Trieste

The first two months of 1945 in Lika and the adjoining areas passed in relative peace: apart from small-scale activity and a handful of fierce skirmishes (e.g. at Ribnik and Pag), there was little else to report. This was largely due to the unexpectedly harsh winter. On the night of 28-29 January, the 10th Dalmatian Brigade was caught in a terrible snowstorm while on march between Knin and Sinj: 46 of its fighters succumbed to cold, while some 200 others were frostbitten, making this perhaps the single biggest NOVJ loss of the war caused by non-violent means. The supply channel leading from Dalmatia to Lika that had been opened in the aftermath of the fall of Gračac, was closed by snow drifts. Each day, up to five battalions of the 35th Division armed with shovels would be sent out to clear the roads in an uphill struggle against the merciless bora. As a result, the 11th Corps was again where it used to be, barely able to provide its fighters with 1,000 calories a day. On the other side of the front, the XV MTC had recovered from the autumn battles by late February and was contemplating a major operation with the aim of capturing the Krbava Field and re-establishing the connection between the 392nd and 373rd IDs. The "Pelikan", as the undertaking came to be know, was the last of its kind and also among the most successful ones. The fighting commenced on 4 March when at least nine German and two NDH battalions (Yugoslav sources speak of seven and thirteen battalions, respectively) made a concentric attack from the east and west against the NOVJ forces in the area Udbina–Plitvice Lakes. The 13th Division got surrounded during the first days of offensive, but somehow managed to escape south, leaving a dozen brand-new cannon behind. Its sister formation, the 35th, also saw some heavy action, but ultimately retained a foothold north of Korenica. Well-satisfied with the results, the XV MTC concluded the offensive on the 17th; in addition to the rich booty obtained at a little cost to themselves, the Germans now occupied a much-straightened front running just south of the line Karlobag–Gospić–Udbina–Donji Lapac.[92]

The task of breaking through the new Axis front in Lika was entrusted to the youngest of the Yugoslav armies, the 4th. The army was formed on 2 March 1945 around the HQ and divisions of the now-defunct 8th Corps. Although not the biggest formation of its kind (67,000 together with the subordinated 4th and 11th Corps), it was probably the most experienced and best supplied one. At its head stood a duo of gifted soldiers. Its CO was the same Petar Drapšin who had been demoted for the "red terror" and subsequent loss of East Herzegovina in May-June 1942. In the intervening years, he redeemed himself by exemplary service in Slavonia (among else, he led the 12th Division, and the 6th Corps) before being given the Dalmatian command

91 NARA/T78/305/6255940 (OKH, Plan and forces for Operation "South", 28.1.1945), 6255883, 6255841-42, 6256074 (OKW to OBSO, 10.2, 23.2, and 29.3.1945, respectively), 6256070-71, (OBSO to OKW, 31.3.1945); TNA/DEFE3/509/BT5338, OBSO to OKW (17.2.1945); TsAMO/500/12450/246/43-48, OBSO to Dönitz (2 and 5.5.1945); Schmidt-Richberg, *Endkampf*, pp. 117–120, 149–151.

92 Anić, *Dvanaesta*, p. 156; Kleut, *Jedanaesti*, pp. 355-56, 364-89; Schraml, *Kriegsschauplatz*, pp. 213-15, 272-74; TNA/DEFE3/515/WA200, HGE, Cable (4.3.1945); NARA/T78/476/6458905, HGE/Intel., Evening report (13.3.1945).

in December 1944. His chief of staff was the prickly but brilliant physicist Pavle Jakšić, who went on to serve as the CO of the 11th Corps and MHQ Croatia's chief of staff after his return from the Sutjeska in the summer of 1943.

In its final form, the plan for the initial phase of the advance on Trieste (officially called Lika-Littoral Operation) was simple. The 4th Yugoslav Army would first use overwhelming force (the 19th, 20th, and 26th Dalmatian Divisions with one tank brigade and extra artillery in the south, 7th Banija and 8th Kordun in the north) to crush the left-wing group of the XV MTC (the 373rd ID and 10th HD) and take Bihać. After that, the main force would veer west, give the same treatment to the right-wing group (the 392nd ID and 11th HD), and advance as far as Rijeka. At the first glance, the plan (and its ultimate fruition) compares favorably to the bloody head-on clashes and bludgeon tactics employed on other sectors of the Yugoslav-German front. It must be born in mind, however, that the 4th Yugoslav Army operated in near-optimal conditions. Unlike in Syrmia or in Eastern Bosnia, there was plenty of space for maneuver and no major water obstacles; the enemy was weaker in almost every respect, be it combat effectiveness (only legionnaire and NDH outfits), numbers (the entire XV MTC had about 40,000 men), or hardware (the Axis had only a handful of armored vehicles).[93]

The great Yugoslav spring offensive began on 20 March 1945. The appearance of the 1st TB's "Stuarts" caused some panic among the legionnaires and contributed to the collapse of the 373rd ID's defenses after only two days of fighting. By the 25th, the Yugoslavs were already at the gates of Bihać, preparing to finish off the remnants of the XV MTC's eastern group. In the last moment, the 104th JD arrived from the Drava and broke through the encirclement ring, allowing the evacuation of ca. 1,100 wounded from the town. Retaining the control over it, however, was out of the question, and the Germans began pulling back in the direction of Karlovac on the 28th, closely followed by the units of the 4th Corps. The presence of von Ludwiger's division along the 4th Yugoslav Army's right flank caused concern in the SHQ: everyone probably remembered how a German veteran formation not unlike the 104th kept the entire 2nd Army occupied in the Drina Valley for weeks on end. Drapšin opposed the idea of halting the drive northwest until this potential threat could be dealt with; instead, he suggested bringing additional reinforcements from Bosnia, as well as leaving in place a strong reserve, all of which was ultimately approved by his superiors.

In the meantime, the bulk of the 4th Army had moved into jump-off positions for the second phase of the operation, which started on 4 April. It was every bit as devastating as the first: the entire Axis front from Karlobag in the south to Jezerane in the north simply ceased to exist within 48 hours. The Yugoslav units deployed in the enemy rear (most notably the 43rd Istrian Division) contributed significantly to this outcome by attacking supply lines. Gospić, which the Partisans had been besieging in vain for almost two years now, fell on the very first day of the offensive. The remnants of the 392nd ID and 11th HD were retreating pell-mell towards Senj; the town itself came under direct attack on 8 and 9 April. This was the last battle the youngest legionnaire formation fought as a cohesive unit; among thousands of casualties was also its much-beloved commander, whose body was taken out of harm's way strapped to a side of an armored car. Had the Yugoslavs properly sealed the northern approaches to the place, the entire

93 Most of the data on the 4th Yugoslav Army's spring offensive comes from Trifković, "Trieste", pp. 10-27. Additional sources will be cited separately, in this case *Zbornik*/XI/4/9, SHQ, Order (2.3.1945).

division would have perished then and there. Ultimately, however, an equivalent of a weak regiment escaped the cauldron and joined the defenders of Rijeka.[94]

The fighting now entered a much more difficult and good deal bloodier phase, known officially as Rijeka-Trst Operation. It took three Yugoslav divisions six days (16-22 April 1945) to pierce the outer defenses held by the all-German 237th ID and cover the last 25 km before Rijeka. The attempt to encircle the city from the north, however, was forestalled by the arrival of the 188th RMTD from Primorska. The division occupied the former border fortifications shielding the interior of the peninsula and the main supply road to Trieste from the east. Altogether, the LXXXXVII AC had about 30,000 effectives; its commander, the scar-faced, energetic General Ludwig Kübler, had only one task, to defend Rijeka "to the last man" (Hitler). The HQ of the 4th Yugoslav Army, eager to open the shortest route to its ultimate objective, decided to commit the bulk of its forces to a full frontal assault; only the 20th Dalmatian Division would be sent on a roundabout march through the mountains towards Trieste. Beginning on 24 April, the 26th Dalmatian Division pounded away against the portion of the enemy defenses located on the ridges outside Klana. By the end of the following week, the village would become known as Bloody Klana in reference to over 700 casualties suffered by the Yugoslavs to no effect; the situation was hardly any better in other sectors as well. In an attempt to break the deadlock, Drapšin decided to encircle the enemy. The Yugoslav Navy, which had taken part in the elimination of the German coastal defenses of the islands of Pag, Rab, Krk, Cres, and Lošinj in the preceding weeks, was now required to ferry the entire 9th Dalmatian Division to the southeastern coast of Istria. Despite immense technical difficulties–the British refused to lend additional shipping space and share the intelligence on German minefields (the latter problem was overcome by using captured charts)–the navy succeeded in bringing over 5,000 men across the Kvarner Gulf. The 9th then proceeded towards Rijeka and Trieste, isolating or destroying smaller enemy garrisons in its path.

Meanwhile, the 20th Dalmatian Division had completed its march, establishing contact with the 30th Division of the 9th Corps on the eastern outskirts of Trieste on 30 April 1945. Together with elements of the 9th and 43rd Divisions, they proceeded with the reduction of enemy strongpoints in the city. The Axis (a mix of Wehrmacht, SS, and Italian personnel) fought fiercely, hoping to surrender to the Western Allies who were known to be advancing rapidly from the west. By this time, the Anglo-Partisan relations had again hit rock-bottom. Churchill imposed an embargo on supplies for the 4th Army and had the Yugoslav squadrons of the BAF grounded. The number of friendly fire incidents had risen so much lately that Tito officially requested that all sorties over Yugoslav territory be canceled (6 May). The arrival of the 2nd New Zealand Division to Trieste on the 2nd was therefore received coldly by the Yugoslavs; the next few days saw several incidents involving the use of firearms and "hijacking" of prisoners. Nevertheless, the hopes for ending in Western Allied captivity would be fulfilled to only a part of the Trieste garrison. In some cases, the New Zealanders even aided the Yugoslavs in reducing the enemy bunkers and abandoned the ca. 3,000 defenders of the last German pocket at Opicina to their fate.

The seizure of the much-coveted main objective did not signal the end of the 4th Yugoslav Army's offensive. The last, dramatic act took place in the hilly border area between Istria and

94 NARA/T78/476/6459119, OBSO, Daily report (28.3.1945).

Primorska. With the enemy already in Trieste and Hitler dead, the holding of Rijeka lost all purpose; consequently, Löhr ordered Kübler to break out and take position on the right flank of the HGE in the area of Postojna. The 7th SS MTD was supposed to aid the maneuver by striking south from Ljubljana, but the division remained entangled in the Moslavina and Karlovac sectors and could not make it. The vanguard of the LXXXXVII AC's "wandering cauldron" surprised the elements of the 13th Primorsko-goranska and 26th Dalmatian Divisions at Ilirska Bistrica on 3 May. The appearance of the 188th RMTD this far north and the simultaneous abandonment of Rijeka had drawn the attention of the Yugoslav high command. In the following days, the encirclement ring would be reinforced by the 7th, 8th, and 43rd Divisions, as well as elements of the 29th Division and the 1st TB. These heavy reinforcements were sorely needed, for Kübler was throwing everything he had in a desperate attempt to save his corps. The fighting of utmost ferocity raged for three full days with heavy casualties on both sides, but lines remained largely in place. By this time, the LXXXXVII AC was at the end of its tethers: its densely packed columns presented a perfect target for Yugoslav artillery, and ammunition had all but run out. With no options left, the Germans did the unthinkable and asked for a truce. On 7 May 1945, some 16,000 soldiers laid down their arms and marched into captivity, a fitting end to the most successful Partisan operation of the war.[95]

7.13 Spring Offensive III: From Mostar to Karlovac

After the loss of the southern parts of Dalmatia and Herzegovina in the first half of October 1944, the Germans withdrew to the so-called "Mostar Position", which ran approximately from Široki Brijeg in the west to Nevesinje in the east. That the lines remained stable throughout the following two months was due to several factors, including the presence of the reinforced veteran 738th JR/118th JD, and the fact that the 29th Herzegovina Division was now stretched to the breaking point. In addition to manning this entire sector by itself, the division also had to devote a significant part of its effectives to combating the main Chetnik army that began arriving from Sandžak to the area of Kalinovik in the first week of December. The V SS MTC used the relative quiet to re-build the decimated 369th ID and make it capable of offensive actions. Starting in mid-November, the division took part in frequent regiment-sized forays into the Partisan-held territory (e.g. Operations "Scharnhorst", "Lützow", "York", "Heuschober") aimed at breaking potentially dangerous enemy concentrations and keeping him off-balance. Although fairly successful, these temporary jabs were not enough for the regime in Zagreb.

Western Herzegovina, which was now controlled by the NOVJ, was one of the few parts of the NDH where the Ustashe enjoyed genuine popular support. Keen to re-claim this region for good, Pavelić requested a green light for a bigger, joint operation already in December, but the HGE, faced with multiple crisis along its huge front, declined. It would not be before late January 1945 when Löhr acquiesced to support the planned NDH attack south of Mostar with one regiment of the 369th. Operation "Bora" lasted from 27 to 29 January; during this time, the 9th HD inflicted heavy losses on the 9th Dalmatian Divsion (which had in the meantime taken over the area west of the Neretva from the 29th) and pushed it to the line Ljubuški–Metković. A prompt counter-attack restored the situation, but the incident convinced the SHQ that its own

95 VAB/GC/71/2/3/2, Josef Kübler/LXXXXVII AC (4.11.1946).

upcoming offensive in this corner of the country would require more resources than previously thought.[96]

From the Yugoslav perspective, the liquidation of the last Axis bridgehead in Herzegovina would have two important results: it would open the southern "door" to Sarajevo and Bosna Valley, and remove a potential threat to the 4th Yugoslav Army's rear during its upcoming drive to Trieste. Earlier plans envisaged cutting the enemy's only retreat route along the Neretva with the 29th Herzegovina, or a direct attack on Mostar Position in cooperation with the 9th Dalmatian. As the result of the "Bora", however, Belgrade decided to commit the bulk of the hard-hitting 8th Corps, which had stood in reserve ever since the great victory at Knin. In a massive and well-prepared operation–which involved, among else, a blanket halt of all civilian traffic and requisitioning of vehicles–two whole divisions, as well as one tank and one artillery brigade, were moved from Northern and Central Dalmatia to Western Herzegovina in only four days. One glance at the map would reveal that, with the new correlation of forces, the Axis position had become a deathtrap. Both its heavily fortified anchors were hanging "in the air" and could be easily outflanked, and that is precisely what the Yugoslavs did. While brigades from three divisions were making diversionary attacks at the front, the reinforced 26th Dalmatian assaulted Široki Brijeg, taking it after two days of extraordinarily fierce fighting (6-8 February 1945). With the right wing disintegrating, the HQ of the XXI MTC ordered the abandonment of the entire Mostar Position.

This was precisely what the 29th Herzegovina was waiting for. As long as it was occupied in strength, Nevesinje was nearly impregnable; once the garrison was out in the open, it was a different matter. Remembering how they used to things in the old days, the Partisans decided to stage a massive ambush along the road leading to Mostar. On 14 February, the 369th GR walked straight in it and was practically annihilated: groups of survivors trod north along the same treacherous paths across the Prenj used by the NOVJ Central Hospital two years earlier during Operation "Weiss". The guerrilla heritage of their foe now played to the Germans' advantage: instead of mounting an immediate pursuit, the victors lingered in the newly-liberated Herzegovinian capital for days, staging parades and organizing rallies. This gave the decimated Axis forces (which lost anywhere between one-half and one-third of their strength, depending on the division) just enough time get out of the harm's way and restore a modicum of discipline and cohesion.

Whilst the units of the 8th Corps were departing for Lika in preparation for the spring offensive, the 29th started moving north through the Neretva Canyon. The going was slow due to the extensive demolitions conducted by enemy sappers. Finally, by the beginning of March 1945, the division stood before the Ivan, a mountain pass sometimes called "The Gates of Bosnia". Exploiting the still-present confusion in enemy ranks, one Partisan company actually managed to occupy this strategically important point but could not be reinforced in time and eventually had to retreat. The Germans made sure such error would not be repeated, as they worked feverishly to establish a deeply-echeloned defense on the peaks surrounding the pass. Having now over 13,000 men and a strong array of heavy weapons at its disposal, the HQ of the

96 This sub-chapter is largely based on Trifković, "Victories", pp. 105-24. As customary, the additional sources will be mentioned separately, in this case Komnenović and Kreso, *Dvadesetdeveta*, pp. 378-414; TsAMO/500/12483/83/265, 283, 291, 306, 320 and 335, 369th Signals Btl., Orders (1, 11, 17, 25.11, and 4 and 10.12.1944, respectively).

29th decided to try its hand in regular warfare. Throughout the month, the Yugoslavs launched repeated, frontal, uphill assaults, all of which were beaten back with heavy casualties (451 on 28 March alone). The inexperience and lack of knowledge did not lead only to human losses, but also to wastage of resources: having fired over 14,000 shells during the final four-day attack, the divisional artillery had practically disarmed itself on the eve of the great offensive against Sarajevo.[97]

The Bosnian capital was the next logical objective of the 2nd Assault Corps ever since it reached the Drina in mid-January 1945. Getting within the striking distance of it turned out to be a lengthy and costly process. Against all expectations, the 181st ID managed to hold onto its positions between Višegrad and Goražde against two NOVJ divisions (the 3rd Assault and 37th Sandžak) for almost seven weeks. In early March, the Germans finally began retreating slowly towards the city's outer defenses located on the western slopes of the Romanija. At this point, the things again went downhill for the XXI MTC and NDH forces under its control (the 8th, 9th, and 17th HDs). One regiment of the 181st was surrounded at Mokro by superior enemy forces, including the 27th and 38th Eastern Bosnian Divisions. The Partisans had also gotten unpleasantly close to the southern outskirts of Sarajevo. Luckily for the XXI MTC, the "Prinz Eugen" was again available after having restored the situation around Zenica. Skillfully utilizing interior lines and the "free hunt" tactics, the division proceeded to conduct perhaps the most successful campaign in its history. After making a brief stop at the heavily-contested Ivan Sedlo, the 13th SS MTR executed a night march across Mount Igman (which was not covered even by patrols) and hit the rear of the 3rd Assault Division around Trnovo on 17 March. The regiment stayed in the area for five days and then retreated just before its opponent could completely change his front and land a massive counterstroke. After Operation "Berggeist", as this small but effective raid was called, the regiment was shipped north, to the area of Vareš. As it turned out, it arrived just in time to engage the 4th and 10th Krajina Divisions, which had crossed the Bosna at Kakanj (where they decimated two LSBs) and were now making their way towards Sarajevo. In several days of seesaw fighting (1-3 April), during which both sides suffered palpable losses, the Germans effectively managed to neutralize this threat. In the meantime, the "Prinz Eugen's" other regiment, the 14th, was deployed around Olovo, from where it was supposed to strike northeast as a part of Operation "Rübezahl". Due to the rapidly worsening situation around the capital, however, the regiment was sent on a relief mission towards Mokro instead. Just as during the "Berggeist", the sudden appearance of the SS troopers in their rear caused the 27th and 38th Divisions to change their front, which, in turn, enabled the encircled regiment of the 181st ID to escape (2 April).[98]

The crossing of the Bosna and the attack on Mokro were, in fact, the opening moves of Sarajevo Operation (28 March-6 April 1945). This complex undertaking, which involved seven Yugoslav divisions with altogether ca. 60,000 fighters, was steered from a specially-created OHQ with General Radovan Vukanović at its helm. In broad strokes, the plan envisaged a concentric, simultaneous advance on the capital from the east and south (2nd Assault and 3rd Corps), as well as from the north (the 5th Corps), which would lead to its liberation and the

97 Komnenović and Kreso, *Dvadesetdeveta*, pp. 487-514; Schraml, *Kriegsschauplatz*, pp. 123-30.

98 Drago Karasijević, "Deseta krajiška divizija u operaciji za oslobođenje Sarajeva", in *Sarajevska*, pp. 459-61; VAB/GC/72/2/17/2, Hans Marth/13th SS MTR (12.7.1947); VAB/GC/72/2/18/2, Gerd Montag/13th SS MTR (15.7.1947).

destruction of the enemy garrison. Shortly before the battle, the local resistance managed to obtain a copy of the defense plan through their Home Guard contacts (interestingly, some "real" Germans were apparently involved as well). Hitler's decision of 31 March to abandon Bosnia, however, negated whatever impact this major intelligence coup might have had on the course of the campaign. In the following days, Axis units began vacating their defensive positions on Mounts Romanija, Ivan and Trebević, and moving through the city towards the northwestern exit from the Sarajevo Plain. Apart from several costly rearguard actions–including the one from 6-7 April during which the ill-fated 181st ID lost a substantial part of its artillery–the evacuation was remarkably successful. The Yugoslavs–again–appeared mesmerized by their primary objective, and once they had the city in their possession, they practically forgot about the retreating enemy. The two Krajina divisions were well poised to cut his main escape route, but due to the fact that they hailed from one of the oldest Partisan strongholds in the country, they were allowed to join the remainder of the army in victory celebrations instead.[99]

The XXI MTC may have avoided encirclement on this particular occasion, but the situation was far from rosy. For the second time in five months, its ca. 50,000 men found themselves virtually cut off from the remainder of their parent army group. The corps now had to cover over twice as many kilometers in order to reach relative safety (Slavonski Brod) than during the breakthrough through Montenegro. The enemy forces were also incomparably stronger and better equipped than before: in addition to Vukanović's OHQ, there were also 45,000 men of the 2nd Yugoslav Army operating from Tuzla. On the other hand, the Germans now controlled the entire length of the route (at least during daylight), and also had the still-functioning Bosna Valley railroad at their disposal. Despite worst fears, the march to Doboj (9-15 April) turned out to be largely uneventful aside from air raids, smaller ambushes, and sniping. The XXI MTC executed a textbook retrograde movement, erecting several temporary defensive lines along the way. Although the SHQ had ordered an "energetic pursuit" aimed at cutting off the enemy before he could reach the Sava, it was clearly not ready to commit any additional resources for this purpose. This is exemplified by the refusal of Popović's request for two more divisions, and in the canceling of ground-attack sorties in favor of the Syrmian Front. To make matters worse, Belgrade sanctioned the use of only two second-tier divisions (the 53rd Central Bosnian and 27th Eastern Bosnian) for the pursuit. These formations gave their best, temporarily cutting the main road at Zavidovići and Žepče, but had to retreat before energetic German intervention led, again, by the veterans of the 7th SS. The progress of the 2nd Yugoslav Army's attack was painfully slow. It took its three divisions two weeks (4-17 April) to subdue Doboj's forward defensive zone on the eastern bank of the Bosna. By this time, however, the bulk of Axis forces had already passed the town and was well on its way to Slavonia. As the Partisans had no troops between Derventa and Bosanski Brod, all they could do was to follow the enemy movements and pick off stragglers. The first part of the campaign ended on 20 April with the withdrawal of the last German rearguards across the Sava.

The XXI MTC's departure and the near-concurrent evacuation of the last remaining NDH outpost on the southern bank of the Sava (Banja Luka) opened the road west for the 2nd Yugoslav Army. Popović now had the task of advancing against Karlovac and Zagreb from the south. The Una sector was largely quiet after the fall of Bihać, thus giving the XV MTC the opportunity

99 Schraml, *Kriegsschauplatz*, p. 126.

to replenish the 373rd ID and strengthen the defenses held by its NDH divisions (at first only the 4th, later also the 6th). The Axis also maintained a lively small-unit activity, often aimed at enemy supply lanes. On 12 April 1945, a group of German sappers made their way into Bihać and blew the recently repaired bridge over the Una (some two weeks later, the 20th JR launched an equally successful raid against the bridge on the Kupa at Vinica). By the end of the month, the newly-created Una OG[100] consisting of the 23rd and 45th Serbian, 28th Slavonian, and 39th Krajina Divisions, began taking up attack positions around the Axis bridgeheads at Dubica, Kostajnica, Dobrljin, and Bosanski Novi. They needed almost an entire week (27 April-2 May) to reduce these fortified towns and gain a firm foothold on the opposite bank. Despite the maximal effort and considerable cost in blood, the Una OG failed to administer a deadly blow to the Axis, who managed to stage an orderly withdrawal to Velika Gorica, just south of Zagreb (2-7 May).[101]

The best opportunity for opening the road to Karlovac came in mid-April 1945, as the entire 4th Yugoslav Corps caught up with the 104th JD's "wandering cauldron" while it was passing through Slunj on its way from the Bihać area. The division, which had been engaged continuously since early March, was demoralized and would have probably been forced to capitulate had it not been for the intervention of Hammerschmidt's unit on 13 April. Although it took additional heavy losses (especially in equipment), the 104th would go on to serve as the mainstay of the LXXXXI AC, whose HQ had recently been made responsible for the defense of Karlovac. The corps also had at its disposal the 13th HD, two German-NDH police regiments, and a handful of support and security battalions. This motley collection of units succeeded in slowing down the 4th Corps' advance but could not stop it. By the end of April, the Yugoslavs were nearing the outskirts of the city from the southwest, south, and southeast. At this time, the 7th Banija and 8th Kordun Divisions were ordered to Istria, their place being taken by Vukanović's old 3rd, 4th, and 10th Divisions (the Karlovac OG), which had just arrived from Bosnia.

On the 30th, these forces, together with the 34th Division on the far right flank, launched a major attack all along the front. Infantry went forward under the cover of self-propelled artillery pieces, causing panic among those Germans who never encountered them before in the Balkans. Two days later, the situation had become so serious that the 13th SS MTR, which was on its way to Slovenia in order to aid Kübler's impending breakthrough from Rijeka, had to be re-routed here instead. The presence of Löhr's "fire brigade"–as well as a pair of well-armed Ustasha guards battalions from Zagreb–did not fail to produce results. By the 4th, the situation was stable enough to allow the unhindered evacuation of the city. Two days later, the LXXXXI AC embarked on a largely uneventful withdrawal towards the northeast, at the same time making sure that its new left wing (the units that formerly belonged to the XV MTC whose HQ had in the meantime been transferred to Ljubljana) kept the Croatian capital covered from the south.[102]

100 Not to be confused with the smaller tactical formation of the same name formed in 1943.

101 Dželebdžić, *Druga*, pp. 337-346, 353-357; Schmidt-Richberg, *Endkampf*, p. 127; VAB/GC/71/1/6/3-4, Hans Wagner/XV MTC (12.7.1947); NARA/T78/304/6255046, OKH, Daily report west (12.4.1945); see the entries for 4th and 6th HDs in https://www.axishistory.com/list-all-categories/380-croatia-army/croatia-army-units/8270-divisions-dec-1944-may-1945-croatia (last accessed on 8.7.2020); VAB/GC/71/1/43/5, Hans Meinicke-Kleint/LXXXXI AC (13.7.1947).

102 Ibid., pp. 4-7; TNA/DEFE3/572/KO2031, HGE, Cable (4.5.1945); Baić, *Četvrti*, pp. 397-404; Colić, *Pregled*, pp. 383-87.

7.14 Spring Offensive IV: From Tovarnik to Zagreb

The plan for the "big push" in Syrmia was finalized in late March and early April 1945. It was to be a massive and complex envelopment operation requiring a high degree of coordination between various task forces from the two armies involved. Bosnian Group, consisting of the 2nd Proletarian, 5th Krajina, and 17th Eastern Bosnian Divisions, plus one tank battalion, would first clear the Bijeljina-Brčko area and then strike across the Sava towards Vrbanja. At the same time, Bosut Group (the 6th Lika and 11th Krajina Divisions, plus one cavalry brigade) would strike towards the same objective by marching through the "no man's land" between the Sava, Bosut, and Spačva. Once combined, these two groups would then attack Vinkovci from the south. The frontal attack against the main enemy line would be carried out by Northern Group (the 1st Proletarian, 21st and 22nd Serbian, 42nd and 48th Macedonian Divisions, reinforced with the bulk of the 2nd TB). The main point of effort would (again) be in the northern sector, with Vukovar as the immediate objective. The 16th, 36th, and 51st Vojvodina Divisions of the 3rd Yugoslav Army would simultaneously cross the Drava and Danube on both sides of Osijek. If Dapčević managed to achieve a breakthrough on his own, these divisions would turn to Našice; if not, they would strike towards Vinkovci, against the enemy rear. In all, the reinforced 1st Army had 110,000 men, and the 3rd Army about 41,000; thanks to the Soviet deliveries the armies had over 500 cannon and 1,500 mortars, and 55 tanks between them. The air support would be provided by both divisions of the GVD. The German XXXIV AC, responsible for the defense of the Syrmian Front and northern Bosnia, had, at best, one-third as many men. They were divided between three German divisions (the 22nd and 41st IDs, and the 11th LWFD) and a similar number of independent brigade-sized formations, as well as at the 3rd and 12th HDs. The Wehrmacht high command was acutely aware of the increasingly exposed position of the old Syrmian line and the adjacent Bosnian "bulge"; in fact, the preparations for the withdrawal to a new line running from Slavonski Brod to Donji Miholjac were well under way when the Yugoslav offensive struck.[103]

Preliminary operations on the Syrmian Front commenced in the first days of April 1945, as Bosnian Group followed the retreating 22nd ID to Brčko. This town would not be surrendered without a fight as Bijeljina: indeed, the street battles here would last until the 7th, when the Axis finally withdrew north. The real prize–the bridge over the Sava–eluded the Partisans: it was blown up by enemy sappers in the last moment. This upset the schedule of the entire undertaking, since the group had no bridging equipment. By the time the infantry units had assembled on the northern bank on 12 April (heavy weapons would need two more days), the main offensive had already begun. Bosut Group was also late. The Germans took care to make any journey through the swamps as unpleasant as possible by blowing up the levee at Stošinci and flooding the entire area. Wet and exhausted, the Partisans reached the Vrbanja clearing on the 4th, only to be engaged by the German reinforcements coming from Brčko. In the costly fighting that lasted a whole week, two Yugoslav brigades were badly damaged, but the lines remained unchanged. Only on the 12th, after the bulk of the 22nd ID had passed through the area on its way north, did the Axis rearguards withdrew. The next objective of Southern Group

103 Trifković, "Carnage", pp. 105-22 will serve as the basis for this sub-chapter. Additional sources will be cited separately, in this case Colić, *Pregled*, pp. 348-53.

of the 1st Yugoslav Army–formed by merging the Bosnian and Bosut groups–was the village of Otok, some 20 km away; much to their discomfort, the infantrymen would again have to wade through the swamps in order to reach it.[104]

The southern pincer of the envisaged encirclement of the Axis forces in Syrmia was thus clearly out of the picture. After having postponed the main assault several times, the SHQ finally chose 12 April 1945 as "D-Day". On 0445 hours, a barrage from some 150 guns heralded the beginning of the much-awaited Yugoslav offensive. Fifteen minutes later, the 1st Proletarian and 22nd Divisions surged forward in the northern-most sector of the front under the protection of the T-34s on the ground and "Shturmoviks" in the air. Unlike on earlier occasions, the Yugoslavs came in well prepared this time. Instead of driving forward herds of cattle, which used to be the only way of neutralizing the notorious German minefields, the sappers now had both the training and equipment needed for the job. Moreover, they dug approach trenches to within 150-200 meters of the enemy forward positions, thereby further reducing the casualty rate among the advancing infantrymen. The improved skill of the Yugoslav Army was also evident from the fact that the attack came as a tactical surprise for the enemy. Within hours, Dapčević's spearheads reached Opatovac (where a landing had been made with the help of the Soviet Danube Flotilla), surrounded the enemy strongpoint of Lovas, and cut the main road west of Tovarnik. By the end of the day, the 1st Proletarian stood in Vukovar, and the 21st Serbian just north of Orolik. In the southern sector, the going was anything but smooth. Tovarnik fell to the 42nd and 48th Divisions only after almost 10 hours of heavy fighting, and the 22nd Serbian, fighting on the extreme left, was nearly overrun in a series of enemy counterattacks. With its northern wing (originally held by the 963rd FB) shattered, however, the only sensible thing for the 41st FD to do was to retire west. An order issued to this effect by the XXXIV AC in the early afternoon hours designated the line Županja–Vinkovci–Osijek as the new main defensive position.

The new line had become untenable practically from the moment it was drawn, for it was already outflanked by the 3rd Yugoslav Army's landings on the southern bank of the Drava. By late 13 April 1945, the Yugoslavs had managed push back the elements of the 11th LWFD and the 1st CCD and connect their bridgeheads at Valpovo and Osijek, thus creating the necessary preconditions for the attack on the city itself (Osijek would be taken one day later). This particular Friday the 13th was especially unlucky for the NDH forces. Their rallying point and one of the main objectives of the 1st Yugoslav Army, Vinkovci, came under direct attack of the 48th Division from the east. In the meantime, the 21st Division and the 2nd TB stormed Nuštar, then veered left and threatened the town from the north (a similar maneuver was performed the day before by the 48th Division at Tovarnik). This proved too much for the already shaken defenders and they began pulling back in the late afternoon hours amidst much confusion and heavy losses. The XXXIV AC, on the contrary, managed to extricate nearly all its forces with little interference from the enemy and occupy the new defensive position Sava–Đakovo–Našice–Donji Miholjac.

From a Yugoslav perspective, Syrmian-Slavonian Operation, as the undertaking was officially called, had gone reasonably well so far; granted, the grand encirclement failed to materialize, but the vaunted Wehrmacht was beaten in open battle, fair and square. The going would

104 NARA/T78/476/6459139, OBSO, Daily report (25.3.1945); Samardžija, *Jedanaesta*, pp. 293-301.

be much tougher from now on. The enemy positions in this part of the country lacked the engineering sophistication of the original Syrmian Front but were far more compact and could not be outflanked. What is worse, the infantry would have to do most of the fighting alone. Due to delays in deliveries from the USSR, the ammunition stocks for heavy guns were practically depleted. During the entire month of April 1945, the 1st Yugoslav Army fired a mere 3,204 122mm howitzer shells (most of them in the short, initial barrage on the 12th) and 6,801 120mm mortar bombs. By far the biggest expenditure was recorded for light mortars and AT guns in the 45-50mm range (78,074 and 45,120, respectively), followed by the 76-82mm ordnance (18,798 and 29,640, respectively). On 18 April, the 2nd TB reported that it needed summer-grade oil or that the tanks would otherwise become unusable. As no oil was forthcoming, the brigade spent two weeks (22 April-5 May) out of action, thereby practically missing out the end of the war. At practically the same moment, the two air divisions ran out of fuel after flying some 508 combat sorties; they would not be able to resume operations before 1 May.

The Germans, for their part, followed the same pattern of action as they did in Eastern Macedonia in October 1944, or more recently in Central Bosnia. Combat units would keep the pursuers at bay long enough to allow the evacuation of baggage train and other rear-area services. They would then retreat under the cover of darkness to a next defensive position, scouted beforehand by staff officers and already partially occupied. The process was repeated 11 times in the period 13 April-7 May along the ca. 250-km stretch of territory between Vinkovci and Zagreb. All said, it is small wonder the last major campaign on the Yugoslav soil lasted as long and was as bloody as it was.[105]

Dapčević was certain he would be in Slavonski Brod within three days of the capture of Vinkovci. These hopes were dispersed, however, as soon as his brigades approached the ancient episcopal town of Đakovo. Contrary to Yugoslav intelligence reports, the 22nd and 41st IDs were far from spent, and they now offered fierce resistance with the sole aim of covering the columns arriving from across the Sava. Consequently, the 1st Yugoslav Army could enter Đakovo only on 16 April 1945, and Slavonski Brod on the 20th, by which time the Germans had already completed the evacuation of Bosnia. This enabled them to reinforce their line in Slavonia with the three divisions of the XXI MTC, which also replaced the XXXIV AC as the most senior Axis command in this part of the country. The Partisans' attempt to cut off the German retreat west of Slavonski Brod by sending four divisions on a flanking movement through the southern part of the Slavonian Mountains culminated in an extraordinarily fierce three-day battle for the small village of Pleternica (17-20 April). On this occasion, the 1st Proletarian Division lost almost 1,000 men (one-fourth of them KIA), while the 22nd ID ended up being forced to disband two of its battalions. Despite the terrible death-toll, the Proletarians failed to open the road to the Sava, and the planned encirclement battle turned into mere frontal pushing.[106]

Concurrent with the 1st Yugoslav Army, the 3rd Yugoslav Army resumed its westward advance in the area between the Drava and Našice. Axis forces, consisting of the 11th LWFD and a motley collection of NDH, security, and police units, were too weak to hold such a wide

105 *Zbornik*/XI/1/560-61 (1st YA, Ammo expenditure April 1945), 362 (1st YA to SHQ, 18.4.1945), 714 (2nd TB, Daily report, 11.5.1945); *Zbornik*/X/2/506, GVD, Activity report (April 1945); VAB/GC/73/1/4/3, Werner Honeck/41st ID (12.7.1947).

106 *Završne operacije za oslobođenje Jugoslavije 1944–5* (Belgrade: VII, 1957), pp. 572-93; *Zbornik*/XI/1/434-40, 1st NOVJD, Diary (17-20.4.1945); von Metzsch, *Geschichte*, pp. 85-86.

front for any length of time. Worse still, the initial Yugoslav advance had severed the division's link with the remainder of the army to the south, and its right flank now stood wide open to a possible thrust from the enemy-held Mount Krndija. Upon realizing this, the Partisans launched a simultaneous attack from the south and west using two divisions of the 6th Corps (which had been ordered to this area in early April 1945), and the 36th Division from the east. In the ensuing battle, the 11th LWFD lost a substantial part of its effectives and was forced to withdraw.

The Yugoslavs repeated the maneuver on several occasions during the following two weeks, but each time failed to exploit the initial success by not making deeper penetrations towards the Drava. Attacking from the front, the 3rd Army's two remaining divisions, reinforced by one Bulgarian regiment, were met with fierce resistance by the 1st CCD and two NDH divisions, and could likewise not achieve a decisive breakthrough. By 27 April, the Germans had managed to extricate their forces to the area southeast of Bjelovar without suffering appreciable losses, where they finally effected a link-up with the main body of the HGE. The new defensive position, called "Giselher", ran approximately along the line Jasenovac–the Ilova–Mount Bilogora–Pitomača. Occupied in strength by six German and five NDH divisions subordinated to the XXI MTC and XV SS CCC, it was meant to be held for at least one week before moving on.[107]

On the opposite side of the front, the 1st Yugoslav Army had decided already on 21 April 1945 to leave only two divisions for operations along the Sava, and shift the focal point of its efforts further north, to the area around Pakrac. This, it was hoped, would not only bring the army closer to its right-hand neighbor, but would also enable the bulk of its forces (five divisions altogether) to take advantage of the favorable terrain there for making either a swift advance towards Čazma, or for another outflanking maneuver in the direction of the Sava. Moving over a single road and being encumbered with all the impedimenta of a modern army, it took the once-light-footed Partisans four days to cross the Požega Basin and the surrounding highlands and arrive to the concentration area. On 25 April, the 5th, 6th, and 48th Divisions hurled themselves against the center of the Axis line, held by one weak German (the 369th ID) and three NDH divisions, and almost immediately gained a foothold on the western bank of the Ilova in the sector between the fish ponds. By the 27th, Löhr was compelled to delay the departure of the "Prinz Eugen" for Karlovac until this new threat could be dealt with. One day later, the SS outfit surprised and shattered the 42nd Division around Poljana (the Yugoslav intelligence had failed again to do its homework), and advanced over 10 km deep into the enemy rear area. Threatened with encirclement, the remaining Yugoslav forces hastily withdrew to the eastern bank of the Ilova, thus allowing the Axis to restore their original front line. Despite this success, the "Giselher" position was becoming untenable owing to the 3rd Army's advances in Mount Bilogora and along the Drava. Consequently, the Germans began gradually evacuating the line and moving towards Zagreb on 1 May.[108]

The brief, almost journal-like description of the next phase of the Axis retreat, as presented in the most important non-Yugoslav account available (authored by the HGE's chief of staff) fails

107 Colić, *Pregled*, pp. 360-61; VAB/GC/72/1/3/16-18, Gerhard Henke/11th LWFD (undated); TNA/DEFE3/572/KO1768, HGE, Situation report (28.4.1945).

108 *Završne operacije*, pp. 683-98; VAB/GC/71/1/14/5, Klaus Schubert/XXI MTC (20.7.1947); TNA/DEFE3/572/WA918, Reports from XV SS CCC and XXI MTC (1-2.5.1945).

to capture the bitterness of the fighting that was taking place during the final week of the war. The news of Hitler's death and the fall of Berlin had no visible effect on the German morale; the Yugoslavs, for their part, had no intention of slackening the pace of their operations even if the end of the war was now plainly in sight. On the right flank, the 3rd Army–now counting eight divisions, including two from the 10th Corps–had to break desperate Axis resistance in the towns of Bjelovar and Koprivnica (4–5 May 1945) before continuing its westward advance. One day later, at Križevci, a Partisan brigade was temporarily cut off by a German counterattack and took such a heavy beating that it had to be rotated to the rear.

Yet the most tragic loss of life occurred during the two days of fighting around the village of Vrbovec, an important crossroads and a forward position of the Zvonimir Line. The battle–which ended just as the German Instrument of Surrender signed at Reims on 7 May was about to go into effect–was one of the bloodiest single engagements of the war, with the 1st Proletarian losing a further ca. 900 KIA, WIA, and MIA. The defenders (the 181st ID and NDH troops) got caught in the open during the retreat and probably suffered just as badly, but somehow managed to find their way to the main defensive line, which ran approximately parallel to the Zagreb–Varaždin highway. By the early afternoon of 8 May, all units of the HGE had been informed of the capitulation of the Third Reich, and of the Partisans' entry into the undefended Zagreb from the south.[109]

7.15 "Bloody May 1945"

The sins of the historiography of the Socialist era were largely ones of omission: delicate or unsavory aspects of "People's Liberation Struggle" were usually either ignored or only mentioned in passing. Contrary to the opinion held in many quarters, both in successor states and in the West, the sins of commission–deliberate distortion of facts and/or fabrication of information for political and propaganda purposes–were few and far between. It may sound surprising, but probably the biggest such case has nothing to do with Draža Mihailović or any other internal political aspect of the war, but the surrender of German occupation forces in May 1945. From the first to the last day of the "Second Yugoslavia", historians and veterans repeated the story of how Löhr's command refused to capitulate with the rest of the Wehrmacht, continuing instead its march northwest in hope of reaching the Western Allies in Austria. The Yugoslav Army managed to catch up with its foes in east-central Slovenia and ultimately force them to surrender through skillful maneuvering. According to the official version, the signed act of surrender was somehow "lost" in the extraordinary confusion that reigned in those days. The survivors of the HGE were telling a very different story. The final outcome was not the result of the Yugoslavs' superior martial skills, but of deceit: the Germans were tricked into surrendering their weapons by false promises of safe conduct to Austria. Each side stuck to its own version of events; the lack of academic interest in the matter, technical difficulties involved in archival research, and acrimonious atmosphere of the Cold War, all contributed to the preservation of status quo

109 Schmidt-Richberg, *Endkampf*, pp. 138-39, 142-44; Colić, *Pregled*, p. 390; von Metzsch, *Geschichte*, pp. 87-88; *Zbornik*/XI/3/548-49, 17th NOVJD, Diary (5-7.5.1945); *Zbornik*/XI/1/675-78, 1st NOVJD, Diary (6-8.5.1945).

in this matter. The topic was entirely neglected by post-Yugoslav historiography, partly also because it could not be utilized for daily political purposes.[110]

The possibility of a negotiated surrender in the Balkans was informally discussed by the German and Partisan representatives during their day-to-day contacts regarding the prisoner exchange throughout late 1944 and early 1945. As the war drew to a close, the Germans were becoming inceasingly keen on achieving some kind of a compromise solution, whereby they would be allowed to depart from the country in exchange for their heavy equipment. With the time on their side, the Yugoslavs procrastinated, but never gave a decidedly negative answer to their opponent's proposals. For the reasons mentioned earlier, Löhr had no intention of honoring the provisions of the articles of surrender signed first at Rheims and then at Zossen. His troops therefore resumed the retrograde movement from the Zvonimir Line, at the same time trying to obtain favorable terms from the Yugoslavs. The latter had every reason to appear open for a negotiated settlement. The course of the recent fighting had shown that their foe could not be forced into submission by force of arms. Each hour the German front remained intact increased the chances of the collaborationists escaping for good, and/or the Western Allies occupying the disputed regions. The Yugoslav flank armies, the 4th and 3rd, were ordered to seal the border with Austria already the week before and hold it until the main force could arrive from the east. Owing to the tense situation around Trieste, Drapšin could spare only one brigade, which he loaded onto captured trucks and sent to Southern Carinthia. This Motorized Detachment reached the provincial capital Klagenfurt by the 10th. At he same time, the 14th Division of the 4th OZ occupied the border crossings in northern Štajerska. Three divisions of Nađ's army were on their way from the east to this sector as well. Their march along the Drava and Mura was facilitated a great deal by the fact that the XV SS CCC, whose men were particularly eager to escape Soviet captivity, was retreating faster than the remainder of the HGE.

Even if all these forces arrived on time, there could be no guarantee that they would be able to hold back the huge mass of enemy soldiers approaching the border. The Yugoslavs therefore agreed to negotiate with Löhr through the HQ of the 4th OZ on 9 May 1945 outside Šoštanj. After several hours of bargaining, the deal was struck; German divisions would halt where they were and deliver their heavy and most of light weapons; they would also hand over their motor vehicles and free up the main roads leading to the border for Yugoslav use. In exchange, they would be allowed to continue towards Austria. Once the Germans had disarmed themselves for the first time, their fate was sealed. During the next four or five days, their formations would be repeatedly stopped and disarmed along the way by the units of all three Yugoslav armies and the Slovene MHQ until they had nothing left. The Yugoslavs would occasionally promise the status of internees, rather than prisoners, and a speedy release home: Convention of Ilirska Bistrica, signed separately with the LXXXXVII AC, is a case in point.

Apathy, fear of reprisals– technically speaking, they were the ones who were unlawful combatants now–and almost childish naivety with which they viewed the arrangement with their mortal foe meant that the Germans offered little resistance. Naturally, there were also

110 The part of this sub-chapter that deals with the capitulation and the subsequent fate of the German forces is based on Gaj Trifković, "The Forgotten Surrender: The End of the Second World War in Yugoslavia", *International journal of military history and historiography*, 37 (2017), pp. 147-172. Additional sources will be cited separately.

those who did not trust their enemy's promises. Some formations, such as the 369th ID and the Cossacks, used calculated threat of force to convince the local Partisans to let them through. Others used blunt force. Retreating before the 29th Herzegovina Division and elements of the 7th Slovene Corps, Rösener's security forces vacated Ljubljana on 9 May. Two days later, they succeeded in hacking their way to British POW camps around Klagenfurt, killing some 200 Slovene Partisans in the process. One other Axis column tried to occupy the border crossing at Poljana, which led to the final German-Yugoslav battle of the war on V-E Day+5 (13 May). This time, the defenders carried the day thanks to their better positions and wealth of automatic weapons and mortars trained on the clogged, narrow road used by their opponents (an estimated several hundred of whom fell or were wounded).

According to the German estimates, some 180,000 members of Löhr's command fell into the Yugoslav captivity. The official Belgrade spoke of altogether 221,287 enemy soldiers born outside the country who were captured in the period 20 March-20 May 1945. The Germans and Austrians constituted about a half of the total (84,453, and 27,398, respectively), followed by the Italians (57,150), "Vlassovites" (26,611), Poles (9,425), Hungarians (4,461), French (3,868), Romanians (3,139), Czechoslovaks (3,849), and others (933). The majority of the Italians belonged either to the RSI forces from Julian March, or used to serve as unarmed auxiliaries attached to the Wehrmacht. However, it is unclear where so many "Vlassovites" came from, given that both capital Russian collaborationist formations, the XV SS CCC and RSK, managed to avoid capture (it also seems unlikely that the figure refers to the *Hiwis* alone). Although they should be taken with a grain of salt, these official statistics represent the only halfway-decent starting point for further research on the post-war Axis POWs in Yugoslavia, another neglected topic.

In fact, Axis prisoners were facing a very uncertain fate. Although the period of worst atrocities had ended by early 1944, the war in Yugoslavia remained a very brutal affair. One of the worst single massacres occurred in April of the same year in Cetinska Krajina, when members of the "Prinz Eugen" murdered roughly 2,000 civilians (most of whom, ironically, had cousins in Axis formations). Three months later, its sister division, the "Skanderbeg" did the same to 428 inhabitants of the village of Velika in Montenegro. In Serbia, the executions of NOP suspects, while not as massive as before, continued almost until the last day of the war: the most perfunctory overview of relevant sources yields the figure of ca. 400 persons shot from January through September 1944 (Sandžak and Vojvodina included). The same is true for Slovenia: the hanging of 99 hostages in reprisal for the aforementioned killing of a Nazi Party functionary outside Celje in February 1945 is the most notorious example. Likewise, the death of SS General Willi Brandner in an ambush in late December 1944 led to the hanging of at least 100 persons in Zagreb. During the retreat from Greece, the Germans were documented shooting hostages in Skopje, massacring at least 70 civilians at Kočansko, and burning down scores of villages in Macedonia and Sandžak.

Thirst for revenge, combined with the headiness of victory and worsening relations with the British (which effectively made the earlier commitments regarding POWs null and void) led to an informal adoption of no-prisoner policy by the NOVJ in large parts of the country, mostly in the south and east. During the liberation of Serbia, the Partisans were shooting prisoners out of hand, and those who survived usually had the Soviets to thank. Very few of ca. 2,000 German prisoners captured at Knin lived through the winter, their numbers decimated by disease and firing squad. The events that transpired in the immediate aftermath of the victory at Nevesinje were disturbing enough to warrant an appeal for more moderation from the top Herzegovinian *politkom*. It should be noted that Yugoslav commands, from SHQ downwards, continued issuing orders concerning humane treatment of captives throughout this period, but these were seldom followed or enforced. It would be fair to assume that May 1945 saw many extrajudicial killings of prisoners immediately after capture or during "death marches" to the camps in the interior, but just how many perished is almost impossible to say, as we have only German eyewitness reports. The claim about the ca. 80,000 dead in the Yugoslav captivity can be safely disregarded. It was based on the subtraction of ca. 90,000 servicemen repatriated to Germany from the already mentioned 180,000-figure, although we have seen that more than a half of the total were non-German citizens who would be returned to their respective countries of origin. We know for certain of 10,000 deaths that occurred in captivity, but the end sum was probably bigger as it would have to include all those declared "missing" and those who never made it to POW camps in the first place. According to Rüdiger Overmans, from some 190,000 members of German armed formations captured in Yugoslavia, 110,000 were repatriated. The difference is made up of the deceased prisoners, the Ethnic Germans (thousands of whom had served on other fronts and were repatriated to Yugoslavia), and those POWs turned over by the Yugoslavs to the Soviets.[111]

The German officer corps paid a high price for the brutal war it waged in Yugoslavia. From 1945 to 1949, Yugoslav military tribunals found 1,392 members (most of them officers) of various German armed formations guilty of war crimes. About a 1,000 of these were tried during 1949. Of the 922 who were found guilty, 40 were executed, while 52 more had the death sentence commuted to prison terms; they would all be released in the early 1950s in course of Yugoslavia's opening towards the West. The highest ranks had the highest mortality. Löhr was executed by firing squad in 1947, primarily for his role in the 1941-bombing of Belgrade. His particularly notorious subordinates and co-defendants, such as August Schmidthuber and Karl von Oberkamp (the 7th SS MTD), Fritz Neidholdt (the 369th ID), Josef Kübler (the 118th JD), and Hans Fortner (the 718th ID), were denied the military courtesy and hanged instead. Also tried and executed were Josef's brother Ludwig Kübler (LXXXXVII AC), Hans von Hößlin (the 188th RMTD), Hartwig von Ludwiger (the 104th JD), Hans-Joachim Gravenstein (the 373rd ID), Adalbert Lontschar (commandant of Belgrade), Heinrich Danckelmann (commander of Serbia), Adolf Fischer (KG "Fischer"), and the *Luftwaffe* General Martin Fiebig. Four generals, Friedrich Stephan (Division "Stephan"), Gustav Fehn (the XV MTC), Werner von Erdmannsdorf (the LXXXXI AC), and Heinz Kattner (commandant of Sarajevo), were murdered without trial immediately after the war. General Gerhard Kühne (the 22nd ID), was shot by a Yugoslav sentry in 1948, allegedly for getting too close to a window.[112]

111 Trifković, *Parleying*, pp. 60-64, 244, 286, 298-302, 340-42, 350; Tone Kregar, "Okupacijsko nasilje na Celjskem", in *Iz zgodovine Celja 1941-1945* (Celje: MNZ, 2004), pp. 150-51; Pavle Dželetović Ivanov, *Dvadesetprva SS-divizija "Skenderbeg"* (Belgrade: Nova knjiga, 1987), p. 193; Trajkovski, *Вермахтом*, pp. 324-26; NARA/T314/1630/605-06, LXXXXI AC, Circular (30.11.1944); Milan Terzić, "Josip Broz Tito i Nemci-ratni zarobljenici", *VIG*, 65:2 (2015), p. 172.

112 Đorđe Lopičić, *Nemački ratni zločini 1941-1945. Presude jugoslovenskih vojnih sudova* (Belgrade: Muzej žrtava genocida, 2009), pp. 17, 35; von Metzsch, *Geschichte*, p. 91; http://lexikon-wehrmacht.de/Personenregister/S/StephanFriedrich-R.htm (last accessed on 15.7.2020). See also the corresponding entries in http://www.smrtnakazna.rs/sr-latn-rs/bazaosudjenika.aspx (last accessed on 15.7.2020).

If April 1945 was bloody for the Partisans, May would be bloodier still for the collaborationists. This refers primarily to the Slovene *Domobranci*, NDH soldiers, and Serbian nationalists who were caught in, or repatriated by the British to, Slovenia. Despite the revenge killings, German servicemen–unless they were members of the Nazi Party or various internal security/intelligence/secret police organizations–were never earmarked for extermination; instead, they were, at least nominally, granted the privileged POW status and used for menial labor. In sharp contrast, the Yugoslav citizens caught on the opposing side were denied any such protection. Partisan commands did not mince words:

> We have to destroy and capture as many fascist butchers and domestic fiends as possible, thus avenging all the crimes they committed against our peoples"; "[...] not a single Ustasha should remain [...] [The HDB] officers who are captured should be dealt with most severely; the ones who surrender [on their own free will] should be treated with more flexibility: the worst among them should be identified and punished most severely, the remainder sent to a camp".

Quenching the thirst for a swift and merciless retribution was considered as means of legitimizing the new regime, especially in the eyes of the biggest ethnic group, Serbs, who also happened to suffer the most during the occupation. The other, more important reason speaking in favor of a bloody showdown had ideological roots. In the Communists' eyes, thousands of collaborationists who had found their way to Austria were die-hards who chose to fight to the bitter end despite all the amnesties and the final outcome of the war in Europe. If released home–which was most likely never seriously discussed–they would take their beliefs with them, thus creating a threat to the internal stability of the new order. Tito was determined not to let this happen.[113]

Before retribution could be meted out, collaborationists would have to be caught first, and this proved to be a difficult task. Löhr, never a friend of the regime in Zagreb and its armed forces, wrote repentantly on 2 May 1945 about the need to support the only remaining ally, "who had been standing on Germany's side for the past thousand years in the struggle against the invaders from the east [*Ansturm vom Osten*]". However, only five days later, he relinquished the control of the remaining NDH combat formations, effectively leaving them to their fate. Pavelić was already trying to find a new mentor in the West, but he underestimated the Western Allies' commitment to the anti-Axis cause and was refused. Nevertheless, the NDH army, followed by large numbers of refugees and camp followers, continued the withdrawal towards Austria parallel to the German forces.

By 15 May, the heads of these huge columns, whose ends stood anywhere between 45 and 65 km to the rear, had passed Celje and were approaching the outskirts of Maribor and the Austrian border town of Bleiburg. During the dramatic talks with the representatives of the British 5th Corps, Pavelić's emissaries requested protection for 200,000 Croat soldiers and 500,000 civilians, who they claimed would otherwise become victims of a Communist-organized genocide. Ironically, these vastly inflated figures that were meant to intimidate the British into accepting the request, were one of the main reasons for its ultimate refusal. First, the British

113 Radanović, *Kazna*, p. 498; *Zbornik*/IX/9/582, 3rd YA/Pol., Circular (24.4.1945).

could not possibly feed so many new mouths; second, they needed the entire area clear in case of an armed confrontation with the Yugoslavs (it is worth remembering that the border crisis was at its height); and third, no one wanted to get killed or injured over those who had faithfully served Hitler throughout all these years. The representatives of the 51st Vojvodina and 14th Slovenian Divisions, who were also present at these meetings, demanded an unconditional surrender within one hour, citing the utterly hopeless position the collaborationists found themselves in. When the NDH envoys began to prevaricate, citing, among else, the shortage of white linen, the Partisans responded icily "Use your shirts and drawers, you surely have those".[114]

News of the capitulation, brought to the stranded columns by parties of Yugoslav and NDH officers, were met with the mixture of emotions. The vast majority of soldiers, who had been held in line "by using every propaganda and disciplinary means available" (according to Löhr's above-cited telegram), were by now thoroughly physically and psychologically exhausted. As a result, they meekly submitted to their fate and began stacking up their weapons. The Ustashe veterans–largely belonging to the still-functional PTS and Francetić's old command, as well as Jasenovac camp guards–headed towards Austria in small groups, moving exclusively through forests and mountains. The Partisans commenced selection process immediately. This usually involved separating soldiers from civilians, members of one branch of the armed forces from the next, officers from men, veterans from conscripts. All those considered not beyond salvation–which included the bulk of the *Domobran* rank-and-file, but also younger, conscripted members of the UV–were sent to the camps in the interior.

Despite the widespread abuse and wanton murders along the way, this group could still hope to survive. The others–classified by the sinister-sounding terms "Category 'C'" or "13th Battalion"–were not as fortunate. The *Politkom* of the 14th Division remembered the case of a Partisan guard who dispatched a group of Ustashe with a knife, the same way his family had perished in. Although it can be safely assumed that such scenes were happening across Slovenia, most of the executions that happened during the "Bloody May" were premeditated, organized affairs. The captives were usually taken to secluded or otherwise convenient places (such as the abandoned coal mine at Huda Jama, the German-made anti-tank ditch at Tezno, or chasms of Kočevski Rog) and executed with machine guns. Veteran brigades, such as the 6th Eastern Bosnian or 15th Majevica, were placed at OZNA's disposal for this task for days on end. The grand total of the former NDH servicemen and camp followers who perished in this way or during the "death marches" is still hotly debated, but the most widely-accepted estimate speaks of ca. 50-60,000. Slovenia is also the final resting place of at least 2,000 members of the "Prinz Eugen", ca. 10,000 Rupnik's *Domobranci*, and 2,000 members of the SFK and some Lika Chetniks. The latter three groups (along with ca. 10-12,000 Croats) were delivered by the British from the holding areas around Klagenfurt.[115]

According to an internal report from 20 February 1946, from 115,415 Yugoslav citizens who were captured at the end of the war as members of collaborationist forces–and this figure

114 TsAMO/500/12450/246/46-48, OBSO to Dönitz (2.5.1945); Đurica Labović and Milan Basta, *Partizani za pregovaračkim stolom* (Zagreb: Naprijed, 1986), p. 317; Tomasevich, *Occuaption*, pp. 751-68.

115 Interview with Ivan Dolničar in: "Tito: posljednji svjedoci testamenta", Episode 8 (Kindodokument/ Hrvatska radio-televizija, 2012); Martina Grahek Ravančić, *Bleiburg i Križni Put 1945: Historiografija, publicistika i memoarska literatura* (Zagreb: HIP, 2009), pp. 196, 204, 218-21, 230, 239, 253, 325-26, 321.

obviously refers only to those who actually made it to the camps– 50,000 *Domobrani* were sent to army labor battalions, 46,355 persons were pardoned in August 1945 and thereafter, 1,562 were handed over to the OZNA, 63 escaped, and 339 died. The remaining 11,096 (mostly Ethnic Germans and the Ustashe) were still toiling in Bor mines and elsewhere. Holders of command authority were particularly hard-hit by the repression. In mid-July 1945, the camps held only 1,699 *Domobran* privates, but 1,738 officers and eight NCOs. The Ustasha leadership corps was practically annihilated: of 16,030 captives, only 74 were officers and one was an NCO. Although many of the highest-ranking NDH officials managed to escape–including Pavelić, whose clandestine flight from Zagreb with a small entourage had a devastating effect on what was left of his reputation–there were still plenty going around for a series of highly-publicized trials. One of the better-known ones ended in a execution of 17 HDB generals and senior UV officers in late September 1945.[116]

In the months leading to final victory, the NOP had to contend with internal threats as never before. Large swaths of territory acquired during this period came with decidedly hostile populations, and the mass mobilization allowed all sorts of characters into the army. The 3rd Corps' censor found suspicious letters written in Morse Code and even in foreign languages. The OZNA of the 10th Corps uncovered a clandestine organization "made up mostly of Croat and Hungarian women", one of whom led the Cossacks onto a Partisan battalion, which lost 16 men in the subsequent surprise attack. Many instances of direct involvement of civilian population in the fighting on the Axis side were recorded during Operation "Bora": among else, women in Čapljina allegedly threw Molotov Cocktails on the passing Yugoslav tanks. Frustration with the inability to pacify Western Herzegovina and the simmering feud with the Catholic Church led to one of the most notorious Partisan crimes of the war. The Franciscan abbey at Široki Brijeg, with its secondary school, had long been considered spiritual home of radical clericalism and extreme Croat nationalism. Incensed over ca. 500 losses they suffered in the two-day battle for the town in early February 1945, and claiming the abbey played a pivotal role in the defense (the NDH and German sources claim exactly the opposite), the Partisans of the 8th Corps executed 28 friars.[117]

Securing the rear of the armies fighting the Germans was the task of the KNOJ: with 120,000 members spread across the country, it was larger than Dapčević's entire command. While these internal security troops usually sufficed for day-to-day operations, several major threats that emerged during late 1944 and early 1945 required a full-blown intervention by the army. The biggest threat to the new order was still coming from Draža Mihailović. By the beginning of spring, the disgraced general still had about 7,000 Serbian and Bosnian Chetniks

116 *Partizanska i komunistička represija i zločini u Hrvatskoj 1944.-1946.–dokumenti* (Slavonski Brod: HIP, 2005), pp. 313-14, Yugoslav MoD, Report on prisoners-our citizens (20.2.1946); *Partizanska i komunistička represija i zločini u Hrvatskoj 1944.-1946.–dokumenti: Zagreb i središnja Hrvatska* (Zagreb: HIP, 2008), pp. 519-20, Dimitrije Georgijević to Ranković (12.7.1945); Tomasevich, *Occupation*, p. 788; Mario Jareb, "Ustaški pukovnik i general Tomislav Sertić", *ČSP*, 32:2 (2000), pp. 300-01; see also the entry for "Tomislav Sertić" in http://www.smrtnakazna.rs/sr-latn-rs/bazaosudjenika.aspx (last accessed on 15.7.2020).

117 *Zbornik*/IV/32/627, 3rd NOVJC/Rear, Activity report (January 1945); *Zbornik*/IX/8/475, 3rd de./Pol. to 32nd NOVJD (3.2.1945); *Zbornik*/IV/33/210, Herzegovina KNOJ Bde. To Bosnian-Herzegovinian KNOJ Div. (7.2.1945); Hrvoje Mandić, "Hercegovačka franjevačka provincija u Drugom svjetskom ratu i poraću" (PhD thesis, University of Zagreb, 2019), pp. 262-88, 375-76.

under his command, plus some 6,000 Montenegrins and Herzegovinians of Đurišić. The latter first followed the XXI MTC through the valleys of Tara and Lim, and then undertook a gruesome winter march across the Bosnian mountains. Now, both groups had to decide where to go next. Although a tentative contact with Pavelić had been established through intermediaries, Mihailović decided against going west. Lured by the overtly optimistic cables sent by the OZNA radio operators posing as Chetniks, he would march to Serbia, where he hoped to incite an anti-communist uprising. Thereupon Đurišić broke away from his erstwhile commander and headed towards Slovenia in order to join hands with Đujić, Ljotić and the others. In order to secure a safe passage through the NDH, Đurišić pledged himself and his army to Sekula Drljević, Montenegrin separatist and Pavelić's ally. Once it became clear that the Chetniks had no intention of honoring their commitments, the Ustashe ambushed them on Lijevča Polje on 4-5 April. On this occasion, several hundred were killed and the remainder was captured; Đurišić and over 130 of his officers were executed in Jasenovac and Stara Gradiška concentration camps. In a moment of supreme irony, most of the survivors would be caught while retreating through Slovenia together with Pavelić's forces and share their ultimate fate (ca. 3,000 were executed).[118]

Even with half of the JVuO forces thus out of the picture, the SHQ did not underestimate the threat. As soon as Mihahilović's main body started its trek from the Motajica to the Vlašić, it came under the attack by the 53rd Division. By the time the Chetniks had reached the southeastern slopes of the Bjelašnica via Fojnica (which they sacked on 4 May) and Bradina, elements of the 27th and 38th Eastern Bosnian, 29th Herzegovinian, 37th Sandžak, as well as the KNOJ, had joined the fray. The royalists' ranks were thinned by combat losses and typhus; the supplies of food were long exhausted and the ammunition was all but gone. On the other side of the front stood the much more numerous and incomparably better equipped and supplied Partisans. In these operations, they applied their own version of the "free hunt" tactics with great success. They were constantly harrowing their foe and did not allow him a moment's rest: they set up blocking lines along the projected route of his movement and utilized trucks to move troops between them. On V-E Day+1 (9 May), the Partisans launched an all-out attack on the southeastern slopes of the Bjelašnica with the help of 15 "Sturmoviks" dispatched to Sarajevo by the GVD just for this occasion. In the subsequent running battle in the Ljuta Canyon, the Chetniks took heavy losses, but still somehow managed to escape towards the Zelengora.

The war had returned to this blood-soaked wilderness for the fourth time in as many years. The small Proletarian army, surrounded by the Italians and their native Serb auxiliaries, departed on its decisive march to Bosanska Krajina from this very area in June 1942. Almost exactly one year later, the Proletarians had nearly met their doom here during Operation "Schwarz", and the 12th Vojvodina Corps avoided the same fate by a hair's breadth in August 1944. It was now the Chetniks' turn to bleed. The final reckoning occurred on 12 May, when the Partisans routed Mihailović's main column: from ca. 3,000 men, only several hundred managed to escape. The secondary column, some 2,000-strong, took a more northerly route, but also broke apart in the

118 Vicko Antić, "Dejstva Korpusa narodne odbrane Jugoslavije na razbijanju kontrarevolucionarnih snaga u poslednjoj godini rata", in *Završne*, pp. 604-11; NARA/T77/775/5501416, Memorandum meeting Lutz Graf Schwerin von Krosigk–Vladimir Košak (10.5.1945); Radanović, *Kazna*, pp. 423-24, 429-30, 472-503.

following days. The general himself went into hiding; he was caught in March 1946 with the help of a high-ranking turncoat and executed in July after a public trial. The Battle of Zelengora has a special significance for the sympathizers of the Chetnik cause even today, much as the Bleiburg surrender has for the Croat nationalists. The Wagnerian narrative usually involves the claim about the alleged murder of thousands of prisoners by the Communists. However, there is little conclusive evidence that the Partisans departed from their standard rules that involved death for officers and captivity for rank-and-file (or at least for those who surrendered freely).[119]

The greatest resistance to the new order was encountered in Kosovo, where troubles started only weeks after the Germans had departed. Knowing full well how precarious the NOP's hold over the province is, the local Party and military authorities tread carefully: amnesty was proclaimed, conscription was kept on voluntary basis, and the disarmament of the population was carried out gradually. Their colleagues in the neighboring Macedonia, however, applied heavy-handed tactics including mass arrests, hard labor, and total disarmament. Fearful of the Slavic revenge and resentful of Yugoslavia, thousands of still-armed Albanians began to organize a full-scale uprising. On 2 December 1944, the rebels attacked the town of Uroševac, followed by Gnjilane three weeks later. On 26-27 January 1945, a full-scale battle involving an equivalent of three Yugoslav brigades took place in and around the Trepča mines. The Partisans now learned the feeling of having to wait for a relief force while being cooped-up in a handful of fortified strongpoints. Although all these attacks were ultimately repulsed, there was no doubt that the province stood in open revolt: couriers were intercepted, smaller detachments ambushed, and high-ranking officials assassinated. On 7 February, martial law was decreed; the OHQ that became responsible for all aspects of life in Kosovo would ultimately control over 40,000 effectives from four divisions and other, smaller units. Despite such a large concentration of troops, it would take almost three months of campaigning (including the application of reprisals) before the situation was stabilized to some extent. In addition to resources that could have been used elsewhere, the Kosovo affair cost the Yugoslavs at least 850 KIA from December 1944 to May 1945.[120]

It should be noted that the rebellion was further fueled by introduction of compulsory mobilization in January 1945. From the authorities' standpoint, Kosovo and its population had to share the burdens of war equally with other regions and ethnic groups. Moreover, the conscription would not only provide fresh replacements for units at the front, but also remove potential rebel recruits from the source of trouble. Many Albanians had no intention of fighting another man's war in the far-flung corners of the Balkans: instead to the depots in Dalmatia and Vojvodina, thousands of them "went to the woods". The troubles did not stop at Kosovo's borders. An entire Albanian battalion mutinied at Vršac on 19-20 February. Faced with a massive intervention by army and KNOJ units, the mutineers laid down their arms. During the subsequent court-martial, eleven ringleaders were sentenced to death, while the remainder was allowed to resume training.

119 Ibid., pp. 433-71; *Zbornik*/IV/34/894-99, 3rd NOVJC, Report battle with Mihailović (17.5.1945); *Zbornik*/X/2/690-91, GVD, Activity report (15-30.5.1945).

120 *DCO*/XXI/234, Miladin Popović to CK KPJ (1.12.1944); Savo Drljević, "Kontrarevolucija na Kosovu i Metohiji– zavođenje Vojne uprave februara 1945", in *Završne,* p. 600; Nenad Miodrag Antonijević, "Ratni zločini na Kosovu i Metohiji 1941-1945. godine" (PhD thesis, University of Belgrade, 2015), pp. 563-609.

All Kosovo recruits destined for the 4th Yugoslav Army would be marched, under armed escort, across Albania to the Montenegrin port of Bar, from where they would be shipped north. While the first and third batches completed the journey without major disturbances, the second met with a tragedy. On 26 March, a scuffle led the guards to open fire on the densely packed mass of recruits, who were held in the courtyard of the town's tobacco monopoly building. Spurred by the rumors of an alleged mutiny, an entire army brigade hurried to the scene accompanied by numerous civilian vigilantes. According to the most moderate estimates, 452 Albanians were killed on this occasion. No official first-hand reports on the massacre had ever been published, and the same goes for an official inquiry that must have taken place in its aftermath. What we do know is that the incident was regarded as an outbreak of sectarian violence serious enough to be discussed at the highest Party levels.[121]

The ultimate battle of the Second World War in Yugoslavia did not occur somewhere along its borders, but at its heart. Nestled in the Bosna-Sava triangle between Modriča and Bosanski Šamac, there is a cluster of Croat settlements centered on the village of Odžak. Writing in early 1944, one Partisan officer described it as a hostile territory and a safe haven for deserters of all colors. He also added that this "miniature NDH" lived its own, secluded existence, and that the local Ustashe rarely ventured out. In the third week of April 1945, the 25th Serbian Division arrived there in the course of the 2nd Yugoslav Army's westward advance. On the 23rd, the Partisans launched an all-out frontal assault, but ran into an unexpectedly strong resistance; the defenders even managed to capture four cannon in one of their many counterattacks. In fact, this particular militia enclave could not be taken from the move; it was held by ca. 2,000 desperadoes who fought from an intricate system of self-made field fortifications. After five days of futile attacks, the 25th Serbian began pulling out pending its transfer towards Zagreb. Its place would soon be taken by three brigades of the 27th Eastern Bosnian and 53rd Central Bosnian Divisions, which had just finished chasing Mihailović's Chetniks. The second Yugoslav attempt to crush the pocket, lasting from 3 to 9 May, fared like its predecessor. Unaccustomed to positional warfare in lowlands, the two divisions suffered heavy losses and yet had little to show for it. The latest setback convinced Belgrade that the objective could not be taken without further reinforcements and thorough preparations; as a result, two additional brigades and some smaller units were dispatched here. Tanks, which were also requested by the 3rd Corps, could not be provided, but the ground attack planes could. In addition to the already mentioned special task force of the GVD, an ad-hoc group of five captured German and NDH machines (the so-called "Mostar Squadron") was made available.

On 22 May–V-E Day+14–the Yugoslavs opened their offensive with air strikes and artillery bombardment. This proved to be too much for the defenders: they tried to break out towards the west but were bloodily repulsed. Despite this success, it took three days until the last pocket of resistance was destroyed. And so, on 25 May 1945, the war in Yugoslavia had finally come to a close, at least in a purely military sense. The final episode was fittingly bloody: the combined losses of the three Yugoslav divisions are estimated at ca. 430 KIA and MIA, and 1,123 WIA. The NDH garrison was all but wiped out. It is known for certain that at least 562 defenders were captured at the end of the battle. Documentary evidence is flimsy, but we can probably trust the eyewitness reports according to which the prisoners were executed in the days after the

121 Ibid., pp. 603-04; Goran Nikolić, "O masakru u Baru 1945.", *Pirotski zbornik* 44 (2019), pp. 87-146.

battle. Indeed, even without mass executions of collaborationists going on in the entire country, it would be hard to imagine that the Partisans would spare the men who caused them so much trouble and losses weeks after the guns had fallen silent in Europe.[122]

122 *Zbornik*/IV/23/311-12, NOVJ Trebava-Posavina area to 36th NOVJD (15.3.1944); *Zbornik*/XI/2/407-24, 25th NOVJD, Activity report (16-30.4.1945); *Zbornik*/X/2/718-19, NOVJ Mostar air base to Air Force HQ (2.7.1945); Đonlagić, *Dvadesetsedma*, pp. 501-20; Mladen Vukosavljević, Drago Karasijević, *Pedesettreća NOU srednjobosanska divizija* (Sarajevo: Zadrugar, 1969), pp. 195-206; Stjepan Marčetić, "Odžak i Odžačka Posavina 1945. godine", *Rostra*, 2:2 (2009), pp. 23-37.

Closing Thoughts

The NOP's ultimate triumph in 1945 was based on several factors.[1] First of all, the entire effort was steered from a single center, the SHQ with Tito at its helm. He enjoyed unquestionable authority thanks to the cult of discipline "transplanted" from the already thoroughly militarized KPJ. For the same reason, the Partisan citizen-officers turned out to be far better in putting grudges and personal issues by side than the colorful mix of civil servants, priests, pre-war politicians, and army professionals who joined the royalist camp. Moreover, the movement pursued a clearly defined and consistent strategy that had two objectives: the liberation of the country from the Axis and carrying out a social revolution. Waiting for the Red Army while engaging in propaganda and a few odd diversions (as was the case in Bulgaria) would simply not do for the Yugoslav Communists.

It was decided early on that this ambitious agenda could be attained only through active campaigning and widest participation of the population. The decision to take the war to the Axis at the time when they were advancing deep into the Soviet Union is often attributed to the Communists' fanaticism, but this explanation fails to take into account the contemporary mindset. Judging by Hitler's actions and words, the Slavic peoples seemed already condemned either to extermination or abject servitude regardless of whether they opposed the Nazis or not. In these circumstances, active resistance was the only option, and the subsequent events in the NDH appeared to confirm the Communists' viewpoint. The genocide against the Serbs–which, incidentally, is probably the single most important factor in the transformation of the KPJ-sponsored insurgency into a true popular uprising–was widely seen as the first step in the realization of the sinister Axis plans, as no one believed the Ustashe were doing anything without an approval from their foreign mentors. The policy of active resistance was also undeniably producing results: with half of the country in flames, with trains being sabotaged, army columns ambushed, and gendarmerie stations sacked, the NDH forces were simply not in the position to raid Serb villages with impunity any longer.

From the very beginning, the NOP leadership knew that the struggle could not be won by small Party-based armed squads, but by a large, modern field force capable of tackling Axis regulars and the myriad of domestic foes. The importance of the early departure from the concept of territorial army and creation of mobile, proto-regular units–cannot be stressed enough. As

1 This chapter is based, in part, on my article "Od ‚bandita' do ‚Jugoslovenske armije': partizanski rat 1941–1945.", published as a part of "Yu historija" project; available at http://www.yuhistorija.com/serbian/drugi_sr_txt01c1.html (last accessed on 31.7.2020). Additional sources will be mentioned separately.

Schmider put it, the creation of brigades not only gave regular traits to the operations against the Axis, "but truly revolutionized the civil war against the Chetniks and Ustashe". The key to their success, apart from higher discipline and motivation, lay in the brigades' ability to operate far from their respective home regions. This leads us to two other pillars on which the NOP's ultimate triumph rested. The first one was the commitment to the Yugoslav idea. Unlike practically all other factions–including the Germans, who treated Slovenia differently from the rest of the country–the NOP viewed the entire territory of Yugoslavia as a single theater of war. The SHQ represented the highest authority from the Karavanke Alps in the north to Mount Kajmakčalan in the south. This allowed for great freedom in planning and execution of complex operations of strategic significance (e.g. incursions into Serbia in 1944) that would otherwise be impossible to contemplate with only local forces at hand. The survival and growth of the NOP could not be imagined without the free flow of troops and supplies between provinces that had been routinely practiced since early 1942 (e.g. between Syrmia and Eastern Bosnia, Slavonia–Moslavina and Banija, etc.).

The other pillar refers to the NOP's policy of integration and inclusion. Being literally the only faction open to all people regardless of their ethnicity, religion, gender, or class, the Partisans could count on finding numerous supporters in every corner of the country. In addition to its already appealing agenda of national liberation and social justice, the NOP's recruiting potential was further increased by discriminate application of violence. Captured rank-and-file of most enemy formations were accepted *en masse* into the NOVJ. Popular demand for justice was satisfied by placing certain hostile groups, such as the Ustashe, outside protection: they would usually be executed right after capture, or, occasionally, after a public trial (e.g. Livno in September 1942). In either case, the movement hoped to achieve the following: to "channel" the fury of vengeance towards relatively small groups rather than entire peoples, and to present itself as a true belligerent with all the prerogatives of a sovereign state. In 1944-45, however, the state-sponsored or tolerated repression would begin to hit the minorities (especially the *Volksdeutsche*), but the war had already been practically won by then and there was little reason to compromise.

At this point we shall again take a look at several other phenomena and/or misconceptions about the Yugoslav insurgency that were hopefully explained/corrected in this book:

- Laying down ambushes and blowing up trains were only a part of the NOVJ agenda. The Partisans were just as well-versed in the art of street fighting and storming of fortifications since the attacks on urban centers represented one of the main forms of their activity; 288 such events were recorded in the NDH alone in the period 27 July 1941 to 27 March 1945 (note: at least 17 attacks from the early period of the uprising were conducted together with the Chetniks).[2] Towns and cities were not only sources of rare commodities such as medicine and fuel, but were essential for the NOP's regularization and state-building efforts. A small band of renegades would have no need for large buildings, workshops, and industrial facilities in Užice, Bihać, Korpivnica, or elsewhere; the NOVJ units, on the contrary, with thousands of men who needed shelter, food, and clothing, would. Urban centers

2 Statistics courtesy of Goran Despotović (private communication, 12.8.2020).

also had the infrastructure needed to run civilian life on liberated territories, a task inseparable from, and complementary to, military operations.

- There is no factual evidence to support the claim that the Partisans deliberately targeted occupation forces near inhabited places in order to provoke reprisals and thus draw the survivors into their ranks. Although their leaders were aware of potential short-term advantages of such actions, the tactic was essentially detrimental to the NOP's war aims in the long run. First of all, reprisals were more likely to stem the tide of an insurgency rather than augment it, as vividly shown in Serbia. Second, the ultimate success depended on a continuous commitment of a large part of the population, not on an odd group or two of desperadoes here and there. A village was not likely to remain loyal or to send its menfolk to far-off provinces without being provided a modicum of protection. The liberated territories were seen as a means to winning the war, but not as its ultimate objective; the Partisans would seldom allow themselves to be drawn into a decisive engagement over a scrap of land (e.g. Užice in late 1941, Mount Kozara in mid-1942). Before leaving, however, they at least had to put up a token fight and make sure that the refugees got out of the harm's way.
- The Partisans' propensity for total war had its limits. Unlike in the Ustasha state, where terror was wanton and unpredictable, the scale of reprisals in Serbia stood in direct correlation with the intensity of guerrilla attacks. The Germans made sure the population knew this as they applied the draconian 1:100 and 1:50 rules that resulted in over 20,000 executions from September 1941 to April 1942 alone. After that, the bulk of the population turned its back on the idea of open confrontation with the occupation forces and embraced the relative stability offered by Nedić's quisling regime. Although their opponents often accused them of callousness, and although they liked to think of themselves as uncompromising enemies of the Nazis, the Partisans, in fact, bowed to the new reality. They stayed clear of the Germans as much as possible throughout 1942 and 1943, directing their efforts to the collaborationists, Chetniks, and Bulgarians instead.
- Various sources of Western provenance often contain the notion that the Partisans "invaded" Serbia in September 1944 with the sole aim of winning the civil war and deliberately refrained from attacking the Germans in the process. It is not surprising when such claims originate from the US observers at Mihailović's HQ: they could not see the big picture and were partial to the party they were attached to, a common occurrence among all liaison personnel. However, even Churchill mentioned "a period of inactivity" on the Partisans' part, and the fact that the Allied supplies were being used against "your [Tito's] own countrymen rather than the Germans". It is a well-established fact–one that was never hidden by the Yugoslav Communists–that the return to Serbia was largely motivated by political reasons. In this respect, it was no different from other major Partisan undertakings of the war, all of which had both military and political objectives. What the Partisans' detractors persistently fail to acknowledge is the fact that the inter-Yugoslav conflict was not taking place in some sort of a vacuum, but was closely, indeed inseparably, interwoven with the occupation of the country and the wider world conflict. This meant that the Chetniks were not simply defined by their anti-communism, but

> also by their relationship with the occupying powers. The truth was, the JVuO had practically become the chief guardian of the western and southwestern borders of Felber's Serbia. The Partisans directed their attention to Račić's and Keserović's group of corps not solely because of ideological animosities, but also because they were the biggest obstacle on the path to the interior of the country. After the bulk of their forces had left for the eastern border, the German contingent in the entire area between the Greater Morava and the Drina had dwindled to an equivalent of two to three regiments. Even so, the Partisans did attack them at Valjevo, Čačak, and Užice (not to mention Zaječar), and around Aranđelovac. Moreover, September was the month of Operation "Ratweek", and Popović's command in the south was as busy as ever. All said, Churchill's comments seem to have been motivated by his increasing frustration over Tito and the waning British influence in the country. Another possible explanation could lay in the fact that the ULTRA decrypts from this period contained less information on the NOVJ activities than usual. At one point even the OKW inquired "if Tito was less active lately", to which von Weichs' chief-of-staff answered: "No, not at all, it is just that we are preoccupied with [the Eastern Front]."[3]

Compared to the NOP, all other Yugoslav factions suffered under one or another self-imposed limitation, usually resulting from their narrow ethnic and/or ideological agendas. Although it might appear otherwise at the first glance, the Chetnik movement had a rather consistent policy throughout the war. After a brief period of co-habitation with the NOP during the first months of the uprising, Mihailović's organization had turned into its implacable enemy by the late 1941. From then on, the Chetniks pursued the "Partisans first" policy, whose aim was to remove the Communists from Yugoslavia's political landscape before the final battle for the liberation of the country could start. This was to be achieved through temporary collaboration with practically every other anti-communist faction, foreign and domestic, including the fiercely anti-Serb Ustashe. The arrangement brought some short-term advantages, especially in 1942 in the Italian occupation zone, but had disastrous consequences in the long run. Despite the attempts to downplay the significance of the dealings with the Axis, the specter of collaboration became impossible to remove. This, combined with Mihailović's reluctance to engage the common enemy more actively, ultimately contributed to the decision made by the Western Allies to drop him in favor of Tito.

In any case, the JVuO was hopelessly unprepared to wage a serious war. Although nominally committed to the Yugoslav idea, the Chetnik movement was in reality almost exclusively Serbian, which drastically reduced the pool of potential recruits and made large parts of the country off-limits. Owing to the lack of authority and forcefulness on the part of its commanding general, it never evolved past the conglomerate of local militias that fought their own small wars against local Partisan groups. On the few occasions when the Chetniks actually managed to put together a larger field force (e.g. at Neretva and Eastern Bosnia in 1943, Western and Southern Serbia in 1944), its performance was decisively impacted by the lack of experience in more

3 NARA/RG226/M1642/R84, Robert McDowell, Report on mission to Yugoslavia, pp. 17-19 (23.11.1944); Biber (ed.), *Strogo*, pp. 314 (Foreign Office to Bari, 16.9.1944.), 327 (Churchill to Eden, 30.9.1944); NARA/T311/193/568, OBSO, Telephone conversations (14.9.1944).

complex operations. On tactical level, the royalists proved themselves as capable scouts and, occasionally, as light infantry, but usually required direct Axis support.

The NDH had not only pushed its Serb minority "into the woods" by its policies of ethnic exclusivity, but also bereaved itself of the service of many Croats and Muslims who sought an alternative to the Ustasha-induced chaos. The armed forces of the puppet state remained a regular army of a rather traditional type; their huge potential for anti-guerrilla warfare remained largely untapped (the UV units in Lika represent a partial exception). What little operational freedom they had left–the bulk of combat formations was subordinated to German field commands–was sacrificed to the need to protect as much territory as possible. As a result, truly mobile formations in the mold of the NOVJ brigades and divisions, practically did not exist. Their closest equivalent, the PTS, remained tied down in northern parts of Croatia for the duration of the war.

This begs the question of overall battlefield performance of the "foreign" Axis armies. The Bulgarians had a large contingent in their occupation zone numbering seven to eight divisions. Thanks to the NOP's numerical and structural weakness in these parts–even in Southern Serbia it had but a couple of thousands of fighters until spring 1944–this was more than enough. Apart from the terror and material losses incurred on the population, classic search-and-destroy operations undertaken by the army most often yielded meager results. The police, which had no qualms about utilizing the Yugoslav anti-guerrilla experiences from the inter-war period, had more success with their *kontračete*. It should be noted, however, that such small, undercover units were of limited use in conditions of massive insurgency (remember *Gegenbanden* in Slovenia, or *Trupps* in the NDH).

The popular image of Rome's armed forces as Berlin's bungling sidekick holds true as far as the Yugoslav front is concerned. In theory, all material preconditions for a successful counterinsurgency were there: the *Regio Esercito* had the numbers and could draw on its own rich experience in colonial warfare. Unfortunately, the army's performance was decisively influenced by its other well-known characteristics, like low morale and poor professional standards of the officer corps. Consequently, the Italians were considered the least dangerous of all foreign Axis regular armies and were frequently beaten in the field. On the other hand, it was the Italians who first introduced dedicated, battalion-sized anti-guerrilla units to the theater and devised a new set of tactics for them. Luckily for the Partisans, the *Arditi* came too late to reverse the course of the insurgency.

The Germans, regardless of their branch of service, were considered by far the most dangerous opponent of the NOP. Until spring 1944, their reputation was largely based on the skill and doggedness they displayed in combat, as well as the utter ruthlessness with which they treated civilians and captured guerrillas alike. By contrast, their theoretical/operational approach to counterinsurgency was far from perfect. Having little experience in guerrilla warfare, the Wehrmacht initially applied the same methods used when dealing with a regular opponent. In short, particularly dangerous guerrilla concentrations–including, nearly always, the one around the SHQ–were to be encircled and destroyed in one massive, decisive battle. Although this tactic had repeatedly failed to deliver results, the Germans stuck to it, as it was practically the only way to counter the superior mobility of the enemy. The other way, the one involving the use of "free hunt"/*Arditi* tactics, required specialist mountain troops, and these were always in short supply. Nevertheless, by the beginning of 1945, the Germans had achieved tactical superiority over their opponent. On the one side, their veteran units (such as the "Prinz Eugen" or 1st JgRR) had by now become well-versed in small-unit tactics, which their opponent chose to neglect in the course of the regularization efforts. The transition to frontal warfare that was taking place at that time also favored the Germans with their incomparably better training and vast experience accumulated on other fronts. In the end, this double supremacy was the key reason for the length and cost of the final Yugoslav campaign of the war.

The effectiveness of Second World War resistance/guerrilla movements can be measured by several factors. The most important one revolves around the question of resources the Axis had to divert from the main fronts in order to conduct COIN campaigns. In this respect, the Yugoslav insurgency stands at the top of the European list. Yugoslavia is often compared with Belarus, the home of the largest and most active branch of the Soviet Partisan movement. The most ambitious Axis operation there, codenamed "Cottbus", which took place at roughly the same time as the "Schwarz", involved a mere 16,000 soldiers. The number of German KIA inflicted by the guerrillas in this Soviet republic from 1941 to 1944 is estimated at ca. 7,000. Hitler's original plan to hold the Yugoslav heartlands with two to four low-quality divisions failed dramatically already in 1941. Historiography of the Socialist era often spoke of 15-20 German divisions tied down in Yugoslavia. In fact, such high troop concentrations were achieved on only several occasions, after the fall of Italy and during the withdrawal of the HGE from Greece. Active campaigning in the interior tied down, on average, "only" five to six divisions. The need to secure the Adriatic coast from a possible landing by the Western Allies required the presence of at least as many divisions, regardless of whether the guerrilla menace existed or not. The absence of large-scale Allied activity, however, ultimately enabled these formations as well to take part in anti-Partisan operations with most of their effectives.

Early chroniclers of "People's Liberation War" also liked to point out that the size of the Wehrmacht's contingent in Yugoslavia was often bigger than the ones in Italy and North Africa. This may have been occasionally true on a strict man-for-man basis, but the claim is misleading since Rommel's and von Kesselring's armies contained a much greater proportion of first-class units (Panzer, motorized, and parachute divisions) than von Weichs' or Löhr's. Maintaining such a force in the field required far more resources than were needed for an "ordinary" security/COIN contingent. Had the circumstances allowed it, the HGF/HGE would have probably been able to supply, at any given moment, at least four divisions whose equipment, training, and morale made them suitable for service on one of the main fronts. Otherwise, the Germans did a fairly good job of holding the Balkans largely with second-class and legionnaire formations. Naturally, it can be argued that even these units would have been much more useful guarding the railways and securing the rear of the main fronts. The truth was, the Germans were having tremendous difficulties in feeding the Moloch-like *Ostfront,* and no source, regardless of how small, was left untapped. According to one survey from early December 1943, there were altogether 20,000 trained recruits spread across occupied Europe. A full 10 percent of them were stationed in the NDH, but not a single one of them could be transferred east, as they were already "fully engaged". Moreover, the Balkans contingent had to be continuously replenished and resupplied. In addition to the human losses discussed earlier, the material losses were also palpable, and frankly, the Germans could do without them. For example, from 1 December 1943 to 30 November 1944, the OBSO recorded the loss of 1,976 passenger cars and 3,890 lorries, and hundreds of other motor vehicles (again, a good part of them were lost to air attacks and to the Red Army, but the Partisans certainly claimed a fair share). This brings us to the fact that the physical size of an occupation contingent alone cannot serve as the basis for determining the influence of a guerrilla/resistance movement. The case in point here is Denmark, where the Germans had about 300,000 men at the beginning of May 1945 (admittedly, many of them sought refuge here from the main fronts in the last weeks of the war). As far as Berlin was concerned, however, the occupation of this country represented a one-time investment: owing to the absence of armed clashes, the troops there required neither extra ammunition nor replacements.[4]

The NOP-led insurgency also crossed the Axis plans for the exploitation of strategic raw materials. Of the four ores the Germans were especially interested in, only the Macedonian chrome could be exported in sufficient quantities; this was, without a doubt, made possible by the weak guerrilla presence in this part of the country. The production aims at the Bor mines were not reached, but the reason for this lay in a combination of several factors. The direct contribution of the Serbian Partisans remained limited to the cutting of coal supply in November 1943, which caused a temporary stop in the refinement of the copper ore. The best results were achieved on the territory of the NDH, where the production of coal in Bosanska Krajina and bauxite in Herzegovina were greatly hampered by the repeated attacks on productions sites and means of transportation. Indeed, the Germans were compelled to import coal in an attempt to stave off the economic collapse of the Croatian puppet state, which always stood menacingly close. In the end, the problems with exploitation of the Yugoslav ores did not lead to major disruptions in war production owing to introduction of economy measures and finding of new sources. This was not for want of effort on the guerrillas' part, as amply shown in the sabotage statistics attached to each chapter. If anything, further research is needed on the fascinating, yet totally neglected, topic of the German rail repair and damage control techniques in the Balkans.

The final verdict: In terms of numbers and armed activity, the Yugoslav Partisans represented the most important independent resistance movement in Europe. Thanks to the combination of enormous self-sacrifice, remarkable resourcefulness, and favorable outside conditions, they went from being a small conspirator-like group to a full-fledged junior member of the United Nations. Through active campaigning, they transformed a sleepy backwater into a small theater of war, forcing the Axis to maintain a disproportionately large troop presence there, with everything that went with it. Would the Allies have won the war without the Partisans? They certainly would. The insurgency, however, should not be viewed as a separate event, but as a part of the gigantic, world-wide effort aimed at crushing Hitler's dystopia. In this scheme of things, the small Yugoslav cog accomplished more than anyone could have hoped for.

4 Kladarin, *Slom*, p. 271; NARA/T77/1421, [both OKW], Memorandum (2.12.1943), and [Balkans deployed divisions] (31.3.1944); NARA/T78/145/6075885, OKH/Motor, Unarmored vehicles (5.1.1945);

Appendix I

The Human Cost

According to public statements made by Tito and other high functionaries already in 1945, the total human losses suffered by Yugoslavia amounted to ca. 1,700,000, which was more than 10 percent of the prewar population (estimated at close to 16 million). The figure was corroborated by Yugoslav experts, conveniently just in time to be used on the Paris Peace Conference as the basis for reparation claims. During the next 40 or so years, it had the validity of a dogma and "social law" for domestic historians. Then, in the latter half of the 1980s, two studies were published that refuted the official figure. Their respective authors, Bogoljub Kočović and Vladimir Žerjavić–the former being a Serb living in France, the latter being a Croat living in Zagreb–used similar methods and reached almost identical results: according to them, the actual number of war deaths was 1,014,000-1,027,000. Even with this huge reduction, the figure is staggering; it represented ca. 6,5 percent of the prewar population and placed Yugoslavia at the very top of the world list, right after the USSR, Poland, and Greece. The bulk of the losses were civilian ones: people died from all the usual war-related causes, such as aerial bombardment, disease, and hunger, but most of them were victims of premeditated actions, of reprisals, wanton killings, and death camps. As in the remainder of Europe, two groups suffered particularly heavy under the Nazi-collaborationist rule: roughly 80 percent of Yugoslavia's Jews, and a similar, if not higher percent of Gypsies within the borders of the NDH, perished during the war. The *Volksdeutsche* also paid a heavy price for their real or perceived role in Hitler's war effort. While hundreds of thousands escaped to the west in late 1944, those who stayed behind–mostly the elderly, and other non-combatants–were declared enemies of the state and suffered heavily at the hands of the victors.[1]

According to the same official statistics, the Partisans suffered a total of ca. 305,000 KIA. Although the relevant document presented by the Yugoslav reparations commission contains a very precise yearly breakdown, its source is unknown. In fact, the number of military deaths was vastly exaggerated. The internal surveys made in 1950 and 1964 yielded much lower figures. According to the latter–whose findings were published only in 1992–the number of those who died as "Members of the [NOVJ] and Allied Armies" amounted to ca. 183,000. The Military Archives in Belgrade still hold "between 170 and 200,000" personal files of deceased Partisans. Taking into consideration the shortcomings of the survey (it was discontinued when it became

1 Tomasevich, *Occupation*, pp. 606-10, 722-24, 729-39.

evident that the 1,700,000-mark could not be even approximated), Žerjavić added ca. 30 percent and arrived to the figure of 237,000, which is probably closest to the truth. For comparison: the number of military deaths suffered by France was 217,600, the UK lost 383,600, and the United States over 416,800.[2]

The shortcomings of the Yugoslav 1964-survey is best seen on the example of Slovenia. According to this document, 17,000 Slovenes died as members of the NOP's various armed formations; in fact, recent research reveals that the real figure lies closer to 28,000. To add to the confusion, it is not always clear whether the numbers in various overviews refer only to fighters in combat units, or do they include other categories of "Participants in People's Liberation War/Struggle". For instance, the above-mentioned recent Slovene research contains two more categories, "Associate of the Partisan Movement" and "OF Activist", with additional 4,900 victims. The 1950-survey, carried out by the federal veterans' association, differentiates between "Fighters and Leaders in Units", "Active Participants in the Rear", and the vaguely-defined "Others"; the latter is, however, grouped with the former two, rather than with NOP's civilian associates, implying the victims had to do something with the military. Although the 1964-survey nominally speaks only of members of combat units, over 70,000 killed could not be associated with any of the divisions and brigades. As the figure is too large to refer to members of independent detachments or village guards, it clearly must include people from some of the said categories. According to Žerjavić, 58 percent of all fallen fighters came from Croatia and Bosnia-Herzegovina, which is not surprising considering the fact that these lands were the hotbed of the insurgency. Nearly a full quarter came from Serbia proper, primarily as the result of the general mobilization from late 1944 and early 1945.[3]

The Communists had won, but at what cost: according to official estimates, over 50,000 KPJ and 100,000 SKOJ members lost their lives in the conflict. The tally included a truly staggering 75 percent of the pre-war Party membership. This book contains numerous examples of high NOVJ officers and NOP leaders who were killed in the line of duty–among else, eight out of 32 members of the CK KPJ–but it should be mentioned that not even the very highest echelons of the movement were spared. Ranković's wife and Đilas' brother were killed by the Chetniks; Kardelj's younger brother perished during one of the Italian offensives in 1942; Tempo famously refused to intervene for his sibling, a priest who was captured with Đurišić's men in Slovenia and who ultimately shared their fate. Occupation and quisling authorities considered family members of the NOP members fair game, regardless of whether they shared political agenda or not. Tito's common-law wife, the wives of Ivan Krajčić-Stevo (the OZNA's first man in Croatia) and Vladmir Dedijer, Ranković's mother and nephew, and the closest relatives of Vladimir Velebit (the NOP's premier diplomat), to name just a few, went through the ordeal of captivity,

2 Estimates of losses can vary greatly; these figures come from the official website of the US National World War Two Museum: https://www.nationalww2museum.org/students-teachers/student-resources/research-starters/research-starters-worldwide-deaths-world-war (last accessed: 2.8.2020).

3 Dragan Ž. Cvetković, "Gubici pripadnika partizanskog pokreta sa teritorije Jugoslavije 1941-1945" (PhD thesis, University of Belgrade, 2016), pp. 3-5, 10; Vladimir Žerjavić, *Opsesije i megalomanije oko Jasenovca i Bleiburga. Gubici stanovništva Jugoslavije u drugom svjetskom ratu* (Zagreb: Globus, 1992), pp. 214-15; *The Verification of Death-toll of World War II and Its Aftermath in Municipal Registry Offices in Slovenia* (Ljubljana: INZ, 2009), pp. 20-21; Mate Rupić, "Ljudski gubici u Hrvatskoj u Drugom svjetskom ratu prema popisu iz 1950. godine", *ČSP*, 33:1 (2001), pp. 7-9, 12; *Žrtve rata 1941-1945. Rezultati popisa* (Belgrade: Savezni zavod za statistiku, 1966), p. 20.

but could ultimately be exchanged; untold number of others was less fortunate. Even without their revolutionary credo that emphasized toughness, the personal experiences made during the war would have left the Yugoslav Communists thoroughly brutalized and well-prepared for the final bloody showdown with their foes.[4]

Record keeping in conditions of guerrilla warfare is a nightmarish job marked by shortages of paper and writing utensils, lack of safe storage, constant movement, ambushes and encirclements, and frequent and unregulated fluctuation of personnel. One should therefore take Yugoslav casualty returns with reserve and be prepared for revisions, usually upwards. For example, initial reports by the units that fought at Belgrade routinely put the losses two to four times lower than they actually were. According to figures contained in their operational documents, the number of KIA suffered by the field armies in 1945 was as follows: the 1st YA–7,433; the 2nd YA–4,477; the 3rd YA–4,705; the 4th YA–2,323 (there were also 61,672 WIA, and at least 4,849 MIA). The sum (18,938 KIA) equals only 40 percent of the yearly total as presented by the 1964-census (47,749). Since it is highly unlikely that the remaining, smaller part of the NOVJ/Yugoslav Army (which included KNOJ and garrison troops, as well as the guerrilla-type formations belonging to provincial commands) bore the brunt of the losses, it is safe to assume that the above-cited figures represent just a fraction of the tally. Otherwise, all sources agree the final 17 months of the war were the bloodiest on record. Whereas there were 7,151 KIA recorded in 1941, 18,627 in 1942, 45,260 in 1943, the grim total for 1944 is 57,988. The figures reflect the steadily increasing involvement of the Wehrmacht, as well as the growth and transformation of the NOVJ into a regular field force. During the late period, even victories were dearly bought: the Partisans lost 956 KIA at Knin (the near-contemporary after-action report spoke of "only" 629 KIA), 515 KIA at Mostar, and a further 637 at Sarajevo. The death toll on the Syrmian Front is still hotly debated (admittedly, more on internet forums than in academic community). According to official data, 13,000 Partisans were killed from late October 1944 to mid-April 1945 in Syrmia (along with 1,100 Soviet and 630 Bulgarian soldiers). Đilas estimates that the NOVJ's path from Belgrade to Zagreb was strewn with ca. 30,000 KIA, while another senior functionary puts the figure at 36,000.[5]

The question of German losses is every bit as problematic as the one concerning the Yugoslavs. Schmider estimates the losses incurred during the "guerrilla phase" of the war (until August 1944) at 10,300 KIA and 3,800 MIA. It should be noted that these figures include Albania, which stood under the auspices of the PzAOK 2, but do not include Slovenia. The losses are denoted as "German", but most probably refer only to the Wehrmacht and those units of other services which were directly subordinated to the army at any given time. This means that the casualties of various local militia, police, or paramilitary formations (e.g., the OT, NSKK) are largely left out from the tally. Judging by the few fragmentary clues available, these were

4 *Povijest Saveza komunista Jugoslavije* (Belgrade: Rad, 1985), pp. 305, 308; Djilas, *Wartime*, pp. 78, 179, 358-59; Tempo, *Revolucija*, Vol. III, pp. 305-06; Trifković, *Parleying*, pp. 124, 175-76, 269; *DCO*/XIX/93, PK Serbia to CK KPJ (8.8.1944); Vladimir Dedijer, *Novi prilozi za biografiju Josipa Broza Tita* (Zagreb: Mladost, 1980), Vol. I [photo caption between pp. 96-97].

5 *Žrtve*, pp. 52-53. For the losses in the above-named individual operations see the following articles by Trifković: "Amateurs", pp. 273-74; "Trieste", p. 10; "Victories", pp. 107, 110; "Carnage", pp. 113-14; see also Anka Petrović's essays on the losses of individual Yugoslav armies in *Završne*, pp. 209-17, 269-75, 323-28, and 463-66.

considerable. A few examples: the *Volksdeutsche* formations in the NDH had altogether 205 KIA during 1942 (Schmider's estimate for the period May 1941-December 1942 speaks of 750 KIA in the entire German-occupied part of Yugoslavia minus Slovenia); Kammerhofer's police lost 517 KIA and 647 MIA in the period April 1943-January 1944 alone.[6]

Things were becoming ever more confusing as the war progressed. The usefulness of the official casualty returns for the period of the heaviest fighting (September-November 1944) is severely diminished by their many shortcomings and inconsistencies. To be sure, these were partly caused by objective reasons: the composition of field commands was changing constantly, some divisions were divided between two or even more sectors (e.g. the 297th ID), and the others lost their archives on the battlefield (e.g. 117th JD). However, plain sloppiness and red tape were definitely also at play. The main survey for the first eleven months of 1944–submitted on 5 January 1945–puts OBSO's losses in October and November at about 30,000. This figure, however, does not include Felber's AAS, which bore the lion's share of the cost in the fighting against the Soviets. The German staff officers who spoke of 50,000 men lost during this period were therefore probably closer to the truth. Returns for individual divisions are often at odds with reports presented by units themselves. For example, the casualties of the 369th ID for October are put at 418 despite the fact that the division's CO computed them at precisely 2,222 in his report from mid-November (the vast majority were incurred at Trebinje and Vukov Klanac). Likewise, the losses of the "Prinz Eugen" for the same month are put at 218. This is nothing short of preposterous given that the division was halved during the battles around Zaječar, Niš, and other towns in Serbia; according to its biographer and former CO, the losses amounted to 7,710. Even contemporary reports from the field dealing with same event sometimes contain major contradictions. For instance, according to one source, the losses of the KG "Allermann" during the breakthrough from Šibenik were 494 men and one cannon, according to the other 764 men and 19 cannon plus five AA guns (Note: Yugoslav sources tend to corroborate higher figures, although official historiography nearly always spoke of ca. 1,400 enemy casualties, which is a gross exaggeration). Sadly, we have very little data on December 1944, the month marked by the Battle of Knin and major Allied offensives in Syrmia. We do know that the 264th ID alone lost at least 4,468 soldiers at Knin, but the precise losses of the 373rd and 392nd ID, as well as the *Kriegsmarine*, are not known. Judging by the quantity of small arms captured by the NOVJ, one can safely add at least several thousand men to the tally. With regards to Syrmia, the intensity of the fighting there is captured by Kübler's statement that his "human and material losses are very high", and the fact that one of his regiment-sized battle groups lost 300 men on 6-7 December alone.[7]

The data for 1945 is fragmentary to say the least. The chief chronicler of the armed forces puts the German losses for the "Wintergewitter" at 188 KIA and 1,047 WIA. Friebe's near-disastrous

6 Schmider, *Partisanenkrieg*, p. 589; TsAMO/500/12451/616/160, GEGC/Leader, Casualty list (1.1.1943); NARA/T314/1548/177, HSSPF Croatia, Activity report (January 1944).

7 NARA/T311/195/99, [all OBSO] (Telephone conversations, 7.12.1944), 264-69, 1025 (Casualty returns, 5.1.1945); NARA/T311/184, Georg Reinicke to Friedrich-Wilhelm Krüger (17.11.1944); NARA/T315/1300/903, KG Lindenblatt, Diary (7.12.1944); NARA/T1022/2551, KM Admiral Adria, Diary (12, 14.11.1944); TNA/DEFE3/308/HP7070, Cables from 264th ID and KM Admiral Adria (12.11.1944); Kumm, *Vorwärts*, p. 312; Anić, *Osmi*, p. 155; Rako and Družijanić, *Jedanaesta*, pp. 221-22. See also the following articles from Trifković: "Trieste", pp. 6, 9-10, "Anabasis", pp. 614-15, "Katastrofa", pp. 564-65.

march through the Drina Valley cost his command 346 KIA, 862 WIA and 22 MIA (for comparison, the breakthrough from Macedonia and Kosovo was paid with 523 men in the first, 1,282 in the second, and 364 in the third category). Sadly, no similar figures exist for the February campaign in Herzegovina, but we do have the casualty returns of individual divisions for March, courtesy of the ULTRA program. The figures provided therein for the 104th JD and 373rd ID–1,300 and 2,900, respectively–reflect the bitterness of the battles on the Drava, in Lika and around Bihać. However, the data on some other formations was either incomplete to begin with or became garbled during transmission/decryption. The losses of the 1st CCD are thus put at 65 killed and wounded. We know from other sources that the division did, in fact, get off lightly during the fighting on the Valpovo Bridgehead, but this estimate seems excessively low. The KIA figure for the 11th LWFD (214) provided in the same decrypt is confirmed in the post-war statement by the division's CO, but the number of wounded (102) is nowhere near the real number (500 to 800, depending on the source). Likewise, the 369th ID was reported having "only" 97 KIA and 317 WIA (along with 193 MIA) during the four weeks of near-constant fighting and artillery bombardment on the Ivan. According to the division's chronicler, the total was about 1,000 men; according to its head doctor, there were 650 KIA and 750 WIA. There are no reliable sources for the final month of the war, which is hardly surprising given the chaos that reigned both at the front and in the corridors of military bureaucracy. The ten-day returns, which were still being issued by the chief medical officer of the army, are evidently flawed and must be taken with reserve. The combined losses for the first three weeks of April are thus calculated at 501 KIA, 2,121 WIA, 2,130 MIA. As a reminder: the period in question saw the breakthrough at Syrmia and first clashes in Slavonia, the evacuation of Bosnia, the debacle in Lika, and the running battle between Bihać and Karlovac (the losses incurred during the first phase of the Battle for Rijeka would not be added to the sum, since the LXXXXVII AC was at that time still subordinated to von Kesselring).[8]

According to the last known official tally, the losses suffered in Southeastern Europe since 22 June 1941 amounted to 20,777 KIA, 65,219 WIA, 23,976 MIA, for a total of 109,972. These figures cover the occupation of Greece and Albania, fighting against the British in the Aegean, losses incurred in air strikes and naval duels, etc, and are therefore of limited use to us. The data from *Volksbund Deutsche Kriegsgräberfürsorge*, the central organization charged by the German government with maintaining the war graves abroad, paint a different picture. According to the *Volksbund*, some 58,600 soldiers are buried on the territory of the former Yugoslavia: ca. 6,300 in Slovenia, 20,100 in Croatia, 15,400 in Serbia, 2,000 in Montenegro, 1,800 in Macedonia; the bulk of the remainder is most likely to be found in Bosnia-Herzegovina, and, to a much lesser extent, Kosovo (for comparison: ca. 15,000 are buried in Greece, at least 2,400 in Albania). This number also includes deaths in captivity and of disease, accidents, and other non-combat

8 NARA/T77/1426/497, OKW, Diary (23.1.1945); von Metzsch, *Geschichte*, p. 82; TNA/DEFE3/568/KO896, OBSO, Casualty return (March 1945); VAB/GC/72/1/3/15, Gerhard Henke, and VAB/GC/72/1/4/4, Hans Bauernstädter (both 11th LWFD, both undated); VAB/GC/71/1/43/2, Meinicke-Kleint/LXXXI AC (13.7.1947); Schraml, *Kriegsschauplatz*, p. 130; NARA/T78/414/6383189, 6383195, 6383211, OKH/Med., ten-day returns (24, 14, and 5.4.1945, respectively).

reasons, but gives a good idea of the price the Third Reich had to pay for its involvement in the "Balkan quagmire" (Schmider).[9]

The losses of other Axis nations and collaborationist forces are in dire need of further research. An estimated 10,631 Italians fell and 5,470 went missing from May 1941 to the first week of September 1943; of these, 7,782 KIA and 4,470 MIA were members of the 2nd ITA, and the remaining 2,849 KIA and ca. 1,000 MIA belonged to the occupation corps in Montenegro. Žerjavić computed the overall losses of collaborationist forces on the pre-war Yugoslav territory at 209,000: 10,000 in Slovenia (the *Domobranci*, MVAC, etc.), 52,000 in Croatia (vast majority were the Ustashe and Home Guards), 70,000 in Bosnia-Herzegovina (the Ustashe and Home Guards, but also Chetniks, and members of Muslim militias), 33,000 in Serbia proper (the SFK, SSW, JVuO, and a part of RSK), 27,000 in Vojvodina (the *Volksdeutsche*), 9,000 in Kosovo (Albanian militiamen), 7,000 in Montenegro (the Chetniks, separatists, Muslim militiamen), 1,000 in Macedonia (members of the VMRO). Only in the rarest of cases do we have a precise breakdown of losses such as the one prepared by survivors of the RSK: according to them, between 1941 and 1945 this formation had 1,132 dead and deceased, 3,280 sick and wounded, 2,297 missing, and 1,057 deserters. Data on other formations is much more fragmented and difficult to come by. For example, the Germans computed the losses among their auxiliaries in Serbia from 15 March to 15 August 1944 as follows (KIA/WIA/MIA): the SFK–140/312/89; the SSW–160/120/28; the JVuO–1,749/2,089/120 (Note: the losses were incurred exclusively in the fighting against the NOVJ). An overiew of the "Croat losses" in the first five months of 1942 (not certain if it refers to the HDB alone, or the UV as well) lists 709 KIA, 874 WIA, 707 MIA. Premier Ustasha formations also suffered heavily. According to one survey prepared on 18 December 1944, the "Black Legion" and its main successor, the 1st UAB, had lost 507 men to all causes since its creation in September 1941 (Note: the survey does not include soldiers of Islamic faith, who were very numerous, at least in the early days of the legion). A similar document exists for Pavelić's bodyguard formations, which lost at least 1,090 soldiers of all faiths until April 1945.[10]

9 NARA/T78/414/6383191, OKH/Med., ten-day return (24.4.1945); for *Volksbund* figures, search for individual regions (keyword: "Landesinformation") in: https://kriegsgraeberstaetten.volksbund.de/friedhof (last accessed: 26.7.2020).

10 Schmider, *Partisanenkrieg*, p. 590; Žerjavić, *Opsesije*, p. 214; Samtsevich, *Марш*, p. 233; NARA/T311/195/968, OBSO, Losses of Serbian units (15.3-15.8.1944); NARA/T501/267/563, DGA, Note (2.6.1942). The Ustasha surveys can be found in HR HDA, fond 205, box 1 (PDF version prepared by members of "Dr. Rudolf Horvat" association). I have not been able to find reliable figures on the Bulgarian and Hungarian losses.

Appendix II

Foreign Weapons Deliveries to the NOP

From mid-1943 to spring 1945, the Yugoslav Partisans received the following quantities of military hardware from their allies in the East and West:

Item	Anglo-American Aid	Soviet Aid
Rifles	137,092	96,515
MGs	15,837	68,423
Automatic Rifles	41,443	-
AT Rifles	1,256	3,797
Pistols	1,626	20,528
AA MGs	132	512
Mortars	2,684	3,364
Field Cannon	388	895
Tanks	107	65
Airplanes	61	421

Table 1: Foreign Weapons Deliveries 1943-45 (Source: Vlado Strugar, *Jugoslavija 1941-1945*, Ljubljana: Partizanska knjiga, 1978, p. 210).

Appendix III

Tables of Organization

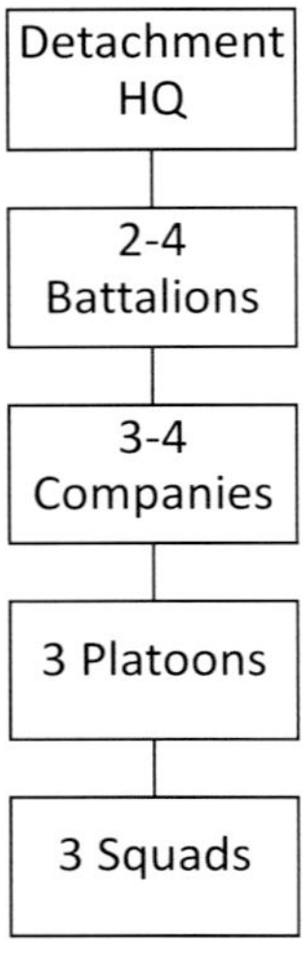

Figure 1: Organization of Partisan Detachment (according to Stolice Ragulations)

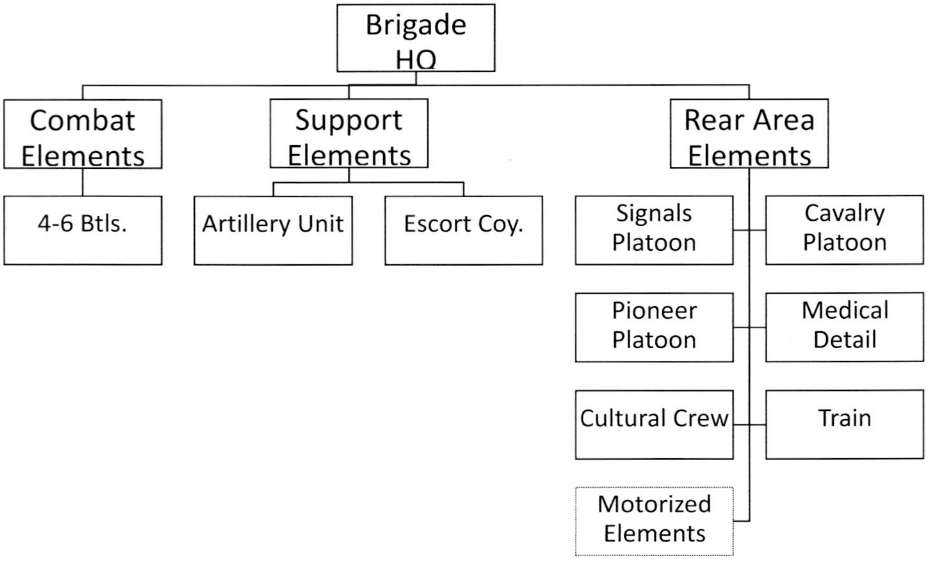

Figure 2: Organization of Proletarian/Assault Brigades (according to Statute of Proletarian Brigades)

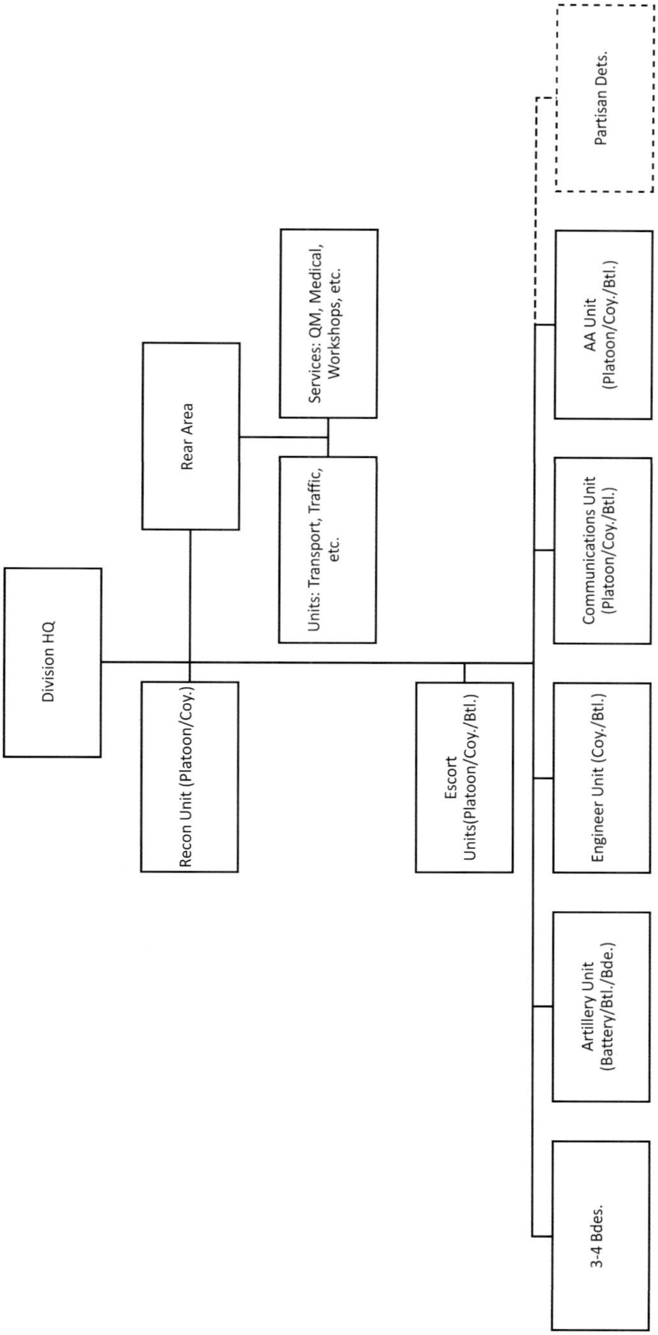

Figure 3: Organization of NOVJ Division

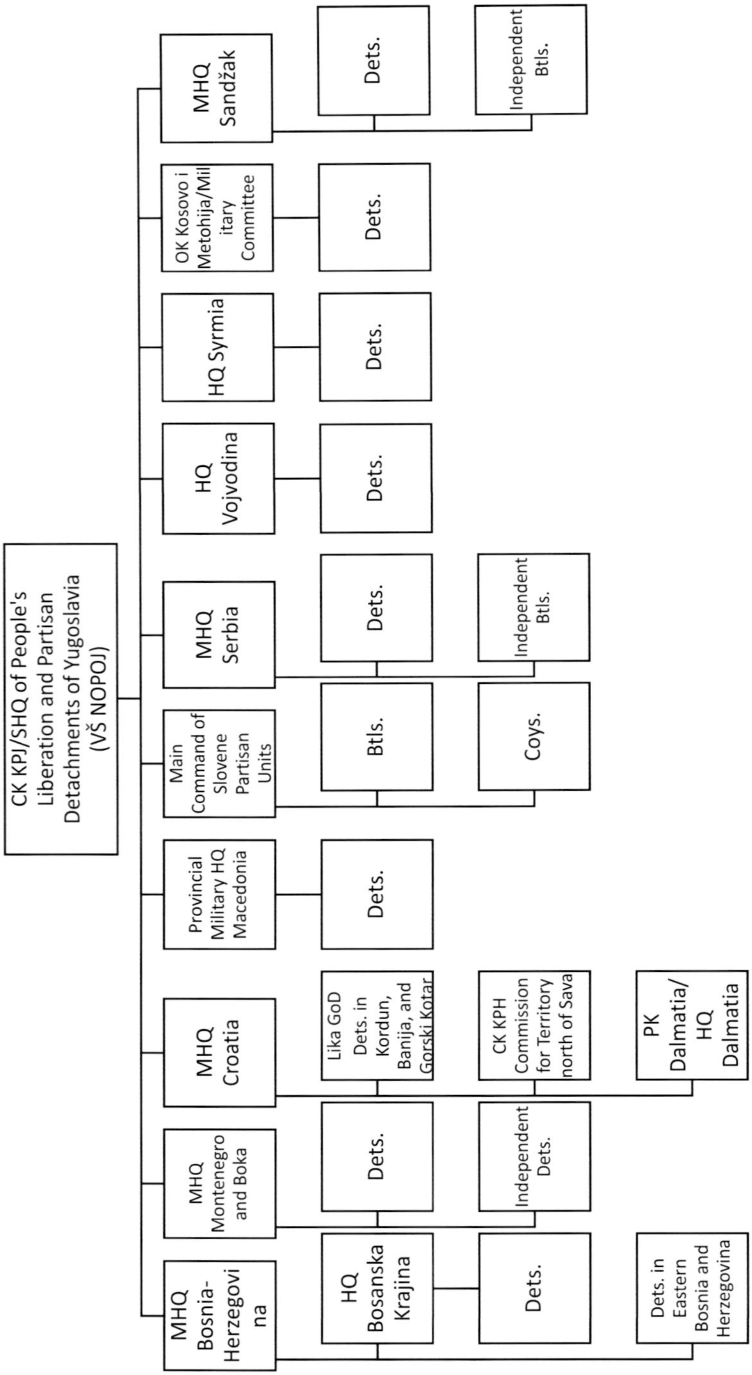

Figure 4: NOPOJ Command-and-Control Arrangements (late 1941)

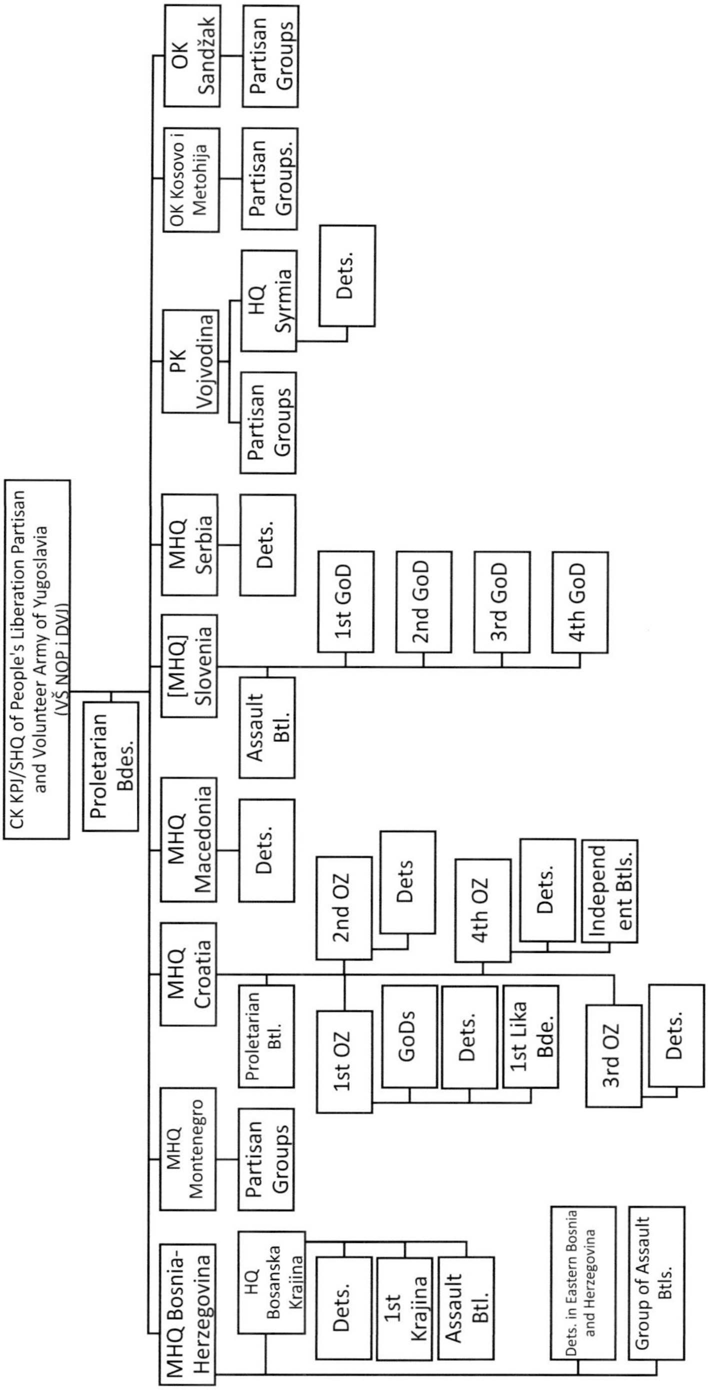

Figure 5: NOP i DVJ Command-and-Control Arrangements (July 1942)

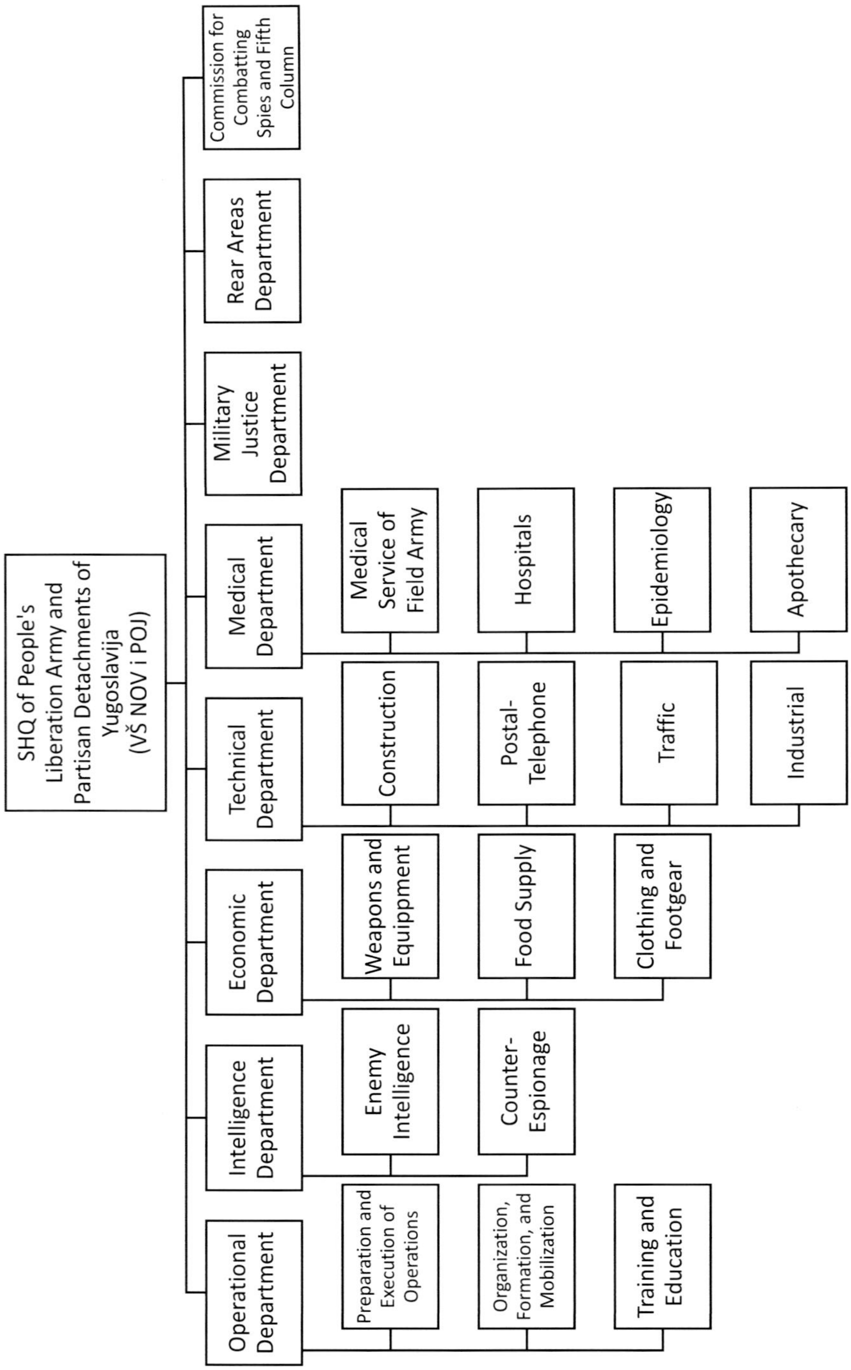

Figure 6: Organization of the SHQ (late 1942)

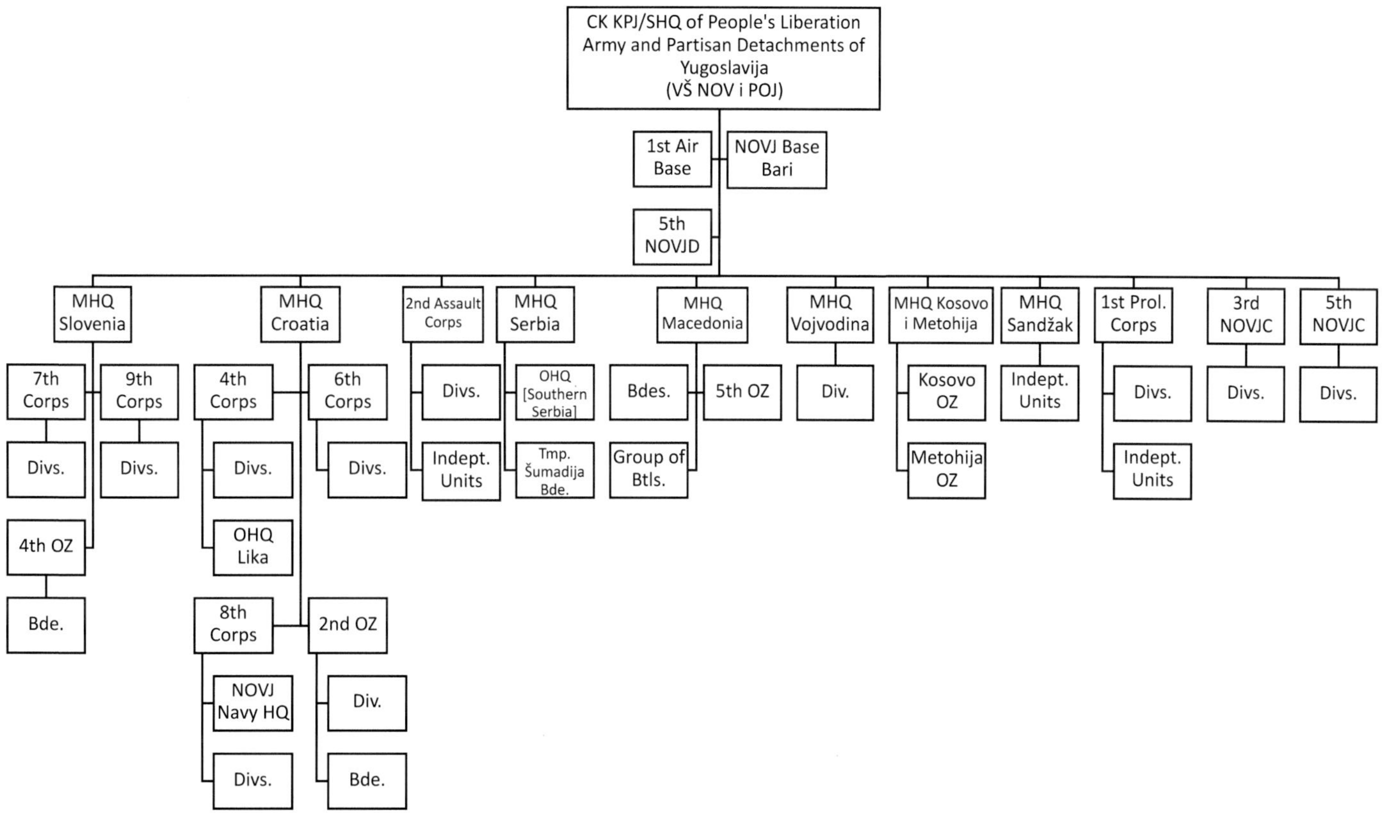

Figure 7: NOV i POJ Command-and-Control Arrangements (late 1943). Note: detachments and rear area commands not shown.

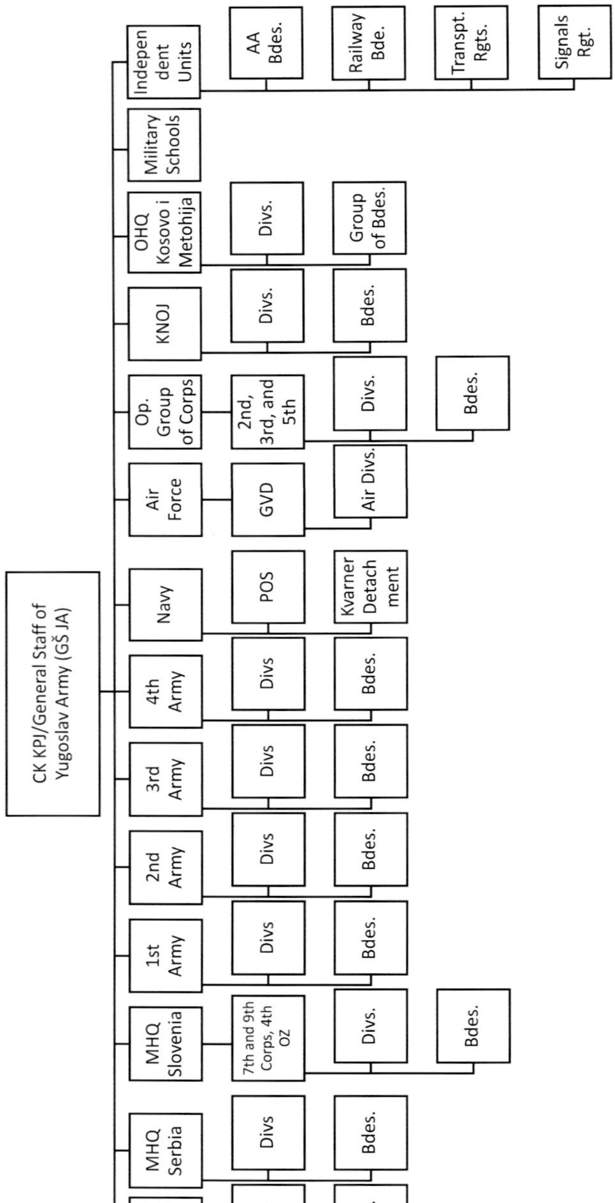

Figure 8: JA Command-and-Control Arrangements (March 1945). Note: detachments and rear area commands not shown.

Bibliography

Unpublished Primary Sources

Arhiv Republike Slovenije (Archives of Republic of Slovenia)
Gendarmerie station Safnitz, Report (28.3.1942).
Arhiv željezničkog muzeja Beograd (Archives of Railway Museum Belgrade)
Serbian State Railways: Materials and summaries 1941-44.
Bundesarchiv-Militärarchiv (German Federal Military Archives)
RH37/4835, 750th JR; RH10/211, Assault Division "Rhodos"; RW29/47, Mining Btl. "Southeast"; N756/182 and 182b Estate Vopersaal/21st SS MTD. BA-MA/RS3-21, 21st SS MTD.
Canadian Department of National Defence/Directorate of History and Heritage
Roll T-2422: LW/Chief of Staff.
Центральный архив Министерства обороны Российской Федерации (Central Archives of the Russian Ministry of Defence)
Red Army Units: [Fond/Opis/Delo (unit): 956/1/142 (64th RC); 956/1/313 (299th RD); 961/1/77 (93rd RD); 975/1/102 (3rd UF); 243/2900/216 (68th RC); 243/2900/791, 839, and 413/10372/400 and 511 (57th Army).
Captured German Documents [all Fond 500, followed by Opis/Delo (unit)]: 12450/183, 226, and 246 (Armed Forces High Command); 12451/616, 621 (German Ethnic Group in Croatia); 12451/457 and 518 (German Railway Units); 12460/43 (KK 847); 12477/679 (42nd JD); 12477/793 (264th ID); 12483/82 and 83 (369th Signals Btl.); 12483/105 (181st Recon Btl.);12483/158 (1025th Sec. Btl.).
Franklin D. Roosevelt Presidential Library and Museum
Safe Files: Box 4, OSS April 1944-45.
President's Secretary Files: Box 154.
Hrvatski državni arhiv (Croatian State Archives)
HR HDA 205 (Ustasha Militia), Box 1.
HR HDA 1689 (German Collection), Document No. 97: Statment of Alexander Löhr (1947).
Istorijski arhiv Beograd (Historical Archives of Belgrade)
Directorate of State Security for Serbia, Interrogation of Božidar Bećarević, (8.6.1949).
Российский государственный архив социально-политической истории (Russian State Archive of Socio-Political History)
Fond 664, Opis 1 and 2: State Defense Committee.

The National Archives of the UK (TNA)
  Military Missions: WO202/196 (Reports from Serbia).
  Ultra Decrypts (collection/folder): HW5/625; DEFE3/234, 242, 302, 308-09, 316, 319, 326, 330-31, 509, 512, 514-16, 565, 568-69, 672, 601, 683, 818, 822.
The US National Archives and Records Administration
  Record Group 242: Captured German Documents [designation (series): unit (roll)]
    Armed Forces High Command (T77): 775, 780, 787, 1421, 1423, 1426.
    Army High Command (T78): 145, 304-05, 331-32, 412, 414, 476, 530, 532.
    Ministry of Foreign Affairs (T120): Gruppe Inland II (5787).
    Reichsführer SS (T175): 20, 124, 126, 140-41, 233.
    Army Groups (T311): E (175, 183-86), F (188-89, 191-97, 285).
    Armies (T312): 12th (425, 460), 14th/von Zangen (1639-40).
    Panzer Armies (T313): 2nd (189-90, 482-87).
    Army Corps (T314): XV (554-55, 557-62, 565-66), XVIII (600), XXI (661-64), XXXIV (849-50), LXV HkDO (1531) LXIX (1544-48), LXXXXI (1630).
    Divisions (T315): 24th Panzer (806), 100th JD (1220), 104th JD (1242), 114th JD (1294-95), 117th JD (1300), 118th JD (1301-02), 181st ID (1544), 187th RD (1533), 369th ID (2154-55), 373st (2170-71), 704th ID (2236-37, 2239, 2241, 2243), 714th ID (2258), 717th ID (2262, 2264), 718th ID (2265-68, 2270-71), Brandenburg" (2281).
    Waffen-SS (T354): 2nd SS Panzer Corps (606).
    Rear Areas (T501): Commanding General in Serbia (245-50, 252, 256-58, 351-52), German General in Zagreb (264, 266-268).
    German Navy (T1022): Admiral Adriatic–Sea Commander North Dalmatia/Albania (2551), Marine Group South (2585), Admiral Adriatic (3956-57).
  Record Group 226 (Office of Strategic Services) [series/roll]
    M1642/84: "Ranger" Mission.
Vojni arhiv Beograd (Military Arhives Belgrade)
  NOVJ Collection [Unit: Box/Folder/Document]: MHQ_ Croatia: 110/7/13, 119-1/2/4, 119-4/2/2-5, 128a//1/31; NOVJ Navy HQ: 2023/2/4-1.
  German Collection/Prisoner Statements [Box/Folder/Document]: 71/1/6, 14, 21, and 43; 71/1/43; 71/2/3; 72/1/3/1 and 4; 72/2/1, 4, 17, and 18; 73/1/4.
Yad Vashem Archives
  Record Group 0.51 (Ludwigsburg, USSR Collection), File No. 176.3.: German Police in Serbia.

Published Primary Sources

Biber, Dušan (ed.), *Tito–Churchill: strogo tajno* (Zagreb: Globus, 1981).

Broucek, Peter (ed.), *Ein General im Zwielicht: Die Erinnerungen Edmund Glaises von Horstenau* (Vienna: Böhlau Verlag, 1988), Vol. III.

Dedijer, Vladimir, *Dnevnik* (Belgrade: Prosveta, 1969), Vols. I-II.

Dokumenta centralnih organa KPJ: NOR i revolucija (1941–1945) (Belgrade: "Komunist", 1986-87), Vols. XV-XIX, XXI.

Dokumenti ljudske revolucije u Sloveniji (Ljubljana: Inštitut za zgodovino delavskega gibanja/Arhiv Republike Slovenije, 1962-2005), Vols. I-III, V, VII-VIII, X.

Ferenc, Tone (ed.), *Fašisti brez krinke: dokumenti 1941-1942* (Maribor: Obzorja, 1987).
Građa za historiju Narodnooslobodilačkog pokreta u Slavoniji (Slavonski Brod: Historijski institut Slavonije, 1960-1984), Vols. IV-VII, X.
Josip Broz Tito: Sabrana dela (Belgrade: Komunist, 1981-89), Vols. VIII, XIV-XXVII.
Jovanović, Dobrivoje, and Dejan Tanić (eds.), *Izveštaji komande Srpske državne straže za Okrug moravski 1941-1944* (Jagodina: Istorijski arhiv Jagodina, 2001).
Коминтерн и вторая мировая война (Moscow: Памятники исторической мысли, 1998), Vol. II.
Matković, Blanka, and Ivan Pažanin (ed.), *Zločin i teror u Dalmaciji 1943.-1948. počinjeni od pripadnika NOV, JA, OZN-e i UDB-e: dokumenti* (Zagreb: n.p., 2011).
Narodnooslobodilačka borba u Dalmaciji 1941-1945: zbornik dokumenata (Split: Institut za historiju radničkog pokreta Dalmacije, 1981), Vols. I-III, V, IX-X.
Orović, Savo, *Ratni dnevnik 1941-1945* (Belgrade: Hronometar, 1972).
Partizanska i komunistička represija i zločini u Hrvatskoj 1944.-1946.–dokumenti (Slavonski Brod: Hrvatski institut za povijest, 2005).
Partizanska i komunistička represija i zločini u Hrvatskoj 1944.-1946.–dokumenti: Zagreb i središnja Hrvatska (Zagreb: Hrvatski institut za povijest, 2008).
Petranović, Branko, and Momčilo Zečević, (eds.), *Jugoslavija 1918.-1988: tematska zbirka dokumenata* (Belgrade: Rad, 1988).
Schramm, Ernst Percy (ed.), *Kriegstagebuch des Oberkommando der Wehrmacht 1940-1945* (Herrsching: Manfred Pawlak Verlag, 1982), Vols. I, IV/2.
Sjeverozapadna Hrvatska u narodnooslobodilačkoj borbi i revoluciji: građa 1941.-1945. (Zagreb: Savjet za izdavanje "Građe za povijest NOP-a i socijalističke revolucije u sjeverozapadnoj Hrvatskoj 1941-1945", 1981), Vols. I-X.
Talpo, Oddone, *Dalmazia: una cronaca per la storia (1943-1944)* (Rome: Ministry of Defense, 1995), Vol. III/3.
The Diary of Georgi Dimitrov, 1933-1949 (London: Yale University Press, 2003).
Zbornik dokumenata i podataka o narodnooslobodilačkom ratu naroda Jugoslavije (Belgrade: Vojnoistorijski institut, 1949-86): Volume I (Fighting in Serbia): books 1-21; Vol. II (Documents of Supreme HQ): books 1-15; Vol. III (Fighting in Montenegro): books 1-10; Vol. IV (Fighting in Bosnia-Herzegovina): books 1-35; Vol. V (Fighting in Croatia): books: books 1-39; Vol. VI (Fighting in Slovenia): books 1-2, 5-19; Vol. VII (Fighting in Macedonia): books 1-4; Vol. VIII (Fighting in the Adriatic): books 1-3; Vol. IX (Documents of KPJ bodies): books 1-9; Volume X (NOVJ Air Force): books 1-2; Vol. XI (Yugoslav armies): books 1-4; Vol. XII (Documents of German Reich): books 1-4; Vol. XIII (Documents of Kingdom of Italy): books 1-3; Vol. XIV (Documents of Chetnik movement): books 1-4; Vol. XV (Documents of Horthy's Hungary): book 1.

Monographs & Edited Volumes

"Borbe protiv okupatora, ustaša i četnika", in *Hercegovina u NOB* (Belgrade: Vojno delo, 1961), Vol. I, pp. 220-34.
Afrić, Vjeko "Sa Kazalištem narodnog oslobođenja u Bihaću", in *Bihaćka republika 4.XI 1942-29.I 1943* (Bihać: Muzej AVNOJ-a i Pounja, 1965), Vol. I, pp. 500-17.
Ambrožič, Lado-Novljan:

Cankarjeva brigada (Ljubljana: Partizanska knjiga, 1975).
Gubčeva brigada (Ljubljana: Borec, 1972).
Petnajsta divizija (Ljubljana: Borec, 1983).
Pohod Četrnaeste (Belgrade: Vojnoizdavački zavod, 1984).

Anić, Nikola:
Dvanaesta dalmatinska udarna brigada (Prva otočka) (Supetar: Domicil 12. dalmatinske NOU brigade, 1984).
"Neka operativno-strategijska razmatranja njemačke odbrane na jadranskom vojištu 1944/45. godine", in *Za pobjedu i slobodu. Jugoslovenska mornarica u završnim operacijama za oslobođenje Jugoslavije. Učesnici govore* (Belgrade: Vojnoizdavački i novinski centar, 1986), pp. 282-99.

Anić, Nikola, Sekula Joksimović, and Mirko Gutić, *Narodnooslobodilačka vojska Jugoslavije: pregled razvoja oružanih snaga Narodnooslobilačkog pokreta 1941.-1945.* (Belgrade: Vojnoistorijski institut, 1982).
Povijest Osmog. korpusa NOVH 1943.-1945. (Split: Udruga antifaštičkih boraca i antifašista grada Splita, 2004).

Antić, Vicko, "Dejstva Korpusa narodne odbrane Jugoslavije na razbijanju kontrarevolucionarnih snaga u poslednjoj godini rata", in *Za pobjedu i slobodu. Završne operacije za oslobođenje Jugoslavije: učesnici govore* (Belgrade: Vojnoizdavački i novinski centar, 1986), pp. 604-11.

Antonić, Zdravko, and Jeremija Perić, *Birač u Narodnooslobodilačkoj borbi* (Tuzla: Univerzal, 1982).

Antonijević, Nenad Miodrag, "Ratni zločini na Kosovu i Metohiji 1941-1945. godine" (PhD thesis, University of Belgrade, 2015).

Arnold, John H., *History: A Very Short Introduction* (Oxford: Oxford University Press, 2000).

Baić, Dušan:
"Oslobođenje Gacke doline", in *Osma kordunaška udarna divizija* (Karlovac: Historijski arhiv, 1977), pp. 373-86.
Četvrti korpus NOV Jugoslavije odnosno Prvi korpus NOV Hrvatske (Belgrade: Vojnoizdavački i novinski centar, 1990).

Balaš, Boris, "Ustanak na Žumberku i u Pokuplju", in *Žumberak-Gorjanci (1941-1945)* (Novo Mesto: Dolenjski muzej, 2005), pp. 303-22.

Banac, Ivo, *With Stalin against Tito: Cominformist Splits in Yugoslav Communism* (Ithaca, NY: Cornell University Press, 1988).

Barker, Elisabeth, *Britanska politika prema jugoistočnoj Evropi u drugom svjetskom ratu* (Zagreb: Globus, 1978).

Baškot, Boško, "Epopeja Kozare u udžbenicima i u enciklopediji Leksikografskog zavoda SFRJ", in Zdravko Antonić, Joco Marjanović (eds.), *Kozara u narodnooslobodilačkoj borbi i socijalističkoj revoluciji (1941-1945)* (Prijedor: Nacionalni park Kozara, 1980), pp. 487-94.

Batanović, Milovan-Batan, "Podrinjski partizanski odred", in *Ustanak naroda jugoslavije 1941.* (Belgrade: Vojno delo, 1964), Vol. I, pp. 171-212.

Batinica, Dušan, "Četvrta neprijateljska ofanziva i njen tok na području kotara Donji Lapac", in *Kotar Donji Lapac u Narodnooslobodilačkom ratu 1941—1945.* (Karlovac: Historijski arhiv, 1985), pp. 325-92.

Batinić, Jelena, *Women and Yugoslav Partisans: History of WW2 Resistance* (New York: Cambridge University Press, 2015).

Bay, Edna G., *Wives of the Leopard: Gender, Politics, and Culture in the Kingdom of Dahomey* (London: The University Press of Virginia, 1998).
Becherelli, Alberto, *Italia e Stato Indipendente Croato (1941-1943)* (Rome: Edizioni Nuova Cultura, 2012).
Beck, Alois, "Sarajevo—Slav. Brod—Donje Miholjac", in Alois Beck (ed.), *Bis Stalingrad...* (Ulm: Helmuth Abt Verlag, 1983), pp. 285-90.
Belinić, Marko, "O Drugoj operativnoj zoni Narodnooslobodilačke vojske i partizanskih odreda Hrvatske", in *Sjeverozapadna Hrvatska u narodnooslobodilačkoj borbi i socijalističkoj revoluciji: zbornik* (Varaždin: zajednica općina, 1976), pp. 120-36.
Biber, Dušan, "Iza kulisa desanta na Drvar", in *Za pobjedu i slobodu. Drvarska operacija: učesnici govore* (Belgrade: Vojnoizdavački i novinski centar, 1986), pp. 489-94.
Bistarelli, Agostino, *La Resistenza dei militari italiani all'estero. Jugoslavia centro settentrionale*, (Rome: Ministry of Defense, 1996).
Bitka na Sutjesci (n.p.: Yugoslav People's Army/Higher Military Academy, 1963).
Bjelica, Obrad, "Nemačka ofanziva na slobodnu teritoriju Zapadne Srbije", in *Užička republika* (Belgrade: NIRO Eksport-Pres, 1978), Vol. II, pp. 215-24.
Bodrožić, Milica, "Radnička klasa užičkog kraja u ratu i revoluciji 1941. godine", in *Užička republika* (Belgrade: NIRO Eksport-Pres, 1978), Vol. I, pp. 91-100.
Böhme, Karl W., *Die deutschen Kriegsgefangenen in Jugoslawien* (Munich: Verlag Ernst und Werner Gieseking, 1962), Vol. I/1.
Bojanić, Miloš, "Broj nastradalih civila u savezničkom bombardovanju Srbije 1943-44. godine: dostupni podaci, procene i analiza", in *Juhorsi zapis: tematski zbornik* (Kruševac: Istorijski arhiv, 2018), pp. 139-50.
Bojić, Milosav, *Posavski partizanski odred: Posavina u oružanom ustanku* (Belgrade: Vojnoizdavački i novinski centar, 1987).
Bokan, Branko J., *Prvi Krajiški NOP odred* (Belgrade: Vojnoizdavački i novinski centar, 1988).
Borković, Milan, *Kvislinška uprava u Srbiji 1941-1944* (Belgrade: Sloboda, 1979), Vol. I.
Boro Mitrovski, Venceslav Glišić, and Tomo Ristovski, *Bugarska vojska u Jugoslaviji 1941-1945.* (Belgrade: Međunarodna politika, 1971).
Borojević, Ljubomir, Dušan Samardžija, and Rade Bašić, *Peta kozaračka brigada* (Belgrade: Rad, 1973).
Bosiočić, Bogdan, *Dvadesetprva slavonska NOU brigada* (Belgrade: Vojnoizdavački zavod, 1981).
Bosiljčić, Slobodan, *Srbija u narodnooslobodilačkoj borbi: Istočna Srbija* (Belgrade: Nolit, 1963).
Bošnjak, Ljubomir:
Bošnjak, Ljubomir, *Diverzantska dejstva u Narodnooslobodilačkom ratu 1941-1945* (Belgrade: Vojnoistorijski institut, 1983).
"Diverzantske jedinice u vrijeme formiranja armija i njihova uloga u završnim operacijama", in *Za pobjedu i slobodu. Armije u strategijskoj koncepciji NOR i revolucije: učesnici govore* (Belgrade: Vojnoizdavački i novinski centar, 1986), pp. 464-70.
Božić, Nikola:
Sedma vojvođanska NOU brigada (Belgrade: Vojnoizdavački zavod, 1984).
Rovovi i mostobrani: Osma vojvođanska brigada (Novi Sad: Institut za savremenu istoriju, 1989).
Božović, Luka, "Narodna vlast u Foči u prvoj polovini 1942.", in *Istočna Bosna u NOB-u: sjećanja učesnika* (Belgrade: Vojnoizdavački zavod, 1971), Vol. I, pp. 544-55.

Bujak, Đorđe, "U bespuću je nikla nova radionica", in *Vojnotehnička radionica Vrhovnog štaba NOV i POJ u Grmeču* (Belgrade: Rad, 1979), pp. 327-54.
Bulat, Rade, *Deseti korpus 'Zagrebački' NOV i POJ* (Zagreb: Globus, 1985).
Bulgakov, Lev, "Череповскии поход", in Vertepov (ed.), *Русский Корпус на Балканах во время II Великой Войны 1941–1945 г.г.* (New York, Nashi Vesti, 1963), pp. 294-99.
Burgwyn, H. James, *Imperija na Jadranu: Musolinijevo osvajanje Jugoslavije 1941-1943* (Belgrade: Službeni glasnik, 2007).
Buturović, Ferid, *Kuća mostarskog kadije: sjećanja skojevca, ilegalca, i partizana* (Sarajevo: self-pub., 2016).
Cafin, James, *Partisan* (Auckland: Harper Collins Publishers, 2019).
Cafuta, Darko, "Ugotavljanje števila padlih pripadnikov okupacijskih sil in partizanov", in Jože Dežman (ed.), *Nemci in partizani: Nemške izgube na Gorenjskem med miti in resnico* (Kranj: Gorenjski muzej, 2016), pp. 61-84.
Colić, Mladenko, *Pregled operacija na jugoslovenskom ratištu 1941-1945* (Belgrade: Vojnoistorijski institut, 1988).
Cvetković, Dragan Ž., "Gubici pripadnika partizanskog pokreta sa teritorije Jugoslavije 1941-1945" (PhD thesis, University of Belgrade, 2016).
Cvetković, Zdravko B., *Osječka NOU brigada* (Belgrade: Vojnoizdavački zavod, 1981).
Čolaković, Rodoljub, *Zapisi iz oslobodilačkog rata* (Sarajevo: Oslobođenje, 1985), Vol. II.
Ćemalović, Enver, *Mostarski bataljon* (Mostar: City municipality, 1986).
Ćetković, Mirko, *Veze u Narodnooslobodilačkoj borbi* (Belgrade: Vojnoizdavački zavod, 1976), Vol. I.
Ćurguz, Dragutin, and Milorad Vignjević, *Drugi krajiški narodnooslobodilački partizanski (kozarski) odred "Mladen Stojanović"* (Prijedor: Nacionalni park Kozara, 1982).
Damjanović, Branko, and Savo Popović, *Šesta krajiška narodnooslobodilačka udarna brigada* (Belgrade: Vojnoizdavački zavod, 1985).
Danilović, Uglješa, "Ustanak u Hercegovini, jun 1941-jun 1942", in *Hercegovina u NOB* (Belgrade: Vojno delo, 1961), Vol. I, pp. 24-37.
Dapčević, Peko, "Završne operacije za oslobođenje Jugoslavije", in *Za pobjedu i slobodu. Završne operacije za oslobođenje Jugoslavije: učesnici govore* (Belgrade: Vojnoizdavački i novinski centar, 1986), pp. 94-98.
Dedijer, Vladimir, *Novi prilozi za biografiju Josipa Broza Tita* (Zagreb: Mladost, 1980), Vol. I.
Deakin, F.W.D., *The Embattled Mountain* (New York: Oxford University Press, 1971).
Devetnaesta birčanska brigada (Belgrade: Vojnoizdavački i novinski centar, 1989).
DeZeng, Henry L. IV, *Luftwaffe Airfields 1935-45: Italy, Sicily and Sardinia* (n.p.: self-pub., 2015).
Dimitrijević, Bojan B., *Vojska Nedićeve Srbije: oružane snage Srpske vlade 1941-1945.* (Belgrade: Službeni glasnik, 2014).
Dimitrijević, Dragoslav-Beli, *Kosmajski partizani* (Belgrade: Beogradski izdavačko-grafički zavod, 1983), Vol. I.
Djilas, Milovan:
Conversations with Stalin (Harmondsworth, UK: Penguin Books, 1967).
Wartime (New York: Harcourt Brace Jovanovich, 1977).

Drljević, Savo, "Kontrarevolucija na Kosovu i Metohiji zavođenje Vojne uprave februara 1945", in *Za pobjedu i slobodu. Završne operacije za oslobođenje Jugoslavije: učesnici govore* (Belgrade: Vojnoizdavački i novinski centar, 1986), pp. 589-603.

Drobac, Milan R., "Razvoj partizanskih jedinica i njihove borbe u kotaru Gračac od aprila 1942. do januara 1943. godine", in *Kotar Gračac u narodnooslobodilačkom ratu 1941-1945.* (Karlovac: Historijski arhiv, 1984), Vol. I, pp. 747-72.

Drulović, Čedo, *Tridesetsedma sandžačka divizija* (Belgrade: Vojnoizdavački zavod, 1983).

Đuković, Isidor, *Prva šumadijska brigada* (Belgrade: Vojnoizdavački zavod, 1978).

Dupalo, Adam, *Banija i Sisak u NOP-u 1941. Događaji, svjedočanstva, dokumenti* (Zagreb: Savez antifašističkih boraca i antifašista Republike Hrvatske, 2014).

Đuretić, Veselin, *Saveznici i jugoslovenska ratna drama* (Belgrade: Veselin Đuretić, 1988), Vol. I.

Đurić, Ljuban, *Banijski partizanski odredi 41-45* (Belgrade: Vojnoizdavački i novinski centar, 1988).

Đurić, Ljubodrag, *Sećanja na ljude i događaje* (Belgrade: Rad, 1989).

Đurišić, Mitar, *Primorska operativna grupa* (Belgrade: Vojnoistorijski institut, 1997).

Dželebdžić, Milovan:

Obaveštajna služba u Narodnooslobodilačkom ratu 1941–1945 (Belgrade: Vojnoistorijski institut, 1987).

Druga jugoslovenska armija (Belgrade: Vojnoizdavački i novinski centar, 1989).

Dželetović Ivanov, Pavle, *Dvadesetprva SS-divizija "Skenderbeg"* (Belgrade: Nova knjiga, 1987).

Džonlagić, Ahmet, *Dvadesetsedma divizija* (Belgrade: Vojnoizdavački zavod, 1983).

Egić, Obrad, "Brigada u bici na Sutjesci", in *Druga dalmatinska proleterska brigada* (Split: Institut za historiju radničkog pokreta Dalmacije, 1982), pp. 125-80.

Ernsthausen, Adolf von, *Die Wölfe der Lika: mit Legionären, Ustaschi, Domobranen und Tschetniks gegen Titos Partisanen: Erlebnisse in Kroatien 1944* (Neckargemünd: Kurt Vowinckel, 1959).

Fajdiga, Mirko, *Zidanškova brigada* (Ljubljana: Borec, 1975).

Fasanotti, Federica Saini, Basilio di Martino, Filippo Cappellano, Andrea Crescenzi, and Alessandro Gionfrida, *L'esercito alla macchia: controguerriglia italiana, 1860-1943 : l'esperienza italiana di controguerriglia dal brigantaggio alla Seconda Guerra mondiale* (Rome : Stato maggiore della difesa, 2015).

Ferenc, Tone, *Kapitulacija Italije in narodnoosvobodilna borba v Sloveniji jeseni 1943* (Maribor: Obzorja, 1967).

Fukarek, Pavle, and Savo Pređa, "Slaviša Vajner Čiča", in *Sarajevo u revoluciji* (Sarajevo: Istorijski arhiv, 1976-81), Vol. III, pp. 812-43.

Galić, Jure, "Zapadnohercegovački odred", in *Hercegovina u NOB* (Belgrade: Vojno delo, 1961), Vol. I, pp. 747-50.

Gallagher, Donat, and Carlos Villar Flor, *In the Picture: The Facts behind the Fiction in Evelyn Waugh's Sword of Honour* (Amsterdam: Rodopi, 2014).

Giron, Antun, *Zapadna Hrvatska u Drugom svjetskom ratu* (Rijeka: Adamić, 2004).

Gizdić, Drago, *Dalmacija 1942: Prilozi historiji Narodnooslobodilačke borbe* (Zagreb: Savez boraca Hrvatske, 1959).

Glišić, Venceslav, and Gojko Miljanić, *Rukovođenje Narodnooslobodilačkom borbom u Srbiji 1941-1945.* (Belgrade: Institut za savremenu istoriju, 1994).

Glišić, Venceslav, *Teror i zločini fašističke Nemačke u Srbiji 1941-1944.* (Belgrade: Rad, 1970).

Goddi, Federico, *Fronte Montenegro: Occupazione italiana e giustizia militare (1941-1943)* (Gorizia: Led edizioni Srl, 2016).

Gončin, Milorad, and Stevo Rauš, *Prva krajiška udarna brigada* (Belgrade: Vojnoizdavački zavod, 1981).

Gončin, Milorad, *Četvrta srpska udarna brigada* (Belgrade: Institut za savremenu istoriju, 1996).

Grahek Ravančić, Martina, *Bleiburg i Križni Put 1945: Historiografija, publicistika i memoarska literatura* (Zagreb: Hrvatski institut za povijest, 2009).

Grgurević, Dragutin, *Devetnaesta dalmatinska divizija* (Zagreb: Institut za historiju radničkog pokreta, 1964).

Guček, Milan, *Šercerjeva brigada* (Ljubljana: Borec, 1973).

Guerrazzi, Amedeo Osti, *The Italian Army in Slovenia: Strategies of Antipartisan Repression, 1941-1943* (New York: Palgrave Macmillan, 2013).

Hamović, Rade, "Deseta hercegovačka", in *Sutjeska: zbornik radova* (Belgrade: Vojnoizdavački zavod, 1959), Vol. II, pp. 267-291.

Hinsley, F. H., *British Intelligence in the Second World War: its Influence on Strategy and Operations* (London: Her Majesty's Stationary Office, 1984), Vol. III/1.

Hlaić, Vladimir, *34. udarna divizija NOV i PO Hrvatske* (Zagreb: Savez antifašističkih boraca Republike Hrvatske, 2002).

Hnilicka, Karl, *Das Ende auf dem Balkan: Die militärische Räumung Jugoslawiens durch die deutsche Wehrmacht 1944/45* (Göttingen: Musterschmidt, 1970).

Hoare, Marko Attila:

Genocide and Resistance in Hitler's Bosnia: The Partisans and the Chetniks 1941-1943 (Oxford: Oxford University Press, 2006).

The Bosnian Muslims in the Second World War: a History (London: Hurst & Company, 2013).

Hribovšek, Mitja, *Prekmurska brigada* (Ljubljana: Partizanska knjiga, 1975).

Hronologija Narodnooslobodilačkog rata (Sarajevo: 27. juli, 1979).

Hurem, Rasim, *Kriza NOP-a u Bosni i Hercegovini krajem 1941. i početkom 1942.* (Sarajevo: Svjetlost, 1972).

Ilari, Virgilio, "L'impiego delle forze armate della RSI in territorio nazionale", in *L'Italia in guerra–il quinto anno* (Rome: Ministry of Defense, 1995), pp. 171-320.

Inđić, Milan, *Borbe za Travnik* (Travnik: Borac, 1979).

Isaić, Vladimir, "Dejstva njemačkih pomorskih snaga na Jadranu protiv mornarice NOVJ", in *Za pobjedu i slobodu. Jugoslovenska mornarica u završnim operacijama za oslobođenje Jugoslavije. Učesnici govore* (Belgrade: Vojnoizdavački i novinski centar, 1986), pp. 272-81.

Ivanović, Miladin, *Dvadesettreća srpska divizija* (Belgrade: Savez udruženja boraca NOR-a, 1994).

Jaković, Milan, "Političko stanje na području okruga Karlovac između Drugog i Trećeg zasjedanja ZAVNOH-a", in *Treća godina narodno-oslobodilačkog rata na području Karlovca, Korduna, Like, Pokuplja i Žumberka* (Karlovac: Historijski arhiv, 1977), pp. 43-82.

Jakšić, Pavle:

"Sećanja na borbeni put Sedme baniske divizije", in *Sutjeska: zbornik radova* (Belgrade: Vojnoizdavački zavod, 1959), Vol. I, pp. 99-136.

"Sedma divizija u IV i V neprijateljskoj ofanzivi", in *Sedma banijska divizija* (Belgrade: Vojnoizdavački zavod, 1967), pp. 173-78.

Nad uspomenama (Belgrade: Rad, 1990), Vol. I.

Janković, Blažo:

Četvrta proleterska crnogorska brigada (Belgrade: Vojnoizdavački zavod, 1975).

"Oslobođenje Kruševca, Trstenika i Vrnjačke Banje i prodor ka Kraljevu", in: Koča Jončićć (ed.), *Borbe sa glavninom nemačke grupe armija E na ibarsko-zapadnomoravskom pravcu u oslobađanju zapadne Srbije 1944. godine (*Belgrade: Vojnoistorijski institut, 1990), pp. 169-85.

Janjić, Tihomir, Đuro Jovanović, and Stevo Opačić-Plavanjac, "Borbena dejstva brigade do oslobođenja Imotskog" in: *Druga dalmatinska proleterska brigada* (Split: Institut za historiju radničkog pokreta Dalmacije, 1982), pp. 47-72.

Javorčić, Ivo, "Borbe u Crnoj Gori, Sandžaku i Zapadnoj Srbiji", in *Druga dalmatinska proleterska brigada* (Split: Institut za historiju radničkog pokreta Dalmacije, 1982), pp. 207-40.

Jelenković, Aleksandar, *Saobraćaj u NOR-u Jugoslavije* (Belgrad: Vojnoizdavački i novinski centar, 1992).

Jerkić, Ivo, "Učešće Zapadne Hercegovine u NOP", in *Hercegovina u NOB* (Belgrade: Vojno delo, 1961), Vol. I, pp. 215-19.

Joksimović, Sekula, "Osnivanje i razvoj oružanih jedinica Narodnooslobodilačke vojske severozapadne Hrvatske 1941—1945.", in *Sjeverozapadna Hrvatska u narodnooslobodilačkoj borbi i socijalističkoj revoluciji: zbornik* (Varaždin: zajednica općina, 1976), pp. 137-59.

Jovanić, Đoko, "Šesta lička proleterska divizija 'Nikola Tesla' u trećoj godini rata (1. Vojnoistorijski institut 1943-30. VI 1944)", in *Treća godina narodno-oslobodilačkog rata na području Karlovca, Korduna, Like, Pokuplja i Žumberka* (Karlovac: Historijski arhiv, 1977), pp. 561-612.

Jovanović, Stanimir, and Dragoljub Mirčetić, *Peta srpska NOU brigada* (Belgrade: Vojnoizdavački i novinski centar, 1989).

Juvančič, Ivo, "Izvodi iz okupatorovih dokumenata", in *Ljubljana u borbi 1941-45: zbornik sjećanja* (Belgrade: Vojnoizdavački zavod, 1978), pp. 326-31.

Južnič, Marjan, "Sanitetska služba u Narodnooslobodilačkoj vojsci i partizanskim odredima Slovenije 1941-1945" in: *Sanitetska služba u Narodnooslobodilačkom ratu Jugoslavije 1941–1945* (Belgrade: Vojnoizdavački i novinski centar, 1989), Vol. III, pp. 9-202.

Kaltenegger, Roland, *Operationszone "Adriatisches Küstenland". Der Kampf um Triest, Istrien und Fiume 1944/45* (Graz: Leopold Stocker Verlag, 1993).

Kannapin, Norbert, Georg Tessin, and Brün Meyer (eds.), *Waffen-SS und Ordnungspolizei im Kriegseinsatz 1939-1945: ein Überblick anhand der Feldpostübersicht* (Osnabrück: Biblio, 2000).

Kapun, Vladimir, "Međimurci na Kalniku", in *Sjeverozapadna Hrvatska u narodnooslobodilačkoj borbi i socijalističkoj revoluciji: zbornik* (Varaždin: zajednica općina, 1976), pp. 542-65.

Karanović, Vukašin:

Od Moslavačkih odreda do 33. divizije (Čazma: Odbor za proslavu 35. godišnjice 33. divizije, 1978)

Moslavački partizanski odred 1941-1945. (Kutina: Savez udruženja boraca NOR-a, 1981).

Karapandžić, Borivoje M., *Građanski rat u Srbiji 1941-1945* (Valjevo: Novo videlo, 2010).

Karasijević, Drago:

"Ustanak i borbe na Kozari do oktobra 1942. godine", in Zdravko Antonić, Joco Marjanović (eds.), *Kozara u narodnooslobodilačkoj borbi i socijalističkoj revoluciji (1941-1945) (Prijedor: Nacionalni park Kozara, 1980),* pp. 133-60.

Peti korpus NOVJ (Belgrade: Vojnoizdavački zavod, 1985).

"Deseta krajiška divizija u operaciji za oslobođenje Sarajeva", in *Za pobjedu i slobodu. Sarajevska operacija: učesnici govore* (Belgrade: Vojnoizdavački i novinski centar, 1986), pp. 456-72.
Četvrta krajiška NOU divizija (Belgrade: Vojnoizdavački i novinski centar, 1988).
Kasaš, Aleksandar, *Mađari u Vojvodini 1941-1946* (Novi Sad: Filozofski fakultet, 1996).
Kazazović, Ćamil, *Travnik u Narodnooslobodilačkom ratu* (Zenica: Naša riječ, 1969), Vol. I.
Kladarin, Đuro:
Slom Četvrte i Pete okupatorsko-kvislinške ofenzive (Zagreb: Kultura, 1956).
Bitka na Sutjesci (Belgrade: Vojnoizdavački zavod, 1959).
Klanjšček, Zdravko, *Narodnoosloboditački rat u Sloveniji 1941-1945* (Belgrade: Vojnoistorijski institut, 1984).
Kleut, Petar:
Partizanska taktika (Belgrade: Vojnoizdavački zavod, 1983).
Jednaesti korpus NOVJ (Belgrade: Vojnoizdavački i novinski centar, 1987).
"Borbe jedinica operativnog štaba za Liku oko Gospića i na teritoriji Perušića (oktobar 1943-januar 1944.)", in *Kotar Gospić i kotar Perušić u Narodnooslobodilačkom ratu 1941—1945.* (Karlovac: Historijski arhiv, 1989), pp. 879-908.
Klukovič, Tilen, *Prisilne mobilizacije v Sloveniji v času 2. svetovne vojne–primerjava med nemško in partizansko vojsko* (M.A. thesis, University of Ljubljana, 2013).
Kljajić, Jovan, *Sedma krajiška brigada* (Belgrade: Vojnoizdavački i novinski centar, 1990).
Kocjančič, Klemen, *Red mrtvaške glave pod Alpami: Enote in ustanove Waffen-SS na Slovenskem med drugo svetovno vojno* (Ljubljana: INZ, 2021).
Komnenović, Danilo, and Muharem Kreso, *Dvadesetdeveta hercegovačka divizija* (Belgrade: Vojnoizdavački zavod, 1979).
Komnenović, Danilo "U napadu za oslobođenje Sarajeva", in *Za pobjedu i slobodu. Sarajevska operacija: učesnici govore* (Belgrade: Vojnoizdavački i novinski centar, 1986), pp. 219-42.
Korać, Dušan, *Kordun i Banija u Narodnooslobodilačkom ratu i socijalističkoj revoluciji* (Zagreb: Školska knjiga, 1986).
Korb, Alexander, *Im Schatten des Weltkriegs: Massengewalt der Ustaša gegen Serben, Juden, und Roma in Kroatien 1941-1945* (Hamburg: Hamburger Edition, 2013).
Kosanović, Radoslav-Braco, "Šesta primorsko-goranska udarna brigada", in *Partizanska Drežnica* (Karlovac: Historijski arhiv, 1982), pp. 191-223.
Košutić, Ivan, *Hrvatsko domobranstvo u Drugom svjetskom ratu* (Zagreb: Matica Hrvatska, 1992).
Krapchanski, V.N, D.D. Vazelov, G.R. Hristov, and I.K. Skachov, *Кратък обзор на бойния състав, организацията, попълването и мобилизацията на българската армия от 1878 до 1944г.* (Sofia: State military publishing, 1961).
Kregar, Tone, "Okupacijsko nasilje na Celjskem", in *Iz zgodovine Celja 1941-1945* (Celje: Muzej novejše zgodovine, 2004), pp. 137-63.
Krizman, Bogdan, *Pavelić između Hitlera i Musolinija* (Zagreb: Globus, 1980).
Krnić, Zdravko, *Tridesettreća divizija NOV Jugoslavije* (Zagreb: Spektar, 1981).
Krunić, Uroš, "Sedma divizija u prvoj polovini 1944", in *Sedma banijska divizija* (Belgrade: Vojnoizdavački zavod, 1967), pp. 583-603.
Kučan, Viktor, *Borci Sutjeske* (Belgrade: Zavod za udžbenike i nastavna sredstva, 1996).
Kühnrich, Heinz, and Franz-Karl Hitze, *Deutsche bei Titos Partisanen: Kriegsschicksale auf dem Balkan in Augenzeugenberichten und Dokumenten* (Schkeuditz: GNN Verlag, 1997).

Kulenović, Hajro, "Nastanak i razvoj sanitetske službe od početka ustanka 1941. do prelaska Vrhovnog štaba NOV i POJ na Vis, juna 1944. godine", in *Sanitetska služba u Narodnooslobodilačkom ratu Jugoslavije 1941–1945* (Belgrade: Vojnoizdavački i novinski centar, 1989), Vol. I, pp. 89-176.

Kumm, Otto, *Vorwärts, Prinz Eugen! Geschichte der 7. SS-Freiwilligen-Divisionza savremenu istorijuon 'Prinz Eugen'* (Dresden: Winkelried Verlag, 2007).

Kvesić, Sibe, *Dalmacija u Narodnooslobodilačkoj borbi* (Zagreb: Lykos, 1960).

Labović, Đurica, and Milan Basta, *Partizani za pregovaračkim stolom* (Zagreb: Naprijed, 1986).

Lampe, John R., *Yugoslavia as History: Twice there was a country* (Cambridge, UK: Cambridge University Press, 2000).

Lazarević, Božo, *Vazduhoplovstvo u Narodnooslobodilačkom ratu 1941-1945* (Belgrade: Vojnoizdavački zavod. 1972).

Leković, Mišo:

Ofanziva proleterskih brigada u leto 1942 (Belgrade: Vojnoistorijski institut, 1965).

"Neki problemi rukovođenja Centralnog komiteta KPJ i Vrhovnog štaba NOPOJ u 1941. godini", in *Užička republika* (Belgrade: NIRO Eksport-Pres, 1978), Vol. I, pp. 183-94.

Martovski pregovori 1943 (Belgrade: Narodna knjiga, 1985).

Lepre, George, *Himmler's Bosnian Division: the Waffen-SS Handschar Division, 1943-1945* (Atglen, PA : Schiffer Military History, 2004).

Lindsay, Franklin, *Beacons in the Night: With the OSS and Tito's Partisans in Wartime Yugoslavia* (Stanford: Stanford University Press, 1993),

Livada, Svetozar, *Kordunski rekvijem* (Zagreb: Euroknjiga, 2006).

Lopičić, Đorđe, *Nemački ratni zločini 1941-1945. Presude jugoslovenskih vojnih sudova* (Belgrade: Muzej žrtava genocida, 2009).

Lučić, Marko, "Borbe Osme divizije u toku neprijateljske operacije 'Panter'", in *Osma kordunaška udarna divizija* (Karlovac: Historijski arhiv, 1977), pp. 492-99.

Lukač, Dušan, *Ustanak u Bosanskoj Krajini* (Belgrade: Vojnoizdavački zavod, 1969).

MacConville, Michael, *A small war in the Balkans: British military involvement in wartime Yugoslavia 1941-1945* (London: Macmillan, 1986).

Mahoney, Kevin A., *Fifteenth Air Force against the Axis: Combat Missions over Europe during World War II* (Lanham, MD: Scarecrow Press, 2015).

Malkovski, Gjorgji, *Профашистичките и колаборационистичките организации и групи во Македонија 1941–1944* (Skopje: Insitut za nacionalna istorija, 1995).

Mamula, Bogdan, Rudi Bašić, Branko Vurdelja, and Dušan Pekić, *Prvi proleterski bataljon Hrvatske* (Historijski arhiv: Karlovac, 1983).

Mandić, Gligo, *Sedamnaesta istočnobosanska divizija* (Belgrade: Vojnoizdavački zavod, 1976).

Mandić, Hrvoje, "Hercegovačka franjevačka provincija u Drugom svjetskom ratu i poraću" (PhD thesis, University of Zagreb, 2019).

Manola, Srećko, "Skica za monografiju razvoja oružane borbe na Kordunu", in *Prva godina narodnooslobodilačkog rata na području Karlovca, Korduna, Gline, Like, Gorskog Kotara, Pokuplja i Žumberka* (Karlovac: Historijski arhiv, 1971), pp. 211-21.

Manoschek, Walter, *Serbien ist Judenfrei: Militärische Besatzungspolitik und Vernichtung der Juden in Serbien* (Munich: Oldenbourg Verlag, 1995).

Marijan,Davor, *Borbe za Kupres: Pohod proleterskih brigade i borbe za Kupres u ljeto 1942. godine* (Zagreb: AGM, 1999).

Marin, Mladen-Mlađo, "O borbama prve krajiške udarne brigade u toku neprijateljske ofanzive na Kozaru 1942. godine" in: Zdravko Antonić, Joco Marjanović (eds.), *Kozara u narodnooslobodilačkoj borbi i socijalističkoj revoluciji (1941-1945)* (Prijedor: Nacionalni park Kozara, 1980), pp. 257-68.

Marjanović, Jovan, *Beograd* (Belgrade: Nolit, 1964).

Martinović, Ratko, *Od Ravne gore do Vrhovnog štaba* (Belgrade: Rad, 1979).

Matetić, Vladimir-Dušan, *Četrnaesta Primorsko-goranska brigada* (Belgrade: Vojnoizdavački zavod, 1972).

Mehtidis, Alexis, *Italian Army 8 September 1943-Regio Esercito 8 Settembre 1943, Part IX: 2nd Army–Slovenia–Croatia–Bosnia-Herzegovina* (unpublished manuscript).

Meyer, Hermann Frank, *Blutiges Edelweiß. Die 1. Gebirgs-Divisionza savremenu istorijuon im Zweiten Weltkrieg* (Berlin: Ch. Links Verlag, 2008).

Mihailovski, Kiril-Grujica, *Treća Makedonska NOU brigada* (Belgrade: Vojnoizdavački zavod, 1976).

Mikašinović, Simo, "Od Saborskog do Drenovače", in *Osma kordunaška udarna divizija* (Karlovac: Historijski arhiv, 1977), pp. 321-26.

Mikić, Vojislav V.:

Italijanska avijacija u Jugoslaviji 1941-1943. godine (Belgrade: Vojnoistorijski institut, 1998).

Nemačka avijacija u Jugoslaviji 1941-1945 (Belgrade: Vojnoistorijski institut, 1998).

Zrakoplovstvo Nezavisne države Hrvatske 1941-1945 (Belgrade: Vojnoistorijski institut, 2000).

Miletić, Antun, "Neke mere i dejstva Vermahta na Kozari 1941-1942. godine", in Zdravko Antonić, Joco Marjanović (eds.), *Kozara u narodnooslobodilačkoj borbi i socijalističkoj revoluciji (1941-1945)* (Prijedor: Nacionalni park Kozara, 1980), pp. 195-214.

Miličević, Žarko, *Kalnički partizanski odred* (Varaždin: TIVA, 2010).

Šumonja, Miloš "Karlovačko-kordunsko područje u doba kapitulacije Italije (vojno-politička razmatranja)", in *Osma kordunaška udarna divizija* (Karlovac: Historijski arhiv, 1977), pp. 443-58.

Milovanović, Nikola, *Kontrarevolucionarni pokret Draže Mihailovića: rasulo* (Belgrade: Slovo ljubve, 1983).

Mlakar, Boris:

Pohod Tridesete divizije NOV i POJ v Beneško Slovenijo (Ljubljana: Partizanska knjiga, 1984).

Mlakar, Boris, *Slovensko domobranstvo 1943-1945: ustanovitev, organizacija, idejno ozadje* (Ljubljana: Matica slovenska, 2003).

Momčilović, Đorđe, *Banat u Narodnooslobodilačkom ratu* (Belgrade: Vojnoizdavački zavod, 1977).

Morača, Milutin, *Peta krajiška divizija* (Belgrade: Vojnoizdavački zavod, 1985).

Mraović, Nikola, *Peta vojvođanska brigada* (Novi Sad: Institut za istoriju, 1985).

Nemačka obaveštajna služba (Belgrade: Savezni sekretarijat unutrašnjih poslova, 1959), Vols. III-V, VIII.

Nenadović, Aleksandar, *Razgovori s Kočom* (Zagreb: Globus, 1989).

Nenezić, Radojica, "Analiza borbenih dejstava u Moslavini i Bilogori od 8. maja do 24. juna 1944. godine", in *Dvadesetosma slavonska NO udarna divizija u Sjeverozapadnoj Hrvatskoj i u dvije borbe za oslobođenje Ludbrega* (Grubišno Polje: Centar za kulturu i informiranje, 1990), pp. 93-146.

Neubacher, Hermann, *Specijalni zadatak Balkan* (Belgrade: Službeni list, 2004).

Nikolić, Kosta, *Istorija Ravnogorskog pokreta* (Belgrade: Srpska reč, 1999), Vol. I.

Nikolić, Živojin-Brka:

Dvadesetdruga srpska divizija (Belgrade: Narodna knjiga, 1972).

Nikolić, Živojin-Brka, *Jugoistočna Srbija u Narodnooslobodilačkom ratu i revoluciji, 1941-1945* (Belgrade: Narodna knjiga, 1979).

Nikoliš, Gojko:

"Ranjenici u bici na Sutjesci", in *Sutjeska: zbornik radova* (Belgrade: Vojnoizdavački zavod, 1959), Vol. I, 271-300.

Nikoliš, Gojko, *Korijen, stablo, pavetina: memoari* (Zagreb: Liber, 1981).

Ninković, Živan M., *Šesta vojvođanska udarna brigada* (Belgrade: Vojnoizdavački zavod, 1973).

NOB Makedonije: Publikacija fotografija, dokumenata i karata sa prigodnim tekstom o Narodnooslobodilačkoj borbi makedonskog naroda (Skopje: Narodna zadruga, 1964).

Novović, Mirko, and Stevan Petković, *Prva dalmatinska proleterska NOU brigada* (Belgrade: Vojnoizdavački zavod, 1986).

Obhođaš, Amir, Zvonimir Despot, Bojan Dimitrijević, and Mario Werhas, *Ustaška vojnica: oružana sila Ustaškog pokreta u Nezavisnoj Državi Hrvatskoj 1941.-1945.* (Zagreb: Despot Infinitus, 2013), Vols. I-II.

Odić, Slavko, and Slavko Komarica, *Partizanska obavještajna služba 1941-1942: šta se stvarno događalo* (Zagreb: Centar za informacije i publicitet, 1988), Vol. II.

Odić, Slavko:

Neostvareni planovi (Zagreb: Naprijed, 1961).

Desant na Drvar (Belgrade: Vojnoistorijski institut, 1981).

"Zašto je nemački plan desanta na Drvar bio pogrešan", in *Za pobjedu i slobodu. Drvarska operacija: učesnici govore* (Belgrade: Vojnoizdavački i novinski centar, 1986), pp. 579-95.

"Savezničke vojne mInstitut za savremenu istorijuje pri Vrhovnom štabu NOV i POJ u desantu na Drvar" in: ibid., pp. 651-80.

Opfer, Björn, *Im Schatten des Krieges. Besatzung oder Anschluss. Befreiung oder Unterdrückung? Eine komparative Untersuchung über die bulgarische Herrschaft in Vardar-Makedonien 1915-1918 und 1941-1944.* (Münster: Verlag Lit, 2005).

Opsenica, Stevan, "Borbe oko Korenice (decembar 1941-mart 1942)", in *Kotar Korenica i kotar Udbina u Narodnooslobodilačkom ratu i socijalističkoj izgradnji* (Karlovac: Historijski arhiv, 1979), pp. 733-47.

Orlović, Đorđe J.:

Druga lička proleterska brigada (Belgrade: Vojnoizdavački zavod, 1983).

"Borbe u zapadnoj Lici (septembar—oktobar 1942.)", in *Kotar Gospić i kotar Perušić u Narodnooslobodilačkom ratu 1941—1945.* (Karlovac: Historijski arhiv, 1989), pp. 586-606.

"Borbe na teritoriji Gospića i Perušića (april-maj 1943. godine)", in *Kotar Gospić i kotar Perušić u Narodnooslobodilačkom ratu 1941—1945.* (Karlovac: Historijski arhiv, 1989), pp. 844-78.

Šesta lička proleterska divizija "Nikola Tesla" (Vojnoizdavački i novinski centar: Belgrade, 1990).

Oslobodilački rat naroda Jugoslavije (Belgrade: Vojnoizdavački zavod, 1957), Vols. I-II.

Pajević, Miloš, *Artiljerija u NOR-u* (Belgrade: Vojnoizdavački zavod, 1970).

Pajović, Ljubivoje:

"Divizion Prve proleterske divizije", in *Sutjeska: zbornik radova* (Belgrade: Vojnoizdavački zavod, 1959), Vol. II, pp. 537-63.

"Prva proleterska divizija", in *Neretva: zbornik radova* (Belgrade: Vojnoizdavački zavod, 1965), Vol. I, pp. 64-125.

Pajović, Ljubivoje, Dušan Uzelac, Milovan Dželebdžić, *Sremski front 1944–1945* (Belgrade: Beogradski izdavačko-grafički zavod, 1979).

Pajović, Radoje, *Kontrarevolucija u Crnoj Gori: četnički i federalistički pokret 1941-1945* (Cetinje: Obod, 1977).

Pantelić, Milojica, *Dvadesetpeta srpska NOU divizija* (Belgrade: Vojnoizdavački zavod, 1977).

Pantelić, Milojica, Radovan M. Marinković, and Vladimir Nikšić: *Čačanski Narodnooslobodilački partizanski odred "Dr Dragiša Mišović"* (Čačak: self-pub., 1982).

Parmaković, Dragoslav, *Mačvanski partizanski odred* (Šabac: Fond narodnooslobodilačke borbe Podrinja iz Šapca, 1973).

Pavičević, Jovan, "Ratni aerodrom na Njegovuđi", in *Durmitorska partizanska republika: materijali sa naučnog skupa održanog u Žabljaku 24, 25 i 26. avgusta 1977. godine* (Titograd: Istorijski institut SR Crne Gore, 1979), pp. 833-37.

Pavlaković, Vjeran, *Yugoslav Volunteers in the Spanish Civil War* (Belgrade: Rosa Luxemburg Stifung Southeast Europe, 2016).

Pavlowitch, Stevan K., *Hitlerov novi antiporedak: Drugi svetski rat u Jugoslaviji* (Belgrade: Clio, 2009).

Perović, Branko, *Borbe Prvog hrvatskog i Prvog bosanskog korpusa NOV I POJ u januaru i februaru 1943.: nemačka operacija "Vajs I"* (Belgrade: Vojnoizdavački zavod, 1977).

Perović, Milivoje, *Srbija u Narodnooslobodilačkoj borbi: Južna Srbija* (Belgrade: Nolit, 1961).

Petelin, Stanko:

Sedma NOU brigada "France Prešern" (Belgrade: Vojnoizdavački zavod, 1973).

Gradnikova brigada (Ljubljana: Borec, 1983).

Petnajsta divizija (Ljubljana: Borec, 1983).

Petković, Radomir, "Borbe desete brigade u Hercegovini, juli-novembar 1943", in *Hercegovina u NOB* (Belgrade: Vojno delo, 1961), Vol. I, pp. 672-82.

Petovar, Rudi, and Miloš Zekić, "Šesta istočnobosanska brigada u bici na Sutjesci", in *Sutjeska: zbornik radova* (Belgrade: Vojnoizdavački zavod, 1959), Vol. I, pp. 205-36.

Petovar, Rudi, and Savo Trikić, *Šesta proleterska istočno-bosanska brigada* (Belgrade: Vojnoizdavački zavod, 1982).

Petranović, Branko:

Istorija Jugoslavije 1918-1988 (Belgrade: Nolit, 1988), Vols. I-II.

Srbija u Drugom svetskom ratu (Belgrade: Vojnoizdavački i novinski centar, 1992).

Petrović, Anka, ["Pregled gubitaka 1., 2., 3., i 4. armije"], in *Za pobjedu i slobodu. Završne operacije za oslobođenje Jugoslavije: učesnici govore* (Belgrade: Vojnoizdavački i novinski centar, 1986), pp. 209-17, 269-75, 323-28, and 463-66.

Phillips, John, *Yugoslav Story* (Zagreb: Mladost, 1983).

Plenča, Dušan, *Međunarodni odnosi Jugoslavije u toku Drugog svjetskog rata* (Belgrade: Institut društvenih nauka, 1962).

Poma, Antonino, *L'ultima carica della cavalleria italiana* (Buseto Palizzolo: Associazione di Lettere, Arti e Sport Dilettantistica Jò, 2007).

Popović-Smoljanović, Zora, "Sa Prvom omladinskom radnom brigadom na žetvi u Saničkoj dolini", in *Bihaćka republika 4.XI 1942-29.I 1943* (Bihać: Muzej AVNOJ-a i Pounja, 1965), Vol. I, pp. 372-75.

Popović, Jovo (ed.), *Bihaćka republika: ratne uspomene Koste Nađa* (Zagreb: Spektar, 1982).
Popović, Jovo, *Prva lička proleterska brigada (Marko Orešković)* (Belgrade: Vojnoizdavački i novinski centar, 1988).
Povijest Saveza komunista Jugoslavije (Belgrade: Rad, 1985).
Pravdić, Stevo, and Nail Redžić, *Šesnaesta slavonska omladinska NOU brigada "Jože Vlahović"* (Belgrade: Vojnoizdavački zavod, 1976).
Pribilović, Kazimir, *Četvrti pomorski obalni sektor Mornarice narodnooslobodilačke vojske Jugoslavije 1943-1945.* (Split: Vojnoizdavački i novinski centar, 1988).
Primorac, Rudolf:
"Treća udarna divizija", in: *Neretva: zbornik radova* (Belgrade: Vojnoizdavački zavod, 1965), Vol. I, pp. 184-231.
Operativno-taktička iskustva iz prve polovine Narodnooslobodilačkog rata (Belgrade: Vojnoizdavački i novinski centar, 1986).
Radanović, Milan:
Oslobođenje: Beograd 20. oktobar 1944. (Belgrade: Rosa Luxemburg Stiftung, 2014).
Kazna i zločin: Snage kolaboracije u Srbiji: odgovornost za ratne zločine (1941-1944) i vojni gubici (1944-1945) (Belgrade: Rosa Luxemburg Stiftung, 2015).
Radošević, Todor:
"Stvaranje i organizacioni razvoj partizanskih odreda u Lici do jula godine 1942", in *Prva godina narodnooslobodilačkog rata na području Karlovca, Korduna, Gline, Like, Gorskog Kotara, Pokuplja i Žumberka* (Karlovac: Historijski arhiv, 1971), *pp. 671-700.*
Trinaesta proleterska brigada "Rade Končar" (Belgrade: Vojnoizdavački zavod, 1984).
Prva proleterska divizija (Belgrade: Sekcija boraca Prve proleterske NOU brigade, 2010), Vols. I-II.
Radovanović, Jovan R., *Požega u NOR i revoluciji* (Požega: Savez udruženja boraca NOR-a, 1986).
Rajčević, Dane "Glavni štab NOV i POH i oficirska škola u Donjem Lapcu", in *Kotar Donji Lapac u Narodnooslobodilačkom ratu 1941.-1945.* (Karlovac: Historijski arhiv, 1985), pp. 628-41.
Rako, Milan, and Slavko Družijanić, Jedanesta *dalmatinska udarna brigada* (Split: Institut za historiju radničkog pokreta Dalmacije, 1987).
Ramet, Sabrina P., *The Three Yugoslavias: State-Building and Legitimation, 1918—2005* (Bloomington, IN: Indiana University Press, 2006).
Ranitović, Boško, "Pobjeda Pete brigade na Drenovači (6. februar 1943. godine)", in *Osma kordunaška udarna divizija* (Karlovac: Historijski arhiv, 1977), pp. 327-35.
Rauš, Stevo, "Bihaćka operacija novembra 1942. godine", in *Bihaćka republika 4.XI 1942-29.I 1943* (Bihać: Muzej AVNOJ-a i Pounja, 1965), Vol. I, pp. 65-87.
Redžić, Nail:
Dvadesetpeta brodska brigada (Belgrade: Vojnoizdavački zavod, 1976).
Telmanovci: Zapisi o njemačkoj partizanskoj četi Ernst Telman (Belgrade: Narodna armija, 1984).
Roglić, Stevan, "Komandovanje i rukovođenje vazduhoplovnim jedinicama", in *Za pobjedu i slobodu. Vazduhoplovstvo u strategiji NOR-a. Učesnici govore* (Belgrade: Vojnoizdavački i novinski centar, 1986), pp. 54-61.

Roksandić, Rade, and Zdravko B. Cvetković, *Osamnaesta slavonska brigada* (Belgrade: Vojnoizdavački zavod, 1974).

Romac, Paško, *Kazivanje o Šesnaestoj vojvođanskoj diviziji* (Novi Sad: Institut za savremenu istoriju, 1979).

Romano, Jaša, *Jevreji Jugoslavije 1941—1945. žrtve genocida i učesnici NOR* (Belgrade: Savez jevrejskih opština Jugoslavije, 1980).

Rossi, Marina, "Obešeni v Ulici Ghega" in: *Po poteh nasilja v 20. stoletju v Tržaški pokrajini* (Trieste: Istituto regionale per la storia del movimento di liberazione nel Friuli Venezia Giulia, 2006), pp. 57-62.

Samardžija, Dušan, *Jedanaesta krajiška NOU divizija* (Belgrade: Vojnoizdavački zavod, 1987).

Samtsevich, Andrei, *Марш Смерти Русского охранного корпуса* (Moscow: Iuza, 2019).

Sarajlić, Abdulah, "Stvaranje dobrovoljačkih jedinica u Istočnoj Bosni", in *Istočna Bosna u NOB-u: sjećanja učesnika* (Belgrade: Vojnoizdavački zavod, 1971), Vol. I, pp. 443-48.

Savić, Sveta *Pedesetprva vojvođanska divizija* (Belgrade: Vojnoizdavački zavod, 1974).

Schmider, Klaus:

Partisanenkrieg in Jugoslawien 1941-1944 (Hamburg: E. S. Mittler & Sohn, 2002).

"The Yugoslavian Theatre of War (January 1943 to May 1945)", in *Germany and the Second World War, Vol. VIII: The Eastern Front 1943–1944: The War in the East and on the Neighbouring Fronts* (Oxford: Clarendon Press, 2017), pp. 1008-88.

Schmidt-Richberg, Erich, *Der Endkampf auf dem Balkan: Die Operationen der Heeresgruppe E von Griechenland bis zu den Alpen* (Heidelberg: Kurt Vowinckel Verlag, 1955).

Schraml, Franz, *Kriegsschauplatz Kroatien: die deutsch-kroatischen Legions-Divisionza savremenu istorijuonen: 369., 373., 392. Inf.-Div. (kroat.) ihre Ausbildungs- und Ersatzformationen* (Neckargemünd: Kurt Vowinckel Verlag, 1962).

Schreiner Božič, Marcus, "Enzian – August bis Oktober 1942 in Gorenjska", in Jože Dežman (ed.), *Nemci in partizani: Nemške izgube na Gorenjskem med miti in resnico* (Kranj: Gorenjski muzej, 2016), pp. 85-100.

Shepherd, Ben:

Terror in the Balkans: German Armies and Partisan Warfare (Cambridge, MA: Harvard University Press, 2012).

Hitler's Soldiers: The German Army in the Third Reich (London: Yale University Press, 2018).

Smirnov, Vladimir, "Surova škola: doživljaji inženjeraca na Neretvi", in *Neretva: zbornik radova* (Belgrade: Vojnoizdavački zavod, 1965), Vol. I, pp. 356-405.

Sokić, Sreten, "Karakter društveno-ekonomskih odnosa u Užičkoj republici", in *Užička republika* (Belgrade: NIRO Eksport-Pres, 1978), Vol. I, pp. 275-86.

Stanković, Milivoje, *Prvi šumadijski partizanski odred* (Belgrade: Narodna knjiga, 1983).

Stiplovšek, Miroslav, *Šlandrova brigada* (Ljubljana: Borec, 1971).

Stišović, Obren-Obrad, "Frontalne borbe i proboj obruča za vreme ofanzive na Kozaru u leto 1942. godine" in: Zdravko Antonić, Joco Marjanović (eds.), *Kozara u narodnooslobodilačkoj borbi i socijalističkoj revoluciji (1941-1945)* (Prijedor: Nacionalni park Kozara, 1980), pp. 227-56.

Stojić, Desanka, *Prva ženska partizanska četa* (Karlovac: Historijski arhiv, 1987).

Strecker, Arthur, "An der Drina", in Otto Weingartner (ed.) *Erinnerungen an die 118. Jäger-Division (frühere 718. Inf.Div.)* (Klagenfurt: self-pub., 1982), pp. 14-23.

Street, Brian Jeffrey, *The Parachute Ward: A Canadian Surgeon's Wartime Adventures in Yugoslavia* (1st electronic version: Edito Online Publishing, 1998).
Strle, Franci, *Tomšičeva brigada* (Ljubljana: Partizanska knjiga, 1986), Vols. II-III.
Strugar, Vlado, *Jugoslavija 1941-1945* (Ljubljana: Partizanska knjiga, 1978).
Sunajko, Stevo, *Sodelovanje slovenskih in hrvaških narodnoosvobodilnih enot 1941-1945* (Ljubljana: Partizanska knjiga, 1971).
Swain, Geoffrey, *Tito: A Political Biography* (New York: I. B. Tauris, 2010).
Šibl, Ivan, *Ratni dnvenik* (Zagreb: Naprijed, 1960).
Škiljan, Filip, *Hrvatsko Zagorje u Drugom svjetskom ratu 1941.-1945.: opredjeljivanja, borbe, žrtve* (Zagreb: Plejada, 2012).
Štaut, Tomaž, "Elitne enote na območju današnje Slovenije med drugo svetovno vojno" (M.A. thesis, University of Ljubljana, 2008).
Tarabić, Joco, "Osma divizija u trećoj godini NOR-a", in *Treća godina narodno-oslobodilačkog rata na području Karlovca, Korduna, Like, Pokuplja i Žumberka* (Karlovac: Historijski arhiv, 1977), pp. 143-76.
Tepavac, Mirko, *Moj Drugi svetski rat i mir: o ratu i posle rata-autobiografski zapInstitut za savremenu istoriju* (Zagreb: Razlog, 2013).
Tepavčević, Borivoje, "Kalinovički NOP odred", in *Sarajevo u revoluciji* (Sarajevo: Istorijski arhiv, 1976-81), Vol. III, pp. 134-66.
Teropšič, Tomaž, *Štajerska v plamenih. Taktika, orožje in oprema štirih vojsk na Štajerskem v drugi svetovni vojni.* (Brežice: Posavski muzej, 2012).
Terzić, Velimir:
"Bitka na Neretvi", in *Neretva: zbornik radova* (Belgrade: Vojnoizdavački zavod, 1965), Vol. I, pp. 13-63.
Slom Kraljevine Jugoslavije 1941: uzroci i posledice poraza (Belgrade: Narodna knjiga, 1982), Vol. II.
Tessin, Georg, *Verbände und Truppen der deutschen Wehrmacht und der Waffen-SS im Zweiten Weltkrieg 1939-1945* (Osnabrück: Biblio Verlag, 1978), Vols. X, XIII.
Thayer, Charles, *Hands Across the Caviar* (London: Michael Joseph, 1953).
The Verification of Death-toll of World War II and Its Aftermath in Municipal Registry Offices in Slovenia (Ljubljana: INZ, 2009).
Timofejev, Aleksei, *Rusi i Drugi svetski rat u Jugoslaviji* (Belgrade: Institut za noviju istoriju Srbije, 2010).
Tomasevich, Jozo:
War and Revolution in Yugoslavia, 1941-1945: The Chetniks (Stanford, CA: Stanford University Press, 1975).
War and Revolution in Yugoslavia, 1941-1945: Occupation and Collaboration (Stanford, CA: Stanford University Press, 2001).
Topalović, Živko, *Srbija pod Dražom* (London: Budućnost, 1969).
Trajkovski, Roberto:
Trajkovski, Roberto, Вермахтот и Македонија (1943-1944 година) (Bitola: SBM, 2018).
Вермахтот и Егејскиот дел на Македонија (1943-1944) (Skopje: Sojuz na antifašsti-Antifa, 2019).
Trew, Simon, *Britain, Mihailović, and the Chetniks, 1941-1942* (London: Macmillan Press LTD, 1998).

Tridesetdruga divizija NOVJ (Zagreb: Globus, 1988).
Trifković, Gaj:
"'Schwarz' auf 'Weiss': Das Jahr der deutschen Großoperationen in Jugoslawien" (M.A. thesis, University of Graz, 2010).
Parleying with the Devil: Prisoner Exchange in Yugoslavia 1941-1945 (Lexington, KY: University Press of Kentucky/Andarta Books, 2020).
Trikić, Savo, and Dušan Repaić, *Proleterski bataljon Bosanske krajine* (Belgrade: Vojnoizdavački zavod, 1982).
Trikić, Savo O., *Treća krajiška proleterska brigada* (Belgrade: Vojnoizdavački i novinski centar, 1987).
Tucker, Spencer C. (ed.), *Battles that Changed History: An Encyclopedia of World Conflict* (Santa Barbara, CA: ABC-CLIO, 2011).
Tus, Andrija, "Četrnaesta primorsko-goranska brigada", in *Partizanska Drežnica* (Karlovac: Historijski arhiv, 1982), pp. 225-53.
Urošević, Sredoje:
Urošević, Sredoje, "Druga proleterska", in Sutjeska: zbornik radova (Belgrade: Vojnoizdavački zavod, 1959), Vol. II, pp. 71-79.
Druga proleterska brigada: ratovanje i ratnici (Belgrade: Poslovna politika, 1988).
Velić, Miroslav, Ante V. Petrić, and Mate Vuletić, *Mosorski partizanski odred* (Split: Institut za historiju radničkog pokreta Dalmacije, 1985).
Vertepov, Dmitri Petrovich (ed.), *Русский Корпус на Балканах во время II Великой Войны 1941–1945 г.г.* (New York: Nashi Vesti, 1963).
Viazzi, Luciano, *La Resistenza dei militari italiani all'estero. La Divisionza savremenu istorijuone "Garibaldi" in Montenegro–Sangiaccato–Bocche di Cataro* (Rome: Ministry of Defense, 1991).
Viazi, Luciano, and Leo Taddia, *La resistenza dei militari italiani all'estero: la divInstitut za savremenu istorijuone "Garibaldi" in Montenegro–Sangiaccato–Bosnia–Erzegovina* (Rome: Ministry of Defense, 1994).
Vidović, Žarko, *Treća proleterska brigada* (Belgrade: Vojnoizdavački zavod, 1972).
Vilhar, Srećko, and Albert Klun, *Prva in Druga prekomosrska brigada* (Ljubljana: Borec, 1967).
Vitorović, Aleksandar, *Srbija u narodnooslobodilačkoj borbi: Centralna Srbija* (Belgrade: Nolit, 1967).
Vojna Enciklopedija (Belgrade: Izdanje redakcije Vojne enciklopedije, 1970-76), Vols. I-X.
Volkogonov, Dmitri A., and Sekula Joksimović (eds.), *Beogradska operacija: 20 oktobar 1944* (Belgrade: Vojnoistorijski institut, 1989).
Von Metzsch Friedrich-August, *Die Geschichte der 22. Infanterie-Divisionza savremenu istorijuon 1939-1945* (Kiel: Verlag Hans-Henning Podzun, 1952).
Von Stering, Erich, *Jeder war ein Stück von uns: Leben und Kampf einer Kompanie auf ihrem Weg von Attika nach Sarajewo Herbst 1944* (Neckargemünd: Kurt Vowinckel Verlag, 1959).
Vrančić, Šime, "Ne pucaj, žive hvataj!", in *Dalmatinci u Prvoj proleterskoj brigadi* (Split: Institut za historiju radničkog pokreta Dalmacije, 1982), pp. 140-44.
Vujasinović, Todor:
"Organizacija ustanka i važnije oružane akcije na Ozrenu", in *Ustanak naroda jugoslavije 1941.* (Belgrade: Vojno delo, 1964), Vol. IV, pp. 543-57.
Ozrenski partizanski odred (Sarajevo: Svjetlost, 1979).
Vukanović, Radovan:

Ratni put Treće divizije (Belgrade: Vojnoizdavački zavod, 1970).
Drugi udarni korpus (Belgrade: Vojnoizdavački zavod, 1982).
Vukčević, Slavko, *Borbe i otpori u okupiranim gradovima Jugoslavije 1941-1945.* (Belgrade: Vojnoistorijski institut, 1985).
Vukmanović, Svetozar-Tempo, *Revolucija koja teče: memoari* (Belgrade: Komunist, 1971), Vols. I and III.
Vukosavljević, Mladen and Drago Karasijević, *Pedesettreća NOU srednjobosanska divizija* (Sarajevo: Zadrugar, 1969).
Vukotić, Jovo, "Druga proleterska divizija", in *Neretva: zbornik radova* (Belgrade: Vojnoizdavački zavod, 1965), Vol. I, pp. 126-85.
Vuksanović, Miloš:
Prva proleterska brigada (Belgrade: Narodna knjiga, 1981).
Koča Popović: beleške uz ratovanje (Belgrade: Beogradski grafičko-izdavački zavod, 1988).
Waller, Douglas, *Wild Bill Donovan: The Spymaster Who Created the OSS and Modern American Espionage* (New York: Free Press, 2011).
Warlimont, Walter, *Im Hauptquartier der deutschen Wehrmacht 1939-1945* (Frankfurt am Main: Bernard&Graefe Verlag für Wehrwesen, 1962).
Weigley, Russel F., *The Age of Battles: The Quest for Decisive Warfare from Breitenfeld to Waterloo* (London: Pimlico, 1993).
Weingartner, Otto, "Errinerungen an die Einheit Dzaack auf die Insel Brac", in Otto Weingartner (ed.), *Erinnerungen an die 118. Jäger-Division (frühere 718. Inf.Div.)* (Klagenfurt: self-pub., 1982), pp. 219-25.
Weise, Hans, "An der Sutjeska", in Oto Weingartner (ed.), *Erinnerungen an die 118. Jäger-Division (frühere 718. Inf.Div.)* (Klagenfurt: self-pub., 1982), pp. 100-05.
Wheeler, Mark C., *Britain and the war for Yugoslavia, 1940-1943* (New York: Columbia University Press, 1980).
Zadnik, Maks, *Istrski odred* (Nova Gorica: Partizanska knjiga, 1975).
Zakić, Mirna, *Ethnic Germans and National-Socialism in Yugoslavia in World War II* (Cambridge, UK: Cambridge University Press, 2017).
Završne operacije za oslobođenje Jugoslavije 1944-5 (Belgrade: Vojnoistorijski institut, 1957).
Žerjavić, Vladimir, *Opsesije i megalomanije oko Jasenovca i Bleiburga. Gubici stanovništva Jugoslavije u drugom svjetskom ratu* (Zagreb: Globus, 1992).
Živković, Milutin D., "Sandžak 1941-1943" (PhD thesis, University of Belgrade, 2017).
Zorić, Rade, *Četvrta krajiška brigada* (Belgrade: Vojnoizdavački zavod, 1980).
Žrtve rata 1941-1945. Rezultati popisa (Belgrade: Savezni zavod za statistiku, 1966).

Journals

Barić, Nikica:
"Položaj Srba u Domobranstvu Nezavisne države Hrvatske, 1941.-1945.", *Polemos*, 5 (2002), pp. 159-175.
"Kozara 1942. — sudbina zarobljenika, civila i djece", *Pilar*, 11:22 (2016), pp. 53-111.
Bojanić, Miloš, "Evakuacija savezničkih avijatičara iz Jugoslavije tokom Drugog svetskog rata", *Zbornik radova Narodnog muzeja Čačak*, 49 (2019), pp. 91-101.

Bokun, Edi, "Operacija 369. njemačke divizije protiv ozrenskih četnika (april 1943. godine)", *Gračanički glasnik*, 18:35 (2013), pp. 58-69.

Demšar, Vinko, "Pregled NOB na Škofjeloškem", *Loški razgledi*, 19:1 (1972), pp. 77-107.

Dulić, Tomislav, "Danish Waffen-SS Soldiers in Croatia, Autumn 1943: The Fighting at Glina and Hrastovica", *Journal of the Danish Commission for Military History*, (2016), pp. 76-94.

Dželebdžić, Milovan, "Dejstva na komunikacije u Jugoslaviji od 1. do 7. septembra 1944. godine— operacija 'Ratweek'", *Vojnoistorijski glasnik*, 3 (1970), pp. 7-61.

Ferenc, Tone:

"Wehrmannschaft v boju proti narodnoosvobodilni vojski na Štajerskem", *Letopis Muzeja narodne osvoboditve LRS v Ljubljani*, 2 (1958), pp. 81-156.

"Množična vstaja na Gorenjskem decembra 1941.", *Borec* 12 (1971), pp. 741-783.

Ferrante, Ezio, "Borghese e la Decima nella bufera (1943-1945)", *Bollettino d'Archivio dell'Ufficio Storico della Marina Militare*, 28 (2014), pp. 81-110.

Guštin, Damijan, "Vprašanja oboroženega odpora 1941", *Prispevki za novejšo zgodovino*, 41:2 (2001), pp. 123-42.

Ivetić, Velimir, "Slučaj partizanskih zločina u logoru na Malom Lošinju 1943. godine", *Vojnoistorijski glasnik*, 1-2 (2004), pp. 137-59.

Jareb, Mario, "Ustaški pukovnik i general Tomislav Sertić", *Časopis za suvremenu povijest*, 32:2 (2000), pp. 271-315.

Jefford, Jeff, "The Balkan Air Force", *Royal Air Force Historical Society Journal*, 46 (2009), pp. 63-80.

Kocjančič, Klemen:

"'Prvi general ujet od nas': zajetje in smrt Konrada Heidenreicha", *Studia Historica Slovenica* 17:1 (2017), pp. 217-36.

"Between Vlasov and Himmler: Russian SS-Sonder-Regiment 1 'Waräger' in Slovenia, 1944–45", *The Journal of Slavic Military Studies*, 30:1 (2017), pp. 50-60.

"Galicijski levi v bojih proti partizanom: 14. grenadirska divizija Waffen-SS (galicijska št. 1) na Slovenskem", *The Studia Historica Slovenica*, 19:3 (2019), pp. 815-46.

Lakić, Zoran, "Razmjena ratnih zarobljenika u Crnoj Gori u toku Narodnooslobodilačkog rata", *Vojnoistorijski glasnik*, 18:1 (1967), pp. 69-116.

Lugarić Vukas, Danijela, "Boško Buha i Pavlik Morozov: novi (jugoslavenski/sovjetski) čovjek u tijelu malenoga dječaka" in *Narodna umjetnost*, 51:2 (2014), pp. 133-54.

Manson, Charles D., "Red Sun: A German Airborne Raid, May 1944", *Journal of Slavic Military Studies*, 13:4 (2000), pp. 101-26.

Marčetić, Stjepan,"Odžak i Odžačka Posavina 1945. godine", *Rostra*, 2:2 (2009), pp. 23-37.

Marijan, Davor:

"Lipanjski ustanak u istočnoj Hercegovini 1941. godine", *Časopis za suvremenu povijest*, 35:2 (2003), pp. 545-576.

"'Livno mora pasti': borbe dijelova V. ustaškog stajaćeg zdruga s II. proleterskom divizijom za Livno u prosincu 1942. godine", *Časopis za suvremenu povijest*, 40:3 (2008), pp. 951-68.

Nikolić, Goran, "O masakru u Baru 1945.", *Pirotski zbornik*, 44 (2019), pp. 87-146.

Rupić, Mate, "Ljudski gubici u Hrvatskoj u Drugom svjetskom ratu prema popisu iz 1950. godine", *Časopis za suvremenu povijest*, 33:1 (2001), pp. 7-17.

Škodrić, Ljubinka, "Vera Pešić i Radoslav Đurić. Jedna ratna epizoda na jugu Srbije", *Leskovački zbornik*, 59 (2019), pp. 361-79.

Terzić, Milan, "Josip Broz Tito i Nemci-ratni zarobljenici", *Vojnoistorijski glasnik*, 65:2 (2015), pp. 164-175.

Timotijević, Miloš, "Sudbina srebra Užičke republike", *Godišnjak za društevnu istoriju*, 1 (2018), pp. 57-81.

Trifković, Gaj:

"A Case of Failed Counter-Insurgency: Anti-Partisan Operations in Yugoslavia 1943", *The Journal of Slavic Military Studies*, 24:2 (2011), pp. 314-336.

"Making Deals with the Enemy: Partisan-German Contacts and Prisoner Exchanges in Yugoslavia, 1941-1945", *Global War Studies*, 10:2 (2013), pp. 6-37.

"The Key to the Balkans: The Battle for Serbia 1944", *Journal of Slavic Military Studies*, 28:3 (2015), pp. 524-555.

"Carnage in the Land of Three Rivers: The Syrmian Front 1944-1945", *Militärgeschichtliche Zeitschrift*, 75:1 (2016), pp. 94-122.

"Damned Good Amateurs': Yugoslav Partisans in the Belgrade Operation 1944", The Journal of Slavic Military Studies, 29:2 (2016), pp. 253-278.

"The Forgotten Surrender: The End of the Second World War in Yugoslavia", *International Journal of Military History and Historiography*, 37 (2017), pp. 147-172.

"'The German Anabasis': The Breakthrough of Army Group E from Eastern Yugoslavia 1944", *Journal of Slavic Military Studies*, 30:4 (2017), pp. 602-629.

"Operacije Crvene armije u sjevernoj Jugoslaviji 1944-1945. iz sovjetskih dokumenata", *Vojnoistorijski glasnik*, 2 (2017), pp. 205-33.

"The German ‚Ultra': Signals Intelligence in Yugoslavia 1943-1944", *Journal of Intelligence History*, Vol. 17:2 (2018), pp. 104-120.

"The Yugoslav Partisans' Lost Victories: Operations in Montenegro and Bosnia-Herzegovina 1944-1945", *Journal of Military History*, 82:1 (2018), pp. 95-124.

"'Katastrofa izbjegnuta za dlaku': njemački izvori o Kninskoj bitci 1944.", *Časopis za suvremenu povijest,* 53:2 (2021), pp. 549-70.

"The Long Way to Trieste: Operations in the Yugoslav Littoral 1944-1945" (forthcoming 2021), pp. 1-39.

"Too Little, Too Late: Evolution in German Counter-insurgency Methods in Yugoslavia, 1943-1944", manuscript, pp. 1-22; will appear in *The Journal of Slavic Military Studies,* 34:2 (2021).

Vasić, Miroljub:

"Komunistička internacionala i KPJ (1929-1941)", *Istorija 20. veka*, 11:1-2 (1993), pp. 147-154.

"Ustanak u Jugoslaviji 1941. godine i Kominterna", Istorija 20. veka, 14:2 (1996), pp. 143-51.

Von Kalben, Heinrich-Detloff, and Constantin Wagner, "Zur Geschichte des XV. Kosaken-Kavallerie Korps", *Deutsches Soldatenjahrbuch*, 18 (1970), p. 106-11.

Ževart, Milan, "Elaborat štaba Treeckove bojne skupine o narodnoosvoboditelnem boju na Štajerskem," *Časopis za zgodovino i narodopisje*, 153:2 (1990), pp. 153-98.

Živković, Milutin, "Uspostavljanje saradnje komandanta Limsko-sandžačkih četničkih odreda Pavla Đurišića i italijanskih vlasti u Crnoj Gori početkom 1942.", *Istorija dvadesetog veka*, 2:34 (2016), pp. 27-44.

Newspapers & Magazines

Doebel, Günther, "Banditen in der Felsenhöhle", *Die deutsche Polizei*, 19 (1942), pp. 284-85.
Miljkić, Milan, "12 dana otpora", *Odbrana*, Special Issue No. 166 (1.4.2017), pp. 1-32.
Schlaug, Georg, "Der Luftwaffen-Einsatz beim 'Unternehmen Rösselsprung'", *Luftwaffe im Focus*, 2 (2003), pp. 37-43.
"Tekst ugovora o prijateljstvu između Kraljevine Jugoslavije i Kraljevine Mađarske", *Politika* (13.12.1940).

Internet

http://www.97legione.siena.it/ (last accessed on 26.8.2018).
http://www.yuhistorija.com/serbian/drugi_sr_txt01c1.html Gaj Trifković, "Od 'bandita' do 'Jugoslovenske armije': partizanski rat 1941–1945." (YuHistory Project, 2016) (last accessed 26.8.2020).
http://www.axishistory.com/axis-nations/croatia/379-croatia-ustasha/croatia-ustasha-units/8198-introduction-to-the-croatian-gendarmerie H.L. deZeng IV, "Introduction to the Croatian Gendarmerie", (accessed 16.3.2018).
https://www.axishistory.com/list-all-categories/135-campaigns-a-operations/anti-partisan-operations-in-croatia/1934-anti-partisan-operations-in-the-independent-state-of-croatia H.L. deZeng IV, "Anti-Partisan Operations in the Independent State of Croatia" (last accessed 26.8.2020).
https://www.axishistory.com/list-all-categories/380-croatia-army/croatia-army-units/8333-introduction-to-the-jaeger-brigades-croatia H.L. deZeng IV, "Introduction to the Jaeger Brigades", (last accessed on 25.9.2019).
https://www.axishistory.com/list-all-categories/380-croatia-army/croatia-army-units/8270-divisions-dec-1944-may-1945-croatia H.L. deZeng IV, "Divisions December 1944-May 1945" (last accessed on 8.7.2020).
http://www.cetinjskilist.com/index.php/drustvo/item/242-obiljezena-76-godisnjica-bitke-na-koscelama (accessed on 10.4.2018).
http://www.cro-eu.com/forum/index.php?topic=1355.0 "Ratni dnevnik Josipa Hübla iz 1943." (last accessed on 20.7.2019).
https://www.danas.rs/drustvo/titov-plan-je-bio-pogresan/ "Titov plan je bio pogrešan", *Danas*, 13.8.2012 (last accessed on 16.9.2019).
http://db.saur.de/DG20/basicFullCitationView.jsf?documentId=rk1443 Nationalsozialismus, Holocaust, Widerstand und Exil 1933-1945. Online-Datenbank. De Gruyter.(last accessed 25.9.2019).
http://www.fasena.de/courage/deutsch/5a.htm and http://www.fasena.de/courage/deutsch/10.htm (last accessed 22.5.2020).
https://kriegsgraeberstaetten.volksbund.de/friedhof (last accessed: 26.7.2020).
http://lexikon-wehrmacht.de/Personenregister/S/StephanFriedrich-R.htm (last accessed on 15.7.2020).
https://www.mladina.si/96492/turjak-60-let-pozneje/ Bernard Nežmah, "Turjak 60 let pozneje", *Mladina*, 3.10.2003. (last accessed on 10.10.2019).

https://www.nationalww2museum.org/students-teachers/student-resources/research-starters/research-starters-worldwide-deaths-world-war (last accessed: 2.8.2020).

http://www.politika.rs/sr/clanak/69738/Drustvo/Zandarmi-iz-Bele-Crkve-zrtve-ideoloskog-terora "Žandarmi iz Bele Crkve žrtve ideološkog terora", *Politika*, 2.1.2009: (accessed on 25.3.2018).

http://www.regioesercito.it/index.htm (last accessed 22.9.2019).

http://www.smrtnakazna.rs/sr-latn-rs/bazaosudjenika.aspx (last accessed on 15.7.2020).

https://www.vreme.com/cms/view.php?id=1100865 Tamara Nikčević, "Ostani kad si navalio da gineš" (last accessed on 24.6.2019).

https://www.youtube.com/watch?v=BKp0tlOEpso (accessed 5.11.2021)

Documentaries

Interviews with Milovan Đilas in TV-documentary *Jugoslavija u ratu 1941-1945* (Radio-televizija Beograd, 1991-92), Episodes 5 and 10.

Interview with Joža Horvat conducted by Damir Horvat and Miljenko Hajdarović, 18.12.2010; video available at https://www.youtube.com/watch?v=EzhdfXKPgCg (last accessed on 3.7.2018).

Interview with Joža Horvat in: *Tito: posljednji svjedoci testamenta*, Episode 5 (Kinodokument/Hrvatska radio-televizija, 2012).

Interview with Ivan Dolničar in: *Tito: posljednji svjedoci testamenta*, Episode 8 (Kinodokument/Hrvatska radio-televizija, 2012).

Miscellaneous

The map prepared by Dušan Dačić and Miloš Bojanić titled "Allied Bombing of Yugoslavia in World War 2 (1941-1945)" (courtesy of Miloš Bojanić).

Private communication from Goran Despotović (12.8.2020).

Index